MONARCHY, MAGNATES AND INSTITUTIONS

According to the Worcester chronicle, when Henry I was crossing the Channel from Normandy to England in August, 1131, his ship was threatened by a great storm. The frightened king vowed that if his ship was granted divine protection he would go on a pilgrimage to St. Edmund at Bury and would suspend the collection of danegeld for seven years. Thereupon the weather turned calm and the ship sailed safely on to England. The chronicler's statement that Henry honoured his vow is perhaps corroborated by a royal act in favour of Bury St. Edmunds issued at Bury c.1132 (*Regesta*, 2, no.1733).

Line drawing in the Chronicle of John of Worcester, MS. Corp. Chri. Coll., Oxon, clvii, fo.383. (*By courtesy of the President and Fellows of Corpus Christi College, Oxford*)

MONARCHY, MAGNATES AND INSTITUTIONS IN THE ANGLO-NORMAN WORLD

C. WARREN HOLLISTER

THE HAMBLEDON PRESS

LONDON AND RONCEVERTE

Published by The Hambledon Press 1986

35 Gloucester Avenue,
London NW1 7AX (U.K.)

309 Greenbrier Avenue,
Ronceverte, West Virginia (U.S.A.)

ISBN 0 907628 50 8

History Series 43

British Library Cataloguing in Publication Data

Hollister, C. Warren
    Monarchy, magnates and institutions in the
    Anglo-Norman world — (History series; 43)
    1. Great Britain — History — Norman period,
    1066-1154
    I. Title   II. Series
    942.02   DA195

Library of Congress Cataloging in Publication Data

Hollister, C. Warren (Charles Warren), 1930-
    Monarchy, magnates and institutions in the Anglo-
    Norman world.

    Essays originally published in various periodicals.
    Includes index.
    1. Great Britain — History — Norman period, 1066-
    1154. Addresses, essays, lectures. I. Title.
    DA195.H673   1986   942.02   85-5552
    ISBN 0 907628 50 8

Printed by WBC Print Ltd., Bristol
Bound by WBC Bookbinders Ltd., Maesteg

CONTENTS

ACKNOWLEDGEMENTS

The articles reprinted here first appeared in the following places and are reprinted by the kind permission of the original publishers.

1   *American Historical Review*, 62 (1968), 708-23.

2   *Speculum* (Medieval Academy of America), 51 (1976), 202-42.

3   *Speculu,n* (Medieval Academy of America), 48 (1973), 637-53.

4   *English Historical Review*, 88 (1973), 315-34.

5   © 1973 by The Regents of the University of California. Reprinted from *Viator*, Vol. 4 (1973), pp. 115-122, by permission of The Regents.

6   *History*, 58 (1973), 18-28.

7   © 1977 by The Regents of the University of California. Reprinted from *Viator*, Vol. 8 (1977), pp. 63-81, by permission of The Regents.

8   *Réflexions Historiques*, 3 (1976), 83-91.

9   *Journal of Medieval History*, 1 (1975), 19-39.

10   *Proceedings of the Battle Conference on Anglo-Norman Studies, 2, 1979*, ed. R. Allen Brown (Boydell Press, Suffolk, 1980), 93-107, 184-88.

11   *Journal of Medieval History*, 6 (1980), 289-306.

12   *English Historical Review*, 93 (1978), 262-75.

13   *American Historical Review*, 83 (1978), 868-91.

14   *Journal of British Studies*, 12 (1973), 1-25.

15   *Anglo-Norman Studies VI: Proceedings of the Battle Conference 1983*, ed. R. Allen Brown (Boydell Press, Suffolk, 1984), 72-88.

16   *Albion*, 10 (1978), 330-40.

17   *Studies in Medieval History Presented to R.H.C. Davis*, ed. Henry Mayr-Harting and R.I. Moore (The Hambledon Press, London, 1985), 303-16.

TO EDITH

INTRODUCTION

The papers reprinted in this book constitute much of what I have published in the field of Anglo-Norman history during the past fifteen years. The first article presents my final published thoughts on the origins of English feudalism, an issue to which I had previously devoted a number of articles and a book.[1] The remaining sixteen papers, published between 1973 and 1985, are products of my research on the reign of Henry I. More than once this research has carried me many decades before and after A.D. 1100–1135, and far beyond the Anglo-Norman frontiers, in an effort to understand Henry I's reign in its larger context. The articles included here will not appear as such in my forthcoming biography of Henry I, but they reflect methodological approaches and points of view that will turn up again in the biography. They by no means exhaust my views of Henry I's reign, yet in some instances they extend well beyond the chronological and geographical limits of a royal biography.

As will be clear from the Table of Contents, I have organized these papers topically. The first looks back at the issue of William the Conqueror's 'feudal revolution,' while the second attempts a sweeping overview of the feudal relationship between the rulers of Normandy and the kings of France from the foundation of Normandy c. 911 to its conquest by Philip Augustus in 1204. The next two papers explore aspects of Henry I's seizure and defense of the English throne in 1100–1101, including a piece of historical detective work on an alleged case of regicide and fratricide. There follows a series of six articles relating primarily to the relationships between the Anglo-Norman kings and their great landholders and *curiales* – as individuals, as groups, and as factions. In pursuing this kind of research, I find myself drifting away from the institutional approach to history that characterized my earlier work (including the first paper in this book) into the newer political history involving prosopographical methods. In the next section I apply similar prosopographical techniques to questions of administrative history, beginning with another piece of detective work involving a forgery case. There follow two papers on adminis-

[1] The previous articles were, by and large, summarized and expanded in my *Military Organization of Norman England* (Oxford, 1965).

trative history, two on diplomatic history, written eleven years apart, and two final papers in the first of which the current dark portrait of Henry I is reevaluated. Here again, as in the regicide and forgery cases, I am an attorney for the defense.

Two of the papers, 'The Rise of Administrative Kingship' and 'The Making of the Angevin Empire' were originally written in collaboration with, respectively, Professors John W. Baldwin and Thomas K. Keefe. Because the Hollister-Baldwin article is divided into two separate parts ('Henry I' and 'Philip Augustus'), and because John Baldwin assumed the entire task of comparing the two regimes, it has been possible to reprint my own part separately here as a non-comparative analysis of Henry I's administration. The Hollister-Keefe collaboration is not so easily undone. Thomas Keefe was a student in my doctoral program at the time we wrote the article, and we did it as a single piece – combining his expertise in the Angevin monarchy with my own interest in the Norman kings. For his permission to reprint the paper here in its original form I am grateful to Tom – my student no longer but a cherished friend.

In rereading these papers I was struck by two things in particular: one good, the other bad. I was relieved to discover that I still agree with most of what I wrote, though whether this reflects past perceptiveness or present stubbornness I would not venture to guess. I was troubled, however, by the repetitiveness that I encountered when reading one article after the other. The problem is common to collections of related papers which the author originally designed as independent, self-contained studies. It was necessary to provide each paper with sufficient historical background to make sense of the topic, and at times I summarized the conclusions of previous papers when they seemed essential to the argument at hand. But I suspect that readers of this book will grow as tired as I did of being reminded, for example, that the last thirty-three years of Henry I's reign in England were peaceful ones.

Let me now comment briefly on each paper in turn. Until recently, I had not reread '1066: The Feudal Revolution' for fifteen years. I returned to it with considerable apprehension but finished it with a sense of relief. I continue to accept its basic thesis, although I was a little jarred by its tone of youthful brashness and by its mistakenly optimistic conclusion that a consensus was developing on the issue of English feudalism. Today, alas, the Freemans and Rounds stand as far apart as ever, and if they are less strident than before it may simply be a sign of intellectual exhaustion. The most recent exchange involved Dr John Gillingham and Professor J. C. Holt, whose papers were identically and daringly titled 'The Introduction of Knight Service into England,' and were presented respectively at the 1981 and 1983 Battle

Conferences.[2] I am firmly in Holt's camp, yet I regret that camps must still exist. One of Holt's many interesting suggestions is that the Conqueror originally assessed knights' quotas on his men rather than on their lands. For my own part, I respectfully request anyone who doubts the existence of customary and exact quotas by A.D. 1101 to explain the Abingdon chronicler's statement that when one knight refused to join the abbatial contingent summoned that year by Henry I, the abbot was obliged to find a substitute.[3]

The second paper, 'Normandy, France, and the Anglo-Norman *Regnum,*' presents a more subtle thesis than its title might suggest. For those who have chided me for insisting that England and Normandy under Henry I 'formed one *kingdom*' (their italics), its republication will afford a convenient opportunity to rediscover what I actually wrote. The paper was first published in 1976, a year that also saw the publication of John Le Patourel's great book, *The Norman Empire*, and his paper, 'Norman Kings or Norman "King-Dukes"?' in which he analyzed a topic closely parallel to mine.[4] At the time, I had not yet met John Le Patourel, but we were already exchanging ideas by correspondence, noting points of friendly disagreement and rejoicing that, by and large, we had independently arrived at similar conclusions about Anglo-Norman unity. We wondered whether our similar views might have stemmed from the similarly neutral backgrounds – neither wholly English nor wholly Norman – of a Channel Islander and an American. At the 1979 and 1980 Battle Conferences, I had the great pleasure of discussing Anglo-Norman history with John Le Patourel on long walks through the grounds of Battle Abbey. His death, at the height of his scholarly powers, deprived medieval historical scholarship of one of its keenest intellects and most generous spirits.

Since the publication of my paper, others have added much to our understanding of the Norman-French relationship. Of particular interest is the as yet unpublished observation by Professor Elizabeth A. R. Brown that the Hyde chronicler, differing from all other sources, has William Adelin rendering homage in 1120 not to King Louis VI but to his son Philip, whom Louis had associated in the royal governance

---

[2] *Proceedings of the Battle Conference*, ed. R. Allen Brown, 4 (1982): 53–64; *ibid.*, 6 (1984), 89–106.

[3] *Chronicon Monasterii de Abingdon*, ed. Joseph Stevenson (Rolls Series, London, 1858), 2:128–29.

[4] Le Patourel, *The Norman Empire* (Oxford, 1976); and 'Norman Kings or Norman "King-Dukes"?' in *Droit privé et institutions régionales: études historiques offertes à Jean Yver* (Paris, 1976), pp. 469–79. Le Patourel concludes with appropriate caution, 'It may well be better therefore to speak of 'Norman kings' rather than Norman 'king-dukes': p. 479. My paper, unlike Le Patourel's, carries the analysis on through the Angevin period to 1204. At his untimely death, Le Patourel was planning a full scale study of the Angevin Empire along the lines of his *Norman Empire.*

just beforehand at the remarkably tender age of three – perhaps for the express purpose of enabling Philip to receive William Adelin's homage.[5] If the Hyde chronicler can be trusted, it would have been one of the odder homage ceremonies of the Middle Ages, and my interpretation of the peace of 1120 would require some modification. On the issue of Anglo-Norman assimilation, Professor David S. Spear has made the valuable point that, even though the English and Norman churches were institutionally distinct, 'there was a vigorous exchange between England and Normandy among the higher clergy,' and that the two churches can therefore be viewed, in many respects, as 'a single, Anglo-Norman configuration.'[6]

Most scholars seem to have been persuaded by my exoneration of Henry I in 'The Strange Death of William Rufus'. Frank Barlow, who was not among Henry I's accusers, adopts an interpretation similar to mine in his important new biography of William Rufus. We differ, however, on the question of whether Rufus intended to defend Normandy against Robert Curthose on his return from the First Crusade.[7] Barlow doubts Orderic Vitalis's statement that Rufus at his death was assembling a military force against Curthose, whereas I continue to regard it as probably correct.[8] Unfortunately, the thinness of the evidence prohibits any clear resolution of the issue; whatever the truth of the matter, I will remain an unabashed admirer of both Frank Barlow and Orderic Vitalis.

'The Anglo-Norman Civil War' turns from the death that permitted Henry I's accession to the crisis that threatened and then consolidated his royal status. Again, my reconstruction of events seems to have found general scholarly acceptance, and Ranulf Flambard is no longer being portrayed as a secret agent. But I would now qualify my argument in several minor respects. In this paper as in the following one, my figures on charter attestations and Domesday values are only approximate. They may depend too heavily on the flawed indices in Henry Ellis's *General Introduction to Domesday Book* and the first (1913) volume of the *Regesta Regum Anglo-Normannorum*, and on H.

[5] On Philip's precocious emergence into the royal government, see Andrew W. Lewis, *Royal Succession in Capetian France: Studies on Familial Order and the State* (Cambridge, Mass., 1981), p. 56. Philip was born on August 29, 1116, and by the time he was three, he was 'consenting' to royal *acta*. He occurs in several *acta* as *rex designatus*, the earliest dated October 4, 1121, shortly after his fifth birthday: Achille Luchaire, *Louis VI le Gros: Annales de sa vie et son règne* (Paris, 1890), nos. 214, 287, 289, 290, 293–94, 302, 310, 365, 408.

[6] David S. Spear, 'The Norman Empire and the Secular Clergy,' *Journal of British Studies*, 21, ii (1982): 1–10.

[7] Frank Barlow, *William Rufus* (London, 1983), pp. 414–32.

[8] Orderic Vitalis, *Historia Ecclesiastica*, ed. Marjorie Chibnall (Oxford, 1969–80), 5:280.

W. C. Davis's thoughtful but now outdated judgmerts regarding the
authenticity of William I's and William II's charters. The figures can
doubtless be refined when David Bates's new edition of William I's
charters and the Santa Barbara Domesday database become available.
But I am confident that errors in my valuation and attestation figures
will turn out to be trivial and, above all, not biased toward the proving
of a thesis. The formidable resources of Robert of Bellême are reduced,
though only slightly, by Marjorie Chibnall's hypothesis that he
probably did not acquire the Builli honor of Blyth, as Orderic states,
but merely held the castle of Tickhill as a royal custodian.[9] It has also
been suggested to me that Wace may have erred in stating that Robert
Curthose was beginning an advance on London when Henry I
encountered him; Robert's forces may have remained encamped near
Winchester while he and his magnates negotiated with Henry I at
nearby Alton. Finally, Paschal II's letter granting Archbishop Anselm
the power of decision in Ranulf Flambard's case is likelier to date from
1102 than 1101 and is probably related to Paschal's letter of 1102
responding to Anselm's request for papal instructions on how to
proceed in Flambard's case now that Henry I had restored him to
Durham.[10]

'Magnates and Curiales in Early Norman England,' like the previous
piece, depends on value and attestation figures that are only
approximate but nevertheless sufficiently accurate to yield reliable
conclusions. Their major weakness appears in Table D. part 2, where
the last two or three names on the list of Rufus's *curiales* attest so few
charters (8 1/2, 8, 7) that the discovery of a few unknown charters
might well put other men in their places. Robert of Montfort, at the
bottom of the list, should be dropped from it altogether. My use of the
anachronistic but convenient term, 'super-magnate,' has raised some
eyebrows, and I would cheerfully abandon it if I could find a synonym
that was more tasteful and equally concise. My central argument, that
Rufus's relations with most of his greatest magnates were unsatisfactory, is at odds with Barlow's more recent judgment of the
matter.[11] I continue to think that Barlow's interpretation is inconsistent
not only with the charter attestation data but with other evidence as
well. Rufus was confronted with two general rebellions during his
thirteen-year reign, whereas Henry I faced only one general English
rebellion in thirty-five years.[12] Henry I's coronation charter promising

[9] 'Robert of Bellême and the Castle of Tickhill,' in *Droit privé et institutions régionales*, pp. 151–56.

[10] *S. Anselmi Cantuariensis Archiepiscopi Opera Omnia*, ed. F. S. Schmitt (Stuttgart-Bad Cannstatt, 1968), 4:Epp. 222–23, 225.

[11] Barlow, *Rufus*, pp. 156–75, 211–13.

[12] I do not regard Henry I's destruction of the Montgomerys in 1102 as a general rebellion; it was undertaken at the king's initiative and directed against a single family.

his nobility relief from Rufus's arbitrary practices corroborates narrative testimony that Rufus's government weighed heavily on rich and poor alike[13] and contrasts sharply with King Stephen's coronation charter promising his nobles all the liberties and good laws that Henry I had conceded them.[14] But here as elsewhere, there is room for honest disagreement.

I must here honestly disagree with my own discussion of tenurial insecurity in the opening paragraph of 'The Misfortunes of the Mandevilles', which I wrote while under the spell of my wise friend, Professor R. H. C. Davis.[15] I have since been persuaded by another wise friend, Professor J. C. Holt, and by my former doctoral student, Professor RaGena DeAragon, that baronial tenures were much more secure during the last two decades of Henry I's reign than at any time since the Conquest.[16] But the Mandevilles' misfortunes remain as I have described them. So, too, do the tribulations and triumphs discussed in the next paper, 'The Taming of a Turbulent Earl: Henry I and William of Warenne'. The fact that nobody has taken exception to anything in this paper may result from its having been published in a small and virtually unknown Canadian journal.

'The Anglo-Norman Succession Debate of 1126' first appeared in the maiden issue of the *Journal of Medieval History*. On rereading it, I find the argument both speculative and plausible. The genealogical chart includes a number of corrections. As originally published, the chart fell victim to the rush to get the first issue of the *Journal of Medieval History* into print before the 1975 medieval studies convention at Kalamazoo. I was in the midst of chairing a panel at that convention when a copy of the journal was handed to me hot off the press. Glancing at my chart, I was flabbergasted to discover that it had been garbled to such an extent that Stephen and Adela of Blois had become the parents of William Clito, and that Henry II was king of England and Aquitaine – an audacious extrapolation of the Anglo-Norman *regnum* idea which I repudiate utterly.

[13] Florence of Worcester, *Chronicon ex Chronicis*, ed. Benjamin Thorpe (London, 1848–49), 2:46; cf. Orderic, 4:178: Rufus bound some to him by generosity and held the rest in check by force or fear, whereas Henry I placated all groups (*ibid.*, 5:296). Rufus was mourned chiefly by his mercenary knights and camp followers: *ibid.*, 5:292; William of Malmesbury, *Gesta Regum Anglorum*, ed. William Stubbs (Rolls Series, London, 1887–89), 2:379.

[14] *English Historical Documents*, 2, 2nd ed., ed. David C. Douglas and George W. Greenaway (London, 1981), pp. 434–35. The correction of Henry's abuses is, however, a major theme in Stephen's charter to the Church: *ibid.*, pp. 435–36.

[15] *King Stephen, 1135–1154* (London, 1967), p. 123 and *passim*; 'What Happened in Stephen's Reign, 1135–54,' *History*, 49 (1964), 1–12.

[16] J. C. Holt, 'Politics and Property in Early Medieval England,' *Past and Present*, 57 (1972): 3–52, and, directly to the point, R. DeAragon, 'The Growth of Secure Inheritance in Anglo-Norman England,' *Journal of Medieval History*, 8 (1982): 381–91.

'Henry I and the Anglo-Norman Magnates' concludes and summarizes the section on the relationships of the Norman kings with their magnates and *curiales*. As an article standing on its own, it was awarded the Walter D. Love Memorial Prize of the North American Conference on British Studies, but as presented here it repeats, regrettably yet unavoidably, some of the ideas and evidence presented in the five preceding papers. A few statements now require correction. Dr David Bates has argued that previous scholars were mistaken in regarding William the Conqueror's Norman magnates as a new aristocracy. He attributes our inability to trace their families back more than a couple of generations to a genealogical optical illusion caused by the transformation of the Norman nobility *c.* 1025–1050 from collateral kinship groups to lineage-based families identified with particular castles.[17] Professor Eleanor Searle will have more to say on the matter, and she has also raised the interesting and as yet unpublished point that the evidence for the Conqueror's mother Herleve being a tanner's daughter is late and unreliable. My former doctoral student, Professor Stephanie Mooers, has demonstrated the error of my statement that Stephen of Richmond 'received no exemption' in the Pipe Roll of 1130.[18] I thank her for doing so; I had mistakenly regarded Stephen of Richmond as an exception to my general thesis that Henry I favoured his great magnates, and by eliminating the exception, Stephanie has strengthened my argument.

Shortly after the publication of 'London's First Charter of Liberties: Is it Genuine?' I had the opportunity to discuss the issue with Dr Susan Reynolds, one of the co-authors of the piece to which I was objecting, when she was visiting Santa Barbara. While generously acknowledging the aptness of some of my arguments, Dr Reynolds correctly observed that surviving copies of Henry I's London charter might yet be interpolated versions of a genuine original. But the same might be said of many charters that have survived only in copies, and I remain convinced that the historical circumstances require no such explanation. Nevertheless, I quite agree with Christopher Brooke, Gillian Keir, and Susan Reynolds that the issue of the charter's genuineness

---

[17] *Normandy Before 1066* (London, 1982), pp. 134–35 and *passim*. Bates is here extending into Normandy the process observed by Duby and others elsewhere on the Continent: e.g. Georges Duby, *The Chivalrous Society*, tr. Cynthia Postan (Berkeley, 1977), Chaps. 6, 9, 10, and *passim*. Bates makes a strong case, but I doubt that the issue will be fully resolved without further prosopographical analysis.

[18] Stephanie L. Mooers, 'Patronage in the Pipe Roll of 1130,' *Speculum*, 59 (1984): 293–94. In actuality, as Professor Mooers demonstrates, Stephen of Richmond's pardons, exemptions, and other benefits from the king place him among the ten most favoured men in England in 1129–30. My error was in calculating danegeld exemptions only: Mooers' research makes it likely that the honour of Richmond was exempt from danegeld by custom and that annual writs of pardon were therefore unnecessary.

cannot be resolved absolutely. If we continue to differ, it is only with regard to degrees of probability or improbability.

In both 'The Origins of the English Treasury' and the paper that follows it, I make the point that Henry I's exchequer was not yet a separate office or ministry but only an occasion – a semi-annual audit. I do not, however, address the question of how long such audits might last. A passage in the Pipe Roll of 1130 suggests that they might run as long as a month and a half or more; Geoffrey the Chancellor accounted for £10 15s. 'for the forty-three days in which he was not at the exchequer with the king's other barons.'[19]

At one point in 'The Rise of Administrative Kingship' I endeavour to distinguish between *curiales* who serve primarily in England (E), primarily in Normandy (N), and frequently in both (X). These calculations, based on attestations of royal charters, have been adjusted to compensate for the much greater number of surviving charters originating in England, but my method of adjustment is admittedly intuitive and could be considerably refined – perhaps by treating Norman and English attestation totals as percentages of the total numbers of surviving royal charters from Normandy and from England. Nevertheless, as before, I am confident that the general conclusions indicated by the attestation data are reliable. My assumption that Henry I turned from his father's policy of appointing magnates as sheriffs must be corrected in two respects. As Dr Judith Green has since shown, William A. Morris was mistaken in believing that the Conqueror routinely appointed magnates as sheriffs.[20] Dr Green makes the important additional point, further developed by Dr David Crouch, that a wealthy curial magnate could sometimes secure the appointment of a friend and client as sheriff of a county in which the magnate was powerful.[21] We must therefore be warned against assuming without further investigation that the choice of sheriffs was always the king's alone. Finally, my observation that Roger of Salisbury functioned as a kind of chief justiciar without title should perhaps be modified in the light of David Bates's stimulating analysis of the origins of the justiciarship.[22]

One of the great problems in discussing Henry I's administrative developments is to determine the point of origin of organizations such as the exchequer – whose earliest surviving pipe roll (1130) reveals for

[19] *Pipe Roll 31 Henry I*, ed. Joseph Hunter, corrected edition (London, 1929), p. 140.
[20] Judith Green, 'The Sheriffs of William the Conqueror,' *Anglo-Norman Studies: Proceedings of the Battle Conference*, 5:129–45; cf. William A. Morris, *The Medieval English Sheriff to 1300* (Manchester, 1927), pp. 41–75.
[21] Green, 'Sheriffs,' pp. 136–38, 145; David Crouch, 'Geoffrey de Clinton and Roger, Earl of Warwick: New Men and Magnates in the Reign of Henry I,' *Bulletin of the Institute of Historical Research*, 55 (1982):113–24.
[22] 'The Origins of the Justiciarship,' *Proceedings of the Battle Conference*, 4:1–12.

the first time a sophisticated accounting system in full operation – or the reformed and intricately regulated royal household that flashes into view in the *Constitutio Domus Regis* of *c.* 1136. Frank Barlow thinks it probable that the household of the *Constitutio Domus Regis* and the exchequer system disclosed in the Pipe Roll of 1130 both existed in recognizable form in Rufus's reign.[23] But although royal audits and royal households can both be traced back many centuries, the forms they had assumed by the 1130s appear to me to have been influenced significantly by Henry I and his great administrator Roger of Salisbury – probably in the years just after Henry's conquest of Normandy in 1106. Eadmer alludes to a drastic reform of the royal household *c.* 1108, and his statement is consistent with the fact that the *Anglo-Saxon Chronicle*, which registers complaints about the depredations of the itinerant courts of William Rufus (1097), Robert Curthose (1101), and Henry I (1104), is silent on the matter thereafter.[24] The late but informed testimony of the *Dialogus de Scaccario* credits Roger bishop of Salisbury with having effected major reforms in the exchequer accounting system, and the earliest allusion to 'barons of the exchequer' occurs in connection with the kingdom-wide aid of A.D. 1110 occasioned by Maud's betrothal to Emperor Henry V[25] – a fiscal operation of great magnitude that may well have prompted Bishop Roger's exchequer reforms.[26]

In writing 'The Making of the Angevin Empire', I was primarily responsible for the Norman period and my co-author, Thomas K. Keefe, for the early Angevin period. The issue of whether Henry I's feudal and matrimonial connections with neighbouring princes represented a policy of defense, as I argue, or of offense as John Le Patourel suggested, is the sort of question that continues to plague international diplomacy to this day. In my own view, although the

[23] Barlow, *Rufus*, pp. 135–55; 222 ff.

[24] Eadmer, *Historia Novorum in Anglia*, ed. Martin Rule (Rolls Series, London, 1884), pp. 192–93; *Anglo-Saxon Chronicle,* A.D. 1097, 1101, 1104; see also William of Malmesbury, *Gesta Regum Anglorum*, ed. William Stubbs (Rolls Series, London, 1887–89), 2:476 where it is said of Henry I: 'In ceteris quoque genitoris aemulus, rapinas curialium, furta, stupra, edicto compescuit'; Walter Map, *De Nugis Curialium*, ed. M. R. James, C. N. L. Brooke, and R. A. B. Mynors (Oxford, 1983), pp. 438, 470.

[25] Richard Fitz Nigel, *Dialogus de Scaccario*, ed. Charles Johnson (London, 1950), pp. 42–43; *Regesta Regum Anglo-Normannorum*, ed. H. W. C. Davis, Charles Johnson, H. A. Cronne, and R. H. C. Davis (Oxford, 1913–69), 2: no. 963; cf. no. 1000, A.D. 1111.

[26] *Anglo-Saxon Chronicle*, A.D. 1110; Karl Leyser, 'England and the Empire in the Twelfth Century,' *Transactions of the Royal Historical Society*, 5th Series, 10 (1960): 64–65, 75–76. The aid, assessed at 3*s.* on the hide, resulted in a betrothal gift to Henry V estimated by Orderic at 10,000 marks (5:200) and by the Winchester annalist at 15,000 marks: *Annales Monastici*, ed. H. R. Luard (Rolls Series, London, 1864–69), 2:43; cf. Henry of Huntingdon, *Historia Anglorum*, ed. Thomas Arnold (Rolls Series, London, 1879), p. 237.

Normans under Henry I continued to win new lands – in Wales and Scotland particularly – Norman expansion was now fueled by individual rather than royal initiative and often, as in Scotland, occurred peacefully. The problem of discerning the intentions of participants in the marriage arrangements between Maud and Geoffrey has been analyzed further by Professor Bernard Bachrach, who agrees with the Hollister-Keefe interpretation but broadens it by exploring Angevin motives and traditions.[27] Whether one can trust William of Newburgh's account of Count Geoffrey's deathbed will is another question that cannot be answered with absolute certainty, but Keefe has provided further persuasive arguments for the affirmative side.[28] And Marjorie Chibnall has demonstrated that my estimate of about a year and a half of warfare in Normandy in 1118–19 may well be too conservative, at least as regards the Vexin frontier.[29]

'War and Diplomacy in the Anglo-Norman State' was published too recently for published reactions or second thoughts. And my 'Royal Acts of Mutilation: The Case against Henry I' has evoked, to the best of my knowledge, no response whatever. Either the readers of the paper have been stunned into silence by its subject matter, or they are saying nothing because they have no reasonable objections to offer. The concluding paper, 'Henry I and the Invisible Transformation of Medieval England', is scheduled to be published more or less concurrently in *Studies in Medieval History presented to R. H. C. Davis.*

In one of my earlier articles, I pointed out with untoward glee a rather trivial error committed by the great Anglo-Norman historian, David Douglas, in his addition of Abingdon knight's fees. Douglas responded with a gracious letter thanking me for correcting him and inviting me to lecture at Bristol and stay at his home on my next visit to England. He concluded by urging that we remain in touch, remarking that there are all too few of us working in the field of eleventh and twelfth century English history, and that we are spread very thinly around the world. I was deeply moved by the letter and I remain so. As a welcome alternative to the warfare of the Freemans and Rounds, Douglas was urging that scholars with kindred interests work

[27] Bernard S. Bachrach, 'The Idea of the Angevin Empire,' *Albion*, 10 (1978):293–99.

[28] Thomas K. Keefe, 'Geoffrey Plantagenet's Will and the Angevin Succession,' *Albion*, 6 (1974):266–74.

[29] Orderic, 6:184–85, n. 4; 186 and n. 1. Chibnall demonstrates that the sources leave it unclear whether the frontier hostilities commenced in 1116, 1117, or 1118. That the warfare did not spread more deeply into Normandy until 1118 is strongly suggested by Orderic's statements that for five years after the peace of 1113 Henry governed both England and Normandy 'in great tranquility' (6:182), and that only after the deaths of William count of Evreux, Queen Edith-Matilda, and Robert count of Meulan (April–June, 1118) did Normandy's great tribulations begin (6:188).

harmoniously together, sheathing their swords and sharing their thoughts. Douglas followed this ideal throughout his celebrated career, as have many others, and they have been an inspiration to me. A close reading of this book will disclose my own debt to a number of historians who have shared their ideas with me – sometimes unpublished ideas – and thereby stimulated and sharpened my own thinking: R. H. C. Davis, J. C. Holt, Sir Richard Southern, Marjorie Chibnall, Eleanor Searle, Edmund King, Elizabeth A. R. Brown, Thomas Waldman, John Le Patourel, Susan Reynolds, Frank Barlow, Andrew Lewis, Denis Bethell, John Baldwin, Robert Patterson, William Reedy, Edward Kealey, Bernard Bachrach, James Alexander, David Crouch, and many others. I have learned much from my own Ph.D. students – an even dozen of whom have defied the formidable odds of the academic marketplace and are now scattered far and wide on college and university faculties.

The thinly spread and widely scattered community of Anglo-Saxon and Anglo-Norman scholars owes a great debt to Professor R. Allen Brown for conceiving and implementing the idea of the annual Battle Conferences, which have become vehicles not only for the exchanging and testing of ideas but for the cementing of friendships and the growth of international scholarly cohesion. Being unable to attend the 1984 Battle Conference, I was deeply touched at receiving a postal card from Battle a few days before writing this, bearing the signatures and greetings of the conferees. In North America, the Charles Homer Haskins Society was established in 1982 and, at this writing, has had three extremely successful annual conferences at the University of Houston. Its membership has soared to some 150 scholars from America, Britain, Canada, France, the Netherlands, and beyond. At this writing, the Battle Conferences and the Haskins Society both appear to have become permanently established, and their relationship to each other is one of confraternity. They are, as Allen Brown expressed it, 'sister houses.' I am certain that David Douglas, were he alive today, would have been delighted.

There is always the danger that an excessive degree of mutual affection might blunt the cutting edge of scholarly analysis and criticism. But I have noticed no such problem in the lively discussions that always follow the presentation of papers at the Battle and Haskins Conferences. It is my great hope that these meetings, and the informal individual contacts that they encourage, will result in narrowing and sometimes resolving scholarly disagreements through rigorous yet courteous debate, conducted in a spirit of mutual regard.

1066: THE "FEUDAL REVOLUTION"

NINE hundred years ago the Normans defeated the Anglo-Saxons at Hastings, and, ever since, historians have been pondering the meaning of this stark event and arguing over its consequences. The historical debate can be traced all the way back into the medieval chronicles, and it still rages hotly today. The present phase of the dispute began with the controversies of the later nineteenth century, centering around such figures as William Stubbs, F. W. Maitland, E. A. Freeman, and John Horace Round. H. G. Richardson and G. O. Sayles have recently demonstrated, to those not already aware of it, that Stubbs was a man of his times, with a historical vision limited by the preconceptions of his own age.[1] It is less widely understood, but equally true, that virtually all the historians of the late nineteenth century involved in the problem of the Norman Conquest were operating with a set of basic assumptions that were then unquestioned and are today unacceptable. To be specific, both Freeman and his bitter antagonist, Round, believed firmly that Anglo-Saxon England contained the seeds of democracy.

Let me reconstruct briefly a fascinating component of the Round-Freeman debate. Here is Freeman writing on Harold Godwinson:

No man ever deserved a higher or a more lasting place in national gratitude than the first man who, being neither King nor Priest, stands forth in English history as endowed with all the highest attributes of the statesman. In him, in those distant times, we can revere the great minister, the unrivalled parliamentary leader, the man who could sway councils and assemblies at his will.[2]

Round comments on this enthusiastic passage as follows:

We know of whom the writer was thinking, when he praised that "irresistible tongue"; he had surely before him a living model [William Gladstone], who, if not a statesman, was, no doubt, an "unrivalled parliamentary leader." Do we not recognize the portrait?[3]

---

[1] H. G. Richardson and G. O. Sayles, *The Governance of Mediaeval England from the Conquest to Magna Carta* (Edinburgh, 1963), 1–21 *et passim*.

[2] E. A. Freeman, *The History of the Norman Conquest of England* (6 vols., Oxford, Eng., 1867–79), II, 352.

[3] J. H. Round, *Feudal England* (2d ed., London, 1964), 304.

Round, while mocking Freeman, is yet agreeing with him. Harold was Gladstone; the Anglo-Saxons were proto-Whigs. The difference between Round and Freeman, here, lay not in the question of whether the Anglo-Saxons were democratic; both Round and Freeman assumed that they were. The difference lay in the fact that Freeman *was* a Whig while Round was a Tory aristocrat with an authoritarian's disdain for democracy. Round continues:

But it was not an "irresistible tongue," nor "the harangue of a practised orator," of which England stood in need. Forts and soldiers, not tongues, are England's want now as then. But to the late Regius Professor, if there was one thing more hateful than "castles," more hateful even than hereditary rule, it was a standing army. When the Franco-German war had made us look to our harness, he set himself at once, with superb blindness, to sneer at what he termed "the panic," to suggest the application of democracy to the army, and to express his character-istic aversion to the thought of "an officer and a gentleman." How could such a writer teach the lesson of the Norman Conquest?[4]

Here is the old Germanist idea turned back on itself. Yes, democracy lurked in the Anglo-Saxon forests, and it destroyed the nation, as it would destroy it again if men like Gladstone had their way. Round continues to berate his dead antagonist, revealing himself in the process:

[Freeman] could not see that the system in which he gloried, a system which made the people "a co-ordinate authority" with their king, was the worst of all trainings for the hour of battle; he could not see that, like Poland, England fell, in large measure, from the want of a strong rule, and from excess of liberty. To him the voice of "a sovereign people" was "the most spirit-stirring of earthly sounds"; but it availed about as much to check the Norman Conquest as the fetish of an African savage, or the yells of Asiatic hordes. . . . Such were the bitter fruits of Old-English freedom.

And finally:

While our fathers were playing at democracy, watching the strife of rival houses, as men might now watch the contest of rival parties, the terrible Duke of the Normans was girding himself for war.[5]

Harold is Gladstone, and William is Bismarck; Harold is Newcastle, and William is the Elder Pitt. One chooses his sides according to his politics. Charles Petit-Dutaillis once said of Stubbs: "He projected into the past the image of the constitutional monarchy which he saw working under his own eyes and to which he attributed the greatness of his country." It might be said of Round that he projected into Anglo-Saxon England the image of Gladstonian liberalism which he despised. Such are the biases that underlie the turbulent historical controversy of the Norman Conquest.

[4] *Ibid.*
[5] *Ibid.*, 303, 305.

No one today believes in Anglo-Saxon democracy, yet throughout the twentieth century to the present, Freeman's theory of continuity across the thin red line of 1066 and Round's theory of feudal revolution have remained the two poles around which the controversy has ranged. English scholars of this century have eschewed the crude political biases of their predecessors, but they have not always succeeded in avoiding a subtler kind of bias, based on the complex antagonisms of conflicting schools of thought, personal followings, and personal loyalties. These delicate interrelationships are rooted firmly in the Round-Freeman controversy, and the biases of these two men are therefore highly relevant today. Round won the battle, though perhaps not the war. His notion of a Norman feudal revolution, asserted so boldly in the 1890's, quickly rose to the Olympian heights of received opinion, and virtually all the research done by scholars in the 1920's, 1930's, and 1940's served only to confirm and strengthen it. The most important book on the subject written in this period, Sir Frank Stenton's *First Century of English Feudalism: 1066–1166* (Oxford, Eng., 1932), incorporated Round's hypothesis in its title.

Since about mid-century, however, Round's feudal revolution hypothesis has come under attack, restrained and modest at first, but, in recent years, vigorous indeed. The past two decades or so have witnessed the emergence of a kind of "neo-Freemanism." Marjory Hollings, in 1948, urged that the Anglo-Saxon five-hide unit survived the Norman Conquest to become the basis of knights' fees in parts of the western Midlands.[6] G. O. Sayles, in 1950, argued generally for the existence of feudalism in late Saxon England.[7] J. O. Prestwich, in 1954, pointed to the neglected mercenary as a significant figure in Anglo-Norman warfare,[8] thereby diminishing the military importance of the Norman feudal settlement in general and the Norman feudal knight in particular. More recently, the books of Eric John, Richardson and Sayles, and Frank Barlow, together with an accelerating flow of controversial scholarly articles in various journals,[9] have reopened the old dispute,

---

[6] Marjory Hollings, "The Survival of the Five Hide Unit in the Western Midlands," *English Historical Review*, LXIII (Oct. 1948), 453–87; see also *The Red Book of Worcester*, ed. id. (4 vols., London, 1934–50), IV, xx–xxxix.

[7] G. O. Sayles, *The Medieval Foundations of England* (Philadelphia, 1950), 199 ff.

[8] J. O. Prestwich, "War and Finance in the Anglo-Norman State," *Transactions of the Royal Historical Society*, 5th Ser., IV (1954), 19–43.

[9] Eric John, *Land Tenure in Early England* (Leicester, 1960), 113–61; Richardson and Sayles, *Governance of Mediaeval England*, 22–135; Frank Barlow, *William I and the Norman Conquest* (London, 1965), 99 ff., and "The Effects of the Norman Conquest," in *The Norman Conquest: Its Setting and Impact*, ed. C. T. Chevallier (London, 1966), 138, and, more generally, 125–61. See also, e.g., C. Warren Hollister, "The Norman Conquest and the Genesis of English Feudalism," *American Historical Review*, LXVI (Apr. 1961), 641–63; J. C. Holt, "Feudalism Revisited," *Economic History Review*, 2d Ser., XIV (Dec. 1961), 333–40; id. and C. W. Hollister, "Two Comments on the Problem of Continuity in Anglo-Norman Feudalism," *ibid.*, 2d Ser., XVI (Aug. 1963), 104–18; Eric John, "English Feudalism

reviving ancient wounds and inflicting new ones, with a result that must be stimulating to some, confusing to others, and unsettling to all. At times the recently reawakened controversy has reached such levels of antagonism that one might well imagine the ghost of John Horace Round still striding fiercely along the thin red line, inspiring both his supporters and opponents with his own distinctive spirit of passionate advocacy. In 1963, Richardson and Sayles could speak of Stubbs as not simply erroneous but "dogmatic and perverse," and of Round himself as "amateurish and undisciplined," "hasty and muddled," one who "fouled the wells of truth."[10] Victorian and Edwardian liberalism are gone, and, with them, the myth of Anglo-Saxon democracy. But the problems of the Norman Conquest are still capable of arousing passions. The debate over the feudal revolution remains not only interesting but explosive.

For the purpose of bringing some limited order out of the present chaos, one can divide current opinion on the question of the Conquest and military service roughly into three schools of thought: the Round school, which includes such modern supporters of the "feudal revolution" as J. C. Holt; the Neo-Freeman or "direct continuity" school represented by Richardson and Sayles, Barlow, and, perhaps, John; and a middle school to which, among other historians, I would subscribe. Advocates of the moderate position will often be found contending among themselves over various points and might well resent being made schoolmates. Their views on the problem have, nevertheless, much in common, as will be seen.

The first of these three schools, that of feudal revolution, is conveniently epitomized in Round's own words, typically lacking in self-doubt:

I am anxious to make absolutely clear the point that between the accepted view and the view which I advance, no compromise is possible. The two are radically opposed. As against the theory that the military obligation of the Anglo-Norman tenant-in-chief was determined by the assessment of his holding, whether in hidage or in value, I maintain that the extent of that obligation was not determined by his holding, but was fixed in relation to, and expressed in terms of, the *constabularia* of ten knights, the unit of the [Norman] feudal host. And I, consequently, hold that his military service was in no way derived or developed from that of the Anglo-Saxons, but was arbitrarily fixed by the king, from whom he received his fief, irrespectively both of its size and of all pre-existent arrangements.[11]

---

and the Structure of Anglo-Saxon Society," *Bulletin of the John Rylands Library*, XLVI (Sept. 1963), 14–41; J. O. Prestwich, "Anglo-Norman Feudalism and the Problem of Continuity," *Past and Present*, XXVI (Nov. 1963), 39–57; John Beeler, "The Composition of Anglo-Norman Armies," *Speculum*, XL (July 1965), 398–414.

[10] Richardson and Sayles, *Governance of Mediaeval England*, 30, 20.

[11] Round, *Feudal England*, 208.

This view, perhaps minus the *constabularia* hypothesis, still finds strong supporters.

The contrary view is aptly summarized by Richardson and Sayles, writing some seventy years later, with equal self-assurance.

The suggestion we have to make is that *servitia debita* [the baronial quotas to the king], far from having been introduced at the Conquest, were gradually established, first by the occasional settlement of disputes . . . and thereafter by reducing those of uncertain amount to something approaching a uniform standard, beginning with ecclesiastical fiefs and culminating in the general review of 1166 [the royal survey of baronial enfeoffments known as the *Cartae Baronum*]. This uniform standard was not derived from Norman practice, but appears to be associated with a widespread, traditional convention.[12]

This careful statement tends to mask the potent emotions that the two authors bring to their study. Like Freeman, they admire the Anglo-Saxons—undemocratic, to be sure, but highly civilized and richly creative. Their attitude toward Normandy can only be described as one of hostility. Normandy was "a small barbaric province" whose inhabitants "had little statecraft and little foresight . . . very little to teach and very much to learn." Thus, "the Norman Conquest introduced no new conceptions of warfare, no new ranks of society."[13] The intellectual debt of Richardson and Sayles to Freeman is perfectly clear, and the two authors recognize it explicitly: "Freeman has long been under a cloud," they write, "but it seems to us that, of all the historians during the last hundred years, he wrote the wisest words on the consequences of the Conquest."[14]

Here are the two polar positions, uncompromisingly asserted, and each rooted firmly in the Round-Freeman controversy of the later nineteenth century. To many historians, including myself, an intermediate position between these two extremes seems closer to reality—that the conquering Normans contributed much and preserved much, that they introduced feudal knights' service, but tamed it by the Anglo-Saxon tradition of royal centralization and brought it into a larger military organization that retained significant Anglo-Saxon components.

The validity of any of these three positions depends of course not on how convincing it sounds in the abstract but on how well it fits the evidence. Limited space prohibits a thorough examination of the evidence on all points at issue, but it might be useful to touch on two specific problems that are central to the general question of revolution versus continuity:

[12] Richardson and Sayles, *Governance of Mediaeval England*, 90.
[13] *Ibid.*, 27, 61.
[14] *Ibid.*, 92.

first, the alleged survival of the Anglo-Saxon "select fyrd" into the Anglo-Norman period; second, the advent of knightly quotas to the king.

Did the Anglo-Saxon five-hide territorial army—the "select fyrd"[15]—persist as a distinct organization in the Anglo-Norman age? This has proven to be an explosive issue indeed, for the survival of the select fyrd presents grave problems to both the "feudal revolution" school and the "direct continuity" school. To the first, an Anglo-Norman fyrd represents an Old English military institution whose existence in post-Conquest times would clearly diminish, at least to a degree, the military impact of the Norman feudal revolution. To those who follow Freeman in assuming a direct evolution of the pre-Conquest five-hide recruitment system into the post-Conquest feudal quota system, it stands as a fatal obstacle. For if the five-hide recruitment system and the arbitrary feudal quotas were employed concurrently by the Norman kings, then, obviously, the one cannot have evolved directly into the other. One must, for example, be under no illusions regarding Richardson and Sayles's rejection of the post-Conquest select fyrd.[16] This rejection is not merely an appendage to their basic argument; it is absolutely essential to it.

There now exist in print studies that trace in a painstaking manner the activities of territorially recruited English troops in Norman England. One such study can be found, for example, in Professor Michael Powicke's illuminating book on military obligation in medieval England.[17] Yet persuasive arguments have been set forth recently to the effect that the evidence on which these studies are built is illusory. Rather than retracing the Anglo-Norman select fyrd once again, let us look briefly at some of the evidence from an analytical rather than a chronological standpoint.

To begin with, something must be said about the general problem of evidence. There is no technical term in medieval Latin or Anglo-Saxon to describe the select fyrd. Indeed, the term "select fyrd" was only coined in 1962. For that matter, there is no contemporary technical term to describe feudal knights serving in the army in return for their tenures. These facts make it exceedingly difficult to cull from the narrative sources specific instances of the military activity of either select fyrd soldiers or feudal knights, and they make it possible for Richardson and Sayles to deny the very existence of both the Anglo-Norman feudal army and the Anglo-

---

[15] On the Anglo-Saxon select fyrd, see C. W. Hollister, *Anglo-Saxon Military Institutions* (Oxford, Eng., 1962), 38–102.

[16] Richardson and Sayles, *Governance of Mediaeval England,* 53–55.

[17] M. R. Powicke, *Military Obligation in Medieval England* (Oxford, Eng., 1962), 37 ff., and, more generally, 26–47; see also C. W. Hollister, *The Military Organization of Norman England* (Oxford, Eng., 1965), 216–67.

Norman select fyrd. Most warriors of that time, they suggest, were mercenaries.

Now with all due respect to those scholars who have done valuable work in tracing the Anglo-Norman mercenary, it must be said that theirs is the happier labor. For there *are* medieval Latin terms for "mercenary," and when one encounters the words *stipendiarii* or *soliderii* in the sources, one knows that he has struck gold. Prospectors seeking traces of the feudal army are doomed to worry over such ambiguous words as *milites, exercitus, equitatio,* and *expeditio.* And the unhappy fyrd scholar (if such a term can be coined) is still less fortunate. *Fyrd* is an Anglo-Saxon word meaning simply "military force." It never appears in the Latin chronicles because it is not a Latin word. It occurs repeatedly in the Anglo-Saxon Peterborough Chronicle, but simply as a synonym for *exercitus*—"army." It is as though some future historian were trying to trace the relative importance of the US Army, Navy, Air Force, and Marine Corps in Vietnam from contemporary Vietnamese chroniclers who tended to refer only to "Those Damned Americans." Similarly, the twelfth-century monks were not interested in the details of military recruitment.

They were, however, interested in the military exploits of native Englishmen. Orderic Vital says that in 1068 the Conqueror summoned the English to his banner for the first time and led them, along with his Norman knights, on an expedition against Exeter.[18] And on a number of occasions thereafter we find Englishmen—*Angli*—as a group receiving special mention in accounts of the military campaigns of the Norman kings. In 1073 and 1078 they fought on the Continent; in 1075, 1088, and 1101 they were summoned to defend the royal interest against rebellion and invasion. And evidence indicates that they were employed at other times as well.[19]

Who were these Englishmen? They must have been recruited somehow. Did the kings send scouts into the countryside to round them up? Were they simply responding to the ancient obligation of freemen to defend their localities in time of crisis? Perhaps on occasion they were, but this would hardly account for their use on the Exeter *expeditio* of 1068 or on the

---

[18] Orderic Vital, *Historia Ecclesiastica,* ed. Auguste Le Prévost (5 vols., Paris, 1838–55), II, 180.

[19] *Ibid.,* 176–77, 193, 254, 256, 387, III, 271–77, IV, 30–31, 174; Florence of Worcester, *Chronicon ex Chronicis,* ed. Benjamin Thorpe (2 vols., London, 1848–49), II, 2–3, 9, 10–11, 22–23, 28, 32, 48–49; William of Malmesbury, *Gesta Regum,* ed. William Stubbs (Rolls Series [hereafter cited as RS], 90, 2 vols., London, 1887–89), II, 312–13, 316, 362, 471–72; *Anglo-Saxon Chronicle,* A.D. 1067 [1068], 1068 [1069], 1071, 1073, 1075, 1079, 1087 [1088], 1091, 1093, 1101; Geoffrey Gaimar, *Lestorie des Engles,* ed. T. D. Hardy and C. T. Martin (RS, 91, 2 vols., London, 1876), I, 232; *Lanfranci Opera,* ed. J. A. Giles (2 vols., Oxford, Eng., 1844), I, 56; *Gesta Normannorum Ducum,* ed. Jean Marx (Rouen, 1914), 270, 282; Henry of Huntingdon, *Historia Anglorum,* ed. Thomas Arnold (RS, 74, London, 1879), 233.

continental campaigns. Were they mercenaries? One would not guess it from the sources, for they are described neither as *stipendiarii* nor as *solidarii*, and in 1088 King William Rufus promised that if they served him he would give them good laws, just taxes, and woods and hunting rights. He did not mention wages.[20]

Even without additional evidence it seems more plausible than not that these Englishmen were recruited by means of the only specifically English system of recruitment that we know of: the five-hide recruitment system described in Berkshire Domesday[21] It has been objected that such a supposition involves an economically crushing double military obligation on the land. But this objection is hardly to the point. The chroniclers leave no doubt that there *was* a double obligation—that on occasion both Englishmen and Normans served and that they were summoned separately. The question is not how much military service the Norman kings were in fact able to wring from their subjects, but, rather, by what means they obtained it.

It can be shown that the identity between the *Angli* of the post-Conquest chronicles and the select fyrd soldiers serving from five hides is not only plausible but, to say the least, exceedingly probable. One can begin with a consideration of two passages from Domesday Book. On the estates of the bishop of Worcester four freemen held ten hides at Bishampton prior to the Conquest, rendering military service by land and sea. (The land and sea combination is characteristic of select-fyrd service but utterly alien to feudal host service.) The holders of these same ten hides in 1086 were responsible for precisely the same service.[22] Again, the town of Bedford was assessed at fifty hides for service by land and sea both at the death of King Edward the Confessor and in 1086.[23] These Domesday passages admit of only two interpretations: They can be taken as demonstrating the total absence of a feudal revolution, as showing that territorial military service in 1086 was identical to that of 1066. Or to those scholars who, for other sound reasons, reject such a drastic conclusion, they can yield the hypothesis that the territorial military service of 1086 described here has nothing to do with the feudal quotas, but was a concurrent select fyrd obligation surviving from the arrangements of the Confessor's day. The passages demolish the extreme "feudal revolution" hypothesis that select fyrd service came to an abrupt end in 1066 or so and that it was then replaced by a totally new sort of service—feudal service. This is merely to say that, if the described service

[20] *Anglo-Saxon Chronicle*, A.D. 1087 [1088].
[21] Domesday Book, ed. Abraham Furley and Henry Ellis (4 vols., London, 1783–1816), I, 56b.
[22] *Ibid.*, 173.
[23] *Ibid.*, 209.

from Bishampton and Bedford in 1066 and 1086 was the same, then it cannot have been different.

In 1086, incidentally, the ten hides of Bishampton were divided between two vast baronial estates: those of Urse d'Abetôt and Roger de Lacy. One reviewer has suggested recently that, if the military service of Bishampton in 1086 is identified with the select fyrd, then one is driven to the absurd conclusion that Urse d'Abetôt and Roger de Lacy were to be found trudging along with the English. The notion of either of these great barons performing personal military service of any sort from these minute holdings is, of course, inconceivable.

Finally there is the well-known Hastings episode of 1094, reported in the Anglo-Saxon Chronicle and repeated, with slight variations, in Florence of Worcester and Henry of Huntingdon.[24] Twenty thousand English foot soldiers were summoned to Hastings purportedly for overseas service. Instead of crossing the Channel, they were fleeced by the King's agent, Ranulf Flambard, of ten shillings each and then sent home. Anyone familiar with the local support system of the select fyrd described in Berkshire Domesday will be struck by the remarkable parallelism of the two passages. Why should each of twenty thousand (or, more safely, "a multitude of") Englishmen have enough money with him that the King's agent could collect a levy of ten shillings per man? To a common foot soldier ten shillings represented, by contemporary standards, a modest fortune. The answer is provided unambiguously in the Berkshire Domesday passage attesting that in 1066 each of the five hides paid the warrior-representative four shillings for his two months of service, giving him a total of five times four shillings or twenty shillings. The parallelism between the Berkshire custom and the 1094 episode extends even to the Latin phraseology. Florence of Worcester, writing of the 1094 episode, and the Domesday scribe, writing of the Berkshire arrangements of 1066, both use the term *ad victum* in explaining why the money was paid to the soldier.[25]

The episode of 1094 is, from the standpoint of the institutional historian, a piece of extreme good fortune, a happy bit of chance. It might not have happened; it might not have been recorded. But it did, and it was, and we are provided with a priceless glimpse of the select fyrd in 1094. Richardson and Sayles suggested that these Englishmen, like all others, were mer-

---

[24] *Anglo-Saxon Chronicle*, A.D. 1094; Florence of Worcester, *Chronicon ex Chronicis*, ed. Thorpe, II, 35; Henry of Huntingdon, *Historia Anglorum*, ed. Arnold, 217.

[25] Domesday Book, ed. Furley and Ellis, I, 56b; Florence of Worcester, *Chronicon ex Chronicis*, ed. Thorpe, II, 35.

cenaries,[26] but their suggestion will not stand close inspection. The ten shillings, quite obviously, are passing in the wrong direction—from the troops to the King, not from the King to the troops. It has even been argued that these Englishmen did not, after all, actually perform military service.[27] To be sure! If they had, we would have been told nothing of the ten shillings *ad victum,* but would have been provided only with another instance of unidentified *Angli* fighting overseas. Finally, it has been argued that, although these Englishmen were admittedly recruited on the Berkshire five-hide basis, they may merely have been victims of a clever bit of "fiscal antiquarianism."[28] This is simply to say that the one case in which a historical accident enables us actually to identify the recruitment system underlying the service of these *Angli* is, in fact, unique and that, in the other instances wherein the recruitment system underlying their service cannot be positively identified, some entirely different and unknown principle was at work. This is a possible interpretation, but an exceedingly unlikely and belabored one.

The other issue to be considered is this: were the feudal quotas of the king's tenants in chief established suddenly by William the Conqueror, or did they evolve slowly and only materialize in 1166 with the great feudal survey of Henry II, the *Cartae Baronum?* Here again there is a problem of evidence. We get no comprehensive data on feudal *servicia debita* until the *Cartae Baronum* and the scutage accounts in the Pipe Rolls of Henry II. There was no general survey of quotas during the century following the Conquest. Strictly speaking, not even the *Cartae Baronum* can be so described, for they recorded enfeoffments, not quotas. All the Pipe Rolls prior to Henry II's reign are lost save one, and that one—the roll of 31 Henry I—does not happen to record a scutage. None of these facts demonstrate that the quotas were Angevin rather than Norman; they leave the question open and send us on to more elusive evidence.

Before looking at examples of such evidence, we must make one crucial point. The five-hide select fyrd principle and the post-Conquest feudal quota principle are fundamentally different. The one was a national system governed by a standardized recruitment arrangement based on the hide; the other was a system of individual, arbitrary quotas based on private contracts and on the fee. Quite apart from the evidence, the hypothesis of an evolution from the one system to the other presents very serious, perhaps

---

[26] Richardson and Sayles, *Governance of Mediaeval England,* 54, n. 7.
[27] Prestwich, "Anglo-Norman Feudalism and the Problem of Continuity," 48.
[28] *Id.,* review of C. W. Hollister, *The Military Organization of Norman England, English Historical Review,* LXXXI (Jan. 1966), 107.

insurmountable, conceptual difficulties. Eric John, arguing vigorously for the direct evolution from Anglo-Saxon hidal recruitment to Anglo-Norman feudal recruitment, makes the candid statement: "At this point I had better confess that I cannot see how this was done."[29]

Turning to the evidence, one finds once again that it is scanty, yet wherever it exists it points to the high antiquity of the 1166 quotas and, in many cases, suggests strongly that they were established by William the Conqueror. A fresh look at the evidence, in other words, suggests that Round's hypothesis concerning the Norman introduction of knights' service, narrowly conceived, still stands.

To be sure, the *Cartae Baronum* of 1166 constitute the first *comprehensive* survey of knightly enfeoffments, but there are many older records that bring the *servicia debita,* in individual cases, back to a much earlier date. There has never been any doubt that some quotas were changed slightly. Some were in dispute for generations (the bishops of Worcester argued with the monarchy for many decades as to whether they owed fifty or sixty knights). Yet the evidence is strongly in favor of a general imposition of quotas by the Conqueror.

The point of the alleged "silence of the chroniclers" has recently been raised once again, so once again the question must be examined briefly. Excluding, for the sake of argument, the thirteenth-century St. Albans chroniclers who place the imposition of quotas in 1070, there remain other far more nearly contemporary reports. The Abingdon Chronicle states that as soon as the disturbances immediately following the Conquest had abated it was noted by the King's order how many knights should be demanded from episcopal sees and abbeys for the defense of the realm. Abbot Athelhelm of Abingdon then granted estates to men who would hold them of the abbey and in each case stipulated the obligations that accompanied the tenures.[30] The Ely chronicler, writing midway through the twelfth century, probably well before the *Cartae Baronum,* stated that in 1088 King William Rufus summoned the knights according to the quotas that his father had imposed on the lands of the Church.[31] Orderic, whose silence on the matter has been specifically and repeatedly alleged, declared that the Conqueror distributed lands to his knights in such a way that the realm should thereafter have sixty thousand men to answer the royal summons. The figure of sixty thousand is of course absurd—Orderic uses that particular figure repeatedly to indicate simply "a great many"—but, discounting the

---

[29] John, *Land Tenure,* 158.

[30] *Chronicon Monasterii de Abingdon,* ed. Joseph Stevenson (RS, 2, 2 vols., London, 1858), II, 3.

[31] *Liber Eliensis,* ed. E. O. Blake (London, 1962), 218.

sixty thousand, we are left with the statement itself, which suggests nothing less than a revolution in military tenures instituted by William the Conqueror. Thus speaks Orderic, and it would be well, once and for all, to acquit this irrepressibly loquacious man of the charge of silence.[82]

So much for the narrative sources. What of the records? First of all, the key date is not 1166 but 1156, the date of the first good Pipe Roll accounts of a scutage. The 1166 *Cartae Baronum* themselves contain comprehensive testimony to enfeoffments not only in 1166 but also in 1135 and show that enfeoffments changed only slightly between these two dates. Thus, the 1166 quotas are, by implication, carried back to 1135. And in individual cases one can carry them back much further. Fixed quotas appear in the Norman Bayeux Inquest of 1133 which almost surely attests to conditions on the Bayeux estates around 1100.

Records relating to particular fiefs sometimes enable us to carry back the 1166 quotas into the reign of the Conqueror. Anyone who is inclined to question the hypothesis that the feudal quotas were established by William the Conqueror should first look closely at the records of such estates as Evesham, Peterborough, and Abingdon. Evesham possessed estates totaling some 160 hides, many of them in Worcestershire, a county wherein the 300-hide Anglo-Saxon ship sokes have been clearly traced and in which, therefore, the related 5-hide rule surely obtained. At the rate of 1 man from every 5 hides, Evesham's 160 hides would yield a quota of 32 men to the Anglo-Saxon select fyrd. But the invaluable military summons of William the Conqueror to Abbot Aethelwig of Evesham of about 1072 alludes to a quota of only 5 men.[33] We know, from a charter of Henry I and from later Pipe Roll evidence, that Evesham's feudal quota wavered a bit, from $4\frac{1}{2}$ knights to 5 knights,[34] but at no time did the knightly quota approach the select fyrd quota of, presumably, 32 warriors. It was 5 knights in 1166; it was 5 knights in 1072.

At Peterborough the fyrd quota is exceedingly difficult to determine because of a widespread and irregular incidence of beneficial hidation combined with the fact that many Peterborough estates were assessed in geld carucates rather than hides. In a previous article I calculated the Peterborough fyrd quota at about 70, but this is decidedly tentative.[35] The feudal *servicium* in Henry II's Pipe Rolls is 60, with 64 fees existing on the

---

[82] Orderic Vital, *Historia Ecclesiastica*, ed. Le Prévost, IV, 7

[33] *Select Charters*, ed. William Stubbs (9th ed., Oxford, Eng., 1913), 97.

[34] *Red Book of the Exchequer*, ed. Hubert Hall (RS, 99, 3 vols., London, 1896), I, 301–302; *Pipe Roll 18 Henry II* (Pipe Roll Society, No. 18, London, 1894), 22; *Calendar of the Charter Rolls* (6 vols., London, 1903–27), I, 257.

[35] See C. W. Hollister, "The Knights of Peterborough and the Anglo-Norman Fyrd," *English Historical Review*, LXXVII (July 1962), 417–36.

estates in both 1166 and 1135.[36] Of these 64 fees, 62 are described by Walter of Whittlesey and John of Peterborough as having been created by Abbot Turold in about 1070.[37] The feudal quota of 60 is very high considering the size of the Peterborough estates, and, in consequence, the individual Peterborough knights' fees are singularly small.[38] It seems most likely that the 60-knight *servicium debitum* was a punitive quota imposed by the Conqueror in reply to the support given by Peterborough tenants to Hereward's rebellion. Indeed, Hereward himself appears to have been a Peterborough tenant.[39]

Abingdon held some 624½ hides in 1066, chiefly in Berkshire—where the 5-hide rule is unquestioned—with some land in Oxfordshire and a little in Gloucestershire. The assessment of 624½ hides in 1066 was reduced by 1086 to 425¼. Dividing these figures by five, one gets 5-hide fyrd quotas of about 125 men in 1066 dropping to about 85 men in 1086. But a knight list of William the Conqueror's time in the Abingdon Chronicle discloses only 31 fees.[40] The same chronicle reports that nearly all the Abingdon knights were required to join King William's Welsh campaign of 1081, and one might reasonably conclude that on this occasion Abingdon must have sent some 30 knights or so to the royal summons.[41] An almost identical number— 33 fees—is disclosed in the *Carta* of 1166, and Henry II's Pipe Rolls attest to a feudal quota of 30 knights.[42] Thus once again the enfeoffments of the Conqueror's time, utterly unrelated to the fyrd quota, are tightly correlated to the feudal quota as it emerges in Henry II's Pipe Rolls.

Robert S. Hoyt, incidentally, has observed in an unpublished paper that at Abingdon the double burden on the land of 5-hide quota and feudal quota is more than balanced by the Conqueror's reduction in hidage. In 1066, at 1 man per 5 hides, Abingdon owed 125 men to the select fyrd. In 1086, with the reduced hidage assessment, the same Abingdon estates owed 85 men to the select fyrd plus 30 knights to the feudal host, or a total of 115 men to both forces. In short, the single obligation in 1066 required 125 men; the double obligation of 1086 required 115 men. It must

[36] *Red Book of the Exchequer*, ed. Hall, I, 329; cf. *Chronicon Petroburgense*, ed. Thomas Stapleton (London, 1849), 168–75, where, in a document dating between 1113 and 1120, 64 Peterborough fees are reported.

[37] Walter of Whittlesey, in *Chronicle of Hugh Candidus*, ed. W. T. Mellows (London, 1949), 84, n. 4; John of Peterborough, *ibid.*, 85 n.

[38] In the Peterborough *Descriptio Militum* of about 1113–1120, fees of less than one hide are reported. (*Chronicon Petroburgense*, ed. Stapleton, 169–75.)

[39] Cf. *ibid.*, 175 (Ansford), with Domesday Book, ed. Furley and Ellis, I, 346, 376b.

[40] *Chronicon Abingdon*, ed. Stevenson, II, 4–6; cf. Domesday Book, ed. Furley and Ellis, I, 566–96.

[41] *Chronicon Abingdon*, ed. Stevenson, II, 10.

[42] *Red Book of the Exchequer*, ed. Hall, I, 305–306; *Pipe Roll 14 Henry II*, 203; *Pipe Roll 18 Henry II*, 15; see also D. C. Douglas, "Some Early Surveys from the Abbey of Abingdon," *English Historical Review*, XLIV (Oct. 1929), 618–25.

be added that other fiefs do not yield such tidy results, but it remains a possibility that there may be some significant connection between the Conqueror's uncharacteristically generous policy of widespread beneficial hidation and the establishment of a twofold military obligation on the land.

The quotas of Evesham, Peterborough, and Abingdon—five knights, sixty, and thirty—are all divisible by five. In this respect they are characteristic of the feudal quotas in general. The *Cartae Baronum* and Henry II's Pipe Rolls disclose a strikingly symmetrical system of round quotas. There are some exceptions to this rule, but the tendency is strong and unmistakable. Quotas of five knights, ten, twenty, forty, sixty, and so on, occur repeatedly. Round associated these figures with his hypothetical ten-knight constabularies. He was doubtless mistaken, yet clearly they suggest the work of a single authoritative assessor. If one can be forgiven for applying a hoary theological argument to this mundane problem, it may be said that such remarkable symmetry as one finds in the English feudal quotas cannot have been the accidental result of individual bargains hammered out over the decades; nor can it have arisen from the older five-hide recruitment system. For if one calculates the hides of the tenants in chief and divides by five, the resulting quotas are not round but bewilderingly miscellaneous. A single assessor was evidently responsible for this coherent structure of feudal quotas, and, in the light of all the evidence, one can confidently identify the assessor as being William the Conqueror.

The Round hypothesis, that the English feudal quotas were established by the Conqueror, has traditionally carried the corollary that William brought the feudal quota system into England from Normandy. Round assumed this without serious investigation, and his assumption was apparently confirmed early in the present century by Charles Homer Haskins.[43] Although Haskins' sources dated for the most part from the post-Conquest period, and largely from the twelfth century, he nevertheless argued persuasively that a coherent and encompassing system of feudal quotas existed in pre-Conquest Normandy and, indeed, served as William's model. Such a conclusion seemed unarguable, for if the Anglo-Norman *servicia debita* were introduced by the Conqueror, and if they had no Anglo-Saxon roots, where else might they have come from besides Normandy?

More recently, however, Haskins' conclusion has been effectively qualified in the writings of David Douglas, Lucien Musset, and Joseph R. Strayer.[44] As Strayer has pointed out, fixed quotas are conspicuously absent

---

[43] C. H. Haskins, *Norman Institutions* (Cambridge, Mass., 1918), vii, 8 ff., *et passim*.
[44] David Douglas, "The Rise of Normandy," in *Proceedings of the British Academy, 1947*

in enfeoffment charters issued by dukes of Normandy prior to the Conquest.[45] And although such quotas may have been developing, at least on Norman ecclesiastical estates, on the eve of 1066, they appear to have been not only far lower but also much less comprehensively established than those imposed by the Conqueror on the estates of post-Conquest England. In short, the feudal quota system of William the Conqueror's England was not a purely Norman importation. Rather, it was a bold extrapolation of limited and undeveloped Norman precedents, greatly expanded and systematized by the Conqueror as he exploited the vast opportunities afforded by his power over a conquered land. It is possible, therefore, to speak not only of the Norman impact on the development of English feudalism but also of the English impact on the development of Norman feudalism. The key word is not "importation" but "interaction." "It may be," writes Strayer, "that Normandy was made to conform to the English model, rather than the reverse."[46] Or, as Douglas has put it, "If English feudalism was essentially Norman, so also was Norman feudalism by the end of the eleventh century, in some sense, English."[47]

Such, then, are the implications of some of the evidence regarding certain crucial issues of the Norman Conquest. There are many other issues, and the diverse interpretations of various historians are apt to convey the impression of confusion and chaos. But, despite this appearance, one can detect a broad consensus developing in the independent and often concurrent investigations of many modern scholars of the Conquest. Agreement is assuredly not complete; far from it! Yet as one examines the works of such men as Michael Powicke, J. O. Prestwich, R. C. Smail, John Beeler, David Douglas (in his *William the Conqueror*), and others, he can see, beneath the surface controversy, a general consensus with varying emphases. All agree that the *servicia debita* were imposed by the Conqueror, that they represent an institutional break from the Anglo-Saxon past, that there were, nevertheless, important elements of institutional continuity between the military organizations of Saxon and Norman England, and that the first century of English feudalism was not so feudal as has sometimes been thought. Sir Frank Stenton himself, of course, was by no

(London, 1948), 101–30, and *William the Conqueror* (London, 1964), 281–84 *et passim;* Lucien Musset, "Aux origines de la féodalité normande," *Revue historique de droit français et étranger,* 4th Ser., XXIX (1951), 150; Joseph R. Strayer, review of *Recueil des actes des ducs de Normandie, 911–1066,* ed. Marie Fauroux, in *Speculum,* XXXVII (Oct. 1962), 609–10.

45 *Recueil des actes des ducs de Normandie, 911–1066,* ed. Marie Fauroux (Caen, 1961), Nos. 80, 140.

46 Strayer, review of *Recueil des actes,* ed. Fauroux, 610.

47 Douglas, *William the Conqueror,* 283.

means insensitive to the continuity of institutions across the line of 1066. Smail has written:

Even from the late-eleventh century, when English feudal institutions were still in process of formation, the Conqueror and his sons after him relied on non-feudal sources of recruitment. It is doubtful whether the military needs of the English kings could ever have been met from feudal sources alone.[48]

Michael Powicke, in his fine book on military obligation in medieval England, stresses both the importance and the limitations of William I's new feudal army and gives due attention to the Anglo-Norman mercenaries and the English.[49] Beeler, in his articles and in his illuminating new book on English medieval warfare, puts slightly greater stress on the service of the knightly feudal contingents, but presents the same heterogeneous picture of the Anglo-Norman army and makes the same distinction between fyrd and feudal host.[50] Prestwich, although hostile to the renewed emphasis on institutional continuity, has himself recently suggested an important and previously neglected example of it in the military households of the Saxon and Norman kings, which constituted the cores of pre- and post-Conquest English armies.[51] Douglas has written recently: "The successful imposition of tenure by service upon his magnates in respect of their English lands must be regarded as one of the most notable of the Conqueror's achievements." But he also states that "the Norman impact upon England was to be drastically modified by English tradition under the direction of the Norman king."[52] And Douglas emphasizes the Conqueror's use of the five-hide fyrd and mercenaries. These statements epitomize the fundamental position that is coming more and more to be accepted.

It is good to have controversy, but it is good, also, to find that the majority of investigators are not looking at the problem in totally diverse ways, to find some reason for believing that, as our knowledge grows, there is developing the tendency for dispassionate scholars to agree on certain fundamental points. And at the moment there is reason for optimism regarding the problem of the Norman Conquest.

[48] R. C. Smail, "The Art of War," in *Medieval England*, ed. A. L. Poole (2 vols., Oxford, Eng., 1958), I, 137.
[49] Powicke, *Military Obligation in Medieval England*, 1–47 *passim*.
[50] John Beeler, "Composition of Anglo-Norman Armies," *passim*, and *Warfare in England, 1066–1189* (Ithaca, N. Y., 1966).
[51] Prestwich, "Anglo-Norman Feudalism and the Problem of Continuity," 50–52.
[52] Douglas, *William the Conqueror*, 273, 265.

2

NORMANDY, FRANCE AND THE
ANGLO-NORMAN REGNUM*

DUDO OF SAINT-QUENTIN, in his half-legendary account of the creation of Normandy c. 911, tells an engaging story about the Viking Rolf and the King of France. Rolf, after receiving the lands of the lower Seine from King Charles the Simple and doing him homage, was told that recipients of royal grants were expected to kiss the king's foot. Rolf replied that he would never bend his knee to anyone or kiss anyone's foot. But in response to further French entreaties he allowed one of his warriors to do the honors. The warrior seized the king's leg, tipped him over backwards, raised the royal foot high in the air and kissed it, amidst the uproarious laughter of the Norse onlookers.[1]

The story may be pure invention.[2] Dudo wrote more than a century after the alleged event, and he always tended to show the dukes of Normandy in the best possible light. But whether real or legendary, the anecdote was believed and enjoyed by Normans of later generations, and it influenced their perception of the Franco-Norman feudal relationship. Hence the up-lifting of King Charles's foot has a significance quite independent of its historical veracity. It suggests that the traditional view of Norman feudal subordination to the French crown may well be oversimplified — that the reality may be more complex.

According to the traditional view, the rulers of England after the Norman Conquest were at once kings and dukes. As kings of England they were subordinate to no one, but as dukes of Normandy they owed homage to the kings of France. This clear-cut formula raises several difficulties. For one thing, the Norman kings shared with other monarchs of their time the deep

* I am grateful to the National Endowment for the Humanities, the American Philosophical Society, the Social Science Research Council, the Fulbright Commission, the John Simon Guggenheim Memorial Foundation, and the Warden and Fellows of Merton College, Oxford, for their help in supporting the research for this paper, to Marjorie Chibnall, Fred A. Cazel, Jr., James W. Alexander, Charles T. Wood, Thomas K. Keefe, John W. Baldwin, Andrew W. Lewis, and John LePatourel for their valuable suggestions (they do not necessarily concur in all that I say), and to my research assistant, Mrs. H. A. Drake. A preliminary version of this paper was presented at the fall, 1973, meeting of the Conference on British Studies, at the Folger Library, Washington, D.C.

[1] Dudo of Saint-Quentin, *De Moribus et Actis primorum Normanniae Ducum*, ed. Jules Lair, Mémoires de la Société des Antiquaires de Normandie, 3rd. series, 3 (Caen, 1865), 169.

[2] The reality of Rolf's homage at Saint-Clair-sur-Epte in c. 911 is itself in doubt: see, for example, Michel de Bouard, "Le Duché de Normandie," in *Histoire des institutions françaises au moyen âge*, ed. Ferdinand Lot and Robert Fawtier, 1 (Paris, 1957), 3–4; and Lucien Musset, "Naissance de la Normandie," in *Histoire de la Normandie*, ed. M. de Bouard (Toulouse, 1970), p. 97. Ferdinand Lot is inclined to accept the lifted foot story: *Fidèles ou vassaux?* (Paris, 1904), p. 181, n. 3, as is Jean-François Lemarignier, *Recherches sur l'hommage en marche et les frontières féodales* (Lille, 1945), pp. 77, 83 and n. 37.

conviction that homage of any sort compromised the royal dignity. Kingship still retained, in the Norman epoch, much of the personal, sacred quality that had characterized it in the early Middle Ages. One did not cease to be a king when he crossed from England to Normandy any more than one ceased to be a priest when he left his parish. Another difficulty is that the kings of England and France seem to have had very different views as to what the traditional Franco-Norman homage meant. The twelfth-century kings of France were coming gradually to regard the Norman dukes as powerful yet essentially ordinary feudal vassals, but the Anglo-Norman monarchs, when they harked back to their ancestor Rolf and the discomfited Charles the Simple, could reasonably raise the question of who was subordinate to whom.[3]

During the century prior to the Norman Conquest of England there is evidence of only one act of homage of a Norman duke to a French king, and even this single instance is a little ambiguous. In 1060 Duke William the Bastard met the young Philip I in the neighborhood of Dreux on the Franco-Norman frontier, where the two princes agreed to a "firm peace and serene amity." Scholars are inclined to believe that Duke William rendered homage to King Philip at that time, and probably he did. But no source refers to homage specifically, and perhaps one should be content with Sir Maurice Powicke's apt observation that "medieval theory did not draw a very clear line between the feudal contract and what we should call a treaty."[4] J.-F. Lemarignier has concluded from the scattered evidence of the tenth and eleventh centuries that the homage occasionally rendered by the Norman dukes to the French kings was homage of a very special kind: *hommage de paix* — homage of peace and concord — always performed on the frontier, never at the lord's court.[5] *Hommage de paix*, Lemarignier argues, was essentially a relationship of equals meeting on neutral ground to negotiate a peace treaty, usually in the presence of their respective armies. The homage rendered to the one prince by the other by no means involved the clear-cut subordination or the full range of feudal obligations that were involved in

---

[3] Lot, *Fidèles ou vassaux?*, pp. 177–235, stresses the subordination of the Norman dukes to the French kings but is challenged by Lemarignier, *Hommage en marche*, pp. 74–93, who emphasizes the reciprocity and ambiguity of the relationship. The debate is of long standing: see H. Prentout, *Étude critique sur Dudon de Saint-Quentin* (Paris, 1916), pp. 207–49; J. Flach, *Les Origines de l'ancienne France*, 4 (Paris, 1917), 111–72; and L. Valin, *Le Duc de Normandie et sa cour* (Paris, 1910), pp. 25–37.

[4] Sir Maurice Powicke, *The Loss of Normandy*, 2nd. ed. (Manchester, 1960), p. 80. On the 1060 meeting see Lot, *Fidèles ou vassaux?*, p. 200; Philip I was a minor at the time. See also David C. Douglas, *William the Conqueror* (London, 1964), p. 38, where it is suggested that William may have been sent to France on his accession in 1035 to do homage to his royal overlord, Henry I. The hypothesis is not unreasonable but it is supported by no contemporary source. The idea first turns up five or six generations later in Wace, *Roman de Rou*, ed. Hugo Andresen, 2 (Heilbronn, 1879), 150.

[5] Lemarignier, *Hommage en marche*, pp. 81–85 and passim; Cf. P. Petot, "L'Hommage servile: Essai sur la nature juridique de l'hommage," *Revue historique de droit français et étranger*, 4th Series, 6 (1927), 82–84.

the more common *hommage vassalique*.[6] Lemarignier cautions, however, that the distinction between *hommage de paix* and *hommage vassalique* became precise only in the twelfth and thirteenth centuries. The concepts overlapped in the period of the earlier Norman dukes, during which time the two parties probably entertained differing notions as to the degree, if any, of Norman subordination.[7] Much depended on specific political circumstances — on the relative military strength of king and duke at particular moments, and on the degree to which they required one another's support. During the turbulent period of William the Bastard's minority, for example, Henry I of France exercised his suzerainty over Normandy in support of the young duke,[8] whereas William in his later years was frequently at odds with the French king and behaved as though no feudal tie had ever existed.

The question of French suzerainty over Normandy is riddled with ambiguities. On the one hand, there was apparently a tradition of French royal participation in the making of a Norman duke. Just before his invasion of England, Duke William formally nominated his son, Robert Curthose, to the ducal succession in the presence of King Philip I and with his consent, and three decades earlier the king of France had given formal sanction to the Conqueror's own accession.[9] On the other hand, the ducal government was altogether immune from French intervention. Normally a feudal lord's more important benefactions received confirmation from his suzerain, but no charter of Duke William's was ever confirmed by the king of France. Indeed, not a single extant act of King Philip I relates in any way whatever to Norman lands or customs. Philip I's acts sometimes bear on Anjou, Flanders, Poitou, the Auvergne and other great vassal principalities, but never on Normandy.[10] In this practical, administrative sense, Duke William had no suzerain.

The singular authority that William exercised over his duchy on the eve of

[6] The custom of *hommage de paix* or *hommage en marche* was not limited to the Franco-Norman relationship; it is also to be found in the feudal relations between, among others, the dukes of Normandy and the counts of Anjou, Maine and Brittany (Lemarignier, *Hommage en marche*, pp. 73–74, 113–22) and between the kings of England and Scotland.

[7] Lemarignier, *Hommage en marche*, p. 84; Petot, "L'Hommage servile," p. 82, n. 1.

[8] Douglas, *William the Conqueror*, p. 45, where it is also pointed out that Duke Robert I, in 1031, assisted King Henry I "per debitum fidei sibi": *Gesta Normannorum Ducum*, ed. Jean Marx (Rouen, 1914), p. 105.

[9] On Robert Curthose's nomination see Florence of Worcester, *Chronicon ex chronicis*, ed. Benjamin Thorpe, 2 (London, 1849), 12; C. W. David, *Robert Curthose, Duke of Normandy* (Cambridge, Mass., 1920), pp. 12–13 and n. 42. By 1067 Curthose began to appear in charters as *comes Normannorum*: ibid., p. 13 and n. 46. On the French consent to Duke William's accession see Douglas, *William the Conqueror*, p. 38; Lot, *Fidèles ou vassaux?*, pp. 193, 196–97. In 1120 and 1137 Louis VI "conferred Normandy" on Anglo-Norman sons and heirs.

[10] *Recueil des actes de Philippe I er roi de France (1059–1108)*, ed. M. Prou (Paris, 1908), nos. 33, 41, 157, 158 (Anjou); 72, 80, 81, 115 (Flanders); 83, 84 (Poitou); 135 (Auvergne); and passim. Philip occasionally grants French lands and privileges to Norman churches (nos. 111, 122, 127, 167), just as the lords of Normandy occasionally grant Norman lands and revenues to French churches. But Philip holds strictly aloof from benefactions and landholding within Normandy, and the same is true of his successor, Louis VI: *Louis VI le Gros: Annales de sa vie et de son règne (1081–1137)*, ed. Achille Luchaire (Paris, 1890), passim. Cf. Powicke, *Loss of Normandy*, p. 79.

the Norman Conquest has been much discussed.[11] To put it briefly, his power substantially exceeded that of any other French territorial prince of his time. Indeed, it exceeded the power of the king of France himself over his own royal domain.[12] The Norman duke exercised ancient regalian rights such as the enforcement of peace and justice; he enjoyed a monopoly on coining; the military service of vassals was assessed more rigorously in Normandy than elsewhere in France and was enforced on a regular basis; William's barons could build castles only with his permission, and he claimed the right to place his garrisons in them at will.[13] Moreover, Normandy differed from all other major principalities of France in the remarkably precise definition of its frontiers and in the uniformity of its legal customs. The duchy was a compact territorial block with boundaries (most of them marked by rivers) that closely approximated the jurisdictional boundaries of the ecclesiastical province of Rouen.[14] Untroubled by the vague frontiers, diverse local customs and internal jurisdictional muddles of other French principalities, pre-Conquest Normandy was politically coherent and autonomous to a degree unmatched elsewhere in feudal Europe. William's singular status is suggested by the fact that he was mentioned by name and ducal title in a special Norman form of the *Laudes Regiae*, traditionally reserved for the acclamation of a king or emperor. In an eleventh-century text of the *Laudes* from the church of Rouen, the traditional words, "Christus vincit, Christus regnat, Christus imperat. Exaudi Christe," are followed first by the normal acclamation of the (unnamed) king of the French, and then by the altogether unique phrase, "Guillelmo, Normannorum duci, salus et pax continua!" — a token, as Ernst Kantorowicz puts it, "of the curious sovereignlike position which the duke of Normandy enjoyed in his duchy."[15] Jacques Boussard, taking all the pre-Conquest evidence into account, concludes that the Norman duke "exercised a power analogous to that of a king."[16]

William's already considerable authority and prestige were enormously

[11] See C. H. Haskins, *Norman Institutions* (Cambridge, Mass., 1918), pp. 3–61; Powicke, *Loss of Normandy*, pp. 38–42; Douglas, *William the Conqueror*, pp. 133–55; M. de Bouard, "Sur les origines de la Trêve de Dieu en Normandie," *Annales de Normandie* 9 (1959), 169–89; Jean Yver, "Les Premières Institutions du duché de Normandie," *Settimane di studio del Centro italiano di studi sull'alto medioevo* 16 (Spoleto, 1969), 299–366; Jacques Boussard, "La Notion de royauté sous Guillaume le Conquérant: ses origines et ses prolongements," *Annali della Fondazione Italiana per la Storia Amministrava*, no. 4 (Milan, 1967), pp. 48–55.

[12] Boussard, "Notion de royauté," p. 49; Charles T. Wood, "Regnum Francie: A Problem in Capetian Administrative Usage," *Traditio* 23 (1967), 125–27; de Bouard, "Le Duché de Normandie," pp. 16, 22; Powicke, *Loss of Normandy*, p. 79.

[13] The duke's rights in William the Conqueror's time are conveniently summarized in the *Consuetudines et Iusticie* of 1091, printed in Haskins, *Norman Institutions*, pp. 281–84; cf. pp. 60, 277–81.

[14] Lemarignier, *Hommage en marche*, pp. 9–72.

[15] Ernst H. Kantorowicz, *Laudes Regiae* (Berkeley, 1958), pp. 166–71. William's reluctance to use the ducal title after his coronation (see below) suggests that this formulary probably antedates the Norman Conquest.

[16] Boussard, "Notion de royauté," p. 55. This power had developed appreciably during William's own regime.

enhanced in 1066 when he acquired the venerable title, *rex Anglorum*. The Christmas coronation at Westminster Abbey did not, of course, make William *rex Normannorum*, yet from that moment onward his rule over Normandy ceased to be simply "ducal." From the perspective of contemporary political theory the royal anointing had transformed William from a mere feudal prince into a priestly figure, an image of Christ the King.[17] He was acclaimed with the *Laudes Regiae* at his coronation and regularly thereafter: "To the most serene William, the great and peacegiving king, crowned by God, life and victory."[18] At every recital of the Mass, in England and Normandy alike, William was mentioned by name and by royal title.[19] And contemporary descriptions of his coronation speak of his exchanging the status of *dux* for that of *rex:* "William determined to wear the crown he had won," writes Guy of Amiens, "and, with the name of duke renounced, be made a King."[20]

At this point one must proceed with the greatest caution. In all likelihood, the *Laudes,* the reference to King William in the Mass, and the ecstatic flights of contemporary writers on William's coronation reflect a sense of awe and jubilation rather than a reasoned solution to a problem of political terminology. Boussard expresses the problem succinctly: "A duke, a feudatory of the kingdom of France, becomes king of England, the equal of the king of France, and achieves an indissoluble union between his fief and his kingdom."[21] What, then, is William's status in Normandy? Having "renounced" his ducal title for a royal one does he now rule Normandy as king? There is no clear answer. Contemporaries do not appear to have thought the matter through, and King William himself took no consistent position. One is left with the impression that the king and his people were content to leave the question open.

The ambiguity permeates William's post-Conquest charters and seal. The legend on his seal describes him as king of the English and "protector"

---

[17] See *Die Texte des normannischen Anonymus*, ed. Karl Pellens, Veröffentlichungen des Instituts für Europäische Geschichte, Mainz, 42 (Wiesbaden, 1966). Among the numerous works on the writings of the Anglo-Norman Anonymous see especially G. H. Williams, *The Norman Anonymous of 1100 A.D.* (Cambridge, Mass., 1951).

[18] Douglas, *William the Conqueror*, pp. 249–50; Kantorowicz, *Laudes Regiae*, pp. 171–79; Guy of Amiens, *Carmen de Hastingae Proelio*, ed. Catherine Morton and Hope Muntz (Oxford, 1972), p. 50.

[19] Douglas, *William the Conqueror*, pp. 259–60 and 260 n. 1; in France the privilege of being included by name in the Mass had been reserved for the king alone and never granted to any of his great vassals: Robert Fawtier, *The Capetian Kings of France*, trans Lionel Butler and R. J. Adam (London, 1960), p. 76.

[20] *Carmen*, p. 48: "disponit ferre coronam, / Et ducis abiecto nomine, rex fieri"; see also p. 4: "Mutasti comitis regali nomine nomen / Quod tibi nobilitas contulit et probitas"; and p. 38: "Nomine postposito ducis, et sic rege locato, / Hinc regale sibi nomen adeptus abit." Cf. William of Poitiers, *Histoire de Guillaume le Conquérant*, ed. Raymonde Foreville (Paris, 1952), p. 222: ". . . novo admirandoque ardore ad honestos et ingentes actus accenditur dignissimus rex: quod nomen, posito ducis nomine, libens acceptat stilus noster" (apparently derived in part from *Carmen*, p. 38, above).

[21] Boussard, "Notion de royauté," p. 47.

(*patronus*) of the Normans.[22] Before the Conquest he usually styled himself in his charters *dux Normannorum* but occasionally he was *comes Normannorum* and, more rarely, *princeps Normannorum.*[23] After his coronation he was titled in his English charters simply *rex Anglorum,* whereas in charters relating to Normandy he seems to have favored the noncommittal *rex Anglorum et princeps Normannorum,* though he also occasionally titled himself *patronus Normannorum et rex Anglorum, rex Anglorum* only, and even *rex Anglorum et dux Normannorum.*[24] His barons occasionally refer to him in their own Norman charters as *rex et princeps* and, rarely, as *rex et dux.*[25] Contemporaries such as William of Poitiers suggested a way of cutting through the problem by eulogizing the Conqueror as an "emperor," pointing out that he had conquered Britain where Caesar himself had failed.[26] And the anonymous writer of a poem on William's death weaves together several of these themes into a dissonant counterpoint: after titling William "Rex Anglorum et Dux Normanniae: / Cenomannis Dominus patriae," he afterward concludes, "Rex de Duce se fecit postea, / Dignissimum Romana laurea."[27] One must beware

[22] "Hoc Normannorum Willelmum nosce Patronum si" (on the equestrian side) "hoc anglis regem signo fatearis eundem" (on the majesty side): *Facsimiles of Royal and Other Charters in the British Museum,* 1, *William I–Richard I,* ed. George F. Warner and Henry J. Ellis (London, 1903), pl. 1.

[23] *Recueil des actes des ducs de Normandie de 911 à 1066,* ed. Marie Fauroux (Caen, 1961), pp. 49–50. One encounters still other titles, such as *marchio et dux* (ibid., no. 219.)

[24] It is possible, though far from certain, that William's sparing use after the Conquest of the titles *dux* and *comes* is connected with Curthose's occasional use of the *comes Normannorum* style after 1066 (above, n. 9). On William's post-Conquest Norman titles see *Regesta Regum Anglo-Normannorum,* ed. H. W. C. Davis, et al., 4 vols. (Oxford, 1913–69), 1, Appendix, nos. 15, 16, 21, 36; *Les Actes de Guillaume le Conquérant et de la Reine Mathilde pour les abbayes caennaises,* ed. Lucien Musset (Caen, 1967), passim, where the normal title is *Willelmus rex Anglorum, princeps Normannorum et Cenomannorum*; but no. 12 (a 12th-century copy) reads *Gwillermus Anglorum rex excellentissimus ac Normannorum dux*; see also R. C. Van Caenegem, *Royal Writs in England from the Conquest to Glanvill,* Selden Society 77 (London, 1959), 143, where it is stated that in trustworthy original charters the Conqueror's style is normally *Willelmus rex Anglorum,* coupled in rare instances with *princeps* or *patronus Normannorum.* His signing formula is *Signum Guillelmi* (or *Willelmi) regis Anglorum* (ibid., and *Actes de Guillaume le Conquérant,* ed. Musset, nos. 3, 5, 8, 9, 15, 17, 19) or, alternatively, *Signum Willelmi regis Anglorum principis Normannorum et Cenomannorum* (Musset, nos. 4, 7, 18), or *Signum Willelmi regis Anglorum et ducis* (or *comitis) Normannorum* [*et principis Coenomannorum*] (Musset, nos. 6, 10).

[25] *Actes de Guillaume le Conquérant,* ed. Musset, nos. 3, 5, 7. No further light is cast on the problem by numismatic evidence. English coins of the Norman kings bear the name *Willelmus* (or *Henricus* or *Stephanus) rex Anglorum* on the obverse and the name of the minter and minting place on the reverse: George C. Brooke, *A Catalogue of English Coins in the British Museum: The Norman Kings,* 2nd ed. (London, 1950), passim. Extant Norman coins of the eleventh and early twelfth centuries are too few to permit exact dating; the great majority of them bear the name of the minter on the reverse and, on the obverse, simply the word *Normannia,* without reference to the ruling prince: Victor Luneau, "Quelques deniers normands inédits de XIe siècle," *Revue Numismatique,* 4th Series, 10 (1906), 306–16; 15 (1911), 86–96; see also Lucien Musset, "A-t-il existé en Normandie au XIe siècle une aristocratie d'argent?" *Annales de Normandie* 9 (1959), 285, 291.

[26] William of Poitiers, *Histoire,* pp. 246–54; Guy of Amiens, *Carmen,* p. 4; Percy E. Schramm, *Geschichte des Englischen Königtums im Lichte der Krönung* (Weimar, 1937), p. 30.

[27] *Scriptores Rerum Gestarum Willelmi Conquestoris,* ed. J. A. Giles, Caxton Society 3 (1845), 73.

of wresting logical distinctions from these accolades. They convey contemporary impressions and nothing more. But the impression of most contemporaries would have been that William's coronation had made him a king and that as a king he governed his dominions — not England alone but Normandy and Maine as well. The impression would have been strengthened by the close etymological tie between the noun "king" and the verb "he governed" — *rex rexit*. For example, the epitaph composed by Thomas archbishop of York for William's tomb reads in part,

> Qui rexit rigidos Normannos, atque Britannos
> Audacter vicit, fortiter obtinuit, . . .
> Rex magnus parva jacet hic Guillelmus in urna;
> Sufficit et magno parva domus domino.[28]

Thus, although William was never formally *rex Normannorum* he was an anointed king who governed the Normans in Normandy and England alike.[29] The chroniclers speak of his Norman followers in England prior to his coronation electing him king.[30] Modern historians would probably be inclined to assume that the Normans acted here in their capacity as future lords of English lands — as Englishmen to be — but the language of the sources makes it doubtful that they had any such distinction clearly in mind. Again one must remember that kingship was regarded as a personal quality — that the best contemporary accounts of the coronation speak of William exchanging his former status as duke for his new status as king. The greater men among William's Norman followers in 1066 held extensive lands in Normandy, to which they hoped to add such English lands as William might give them, but the distinction between their Norman and English holdings was altogether secondary to the central reality: that William, the lord to whom they had done personal homage for all their lands, was about to be transformed from a mere duke into a consecrated king. And in order for a lord to become a changed man, his vassals must give their consent.

So it was that when William crossed to Normandy in 1067 he returned to his homeland as a king. At his Easter court at Fécamp he astonished visiting French noblemen with the regal treasures that he had brought from England — vessels of gold and silver for his banquet table, splendid garments woven and crusted with gold, "befitting the magnificence of a king."[31] Displays of this sort, despite their constitutional irrelevance, would have inten-

---

[28] Orderic Vitalis, *Historia Ecclesiastica*, ed. Auguste Le Prévost, 5 vols. (Paris, 1838–55), 3: 257; *Gesta Normannorum Ducum*, p. 148.

[29] This point is skillfully discussed in Douglas, *William the Conqueror*, pp. 263–64.

[30] *Gesta Normannorum Ducum*, p. 136: "ab omnibus tam Normannorum quam Anglorum proceribus rex electus"; the "election" by the Normans is discussed in fuller detail by Guy of Amiens (*Carmen*, p. 52) and by William of Poitiers (*Histoire*, pp. 216–20), who speaks of a preliminary "election" by William's Normans at Berkhampstead followed by their formal acclamation at the Westminster coronation. See Schramm, *Königtums*, pp. 27–28; Douglas, *William the Conqueror*, pp. 206, 249.

[31] Orderic, *Historia*, 2: 168; William of Poitiers, *Histoire*, pp. 260–62.

sified the feelings of contemporary Normans that their ruler was a king indeed. And as one might expect, the chroniclers who describe William's post-coronation activities in Normandy refer to him always as *rex*, never as *dux*. The gold-encrusted garments were worn at the Fécamp Easter court by "the king and his companions."[32] "All Normandy was overjoyed at the arrival of *Guillelmo rege*."[33] Lanfranc was elected to the archbishopric of Rouen, "et rex Guillelmus cum optimatibus suis . . . concessit."[34]

It might be argued that these writers are simply honoring William with his highest title. Indeed, precisely this explanation is offered by a Poitevin writer of the later twelfth century in reference to Henry II. Listing Henry's various lordships — Poitou, Aquitaine, Anjou, Touraine, Maine, Normandy and others — he adds, "but in consideration of the honor and reverence of the royal name he is called king of the English."[35] But if any such thought lurked in the minds of Norman writers a century earlier, it never became explicit. And there is danger in attributing to the mental processes of eleventh-century Normans and Anglo-Normans the analysis of a later writer of Poitiers, speaking of a foreign prince whose various jurisdictions were far more numerous and more consciously defined than those of William the Conqueror. The legal and logical difficulties surrounding William's royal status in Normandy seem scarcely to have occurred to his own Norman followers. Their response to the coronation was deeply emotional: proudly aware that their leader had been anointed a king, and that he dressed, acted, and governed like a king, they regarded him as their king.

In the years following the Conquest, England and Normandy became in many respects two parts of a single political unit. The greatest post-Conquest magnates of England, or their close kinsmen, were major landholders in Normandy as well. Most of the larger Norman abbeys acquired properties and daughter houses in England. The single Anglo-Norman ruler was, in short, supported by a single, homogeneous feudal aristocracy that shared with him the responsibility of governance and formed the core of his royal court and household. The court was of course itinerant, and it changed in no significant way as it moved back and forth across the Channel. In England and Normandy alike it consisted of the ruler, his great men, and their retainers, all of whom shared not only a single language, culture and feudal ideology but likewise, as Normans, a deep awareness of common achievement and ethnic identity. William of Poitiers conveys the sense of pride that must have animated the whole Norman nobility when he acclaims the triumphant race that conquered Apulia, subjected Sicily, attacked Constantinople, struck fear in Turkish breasts and brought King Harold of England to his

---

[32] William of Poitiers, *Histoire*, pp. 260–62.

[33] Orderic, *Historia*, 2: 168.

[34] Orderic, *Historia*, 2: 170; Lanfranc declined the honor. William is likewise called *rex* in Normandy by William of Jumièges (*Gesta Normannorum Ducum*, pp. 138, 139 and passim) and by the author of *De obitu Willelmi* (ibid., p. 145).

[35] Richard of Poitiers, in *Recueil des historiens des Gaules et de la France* ed. Martin Bouquet, et al. 24 vols. (Paris, 1738–1904), 12: 417 (hereafter cited as HF).

destruction.[36] Two generations later, at the onset of the battle of the Standard in 1138, the chords could still be struck: "Nobles of England, most illustrious Normans — for it is proper that on the eve of battle you should recall your name and your ancestors — no one ever stood successfully against you. Audacious France you have often humbled, fertile England succumbed to you, wealthy Apulia you caused to flourish again, renowned Jerusalem and noted Antioch you subjected."[37] The eleventh-century Norman world produced more than its share of celebrated heroes, but William alone had won a crown. And the admiration of his Norman contemporaries finds expression in the words of the Conqueror's biographer: "Vivet, vivet in longum rex Guillelmus."[38]

The cohesion of William's two dominions must not be exaggerated. Each had its own ecclesiastical primate and its own episcopacy. Norman and English legal customs remained distinct (as did, to a lesser extent, the customs of Wessex, Mercia and the Danelaw).[39] English feudal military quotas, though framed more or less on the Norman model, were much heavier than those of Normandy. The hereditary status of Norman vicomtes was far more solidly entrenched than that of English sheriffs. There were no Norman hundreds or hundred courts. Money might be moved back and forth between the treasury at Winchester and the treasury at Rouen, yet the two retained their separate identities and officials, and in later years became the foci of two separate exchequers. Finally, the English and Norman judicial systems, although subordinate to the single itinerant court, were in many respects distinct, even to the point that, in the twelfth century, separate English and Norman justiciars emerged.[40] Nevertheless, from the administrative standpoint the two dominions had much in common. Above all else, the traditional regalian rights of the kings of England were closely approximated by the unprecedented ducal authority over pre-Conquest Normandy. Thus William, as heir to both traditions, could govern England and Normandy with almost equal authority and independence. He could rule as a king throughout his dominions, surrounded by a single *curia*, served by a single chancellor, a single scriptorium, a single household.

Just as William continued to be perceived as a king when he was in Normandy, so also he was viewed as ruling Normandy by his royal authority. In 1082 a suit between Gilbert abbot of Saint-Wandrille and William archbishop of Rouen was heard in Normandy *coram Rege*.[41] In 1080, at the Council of Lillebonne, William took in hand the reform of the Norman

---

[36] William of Poitiers, *Histoire*, pp. 228–30; cf. David C. Douglas, *The Norman Achievement* (Berkeley, 1969), pp. 110–12.

[37] Henry of Huntingdon, *Historia Anglorum*, ed. Thomas Arnold, Rolls Series (1879), p. 262.

[38] William of Poitiers, *Histoire*, p. 230.

[39] *Leges Henrici Primi*, ed. L. J. Downer (Oxford, 1972), pp. 106–108 and passim.

[40] See H. G. Richardson and G. O. Sayles, *The Governance of Mediaeval England* (Edinburgh, 1963), pp. 224–25; G. H. White, "The Household of the Norman Kings," *Transactions of the Royal Historical Society*, 4th Series, 30 (1948), 127–55; Haskins, *Norman Institutions*, pp. 112–14.

[41] Ferdinand Lot, *Études critiques sur l'abbaye de Saint-Wandrille* (Paris, 1913), no. 39.

Church. Orderic Vitalis, who provides the most detailed description of the council, views it as a product of the royal will: "The king's mandate was obeyed," he writes, "and by the king's foresight and the advice of his barons sound provision was made for the prosperity of God's church and the whole realm (*totiusque regni*)."[42] Throughout the canons of the council William is referred to consistently as *rex*, and the point is hammered home by the recurring phrase, *tempore Rodberti comitis* [A. D. 1027–35] *vel Guillelmi regis*.[43] After quoting the canons, Orderic concludes by saying that the council was held in a "royal village" on the Seine.[44]

The statement that this Norman synod, dealing chiefly with Norman affairs, was providing for the prosperity of "the whole realm" suggests that Orderic was thinking of Normandy as a part of an Anglo-Norman *regnum*. Doubtless he used the term in a non-technical sense and without serious reflection; he does not apply it to Normandy consistently throughout his history, nor do other writers of the period.[45] Nevertheless, Orderic's terminology was by no means unprecedented. Dudo of Saint-Quentin, writing generations before, had occasionally called the Norman duchy a *monarchia* or a *regnum*, and the latter term occurs in other early Norman sources as well.[46] It had been used now and then in Norman ducal charters ever since A.D. 968,[47] and Duke William himself employed it on occasion. The dating clause of a charter of 1038 concludes, "Quo tempore, monarchiam regni Nortmannorum Vuillelmus, Rotberti comitis filius, obtinebat."[48] William's charter of 1050 in favor of Saint-Évroul describes Normandy as *regnum nostrum*.[49] And a grant to Saint-Ouen, dated 29 June 1053, is confirmed by Duke William, Matilda his wife, "et Rodberti eorum filii, quem elegerant ad gubernandum regnum post suum obitum."[50]

[42] Orderic, *Historia*, 2: 315; I am using here the excellent translation in Marjorie Chibnall's as yet incomplete new edition of Orderic: 3 (Oxford, 1972), 25–35.

[43] Orderic provides a good text of the canons of Lillebonne: *Historia*, ed. Le Prévost, 2: 316–23; see also *Sacrorum Conciliorum*, ed. J. D. Mansi, et al. (Florence and Venice, 1759–98), 20: 67–74, 555; see further Haskins, *Norman Institutions*, pp. 32–35; Boussard, "Notion de royauté," p. 55; Heinrich Böhmer, *Kirche und Staat in England und in der Normandie im XI. und XII. Jahrhundert* (Leipzig, 1899), p. 32 and n. 3.

[44] Orderic, *Historia*, 2:323: *in vico regali*.

[45] E.g., William of Poitiers, *Histoire*, pp. 258–60, on the Conqueror's return to Normandy in 1067: "Patriam, non minus regno caram sibi . . . in statu quem volebat, invenit"; Orderic, *Historia*, 4: 309: "Henricus . . . in magna tranquillitate regnum ultra mare et ducatum citra gubernavit"; but on other occasions Orderic uses *regnum* in the Anglo-Norman context: below, notes 98–100.

[46] Dudo, *De Moribus*, p. 281 and passim; Lot, *Fidèles ou vassaux?*, pp. 191 n. 4, 198 n. 5; E. A. Freeman, *The History of the Norman Conquest of England*, 6 vols. (Oxford, 1870–79), 1: 167, 609–12.

[47] *Recueil des actes des ducs de Normandie*, pp. 71 (Duke Richard I, 968: *in regno nostro*), 186 (Duke Robert, 1030: *temporalis regni statum*), 203 (Duke Robert, 1028–33: *regni nostri*), 215 (Duke Robert, 1027–35: *Monarchiam regni Normannorum*), 247 (Gradulf abbot of Saint-Wandrille, c. 1038–40: *in regno Robertus*).

[48] Ibid., p. 243: charter of Richard of Évreux, subscribed by Duke William.

[49] Ibid., p. 289.

[50] Ibid., p. 344: an original.

The word *regnum,* as it appears in these pre-Conquest Norman sources, must not be interpreted too strictly. Norman dukes might claim to rule a *regnum* but they did not yet style themselves *reges.* Indeed, one finds *regnum* applied in tenth and eleventh-century sources to such feudal principalities as Brittany, Burgundy and Aquitaine.[51] Nevertheless, at least by Duke William's time the notion of a *regnum Normanniae* was coming to signify Normandy's growing independence from the *regnum Franciae.* William of Poitiers illuminates the contemporary meaning of the term in an important passage describing Normandy's rise to a position of political autonomy. The passage begins with the proud assertion that William had never been the French king's *miles.* Normandy, William of Poitiers explains, had long before been subject to the kings of France, but in his own time it had been raised virtually to a kingdom (*prope in regnum evectam*) — a thing which its early dukes had never dared attempt.[52] The term *regnum,* cautiously qualified by *prope,* is used here as nowhere else with obvious deliberation and a sense of technical precision — as a sign of the new ducal freedom from French royal suzerainty, and perhaps also as an allusion to the duke's comprehensive powers over his duchy.

Such was the status of Normandy prior to William's coronation. Returning as *rex* to a duchy that had already been regarded at times as a *regnum,* he proceeded to govern it by his royal authority and was hailed as a king wherever he went. Under these circumstances it is understandable that William's *regnum Angliae* and his *regnum Normanniae* might sometimes merge in the minds of post-Conquest writers such as Orderic into a single Anglo-Norman *regnum.* As for the traditional subordination to France (such as it was), King William would have nothing to do with it. His royal anointment had inaugurated a new order of affairs in northern Europe. In the one known charter of King Philip I that the Conqueror signs (at the siege of Gerberoy in 1079), his *signum* appears at the same level as the French king's own, and he uses only the title *rex Anglorum.*[53]

The evidence from William the Conqueror's time, varied and ambiguous though it is, demonstrates Normandy's gradual drift from the fitful French suzerainty of earlier days toward complete independence and, after the Conquest, toward a kind of half-conscious absorption into the larger kingdom. But the drift was abruptly reversed at the Conqueror's death in 1087 when his two great dominions were split between his eldest sons. William

[51] Lot, *Fidèles ou vassaux?,* p. 198 n. 5: "Le mot avait le sense vague de 'province,' ou 'gouvernement.'" Cf. Wood, "Regnum Francie," pp. 117–47 passim, and especially pp. 122–23, 128–37 and 142–43, where the various shades of meaning are expertly discussed; *Recueil des actes des ducs de Normandie,* p. 90 (. . . *in Aquitaniae regno locata:* A.D. 1012.) Coins of Alan III count of Brittany (1008–40) bear the legend "Alan Rix": Faustin Poey d'Avant, *Monnaies féodales de France,* 1 (Paris, 1858), 45.

[52] William of Poitiers, *Histoire,* p. 66; cf. J.-F. Lemarignier, *Le Gouvernement royal aux premiers temps capétiens (987–1108)* (Paris, 1965), p. 118.

[53] Lemarignier, *Gouvernement royal,* p. 118; *Recueil des actes de Philippe I,* no. 94.

seems to have sanctioned this division only with considerable reluctance. With Robert Curthose in open rebellion, the Conqueror might very well have preferred to bequeath everything to his second son, William Rufus.[54] But Robert Curthose's supporters urged the right of the first-born son, and their arguments were strengthened by the fact that Curthose had already been formally installed years before as the Conqueror's successor in the duchy.[55] The result was that Normandy passed once again under the rule of a prince who was unambiguously a *dux*, whose calamities forced him repeatedly to acknowledge the overlordship of the king of France, and who almost certainly did him homage.[56] Three times Curthose called on Philip I to aid him against Rufus, though on at least two of these occasions Rufus bought the French king off.[57] And according to one (slightly doubtful) source Philip was called on to mediate between the brothers in 1091.[58]

In 1096, however, Normandy's relationship with France changed drastically once again when Curthose pawned the duchy to Rufus and departed on the First Crusade. Without the advice or consent of Philip I, Normandy now passed under the governance of the king of England — a man who had never done homage to a French king and never intended to. Curthose took his ducal title with him to the east, and Rufus ruled the duchy as *rex Anglorum*, much as his father had done, but unencumbered with the ambiguities that had surrounded the Conqueror's status in Normandy. The new situation was supposed to be temporary, but in all probability Rufus did not expect Curthose to return and intended to hold the duchy against him if he did.[59] Rufus seems to have had it in mind to rule Normandy indefinitely in his royal capacity. He issued charters for both England and Normandy under the sole title, *rex Anglorum;* his one seal bears the identical legend on both sides: Willelmus Dei gratia rex Anglorum.[60] And far from respecting the overlordship of Philip I, Rufus devoted several years to aggressive campaign-

[54] See John Le Patourel, "The Norman Succession, 996–1135," *English Historical Review* 86 (1971), 225–50. But compare L. J. Engels, "De obitu Willelmi," *Melanges Christine Mohrmann* (Utrecht, 1973), pp. 209–255.

[55] David, *Robert Curthose*, pp. 11–12; Haskins, *Norman Institutions*, p. 67 and n. 19, where charters of Curthose as duke of Normandy date his reign from 1077–78; cf. *Anglo-Saxon Chronicle, s.a.* 1079.

[56] Curthose appeals for military aid to Philip I as *dominus suus rex Francorum* (or *Franciae*): William of Malmesbury, *Gesta Regum Anglorum*, ed. William Stubbs, 2 vols., Rolls Series (1887–89), 2: 363; Florence of Worcester, *Chronicon*, 2: 34.

[57] *Anglo-Saxon Chronicle, s.a.* 1090, 1094; *Gesta Normannorum Ducum*, p. 270; Florence, *Chronicon*, 2:26–27; Malmesbury, *Gesta Regum*, 2:363–64; Henry of Huntingdon, *Historia Anglorum*, p. 217.

[58] *Gesta Normannorum Ducum*, p. 270.

[59] See David, *Robert Curthose*, p. 124; E. A. Freeman, *The Reign of William Rufus*, 2 vols. (Oxford, 1882), 1:555–56; 2:312–13; C. W. Hollister, "The Strange Death of William Rufus," below, 66-7.

[60] Pierre Chaplais, "The Seals and Original Charters of Henry I," *English Historical Review* 75 (1960), 265 n. 1; *Regesta*, 1, Appendix, nos. 73, 74; *Actes de Guillaume le Conquérant*, ed. Musset, p. 133.

ing against the French Vexin. He is even said to have aspired to Philip's throne.[61]

Rufus's death and Curthose's return in 1100 left England and Normandy divided once more, but only briefly.[62] In September 1106 the Conqueror's youngest son, King Henry I of England, routed Curthose's forces at Tinchebray and assumed control of the duchy. Curthose was consigned to lifelong imprisonment, and Henry began his eventful twenty-nine year rule of the Anglo-Norman state.

At the time that Henry conquered Normandy from his brother, no crowned king of England had ever done homage to a king of France. The Conqueror, as we have seen, had probably done homage to Philip I in 1060, but after 1066 he viewed his relationship to Philip as that of a fellow king and an equal.[63] And Philip would have had no strong grounds for demanding William's homage as king if he had already received William's homage as duke. The Conqueror could believe that he was Philip's peer whereas Philip might well assume that William remained bound by a homage that he had rendered years before the Conquest.[64] A similar ambiguity underlay the good relations between Henry I and King David of Scotland: before becoming King of Scots in 1124, David had done homage to Henry for the earldom of Huntingdon; after David's coronation neither king seems to have pressed the issue of the traditional Scottish royal homage to the English crown. The feudal relationship between Henry and David had previously been made clear. Whatever the legal niceties, Henry could regard the king of Scotland as his feudal man, and David was spared the embarrassment of doing homage to a fellow king.[65] Henry's conquest of Normandy, however, created a problem of feudal relationships that could not be screened by any such ambiguities. For when Henry took control of the duchy he was already crowned and had never done homage to a king of France.

In order to sever the ancient tie between France and Normandy, Henry I quite consciously eschewed the ducal title altogether and ruled simply as *rex Anglorum*. William the Conqueror had advanced toward this goal, and Wil-

---

[61] Suger, *Vie de Louis VI le Gros*, ed. Henri Waquet (Paris, 1964), p. 10.

[62] It is possible that sometime between 1100 and 1106 Curthose did homage to Philip I's son, the future Louis VI. Orderic "quotes" Louis as claiming in 1119 that Curthose had become *hominem meum* (*Historia*, 4:376). Louis became *rex designatus* in 1098–1100 (*Louis VI*, ed. Luchaire, no. 8 and pp. 289–93) and king in 1108; Curthose was away on the Crusade in 1096–1100 and in captivity from 1106 until his death in 1134. In c. 1105 Curthose is said to have called vainly for help from *dominum suum regem Francorum*: Malmesbury, *Gesta Regum*, 2:463.

[63] Above, note 53.

[64] It is likely, though not certain, that William did homage to Philip in 1060: above, notes 4, 8.

[65] See R. L. G. Ritchie, *The Normans in Scotland* (Edinburgh, 1954), p. 388; cf. W. L. Warren, *Henry II* (Berkeley, 1973), pp. 177–80. In a somewhat similar case, Anselm archbishop of Canterbury agreed in 1107 not to press for the profession of obedience from Gerard archbishop of York because Gerard had earlier professed obedience to Canterbury in his suffragan capacity as bishop of Hereford: Eadmer, *Historia Novorum in Anglia*, ed. Martin Rule, Rolls Series (1884), pp. 186–87.

liam Rufus had achieved it, but only in the absence of a recognized duke
who was alive and free and might return. After 1106, however, with Curthose in strict captivity, Henry's rule over Normandy could hardly be regarded
as temporary. It is tempting, nevertheless, to speculate that Henry I's idea
may have been to recreate the legal situation of 1096–1100, continuing to
recognize the captive Curthose as a kind of phantom duke and governing
Normandy as king in his "absence," declining homage to France on the
grounds that the real duke still lived and had already done the homage. One
can perhaps detect hints of such an attitude in the writings of Henry's
apologist, Orderic Vitalis, who has Henry say to Curthose on the eve of the
battle of Tinchebray, "I have come here not out of the cupidity of worldly
ambition, nor to take away your right to your duchy, but in response to the
tearful complaints of the poor," etc.[66] Orderic continues to call Curthose *dux*
after the battle and, indeed, throughout his life.[67] At his death in 1134, he is
Robertus II dux Normannorum to both Orderic and Robert of Torigny.[68]
Moreover, both these Norman writers invariably call Henry *rex* throughout
his reign, until his death in 1135 when he is styled *Henricus rex Anglorum et
dux Normannorum*.[69] It is almost as though the ducal title, like some unwanted
bequest, passed to Henry only on Curthose's death.

Such a notion, though superficially plausible, does not bear close scrutiny.
Henry I, as we shall see, was willing by 1120 or 1121 to claim the ducal title
for himself when it suited his purposes. And when the Norman writers give
the captive Curthose his ducal title it is much more likely a spontaneous act
of courtesy than a calculated statement of legal right.[70] John of Worcester, in
his passage on Curthose's death, refers to him as "brother of King Henry
and formerly duke of Normandy, but afterwards captured in battle by the
king while in Normandy at a certain castle called Tinchebray."[71] Perhaps
John of Worcester is proposing an alternative theory to Orderic's, but it
seems likelier that he is simply being more precise. Likelier still, Henry I and
his contemporaries had no coherent position on the matter at all.

However this may be, Henry eschewed the ducal title for a number of
years and always refused homage to the king of France. Like William the
Conqueror, Henry regarded kingship more as a personal quality than as a
territorial authority. And like his Capetian contemporaries, he was firmly

[66] Orderic, *Historia*, 4:227.

[67] Ibid., pp. 232–34, 403, 486.

[68] Ibid., 5:18, 42, 161; *Gesta Normannorum Ducum*, p. 292.

[69] Orderic, *Historia*, 1:190; *Gesta Normannorum Ducum*, p. 314.

[70] One finds contemporary instances of men being honored with titles which they no longer
legally bear: Eudes count of Champagne had been convicted of murder and deposed from his
comital office c. 1063, but both he and his son, Stephen of Aumale (who died in the 1120s)
continued to be titled *comes* by Orderic and others (Orderic, *Historia*, 3: 319, 346; 4:199, 315–16,
473 and passim), while at the same time Orderic also gave the title *comes* to Hugh, the ruling
count of Champagne between 1093 and 1125 (3:390–91; 4:213, 373.)

[71] John of Worcester, *Chronicle*, ed. J. R. H. Weaver (Oxford, 1908), p. 38: "Rotbertus frater
regis Heinrici, quondam comes Normannie sed postmodum ab illo Normannie morante apud
quoddam castrum quod Tenercebrei dicitur in bello captus. . . ."

committed to the notion that a king can do homage to no one [72] His English and Norman dominions remained, as in the days of his father, bound together by a single Anglo-Norman baronage and ruled by a single itinerant court and household. In the twenty-nine years of Henry's rule, even more than in the twenty-one years of William I's, Normandy was governed as if it were the southern part of a trans-Channel kingdom.

It is not to be thought, of course, that a ruler as cautious as Henry I would challenge the French monarchy by proclaiming publicly his own kingship over Normandy. Rather, he simply avoided claiming the ducal title and proceeded to rule as king. Following the lead of William Rufus, he issued his writs for England and Normandy alike as *Henricus rex Anglorum*. He seems to have raised no serious objection to others referring to him as *rex et dux;* in original royal diplomas of the period drawn up in the scriptoria of the benefited religious houses, Henry is occasionally styled *rex Anglorum et dux Normannorum*. [73] The fact that he was willing to sanction charters in this form suggests that his approach to the matter of the ducal title was not altogether consistent. Certainly the occasional appearance of the *rex et dux* formula belies the existence of any firm notion among Henry's ecclesiastics that Curthose retained the office in captivity. Even the letters of Archbishop Anselm reveal at least a temporary confusion over Henry's title. In answer to a letter of *Henricus rex Anglorum* announcing his conquest of Normandy, Anselm replied *Henrico, gratia Dei glorioso regi Anglorum et duci Normannorum*, [74] and again, just afterwards, he addressed the king in similar words. [75] But by 1109 Anselm seems to have gotten his signals straight: in response to a letter of *Henricus gratia Dei rex Anglorum, Anselmo*, etc., the archbishop replies *Domino suo carissimo Henrico, gratia Dei glorioso regi Anglorum, Anselmus*, etc. [76]

The practice of Henry's own chancery is quite consistent. Among the

---

[72] Suger, *Louis VI*, p. 221, n. 2; cf. Fawtier, *Capetian Kings*, p. 80. In his agreement with Curthose in 1101, King Henry had taken pains to obtain a formal release from the homage he had rendered some years before his coronation: Orderic, *Historia*, 4:114.

[73] Van Caenegem, *Royal Writs*, p. 153; *Regesta*, 2, nos. 809, 919, 1183, 1468, 1470, 1569, 1587, 1588, 1591, 1726, 1927. The earliest of these — no. 809, Rouen, 1106–7 — is regarded as a forgery by Henri Chanteux: "Recueil des actes de Henri Ier Beauclerc," (unpublished MS in the Archives du Calvados), no. 170*, on the grounds that the subscriptions are not autographs, the handwriting is of the late twelfth century, and the charter contains diplomatic archaisms and anomalies in form. See also *Regesta*, 2, no. 1548, a charter of John bishop of Sées (A.D. 1127): Henry signs as *Henrici regis Anglorum* but appears in the dating clause: *duce autem Normannorum Henrico rege Anglorum*: ibid., p. 361; and cf. ibid., no. 1742 (p. 376). All the above charters are originals (later copyists sometimes altered the royal styles of their originals) but none are products of Henry's chancery. Two, however, have been annotated by chancery scribes (nos. 919, 1588): see T. A. M. Bishop, *Scriptores Regis* (Oxford, 1961), nos. 368, 625; Chaplais, "Seals and Original Charters," p. 272 (B. 4); C. N. L. Brooke and G. Keir, "Henry I's Charter for the City of London," *Journal of the Society of Archivists* 4, no. 7 (1973), 563.

[74] S. *Anselmi Cantuariensis Archiepiscopi Opera Omnia*, ed. F. S. Schmitt (Edinburgh, 1946–61), 5, ep. 401, 402.

[75] Ibid., ep. 404 (A.D. 1106/1107.)

[76] Ibid., ep. 461, 462.

considerable number of extant original charters prepared by identifiable chancery scribes, only one adds the ducal title to the normal *Henricus rex Anglorum* in the address clause. That one exception is dated A.D. 1133, twenty-seven years after Henry's conquest of Normandy, and it was drawn up by a royal chancery scribe noted for his idiosyncratic formulae (Scriptor xiii). Moreover, apart from the *rex et dux* address clause, the charter testifies in the strongest possible terms to Henry's royal status in Normandy: *Henricus rex Anglorum et dux Normannorum* has, for the prosperity and preservation of his kingdom (*regni mei*), taken the hospital of Falaise "into the custody and protection of the royal hand" (*manus regie*), and he has done so by his royal authority (*regia auctoritate*).[77] The subject of the charter is exclusively Norman, and it is addressed to the archbishop of Rouen, yet the protection of the *manus regis,* at least in contemporary Capetian usage, bound the recipient directly and officially to the crown.[78] Such protection could never be given by a duke or count, for only the king had a "royal hand." Yet in this late charter alone, of all surviving products of royal chancery scribes, Henry is *rex et dux.* In all others, even when the charter is issued from Normandy and deals solely with Norman matters, he is simply "king of the English."[79]

The charter evidence is corroborated by the evidence of Henry's seals. The legend on the Conqueror's seal, as we have seen, expresses his dual role as "king of England" and "protector of the Normans," whereas William Rufus's seal, which remained in use during his 1096–1100 occupancy of Normandy, titles him on both sides *Dei gratia rex Anglorum.*[80] Rufus's *rex Anglorum* style doubtless reflects the perception that he was ruling in the place of a legitimate but absent duke, and it is likewise no surprise that Henry I, on his accession to the English throne in 1100, employed a similar legend: *Henricus Dei gratia rex Anglorum,* on both sides of his seal.[81] Much more significant is the fact that when Henry replaced this seal in 1106 or 1107, probably just after his conquest of Normandy, the legends on the new seal were identical to those of the former one which he had used while ruling England alone.[82] Not until c. 1120 did he replace the seal of 1106/1107 with a new seal reading *Henricus Dei gratia dux Normannorum* on the equestrian side (with the traditional *Henricus Dei gratia rex Anglorum* on the

[77] Archives départementales du Calvados, H. 4033 (original): *Regesta,* 2, no. 1764 and Appendix, no. 270: a somewhat corrupt text from P. R. O. Transcripts 8/140 B, II, p. 4; Chaplais, "Seals and Original Charters of Henry I," pp. 265, 267; Bishop, *Scriptores Regis,* no. 65. On Scriptor xiii see ibid., pl. 17(a), and *Regesta,* 4:19.

[78] I am grateful to Professor Andrew W. Lewis for calling this point to my attention.

[79] E.g., *Regesta,* 2, no. 1200; Bishop, *Scriptores Regis,* pl. 11(b): *H. rex angl'* to Richard bishop of Bayeux and all his barons and *fideles* of the Hiémois, in favor of the abbey of Saint-Martin, Troarn, issued at Rouen [1110–18]. Similarly, *Regesta,* 2, nos. 1229, 1689, 1690, etc.

[80] Chaplais, "Seals and Original Charters of Henry I," p. 265 and n. 1.

[81] Ibid., p. 264: This is the so-called "second seal" of Henry I, the "first seal" being a forgery.

[82] Ibid., the so-called "third seal," used between 1006/7 and c. 1120–21: *Henricus Dei gratia rex Anglorum* on both sides. Chaplais makes the very plausible suggestion that the previous, virtually identical "second seal" may have been lost or damaged during the battle of Tinchebray, in which Waldric the chancellor played an active military role (Orderic, *Historia,* 4:230.)

majesty side as before).[83] And as will presently be shown, there was a reason for this later change. For now, suffice it to say that until c. 1120 the evidence of Henry's seal legends supports the testimony of the charters — that Henry ruled Normandy by his authority as "king of the English."

This notion finds further support in the contemporary Norman chronicles. In an age obsessed with ceremonies of initiation — investiture, consecration, coronation and the like — it is striking that no writer alludes to any sort of formal installation of Henry I as duke of Normandy. Robert Curthose had received solemn oaths from the Norman barons c. 1066 at a ceremony in which Duke William formally proclaimed him his heir and successor in the duchy and Philip I gave his consent.[84] The ceremony was repeated at Bonneville after the Conquest, and still later, in 1077 or 1078, Curthose seems to have been officially invested with the Norman duchy.[85] In subsequent generations of the twelfth century Geoffrey of Anjou, the future Henry II, the young Henry his son, Richard I and John were all, in one way or another, formally installed in the ducal office.[86] But no such formalities accompanied Henry I's assumption of power over Normandy. His avoidance of ceremony, and of the ducal title, brought the immediate advantage of enabling him to sidestep the tradition of French royal participation in the making of a Norman duke.[87] As the first ruler to acquire unqualified control of Normandy after acceding to the English throne, Henry would have nothing to do with any such tradition. And by ruling the duchy through his existing authority as *rex* he could evade the formalities of the ducal initiation, in connection with which the French king might either have asserted unwanted prerogatives or taken offense if they had been denied him.

It was politically essential, of course, that Henry obtain oaths of homage and fealty from his Norman tenants-in-chief, but he seems to have received them over a period of time rather than in the ceremonial atmosphere of a single great council. The most formal assembly in the aftermath of Henry's victory at Tinchebray was convoked at Lisieux, probably in October, 1106. Here Henry established regulations against violence in Normandy and took into his hands the ducal estates that Curthose had alienated. Henry acted not as Normandy's new duke, but, as Orderic puts it, "by royal authority."[88] The

---

[83] Orderic, *Historia*, 4:264–65. The extreme date range for the introduction of this "fourth seal" (which remained in use until Henry's death) is 1114–21; Chaplais argues persuasively for 1120 or 1121. The "fourth seal" first occurs on a charter dated at Windsor, 30 January, 1121 (*Regesta*, 2, no. 1247). The "third seal" last occurs on a charter issued at Mortain sometime between 1114 and 1118 (ibid., no. 1187); the *Regesta* editors tentatively assign it to 1118 on the grounds that Henry I is known to have campaigned in southern Normandy in that year.

[84] Florence of Worcester, *Chronicon*, 2:12; David, *Robert Curthose*, pp. 12–13.

[85] David, *Curthose*, pp. 15, 18; *Gesta Normannorum Ducum*, p. 268; Haskins, *Norman Institutions*, p. 67 n. 19.

[86] Schramm, *Königtums*, pp. 46–48; Lot, *Fidèles ou vassaux?*, pp. 204, 217–18; Haskins, *Norman Institutions*, p. 130; Robert of Torigny, *Chronicle*, in *Chronicles of the Reigns of Stephen, Henry II and Richard I*, ed. Richard Howlett, 4 vols., Rolls Series (1884–89), 4:148, 161, 216; Roger of Hoveden, *Chronica*, ed. William Stubbs, 4 vols., Rolls Series (1868–71), 3:3; 4:87.

[87] Above, note 10.

[88] Orderic, *Historia*, 4:233: *regali sanctione*. At a second Lisieux council dated March, 1107,

English historian Eadmer of Canterbury, writing of the same period, speaks of Normandy being set in order "under the king's peace."[89] And Archbishop Anselm seems to reflect a similar view when he describes Henry, in a letter of 1107 or 1108 to Pope Paschal II, as "the king who is lord of England and Normandy."[90]

The notion of Henry's "royal jurisdiction" over Normandy is a recurring theme in the histories and records of the period. Orderic reports that in 1112 Henry arrested Robert of Bellême on the charge of having made no rendering, as "the king's vicomte and official," of the "royal revenues" from his Norman vicomté of Argentan, Exmes and Falaise.[91] Throughout the great Norman war of 1118–19 Henry maintained firmly "his royal authority."[92] His local officials in Normandy are *regii satellites* and *justiciarii regis*, and the castellan of Gisors is *munio regii dangionis*.[93] Likewise, a Norman road is "the king's road," and Norman knights are *regii milites*.[94] Normans do homage to Henry "in right of his crown,"[95] and Norman prelates are summoned to a council at Rouen *jussu regis*.[96] That such terms are more than mere stylistic idiosyncrasies of contemporary historians is made clear by the express statements in Henry's own charters for Normandy that he is acting "by royal authority" or "by royal power."[97] Recurring throughout the reign, in charters for England and Normandy alike, these formulae demonstrate that the impressions of Orderic and Robert of Torigny were shared by the royal chancery itself.

In the years of Henry's Anglo-Norman rule, as in those of his father, the idea of a trans-Channel *regnum* hung in delicate balance alongside that of a *regnum Angliae et ducatus Normanniae*. Orderic can refer to Henry's English kingdom and Norman duchy, but he can also speak of Henry, at a council at Rouen, making arrangements "for the peace of his *regnum*."[98] He reports that Henry permitted the prelates of his *regnum* — including Geoffrey archbishop of Rouen and his Norman suffragans — to attend the papal

---

which may well be a confused duplicate notice of the first, Orderic has Henry establish edicts for the enforcement of peace *regali potestate*: p. 269.

[89] Eadmer, *Historia Novorum*, p. 184: "Normannia ergo sub regia pace disposita. . . ."; but immediately afterwards, "rex ipse in regnum suum reversus est."

[90] *S. Anselmi Opera*, 5, ep. 430: "rex qui dominatur Anglis et Normannis."

[91] Orderic, *Historia*, 4:305: ". . . cur de regiis redditibus ad vicecomitatum Argentomii et Oximorum, Falesiaeque pertinentibus, ut regis vicecomes et officialis, rationem non reddiderit. . . ."

[92] Ibid., p. 346: ". . . sceptriger Henricus regio stemmate rigidus perstitit. . . ."

[93] Ibid., pp. 448, 451, 453.

[94] Ibid., pp. 456–58; similarly in Robert of Torigny, *Gesta Normannorum Ducum*, p. 295: the victory at Rougemontier in 1124 was won by the *exercitus regis* led by King Henry's commanders ("a ducibus Henrici, regis Anglorum.")

[95] Orderic, *Historia*, 4:484: "rex Henricus ei subjugavit regali justitia."

[96] Ibid., p. 495.

[97] Among Henry's charters concerning Norman affairs that include the terms *regia auctoritate* or *regia potestate* are Regesta, 2, Appendix, nos. 177, 178, 248, 266, 270, and Haskins, *Norman Institutions*, pp. 107, 298, 299, 307.

[98] Orderic, *Historia*, 4:309, 329: "Ibi rex Henricus de pace regni tractavit" (1118).

council of Reims in October, 1119,[99] and shortly afterwards Henry explained to Pope Calixtus II that he was keeping his brother and other Tinchebray captives in prison "for fear of their causing disturbance to me or my *regnum*."[100] Henry's own Norman charters disclose the same ambiguities. One encounters such phrases as *regnum meum Anglie et ducatum Normannie*,[101] but also such phrases as *pro statu regni mei* or *pro statu totius regni mei*.[102] Indeed, a charter of 1131 is issued *pro statu totius regni mei* with the approval of *episcopis, baronibus, et personis regni mei et Normanniae* — and the culprit is once again Scriptor xiii.[103]

Thus, although contemporary historians and chancery scribes speak pointedly and unanimously of Henry's "royal authority" over Normandy, they are uncertain whether Normandy is within the *regnum* or distinct from it. Their choice can turn either way, depending on whether they are emphasizing the ancient realm of *Henricus rex Anglorum* or the wider realm of *Henricus rex*. But it is out of precisely such uncertainty that a basic change in political status might silently occur. A duchy ruled by a duke had become a land (sometimes *ducatus*, sometimes *regnum*) ruled by the royal authority of an anointed king and might in time have become, unambiguously, a kingdom — or, rather, a part of a greater Anglo-Norman kingdom. A century before, Hugh, avoué of Saint-Riquier, had received Abbeville and its surroundings from the king of France; Hugh's son and heir, Enguerran, had married the widow of a count of Boulogne, and their son, Hugh II, began styling himself "count of Ponthieu," deriving his title from his mother's status as a count's widow — and therefore a "countess."[104] Thus did the lordship of Ponthieu, ruled by a countess's husband, become the county of Ponthieu — a product of just such ambitions and ambiguities as existed in the Anglo-Norman court of William I, William II and Henry I.

In retrospect, we know that Normandy was eventually absorbed into France, and we must beware of permitting this knowledge to mislead us. The conquest by Philip Augustus in 1203–1204 could not have been anticipated a century earlier, when the French kings were just beginning the systematic exploitation of their feudal rights over the great principalities. The example of Ponthieu illustrates the political fluidity of an age in which suzerainties were uncertain and shifting — an age of the birth and unpredictable expansion of monarchies. In such an age, the destiny of Normandy — whether as

---

[99] Ibid., p. 373; cf. p. 378.

[100] Ibid., p. 402: ". . . mihi vel regno meo."

[101] *Regesta*, 2, no. 1742 and Appendix, no. 266 (as corrected from the original charter; the hand is that of Scriptor xiii: Bishop, *Scriptores Regis*, no. 64). See also *Regesta*, 2, nos. 1688 ("pro statu et incolumitate regni nostri et ducatus Normanie") and 1917; printed in Haskins, *Norman Institutions*, pp. 299 and 107 (both are copies).

[102] *Regesta*, 2, no. 1687 (Appendix, no. 248): "pro statu totius regni mei"; cf., no. 1764 (Appendix, no. 270): "pro statu quoque et incolumitate regni mei"; both are from the hand of Scriptor xiii: Bishop, *Scriptores Regis*, nos. 675, 65; see also *Regesta*, 2, no. 1700 (Appendix, no. 252): "pro statu regni mei" (a copy; the original is lost.)

[103] Ibid., no. 1687, as above.

[104] *Recueil des actes des comtes de Pontieu (1026–1279)*, ed. Clovis Brunel (Paris, 1930), pp. iii-iv.

a part of the French *regnum* or the English — was a wide open question. Indeed, it was one of many open questions. Who could tell, for example, whether the Holy Roman Emperors would succeed in their effort to assert their suzerainty over the kings of France?[105] Who could have predicted that the papal attempt at suzerainty over England, so firmly rejected by William I, would succeed in the reign of John? The Capetians held title to Bourges as successors to vicomtes yet ruled it as kings. The twelfth-century kings of Scotland ruled their English earldoms of Huntingdon and Northampton as "kings of the Scots," issuing charters under the royal Scottish seal and styling themselves *rex Scottorum* in all their dealings with their English honor.[106] Their authority over these possessions was so extraordinarily broad as to bring to mind the Norman analogy. But because the honor of the Scottish kings was scattered across ten English shires and even included property in London, there could be no question of its ever drifting *en bloc* out of the English *regnum* into the Scottish.[107]

A much closer parallel to the Anglo-Norman configuration is to be found in the Norman kingdom of Sicily, which had its formal inception with the coronation of Roger II in 1130. Like Henry I, Roger had used the resources of a wealthy and well-organized island-state (Sicily) to conquer a mainland duchy (Apulia) formerly ruled by his kinsmen. Roger's uncle, Robert Guiscard, had earlier united Sicily and Apulia under his supreme rule.[108] But at Guiscard's death in 1085 (as at William I's in 1087) the island and the mainland duchy were divided, and they remained so until Roger II's conquest of 1127–1130. Since Roger's 1130 coronation was performed by the "antipope" Anacletus II, it was not recognized by Pope Innocent II and his supporters until 1139, when Roger and Innocent came to terms. At that time the theory was advanced, and accepted by king and pope alike, of a *restitutio regni Siciliae:* Roger's kingdom of Sicily was viewed not as a new creation but as the revival of "a kingdom that according to ancient historians had existed of old."[109] And Roger II's official biographer, Alexander of Telese, writing at the same time, asserts that it had always been Sicily's prerogative to be ruled by kings from Palermo.[110] Whatever the historical merit of this *re-*

---

[105] Luchaire, *Louis VI*, nos. 349, 358; the effort continued into the reign of Frederick Barbarossa: Fawtier, *Capetian Kings*, pp. 83–85.

[106] *Regesta Regum Scottorum*, 1, ed. G. W. S. Barrow (Edinburgh, 1960), pp. 98–100; cf. Warren, *Henry II*, p. 177; Warren (p. 179) draws the analogy between Scotland-Huntingdon-England and England-Normandy-France.

[107] William Farrer, *Honors and Knights' Fees*, 3 vols. (London, 1923–25), 2:294–416.

[108] Helene Wieruszowski, "Roger II of Sicily, *Rex-Tyrannus*, in Twelfth-Century Political Thought," SPECULUM 38 (1963), 47–48. Robert Guiscard, duke of Apulia, controlled Palermo but granted much of Sicily to Roger his brother, Roger II's father, to be held under Guiscard's suzerainty.

[109] Ibid., p. 51; from the bull *Quos dispensatio* (27 July, 1139): PL 179:479; cf. David Douglas, "Two Coronations," *Économies et sociétés au moyen âge*, Mélanges offerts à Edouard Perroy, Études, 5 (1973), 95–96.

[110] Alexander of Telese, "De Rebus Gestis Rogerii Siciliae Regis," in *Cronisti e scrittori sincroni della dominazione normanna*, ed. G. Del Re, 1 (Naples, 1845), 101; Wieruszowski, "Roger II," p.

stitutio theory, it created a legal fiction that parallels to a remarkable degree the constitutional situation of Henry I's Anglo-Norman state: Roger II, king of the "ancient" *regnum Siciliae,* likewise ruled mainland territories that had not traditionally been a part of his *regnum.* Moreover, he ruled them as king, adopting the marvelously ambiguous title, "King of Sicily, of the duchy of Apulia and of the principality of Capua."[111] Alexander of Telese reports that Roger's barons suggested the extension of his Sicilian *regnum* to his mainland dominions,[112] which were in fact commonly called after 1130 the "kingdom of Italy."[113] Before long the *regnum Siciliae* had come to embrace in common opinion both the island and mainland territories of the *rex Siciliae,* and this situation continued until the wars of the Sicilian Vespers (1282–1302). In 1302, the island and mainland split into two separate kingdoms — the *regnum Siciliae* of the Aragonese kings of the island, and the *regnum* of the Angevin kings of Naples, who likewise employed the title *rex Siciliae* — thus leading to the creation of the fifteenth-century "kingdom of the Two Sicilies."[114]

The absorption of a mainland duchy into an island *regnum* might well have occurred in the Anglo-Norman state just as in the Norman kingdom of the South. That Normandy eventually joined the French *regnum* rather than the English is in large measure a consequence of the Capetian kings' tenacity and luck in clinging to the rights of their ancient suzerainty and gradually expanding them. At first, however, the Norman drift from *feodum* to *regnum* roused little or no opposition from the king of France. For the power and prestige of the French monarchy were far less evident in 1100 than they would become a century later. Recent scholarship has emphasized the fact that the disintegration of the Carolingian Empire did not immediately produce a French feudal monarchy on the high-medieval pattern. On the contrary, Carolingian Frankland broke up into territorial principalities such as Flanders, Anjou, Aquitaine and Normandy, whose rulers were all but independent. The *rex Francorum,* as an anointed king, was pre-eminent among the princes, but his actual power was restricted largely to his own domains, which were neither larger nor wealthier than various neighboring principalities.[115] The later eleventh century marks the nadir of Capetian

---

52; cf. E. Caspar, *Roger II (1101–1154) und die Gründung der normannisch-sicilischen Monarchie* (Innsbruck, 1904), p. 231, and M. Fuiano, "La fondazione del '*Regnum Siciliae*' nella versione di Alessandro Telese," *Papers of the British School at Rome* 24 (1956), 65–77.

[111] "Rex Siciliae, ducatus Apuliae et principatus Capuae": Wieruszowski, "Roger II," p. 49.

[112] Alexander of Telese, "De Rebus Gestis Rogerii," p. 102.

[113] K. A. Kehr, *Die Urkunden der normannisch-sicilischen Könige* (Innsbruck, 1902), p. 248; Wieruszowski, "Roger II," p. 49: prior to 1139 Roger is often entitled in his charters *Siciliae et Italiae rex* or simply *Italiae rex,* Anacletus having given to him and his heirs in 1130 the royal title for Apulia and Calabria which Innocent withdrew in 1139.

[114] Ibid.

[115] J. Dhondt, *Études sur la naissance des principautés territoriales en France du IXe au Xe siècle* (Bruges, 1948); K. F. Werner, "Untersuchungen zur Frühzeit des französischen Fürstentums (9.-10. Jahrhundert)," *Die Welt als Geschichte,* 18 (1958), 256–89; 19 (1959), 146–93; 20 (1960), 87–119; Lemarignier, *Gouvernement royal.* Here again I am indebted to Professor Andrew Lewis for his help.

power: the great territorial princes were almost never at the king's court, and many of them did not bother to do him homage.[116] The idea of a feudal hierarchy, with great vassals bound by homage and fealty to the French royal suzerain, was so faint in these years as to be virtually nonexistent. And the French kings themselves seem only sporadically concerned with the direction of events outside their own domain. As late as 1106, Henry I could buy France's neutrality and its kings' assent to his conquest of Normandy.[117]

By 1106, however, the French monarchy was on the threshold of recovery. Some signs of new energy can be perceived in Philip I's reign, but it was not until the accession of Louis VI "the Fat" in August 1108 that the process of revitalization truly commenced.[118] Louis VI was the first French king to advance systematically the Capetian policy of ruling a pacified domain surrounded by fiefs of dependent princes who were "prepared to respect their feudal obligations."[119] He was not rigidly opposed to England and Normandy being ruled by a single person, for it was apparently his decision rather than his father's to assent to Henry's conquest of 1106, and in the closing years of his life he willingly conceded King Stephen's right to the duchy.[120] What the twelfth-century Capetians desired was a friend and obedient *fidelis* ruling Normandy, who might, if these conditions were met, rule England as well. But the dukes of Normandy had seldom if ever been obedient *fideles* in the sense that Louis VI seems to have had in mind. And Henry I, with his strong sense of Anglo-Norman unity and kingly station, could not tolerate the subordination that the new Capetian feudalism implied — or, indeed, any subordination whatever. Accordingly, Henry's conquest of 1106 and Louis's accession of 1108 set the stage for a climactic struggle over the status of Normandy.

In the opening year of his reign, Louis VI moved decisively to obtain the homage of the French territorial princes — among them, Henry I.[121] Henry refused outright, "because of the loftiness of his authority," so William of Malmesbury explains.[122] At the moment when the Capetian monarchy was

[116] Lemarignier, *Gouvernement royal*, pp. 46–50, 67–72, 114–18, 170–76.

[117] *La Chronique de Morigny (1095–1152)*, ed. Léon Mirot (Paris, 1912), p. 21; Malmesbury, *Gesta Regum*, 2:480; cf. Orderic, *Historia*, 4:210.

[118] Lemarignier, *Gouvernement royal*, pp. 67–72.

[119] Fawtier, *Capetian Kings*, p. 162; J. W. Thompson, *The Development of the French Monarchy under Louis VI le Gros (1108–37)* (Chicago, 1895), pp. 39–41.

[120] Luchaire, *Louis VI*, no. 583; Orderic, *Historia*, 5:81; Henry of Huntingdon, *Historia Anglorum*, p. 260.

[121] Suger, *Louis VI*, p. 184, accuses Henry I of stirring up the French kingdom "ut ejus dominio derogaret"; "Chronica Monasterii de Hida juxta Wintoniam," in *Liber Monasterii de Hyda*, ed. Edward Edwards, Rolls Series (1866), p. 309, presents the case from the other side: Louis VI "ira commotus [ob] antiquum antecessorum suorum in Normannia dominatum debitam subjectionem ab Henrico exigere coepit"; Clarius of Sens, "Chronicon S. Petri Vivi Senonensis," HF 12:281 (again from the French side): Louis VI had entered into hostilities with the king of the English and duke of the Normans, "qui contra jus et fas denegabat facere hominium quod debebat et debet Regibus Francorum."

[122] Malmesbury, *Gesta Regum*, 2:496, refers to William Adelin's rendering in 1120 the homage that Henry I "pro culmine imperii fastidiret facere"; cf. Suger, *Louis VI*, pp. 182–84.

beginning to tighten the feudal bonds, the Anglo-Norman king was endeavoring to break them altogether. And the result was war.

Crossing to Normandy in summer, 1108, Henry resisted the demands of the newly-crowned Louis VI — the neutralization of Henry's frontier strongholds of Gisors and Bray-et-Lû, and the act of homage.[123] In spring, 1109, the two kings, surrounded by their armies, negotiated from opposite sides of the river Epte, much as Rolf and Charles the Simple were said to have done in c. 911.[124] The interview was a stormy one, yet it ended with a truce. None of the issues was resolved, but the kings exchanged hostages and for the next two years attended to their own affairs, each contenting himself with encouraging the disloyalty of the other's barons.[125] In c. 1110 or 1111 Henry, evidently fearing a rebellion, banished a number of his English and Norman vassals and made an effort to arrest Robert Curthose's son, William Clito, who barely managed to elude the royal officers and flee Normandy.[126] Hostilities between the kings resumed in 1111, ending with another interview and truce in March, 1113, near Gisors on the Franco-Norman frontier. Henry had done well in the warfare and had won over Anjou by betrothing his only legitimate son, William Adelin, to the daughter of the Angevin count. Accordingly, the peace terms of 1113 were highly favorable to the Anglo-Norman monarch, and Louis is not reported to have raised the touchy question of Henry's homage. Indeed, Louis conceded to Henry the right to receive homage from the count of Anjou (for Maine) and the count of Brittany.[127] All considered, the peace of Gisors can only be regarded as a treaty between two sovereign princes.

Still, Henry I's authority over Normandy remained insecure. His brother, Robert Curthose, was safely in captivity, but Curthose's son, William Clito, remained at large. Clito, as son and heir of the Conqueror's eldest son, had a persuasive legal claim to the Anglo-Norman state — a claim that threatened to compromise not only the succession of Henry's son, William Adelin, but the legitimacy of Henry's own rule as well. As a viable pretender to Normandy and England, Clito was the obvious focus of French, Flemish, Angevin and domestic opposition to Henry I. And since the treaty of Gisors avoided any hint of a feudal bond between Louis VI and Henry I, it in no way committed the French king to future support of Henry's rule or William Adelin's succession. Louis VI was free to throw his support behind Clito whenever circumstances might favor such a course. Thus, the threat of Clito

---

[123] Suger, *Louis VI*, p. 106; Clarius of Sens, "Chronicon," p. 281; *Liber de Hyda*, p. 309.

[124] Luchaire, *Louis VI*, no. 72; cf. Lemarignier, *Hommage en marche*, pp. 39–40, 44.

[125] The meeting took place near Neaufles-Saint-Martin (Eure), where the Epte was spanned by a small, dilapidated bridge. Suger's account (*Louis VI*, pp. 104-110) is the most detailed but is misleading in its suggestion that the interview resulted not in a truce but in two years of warfare. Henry I spent the two years in England (June, 1109-August, 1111), while Louis VI was occupied elsewhere in France (Luchaire, *Louis VI*, nos. 73, 79, 87, 90, 91, etc.). On the truce and hostage exchange see Clarius of Sens, "Chronicon," p. 281; and *S. Anselmi Opera*, 5, ep. 461.

[126] Orderic, *Historia*, 4:292; *Liber de Hyda*, p. 309.

[127] Orderic, *Historia*, 4:306–308.

created a powerful practical motive for Henry I to reestablish the feudal relationship with France. As Henry's feudal suzerain, Louis would be morally bound to back him against all opposition, or at the very least to refrain from supporting Clito.

In September, 1114, Henry crossed to Normandy with the intention of safeguarding his son's succession. Clito was then a refugee at the court of Baldwin VII, count of Flanders, who may already have begun his series of raids against Normandy in Clito's behalf.[128] In late 1114 or early 1115, at Rouen, Henry made his Norman magnates swear fealty to William Adelin.[129] At some point during this brief Norman visit (ending in July, 1115), Henry sent envoys to the French royal court, offering a large sum of money in return for Louis's conceding Normandy to William Adelin and receiving William's "profession" (*professio*) for the duchy.[130] Louis, who was by no means immune from the influence of silver,[131] was on the point of agreeing to the proposal but was dissuaded by one of his counts. Instead of accepting William Adelin's submission he gave his full support to William Clito,[132] thereby rejecting the legitimacy of Henry's authority and instigating a war that would disrupt Normandy and France for the next four years.

Henry's rejected offer constituted a new strategy, adapted to the danger posed by Clito's pretensions and the need of French support. It was a compromise, characteristic of Henry's calculating policy. Without humbling himself by rendering homage personally, he would place Louis VI under the moral obligation of a good feudal lord to reject the pretensions of Clito and accept the legitimacy of Henry's rule and the succession rights of his son and heir. This strategy was not altogether without precedent. Two centuries before, Rolf, having himself done homage to the king of France, subsequently associated his son William Longsword with him in the duchy and had William do homage to Charles the Simple at the frontier castle of Eu.[133] And Robert Curthose had, in his father's lifetime, done homage for Maine to the count of Anjou c. 1063 and again in 1081, thereby legitimizing

---

[128] Herman of Tournai, "Liber de Restauratione Monasterii Sancti Martini Tornacensis," MGH SS 14:284; *Actes des comtes de Flandre, 1071–1128,* ed. Fernand Vercauteren (Brussels, 1938), no. 66: Charter of Baldwin VII dated 1114 at Ypres, "ubi conventus plurimorum clericorum ac laicorum ad disponendam expeditionem in Nortmanniam convenerat."

[129] *Anglo-Saxon Chronicle, s.a.* 1115; *Regesta,* 2, no. 1074. Haskins, *Norman Institutions,* p. 312, dates the oath-taking at Christmas, 1114; but cf. William Farrer, *An Outline Itinerary of Henry I* (Oxford, 1920), p. 73, suggesting early spring, 1115.

[130] *Liber de Hyda,* p. 309. The date is not provided, but the Hyde chronicler places the offer at some time subsequent to the Gisors peace of 1113. He also alludes to the advice given Louis VI by William II count of Nevers, who became a captive of the count of Blois sometime between 11 April and 8 November, 1115, and remained in captivity until late 1119 or 1120: Orderic, *Historia,* 4:377, 404; Luchaire, *Louis VI,* no. 203.

[131] Luchaire, *Louis VI,* pp. xxxv–xxxvi.

[132] *Liber de Hyda,* pp. 309, 319; cf. p. 308, stating that Louis VI had granted Normandy to Clito on a prior occasion, apparently in 1111 or 1112 — but the chronicler's chronology is by no means clear.

[133] Lot, *Fidèles ou vassaux?,* pp. 183–84.

William the Conqueror's own *de facto* power over Maine without obliging William to humble himself before an Angevin count.[134] But the Norman claim to Maine at that time had its immediate basis in Curthose's betrothal to Margaret, daughter of Count Herbert of Maine, and there was thus a special reason why the Conqueror should choose to rule Maine in Curthose's name. It is possible that Curthose did homage to Philip I for Normandy in the Conqueror's lifetime and with his approval, conceivably just before the Conquest when William formally proclaimed him his heir and successor in Philip's presence,[135] but no evidence of any such homage exists. In any event neither Robert Curthose nor William Longsword had played the role that Henry was calling on his son to play in 1115. For Curthose's and William Longsword's fathers had themselves done homage to the French kings on previous occasions, whereas Henry I had not. Thus Henry I, in urging that his son should render homage in his place, was proposing an essentially novel approach to the restructuring of Normandy's feudal relationship with France.

After four years of war, Louis VI was persuaded to accept Henry's proposal. The formalities took place at an unrecorded point on the Franco-Norman frontier sometime between 30 May and 29 September, 1120.[136] Persuaded by Henry's military triumphs, and his money, Louis VI granted Normandy to William Adelin to be held of him, and William did homage to Louis, "just as Rolf, the first duke of Normandy, had promised in perpetual right."[137] Lemarignier interprets the homage of 1120 as in one sense a traditional *hommage de paix*, ending a war with a frontier treaty of peace and reconciliation; but in another sense he sees it as a shift from the earlier personal relationship between duke and king to a new emphasis on territorial vassalage — a concession *en fief*.[138] Lemarignier, however, may well be underemphasizing the territorial aspect of earlier Franco-Norman feudal arrangements, which clearly carried with them, for example, some obligation to render military service to the king of France in return for the ducal fief.[139] The striking fact about the peace of 1120 is that Henry had managed

---

[134] David, *Robert Curthose*, pp. 9–11, 34; Orderic, *Historia*, 2:253, 257. Curthose occasionally attested as count of Maine, but Duke William actually kept the province in his own hands.

[135] David, *Robert Curthose*, p. 12; above, n. 9.

[136] Hugh the Chantor, *The History of the Church of York, 1066–1127*, ed. Charles Johnson (London, 1961), p. 97; cf. p. 95. The treaty may well have been concluded in June near the Norman frontier stronghold of Vernon. Hugh speaks of a meeting between Henry I and the papal legate Cuno at Vernon on 30 May, and adds that the peace with France was concluded "non longo post tempore."

[137] "Ex Anonymi Blandinensis appendicula ad Sigbertum," HF 14:16, "sicut Rollo primus Normanniae dux jure perpetuo promiserat." See also *Liber de Hyda*, p. 319, mentioning Henry's concession of an annuity to Louis VI from the English royal revenues. Cf. Malmesbury, *Gesta Regum*, 2:496; Simeon of Durham, *Opera Omnia*, ed. Thomas Arnold, 2 vols., Rolls Series (1882–85), 2:258.

[138] Lemarignier, *Hommage en marche*, p. 92.

[139] The provisions for military service to France in the Bayeux Inquest of 1133 seem to date back at least to the time of the Conqueror: HF 23:699–700; Haskins, *Norman Institutions*, pp.

to win the full benefit of Louis's lordship while eluding the responsibility and embarrassment of personal vassalage. The solution was attractive, if not thoroughly logical, and served as the chief precedent for future acts of homage — of King Stephen's son Eustace to Louis VI in 1137 and Louis VII in 1140; and of Henry, son of David king of Scots, to King Stephen in 1136.[140]

When William Adelin "received Normandy" from Louis VI did he thereby become "duke," or co-ruler with his father, or was his status in the duchy merely nominal? The question is a vital one in comprehending the full significance of the 1120 homage, but the answer is not easily obtained. William's name appears in no extant charter that can be dated securely within the brief period between the peace of mid-1120 and the death of the young prince on 25 November of that year in the wreck of the White Ship. The Hyde writer speaks of Henry's desire to relinquish the realm to his son, and the Winchester annalist goes so far as to say that, at the time of the homage to Louis, William received Normandy by his father's grant.[141] But this last phrase cannot be interpreted strictly without corroborative evidence, and there is none. Much more valuable is the evidence of Hugh the Chantor, who was in Normandy in 1120 and was closely involved in the high politics of the period. Hugh calls William Adelin, in the closing days of his life, *rex et dux designatus*.[142] The possibility that this term may indeed have been an official title is suggested by William's attestation of a royal charter of June, 1119, as *Dei gratia rex designatus*,[143] at a time when he had not yet received Normandy from Louis but had previously been named Henry's heir to the kingdom of England.[144] One might seek an analogy in Eustace, son of King Stephen, who in 1137 did homage for Normandy to Louis VI as a part of a treaty that Stephen concluded with Louis "on the same terms" as Henry I

15–20; cf. H. Navel, "L'Enquête de 1133 sur les fiefs de l'évêché de Bayeux," *Bulletin de la Société des Antiquaires de Normandie* 42 (1934), 5–80. On the Norman military obligation to France see further, Lot, *Fidèles ou vassaux?* pp. 189–90, 193–94, 198.

[140] Henry of Huntingdon, *Historia Anglorum*, pp. 259, 260; Gervase of Canterbury, *Historical Works*, ed. William Stubbs, 2 vols., Rolls Series (1879–80), 1:112. Fawtier, *Capetian Kings*, p. 81, cites an interesting instance of a Capetian son and heir, the future Philip IV, doing homage in 1285 to the bishop of Langres for certain fiefs in Champagne, "on condition that, should we become King of France, the homage will disappear. . . ."

[141] *Liber de Hyda*, p. 319; "Annales Monasterii de Wintonia," in *Annales Monastici*, ed. H. R. Luard, 5 vols. Rolls Series (1864–69), 2:46.

[142] Hugh the Chantor, *History of the Church of York*, p. 99. Hugh was in Normandy and France in the company of Thurstan archbishop of York, who played a key role in arranging the peace. Hugh and Thurstan were at Vernon on 30 May, 1120 (cf. above, n. 136): ibid., pp. 95–97; Donald Nicholl, *Thurstan Archbishop of York (1114–1140)* (York, 1964), p. 72. Hugh the Chantor may or may not intend the implication that Henry I is himself *rex et dux*.

[143] *Regesta*, 2, no. 1204 (at Rouen, 1119, ? June).

[144] *Anglo-Saxon Chronicle*, s.a. 1115; Eadmer, *Historia Novorum*, p. 237: at Salisbury, on 19 March, 1116, Henry made known his wish to make William heir to the kingdom. The magnates thereupon rendered homage and fealty to the prince, and the prelates promised to do him homage when he became king after Henry's death. He had previously received oaths of homage in Normandy.

had done.[145] Eustace lived on for some years, subsequently acquiring Boulogne and adopting the comital style, but he played no significant role in the governance of either Normandy or England and was never styled *dux Normannorum* or even *dux designatus*.[146] Conversely, sometime between 1098 and 1100 the future Louis VI was associated with his father on the throne and entitled *rex designatus,* after which time he used the title regularly and took a vigorous part in the royal governance, either jointly with his father or on his own initiative.[147]

But one cannot safely equate Capetian with Anglo-Norman customs, nor can one define the position of a *designatus* without taking into account the relative age, vigor and ambition of father and son. Eustace was a child when he did homage to Louis VI, and a few years thereafter the province of Normandy was lost to Geoffrey of Anjou. Louis became *rex designatus* at about seventeen or eighteen and continued in that capacity for nearly a decade, while his father slipped into premature senility. At the peace of 1120 William Adelin was probably just turning eighteen, while Henry I was a vigorous fifty-one and was apparently not in the least prepared to relinquish his control of Normandy or England. At some time after the meeting with Louis, he arranged for William to receive renewed oaths from the Norman barons,[148] but charter evidence makes it clear that on the eve of the White Ship disaster William had no real authority. In a charter of 1119-20 Henry and his son jointly grant Norman lands to the bishop of Angers (William having just been wed to Matilda of Anjou), and in 1120 William concurs in Henry's confirmation of a benefaction to an English Tironian house.[149] But Henry remained very much in control. On 21 November, 1120, at the Norman embarkation port of Barfleur, he convoked a council "of my bishops and barons," at which time a charter was issued confirming the lands and privileges of the Norman abbey of Cerisy. The confirmation was granted neither by William Adelin, nor by William and his father jointly, but by the king alone — by *Henricus rex Anglorum*.[150] What titles and authority William might subsequently have received we do not know. But when his

---

[145] Henry of Huntingdon, *Historia Anglorum,* p. 260; Orderic, *Historia,* 5:81. Orderic mistakenly has Louis grant Normandy directly to Stephen, "sicut antecessor ejus tenuerat."

[146] *Regesta,* 3, passim. He is normally *filius regis* or *comes* (of Boulogne); no. 921 (A.D. 1140) is attested *Eustachio filio et herede meo*; Stephen subsequently attempted without success to have Eustace crowned.

[147] Luchaire, *Louis VI,* nos. 4–55 passim, and pp. 289–93. On the use of the term *rex designatus* in Norman Sicily see L.-R. Ménager, "L'Institution monarchique dans les états normands d'Italie," *Cahiers de civilisation médiévale* 2 (1959), 448.

[148] "Annales de Wintonia," *Annales Monastici,* 2:46; Simeon of Durham, *Opera Omnia,* 2:258.

[149] *Regesta,* 2, nos. 1204a, 1223. William had previously served briefly and nominally as regent in England between Queen Matilda's death in May, 1118, and his own departure for Normandy a year thereafter to join his father; the actual work of government was performed by seasoned royal administrators: nos. 1189, 1191–92, 1201–1202.

[150] *Monasticon Anglicanum,* 6:1075 (*Regesta,* 2, no. 1233): "Ego Henricus rex Anglorum ab abbate requisitus coenobii Cerasiensis," etc.; ". . . inito consilio episcoporum meorum, simul et baronum. . . ." William Adelin's name appears nowhere in the charter.

White Ship set off from Barfleur he was still a mere *designatus;* his father remained the master of the Anglo-Norman state. And this being true, the significance of the 1120 homage becomes clear: it bound the king of France to Henry's succession plan without binding the lord of Normandy to the king of France.[151]

William Adelin's death released Louis VI from his commitment and threw the Anglo-Norman succession into chaos. Now as never before, Henry's nephew and enemy William Clito stood out as the obvious heir. It was perhaps to oppose the claim of this son of a Norman duke that Henry, quietly and unobtrusively, began styling himself *rex et dux:* the earliest known example of the "fourth seal" — bearing the twofold title — is on a charter dated 30 January, 1121.[152] But the seal may well have been in use prior to that date — conceivably as early as 1118 or before — and without knowing the precise moment of its introduction one cannot safely associate it with any specific event. Indeed the change from *rex* ("third seal") to *rex-dux* ("fourth seal") may simply have represented a delayed, half conscious response to Henry's decision of 1114/15 to modify his post-Tinchebray position of absolute Norman independence.

Whatever the case, Henry's "fourth seal" by no means resolved the ambiguities surrounding his title in Normandy. There was of course no ceremony of ducal installation, and he continued to issue charters for Normandy as *rex Anglorum* and to rule it by his "royal authority." Most important of all, he remained firmly opposed to doing personal homage to the French king, and after 1120 he had no legitimate son to act in his place. Still, the very title of *dux* created a certain implication of French suzerainty, evoking as it did the memory of homages long past and the more recent homage of William Adelin to Louis VI. It was in Henry's interest, therefore, to define the ducal title in such a way as to deemphasize the notion of Norman subordination. And two Anglo-Norman writers of 1120–35, both subject to the influence of Henry's court, produced the appropriate texts.

The first of these passages is an account in the anonymous *Brevis Relatio* defining the Franco-Norman relationship of the author's own time in terms of a Franco-Norman treaty executed c. 945 between King Louis IV "d'Outremer" and Duke Richard I. Louis IV is alleged to have agreed that the duke should not be required to perform feudal service for Normandy or otherwise serve the French monarchy unless the king should grant him a fief within the royal domain. Thus the duke renders (*facit:* shifting to the present

[151] Cf. the case of Robert Curthose's investiture in Normandy and his use of the title *comes Normannorum* while his father exercised the real authority: above, n. 9. The 1120 agreement of course cost Henry the concession that when William Adelin eventually succeeded to the rule of Normandy he would do so as Louis VI's *fidelis* — assuming that Louis VI still lived and reigned (and he was Henry I's junior by thirteen years). William Adelin could then either have ignored the homage (as William I had done), or have had it transferred to his own son (as William I also may possibly have done), or simply have waited for the bond to be severed by Louis VI's death.

[152] Chaplais, "Seals and Original Charters," pp. 265, 273; *Regesta*, 2, no. 1247: written in the hand of a chancery scribe. On the date of the seal's introduction see above, n. 83.

tense) nothing to the king except homage for Normandy and fealty during his lifetime and for his earthly honor. And likewise the king does fealty to the duke during his lifetime and for his earthly honor. And there is no distinction between them except that the king of the French does no homage to the duke of the Normans as the duke does to the king.[153]

This pointed assertion of Norman feudal doctrine through historical reinterpretation is obviously a text of extraordinary value. Its significance has been duly recognized by Ferdinand Lot and, most particularly, by J.-F. Lemarignier, who sees it as marking a fundamental turning point in the Franco-Norman relationship.[154] But both Lot and Lemarignier misdated the passage by a generation and thus placed it in the wrong historical context. The *Brevis Relatio* may well have been composed at Rouen — Henry's chief administrative center in Normandy — and the account can be placed firmly in the second half of Henry's reign (1120–35).[155] Considerable portions of the *Brevis Relatio,* including the passage in question, turn up almost verbatim in the interpolations that Robert of Torigny added in the mid-twelfth century to William of Jumièges's *Gesta Normannorum Ducum.*[156] Unfamiliar with the earlier text, the French writers assumed that the passage was composed by Robert of Torigny in connection with tensions between Louis VII and the Angevin dukes of Normandy. But while Robert of Torigny may well have had such tensions in mind when he reproduced the account, its original composition was evidently related to Henry I's problem of employing the ducal title without conceding his subservience to France.

The tone of the *Brevis Relatio* text is echoed in a contemporary passage from the first edition of Henry of Huntingdon's *Historia Anglorum,* written between 1125 and 1130.[157] Henry of Huntingdon weaves the idea into a speech allegedly delivered by Duke William at the onset of the battle of Hastings. William speaks of his Viking ancestors who took whatever French lands they chose, despite the French king — of Rolf, who conquered a French monarch at Paris and forced him to offer humbly the province of

---

[153] "Brevis Relatio de Willelmo Nobilissimo Comite Normannorum," in *Scriptores Rerum Gestarum Willelmi Conquestoris,* ed. Giles, p. 19. The story is based on Dudo, *De Moribus,* p. 247: King Louis IV renounces the feudal service of Duke Richard I and his successors: "et nullis, nisi Deo, servitium ipse et successio ejus reddat."

[154] Lot, *Fidèles ou vassaux?* pp. 231–35, 258–63; Lemarignier, *Hommage en marche,* pp. 96–100; cf. Powicke, *Loss of Normandy,* p. 79, and Warren, *Henry II,* pp. 225–26.

[155] The text contains a reference to William's death in the White Ship and refers to Henry I as still living: "Brevis Relatio," pp. 12, 14. Marjorie Chibnall has expressed to me some doubt that the various parts of the text are of the same origin, though they were clearly put together in the latter part of Henry I's reign. The four extant MSS and their differences are discussed in T. D. Hardy, *Descriptive Catalogue of Materials Relating to Great Britain and Ireland,* 3 vols., Rolls Series (1862–71), 2:6–7. For the argument that the work is of Rouen provenance see Howlett, *Chronicles of the Reigns of Stephen, Henry II, and Richard I,* 4:xxxvii. L. J. Engels, however, suggests that the work may have originated in England: "De obitu Willelmi," p. 243 and n. 101.

[156] *Gesta Normannorum Ducum,* pp. 338–39. Howlett suggests that the related passages in Robert of Torigny and the "Brevis Relatio" may have been drawn from a third chronicle, now lost: *Chronicles of Stephen, Henry II, and Richard I,* 4:xxxvi–xxxviii.

[157] P. 201, and on the date of composition, pp. x–xi.

Normandy — of Duke Richard I, who obtained a renewed title to the duchy from a French king (Louis IV) held captive in Rouen, and won the further concession "that in all meetings of the king of France and the duke of Normandy, the duke should be armed with a sword while the king should be allowed to bear neither a sword nor even a dagger. This stipulation your ancestors compelled the great king to accept for all eternity."

These words suggest that the Normans of 1066 were about to do battle with the French rather than the English. Their author was of course not Duke William but Henry archdeacon of Huntingdon. Henry of Huntingdon's patron and ecclesiastical superior — and the man to whom he dedicated his *Historia Anglorum* — was Alexander bishop of Lincoln, an intimate at Henry's court and favored nephew of Henry I's chief administrator, Roger bishop of Salisbury. It is to be presumed, therefore, that the words that Henry of Huntingdon put into the Conqueror's mouth expressed the viewpoint of the Anglo-Norman royal court in the 1120s. They are reminiscent of the ideas in the *Brevis Relatio* but go even farther, suggesting not ducal equality but ducal ascendancy. The image of a vanquished French king humbly conceding Normandy to a victorious duke neatly reverses the contemporary Capetian notion of the Anglo-Norman ruler receiving Normandy in fief from the "munificent hand," and by the "generous liberality," of the king of France.[158] The concepts of *hommage de paix* and *hommage vassalique* were hardening into rival, irreconcilable doctrines.

Behind the new Anglo-Norman propaganda lay the reality of a wealthy and powerful trans-Channel sovereign who, with Clito still at large, valued the support of Louis VI yet would not do him homage — and certainly not on Capetian terms. Henry was prepared to compromise on the matter of military service: in 1126 he sent knights to Louis's Auvergne expedition, but since he declined to lead them personally his act could be interpreted as a gesture of amity rather than a vassalic service.[159] And after Clito's death in 1128 the necessity of such gestures ceased altogether. During the closing years of the reign, Henry I and Louis VI lived in peace with one another, yet without any pretense of a defined feudal relationship. The issue on which they could never agree was at length left unresolved and ignored.

In the meantime the notion of an Anglo-Norman *regnum* had never died. Henry's half-hearted assumption of the ducal style on his seal might seem logically to have ruled out the earlier notion of a trans-Channel kingdom, but Henry I was never a captive of logic when it did not suit his purposes. In the very years when Henry of Huntingdon and the *Brevis Relatio* were emancipating the ducal title, an anonymous writer at Hyde Abbey, just across the town wall from Henry's Winchester treasury and exchequer, was exploring the idea of a "*regnum Norm-Anglorum.*"[160] A. L. Poole, calling

---

[158] Suger, *Louis VI*, p. 106.

[159] Suger, *Louis VI*, p. 236, and, on the date, p. 234 n. 2. It is perhaps equally significant to note the several major expeditions of Louis VI to which Henry did not send knights: e.g., Luchaire, *Louis VI*, nos. 318, 349, 452, 461, 558.

[160] *Liber de Hyda*, pp. 283–321 passim. This important anonymous account, written in the

attention to this novel phrase, seems to have interpreted it as referring to the English and Norman inhabitants of England alone.[161] But the Hyde writer devotes the bulk of his account of Henry I to the activities of the *rex Norm-Anglorum* in Normandy, and among the men whom he describes as *principes Norm-Anglorum* are such predominantly Norman figures as Elias de Saint-Saens, Hugh de Gournay and Henry count of Eu.[162] His phrase may well be intended as a play on words — *Norm-Anglorum* for *Normannorum* — but it also has the weight of a calculated political theory: that the *regnum Norm-Anglorum* was the realm of the *rex Norm-Anglorum* — actually or potentially, England and Normandy. William I, William II, and Henry I are all given the title *rex Norm-Anglorum;* Henry I's queen is *regina Norm-Anglorum domina Matildis,* and his son is *Willelmus rex Norm-Anglorum, ut putabatur futurus.*[163] Thus the peoples of the two lands, ruled by one monarch and his homogeneous feudal aristocracy, were viewed by the Hyde writer as comprising a single, indivisible *regnum.*

The idea had long been in preparation. Dudo of Saint-Quentin, William of Poitiers, and the charters of the pre-Conquest dukes could, as we have seen, apply the term *regnum* to Normandy. And the notion of the greater, trans-Channel *regnum* occurs off and on, as we have also seen, in the writings of post-Conquest authors such as Orderic, and even in the charters of Henry I. The Hyde writer did not invent the idea, but he did use it more consciously and systematically than anyone else, and he freed it of its customary ambiguity. In the world that he describes, there is no such thing as a *dux Normannorum* or a *ducatus Normanniae.* The ancient *ducatus* has become absorbed unqualifiedly into an integrated *regnum* of the Normans and English, ruled by a crowned and anointed king whose title ran back into the mists of ancient Wessex.

Far from being an eccentricity peculiar to the chronicler of Hyde, the notion of an Anglo-Norman *regnum* is a natural corollary to Henry I's determined policy of ruling England and Normandy as a unit, and passing them on as a unit to his heirs. On 1 January, 1127, Henry's magnates and prelates, meeting at London, swore to give England *and Normandy* to the Empress Maud after the king's death.[164] There is no record of separate oaths being rendered to Maud in Normandy. Indeed, there was no need of

---

1120s (it breaks off abruptly while describing the sinking of the White Ship) is traditionally associated with the abbey of Hyde (ibid., pp. xcvi–xcvii), but the considerable attention that it devotes to the Warenne earls of Surrey suggests the alternative possibility that it was produced at the Warenne foundation of St. Pancras, Lewes (Sussex). William II of Warenne (earl of Surrey, 1088–1138) was an intimate counselor of Henry I, attesting sixty-nine extant royal charters in the course of the reign.

[161] A. L. Poole, *From Domesday Book to Magna Carta,* 2nd ed. (Oxford, 1955), p. 1.

[162] *Liber de Hyda,* pp. 308, 313; the phrase occurs also on pp. 296, 297, 311, and 319.

[163] *Liber de Hyda,* pp. 296–319 passim; note the parallel on p. 315 of "Lodowicus rex Francorum et Henricus rex Norm-Anglorum." For *Norm-Anglorum* the writer occasionally substitutes *Norman-Anglorum.*

[164] *Anglo-Saxon Chronicle, s.a.* 1127.

such oaths. The Anglo-Norman *principes*, at the king's council in London, could act definitively for the entire *regnum*. And in the closing years of his reign, Henry ruled Normandy, as before, by his royal authority. In 1133 he ordered an important inquest of the feudal obligations of the bishopric of Bayeux: "Henry, king of England (*rex Angliae*) made an inquiry of the fees of knights and vavassors holding of the church of Blessed Mary of Bayeux, and of their service."[165] Again, in the final year of his life Henry proclaimed his great ordinance defining the role of his court in the enforcement of the Peace and Truce of God in Normandy. The decree was issued at Rouen, with the counsel and consent of his barons, by Henry *rex Anglorum*.[166] The fact that "Duke" Robert Curthose had been dead for several months in no way deterred Henry from issuing the most significant Norman ordinance of his reign under his royal title alone. Finally, the tradition of trans-Channel kingship receives its clearest possible expression in the *Gesta Stephani* account of Stephen's coronation in December, 1135: William archbishop of Canterbury anointed Stephen in Westminster Abbey as "king in England and Normandy."[167]

The appropriateness of this expression is shown by the fact that Stephen proceeded without further formality to claim and exercise lordship over Normandy. Like his patron and mentor, Henry I, he saw no necessity of a separate ducal installation. His first great royal court, of Easter 1136 at Westminster, was attended by the archbishop of Rouen and three of the five Norman suffragan bishops,[168] and when Stephen made his one royal crossing to Normandy in 1137 he came as its acknowledged ruler. When the Angevins appealed their case against Stephen to the papal court in 1139, Stephen's claims to England and Normandy were regarded as inseparable, and the pope confirmed both claims as though they were one.[169] If Stephen was the first Anglo-Norman monarch to be anointed "king in England and Normandy," he was also, it must be remembered, the first person ever to accede concurrently to the lordship of the two lands. The second such

---

[165] HF, 23:699; Henry I is referred to in the body of the document as *rex* or as *dominus Normanniae*, but never as *dux*. Cf. ibid., p. 703: The Norman feudal inquest of 1172 is undertaken "ex praecepto domini regis Henrici secundi," but its original rubric begins: "Infeudationes militum qui debent servitia militaria duci Normanniae," and it concludes, "Summa militum omnium praecedentium qui debent servitia duci": *Red Book of the Exchequer*, ed. H. Hall, 3 vols., Rolls Series (1896), 2:624, 647.

[166] *Coutumiers de Normandie*, ed. E.-J. Tardif, 2 vols. (Rouen, 1881–1903), vol. 1, part 1, p. 65: "Henricus rex Anglorum archiepiscopis . . . et fidelibus sancte ecclesie per Normanniam constitute, salutem."

[167] *Gesta Stephani*, ed. K. R. Potter (London, 1955), p. 8: "archiepiscopus, regem eum in Angliam et Normanniam . . . sacrauit et inunxit." Cf. the letter of Innocent II confirming Stephen's throne, referring to the peace and blessings under Henry I "in regno Angliae et ducatu Normanniae," and adding, "te in regem eligere et a praesulibus regni consecrari providit": Richard of Hexham, "Gesta Regis Stephani," in *Chronicles of Stephen, Henry II and Richard I*, 3:147.

[168] Schramm, *Königtums*, p. 46; *Regesta*, 3, nos. 46, 944.

[169] J. H. Round, *Geoffrey de Mandeville* (London, 1892), p. 257 and n. 4: "ei familiaribus litteris regnum Angliae confirmavit et ducatum Normanniae."

person was the Empress Maud who, on Stephen's capture in 1141, took into her possession the royal crown and was elected at Winchester "lady of England and Normandy."[170] Thus the lordship of the Anglo-Norman state was conveyed once again by a single act. Stephen's Norman charters are normally issued under the traditional Anglo-Norman title, *rex Anglorum*,[171] and in several of them he states explicitly, following Henry I's formula, that he is acting by his royal authority.[172] Of the few charters in which he is styled *rex Anglorum et dux Normannorum*, the majority are copies of lost originals.[173] The *rex et dux* formula occurs in only two of Stephen's original charters, and neither is in the hand of an identifiable scribe of the royal chancery.[174] In short, there is no certain evidence that Stephen's own scribes ever titled him anything but *rex Anglorum* in the address clauses of his charters. And it is apparently by this title alone that he reissued, at Evreux in 1137, the ordinance on the Norman Truce of God that had originally been issued in 1135 by *Henricus rex Anglorum*.[175]

And yet the ambiguity persisted. Stephen's seals, like the last seal of Henry I, bear the legend on the equestrian side, *Dei gratia dux Normannorum*. Anglo-Norman writers could still refer alternatively to the *ducatus Normanniae* and the *regnum* of Normandy and England, and to the suzerainty, however limited, of the king of France.[176] Stephen himself permitted his son to do homage to Louis VI in 1137 as Henry's son had done in 1120. And Stephen's charters continue to equivocate as to the nature of the *regnum* — *pro statu totius regni mei*, or *pro statu regni mei Anglie et ducatus Normannie*.[177] In

---

[170] Malmesbury, *Historia Novella*, p. 54: "in Anglie Normannieque dominam eligimus et ei fidem et manutenementum promittimus"; cf. *Gesta Stephani*, p. 79: Henry bishop of Winchester enjoins his people to salute Maud as their *dominam et reginam*.

[171] *Regesta*, 3, nos. 67, 69, 73, 75, 117, 280, 281, 282, 298, 327, 594, 598, 727, 733; cf. Haskins, *Norman Institutions*, p. 124.

[172] *Regesta*, 3, nos. 69, 327, 594, 749 (*regia auctoritate confirmo*).

[173] *Regesta*, 3, nos. 74, 213 (suspicious), 261, 609, 621, 622, 675. The original of no. 74, in the hand of Scriptor xix, survives in fragments, with the address clause missing: ibid., 4, pl. 26; cf. Bishop, *Scriptores Regis*, no. 205; Brooke and Keir, "Henry I's Charter for London," p. 563, n. 18. *Regesta*, 3, no. 118 (*Stefanus rex Anglorum dux Normannorum*) is a pretended original and almost certainly forged.

[174] *Regesta*, 3, nos. 262, 749 (Bishop, *Scriptores Regis*, nos. 193, 52.) *Regesta*, 3, no. 749 is written mostly in an unidentified hand but the final 3½ lines are in the hand of Scriptor xiii. See also *Regesta*, 3, no. 964 (Bishop, *Scriptores Regis*, no. 773), apparently another *rex et dux* original in an unidentified hand, but bearing a forged seal and of very doubtful authenticity.

[175] *Regesta*, 3, no. 608: from two copies; Stephen's ordinance is an almost verbatim transcript of Henry I's (*Regesta*, 2, no. 1908), with Stephen's initial in place of Henry's and a fresh witness list.

[176] *Regesta*, 4, pl. 2; Henry of Huntingdon, *Historia Anglorum*, p. 260, speaks of Eustace doing homage for Normandy, "quae Francorum adjacet imperio," (from the "third edition" written c. 1139: ibid., pp. xii–xiii.)

[177] *Regesta*, 3, nos. 69, 327, 594; cf. no 609. No. 327, an original in an unidentified hand, abounds in ambiguities: Stephen *rex Anglorum*, at Rouen, greets his English subjects and informs them that "ego Stephanus rex Anglorum et dux Normannorum . . . pro statu totius regni mei" confirm a pension originally granted to the abbey of Fontevrault by Henry I from the farms of London and Winchester: "regia auctoritate confirmo et a deo mihi concessa corroboro." Much

short, the concept of a *regnum Norman-Anglorum* never became the official position of the royal court. It was only a hope — a captivating possibility. It floated through court circles much as the doctrine of the Virgin's Immaculate Conception was floating just then through English ecclesiastical circles — not as dogma but as pious opinion aspiring to canonical acceptance.

In the 1120s and 1130s the two traditions coexisted — *ducatus-regnum* and *regnum Norm-Anglorum, rex-dux* and *rex* only. From the perspective of this era, either tradition might have prevailed in future generations. During the years when Henry I's ducal government was blurring more and more into his title and authority as king, a true Anglo-Norman kingdom, free of France, was a very real possibility. But in the course of the brutal succession struggle between the houses of Blois and Anjou and the consequent separation of Normandy from England, the opportunity dissolved. Both sides needed the support of France, and when Geoffrey count of Anjou mastered Normandy in 1144 he did personal homage for it to King Louis VII.[178] Henry Plantagenet likewise did homage to Louis VII in 1151 after receiving the duchy from his father, and again in 1156 as King Henry II.[179] Subsequently, homage for the duchy was rendered by Henry the Younger in 1160, by Henry II again in 1169 and 1183, by Richard I in 1188 and 1189, by Arthur of Brittany in 1199, and by John in 1200 — usually in the context of wars, family squabbles and succession conflicts.[180] A French alliance, for example, was vitally necessary to Henry II in February, 1156, when he was endeavoring to consolidate his authority over his immense new "Angevin Empire" against his brother Geoffrey's claims to the counties of Maine, Touraine and Anjou. Henry II managed to obtain Louis VII's formal concession of Normandy, Anjou, Touraine, Maine and Aquitaine, but at the cost of becoming England's first crowned king to do homage to a king of France.[181] In a very real sense, the homage of February 1156 marks both the formal inception of Henry II's feudal "empire" and the death of the Anglo-Norman *regnum*.

For Henry II's "Angevin Empire" was not merely an expanded version of the Anglo-Norman state; it was something quite new. If Henry II's dominions were more imposing than Henry I's, they were also more heterogeneous and unwieldy. In some respects Henry II continued to rule in the royal tradition of the Anglo-Normans. He was commonly called "King Henry"

---

of the text follows the language of Henry I's original grant (*Regesta*, 2, no. 1687; above, notes 102, 103) which is in the hand of Scriptor xiii.

[178] Josèphe Chartrou, *L'Anjou de 1109 à 1151* (Paris, 1928), p. 65.

[179] Lot, *Fidèles ou vassaux?*, pp. 204, 212–13.

[180] Ibid., pp. 214–19; Lemarignier, *Hommage en marche*, pp. 101–102, 105, 108–109.

[181] Hoveden, *Chronica*, 1:215; R. W. Eyton, *Court, Household and Itinerary of King Henry II* (London, 1878), p. 17. Earlier historians were unable to explain satisfactorily the motive underlying Henry II's feudal submission of 1156; e.g., Lot, *Fidèles ou vassaux?*, p. 213. The vital connection between this unprecedented act of royal homage and Henry II's war against his brother Geoffrey over the inheritance of Anjou and Maine was recently demonstrated by the penetrating analysis of Thomas K. Keefe, published in C. W. Hollister and T. K. Keefe, "The Making of the Angevin Empire," *Journal of British Studies* (1973); see below,: 267-71; see also T. K. Keefe, "Geoffrey Plantagenet's Will and the Angevin Succession," *Albion* 6 (1974), 266–74.

whether he was in England or not, but it was now recognized more clearly than before that in fact he ruled Normandy and Aquitaine in his capacity as duke and Anjou in his capacity as count.[182] Like his royal predecessors, he issued charters for all his lands from a single chancery and ruled them through a single itinerant court, which was known wherever it went as the *curia regis*.[183] It has even been suggested that the 1172 re-coronation of Henry the Young King may have been thought of as applying to Normandy as well as England.[184] But if this was so — and the evidence is far from clear — it was the last expression of a waning tradition. For the nature of the king's dominions had changed vastly since Anglo-Norman times. The "empire" of the Angevin monarchs was, in the words of Henry II's most recent and astute biographer, "no more than a loose confederation of client states."[185] Each continental province had its own aristocracy and its own government. With the later-twelfth-century trend toward administrative departments drifting out of the itinerant court to fixed centers, even the English and Norman administrations were becoming more distinct. This process of departmentalization increased the administrative efficiency of the Angevin dominions but diminished the unifying role of the central curia. Henry II might endeavor now and then to govern his continental possessions as a unit, issuing an ordinance, for example, that was binding in Anjou, Normandy and Aquitaine alike.[186] But the task of amalgamating such diverse principalities was hopelessly unrealistic, and the Angevin kings were wise enough not to attempt it seriously. Indeed, Henry II's father had cautioned him specifically against such a policy.

The early Angevin monarchs were doubtless influenced too, at least unconsciously, by the gradual erosion of the ancient concept of numinous kingship. The later twelfth century witnessed a growing emphasis on the monarch's territorial authority as against his personal, priestly status. This change, combined with a heightened sensitivity to subtle legal distinctions, made it easier for Henry II and his sons than for their Anglo-Norman predecessors to see how a single person might be king in England, duke in Normandy and count in Anjou. The new perception is exemplified in the contrast between the charters of *Henricus rex Anglorum* and those of his grandson, *Henricus rex Anglorum et dux Normannorum et Aquitanorum et comes Andegavorum*.[187] It is further exemplified in the contrast between Henry I's

---

[182] Above, note 35.

[183] Haskins, *Norman Institutions*, pp. 191–93; Warren, *Henry II*, p. 301.

[184] Schramm (*Königtums*, p. 47) deduces this from the fact that Henry the Younger was crowned in Westminster by the archbishop of Rouen. It should be borne in mind, however, that Canterbury was vacant just then and that Henry II may well have been concerned not to anger the Canterbury monks by permitting the archbishop of York to officiate. On the political background see Warren, *Henry II*, p. 111. Henry the Younger had done homage and been invested in Normandy by Louis VII in 1160 and had received oaths of homage and fealty from the Norman barons c. 1162: Robert of Torigny, *Chronicle*, pp. 208, 216.

[185] Warren, *Henry II*, p. 230.

[186] Powicke, *Loss of Normandy*, p. 25; but cf. Warren, *Henry II*, pp. 228–30.

[187] *Recueil des actes de Henri II, roi d'Angleterre et duc de Normandie, concernant les provinces*

and Stephen's avoidance of a ducal installation and the emergence in the late twelfth century of a majestic *Ordo* for the consecration of the dukes of Normandy. The new *Ordo* was, in Kantorowicz's words, "a cutting taken from an ancient English coronation ritual," but with the careful omission of every element that was distinctively royal: the anointing, the crown, the rod, the scepter, and the enthronement.[188] Richard I and John were both solemnly installed as Norman dukes in Rouen cathedral just prior to their coronations at Westminster. They were girt with the ducal sword by the archbishop of Rouen, who is said to have placed on John's head a golden circlet adorned with golden roses.[189] These were impressive matters — the multiple titles, the splendid ducal installations — and yet the earlier, Anglo-Norman style of ruling by the authority of the royal anointment and coronation alone is impressive in a very different sense, and perhaps more deeply so.

The great problem faced by the early Angevin kings was to hold together their various titles and authorities. Lacking the homogeneity and relative compactness of the Anglo-Norman state, and lacking the firm territorial and jurisdictional frontier that had formerly separated Normandy from its neighboring principalities, the "Angevin Empire" could not be governed in the Anglo-Norman tradition. Its vastness and diversity challenged the effectiveness of personal, itinerant rule. And the Anglo-Norman sense of independence, derived from both English and Norman traditions, was compromised by the acquisition of titles to less autonomous provinces. The extraordinary rights of the duke of Normandy could all too easily blur into the more dependent status of the other continental dominions.[190] The Angevin kings tried to impede this process by a policy of doing separate homage for each principality, but Roger of Hoveden asserts that in 1183, when Henry II made his final feudal submission to the French crown, he did so with a single act of liege homage "for all his overseas holdings."[191]

Despite these homages, Normandy's domestic government remained as autonomous as ever. The French monarchy continued its traditional policy of holding strictly aloof from the internal administration of the duchy, and the Angevin dukes carried on and systematized the remarkable regalian powers of their Norman predecessors. Norman writers could still refer on occasion to their *justiciae regis* and could call their feudal service to the duke

---

françaises et les affaires de France, ed. L. Delisle and E. Berger (Paris, 1909–27), passim. Henry II's seal likewise bears the legend on the equestrian side, *Henr[icus] Dei gratia dux Norm[annorum et] Aquit[anorum] et com[es] Andeg[avorum]* (with *Henricus Dei gratia rex Anglorum* on the majesty side): Warren, *Henry II*, Frontispiece. Cf. also the address-clause styles of Henry I's queen — *Matilda regina Anglorum* or *Matilda regina* — with *Alienora regina Anglorum et duchissa Aquitanorum et Normannorum et comitissa Andegavorum*. Richard I uses the same titles as Henry II; John is *rex Angliae dominus Hiberniae dux Normanniae et Aquitaniae comes Andegaviae*.

[188] Kantorowicz, *Laudes Regiae*, p. 178; cf. p. 170; and Schramm, *Königtums*, p. 47.
[189] Schramm, *Königtums*, pp. 47–48; Kantorowicz, *Laudes Regiae*, pp. 170–71; Hoveden, *Chronica*, 4:87–88.
[190] Warren, *Henry II*, pp. 227, 609.
[191] *Gesta Regis Henrici Secundi*, ed. William Stubbs, 2 vols., Rolls Series (1867), 1:306.

their *servicium regis,* although much less consistently than before.[192] On no known occasion, however, did Henry II follow the Anglo-Norman custom of confirming Norman lands and privileges by his "royal authority."[193]

Normandy under the Angevins was clearly a duchy, whose dukes acknowledged the lordship of the kings of France. One must not overlook the obvious point that the Angevin rulers were, after all, Angevins. Henry II's injection of Angevin institutions into the political structure of Normandy is well known,[194] and it should be remembered, too, that Anjou lacked Normandy's tradition of independence from France and its sensitivity on the matter of homages. "The continuous dependence of Anjou upon the kings of France," writes Powicke, "was not unimportant in the history of the Angevin Empire as a whole."[195] Thus, Henry Plantagenet's initial homage, in 1151, is the first certain instance of a Norman duke performing the ceremony at Paris rather than *en marche.*[196] An agreement between Henry II and Louis VII at Ivry in 1177 reminds one in some ways of Henry I and Louis VI at Gisors in 1113 negotiating as two sovereign princes, except that at Ivry Henry II called Louis VII his *dominus* and Louis called Henry his *homo et fidelis.*[197] And two years thereafter Henry the Younger journeyed to Paris to serve at Philip Augustus's coronation, carrying Philip's crown in the procession *de jure ducatus Normanniae.*[198] The pride that the Angevin monarchy seems to have taken in its right to serve at the French coronation reflects an attitude more in harmony with the claim of the counts of Anjou to the hereditary seneschalship of France than with ambitions of earlier dukes of Normandy.[199] Now as never before the king of England viewed the French monarchy as the ultimate source of his authority on the continent, and a

---

[192] Robert of Torigny, *Chronicle,* p. 349: on the feudal inquest of 1172; but cf. *Red Book of the Exchequer,* 2:624, 647, where the term is *servicium ducis* (above, n. 165). On Normandy's powerful and autonomous administration in Angevin times see Powicke, *Loss of Normandy,* pp. 50–67; Haskins, *Norman Institutions,* pp. 156–95.

[193] To my knowledge, the formula occurs in only two Norman charters attributed to Henry II. The first, in favor of the abbey of Blanchelande, is almost certainly forged: Delisle and Berger, *Recueil,* 1:135–36; cf. ibid., Introduction, p. 295; the second, in favor of Notre-Dame-du-Pré, Rouen, has an impossible witness list and is an almost verbatim copy of a charter of Henry I dated 1122 (whose witnesses likewise create problems): ibid, 2:104–107.

[194] See Powicke, *Loss of Normandy,* pp. 18, 28, 29, 50–78.

[195] Powicke, *Loss of Normandy,* p. 14.

[196] Robert of Torigny, *Chronicle,* p. 162.

[197] Lemarignier, *Hommage en marche,* pp. 98–99; similar phrases occur in the treaty of 1180 (ibid.); cf. HF, 16:16–17: "Ego rex Henricus assecurabo regi Francorum sicut domino vitam suam et membra sua, et terrenum honorem suum: si ipse mihi assecuraverit sicut homini et fideli suo vitam meam et membra mea, et terras meas quas mihi conventionavit, de quibus homo suus sum" (1158). Despite the contrast of *dominus* with *homo* there is an obvious emphasis on reciprocity here, and some of the phraseology is strongly reminiscent of the *Brevis Relatio* text (above, n. 153; cf. Lemarignier, *Hommage en marche,* p. 98, n. 95).

[198] Hoveden, *Chronica,* 2:94; the episode alarmed Ralph of Diceto: *Opera Historica,* ed. William Stubbs, 2 vols., Rolls Series (1876), 1:438–39; cf. Warren, *Henry II,* p. 227.

[199] See Robert of Torigny, *Chronicle,* pp. 240–41: in 1169 Henry the Younger had served Louis VII as his seneschal at Paris. Cf. Powicke, *Loss of Normandy,* p. 14; Lot, *Fidèles ou vassaux?,* p. 234.

Norman spokesman of Henry II could freely admit that Normandy was *de regno Franciae*.[200]

The implications of this evidence are clear enough: whereas homage to France had been an unacceptable infringement on Henry I's authority on the continent, it was the foundation of Henry II's. And whereas the Anglo-Norman kings would do homage to no one, the Angevins did homage frequently, and not to France alone. In a letter written in 1157 to Frederick Barbarossa, Henry II declared that he put all his lands at the emperor's disposal, and some years later King Richard I, in obtaining release from his imprisonment, did homage for his dominions to Barbarossa's son and heir, Henry VI.[201] Richard was obviously acting out of necessity rather than policy, but this was less clearly the case in 1213 when King John unwittingly marked the centenary of Henry I's triumphant treaty of Gisors by declaring England and Ireland a papal fief and swearing homage to Innocent III.[202] Years before, during Richard I's imprisonment, John had journeyed to Paris and done homage to Philip Augustus for Richard's lands, including, so it was widely believed, the kingdom of England itself.[203]

These cases are of course highly atypical. Henry II's long-range plan seems to have been to concede the formal French suzerainty over his continental lands while at the same time uniting them by means of a family pyramid of authority — granting them out to his sons on the understanding that they would do homage to him and to each other.[204] The plan was a sensible solution to the problem of governing far-flung dominions. Its failure was due in part to the quarrels of Henry's sons with their father and with one another, and in part to the rising feudal demands of the French crown.

More and more, the Capetians were coming to view Normandy as an ordinary feudal dependency, differing in no way from other great fiefs.[205] At the same time, the French monarchy was investing the concept of feudal suzerainty with ever increasing authority and precision. In defiance of Henry II's wishes, Philip Augustus accepted Geoffrey's homage for Brittany in 1186 and Richard's for Aquitaine in 1188.[206] On Geoffrey's death, Philip demanded custody of Brittany and wardship over Geoffrey's daughter.[207] Hostilities between Richard and Henry II provided Philip the opportunity of

[200] Robert of Torigny, *Chronicle*, p. 208 (A.D. 1160); cf. Henry of Huntingdon's account of Eustace doing homage in 1137 for Normandy, "quae Francorum adjacet imperio" (above, n. 176). Robert of Torigny recasts this passage as "quae adjacet regno Francorum (ibid., p. 132), and sharpens it in 1160 to "qui est de regno Franciae."

[201] K. Leyser, "Frederick Barbarossa, Henry II and the Hand of St. James," *English Historical Review* 90 (1975), 481–506.

[202] Schramm, *Königtums*, pp. 55–56.

[203] Hoveden, *Chronica*, 3:204, 207.

[204] Powicke, *Loss of Normandy*, p. 82.

[205] Ibid., pp. 79, 291.

[206] Ibid., p. 82; Warren, *Henry II*, pp. 613, 621.

[207] Warren, *Henry II*, p. 610; Henry II refused Philip's demand. Recall that in 1113 at Gisors Louis VI had conceded the overlordship of Brittany to Henry I.

playing the overlord's role as arbiter between them, and when Henry refused to surrender the Norman fortress of Gisors in 1186 Philip is said to have summoned him as a disobedient vassal to the court of the royal suzerain.[208] Henry refused to come, just as he had likewise refused to yield the custody of Brittany. But Philip continued to press. In 1189 he compelled the defeated and dying Henry II to agree to do homage once again for all his continental territories, to submit entirely to Philip's will, to pay him an indemnity of 20,000 marks, and to acknowledge Richard as the Angevin heir.[209] On Henry II's death, Philip obliged Richard I to relinquish his claims to Auvergne and portions of Berry and to add 4,000 marks to the 20,000 that Henry II had agreed to pay.[210] In 1200 Philip forced John to render 20,000 marks as a relief for his French lands.[211] And in 1202 he declared these same lands forfeit, alleging that John had declined a summons to the overlord's court at Paris, and that the dukes of Normandy had long ignored their service and obedience to the kings of France.[212] John claimed immunity from the summons on the grounds that Norman dukes had traditionally dealt with their French suzerains only on the frontier. The claim was clearly rooted in ancient custom, and yet John's father had gone to Paris in 1151 to render homage for Normandy, Henry the Younger had carried Philip's crown in the 1179 coronation *de jure ducatus Normanniae*, and John himself had done homage in Paris during Richard's captivity. But the decisive point was that Philip summoned John in 1202 not as duke of Normandy but as duke of Aquitaine.[213] Thus did Philip Augustus exploit the fundamental weakness of the Angevins' position as kings, counts, dukes and *fideles*. And when John refused the summons Philip, marching into Normandy, resolved the ancient issue by force of arms.

The loss of Normandy and Anjou in 1203–1204 was not, of course, an inevitable consequence of the Angevins' feudal subordination to France. In a more immediate sense it resulted from John's personal shortcomings as a commander and leader. Five decades earlier Henry II, as duke of Normandy, had refused a summons to Louis VII's court; when Louis thereupon decreed the confiscation of Henry's possessions, Henry had defended them

---

[208] Lot, *Fidèles ou vassaux?*, pp. 81–83, 230 and n. 1.

[209] Hoveden, *Chronica*, 2:365–66; *Gesta Regis Henrici*, 2:70–71.

[210] *Gesta Regis Henrici*, 2:73–74; in 1191 Richard formally recognized Philip as his liege lord for all his continental lands and agreed to make their succession a matter of public treaty: *Recueil des actes de Philippe-Auguste*, ed. H.-F. Delaborde, 1 (Paris, 1916), no. 376.

[211] For the provisions of John's treaty with Philip Augustus of 22 May, 1200, at Le Goulet on the Franco-Norman frontier, see ibid., 2, no. 623; Hoveden, *Chronica*, 4:148; *Cartulaire normand de Philippe-Auguste, Louis VIII, Saint Louis, et Philippe-le-Hardi*, ed. Léopold Delisle, in Mémoires de la Société des Antiquaires de Normandie 16 (1852), no. 1063.

[212] Lot, *Fidèles ou vassaux?*, p. 221.

[213] Ralph de Coggeshall, *Chronicon Anglicanum*, ed. Joseph Stevenson, Rolls Series (1875), pp. 135–36; see also Lot, *Fidèles ou vassaux?*, pp. 228–30; Powicke, *Loss of Normandy*, pp. 79–80; Lemarignier, *Hommage en marche*, pp. 109–111, and p. 101, for additional Angevin exceptions to the Norman *hommage en marche* tradition (Henry II in 1169, Arthur of Brittany in 1199).

energetically and forced Louis to relent.[214] Whatever the merits of Philip's case against John in feudal law, the Angevin dominions could pass into French hands only through conquest. For half a century the Angevin kings had more than held their own, and their policy of using the French suzerainty as the foundation of their own authority had served as an effective accommodation to political circumstances. But these circumstances were such that the Angevin territorial ensemble necessarily suffered from a certain instability, and although the French suzerainty was an essential support it was also a dangerous one. For ultimately the recognition of a feudal overlord involved the risk that the overlord might exercise his right of forfeiture against a disobedient *fidelis*. And while it is true that Philip took Normandy by military force, and that John defended it badly, it is likewise true that Philip's military designs were decisively reinforced by the appearance of feudal right. From the beginning the Angevin kings had, for their own purposes, recognized the Capetian suzerainty; in the end it was the instrument of their undoing.

In summary, the possibility of an independent trans-Channel *regnum* was created by the Norman Conquest, advanced by the Norman kings, and abandoned by their Angevin successors. The height of Norman independence was achieved in the years just following the conquest of 1106, when Henry I governed the province through his royal title and refused any feudal relationship whatever with the king of France. Henry I and his successors enjoyed the advantage over their Capetian rivals of much superior power and wealth. But they suffered the crippling disadvantage of contested thrones and perilous successions, which drove them to seek the security of the French royal suzerainty. The claims of William Clito forced Henry I to fight and bargain with Louis VI to accept the homage of William Adelin. The claims of Maud and Geoffrey drove Stephen to a similar compromise. And it was in the midst of their trans-Channel conflict with Stephen that Geoffrey and Henry Plantagenet did homage for Normandy in 1144 and 1151. Likewise, Henry II rendered his precedent-shattering homage of 1156 during his brother's rebellion in Anjou. And subsequent homages occurred amidst the quarrels of Henry II and his sons, Richard's struggle with John, and John's with his nephew Arthur of Brittany. These Norman and Angevin family rivalries contrast dramatically with the congenial domestic relations and uncontested successions of the twelfth-century Capetians, whose success owed much to their talent for producing healthy and patient heirs.

Henry II's accession in 1154 marked the expansion and transformation of a tightly-integrated Anglo-Norman state into a cluster of diverse provinces. Over the decades that followed, Henry and his sons had to contend with an

[214] HF 12:127, 202, 208; Robert of Torigny, *Chronicle*, pp. 165, 167, 172, 180. See also the summons of 1186: above, n. 208.

increasingly aggressive and self-confident sense of suzerainty in France, and with the escalating feudal demands of their French overlords. Under the circumstances, a multi-faceted Angevin *regnum* was out of the question. Henry II turned instead to publicizing his comital and ducal titles, listing them in his charters, and doing homage for them all. The notion of an "Angevin Empire" is nothing more than a convenient invention of modern historians. But the concept of an Anglo-Norman state is rooted in the political ideas and realities of the Norman kings themselves, who governed England and Normandy alike by their royal authority. The concept began with William the Conqueror, who exchanged his ducal status for that of *rex*. And it reached full bloom in the days of Henry I, who ruled as king over the Normans and English and called no mortal his lord.

3

THE STRANGE DEATH OF WILLIAM RUFUS

"The death of William Rufus," writes E. A. Freeman, "is one of those events in English history which are familiar to every memory and come readily to every mouth."[1] The Red King, master of England and Normandy and terror of the Church, was still in his early forties — vital, flamboyant, and planning great deeds — when he was killed by an arrow while hunting in the New Forest. He died in the late afternoon of Thursday, August 2, 1100, and on the following Sunday his younger brother, Henry I, began an eventful reign of thirty-five years with a hurried coronation in Westminster Abbey.

The sudden demise of a powerful, exuberantly anticlerical king in his prime made a deep impact on the age. Here was a spectacular illustration of that favorite medieval theme, "pride falleth," and the point was made by nearly every chronicler. Out of the deep conviction that God does not change the course of history without warning or reason, contemporaries sought out portents — dreams, visions, a spring bubbling with blood — and took comfort in the belief that divine judgment had struck down a wicked sovereign.

The drama of Rufus's death catches our imaginations even today and has set modern investigators on a search for some significance in the event beyond mere chance. We still search for meaning in history, though meaning of a different kind than Rufus's contemporaries sought, and we are uncomfortable with the notion of totally fortuitous causes for great events. Now, as then, it is the magnitude of the occurrence — the dramatic impact of a strong king's fall, the jolting redirection of English history — that tempts us to look for some hint of human calculation such as we would not seek in the reportedly accidental deaths of lesser men. Accordingly, the explanation of divine judgment through human accident, which provided Rufus's death with satisfactory meaning in the middle

I am grateful to the American Council of Learned Societies, the American Philosophical Society, the Social Science Research Council, the Fulbright Commission, the John Simon Guggenheim Memorial Foundation, and the Warden and Fellows of Merton College, Oxford, for their help in supporting the research for this paper, and to my research assistants, Miss Carol E. Moore and Mr Jonathan Kaplan.

[1] E. A. Freeman, *The Reign of William Rufus* (Oxford, 1882), ii, 336.

ages, has given way in recent times to theories of human conspiracy involving clandestine witchcraft rites or a secret assassination plot.

The possibilities of witchcraft and murder have added spice to the now-considerable twentieth-century literature on the killing. The murder hypothesis — involving a plot between King Henry I and the Clare family — was affirmed with little qualification in an old but still-cited scholarly article by F. H. M. Parker[2] and is the central theme of a recent book by Duncan Grinnell-Milne.[3] It has been advanced as a possibility, sometimes as a very distinct possibility, in virtually all serious historical discussions of the matter since the end of the last century.[4] The witchcraft hypothesis — involving a ritual royal killing which Rufus accepted voluntarily as a secret initiate in the "Old Religion" — was advanced and developed by the anthropologist Margaret Murray,[5] and although poorly received by historians it has not been altogether undefended.[6]

These historians, anthropologists and interested laymen — some cautious, others not — would all agree that there are at most three possibilities: witchcraft, murder, and accident. It will be argued here that the third of these possibilities, although the least entertaining, is far the most likely.

The witchcraft theory depends on the assumption that William Rufus's anticlericalism was a sign of his membership in a non-Christian fertility cult that had survived from olden days under the Christian surface of medieval society. This "Old Religion," so it is argued, taught that the king was a nature god whose fructifying powers might wane with time, requiring his sacrificial slaying after a period of years. Rufus, facing up to his duty, allowed himself to be shot by his knight and companion, Walter Tirel. The historical sources are silent on the ritual aspect of the killing because they were written by clerical enemies of the "Old Religion," but hints are to be found in such matters as the portents surrounding the royal death, the report that Rufus's bier was strewn with flowers in pagan style, and William of Mortain's vision of Rufus astride a hairy black goat who announced that he was the devil carrying the king to his judgment. Dr Murray believes that similar sacrificial slayings account for the deaths of King Edmund (946), Prince Edmund Ironside (1016), King Canute (1035), Walchere bishop of Durham (1080), Thomas Becket (1170), Gilles de Rais (1440), and Joan of Arc (1431).[7]

---

[2] "The Forest Laws and the Death of William Rufus," *English Historical Review*, xxvii (1912), 26–38.

[3] *The Killing of William Rufus* (Newton Abbot, 1968).

[4] For recent examples, see W. L. Warren, "The Death of William Rufus," *History Today*, ix (January, 1959), 22–29; Christopher Brooke, *The Saxon and Norman Kings* (New York, 1963), 175–96; A. L. Poole, *From Domesday Book to Magna Carta* (2nd ed., Oxford, 1955), 113–14.

[5] The theory is set forth in Dr Murray's *God of the Witches* (rev. ed., London, 1952); cf. *The Divine King in England* (London, 1954).

[6] See Hugh Ross Williamson, *The Arrow and the Sword: An Essay in Detection* (2nd ed., London, 1955), 105–19.

[7] Murray, *God of the Witches*, 161–97.

This remarkable thesis is supported by extensive analysis of the source materials to which the above paragraph has done scant justice. But neither Dr Murray nor her follower, Mr Ross Williamson, have handled their sources as a historian would. The flower-strewn bier story comes from the fanciful twelfth-century poet-historian Geoffrey Gaimar and is flatly contradicted by more serious and better-placed writers.[8] The hairy black goat story was written a century and a half after the event[9] and does not harmonize particularly well with what we know of early cultism. We know, in fact, very little about it, and that is the chief difficulty. There are reports of witchcraft and devil worship here and there in medieval Europe but no specific evidence as to the forms it might have taken in the Anglo-Norman state at the close of the eleventh century. Of necessity, therefore, much of Dr Murray's evidence dates from the sixteenth and seventeenth centuries when witchcraft was not only better recorded but also probably much more widespread than in the high middle ages. Like most things, the doctrines of witchcraft would doubtless have evolved considerably over four or five hundred years, and it is hazardous to use such evidence to reconstruct unrecorded beliefs of the year 1100.[10]

Even if one grants, for the sake of argument, that a divine-victim doctrine existed in Rufus's society, it would remain wildly unlikely that Rufus himself subscribed to any such belief. True, he abused his churches, blasphemed more than occasionally, and seems to have generally disliked the ecclesiastical establishment. But swearing and fleecing churches were not uncommon royal sins in the middle ages, and anticlerical Christians have abounded in the annals of Europe. Rufus was a type of irreligious, self-aggrandising cynic such as often emerges from a religious society — a man who shared the common faith but usually ignored it in his worldly activities. And true to type, he did behave as a Christian now and then, especially in times of crisis. He was a generous benefactor to Battle Abbey.[11] In 1093, as he lay ill and thought he was dying, he appointed St. Anselm to the archbishopric of Canterbury — much to his later regret.[12] In 1099, when his troops were besieging the castle of Mayet near Le Mans, he agreed to a disadvantageous weekend truce "out of respect for the day of the Lord's burial and resurrection."[13] Moreover, contemporary writers describe Rufus on the eve of the shooting as being filled with great hopes and

[8] Geoffrey Gaimar, *Lestorie des Engles*, ed. T. D. Hardy (Rolls Series, London, 1888–89), I, 270. Orderic Vitalis, *Historia Ecclesiastica*, ed. A. Le Prévost (Paris, 1838–53), III, 89, says that servants wrapped the corpse in an old piece of cloth and carted it like a pierced boar to Winchester. Cf. William of Malmesbury, *Gesta Regum Anglorum*, ed. William Stubbs (Rolls Series, London, 1887–89), II, 379.

[9] Matthew Paris, *Chronica Majora*, ed. H. R. Luard (Rolls Series, London, 1872–83), II, 113. Murray also draws from Henry Knighton who wrote three centuries after A.D. 1100.

[10] These matters are discussed more fully in Brooke, *Saxon and Norman Kings*, 177–85, and Warren, "Death of William Rufus," 27–28. For an excellent, measured discussion of pre-Christian influences on Old English kingship see William A. Chaney, *The Cult of Kingship in Anglo-Saxon England* (Manchester, Engl., 1970).

[11] *Regesta Regum Anglo-Normannorum*, ed. H. W. C. Davis, C. Johnson, H. A. Cronne, and R. H. C. Davis (Oxford, 1913–69), I, nos. 290, 348, 401, 458; II, no. 290a (pp. 399, 409).

[12] Eadmer, *Historia Novorum in Anglia*, ed. Martin Rule (Rolls Series, London, 1884), 29–38.

[13] Orderic, *Historia*, IV, 60.

designs, about to depart to the Continent to assume the governance of Aquitaine while its troubadour-duke was crusading, and boasting that he would hold his Christmas court in Poitiers.[14] That such a man would willingly cast himself as a divine victim seems beyond belief.

Historians have rightly questioned the witchcraft theory but have taken the murder theory very seriously indeed. The more careful scholars present it merely as a hypothesis, recognizing that the case is circumstantial only and that nothing can be proven. But we are left with our doubts: "There is," writes A. L. Poole, "at the least, enough evidence to arouse the suspicion that the sudden end of Rufus was the result of a conspiracy . . . of which Henry himself was cognizant."[15] And Norman Cantor asserts, "There is circumstantial evidence that Henry, who was in the hunting party, participated in a plot to assassinate his brother."[16] Frank Barlow recognizes the hazards of the thesis: "If Rufus did not die through a common hunting accident we may think Henry guilty. But circumstantial evidence presented so long after the event is insufficient to fasten upon him responsibility for so monstrous a crime."[17]

The circumstantial evidence is this: first, tales of the killing being prophecied in dreams and sermons have suggested to some interpreters that the "prophets" were, in fact, privy to a murder plot. Second, Henry's response to the shooting was so swift and effective as perhaps to imply premeditation. Third, there is motive: with Henry's and Rufus's elder brother, Robert Curthose, about to return to Normandy from the Crusade, August 1100 might perhaps have represented a desperate younger brother's last hope for the English throne. Finally, there is the argument that Walter Tirel, the reputed shooter of the fatal arrow, was connected by marriage to two powerful, related Anglo-Norman families — the Clares and Giffards — which Henry thereafter held high in his favor.

Such, briefly, is the circumstantial case against Henry I. The four elements in the case have long been recognized and endlessly repeated. Yet upon close analysis each of them dissolves. The charge of assassination through conspiracy is, by its very nature, impossible to disprove: how can the notion of an unreported plot be positively refuted? The evidence for such a plot, however, can be shown to be not merely circumstantial but fallacious.

A number of modern historians have wisely ignored the prophecy argument, but it does turn up occasionally and cannot be passed over. William of Malmesbury relates that on the morning of the shooting a certain foreign monk came to the hunting court and reported dreaming that Rufus had been gnawing on the

---

[14] *Ibid.*, iv, 80; Malmesbury, *Gesta Regum*, ii, 379. Cf. Gaimar, *Lestorie*, i, 268–69.

[15] Poole, *Domesday Book to Magna Carta*, 114.

[16] Norman F. Cantor, *The English* (New York, 1967), 122. Cf. C. W. Hollister, *The Making of England* (2nd ed., Lexington, Mass., 1971), 107: "Henry must stand acquitted, though a lingering doubt remains." G. O. Sayles, *The Medieval Foundations of England* (rev. ed., New York, 1961), 294, speaks of William II's "assassin."

[17] Frank Barlow, *The Feudal Kingdom of England* (London, 1955), 170.

arms and legs of a crucifix. At length the crucifix kicked the king, who fell backwards and began breathing out flames and smoke that rose to the sky.[18] Orderic
tells another story — or perhaps another version of the same story: a Gloucester
monk had a vision of a young virgin (representing the Church) begging the
Lord Jesus in heaven to strike out in vengeance against her oppressor, the king
of England. Jesus replied that the virgin should bear her oppression patiently
and would soon be avenged.[19] On August 1, so we are told, Abbot Fulchered of
Shrewsbury, preaching at the same abbey of Gloucester, prophecied a sudden
change in affairs that would soon free England from iniquity: "The bow of divine
vengeance is bent on the sinner, and the swift arrow is out of its quiver, ready to
wound. The blow will quickly be struck."[20] On the following morning Rufus
received a message from Serlo abbot of Gloucester warning him of these premo-
nitions. Exploding with laughter the king declared that he had more to do than
listen to the dreams of snoring monks. Giraldus Cambrensis, writing in the later
twelfth century, ascribes the vision to the prior of Dunstable — a house, Giraldus
explains, which Rufus had built at his own cost and for which he had a special
love.[21] In point of fact, Dunstable was founded a generation later by Henry I.[22]

Reports such as these, Parker argues, may well have been spoken "with guilty
knowledge."[23] But if we are to include the abbots of Shrewsbury and Gloucester
and the (non-existent) prior of Dunstable in the conspiracy, we cannot stop
there. Foreknowledge of Rufus's death was attributed by various writers of the
early twelfth century to St. Hugh abbot of Cluny,[24] St. Anselm in his French
exile,[25] Merlin the Magician,[26] and Rufus himself, who on the night before his
death is said to have dreamed that his blood was gushing heavenward, darkening
the sky.[27]

None of these stories contains any hint of human premeditation. They are all
grounded in the faith that God directs history. They were told by men who
believed in divine portents and, seeking them, found them. For an event of the

---

[18] Malmesbury, *Gesta Regum*, ii, 377–78.

[19] Orderic, *Historia*, iv, 83–84.

[20] *Ibid.*, iv, 85–86.

[21] Giraldus Cambrensis, *Opera*, ed. J. S. Brewer *et al.* (Rolls Series, London, 1861–91), viii, 324–25.

[22] *Cartulary of Dunstable*, ed. R. C. Fowler (Bedfordshire Record Soc., 1926), 342; "Annales Prio-
ratus de Dunstapalia," in *Annales Monastici*, ed. H. R. Luard (Rolls Series, London, 1864–69), iii, 15;
Regesta, ii, nos. 1826–27; David Knowles and R. N. Hadcock, *Medieval Religious Houses, England
and Wales* (2nd ed., London, 1971), 156.

[23] Parker, "Forest Laws," 32; cf. Grinnell-Milne, *Killing of Rufus*, 56, 61.

[24] Eadmer, *Vita Sancti Anselmi*, ed. R. W. Southern (London, 1962), 123; Gilo, *Vita Sancti Hugonis*,
ed. Albert L'Huillier in *Vie de S. Hugues, abbé de Cluny* (Solesmes, 1888), 588–89. Cf. "Chronica
Monasterii de Hida juxta Wintoniam," in *Liber Monasterii de Hyda*, ed. Edward Edwards (Rolls
Series, London, 1866), 304.

[25] Eadmer, *Vita Anselmi*, 124. Despite Anselm's foreknowledge, when the news of Rufus's death
reached him by earthly messengers some days later, "It came as a great shock" and "he wept most
bitterly": Eadmer, *Historia Novorum*, 118.

[26] "Succedent duo dracones, quorum alter invidiae spiculo suffocabitur": Orderic, *Historia*, iv, 490,
quoting from the prophecies of Merlin in Geoffrey of Monmouth, *Historia Britonum*, ed. J. A. Giles
(Caxton Soc., London, 1844), lib. 7, ch. 3.

[27] Malmesbury, *Gesta Regum*, ii, 377.

magnitude of Rufus's death a comet or eclipse would have been preferable, but in
their absence contemporaries had to make do with dreams, visions, and mysterious messages. Similar tales had circulated after the deaths of former kings —
Aethelbald of Mercia, Ecgfrith of Northumbria, Eadred of Wessex, Harold I,
William the Conqueror, and others.[28] Indeed, they recur throughout history and
turn up in family legends even today. In the middle ages every cataclysmic
event was quickly entangled in a thicket of legend. In the case of Rufus, if there
is any reality at all behind these stories it probably lies in Florence of Worcester's
statement that sinister portents were being discovered constantly throughout
the reign.[29] Rufus was no friend of the Church, and clerics must often have
dreamed of his death and damnation. Perhaps he actually did receive a warning
before setting out on his last hunt; he had doubtless been receiving them for
years.

The next charge against Henry I relates to his swiftness and presence of mind
during the three days following the shooting. The arrow struck late in the day on
August 2. By evening he was in Winchester — some 22 miles distant — where,
after a lively argument with William of Breteuil, he came into possession of the
royal treasure.[30] On the next day Rufus was entombed at Winchester and Henry
was elected king by a hastily-assembled council. He promoted Rufus's chancellor, William Giffard, to the vacant bishopric of Winchester and shortly afterward
set out for London, some 70–75 miles distant, perhaps breaking his journey and
arriving on August 4. On Sunday, August 5, he was crowned in Westminster
Abbey by Maurice bishop of London (with both archbishops absent) and issued
his Coronation Charter.[31] Grinnell-Milne concludes, "Only premeditation can
account for such speed."[32]

But at the death of a Norman king, speed was always of the essence. At Henry
I's own death in 1135, Stephen of Blois dashed from Boulogne to London, was
elected king, rushed to Winchester for the treasure, then back to Westminster
for the coronation: "The speed of Stephen's action has not ceased to provoke
amazement and admiration," writes one of his recent biographers,[33] and even
before he received the news of Henry's death, Norman magnates were already

[28] Orderic tells us that on the day William I died in Rouen, his death was known to Norman
exiles in Rome and Calabria: *Historia*, III, 249. On the earlier kings see Chaney, *Cult of Kingship*,
153–55.

[29] Florence of Worcester, *Chronicon ex Chronicis*, ed. Benjamin Thorpe (London, 1848–49), II,
45–46. Among other things, the devil often appeared to people in the woods, assuming a horrible form
and talking about Rufus.

[30] Orderic, *Historia*, IV, 87–88.

[31] A simple, trustworthy itinerary is provided in the *Anglo-Saxon Chronicle*, A.D. 1100: *The Peterborough Chronicle, 1070–1154*, ed. Cecily Clark (2nd ed., Oxford, 1970), 28. Grinnell-Milne, *Killing
of Rufus*, 122–41, provides an extraordinarily precise and detailed account of Henry's movements,
but it rests on far too many unverifiable assumptions to be dependable.

[32] *Ibid.*, 141; cf. Cantor, *The English*, 122; Brooke, *Saxon and Norman Kings*, 188–89.

[33] R. H. C. Davis, *King Stephen* (London, 1967), 17. Stephen's speed has suggested to another
recent biographer the possibility of a plot — but not an assassination plot: H. A. Cronne, *The Reign of
Stephen* (London, 1970), 86–87.

rushing about "like ravening wolves to the prey."[34] They had behaved in similar fashion half a century earlier on William I's death, mounting their horses and dashing off to secure their property, and Rufus had left Rouen to take the English crown even before his father expired.[35]

Thus the absence of mourning and prolonged solemnities at Rufus's death should be no surprise. Only the most dull-witted magnate could fail to grasp the political options: immediate commitment to Henry, opposition to Henry in behalf of the absent Curthose, or non-commitment until the situation cleared. There is nothing suspicious in the fact that certain magnates, such as the traditionally royalist Beaumonts, immediately opted for Henry, or in the support he received from the royal administration and the clergy, who had much to gain from a speedy settlement of the succession issue. As for Henry himself, everything we know of his capacity for swift decision and effective action suggests that with or without advance knowledge of the shooting he would have acted as he did. Within moments he would have understood the full significance of the situation, and his strategy of dashing to Winchester for the treasure and to Westminster for the coronation was both practical and obvious. Henry's much-admired Coronation Charter is in fact a brief list of fourteen promises, aimed chiefly at rectifying well-known abuses of the previous reign. It was a clever bid for needed support from magnates and prelates, and, requiring no prolonged negotiations, could have been drawn up quickly by an alert, well-counselled king.

Far more serious is the matter of motive. There were many, of course, who gained from Rufus's death: Robert Curthose could now reenter Normandy unhindered, without repaying the 10,000 marks for which he had pawned the duchy to Rufus; Anselm could return from exile; King Philip of France and Pope Paschal II were rid of a dangerous enemy; the monks of Malmesbury, Ely, Winchester, Bury, and Canterbury were free of their avaricious royal administrators. But it is argued that Henry stood to gain the most. "When Robert set off for the First Crusade," Brooke explains, "he made an arrangement with Rufus whereby each was the other's heir."[36] In August, 1100, Robert Curthose was on his way home from the Holy Land. Passing through Italy he had taken a beautiful, well-born wife — Sibylla of Conversano — whose dowry was more than sufficient to redeem Normandy from Rufus. Until then none of the three brothers had married — although Rufus and Curthose were both in their forties — but now Curthose might well beget a male heir who would remove Henry's last, slender chance at the throne. Seemingly, then, Henry would have been desperate. From his point of view the shooting occurred in the nick of time, and in just the right spot for a short dash to Winchester: "Is it not a strange coincidence that Rufus died in that month, and in that part of England?"[37]

---

[34] Orderic, *Historia*, v, 53. The English were equally turbulent: *Gesta Stephani*, ed. K. R. Potter (London, 1955), 1–4, 7–8.

[35] *Ibid.*, III, 244, 249.

[36] Brooke, *Saxon and Norman Kings*, 189.

[37] *Ibid.*

The crown of England was an alluring prize for a last-born son, but one must not forget that the duchy of Normandy was alluring, too. Rufus, Curthose, and Henry were all Normans, and, as Professor Le Patourel has recently demonstrated, all three of them thought in terms of an undivided Anglo-Norman state.[38] Rufus and Curthose had battled for one another's dominions for eight years before Curthose left for the Crusade, and Henry was to struggle with Curthose for another six before routing him at Tinchebray and joining the duchy to the kingdom. Seen in this light, August 2, 1100 was not, from Henry's viewpoint, a particularly advantageous moment for Rufus's death. Had it occurred at any other time over the previous four years, Henry might well have avoided the immediate baronial opposition that he faced in England. He would have been given the time to consolidate his position and organize his government and might also have annexed Normandy without serious difficulty.[39] Far better for Henry if Rufus had been killed — as he nearly was — at the siege of Mayet in July, 1099,[40] or in his Vexin campaigning in 1097 and 1098.[41] With Curthose in Syria there would have been ample opportunity for Henry to travel to Winchester from anywhere in the Anglo-Norman state.

It might nevertheless be argued that August, 1100, if not the best moment, was the last moment. But the notion of Henry's desperation at Robert's imminent return breaks down under close analysis. To begin with, in 1100 there existed no agreement between Rufus and Curthose that each should be the other's heir. The two brothers did agree to a survivor arrangement of this sort in their truce of 1091, but, in the words of the Anglo-Saxon chronicler, "It lasted only a little while."[42] It was repudiated by Curthose at Christmas, 1093, and was followed by renewed hostilities between the brothers in the course of which Rufus, with Henry's help, extended his dominion over considerable portions of Normandy.[43] In 1096 Rufus agreed to loan Curthose 10,000 marks for his crusade taking all of Normandy as security, but in the several fairly detailed accounts of this transaction not a word is said about England going to Curthose on Rufus's death.[44]

It is most unlikely, therefore, that Curthose was Rufus's designated heir to the English throne in August, 1100.[45] More important, Rufus seems to have had

---

[38] John Le Patourel, *Normandy and England, 1066–1144* (Reading, 1971), and "The Norman Succession, 996–1135," *English Historical Review*, LXXXVI (1971), 225–50.

[39] Even after Curthose's return, many Norman barons wished to have Henry as their duke: Orderic, *Historia*, IV, 106.

[40] *Ibid.*, IV, 61.

[41] *Ibid.*, IV, 19–26.

[42] *Peterborough Chronicle*, 18–19; Henry of Huntingdon, *Historia Anglorum*, ed. Thomas Arnold (Rolls Series, London, 1879), 215–16.

[43] *Ibid.*, 218; *Peterborough Chronicle*, 21–25; Orderic, *Historia*, III, 475–76.

[44] *Ibid.*, III, 483, IV, 16; *Peterborough Chronicle*, 25; Florence of Worcester, *Chronicon*, II, 40; Henry of Huntingdon, *Historia Anglorum*, 219; Malmesbury, *Gesta Regum*, II, 371; Eadmer, *Historia Novorum*, 74–76; Simeon of Durham, *Opera Omnia*, ed. Thomas Arnold (Rolls Series, London, 1882–85), II, 227; Hugh of Flavigny, in *Monumenta Germaniae Historica, Scriptores*, ed. G. H. Pertz *et al.* (Hanover, 1826 ff.), VIII, 474–75; *Gesta Normannorum Ducum*, ed. Jean Marx (Rouen and Paris 1914), 274–75.

[45] When Curthose made his bid for the crown in 1101 he asserted no prior agreement with Rufus but based his claim on primogeniture alone: Orderic, *Historia*, IV, 113.

no intention of permitting Curthose to repurchase Normandy on his return. On the contrary, Rufus was just then in the process of assembling an extensive continental empire. William IX, duke of Aquitaine and count of Poitou, had sent messengers to England with his offer to mortgage all his domains to Rufus in return for money with which to lead a crusading army to the Holy Land, and Rufus had accepted the proposal "with great satisfaction," because, Orderic says, he longed to add Aquitaine to "his father's duchy and kingdom."[46] Indeed, rumors were circulating that Rufus aspired to the throne of France itself.[47] At the time of his death he had collected a huge treasure with which to consummate the agreement with William IX. He was on the point of leading an army across the Channel to occupy William IX's domains and, as Orderic explicitly states, to oppose by war Robert Curthose's return to Normandy.[48]

What the outcome of such a war might have been we cannot know, but on their past records Rufus's prospects of holding Normandy against Curthose were excellent. As it turned out, Curthose was able to return unopposed, benefiting as much from Rufus's death as Henry himself. Had Rufus lived on, and had he succeeded in exiling his crusader-brother from Normandy, his death at some later time would have offered Henry much the same opportunity for seizing the crown and perhaps a good chance at the duchy as well. All this is hypothetical, but it demonstrates clearly enough that August 2, 1100 represented neither Henry's first chance at the throne nor his last.

The final charge against Henry I is based on evidence originally presented in 1895 by John Horace Round, showing that Walter Tirel, the alleged assassin, was related by marriage to the Clares and Giffards, and that Henry favored these families throughout his reign.[49] Round makes his suggestion almost offhandedly, in the process of a characteristically brilliant paper on genealogy — a subject that fascinated him. The theory of a Clare-Giffard plot has since been introduced as evidence in almost every discussion of Rufus's death, and its serious flaws have never been pointed out. With the hope of uprooting it from our history books once and for all, it will be subjected here, for the first time, to detailed criticism.

In its fully elaborated form[50] the theory runs as follows: Walter Tirel's wife

[46] *Ibid.*, IV, 80. The arrangement was aborted by Rufus's death, but William IX managed his crusade notwithstanding, departing in 1101: *ibid.*, 118; *A History of the Crusades*, I, ed. Marshall W. Baldwin (2nd ed., Madison, Wisc., 1969), 348, 352.

[47] Suger, *Vie de Louis VI le Gros*, ed. Henri Waquet (Paris, 1964), 10.

[48] Orderic, *Historia*, IV, 80: " . . . fratrem ab introitu Neustriae bello abigeret . . . " Cf. *ibid.*, 83. Orderic alone is specific on this point, but it can also be inferred from other sources, e.g., Malmesbury, *Gesta Regum*, II, 379. Cf. Gaimar, *Lestorie*, I, 268–69. Rufus's vast ambitions at this moment are widely reported, and the notion that he was prepared to surrender Normandy on Robert's repayment of the 10,000 marks is unlikely in the extreme. See, on this point, C. W. David, *Robert Curthose, Duke of Normandy* (Cambridge, Mass., 1920), 124, and Freeman, *William Rufus*, I, 555–56, II, 312–13.

[49] John Horace Round, *Feudal England* (London, 1895), 468–79.

[50] See, for example, Brooke, *Saxon and Norman Kings*, 189–90. Brooke presents the theory fully but cautiously, demonstrating his usual sensitivity in handling historical evidence. See also Parker, "Forest Laws," 33; Sidney Painter, "The Family and the Feudal System in Twelfth Century England," SPECULUM, XXXV (1960), 5–6; Warren, "Death of William Rufus," 29; Poole, *Domesday*

was Adeliza, daughter of Richard of Clare and Rohese Giffard. Adeliza's brothers, Gilbert and Roger were, in 1100, the major Clare landholders in England and Normandy respectively and both were members of Rufus's hunting party. Adeliza's uncle, Walter II Giffard, was the major representative of the Giffard house in both England and Normandy. A sister of Adeliza's was wed to Eudo *Dapifer*, a royal steward of William I, William II, and Henry I, and a substantial Domesday landholder. (See the Genealogical Chart.) The Clares and Giffards were close associates of Henry I, and Eudo *Dapifer* was one of his favorites. Walter Tirel fled to France immediately after the shooting but his English lands were not seized, nor was any investigation of Rufus's death ever conducted. Within a few days Henry had made Adeliza's brother Richard abbot of Ely, had given her uncle William Giffard the bishopric of Winchester, and (so it is sug-gested) had bestowed the title "earl of Buckingham" on Walter II Giffard. In later years the Clares, who "were in constant attendance at Henry's court,"[51] received further favors from him.[52]

One element in this theory — Round's genealogy — is almost surely correct, but the remaining elements are either wrong, doubtful, or misleading. First of all, there is nothing to suggest that prior to the shooting Henry had any relationship whatever with the Clares, the Giffards or Walter Tirel.[53] We know that Henry's close associates before his accession came chiefly from the areas in Normandy where Henry held lands: the Cotentin, the Avranchin (and neighboring Brittany), the Bessin, and the region around Domfront.[54] The Giffards, however, came from Longueville, far off in *Haute Normandie*, and the Clares' Norman bases were Orbec and Bienfaite in central Normandy, again far removed from the districts where Henry had been active.

Moreover, it is by no means certain that Gilbert and Roger of Clare were in the hunting party at all. Their presence is reported in no contemporary chronicle but only in Geoffrey Gaimar's rhyming, error-ridden *Lestorie des Engles*.[55] Gaimar places Gilbert, Roger, and Walter Tirel at Rufus's side when he was shot, whereas the chroniclers report that Rufus was alone except for Tirel and perhaps a few servants.[56] Gaimar calls Gilbert of Clare "Earl Gilbert," thereby confusing

Book to Magna Carta, 113–14; Michael Altschul, *A Baronial Family in Medieval England: The Clares* (Baltimore, 1965), 19–20.

[51] Round, *Feudal England*, 472.

[52] See *ibid.*, 468–79; Altschul, *Clares*, 20; Painter, "Family and Feudal System," 5–6.

[53] No chronicle associates them. Prior to his accession Henry attests with Walter Giffard on only one occasion, along with numerous other witnesses and at a time when Henry was 12 or 13 years old: *Regesta*, I, nos. 170 (29 witnesses) and 171 (21 witnesses), issued concurrently, A.D. 1080–82. Henry attests once with Richard Fitz Gilbert of Clare (43 witnesses) and twice with Gilbert Fitz Richard (1088: 13 witnesses; 1091: 16 signators): *ibid.*, nos. 220, 301, 320.

[54] See Le Patourel, *Normandy and England*, 28, 33; John Horace Round, *Studies in Peerage and Family History* (New York, 1901), 124–25. These districts produced such royal favorites as Hugh of Avranches earl of Chester, Richard of Redvers, Roger bishop of Salisbury, John bishop of Lisieux, the Veres, Bassets, Pomeroys, Courcys, Hayes, St. Johns, Paynels, and Breton and Cotentin Albinis.

[55] Gaimar, *Lestorie*, I, 271. Round, uncharacteristically, accepts this as good evidence (*Feudal England*, 272; *Dictionary of National Biography*, IV, 377) as does Freeman (*William Rufus*, II, 321).

[56] Orderic, *Historia*, IV, 87; Malmesbury, *Gesta Regum*, II, 378.

CLARE-GIFFARD GENEALOGICAL CHART SHOWING RELATIONSHIPS WITH WALTER TIREL AND GIFTS OF HENRY I

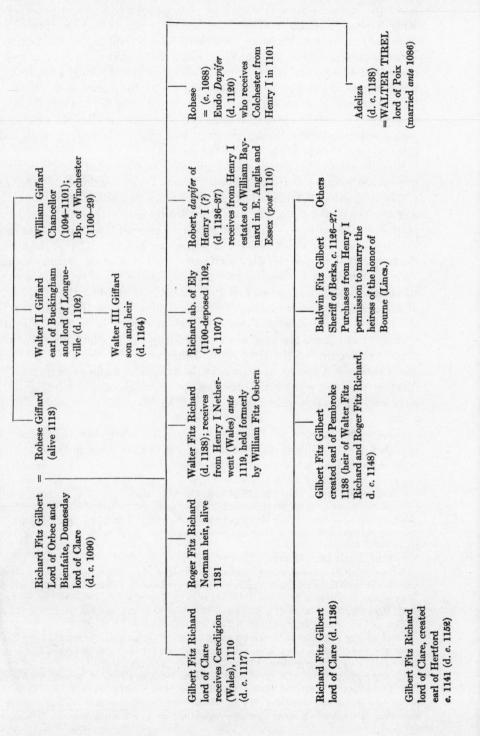

him with his son who was made earl of Pembroke thirty-eight years later by King Stephen.[57] Gaimar has the Clares and other barons linger long over Rufus's dead body, having an elaborate bier built, then accompanying the bier on foot as it was carried in great state to Winchester. Better sources report that everyone dashed off to his own affairs immediately after the shooting, abandoning the royal corpse which was brought to Winchester by rustics in a crude cart.[58] Gaimar reports that when the barons reached Winchester Cathedral they were joined by Walkelin, bishop of Winchester, who kept an all-night vigil over the king's body. In reality Bishop Walkelin had died on January 3, 1098 and the bishopric was vacant at the time of the shooting.

Round, moreover, is a little misleading when he states that the Clares were "in constant attendance at Henry's court."[59] From the coronation in 1100 to Gilbert of Clare's death c. 1117, he attests sixteen known royal charters — an unimpressive average of about one per year, exceeded by no less than eighty-eight other persons during the reign. (Robert of Meulan witnessed 112 charters over roughly the time span in which Gilbert was witnessing his sixteen.[60]) Throughout the thirty-five year reign seven Clares witness a total of 55 royal charters, compared with 111 charters witnessed by four members of the Bigod family, 164 charters witnessed by five Beaumonts, and 236 charters witnessed by the brothers Nigel of Albini and William *Pincerna*.[61] These statistics suggest that Clares attended the royal court no more frequently — and perhaps a little less frequently — than one might have expected of such a wealthy and prolific family. There were others much closer to the king — the Beaumonts, Fitz Johns, Albinis, Bigods, and Tancarvilles, not to mention royal bastards and nephews, important court functionaries, and ecclesiastical families such as those of Roger bishop of Salisbury and Thurstan archbishop of York. The Clares never reached this inner circle.

Clares were favored by Henry but, again, no more than might have been expected. In 1110 Gilbert received the lordship of Ceredigion in Wales but had to tame the wild land before reaping its profits.[62] Two of Gilbert's younger brothers,

---

[57] *The Complete Peerage* (London, 1910–59), x, 349–51.

[58] Orderic, *Historia*, iv, 88–89; Malmesbury, *Gesta Regum*, ii, 379. Malmesbury's account suggests that the shooting occurred late in the day. A walk to Winchester would have required about 7 hours, assuming that the latter part of the route could be negotiated in pitch darkness at normal walking speed.

[59] Round, *Feudal England*, 472.

[60] These attestation statistics are based on my analysis of c. 1500 royal charters in *Regesta*, ii, excluding obvious forgeries. Other frequent witnesses are Brian Fitz Count (42 charters in 10 years), Miles of Gloucester (44 in 14), Urse of Abitôt (46 in 8), Robert of Vere (50 in 14), Roger Bigod (58 in 7), Payn Fitz John (60 in 21), William of Warenne (69 in 35), Geoffrey Fitz Payn (74 in 28), William of Tancarville (90 in 22), and Robert earl of Gloucester (93 in 22).

[61] *Ibid.* Walter and Miles of Gloucester attest a total of 74 charters, Eustace and Payn Fitz John attest 84 (over 21 years), and 2 Tancarvilles attest 97. (In calculating these figures, I have counted each charter only once, regardless of how many family members attest it.)

[62] J. E. Lloyd, *A History of Wales* (3rd ed., London, 1939), ii, 420; L. H. Nelson, *The Normans in South Wales* (Austin, 1966), 122. Henry's boons to the Clares in c. 1110 are best viewed in the context of the widespread forfeitures and gifts associated with the international crisis of 1109–13. This reshuffling of the Anglo-Norman baronage ruined such men as William Baynard, William Malet,

Walter and Robert, also received fiefs from Henry — one in Wales, the other centering in Essex — but it was not until Stephen's reign that Clares were made earls of Pembroke and Hertford.[63] The family had been richly favored by William I and William II[64] and would continue to be favored by Stephen and Henry II. The Clares traced their lineage back to Duke Richard I of Normandy, and the Conqueror had given the first lord of Clare the eighth wealthiest lay honor in England.[65] By 1100 the honor had risen to sixth,[66] and during Henry I's reign it probably dropped to seventh. Robert of Bellême and William of Mortain, the wealthiest barons of all, were disinherited early in the reign, but Henry raised up others in their place. Robert earl of Gloucester, Stephen of Blois, and the earl of Leicester all catapulted past the lord of Clare, and by the end of the reign Hugh Bigod and Brian Fitz Count were drawing abreast of him.[67]

The Clares received such favors as might ordinarily be bestowed on a great family over thirty-five years, and in return they rendered good service to the king. Gilbert of Clare struggled to pacify Ceredigion; his brother Roger escorted Henry's daughter Maud to Germany in 1110 and was a commander of Henry's army at the crucial battle of Brémule in 1119. Their younger brother Robert was apparently a royal steward, and Gilbert's son Baldwin seems to have served briefly as sheriff of Berkshire.[68] The relationship is a perfectly characteristic case

Robert of Lacy, Roger of Abitôt, and Elias of Saint-Saens, and enriched others such as Stephen of Blois, William of Warenne, Walter of Beauchamp, Hugh of Laval, and Gilbert and Robert of Clare.

[63] Altschul, *Clares*, 22–23.

[64] On the role of the Clares under William II: R. W. Southern, "Ranulf Flambard and Early Anglo-Norman Administration," *Transactions of the Royal Historical Society*, 4th Series, xvi (1933), 117. Gilbert of Clare was probably a steward of William Rufus: *Regesta*, i, xxiv and nos. 318, 320. Rufus likewise favored Eudo *Dapifer: ibid.*, nos. 399, 435, 442.

[65] W. J. Corbett in *Cambridge Medieval History*, v (Cambridge, Engl., 1926), 511. Corbett ranks Richard sixth, but excludes Odo of Bayeux, Robert of Mortain, and Stephen lord of Richmond, all of whom were wealthier than the lord of Clare as measured by the values of their manors in Domesday Book. Eustace of Boulogne, on the other hand, was slightly less wealthy according to my calculations.

[66] The immense earldoms of Hereford and Kent were now in royal hands.

[67] Under Henry I the Beaumonts acquired the earldom of Leicester, the lordship of Gower (Wales), and the great Norman frontier fief of Breteuil. In 1135, according to Henry II's *Cartae Baronum*, the honor of Clare had 127¼ knight's fees, the earldom of Gloucester 265½ excluding Wales, the Bigod fief 125, and the honor of Brian Fitz Count 100½: I. J. Sanders, *English Baronies* (Oxford, 1960), 6, 35, 47, 93. The earldom of Leicester had *c.* 160 fees in 1166, and the lands formerly held by Stephen of Blois (honors of Boulogne, Eye, and Lancaster) had 225–50 (*ibid.*, 43, 61, 126, 151). On Stephen's lands see Round, *Peerage and Family History*, pp. 167–68, and Davis, *King Stephen*, 7–10; on the Gloucester earldom, R. B. Patterson, "William of Malmesbury's Robert of Gloucester," *American Historical Review*, lxx (1965), 994. The danegeld exemptions in the *Pipe Roll of 31 Henry I* (ed. Joseph Hunter, London 1833, reprinted 1929) have sometimes been used to estimate the extent of baronial demesne lands, but these figures seem to depend very much on royal favor and administrative office. In the year 1130, the lord of Clare had a total exemption of only £10-1-0. All members of the Clare family together had £25-16-5. Walter Giffard had no exemption whatever. Compare the 1130 exemptions of Robert of Gloucester (£125), Stephen of Blois (£66, but £134 in 1129), Roger bishop of Salisbury (£153), William of Warenne (£104), Brian Fitz Count (£72), Hugh Bigod (£20), and Robert earl of Leicester (£29).

[68] Orderic, *Historia*, iv, 296–97, 356; "Chronica de Hida," 317; *Monasticon Anglicanum* vi, 147; *Regesta*, iii, xviii and no. 944; *Pipe Roll 31 Henry I*, p. 122.

of king and barons cooperating to their mutual advantage; there is nothing in it
to attract suspicion.

It might be argued, however, that the case for a Clare-Giffard conspiracy must
rest on events during the opening year of the reign, when Henry appointed
William Giffard to the bishopric of Winchester, raised Walter Giffard to the
earldom of Buckingham, and gave Richard of Clare the abbey of Ely. But it is
precisely during the first year that the hypothesis breaks down most completely.
In 1100, Henry might well be expected to have favored powerful families. His
brother was contemplating an invasion of England, and Henry's throne was
desperately insecure. His position was not that of a successful monarch distribut-
ing largesses to deserving friends but that of a man in serious difficulties, casting
about for support wherever he could find it. His appointment of a Clare to the
abbacy of Ely, like his appointment of Earl Hugh of Chester's bastard son
Robert to the abbacy of Bury St. Edmunds, was an attempt to win powerful support while filling the numerous ecclesiastical vacancies left by Rufus. The
appointment of William Giffard to Winchester, however, was quite another
matter. William had been Rufus's chancellor and was due for a bishopric. Every
one of the six previous chancellors appointed by William I or William II had
been promoted to bishoprics, and Henry was only doing what Rufus himself
would probably have done soon.[69] At the moment of the appointment (August 3)
Henry had just dashed to Winchester from the catastrophe in the New Forest
and was in the most urgent need of curial support. His on-the-spot promotion of
William Giffard was a timely bid for backing, not so much from the Giffard
family as from the royal administration and the Church. As for Walter Giffard,
the head of the family, the evidence suggests that he had already been appointed
earl of Buckingham by Rufus *c.* 1097[70] and gained nothing whatever from the
change of kings.

King Henry's initial year was a time of extreme danger, culminating in Robert
Curthose's invasion in July, 1101. Curthose's bid for the English crown was
accompanied by a widespread rebellion of such great English barons as Robert
of Bellême earl of Shrewsbury, William count of Mortain, and William of
Warenne earl of Surrey. Orderic names Henry's closest advisers at this time:

---

[69] *Regesta*, I, xviii. Herfast became bishop of Elmham, Osbern bishop of Exeter, Osmund bishop of
Salisbury, Maurice bishop of London, Gerard (whom *Regesta* I omits) bishop of Hereford (later arch-
bishop of York), and Robert Bloet bishop of Lincoln. William Giffard was chancellor 1094–1101.
Three other chancellors of Henry I also became bishops: Roger to Salisbury, Waldric to Laon, and
Geoffrey Rufus to Durham (*Regesta*, II, ix–x). The fourth died in office.

[70] *Complete Peerage*, II, 386–7; *Victoria History of the County of Buckingham* (London, 1905–28), I,
248. Orderic (*Historia*, II, 221) is surely mistaken in saying that William I conferred the earldom on
Walter Giffard. Writing of Walter's activities in 1097, Orderic calls him *comes Bucchingehamensis*
(*ibid.*, IV, 20–21) but does not give him the comital title in 1089–90 or 1095 (*ibid.*, III, 319, 475).
Walter does not appear as earl in *Domesday Book*. Later on he sometimes attests as earl, sometimes
not. He does not so attest for William II, but his last attestation in that reign is *Regesta*, I, no. 474
[1093–1100]. All other attestations are 1091 or before. He appears as a witness in 6 versions of Henry I's
Coronation Charter (August 5, 1100: *ibid.*, II, no. 488) — as earl in three but simply as Walter
Giffard in the other three. Before his death in 1102 he witnessed three additional charters of Henry I:
no. 492 not as earl; no. 510 as earl; no. 524 not as earl.

Robert count of Meulan, Hugh earl of Chester, Richard of Redvers and Roger Bigod.[71] If the Clares and Giffards had just completed a successful conspiracy to place Henry on the throne, one might reasonably expect to find them at his side during the critical months that followed. Where were they? Walter Giffard, earl of Buckingham and lord of Longueville, was among the rebels backing Robert Curthose.[72] Gilbert of Clare and his relatives were apparently on the fence. They are mentioned by no chronicler during Henry's first year. They are conspicuously absent from contemporary lists of royal supporters in 1101. Until Henry's reconciliation with Curthose they attest no known royal charters.[73] Their leanings are suggested by the fact that in the following year Henry deposed Richard of Clare from the abbacy of Ely for, among other offenses, failing to obey royal commands with sufficient punctuality.[74] The king may well have had in mind his command to his tenants-in-chief in June, 1101, to bring their knights to the army that he was assembling to meet Curthose's invasion.[75] The behavior of the Clares and Giffards in the great crisis of 1101 cuts through any vague speculation as to their participation with Henry in a hypothetical murder plot.

As for Walter Tirel himself, he evidently enjoyed high favor at Rufus's court. Orderic describes him as the king's constant companion.[76] It is incomprehensible that a man would sacrifice such an enviable position for the sake of his in-laws — fleeing England and leaving his wife's relatives to reap the alleged benefits. Medieval families were often close-knit, but their relationships were characterized by the mutual pursuit of mutual interests, not by self-sacrifice. Moreover, there has long been serious doubt that Tirel actually fired the fatal arrow, and if he did not, the Clare-Giffard hypothesis collapses at its base. The earliest accounts of the shooting — those of the Anglo-Saxon chronicler and Eadmer — omit the archer's name,[77] and although most later accounts identify Tirel as the

---

[71] Orderic, *Historia*, IV, 95; cf. Malmesbury, *Gesta Regum*, II, 471: "Only Robert Fitz Hamon, Richard of Redvers, Roger Bigod, and Robert of Meulan with his brother Henry [earl of Warwick] declared on the side of justice."

[72] Orderic, *Historia*, IV, 103.

[73] Gilbert of Clare appears only once in this period, as one of eleven guarantors for Henry I in the treaty of March 10, 1101 with Robert count of Flanders. Since the list of royal guarantors also included Arnulf of Montgomery, who was in rebellion four months later, nothing much can be deduced from it: *Diplomatic Documents preserved in the Public Record Office*, ed. Pierre Chaplais, I (London, 1964), 1–4.

[74] *Liber Eliensis*, ed. E. O. Blake (Royal Historical Society, London, 1962), 226–27.

[75] *Chronicon Monasterii de Abingdon*, ed. Joseph Stevenson (Rolls Series, London, 1858), II, 128; Eadmer, *Historia Novorum*, 126–27. The Clare in-law Eudo *Dapifer* did support Henry in 1101: *Regesta*, II, nos. 529, 531, 533, 536. But Eudo and Henry were apparently at odds in 1100. The *Historia Fundationis* of St. John's Abbey, Colchester, states that in the immediate aftermath of Rufus's death Henry doubted Eudo's loyalty and turned against him, later restoring him to favor at the urging of Eudo's two curial kinsmen, Bishop William Giffard and Peter of Valognes: *Monasticon Anglicanum*, IV, 608.

[76] Orderic, *Historia*, IV, 86.

[77] *Peterborough Chronicle*, 27: "King William while hunting was shot with an arrow by one of his own men." I find no hint of murder in these words, as others have. Eadmer (*Historia Novorum*, 116) leaves it unsettled whether the arrow struck him in flight or whether, "as the majority say," he stumbled and fell on it. Malmesbury, *Gesta Regum*, II, 378, reports that Rufus hastened his death by

accidental slayer,[78] he himself denied the story. Abbot Suger of Saint-Denis reported that he had often heard Walter Tirel swear by oaths that on the day of the shooting he had not even been in the section of the forest where Rufus was hunting.[79] Tirel was safely in France when he made these denials. As Suger points out, he was free of fear and hope and had no motive to lie.[80] Rumors that Tirel had shot Rufus were evidently in circulation immediately after the king's death, but they may well have been groundless. If so the actual culprit, whoever he was, wisely kept his silence.

A few questions remain to be answered. If Tirel was innocent why did he flee? He doubtless did so to escape the vengeance of Rufus's familiars who, acting on the rumors — accurate or not — were threatening to tear him to pieces. Earlier in the same year the accidental slayer of Curthoses's illegitimate son had escaped vengeance by becoming a monk.[81] Why was there never an official inquiry into the shooting? Perhaps there was, for a proceeding of this sort might well be passed over by the chroniclers.[82] Or perhaps contemporaries were sufficiently convinced of the accidental nature of the deed that no such inquiry was indicated. This may also provide the explanation for Tirel's English lands not being confiscated. The lands in question consisted of a minuscule estate of $2\frac{1}{2}$ hides at Langham, Essex, which Tirel held not as a feudal tenant of the king but as a subtenant of his in-law, the lord of Clare. Responsibility for disinheriting Tirel — if any — would have fallen on Gilbert of Clare, not on Henry I.[83] But in any event, a hunting accident, even if it resulted in the death of a king, would probably call for no legal indictment. Rufus's cronies might curse Tirel, but the law usually required evidence of bad intention, and no such evidence is suggested by any contemporary observer.[84]

---

falling on the wound after Tirel's arrow had struck him. *Chronicon Abingdon*, ii, 43, also leaves the archer unnamed, as does Robert of Torigni (*Gesta Normannorum Ducum*, 278–79: *a quodam suo familiari in corde percussus*).

[78] Malmesbury, *Gesta Regum*, ii, 378; Orderic, *Historia*, iv, 86–87; "Chronica Hida," 302–03; "Annales de Wintonia," in *Annales Monastici*, ii, 40. Cf. the continental accounts in *Monumenta Germaniae Historica, Scriptores*, xiii, 647; xiv, 280. Geraldus Cambrensis identifies the archer as Ralph *de Aquis* (*Opera*, viii, 325–26), but the details of his story suggest a confusion with earlier accounts of Walter Tirel. The name "Ralph de Aquis" (of Aix?) defies identification.

[79] Suger, *Louis VI*, 12.

[80] Suger's story was corroborated later in the century by John of Salisbury in his "Vita Anselmi"· *Anglia Sacra* [ed. Henry Wharton] (London, 1691), ii, 169–70.

[81] Orderic, *Historia* iv 81 90–91.

[82] The chroniclers, for example, report no inquiry and no charges in connection with Ranulf Flambard's arrest in 1100. That formal charges were indeed brought against him we learn quite accidentally from a letter of Archbishop Anselm to Pope Paschal II: *S. Anselmi Opera Omnia*, ed. F. S. Schmitt (Edinburgh, 1946–61), iv, 112–13.

[83] *Domesday Book*, ii, 41. The estate turns up in 1130 in the hands of Tirel's widow, Adeliza of Clare: *Pipe Roll of 31 Henry I*, 56. Tirel was a large landholder on the Continent: lord of Poix and castellan of Pontoise.

[84] Customary law was not altogether consistent on the question of intention: *Leges Henrici Primi*, ed. L. J. Downer (Oxford, 1972), Chs. 5.28b, 70.12, 88.6, 90.2, and 90.11. Professor Joseph M. Tyrrell of Old Dominion College (Norfolk, Va.) has suggested to me still another possible explanation for Rufus's death: that he was assassinated, by Walter Tirel or somebody else, for some personal grievance unconnected with Henry's accession and unknown to us.

Medieval accounts of the shooting differ on many points, but no writer suggests deliberation or conspiracy. The notion that all the writers of the age were involved in a vast deception cannot be taken seriously.[85] Not the slightest breath of scandal ever touched Henry I from any contemporary or nearly contemporary writer — not from Suger of Saint-Denis who had little to fear from Henry, or from the able historians writing in Stephen's reign. Henry of Huntingdon, in his *De Contemptu Mundi*, catalogued most of the scandals of the era and was by no means gentle with Henry I, but the notion of fratricide never dawned on him. King Henry was accused of dark deeds that he may actually have committed, such as the blinding of William of Mortain,[86] and of other crimes that he did not commit, such as the alleged mutilation of Robert Curthose.[87] But he was never accused, even by indirection, of involvement in Rufus's slaying.[88]

Hunting in the middle ages could be a dangerous sport, and Rufus was not the only man of his period to meet with death while engaged in the chase. Some years earlier, Richard, son of William the Conqueror, had been mortally injured by colliding with a tree while riding swiftly after a stag in the New Forest. In about May, 1100, Curthose's bastard son Richard had been shot accidentally while hunting in the same forest.[89] In 1143 the earl of Hereford, hunting deer on Christmas Eve, "was pierced through the breast by a knight, who shot an arrow wildly at a stag, and died wretchedly without profit from repentance."[90] At about the same time Malcolm of Morville perished in a hunting accident in Scotland, the victim of Adulf of St. Martin's poor aim.[91] There is no evidence that these deaths were anything but accidental, nor in the long run is there any evidence that Rufus's was. Theories of witchcraft, conspiracy, and murder only demonstrate how a fortuitous chain of events can sometimes acquire a misleading aura of premeditation when viewed in retrospect.

But one cannot lay such theories aside without a touch of regret. Henry emerges less repellent than before but also, in a sense, less interesting. For in all probability his accession in 1100 can be ascribed to neither human calculation nor divine, but only to the misaimed arrow of some blundering archer.

---

[85] Parker ("Forest Laws," 31) seems to have this notion.

[86] Henry of Huntingdon, *Historia Anglorum*, 255.

[87] David, *Robert Curthose*, 200–02.

[88] Cf. the killing of Geoffrey Martel of Anjou at the siege of Candé (May 19, 1106), which immediately generated rumors accusing his stepmother, Queen Bertrada of France, and his father, Fulk IV count of Anjou: Josèphe Chartrou, *L'Anjou de 1109 à 1151* (Paris, 1928), 3 and n. 3.

[89] *Gesta Normannorum Ducum*, 279; Malmesbury, *Gesta Regum*, II, 332; Orderic, *Historia*, II, 391, IV, 81; Florence of Worcester, *Chronicon*, II, 45.

[90] *Gesta Stephani*, 106; cf. *ibid.*, 16, 98; John of Hexham, in Simeon of Durham, *Opera Omnia*, II, 315; Gervase of Canterbury, *Historical Works*, ed. William Stubbs (Rolls Series, London, 1879–80), I, 126.

[91] *Liber S. Marie de Dryburgh* (Bannatyne Club, 1847), 68–69.

4

THE ANGLO-NORMAN CIVIL WAR: 1101[1]

DUKE Robert Curthose's invasion of England in 1101 might have changed the course of twelfth-century history. But in fact it ended anticlimactically, in a truce rather than a battle, and the newly-won crown of Henry I was saved without a blow. The campaign was the key to Henry's future and to the generation of peace that England enjoyed from 1102 to 1135. Its outcome would have seemed far from certain, however, during the first, troubled year of Henry's reign (August, 1100–July, 1101). In the month following his coronation his elder brother, Robert Curthose, had returned to Normandy in triumph from the First Crusade with a strong claim of his own to the English throne.[2] The greatest magnates in England were ready to support Curthose's cause, and Henry, with only a handful of firm baronial supporters, was threatened with catastrophe – or with a prolonged insurrection such as was later to cloud King Stephen's reign. Henry was shrewder than Stephen, and luckier too. But in July, 1101, his crown, his life, and the peace of England were all at stake, and the prospect was not encouraging.

E. A. Freeman described the campaign of 1101 as the last Norman invasion of England. More than that, he saw it as the last occasion on which Englishmen would be called to defend their land against foreigners.[3] But the episode cannot be seen simply as a struggle between English patriots and Norman invaders; the reality was much more complex. True, most of the native English supported Henry against his brother.[4] But there were Normans, too, who favoured Henry, both in England and in Normandy.[5] Freeman notwithstanding, Henry was far more Norman than English, and his friends and enemies alike were apt to hold lands on both sides of the Channel. As Professor Le Patourel has so persuasively demonstrated,

---

1. I am grateful to the American Council of Learned Societies, the American Philosophical Society, the Social Science Research Council, the Fulbright Commission, the John Simon Guggenheim Memorial Foundation, and the Warden and Fellows of Merton College, Oxford for their help in supporting the research for this paper, to the British Museum for providing a photocopy of portions of Cottonian MS. Caligula, A. viii, and to my research assistants, Mrs. H. A. Drake, Miss Carole E. Moore, and Mrs. Jean Saulter.

2. Ord[ericus] Vit[alis], *Historia Ecclesiastica*, ed. A. Le Prévost (1838–55)], iv. 113, reports that Robert Curthose claimed England on the grounds of primogeniture. Rules of succession were murky in 1100, and Henry had colourable claims of his own. See C. W. David, *Robert Curthose, Duke of Normandy* (1920), pp. 120–1, and Christopher Brooke, *The Saxon and Norman Kings* (1963), pp. 194–6.

3. E. A. Freeman, *The Reign of William Rufus* (1882), ii. 402, and *Norman Conquest*, v (1876), 172.

4. Robert of Torigny, in *Gesta Normannorum Ducum*, ed. J. Marx (1914), p. 282; Florence of Worcester, *Chronicon ex Chronicis*, ed. B. Thorpe (Engl. Hist. Soc., 1848–9), ii. 48–9; William of Malmesbury, *Gesta Regum Anglorum*, ed. W. Stubbs (R.S., 1887–9), ii. 471–2. Some English sailors defected to Curthose: Florence, ii. 48.

5. Malmesbury, *Gesta Regum*, ii. 471; Ord. Vit., iv. 106.

the larger landholders of Normandy and England are best regarded as members of a single society. These were men with common customs, a common tongue, a common culture, a strong sense of ethnic identity, trans-Channel holdings and family interests, and a preference toward being governed by a single ruler.[1] From 1066 to 1204, Anglo-Norman unity was the norm and division the unstable exception. Curthose's supporters in England and Henry's in Normandy were both, in effect, working toward the reunification of what one contemporary called the *regnum Norman-Anglorum*.[2] The campaign of 1101 was not an abortive Norman invasion of England but a crucial episode in an Anglo-Norman civil war that had begun the previous year when William Rufus died, Henry seized the throne, and Curthose returned to his duchy. The truce that ended the campaign left the Anglo-Norman state divided until 1106 when Henry routed Curthose at Tinchebray and assumed the government of Normandy.

The events of the 1101 campaign are touched on in every history of medieval England. In the last century they have received two detailed treatments – the first by Freeman (1882), the second by C. W. David (1920).[3] Both accounts make thorough use of the published sources and both remain valuable. But both require revision on the basis of interpretations and documents that have emerged in the past fifty years. For one thing, analysis of the holdings of important lords in England permits a more precise estimate than before of the nature and relative strength of the opposing baronial factions. Further illumination is cast by the charters relating to Ranulf Flambard published for the first time in 1930 by Sir Edmund Craster.[4] Finally, a previously unused Durham manuscript provides fresh information on the campaign. This manuscript, which forms a portion of British Museum Cottonian MS. Caligula, A. viii, is a condensed version of Simeon of Durham's *Historia Regum* with certain valuable additions.[5] The annal for 1101 departs almost

1. John Le Patourel, 'The Norman Succession, 996–1135', *ante*, lxxxvi (1971), 225–50, and *Normandy and England, 1066–1144* (Stenton Lecture, Reading, 1971), *passim*. Orderic (iii. 268–9) lays bare the difficulties faced by Anglo-Norman barons in trying to keep the favour of two antagonistic masters. The English, of course, had very different perceptions, but Freeman's picture of their accepting Henry I as one of their own is overdrawn. Having no choice but to be ruled by a Norman, they were more interested in their king's ability to keep the peace than in his place of birth. They supported William II no less than Henry I: *e.g.*, *A[nglo] S[axon] C[hronicle]*, A.D. 1087 (= 1088).

2. 'Chronica Monasterii de Hida juxta Wintoniam', in *Liber Monasterii de Hyda*, ed. Edward Edwards (R.S., 1866), pp. 300, 305; *cf. ibid.*, pp. 296–319, *passim*.

3. Freeman, *Rufus*, ii. 392–415, 688–91; David, *Curthose*, pp. 127–37.

4. H. H. E. Craster '[A Contemporary Record of the Pontificate of Ranulf]Flambard,' [*Archaeologia Aeliana*, 4th series, vii (1930)], 33–56.

5. The manuscript, written in a twelfth-century hand, is the second of 17 items in MS. Caligula, A. viii. It is entitled *Chronicon Simeonis monachi Dunelmensis, de primis Angliae gentis regibus; sive a primo Saxonum adventu, h.e. ab A.D. 449, ad annum 1119.* T. D. Hardy noticed it in his *Descriptive Catalogue of Materials Relating to the History of Great Britain and Ireland* (R.S., 1862–71), ii. 176–7, where brief excerpts are printed.

totally from the *Historia Regum,* omitting most of the information
contained in the original (which is drawn chiefly from Florence of
Worcester)[1] and inserting in its place an account that provides new
facts and clarifies former ambiguities. The fresh data seem consistent
with all that we know of the campaign. One cannot help but suspect
that the passage is based on the eyewitness report of Ranulf Flambard, bishop of Durham, who was Curthose's chief adviser in 1101.[2]
Together with other evidence, unused by Freeman and David, it
provides the basis for a reappraisal.

Freeman saw the invasion-rebellion of 1101 as a duplicate of the
uprising of 1088 against King William Rufus.[3] In many ways, the
two episodes were similar. Each occurred in the opening year of a
new reign. Each was an abortive attempt to reunify England and
Normandy under Robert Curthose. And in each a new king of
England was opposed by a coalition of the realm's greatest barons.
In 1088 the three wealthiest magnates of England were in rebellion:
Odo bishop of Bayeux and Robert count of Mortain – the Con-
queror's half brothers – and Roger of Montgomery, earl of Shrews-
bury. All three had extensive holdings in Normandy as well as in
England, and they were supported by other important Anglo-
Norman magnates such as Eustace of Boulogne, Roger Bigod,
Hugh of Grandmesnil, Geoffrey bishop of Coutances, and Geoffrey's
nephew Robert of Mowbray, earl of Northumberland.[4] In 1101 the
anti-royal coalition was at least as formidable. In place of Robert of
Mortain and Roger of Montgomery were their sons and heirs,
William of Mortain and Robert of Bellême. William was earl of
Cornwall, count of Mortain, and lord of vast dominions on both
sides of the Channel.[5] Robert of Bellême had inherited the Builli

---

Excerpts have also been provided by Hodgson Hinde, *Symeonis Dunelmensis Opera et
Collectanea,* i (Surtees Soc., li, 1868), 105. The annal for 1101 (fo. 41, new foliation) is
printed in full in the appendix to this article.

1. See Simeon of Durham, *Opera Omnia,* ed. Thomas Arnold (R.S., 1882–5), ii. 232–3.
2. Ord. Vit., iv. 110; Florence, ii. 48; *A.S.C.,* A.D. 1101; Henry of Huntingdon,
Historia Anglorum, ed. Thomas Arnold (R.S., 1879), p. 234. Ranulf's exact connection
with the unknown annalist is beyond discovery. Conceivably, the intermediary may have
been the Durham Book of the High Altar (now lost): see Craster, 'Flambard', p. 34,
and 'The Red Book of Durham', *ante,* xl (1925), 504–32.
3. Freeman, *Rufus,* ii. 392–3.
4. On the 1088 campaign see *ibid.,* i. 22–89; ii. 465–83.
5. On the immense Mortain *apanage* in England – concentrated in Cornwall and
Somerset but extending across the land (Yorks., Northants., Devon, Sussex, Dorset,
Bucks., and twelve other counties) – see Domesday Book, *passim;* Henry Ellis, *A
General Introduction to Domesday Book* (1833), i. 455; ii. 356; and W. J. Corbett in
Camb. Med. Hist., v. 506, 508. In 1086 the Mortain barony in England was worth about
£2100 a year, almost one fifth the demesne income of the king and queen (c. £11,000:
ibid., p. 508). In 1172 the Mortain fief in Normandy owed about 30 knights to the
duke, exceeding by 50 per cent the obligation of any other Norman lord: *R[ed] B[ook
of the] E[xchequer],* ed. Hubert Hall (R.S., 1896), ii. 643; *Recueil des historiens des Gaules
et de la France,* ed. M. Bouquet *et. al.,* xxiii. 698. For William of Mortain's role in 1101
see 'Chron. Hida', pp. 304–5; Wace, *Roman de Rou,* ed. Hugo Andresen (1877–9), ii.
445; and Malmesbury, *Gesta Regum,* ii. 431.

dium uſuſ · a duob; pꝼ ſcrand̄ clerci apud heretochiam a laudiſ; nocꞇurniſ ercuꞇuſ ſplendor in
ſoleſ ad menſuram unuſ gnue porectuſ · m illa celeſꞇi ſpe parte qua ſol eſſe ſolec circa hinem
h eꝯ · cum in eſꞇuo ſolſꞇiꞇio uergit Adoccaſum · Eric aūt conſꝓ illud unde ſplendor erchar ille alba
ꞇerum rubie · ꝓ breuia ꞇemꝑuſ ineruallia ſepi augibe ſſara quaſi erciliens Ad ſupiora emer
gebac · ꝓ breuem moꞇa ꞇerum rubi immergebac · qd non ſine meu de ſtupore cernebauꞇ ·
Coler · ꝙ; eiuſ erac · quaſi de coloub; plene lune ꝓ lucid̄q flamme eſſe confecꞇ· formali ec quivaſ
euſ ſic breuiſ piꞇamiſ · in inferioub; laꞇa · ꝓ in ſuperioub; Anguſta · Cumꝙ; illi ꝙ hec uidiere in
clamaſſenꞇ · uc pluriſ in laic re reſteſ habe poſſenꞇ· ꞇabula mediocriſ in longum ercta ſtare in
ſaꝯ ſupiniubem · in qua ſplendid̄ conſꝓ illud fuerac qd ſupꞇſiam nubie lumen Abinꞇuo ſpaꞇſerac ·
ꝓ in ſinc primaſ ſibi aquilonis partes inferni magna er parte ꞇenui luce repleuerac · mui luciidaꝙ
qua loꝯ in ꝙ ſtabar · Inꝛ hec ueneir qd̄ qui in clinian fuerant · ꝓ moꝛ in eotum aduencu omiſ
luc illa pene; ercinctu · n̄ paucuſſima ipſi ueſtiga que uiu imparc· Aquiloniſ tenui porerare
uider · Qui uuce priuſ ſtarꞇ lucem uidir· duaſ· eciam nuncio uiſtoniſ lineaſ quaſi aurorali lu
ce plenuſ Abquinoctuali ſolſ omi—uſꝙ· Abquinoctale ci occaſum porecꞇaſ aſpecꞇ· h; propauore
quem inde in currie; ꝓ Altera de qua dictuſ uiſtone cu tre muiende· naꝙ; quancum ille ꝓſtare
due lineꝯ dinauerꞇ · neꝙ; ꝙdo diſceſſere poꞇuit agnoſcei · Viſa ſunt iſta in caſtello herehonclenſi· 1
a clerciſ ſi queſtaci · Viſa ſt eciam a multiſ; brecena in menſi caſtelli · inſup in pago herehonden̄ſir
ap oſtercu; in ipla nocte ſup gregem ſui uigilanꞇub; Que dici ſcripſi · ſaluec noſ gꞇ na · ꝟꝯ·

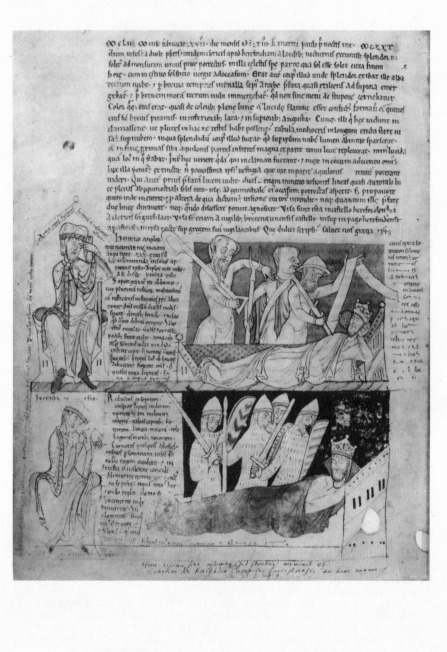

The Worcester chronicle, on the authority of Henry I's physician Grimbald, reports that the king, while in Normandy in 1130, was alarmed by three successive nightmares in a single night. In the first, a great crowd of angry peasants advanced threateningly toward him brandishing their tools and gnashing their teeth. In the second, Henry's life was similarly menaced by an array of knights brandishing their weapons. In the third, Henry was terrified by hostile prelates attacking him with the points of their pastoral staves. Afterwards, relating his dreams to Grimbald, Henry followed his physician's advice to atone for his sins by almsgiving.

Line drawing in the Chronicle of John of Worcester, MS. Corp. Chri. Coll., Oxon, clvii, fo. 382–83. (*By courtesy of the President and Fellows of Corpus Christi College, Oxford*)

honour of Tickhill (Yorks.) in addition to the Montgomery earldom
of Shrewsbury and lordship of Arundel. He was count of Ponthieu
by marriage, vicomte of the Hiémois in southern Normandy, lord
of Bellême in Perche, and master of thirty-four continental castles.
He was also William of Mortain's uncle.[1] Odo of Bayeux's lands
having been forfeited under Rufus, Robert of Bellême and William
of Mortain remained the two wealthiest landholders in England and
Normandy alike. They were joined in their conspiracy by Robert
of Bellême's two brothers, Roger the Poitevin lord of Lancaster and
count of La Marche, and Arnulf of Montgomery lord of Pembroke
(South Wales) and Holderness (Yorks).[2] Allied with William of
Mortain and the Montgomerys were other formidable magnates:
William II of Warenne earl of Surrey, Walter II Giffard earl of
Buckingham, Ivo of Grandmesnil, Robert of Lacy lord of Ponte-
fract, and Eustace III count of Boulogne.[3]

All nine of these magnates belonged to powerful older families
that had acquired extensive English lands from William the Conqueror. Each man, as it happened, was a son of the original recipient of the family's English estates. Most of them were young in
1101, and all were fiercely independent, accustomed to wealth and
power, suspicious of royal centralization, and disinclined to frequent
the king's court or serve in his administration. Their attestations
appear in Rufus's surviving charters only seven times.

Henry's baronial partisans were older, less wealthy, and far
more devoted to the royal service. The nine who can be identified
were responsible for some 123 attestations of Rufus's charters.
These were men who had prospered, or hoped to prosper, in the

1. William of Mortain's mother was Matilda, daughter of Roger of Montgomery
and sister of Robert of Bellême. Robert's English inheritance from his father, Roger of
Montgomery (Shrewsbury, Arundel and elsewhere), was worth about £2100 a year;
the Builli honour of Tickhill added c. £267 (Edmond C. Waters, 'The Counts of Eu',
Yorks. Archaeological and Topographical Journal, ix (1886), 287). On the Hiémois (Sées,
Argentan, and the Forest of Gouffern): Ord. Vit., iv. 104 and n., 305; V, 4. See Sidney
Painter, 'The Family and the Feudal System in Twelfth-Century England', *Speculum*,
xxxv (1960), 14, and J. F. A. Mason, 'Roger de Montgomery and his Sons', *Trans.
Royal Hist. Soc.*, 5th series, xiii (1963), 4–5, 22–3. Cf. Vct. du Motey, *Robert II de Belleme*
(1923), *passim*.
2. On Roger's countship of La Marche: *Reg[esta Regum Anglo-Normannorum*, ed.
H. W. C. Davis, Charles Johnson, H. A. Cronne, and R. H. C. Davis (1913–69)], ii,
no. 919 (but *cf.* P. Chaplais, *E.H.R.*, lxxv (1960), p. 272). See also Painter, 'Family and
Feudal System', p. 14. Mason, 'Roger de Montgomery', p. 23, calls the holdings of
Robert of Bellême and his brothers 'one of the largest, if not the largest, accumulations
of power ever wielded by a single English baronial family'.
3. Ord. Vit., iv. 103–4, 161; *A.S.C.*, A.D. 1101 (on Eustace of Boulogne). William II
of Warenne, with estates in Sussex and elsewhere worth c. £1165 a year in 1086, was
the third wealthiest English landholder among the Anglo-Norman baronage, behind
Robert of Bellême and William of Mortain (and the archbishop of Canterbury).
Eustace of Boulogne (Essex and elsewhere), who had crusaded with Curthose, ranked
eighth among laymen with c. £770 but was apparently not in possession of his English
patrimony until the settlement of August, 1101 (*ibid.*) Orderic places Robert Malet in the
Curthose faction, but wrongly I believe (below, pp. 129-36).

service of a strong, successful king. They came from two overlapping groups: (1) old friends of Henry's prior to his accession – Hugh earl of Chester (who had also been close to Rufus) and Richard of Redvers – and (2) administrators, *familiares*, and 'new men' of the previous regime. Of these latter, Robert count of Meulan had been for several years a leading royal counsellor. His brother, Henry earl of Warwick, had received his lands and title from Rufus. Roger Bigod, sheriff of Norfolk, had been made a royal *dapifer* by Rufus and attested 26 of his charters. Robert fitz Hamon, conqueror of Glamorgan, had received from Rufus a large honour in western England and attested 18 of his charters. Robert's brother, Hamo *Dapifer*, who had inherited a royal stewardship and the shrievalty of Kent, had been one of Rufus's most active administrators (though it is possible that the Hamo of 1101 was Hamo I's son, Hamo II). Eudo *Dapifer*, steward of both Williams and a large Domesday holder, had been another of Rufus's chief administrators (31 attestations) and had received from him substantial lands in Bedfordshire. Finally, Urse of Abitôt, constable and sometime sheriff of Worcestershire, had been still another of Rufus's *familiares* and administrative lieutenants (15 attestations).[1]

The wealthiest of these royalist barons, Hugh earl of Chester (*c.* £800 a year) was dying in his monastery of St. Werburgh at the time of the 1101 invasion, and his son Richard was only about seven years old.[2] Hugh alone had an English income comparable to those of Curthose's leading supporters, and he was incapable of aiding the king. Roger Bigod's English holdings were substantial (*c.* £450 a year) but only after 1101 did they grow into one of the kingdom's leading honours.[3] The wealth of the Beaumonts likewise lay largely

---

1. For the names of Henry's partisans: Malmesbury, *Gesta Regum*, ii. 471; Ord. Vit., iv. 95, 110; Florence, ii. 49; *Reg.* ii, nos. 534–6. On their administrative role: *Reg.* i, pp. xvi, xxiii–iv, and nos 337, 387, 416, 418, 422, 424; ii, no. 377a; Ord. Vit., iv. 51. On their holdings: *Monasticon Anglicanum*, ii. 60; Ord. Vit., iii. 273, 350; I. J. Sanders, *English Baronies* (1960), pp. 6, 92, 93. Hugh of Chester and Robert fitz Hamon were among Rufus's few baronial supporters in 1088: Ord. Vit., ii. 436–7. Most of these *familiares* of Rufus were also acquaintances of Henry I prior to Rufus's death. The Norman patrimonies of Robert fitz Hamon, Hamo *Dapifer*, Eudo *Dapifer* (all in the Bessin), and Roger Bigod (Bocage) were in Norman districts where Henry had been and remained influential. Their Norman family lands were thus shielded to a degree from the ducal vengeance. But this point must not be pressed too far: *e.g.*, the Beaumont lands were vulnerable as was Richard of Redvers' Vernon fief. Henry I and Henry earl of Warwick had long been intimate friends (Malmesbury, *Gesta Regum*, ii. 470). Henry I was also backed by the great prelates (apart from Ranulf of Durham and perhaps Richard of Ely). Anselm supported him ardently: Eadmer, *Historia Novorum in Anglia*, ed. Martin Rule (R.S., 1884), pp. 126–8; William of Malmesbury, *Gesta Pontificum Anglorum*, ed. N. E. S. A. Hamilton (R.S., 1870), pp. 104–6.

2. Hugh of Chester held lands in 21 counties: Ellis, *Introduction to Domesday*, i. 437. On his last illness and death (27 July 1101) see Ord. Vit., iv. 111. *Cf. Complete Peerage*, iii. 165.

3. Roger Bigod (d. 1107) held in Essex, Norfolk, and Suffolk: Domesday Book, ii. 87b, 173, 330b; *cf. V[ictoria] C[ounty] H[istory], Suffolk*, i. 468; R.B.E., i. 395–7; and *Complete Peerage*, ix. 575–80. The honour claimed (in 1166) to have enfeoffed 125 knights by 1135.

in the future: Henry's Warwick earldom was based on lands held formerly by Thurkill of Arden and Robert of Meulan, worth about £327 a year in 1086; and Robert of Meulan – with rich fiefs in Upper Normandy and the French Vexin – had not yet acquired the Grandmesnil lands that were to form the core of the later Beaumont earldom of Leicester. Robert fitz Hamon's English holdings consisted chiefly of lands belonging originally to the thegn Brictric and later to Queen Matilda, which had a total Domesday value of c. £260–320 a year.[1]

In 1101 twelve lords held English lands worth £750 a year or more. I have compiled a list of these twelve based on Domesday values of the lands that they or their predecessors held of the king in 1086. These figures should not be taken as precise indices of wealth: they exclude non-landed income; they lump together demesne and subinfeudated portions of the various honours; they do not take into account the sub-tenancies that great magnates often held from other tenants-in-chief; and, of course, they ignore continental holdings.[2] Nevertheless the figures are suggestive. Of the twelve leading English landholders, eight are laymen, and of the eight, four (including the three wealthiest) favoured Curthose in 1101. Of the four remaining laymen, one – Hugh of Chester – was incapacitated, and the leanings of the other three are not reported.[3]

1. On the origins of the Warwick earldom see *Chronicon Monasterii de Abingdon*, ed. Joseph Stevenson (R.S., 1859), ii. 20; *V.C.H., Warwicks.*, i. 276–9; Domesday Book, i. 160b, 239b–241b. The earldom owed 63 knights in 1159 and claimed (in 1166) to have enfeoffed 102 by 1135: *R.B.E.*, i. 18, 324–6. On the earldom of Leicester see Ord. Vit., iv. 168; *V.C.H., Leics.*, i. 291, 301; *Complete Peerage*, vii. 524–5. On the fitz Hamon lands (Glos., Bucks., Cornwall, and possibly Wilts. and Somerset) see *Complete Peerage*, v. 682–3; Domesday Book, i. 73b, 98b, 99, 120, 152b, 163b, 164, 170b.

2. Their names are as follows (the asterisk indicates a ducal supporter in 1101; approximate 1086 land revenues in pounds a year are bracketed): (1) Robert of Bellême* [2365]; (2) William of Mortain* [2100]; (3) Anselm abp. of Canterbury [1635]; (4) William of Warenne* [1165]; (5) Count Stephen lord of Richmond [1100 plus much Yorks. waste]; (6) William Giffard bp. of Winchester [1000]; (7) Herluin ab. of Glastonbury [828, but in financial difficulties c. 1101]; (8) Hugh earl of Chester [800]; (9) Gilbert of Clare [782]; (10) William of Mandeville [780]; (11) Eustace count of Boulogne* [770, but probably not in possession in 1100]; (12) Richard of Clare, ab. of Ely [770]. The relative wealth of churchmen on this list tends to be exaggerated because, unlike laymen, they held no continental lands and held no lands as tenants of other lords. The preparation of this list was facilitated by the calculations of David Knowles, *The Monastic Order in England* (2nd ed., 1966), p. 702; Corbett in *Camb. Med. Hist.*, v. 508–11; Mason, 'Roger de Montgomery', pp. 4–5; F. R. H. DuBoulay, *The Lordship of Canterbury* (London, 1966), p. 58 n.; and my research assistant, Miss Carole E. Moore.

3. The three are Stephen of Richmond, Gilbert of Clare, and William of Mandeville. William was lord of the Tower of London at the time of Ranulf Flambard's escape (Ord. Vit., iv. 108–9), and it may well be significant that shortly thereafter key portions of the Mandeville demesne were seized for non-payment of a huge debt to the king: C. W. Hollister, 'The Misfortunes of the Mandevilles', below, pp. 117-27.   From the beginning of the reign to the time of Henry I's reconciliation with Curthose William attests no royal charters. The other two men, Stephen of Richmond and Gilbert of Clare, do not attest in this period, but both are among Henry I's sureties at the treaty of Dover (10 March, 1101: *Reg.* ii, no. 515). Since Arnulf of Montgomery also appears in this group of sureties, not much can be inferred from it regarding loyalties. It may

The appearance of Gilbert fitz Richard's name among these three unreported magnates is a matter of considerable interest. Neither Gilbert nor his Clare kinsmen turn up in any contemporary discussion of Henry's supporters. Their inconspicuousness at this moment of crisis, combined with the known anti-royal stance of Gilbert's uncle, Walter Giffard, should give pause to anyone inclining toward John Horace Round's suggestion of a Clare-Giffard conspiracy to murder William Rufus and crown Henry in his place.[1]

The list also points to the importance of churchmen, not only in providing Henry with moral support – as Anselm did so conspicuously – but also in supplying armed help. Anselm's archiepiscopal lands were more valuable than those of any layman except Robert of Bellême and William of Mortain. Anselm owed 60 knights to the crown,[2] and by the late eleventh century Canterbury tenants owed the archbishop 98–1/2 knights.[3] We know that Henry I summoned the full *servicia debita* for the 1101 campaign,[4] and given the extreme emergency, Anselm may well have brought considerably more than his required 60 knights to Henry's army.[5] Altogether the four prelates among the twelve largest landholders owed, according to later figures, a total of 220 knights. English churchmen as a whole owed over 740 knights, and even though their actual contribution probably fell below that figure, it must have been considerable.[6]

From the moment of his accession Henry had courted the Church – filling bishoprics and abbacies long kept vacant by Rufus, bringing Archbishop Anselm back from exile and handling him with cautious restraint, imprisoning Ranulf Flambard, bishop of Durham, who as head of Rufus's government in England had bled churchmen of

be suggestive that Gilbert's uncle was the known rebel Walter II Giffard (J. H. Round, *Feudal England* (1895), pp. 468–73) and that Gilbert's brother Richard was deprived of his abbacy of Ely in 1102 for, among other things, failing to respond promptly to royal commands: *Liber Eliensis*, ed. E. O. Blake (Royal Hist. Soc., 1962), pp. 226–7. The Mandeville and Boulogne families were connected by the marriage (*ante* 1085) of William of Mandeville's sister to Geoffrey, natural son of Eustace II of Boulogne: *Reg.* i, no. 202; *ante*, xxix (1914), 356; J. H. Round, in *The Genealogist*, new series, ii. 145–6.

1. Round, *Feudal England*, p. 472. Apart from Gilbert of Clare's one appearance, in the treaty of Dover, no Clare turns up in a royal charter until after the 1101 settlement, and none is mentioned in any chronicle. See C. W. Hollister, 'The Strange Death of William Rufus', above, ch. 3, pp. 59–75.

2. *R.B.E.*, i. 22.

3. *The Domesday Monachorum of Christ Church, Canterbury*, ed. D. C. Douglas (1944), p. 105.

4. *Chron. Abingdon*, ii. 128.

5. On the obligation to provide, in time of emergency, the full armed strength rather than the quota, see C. W. Hollister, *The Military Organization of Norman England* (1965), pp. 75–81, 216–19, and *Anglo-Saxon Military Institutions* (1962), pp. 25–37.

6. H. M. Chew, *The English Ecclesiastical Tenants-in-Chief and Knight Service* (1932), pp. 19–20. See Ord. Vit., iv. 106: 'Venerabilis Anselmus archiepiscopus et omnes episcopi et abbates cum sacro clero et omnes Angli indissolubiliter regi suo adhaerebant ....'

their treasures and earned their hostility. Accordingly, the prelates supported Henry as a friend who would treat them generously and as a ruler who would keep domestic peace. Likewise the curial barons and administrators, who had prospered in Rufus's service, evidently hoped to prosper more in the court of another strong king. Henry tried to win the support of the wealthy non-curial barons as well. He obtained oaths of allegiance from his major tenants-in-chief on more than one occasion during his first year.[1] It was perhaps at this time, too, that he promoted Robert Malet to the master chamberlainship, offered his sister-in-law in marriage to William of Mortain, and tried to arrange the marriage of one of his natural daughters to William of Warenne.[2] But neither marriage took place: William of Mortain is said to have refused disdainfully, and William of Warenne's marriage was blocked by consanguinity. In general, the non-curial magnates preferred the rule of a genial, undemanding monarch who would not compromise their independence. As in 1088, so in 1101 most of them supported Curthose, 'seeming to follow King Henry but far removed from him in spirit'.[3] The one great difference between the campaigns of 1088 and 1101 lay in their execution. In 1088 the rebellion was wretchedly co-ordinated and Curthose provided no effective leadership. He was planning to cross to England but never quite managed it, and Rufus was able to put down the revolt castle by castle.[4] Curthose's aimlessness in 1088 typified the quality of his leadership throughout his career, except for the months between February and July, 1101. Then, for the first and last time, his administration functioned with rare effectiveness, raising and organizing a sizeable army and fleet and directing them with shrewd intelligence. No baron rebelled in England until Curthose had landed, and even then the rebels acted in close co-ordination with the invasion force.

1. Ord. Vit., iv. 94; Hugh the Chantor, *The History of the Church of York, 1066–1127*, ed. Charles Johnson (London, 1961), p. 10; Eadmer, *Historia Novorum*, p. 126; *Reg.* ii, no. 531.

2. At some point in his career Robert Malet was appointed master chamberlain: *Sir Christopher Hatton's Book of Seals*, ed. L. C. Loyd and D. M. Stenton (Oxford, 1950), no. 39; *Reg.* ii, no. 1777; *cf. Reg.* iii, nos. 634–5. Since Robert attests no known charters of William II the appointment must have been made by Henry I (of whose charters Robert attests at least 19 between 1100 and c. 1105), but whether before or after the crisis of 1101 is uncertain. He attests as *camerarius* only once: *Reg.* ii, no. 682: 13 Feb. [1105]. 'Chron. Hida', p. 306, mentions under the year 1104, perhaps retrospectively, that Henry offered his wife's sister, Mary of Scotland, in marriage to William of Mortain; if the offer was indeed made it must have been before Mary's marriage to Eustace of Boulogne in 1102. On Henry's attempt to arrange a marriage between one of his bastard daughters and William of Warenne see *S. Anselmi Cantuariensis Archiepiscopi Opera Omnia*, ed. F. S. Schmitt (1946–51), v. 369–70. Anselm's letter on the matter must have been written in 1100–01 or 1105–9, when Henry was on good terms with both Anselm and William of Warenne. The earlier period seems the more likely because of the circumstances of 1101 and because in later years Henry did not marry his daughters to Anglo-Norman barons (see *Complete Peerage*, xi, App., pp. 112–21).   3. 'Chron. Hida', p. 305.   4. See David, *Curthose*, pp. 47–52.

The source of this suddenly effective leadership was Ranulf Flambard, administrative lieutenant of the late William Rufus, who managed a spectacular escape from the Tower of London on February 2 or 3 and, hastening to Normandy, became Curthose's chief adviser for the next half year.[1] Curthose had already been considering a move against Henry at the secret urging of prominent barons in England and had sent a complaint against his seizure of the throne to Pope Paschal II.[2] But until the arrival of Flambard one gets the impression of lethargy and non-direction at the Norman court. Curthose's movements in these months seem unhurried and politically aimless. He went on a short pilgrimage to Mont-Saint-Michel, perhaps paid a visit to his sister Cecilia, abbess of Caen, and lavished money, strategic castles and huge tracts of land on his favourites.[3] It is at this point that Orderic inserts his remarks about Curthose surrounding himself with harlots, buffoons, and idlers who consumed all his money and even stole his clothes, preventing him from going to mass because he had nothing to wear.[4] Orderic's enthusiasm toward Henry I doubtless prompted him to exaggerate the duke's shortcomings, yet we are left with the impression that without Flambard's guidance Curthose would have had serious difficulty organizing a major cross-Channel invasion.

In the months following Flambard's arrival everything changed. By mid-July a sizeable army and fleet had been assembled at Tréport in northeastern Normandy, ready to cross to England.[5] Flambard was well informed on Henry's defensive arrangements and had an effective plan to circumvent them. By Whitsunday (9 June), rumours of Curthose's preparations had reached England, and the chronicles report that Henry's chief men turned openly hostile.[6]

At his Whitsun court at St. Albans, the king struck out at his brother's new counsellor. Having already arranged for an extension of his truce with Anselm on the investiture and homage issues,[7] he disseised Ranulf Flambard, with Anselm's backing, of the lands of

1. *A.S.C.*, A.D. 1101, dates the escape at Candlemas (2 Feb.); the first continuer of Simeon's 'Historia Dunelmensis Ecclesiae,' (*Opera*, i. 138), and MS. Caligula, A. viii (below, Appendix), both render the date 3 Feb. On the escape see Ord. Vit., iv. 108–110 and Malmesbury, *Gesta Regum*, ii. 471. Flambard's role as Curthose's chief adviser in 1101 is affirmed by all the contemporary writers; Orderic states that Flambard was charged with the administration of Normandy and that Curthose, as far as his laziness permitted, was guided by his advice (iv. 110).

2. Malmesbury (*Gesta Regum*, ii. 471) and others make it clear that invasion plans were afoot several months before Flambard's escape. Curthose's appeal to Rome is alluded to by Paschal II in a letter to Anselm of 24 Feb. 1101; *Anselmi Opera*, iv. 110–11. The appeal was fruitless.

3. *Ord. Vit.*, iv. 98, 103–4; David, *Curthose*, pp. 124–7.

4. *Ord. Vit.*, iv. 105–6.

5. Florence, ii. 48.

6. *A.S.C.*, A.D. 1101; Henry of Huntingdon, p. 233. These writers put the arrival of the rumour soon after Easter (April 21). Eadmer (*Historia Novorum*, p. 127) places it at Whitsuntide and adds that it alarmed the king's Whitsun court.

7. At the Winchester Easter court: *ibid.*, p. 126.

the bishopric of Durham.[1] This act was the culmination of a series of sanctions, secular and ecclesiastical, taken against Flambard at Henry I's instigation. At the time of the arrest, in August, 1100, Henry had charged Flambard with misappropriating funds relating to his administrative office. At the same time, Thomas archbishop of York had testified before the curia that Flambard had violated the promises he had made at his episcopal consecration. Anselm was no friend of Flambard's, having been driven into exile by Flambard's former master, yet on his return from exile in 1100 the archbishop had appointed an ecclesiastical commission to hear Flambard's defence. The commission reported back to Anselm that Flambard had failed to clear himself, and shortly afterwards Flambard fled to Normandy. Anselm responded by writing a letter to Paschal II summarizing the case and requesting papal support. He charged the bearer of the letter with detailing to the pope specific accusations of simony and other offences which Flambard had committed before and after his elevation to the bishopric.[2] Paschal responded by granting Anselm power of decision in the case[3] and wrote a firm letter to Flambard in Normandy ordering him to return to England and give satisfaction to Anselm or be defrocked by canonical sentence.[4] Having lost the bishopric of Durham, Flambard now found his whole ecclesiastical career placed in jeopardy. The key to his future in the European Church was Henry's own friend and archbishop – a man unlikely to be swayed even if Curthose should conquer England. Flambard's best hope now lay in reconciliation with the man whom he was preparing to attack.

At the same Whitsun court, Henry, through Anselm's mediation, obtained renewed pledges of loyalty from the magnates assembled at St. Albans for the thrice-yearly ceremony of the royal crown-wearing. Immediately thereafter news arrived that Curthose's invasion was imminent, and Henry sent word throughout England summoning his subjects to arms.[5] Many of his baronial enemies failed to respond despite their oaths, and others joined him with faint enthusiasm, but the great ecclesiastical fiefs were strongly represented. Eadmer tells us proudly that Anselm camped with his own men in the field. From the Abingdon Chronicle we learn that

1. Craster, 'Flambard', no. xxx, pp. 55–6.

2. *Anselmi Opera*, iv. 112–13. At some point in the proceedings, Flambard seems to have been deprived of the bishopric of Durham by his ecclesiastical superior, the archbishop of York (Thomas I or Gerard): Craster, 'Flambard', p. 49.

3. The letter is lost but is alluded to in Paschal's letter to Flambard: *ibid.*, pp. 41–2.

4. *Ibid.* This letter, in response to Anselm's of *post* 3 Feb., cannot have reached Flambard much earlier than mid-May. It is barely possible that he did not receive it prior to the invasion, but even if so, the general situation would have been clear to him by July.

5. Eadmer (*Historia Novorum*, p. 126) places the summons after the Whitsun Council. It cannot have been long after, since Henry led his army to the Sussex coast 'at Midsummer' (*A.S.C.*, A.D. 1101). On the baronial oaths see Ludwig Riess, 'The Reissue of Henry I's Coronation Charter', *E.H.R.*, xli (1926), 324.

the full *servicium debitum* was demanded from tenants-in-chief: when the holder of one of the abbey's knight's fees refused service, the abbot had to find a substitute.[1] The English were summoned, too, and large numbers of them responded.[2] As the army gathered, Henry sent a fleet out into the Channel, manned by English sailors, to guard the coast.[3]

On about 24 June – Midsummer's Day – Henry led his army to the Channel shore and encamped in the neighbourhood of Pevensey Bay to await his brother.[4] The site of the Conqueror's landing in 1066 doubtless seemed a likely place to guard, and Henry may well have had specific intelligence that Curthose was planning to land there. Pevensey was on the section of the English coastline nearest Tréport, where Curthose was assembling his army, and Pevensey Castle, belonging to the dangerous magnate William of Mortain, was best not left unwatched.

Eadmer writes at considerable length of Anselm's indispensable role in strengthening the wavering loyalties of the king's barons. The archbishop persuaded them individually and preached to them collectively. Had it not been for Anselm's intervention, Eadmer writes, 'King Henry would at that time have lost the English throne'.[5] The king is said to have made sweeping promises to his archbishop on matters of ecclesiastical policy and to have brought untrustworthy barons to him for lectures on loyalty. But Henry was also busy with his troops, moving frequently through their ranks, instructing English foot soldiers in the art of meeting a cavalry charge with shields and blows.[6] The situation was grave, but with a large army on the coast and a fleet in the Channel Henry was in a powerful defensive position.

He was outwitted, however, by Flambard. Curthose, 'advised by Bishop Ranulf', bribed a number of Henry's English sailors to join his side and, using some of them as pilots, sailed his fleet past Pevensey to Portsmouth where his army of horsemen, archers and foot soldiers landed unopposed.[7] It was a far smaller army than the

---

1. *Chron. Abingdon*, ii. 128. *Cf. ibid.*, p. 129.

2. Hollister, *Military Organization*, pp. 226–7, 252.

3. On the naval obligation of the men of Dunge Marsh and Hastings, see *Reg.* ii, no. 1135. In general see Hollister, *Anglo-Saxon Military Institutions*, pp. 103–26.

4. *A.S.C.*, A.D. 1101. Some sources say Pevensey, others Hastings. If the editors of *Reg.* ii are correct in their supposition that nos. 529 and 530 [A.D. 1100–16] are to be dated *c.* June 24 1101, the actual place of Henry's encampment may have been Wartling (Sussex), about 11 miles west of Hastings and 3 miles north of Pevensey Bay. The matter is expertly discussed in Eleanor Searle's forthcoming book on Battle Abbey.

5. *Historia Novorum*, p. 127. *Cf.* Malmesbury, *Gesta Pontificum*, pp. 104–6.

6. Malmesbury, *Gesta Regum*, ii. 472. Twenty-two years later, at the siege of Pont-Audemer, Henry is reported to have run about like a young soldier, urging everyone on, instructing carpenters in the building of a siege tower, and giving encouragement to those who worked hardest: Ord. Vit., iv. 449.

7. Florence, ii. 48–9. The episode is mentioned in nearly all the chronicles. Anselm reported to Paschal in *c.* Feb. 1101, that Flambard, after his flight to Normandy,

Conqueror's in 1066[1] – the Winchester annalist reports that it
crossed in 200 ships whereas the Conqueror's fleet may have
numbered 1,000,[2] and a Worcester annal reports that it included
260 knights.[3] But its numbers were quickly swelled by baronial
forces in England, and once safely ashore at Portsmouth it was
ideally poised to move on Winchester and the royal treasure, with
Henry's army some eighty miles to the east.

The date of the duke's landing was variously reported by contemporary chroniclers as 20 July, 'before 1 August', 'about 1
August', 'in the month of August', and 'in the autumn'.[4] Caligula,
A. viii provides the date *xiii Kalendas Augusti* (20 July)[5] which
matches the date in the Anglo-Saxon Chronicle (twelve nights
before Lammas) and is therefore almost certainly correct. More
significantly, Caligula, A. viii states that Curthose was accompanied
to England by Ranulf Flambard. Historians have heretofore
assumed that Flambard remained in Normandy until the brothers'
reconciliation when he was summoned to England under a safe
conduct from Henry I.[6] The safe conduct, however, does not mention Normandy but simply orders Flambard to appear at the royal
court, assuring him that he can 'come and return in safety and
security'. The bishop was probably with Curthose's men somewhere
in southern England when he received it.[7]

Flambard's presence in the invasion force raises a new problem
in interpreting the campaign. Until the time of the Portsmouth

became a lord of 'pirates' whom he sent out to sea (*Anselmi Opera*, iv. 113), which might
explain his means of contacting Henry's shipmen.

1. Ord. Vit., iv. 110.

2. 'Annales Monasterii de Wintonia', in *Annales Monastici*, ed. H. R. Luard (R.S.,
1864–9), ii. 41. For the size of the 1066 armada see David C. Douglas, *William the
Conqueror* (1964), p. 190 n.

3. B.M. Cottonian MS. Vespasian, E. 4: *Annales Monastici*, iv. 374. This would be
somewhat under half the *servicium debitum* of Normandy as reported in the inquest of
1172, which is given as 581 in *Recueil des historiens des Gaules*, xxiii. 698, and as *c.* 773
in R.B.E., ii. 647. My own calculations support the former figure. In 1101 substantial
portions of western Normandy seem to have favoured Henry I.

4. *A.S.C.*, A.D. 1101; Henry of Huntingdon, p. 233; Florence, ii. 48–9; Malmesbury,
Gesta Regum, ii. 471; Ord. Vit., iv. 110.   5. See Appendix.

6. See, for example, Craster, 'Flambard', p. 43, and R. W. Southern, 'Ranulf Flambard
and Early Anglo-Norman Administration', *Trans. Royal Hist. Soc.*, 4th series, xvi
(1933), 118–19.

7. Craster, 'Flambard', no. x, p. 44. In *ibid.*, no. xi (p. 45), Henry I orders that
Flambard be allowed to hold his Durham lands in peace 'until he comes again from
Normandy'. The editors of *Reg.* ii (no. 540), following Craster, suggest the date August,
1101. But Craster xiii (*Reg.* ii, no. 545, Windsor, probably 3 Sept. when Flambard was
in England) is a vaguer, less specific, and therefore probably earlier restoration of
Flambard's lands than Craster xi. Moreover, it seems unlikely that Henry would have
begun the process of reseising Flambard before the two had met. Thus, Craster xi
(attested by Robert of Bellême) should be redated Oct. 1101–May 1102 – after the
return of Curthose and Flambard to Normandy and before Henry's summons to
Robert of Bellême (1102, *c.* May). Flambard's presence in the invasion army is corroborated by two other well-informed writers: 'Historiae Dunelmensis Ecclesiae Con-
tinuatio', p. 138, and 'Annales de Wintonia', p. 41.

landing Curthose's strategy bears the mark of skilful direction; after 20 July his leadership faltered. He advanced on Winchester, encamped, wasted several days, then reconsidered and moved toward London, was confronted by Henry's army, and entered into a disadvantageous truce. One of two things must have happened: either Flambard's influence declined or Flambard was himself manoeuvring for an accommodation with Henry and Anselm through which he might salvage his ecclesiastical career. The first alternative is suggested by Orderic's account of how Robert of Bellême, William of Warenne and other baronial confederates met Curthose when he landed, conducted him toward Winchester, and persuaded him to send a formal message to Henry challenging him to abdicate or fight.[1] The implication is that Robert of Bellême and his allies were now the duke's chief counsellors and that Flambard's voice was muted accordingly. To the extent that the decisions to turn from Winchester and to accept a truce were Curthose's own, they were probably muddied by considerations of chivalry and sentiment. But Flambard cannot have lost his influence altogether, and it is suggestive that the final outcome of the affair was by no means to his personal disadvantage.[2]

Advancing north-northwestward from Portsmouth toward Winchester, the ducal army pitched camp 'on a suitable spot',[3] which Caligula, A. viii describes as *in rivaria de Walmesforde*. The site in question may possibly be Warnford, Hants., on the River Meon, about 9½ miles southeast of Winchester and two miles northwest of the ancient earthworks atop Old Winchester Hill.[4] Henry reacted swiftly. The moment he heard of his brother's landing, he led his force northwestward into Surrey, then southwestward into Hampshire, following a great arc that would shield the approach to London as he hastened toward Winchester.[5] Henry's strategy was well conceived, for at this point Curthose turned from Winchester and began his march on London.[6]

1. *Ord. Vit.*, iv. 110.
2. Within a few months not only had he recovered his see of Durham but he also had a firm hold on the see of Lisieux in Normandy: *ibid.*, pp. 116–17.
3. Florence, ii. 49.
4. Hubert Hall, in *R.B.E.*, iii. 1342 (index; *cf. ibid.*, ii. 579) identifies 'Walmeforde' as Warnford. No such rendering is noted by Ekwall in his place-name dictionary; at the time of this writing the English Place-Name Society's volume on Hampshire was not yet available.
5. MS. Caligula, A. viii: see Appendix.
6. So writes Wace (ii. 440), and his testimony is confirmed by the fact that the two forces met at Alton (Hants.), on the road from Winchester (and Warnford) to London. Wace adds that the change of plan was dictated by Curthose's respect for Henry's queen who was in Winchester (*cf. Reg.* ii, no. 534) and pregnant. (She was, as Malmesbury tells us, Curthose's goddaughter: *Gesta Regum*, ii. 462; Curthose had been in Scotland in 1080, the probable date of the queen's birth: Simeon, *Opera*, ii. 211). But barring treason, Winchester could easily have held out until the arrival of Henry's swiftly-approaching army, which would soon be at Curthose's encampment and could not be ignored.

The duke had advanced less than fifteen miles from his encampment when the two armies met.[1] On the authority of Wace alone, modern historians have placed this meeting at Alton (Hants.).[2] It is now possible to confirm Wace's statement with the independent account in Caligula, A. viii: *Rex . . . venit ad Auwltune*.[3] Here, as often happened in medieval warfare,[4] the two sides held back from pitched battle and negotiated. The English chroniclers report that the barons mediated a peace between the brothers.[5] But Orderic declares that the barons were bent on war and that the peace was worked out by Henry and Curthose face to face.[6] Freeman, scrutinizing the various accounts in detail, attempts to reconcile them with the suggestion that some barons favoured battle while others favoured negotiation, and that men of the latter persuasion, on both sides, agreed upon terms which the brothers then ratified at a personal meeting.[7] David rejected this suggestion, discounting Orderic and doubting that Henry and Curthose played any role at all in the negotiations.[8] But the account in Caligula, A. viii demonstrates that Freeman was more or less correct after all: 'There, with the barons of both sides mediating, the king and the count conversed with one another, and a concord was declared between them'.[9] Wace names three of the baronial negotiators: Robert of Bellême, William of Mortain, and Robert fitz Hamon.[10]

 By the agreement at Alton, Curthose surrendered his claim to the English throne, the prize that had drawn him to England. His exact motives are beyond recovery, but it should be borne in mind that in this era of siege warfare a major battle was a rare and terrifying

---

1. Warnford to Alton: *c.* 12 miles; Winchester to Alton: *c.* 15 miles. Henry had marched some 70 or 80 miles from Pevensey to Alton via Surrey. Some of the barons discussed earlier as ducal supporters may well have been in Henry's army rather than Curthose's. The chroniclers make it clear that many barons in the royal host were actually or potentially disloyal. Malmesbury's account of William of Mortain suggests that, despite his sympathies, he may have been with the king (*Gesta Regum*, ii. 473). Orderic says that a number of barons joined Curthose's force but names only Robert of Bellême and William of Warenne (iv. 110).

2. The Wace manuscripts are themselves inconsistent. In the Andresen text the meeting place is first given as *Hantone* (ii. 440), then *Altone* (ii. 441); the French editor gives the reading *Hantone* in both instances: *Le Roman de Rou et des Ducs de Normandie par Robert Wace*, ed. F. Pluquet (1827), ii. 357, 358. *Cf.* Freeman, *Rufus*, ii. 408 n.

3. See Appendix.

4. *A.S.C.*, A.D. 1052; Ord. Vit., iv. 174 (1102), 226–8 (1106); Henry of Huntingdon, pp. 287–8 (1153).

5. *A.S.C.*, A.D. 1101; Malmesbury, *Gesta Regum*, ii. 472; Florence, ii. 49; Henry of Huntingdon, p. 233; Wace, ii. 442–3; 'Chron. Hida', p. 306.

6. Ord. Vit., iv. 113–14.

7. *Rufus*, ii. 688–90.

8. *Curthose*, pp. 133–4 and n.

9. See Appendix. Contrary to Freeman's reconstruction, the brothers seem to have done more than merely ratify. They probably worked out final details face to face and may, as Orderic suggests, have added a clause or two on their own.

10. Wace, ii. 442. In this passage Robert of Bellême is the only one of the three to be identified explicitly with one of the two sides. Wace adds that there were other negotiators whose names he did not know.

thing, sufficient perhaps to make even a former crusader apprehensive. The barons on both sides risked losing their lands if the battle turned against them. The former crusader would probably also have been sobered by Anselm's threat to excommunicate him if he persisted in his campaign.[1] And it may well be, as Eadmer suggests, that disloyalty within the royal ranks was far less widespread than Curthose had hoped.[2] Finally, one must not discount the role of Flambard who, despite the silence of the chroniclers, was surely present at Alton. The first continuer of Simeon's history of Durham implies that Flambard's reinstatement was part of the agreement,[3] and whether he was mentioned by name or not he was evidently included in the general amnesty. Flambard had won what he came to England to seek and would doubtless have influenced the impressionable duke toward accommodation.

We learn from Caligula, A. viii that the agreement between the brothers in the field was merely verbal. The document known in our histories as the treaty of Alton was in fact a treaty of Winchester. By 31 July Henry and his faithful barons had traversed the fifteen miles from Alton to Winchester[4] where, on 2 August 1101 – the first anniversary of William Rufus's death – the treaty was solemnly ratified by oaths between the king and his brother and confirmed by oaths of twelve leading men from each side.[5]

The new information in Caligula, A. viii, added to other narrative accounts, makes it possible to trace step by step the process that produced the settlement of 1101: baronial negotiations, the meeting and agreement of the brothers on the field, and the subsequent ratification of the treaty, in more formal surroundings, by mutual oaths and pledges of faith between the brothers, supported by the oaths of their chief barons. The procedure is reminiscent of other political settlements of the age. In 1052, for example, when the armies and fleets of King Edward and Earl Godwine faced one another at London, intermediaries on both sides arranged the terms of a peace, and on the following day, perhaps at Westminster, the formal settlement was effected between king and earl, Godwine swearing to his and his son's innocence, and Edward formally restoring them to favour.[6] In 1091 Rufus invaded Normandy 'for his brother's undoing' but subsequent negotiations brought the brothers together, and their mutual promises were secured by the

1. Eadmer, *Historia Novorum*, pp. 127–8.
2. *Ibid.*
3. Simeon, *Opera*, i. 138.
4. *Reg.* ii, nos. 534–6, recording the presence at Winchester on 31 July of King Henry, Queen Matilda, Roger Bigod, Hamo *Dapifer*, Urse of Abitôt, Henry earl of Warwick, and Eudo *Dapifer*.
5. See Appendix. Wace, the only other writer to mention Alton, does not say that the treaty was ratified there: ii. 442–5. On the 24 oath-taking barons see *A.S.C.*, A.D. 1101.
6. *A.S.C.*, A.D. 1052; Frank Barlow, *Edward the Confessor* (1970), pp. 123–4.

oaths of twelve chief men from each side.[1] In 1153, after the intervention of the leading men of each army, King Stephen and Duke Henry exchanged views across the river at Wallingford. The interview was unsuccessful, but some months later, after further negotiations, the two rivals met at Winchester and worked out their accord. Shortly afterwards at Westminster, probably after final negotiations on details, they sealed their treaty with mutual oaths and published it in the form of a royal charter attested by men from both sides.[2]

The treaty of 1101 has not survived and must be reconstructed from chronicle accounts. The chroniclers are in general agreement that Curthose renounced his claim to England, recognized his brother's royal title, and released Henry from an oath of homage – probably taken when Henry purchased the Cotentin from the duke in 1088. The king in return undertook to pay Curthose 3,000 marks a year for life and to give up the Cotentin and other continental possessions except the castle of Domfront, which Henry had sworn years before never to abandon. A surviver clause provided that if either Henry or his brother should die without a lawful male heir, the other should inherit the entire Anglo-Norman state.[3] Since Henry's queen was probably approaching her fourth month of pregnancy at the time,[4] the clause was to the king's advantage. The duke's only legitimate child, William Clito, is generally thought to have been born in 1101,[5] but Caligula, A. viii provides for the first time the exact date of Clito's birth: 25 October 1102.[6] At the time of the Winchester treaty Curthose had no heir on the way.

The treaty also provided that barons who had been disseised for supporting either side in 1101 should have their lands restored.[7] This is a curious clause for several reasons. Henry began disseising ducal supporters before Curthose left England, at a time when the

1. *A.S.C.*, A.D. 1091; David, *Curthose*, pp. 59–61.
2. R. H. C. Davis, *King Stephen* (1967), pp. 120–2; *Reg.* iii, no. 272.
3. See David, *Curthose*, pp. 134–6 and the references cited therein.
4. The Winchester annalist (*Annales Monastici*, ii. 43) reports that when Henry I sent Maud to Germany in 1110 to be betrothed to the Emperor Henry V she was exactly 8 years and 15 days old. Simeon of Durham (ii. 241) states that she left England *in initio Quadragesimae*, 1110, and *A.S.C.*, A.D. 1110, states that she left *foran laengtene* ('before Lent' or 'before spring'). If she left *c.* Ash Wednesday – 23 Feb. 1110 – and if the Winchester figure is accurate, she was born *c.* 8 Feb. 1102.
5. See, for example, David, *Curthose*, pp. 180–1 and n.
6. Fo. 41: A.D. 1102: 'Eodem anno natus est Guillelmus filius R[odberti] comitis die sanctorum Crispini et Crispiniani in turre Rotomagensi'. Orderic's data on Clito's age are mutually inconsistent, implying birth dates ranging from 1100 to 1103. The date of 25 Oct. 1102, harmonizes well with the chronology of Clito's career provided by Herman of Tournai: *M.G.H., Scriptores*, xiv. 284 (10 years old in *c.* 1113, 14 in *c.* 1117). Malmesbury (*Gesta Regum*, ii. 461) discloses that Curthose's wife, Sibylla of Conversano, died soon after giving birth to Clito. Orderic (iv. 183–4) says that she died in Lent, not long after the death of Walter Giffard who died on 15 July 1102.
7. Caligula, A. viii: Appendix; *A.S.C.*, A.D. 1101; Florence, ii. 49.

two were on the best of terms.[1] Orderic ignores the amnesty clause altogether but asserts that the brothers swore to punish wicked sowers of discord and to render mutual aid in recovering all their father's lands.[2] These apparently contradictory provisions for amnesty and punishment of traitors are both well corroborated. The amnesty provision is described in the Anglo-Saxon Chronicle, related Latin chronicles, and the independent account of Caligula, A. viii, while the treason clause becomes a fundamental issue in the diplomacy of 1103–6.[3] The solution seems to be that the amnesty clause, as the chronicles make clear, applied to the past – to those disseised before Alton – whereas the treason clause evidently applied to the future. Together they embodied the principle, vital to the peaceful functioning of the proposed condominium, that the brothers would follow a uniform policy toward their trans-Channel baronage.

But there is a further problem. If, as seems likely, nobody had been disseised before Alton except Ranulf Flambard, why was the amnesty expressed in terms of restoring confiscated lands? The inappropriateness of wording to circumstance probably arises from the fact that this was one of several clauses patched into the treaty of Winchester from the Norman treaty of 1091 between Curthose and William Rufus. As the one previous effort to work out terms for an Anglo-Norman condominium, the 1091 agreement was an obvious model for negotiations in 1101. The two treaties, both ratified by twelve barons from each side, had parallel survivor agreements, parallel commitments to recover William the Conqueror's lands (virtually meaningless in 1101), and parallel amnesty provisions.[4] In 1091 the restoration of confiscated lands had benefited English barons disseised in 1088, but when the clause was copied into the Winchester treaty it was ambiguous toward all except Flambard. By implication it would bar subsequent action against barons simply for having cast with one side or the other in 1101, but it would not protect them against charges for other crimes, past or future.

Henry quickly began to exploit these loopholes. William of Warenne, still earl of Surrey in early September, 1101, was disseised soon afterwards, perhaps for acts of violence committed by his men in Norfolk,[5] and in time certain other ducal sympathizers were

1. Ord. Vit., iv. 116.
2. *Ibid.*, p. 115. The latter statement is embroidered by Wace: ii. 444.
3. Ord. Vit., iv. 192, 199–200. *Cf. Gesta Normannorum Ducum*, p. 283.
4. On the 1091 treaty see *A.S.C.*, A.D. 1091; Freeman, *Rufus*, i. 275–83; David, *Curthose*, pp. 59–61.
5. See *Reg.* ii, no. 542 and p. 306. Earl William might also have faced a charge relating to his earlier taunts toward Henry I (Wace, ii. 446–7; Malmesbury, *Gesta Regum*, ii. 471). In English customary law slander against the king's person was a high crime: *Leges Henrici Primi*, chaps. 10, 1 and 13, 1. William attests as earl at Henry I's Windsor court of 3 Sept. but is with Curthose in Normandy in 1102 – still claiming to be earl: *Reg.* ii, nos. 544, 548–9, 621; see Ord. Vit., iv. 116.

punished on charges other than that of following Curthose in 1101.
It is true that Orderic exaggerates the speed and thoroughness with
which Henry acted against these men. Several of them lost their
lands for complex reasons or held them far longer than Orderic
implies: Robert of Lacy held until about 1113; Ivo of Grandmesnil,
under royal pressure, pledged his lands to Robert of Meulan and
went crusading; William of Mortain may have left England voluntarily to cast with Curthose in Normandy; and Robert Malet did
not fall from favour at all.[1] Nevertheless, Henry's actions violated
the spirit if not the letter of the amnesty provision. 'Soothe them
with promises', Robert of Meulan had advised the king on the eve
of Alton; afterwards the traitors can be disseised and 'driven into
exile'.[2] This sharp practice on Henry's part was aimed not at eliminating great magnates as such but at destroying or converting particular
magnates whom the king did not trust. The creation of a loyal
baronage, at home in the royal court, was the essential step in
Henry's pacification of England. Accordingly, the decade following
Alton and Winchester witnessed a substantial reordering of the
English aristocracy, with the fall of such dominant eleventh-
century families as the Mortains, Montgomerys, Grandmesnils and
Malets, to be replaced in time by great royalist landholders such as
Roger bishop of Salisbury, Robert of Meulan, the Albinis, Brian
fitz Count, Stephen of Blois and Robert of Gloucester.

The treaty of Winchester had a short life. On an impulsive visit
to England in 1103, Curthose was persuaded – probably by the
threat of imprisonment – to relinquish the 3,000-mark annuity.[3]
And despite the treaty provision regarding the Cotentin, Henry
retained a strong influence there. In 1104 he crossed to Normandy,
visiting Domfront 'and other castles which were under his rule'.
In 1105 he brought an army unopposed to Barfleur in the Cotentin,
spent a quiet Easter at Carentan, and met no opposition from
Curthose's men until he reached the wall of Bayeux.[4]

Robert Curthose lingered on in England for two or three months
after the treaty of Winchester. He was at Henry's court in London,
probably sometime in August, 1101, and attended a great royal
council at Windsor on 3 September in company with a distinguished

---

1. Ord. Vit., iv. 161–3, 167–9; *Reg.* ii, no. 682 (Robert Malet); *A.S.C.*, A.D. 1104
(William of Mortain); W. E. Wightman, *The Lacy Family* (1966), p. 66. Orderic seems
to confuse Robert Malet with his heir, William Malet: *A.S.C.*, A.D. 1110. See C. W.
Hollister, 'Henry I and Robert Malet', (below, pp. 129–36).

2. Ord. Vit., iv. 112–13.

3. *A.S.C.*, A.D. 1103; Ord. Vit., iv. 161–2; *cf.* Wace's detailed account: ii. 448–55.
William of Warenne was restored to his earldom at this time, and the treaty of Winchester was renewed, minus the annuity.

4. Ord. Vit., iv. 199, 204–10, 218–19. Curthose may conceivably have receded the
Cotentin on his visit to England in 1103. In the following year Henry broke with his
brother on the grounds of the duke's coming to terms with Robert of Bellême whom
Henry had exiled for treason in 1102: *ibid.*, pp. 199–200; *cf.* pp. 162–3.

assemblage of magnates and prelates.[1] He and his friends are said to have been instrumental in persuading Henry to take an unyielding stand against the archbishop of Canterbury, 'boiling with hatred toward Anselm because he had caused them to lose the kingdom'. And the Anglo-Saxon chronicler complains that Curthose's men 'always did much damage wherever they went while the duke remained in the land'.[2] Orderic writes that after two months with Henry I, Curthose returned to his duchy as winter approached. English writers place his departure sometime after Michaelmas, and Caligula, A. viii dates it around All Saints' Day (1 Nov.).[3]

Among the men who accompanied Curthose to Normandy was Ranulf Flambard. He had made his own peace with the king, and as he left England the process of restoring him to the bishopric of Durham was already under way.[4] He left neither as an exile nor (as has been suggested) as a clandestine royal agent at the ducal court. His reinstatement was not kept secret but was well known to Curthose and his supporters,[5] and on returning to Normandy he attended to his own interests rather than the duke's. He obtained the bishopric of Lisieux first for his semi-illiterate brother, then for his own son, and for the next several years he functioned as bishop of Durham and provost of Lisieux, enjoying the revenues of both sees.[6] His activities at Lisieux were a source of scandal in the Church, and eventually he lost his hold on the see. He never resumed his viceregal role in England; but he remained bishop of Durham until his death in 1128.

In restoring Flambard, Henry was not buying himself a secret agent. Rather he was making a concession essential to obtaining the truce with Curthose. From Henry's standpoint, the rehabilitation of Flambard was a key to the peace and security of England. And from Flambard's standpoint, the invasion of 1101 had accomplished its purpose.

Flambard's fate

---

1. *Reg.* ii, nos. 539, 544–50.
2. Eadmer, *Historia Novorum*, p. 131; Malmesbury, *Gesta Pontificum*, p. 106; *A.S.C.*, A.D. 1101.
3. Ord. Vit., iv. 116; *A.S.C.*, A.D. 1101; Henry of Huntingdon, p. 233; Appendix.
4. Craster, 'Flambard', nos. x–xiii, *cf.* nos. xiv–xxx.
5. *Ibid.*, nos. x (Curthose attests Henry's safe-conduct for Flambard); xi–xiii (Robert of Bellême attests charters restoring the lands and customs of Durham to Flambard); *Reg.* ii, nos. 544, 548 (Flambard attests charters of Henry I as bishop of Durham at Windsor, 3 Sept. 1101, in the presence of Curthose, Robert of Bellême, William of Mortain, and a great company of magnates and prelates).
6. Ord. Vit., iv. 116–17.

APPENDIX

British Museum MS. Caligula, A. viii, fo. 41 (fo. 38, old foliation). Chronicon Simeonis monachi Dunelmensis, de primis Angliae gentis regibus; sive a primo Saxonum adventu, h.e. ab A.D. 449, ad annum 1119: Annal for A.D. 1101.

Millesimo ci.*

Rex Anglorum Henricus tenuit curiam suam in natale Domini apud Westmonasterium. Huic curiae interfuit Lothowicus electus rex Francorum et ad mensam sedebat ad dexteram regis inter regem scilicet Henricum et Anselmum Archiepiscopum. Eodem anno die sequenti post purificationem Sanctae Mariae exivit Rannulfus Dunelmensis episcopus de turre Lundoniae et ad comitem Rodbertum in Normanniam venit. Civitas Glauvornia cum principali monasterio et aliis 8 Idus Junii feria 5 incendio consumitur. Eodem anno in aestate 13 Kalendas Augusti applicuit Rodbertus comes Normanniae cum navali exercitu ducens secum Rannulfum Dunelmensem episcopum aliosque proceres in loco qui Portesmuthe dicitur. Ibique in rivaria de Walmesforde figi tentoria praecepit. Rex autem eius adventum apud Hastingas expectans, cum comitem venisse audisset, cum exercitu suo maximo per Surreiam venit ad Auwltune, ibique et ipse sua tentoria figi fecit. Ibique mediantibus utrorumque baronibus locuti sunt ad invicem rex et comes; concordiaque inter eos prolocuta, venerunt Guintoniam secundo die Augusti, et ibi sacramento et affidatione inter eos facta, redditae sunt unicuique baronum utrorumque terrae quas vel in Anglia vel in Normannia tempore diffensionis perdiderant sicut praelocutum inter eos fuerat. Eodem anno circa festum omnium sanctorum rediit comes pacifice in Normanniam.

* The year is written in a later hand at the bottom of fo. 40.

5

MAGNATES AND "CURIALES"
IN EARLY NORMAN ENGLAND

The Norman Conquest, R. H. C. Davis recently remarked, transformed England into "the first and most perfect example of a feudal monarchy."[1] The Old English ruling class was swept away and its lands passed to William the Conqueror, to be kept or granted out much as ₒie chose. William was thus given the opportunity, never·to be repeated, of creating a new English landed aristocracy *ex nihilo*. In this sense (to misquote Burckhardt), Norman England was William the Conqueror's work of art.

The outlines of William's new design are disclosed in Domesday Book (1086): he kept about seventeen percent of the lands as *terra regis*, permitted the churches to retain about twenty-seven percent, and granted fifty percent to some 180 homage-bound lay tenants-in-chief, almost all of whom were Normans or other Frenchmen.[2] Of these lands granted to laymen, well over a third was reserved for an elite group of ten powerful magnates, all of whom held lands with annual values in excess of £750. At the top of this list of ten stood three super-magnates: the Conqueror's half-brothers Odo bishop of Bayeux (about £3000 per year) and Robert count of Mortain (about £2100), and a more distant royal kinsman, Roger of Montgomery (about £2100).

William's ten leading magnates together controlled nearly twenty percent of the land revenues of all England. These men were drawn largely from the new nobility that the Conqueror had earlier raised to positions of wealth and power in Normandy,[3] but they also included two neighboring magnates who had fought for him at Hastings: Eustace count of Boulogne and Alan of Brittany (who became lord of

I am grateful to the National Endowment for the Humanities, the American Philosophical Society, the Social Science Research Council, the American Council of Learned Societies, the Fulbright Commission, the John Simon Guggenheim Memorial Foundation, and the Warden and Fellows of Merton College, Oxford, for supporting research on this paper, to Professors Emily R. Coleman and W. Elliot Brownlee for their valuable suggestions (they do not necessarily concur in all that I say), and to my research assistants Jean Saulter, Carole Moore, Joseph Navari and Thomas Keefe.

[1] R. H. C. Davis, *The Normans and their Myth* (London 1976) 110.

[2] These percentages are derived from information gathered by W. J. Corbett, *Cambridge Medieval History* 5 (1926) 508ff., and represent land values as recorded, manor by manor, in Domesday Book. About 6% of the land was in the hands of miscellaneous smallholders.

[3] D. C. Douglas, *William the Conqueror* (Berkeley 1964) 83-104.

Richmond).[4] Although the loyalty of these ten proved to be less than total,[5] most of them remained faithful companions of the Conqueror throughout his reign.

Their activity at William's court can be measured roughly by the frequency with which they attested his charters. For obvious reasons, the correlation between charter attestations and attendance at court is imperfect: one could be at court and not attest, and it is possible that a person's name might occasionally appear on a witness list without his having been present at the time the charter was issued. Nevertheless, attestations remain our surest means of determining which people were habitually in the royal entourage. And the wealthiest of William the Conqueror's magnates were also among his most frequent attestors.

This close connection between wealth and court activity can best be shown in tabular form. Table A lists England's ten greatest lay landholders at the Conqueror's death in 1087, roughly in the order of their wealth as measured by the annual values of their Domesday manors.[6] These values are provided in column 1; column 2 lists the total number of their attestations of extant royal charters; and column 3 provides their rank-order based on the frequency of attestation among all lay witnesses of royal charters. Thus, Roger of Montgomery attested more charters of William I than any other layman; Odo of Bayeux, Geoffrey of Coutances and Robert of Mortain were second, third and fourth, and so on. In other words, William I's three supermagnates were among the four most frequent attestors of his charters. If for our purposes here we define as a *curialis* anyone among the fifteen most frequent lay witnesses of royal charters, it results that seven of William I's ten wealthiest barons in 1087 were also *curiales*. Of the remaining three, William of Warenne attested with reasonable frequency (eight known charters), Geoffrey de Mandeville served as sheriff of several counties and was the addressee of five royal charters, and Eustace count of Boulogne had responsibilities in his homeland. Table A thus presents a highly simplified profile of the model feudal monarchy to which R. H. C. Davis alludes — a polity in which

[4] Alan's presence at Hastings is not certain but is highly probable: *Complete Peerage* 10 (1945) 783.

[5] Eustace of Boulogne rebelled in 1067 but was reinstated; Odo of Bayeux was arrested by the king in 1082, for reasons that are not altogether clear, and was restored as the king lay dying in 1087: see David R. Bates, "The Character and Career of Odo Bishop of Bayeux (1049/50-1097)," *Speculum* 50 (1975) 15-18. Another very large landholder, William I's kinsman William fitz Osbern (earl of Hereford), was killed while fighting in Flanders in 1070 or 1071; his son and English heir, Roger earl of Hereford, rebelled in 1075 and was disseised and imprisoned: *Complete Peerage* 6 (1926) 447-450.

[6] Two of the ten, Odo of Bayeux and Geoffrey of Coutances, were bishops in Normandy but held their English lands as laymen. The Domesday manorial values represent the gross revenues from all lands held of the king, whether retained as demesne or granted out as fiefs; to have provided only demesne values would have been to overlook the income that a tenant-in-chief derived from his vassals. On the other hand, manors held in mesne tenancy of some other tenant-in-chief have been excluded, as have sources of income not associated with land. For these and other reasons, the figures are imprecise — yet they remain our best available indexes of English baronial wealth. For a discussion of the problems involved in using Domesday manorial values see Reginald Lennard, *Rural England, 1086-1135* (Oxford 1959) 25-29.

TABLE A

Relationship between Landed Wealth
and Frequency of Attestations among
English Magnates Alive in 1087

10 greatest Engl. lay landholders	pounds/year	Wm. I attests.	rank/lay attestors
Odo of Bayeux (deprived 1082)	3000	34	2
Robert of Mortain	2100	30½	4
Roger of Montgomery	2100	40	1
Wm. I of Warenne	1165	8	
Alan ld. of Richmond	1100 + waste	21	7
Hugh e. of Chester	800	15½	9
Richard of Clare	780	11	11
Geoffrey of Coutances	780	34	3
Geoffrey de Mandeville	780	0*	
Eustace II c. of Boulogne	770	0**	
Total of attestors in top 15: 7 of 10			

*Sheriff: 5 charters of Wm. I addressed to him.
**Spends much of the reign in Boulogne.

the greatest lords are joined to their king not only by homage but by companionship and royal service as well.

As in the case of many such statistical demonstrations, however, one might have guessed as much without the figures. That most of William I's wealthiest barons were also *curiales* is a predictable result of the Conqueror's having given huge English honors to his kinsmen and associates and having continued his intimacy with most of them throughout his reign. Orderic Vitalis writing some decades later, speaks with reverence of "those wise and eloquent men who for many years lived at King William's court, observed his deeds and all the great activities there, were privy to his deepest and most secret counsels, and were endowed by him with wealth that raised them above the condition to which they were born."[7]

The Conqueror's successors on the English throne, lacking his fresh start, had to deal with powerful, entrenched families not of their own choosing. The trouble began as soon as the close associations between William I and his magnates were

[7] Orderic Vitalis, *Historia ecclesiastica*, ed. Marjorie Chibnall (Oxford 1969-1975) 2.190.

severed by death. It was a classic problem of feudal regimes, bound together by personal relationships and based on the idea of governance through the cooperation of prince and magnates. Repeating the homage and fealty oaths on the succession of a new lord or vassal might restore the former moral and legal bond, but it did not guarantee the close cooperation that enabled the political order to function smoothly.

The Conqueror's successor in England, William II "Rufus," faced this problem and others as well. At William I's death in 1087, the Anglo-Norman realm was divided: England passed to William Rufus and Normandy to his older brother, Robert Curthose. Neither brother was satisfied with only half the patrimony, and to make matters worse, the great magnates – most of them with extensive lands on both sides of the Channel – now owed allegiance to two princes. From the standpoint of the princes, the undivided loyalty of their magnates could no longer be assumed. And from the magnates' standpoint, allegiance to one prince against the other involved the risk of forfeiting either their English or Norman honors. The separation of England from Normandy thus produced political instability in both lands.

Accordingly, William Rufus, in the first year of his reign (1088), faced a major rebellion involving at least six of the realm's ten wealthiest magnates (see Table A): Odo of Bayeux, his brother Robert of Mortain, Roger of Montgomery (with three of his sons), Gilbert fitz Richard of Clare, Geoffrey of Coutances (with his nephew Robert of Mowbray), and Eustace count of Boulogne (son and heir of William I's Eustace). Other wealthy landholders supporting Curthose included Roger Bigod (lands worth ca. £450 per year), William of Eu (ca. £400), Roger of Lacy (ca. £400) and Hugh of Grandmesnil (ca. £340). Only two of the magnates in Table A, William of Warenne and Hugh earl of Chester, are known to have supported Rufus.[8]

The rebels hoped to reunite the Anglo-Norman realm by putting Robert Curthose on the English throne. Their motives are suggested (in simplified form) by a speech that Orderic Vitalis puts in their collective mouths:

> What are we do? Behold that on the death of our lord two youths succeed him, and the lordship of England and Normandy is suddenly divided. How can we properly serve two lords who are so different and live so far apart? If we serve Robert duke of Normandy as we ought, we shall offend his brother William, who will then despoil us of our great incomes and mighty honors in England. Conversely, if we adhere to King William, Duke Robert will deprive us of our paternal estates in Normandy . . . . Thus let us join in a firm, inviolable agreement, and having ousted or killed King William, who is the younger and more impudent, and to whom we owe nothing, let us make Duke Robert – who is the firstborn and of pliable temper and to whom we have already sworn

[8] The rebellion is discussed in some detail in E. A. Freeman, *The Reign of William Rufus* (Oxford 1882) 1.22-89, and C. W. David, *Robert Curthose, Duke of Normandy* (Cambridge, Mass. 1920) 44-52.

fealty in his father's lifetime — prince of England and Normandy, to the end of preserving the unity of the two realms.[9]

Although Orderic's quotation is not to be taken literally, it does represent an informed, nearly contemporary judgment of baronial motives. In 1088 the reunification of the Anglo-Norman state would clearly have been a convenience to major trans-Channel magnates, but this goal could have been achieved as well by establishing Rufus in Normandy as by enthroning Robert in England. The passage raises two points of feudal ethics in Robert's favor: that he had previously received the barons' oaths of fealty,[10] and that he deserved to inherit his father's dominions in accordance with the Norman custom of primogeniture.[11] But against these arguments there might well have been raised the *fait accompli* of Rufus's coronation and the Conqueror's deathbed designation. One gets the impression that, within the customary framework of kin-right, the magnates were apt to consult their own interests first and discover moral justifications afterwards. The leaders of the ducal party in 1088 were at once intimate advisers of the previous ruler and great territorial lords in their own right. Although they had been *curiales* of William the Conqueror, they now had the potential of exercising quasi-independent power, and one can understand how they might have preferred the pliability of Curthose to the "impudence" of Rufus. William of Malmesbury expresses this idea when he writes that the ducal faction preferred Robert, "who was of milder spirit and whose youthful follies had been melted away by many hardships," to Rufus, "fastidiously reared, ferocious in spirit, whose scornful look discloses his overbearing nature, who would risk all in defiance of faith and justice."[12] Curthose could be manipulated; Rufus could not — or not so easily. Rufus was arrogant, unpredictable, and therefore less apt to consult or defer to the wealthy, established magnates of the previous reign.

Rufus survived the 1088 rebellion as a consequence of his own skill and his brother's incompetence (Curthose, who was supposed to join his supporters in England, never quite made it across the Channel). But even though the rebellion failed, it dramatized the worrisome fact that Rufus could not trust most of his greatest magnates. Robert Curthose learned the same lesson during the next few years when Rufus campaigned with some success in Normandy, drawing a number of major Norman and Anglo-Norman barons into his camp. But despite Rufus's advances in Normandy, his hold on England remained far from secure. In 1095 there

---

[9] Orderic, 4.122-124. These thoughts are attributed to Odo of Bayeux, Eustace of Boulogne (who held nothing in Normandy), Robert of Bellême (who stood to inherit vast Norman lands from his father, Roger of Montgomery), *aliique plures.*

[10] Indeed he had: see David (n. 8 above) 12, 15, 18.

[11] On the 1087 inheritance see John Le Patourel, "The Norman Succession, 996-1135," *English Historical Review* 86 (1971) 225-250; cf. John S. Beckerman, "Succession in Normandy, 1087, and in England, 1066: The Role of Testamentary Custom," *Speculum* 47 (1972) 258-260.

[12] William of Malmesbury, *Gesta Regum Anglorum,* ed. William Stubbs, Rolls Series (1887-1889) 2.360.

came to light a widespread conspiracy of Rufus's magnates to depose or assassinate the king and to enthrone in his place Stephen of Aumale, a son of one of William I's sisters.

Fortunately for Rufus, the rebellion-conspiracy of 1095 misfired. The only magnate actually to rebel was Robert of Mowbray earl of Northumberland, who had inherited the huge Conquest honor of his uncle Geoffrey bishop of Coutances (d. 1093). Robert seems to have defied Rufus prematurely, and when the king moved swiftly against him, his fellow conspirators held back. They had expected a supporting invasion from Normandy, but it never materialized. And Rufus was saved from being assassinated in a well-planned ambush by the timely confession of one of the conspirators.[13] Once again Rufus survived, and once again he did so despite the wishes of his major magnates. The sources do not reveal the names of every baron involved in the conspiracy, but they do suggest that it was a large and very serious affair: "Earls and men of similar rank," writes Orderic, "had knowingly been parties to the treacherous confederacy."[14] Among the conspiring magnates whose names are disclosed were the heirs of three of William I's ten wealthiest magnate-*curiales*: Hugh of Montgomery earl of Shrewsbury, Gilbert fitz Richard of Clare and (as we have seen) Robert of Mowbray earl of Northumberland.[15] Among the other wealthy magnates known to have been involved were two more veterans of the 1088 uprising: William of Eu and Roger of Lacy. The sources fail to identify any major lay landholders who gave Rufus their unqualified support.

The magnates who conspired in 1095 were distinctly noncurial.[16] Attestations of the eight lay conspirators whose names are disclosed occur only nine times in Rufus's surviving charters. Table B provides a list of the known conspirators with their total attestations (A.D. 1087-1100) and an indication of their landed wealth. They were a rich, powerful group, and none of them was ever drawn fully into Rufus's court circle either before or after 1095.

Clearly Rufus had inherited a troublesome landholding elite. But he was by no means helpless to change the situation. Rebellious magnates might be disseised, and the king might use their forfeited lands (or his own demesne) to raise up new magnates from among his friends. Through such means a new elite group of magnate-*curiales* might in time have been created.

---

[13] The narrative sources on the 1095 rebellion are woven together (with abundant nineteenth-century constitutional interpretation) in Freeman (n. 8 above) 2.37-69. On the projected invasion from Normandy see *S. Anselmi Opera omnia*, ed. F. S. Schmitt (Edinburgh 1946-1961) 4.77-78, epistle 191.

[14] Orderic (n. 7 above) 4.284.

[15] Of the remaining seven magnates in Table A, Odo of Bayeux and Eustace of Boulogne had forfeited their English honors in 1088 and Robert of Mortain had died leaving a son not yet of age. The allegiances of the other four (or their heirs) are unknown.

[16] The one *curialis* who may have been involved in the conspiracy is William bishop of Durham, who attested 28 of Rufus's charters.

TABLE B
Laymen Known to have been Rebels or Conspirators, 1095

Name	Attestations for Rufus	Lands worth over £750	Lands worth £400-750	Disposition of lands	Family rebelled in 1088
Robert of Mowbray	2	X		to king	X
Hugh of Montgomery	2	X		retained	X
Philip of Montgomery	0			none	X
Gilbert of Clare	4	X		retained	X
William of Eu	0		X	to king	X
Roger of Lacy	0		X	to his brother Hugh	X
Odo of Champagne	1		[£200]	to Arnulf of Montgomery	
Stephen of Aumale	0			none	

There is some evidence that Rufus moved in this direction, though apparently not very far. In the aftermath of the 1088 rebellion he seized the lands of Odo of Bayeux and (probably) Eustace of Boulogne,[17] keeping their demesnes in his own hand throughout the remainder of his reign. But Rufus forgave Robert of Mortain,[18] Roger of Montgomery and his sons, Geoffrey of Coutances, Robert of Mowbray, Gilbert of Clare, William of Eu, Robert of Lacy, Roger Bigod and the rest. According to Orderic,

[17] On Eustace see the *Anglo-Saxon Chronicle*, A.D. 1101: a clause in the treaty of that year between Robert Curthose and Henry I provided that Eustace's English lands be restored to him; it seems most likely that Eustace had lost them in 1088.

[18] A. S. Ellis, "Biographical Notes on the Yorkshire Tenants Named in Domesday Book," *Yorkshire Archaeological and Topographical Journal* 4 (1875-1876) 129, states mistakenly that Robert of Mortain was disseised and banished from England in 1088, citing the *Anglo-Saxon Chronicle* (which says nothing about Robert of Mortain). William Farrer made the same point in *Victoria County History* (hereafter VCH) *Yorkshire* 2 (1912) 155 and in *Early Yorkshire Charters* 2 (1915) 236, citing Ellis and (again wrongly) the *Anglo-Saxon Chronicle*. The error was repeated by, among others, C. T. Clay (*Early Yorkshire Charters* 6 [1939] 57) and I. J. Sanders (*English Baronies* [Oxford 1960] 66), both citing Farrer, and F. J. West (*The Justiciarship in England* [Cambridge 1966] 35-36). The decisive text is Orderic (n. 7 above) 5.208, reporting that after Robert surrendered Pevensey Castle in 1088 he was restored to Rufus's friendship.

He shrewdly spared the older barons . . . out of love of his father whom they had served long and faithfully, and out of respect for their gray hairs. In any event he knew that illness and speedy death would soon put an end to their activities.[19]

But when the Conqueror's magnates died — as most of them did during the new reign — Rufus took no steps to prevent their lands from passing to their heirs. And many of the reinstated rebels of 1088, or their heirs, were involved in the conspiracy of 1095 (see Table B).

Rufus acted with greater severity in 1095-1096, though once again he failed to break the power of the great Conquest families. His treatment of the known conspirators of 1095 is shown in Table B. Robert of Mowbray was imprisoned, and the vast honor that he had inherited from Geoffrey of Coutances remained in Rufus's possession until his death. William of Eu was blinded and castrated, and his Domesday lands likewise passed into the king's hands and remained there.[20] Roger of Lacy was banished, and his lands passed to his brother Hugh.[21] Another conspirator, Odo of Champagne (father of the 1095 pretender, Stephen of Aumale), also lost his lands; and Rufus surprisingly gave large portions of them to Arnulf of Montgomery, whose powerful family had supported Curthose in 1088 and Stephen of Aumale in 1095.[22] The other conspirators were forgiven, "out of respect," says Orderic, "for their exalted kinsmen who might have sought vengeance in Normandy." Of the very wealthiest of the conspirators, Orderic states that Rufus "spared men of this kind."[23]

Can any pattern be discerned in Rufus's policy of punishing a few rebels or conspirators and reinstating the rest? One can comprehend the harsh treatment of Bishop Odo, the leader of the 1088 rebellion,[24] and of Robert of Mowbray who alone took up arms in 1095. But beyond this, the king's motives seem to have consisted largely of vengeance (sometimes for obscure reasons) and greed. Rufus is said to have received huge fines from those whom he forgave in 1095, and we are told explicitly that he took Hugh of Montgomery back into his favor for £3000.[25]

---

[19] Orderic (n. 7 above) 4.134, based on Chibnall's translation.

[20] William of Eu's Domesday honor was eventually granted by Henry I to Walter fitz Richard of Clare: see Sidney Painter, *Studies in the History of the English Feudal Barony* (Baltimore 1943) 178-179; E. C. Waters, "The Counts of Eu," *Yorkshire Archaeological and Topographical Journal* 9 (1885-1886) 257-302. This honor is not to be confused with the Rape of Hastings — held in 1086 by William's father, Robert count of Eu — which remained in the hands of the counts of Eu for several generations: see Henry Ellis, *A General Introduction to Domesday Book* (London 1833) 1.463; Sanders (n. 18 above) 119-120.

[21] Orderic (n. 7 above) 4.284.

[22] J. F. A. Mason, "Roger de Montgomery and His Sons (1067-1102)," *Transactions of the Royal Historical Society,* ser. 5, 13 (1963) 16-17.

[23] Orderic (n. 7 above) 4.284.

[24] Odo's treason was compounded by his defiance of Rufus at Rochester Castle after submitting to him at Pevensey: *Anglo-Saxon Chronicle,* A.D. 1088.

[25] Orderic (n. 7 above) 4.284.

The king seems to have been interested chiefly in collecting money rather than friends from among the great families, for the sons and heirs of the wealthiest Conquest magnates are seldom found on the witness lists of Rufus's surviving charters (see Table C). William son of Robert of Mortain and Stephen son of Alan of Richmond are not known to have attested at all; William II of Warenne, adult and active throughout Rufus's reign, attested only twice; Gilbert of Clare attested only four times. The sons and heirs of Roger of Montgomery gained much land under Rufus (usually for a stiff price), yet they rarely attested.[26] In short, many magnates purchased Rufus's forgiveness, but — whether by their choice or his — they were seldom in his entourage.[27]

It is clear enough that Rufus did not make *curiales* of his magnates. But the question remains, did he give lands to his friends on such a scale as to make magnates of his *curiales*? As we have seen, the greatest honors forfeited under Rufus (by Odo of Bayeux, Eustace of Boulogne, Robert of Mowbray and William of Eu) were not granted out to royal favorites but remained in the king's hands. Nevertheless, frequent attendance and service at court doubtless brought its rewards. Indeed, Orderic goes so far as to say,

> Many of his father's nobles ... died during his reign, and the king raised
> up in their place not magnates but certain underlings, whom he exalted
> by granting them wide honors as a reward for their flattery.[28]

In the absence of Pipe Rolls or another Domesday survey, it is difficult to tell how much Rufus gave to his *curiales*. His administrative lieutenant, the cleric Ranulf Flambard, surely grew wealthy in the king's service, and other members of Rufus's court circle prospered as well. His faithful steward Eudo is known to have received some lands,[29] and the *curialis* Robert fitz Hamon was given a substantial barony of

---

[26] Mason (n. 22 above) 13-20. Hugh of Montgomery, earl of Shrewsbury 1093/4-1098 (a 1095 conspirator) attested twice. His brother Robert of Bellême (a 1088 rebel) served as a military commander for Rufus in Normandy when Curthose was on Crusade and became earl of Shrewsbury in 1098, yet attested no known charter of Rufus's. Another brother, Roger the Poitevin (a 1088 rebel and major landholder under Rufus), attested only twice. Still another brother, Arnulf of Montgomery (a 1088 rebel to whom Rufus granted extensive lands seized from Odo of Champagne in 1095), attested only once.

[27] One notable exception was Roger Bigod, a 1088 rebel with Domesday lands worth about £450 per year. Roger became a royal steward under Rufus and attested twenty-six of his surviving charters.

[28] Orderic (n. 7 above) 5.202.

[29] Eudo held a considerable Domesday honor, valued at £383; Rufus granted him the manor of Dereman, Hertfordshire (worth £15 in 1086), and some minor properties in Essex; plus perhaps other lands for which the charters have not survived: *Regesta regum Anglo-Normannorum,* ed. H. W. C. Davis and others (Oxford 1913-1969) 1, nos. 399, 435, 442; William Farrer, *Honors and Knights' Fees* (Manchester 1925) 3.166; cf. Lennard (n. 6 above) 99-104. Henry I seems to have treated Eudo much more generously, granting him the city of Colchester (worth £88 in 1086), the manor of Witham, Essex (£12-9-0 in 1086) and control of three valuable manors of the Mandeville family (£163 in 1086): *Regesta* 2, nos. 519, 553, 661, 688.

TABLE C

Relationship between Landed Wealth and Frequency of
Attestations among English Magnates Alive in 1100

10 greatest Engl. lay landholders	pounds/ year	Wm. II attests.	rank/lay attestors	succeeds
Robt. of Bellême	2430	0 (2)*		1098 (1093/4)*
Wm. of Mortain	2100	0		1090
Wm. II of Warenne	1165	2		1088
Stephen ld. of Richmond	1100 + waste	0**		c. 1093
Hugh e. of Chester	800	8½	8	ante 1087
Gilbert of Clare	780	4		1086/8
Geoffrey de Mandeville	780	1		ante 1087
Robert Malet	600	0		ante 1087
Henry of Ferrers	545	3		(d. 1093/1101; no attests. by heir)
Philip of Braose	455 + Wales	0		1093/6
Total of attestors in top 15: 1 of 10				

*The figure in the parentheses applies to Robert of Bellême's brother, Hugh of Montgomery, who was Robert's immediate predecessor as earl of Shrewsbury.
**Spends much of the reign in his honor in Brittany.

about £300 a year.[30] Additional acts of royal generosity have doubtless gone unrecorded, yet it does seem clear that Rufus raised nobody to the level of the greatest Conquest magnates. Occasionally he might grant earldoms to men who supported him in times of trouble: in 1088 he made William I of Warenne earl of Surrey and Henry of Beaumont earl of Warwick; and Walter Giffard was later raised to the earldom of Buckingham. But neither William of Warenne nor Walter Giffard

[30] Robert fitz Hamon, who attested 21 of Rufus's charters, had been landless in 1086; he supported Rufus in the 1088 rebellion and soon thereafter was given the estates of the late Queen Matilda (Orderic [n. 7 above] 4.220). The lands ascribed specifically to the queen in Domesday Book have a total annual value of £261, but to them should probably be added additional lands

seem to have received any additional lands in the process.[31] Henry of Warwick, landless in 1086, was enriched with the Warwickshire estates of the Englishman Thurkell of Arden (worth about £120 per year) plus the Warwickshire and North-amptonshire lands of Henry's brother, Robert of Meulan (worth about £210 per year).[32] The total value of the lands in Henry's earldom apparently came to the tidy but unspectacular figure of about £330 per year. If he received any additional lands, for which the evidence has vanished, they cannot have been worth a great deal.[33] In any event, the three new earls came from families already wealthy: the Giffard honor had a Domesday value of about £420; Henry of Warwick's Beaumont kinsmen held lands in 1086 worth about £300; and William of Warenne was, as we have seen, one of William I's ten greatest landholders (about £1165). And of the three, only Henry of Warwick can be regarded as a *curialis* of William II (eight attestations). Walter Giffard and William II of Warenne (whose father, William I, died in 1088 just after receiving his earldom) each attested only two known charters of William Rufus.

The shape of Rufus's policy toward his great men is suggested by the contrasting careers of two major magnates of his reign: the curial baron Robert count of Meulan and the eldest of the Montgomery brothers, Robert of Bellême. Robert of Meulan was one of Rufus's most active *curiales* (sixteen attestations), yet his English holdings appear from the available evidence to have actually diminished during the reign. Robert received his maternal grandfather's county of Meulan in the French Vexin and inherited the extensive Norman honor of his father Roger of Beaumont (d. ca. 1094) plus Roger's English estates in Dorset and Gloucestershire, worth about £77 per year. But Robert gave his own Domesday lands in Warwickshire and Northamp-tonshire (ca. £210 per year) to his brother Henry earl of Warwick.[34] It is difficult to believe that Robert of Meulan received no additional English lands under Rufus, and some acquisitions doubtless went unrecorded. But Robert became a dominating magnate only under Henry I, who gave him large chunks of the super-honor of

---

ascribed to the queen's *antecessor*, the thegn Brictric, valued at £55. Robert fitz Hamon extended his power into Wales during the reign, becoming the conqueror and lord of Glamorgan. Cf. also Urse of Abitôt, sheriff of Worcester and a *curialis* of William II (11 attestations), whose aggressions against the bishropric of Worcester during William I's reign are well recorded, and who "seems to have secured fresh lands between the survey and his death" (in 1108): VCH *Worcestershire* 1.264.

[31] *Complete Peerage* 2.386-387; 12.1.493-495; Orderic (n. 7 above) 4.180 n. 1.

[32] *Chronicon Monasterii de Abingdon,* ed. Joseph Stevenson, Rolls Series (1858) 2.20; *Complete Peerage* 12.2.358; VCH *Warwickshire* 1.277; VCH *Northamptonshire* 1.371.

[33] The Northamptonshire Survey (temp. Henry I – Henry II: *ibid.* 1.387) shows that the earl of Warwick received a crumb or two of *terra regis* in Northamptonshire from either William II or Henry I. At some point the earls of Warwick received lordship over the Domesday fee of William fitz Corbucion, worth £28 per year in 1086: VCH *Warwickshire* 1.278. Henry I made Henry of Warwick lord of Gower (South Wales): Lynn H. Nelson, *The Normans in South Wales* (Austin 1966) 122.

[34] Levi Fox, "The Honor and Earldom of Leicester: Origin and Descent," *English Historical Review* 54 (1939) 386-387; Robert's role as one of Rufus's key advisors emerges clearly in Eadmer, *Historia novorum,* ed. Martin Rule, Rolls Series (1884) 40, 62, 86.

Mortain (forfeited ca. 1104) and permitted him in 1102 to acquire extensive lands from the Grandmesnil family in and around Leicestershire.[35]

Robert of Bellême, on the other hand, had fought against Rufus in the rebellion of 1088, and two of his brothers (at least) had joined the secret confederacy of 1095 and been pardoned afterwards. Robert of Bellême himself had always tended to support Curthose against Rufus.[36] When Curthose departed for the Holy Land in 1096, pawning Normandy to Rufus, Robert of Bellême fought in the king's behalf along the Norman frontiers. In April 1098 Robert of Bellême captured Rufus's enemy (and his own), Elias count of Maine.[37] But Robert must seldom have been in the royal entourage, for he attests no known charter of William Rufus. Nor could Rufus depend on Robert's unfailing allegiance. In August 1100, when Rufus was killed in the New Forest, Curthose was known to be returning from the Holy Land, and the king was about to lead an army across the Channel to hold Normandy against its crusader-duke.[38] In the warfare that would have ensued had Rufus dodged the fatal arrow, nobody can predict what Robert of Bellême might have done. Yet Rufus had, in the meantime, raised Robert to a dominating position among the magnates of England. On the death of his brother Hugh earl of Shrewsbury in 1098, Robert of Bellême bought the earldom from Rufus for £3000 (to the disadvantage of two younger brothers).[39] This vast honor, plus the estates of Roger of Builli which he purchased "from the king for a great sum of money,"[40] made Robert of Bellême the wealthiest lord in England. He was also a tremendously powerful magnate on the continent — lord of his father's great estates in Normandy, his mother's inheritance of Bellême and his wife's county of Ponthieu. In raising him to the pinnacle of the English landholding nobility, Rufus was playing a hazardous game.

Taken altogether, the evidence from Rufus's reign suggests very strongly that the king granted lands to his *curiales* on only a relatively modest scale.[41] Most of the great Conquest families, though prone to rebellion and seldom at court, retained their honors or (*vide* Robert of Bellême) expanded them. Only a few fell, and Rufus raised up no *curiales* to take their places.

Between the Conqueror's death in 1087 and Rufus's in 1100, the royal *curia* was

---

[35] Fox 387-388; J. F. A. Mason, *William the First and the Sussex Rapes,* The Historical Association, Hastings and Bexhill Branch (1966) 20; VCH, *Northamptonshire* 1.371, 374, 377-378, 381-383 (Northamptonshire Survey).

[36] Mason (n. 22 above) 19-20.

[37] Orderic (n. 7 above) 5.214, 238, 242, 254.

[38] *Ibid.* 5.280.

[39] *Ibid.* 5.224.

[40] *Ibid.* 5.224-226. Robert of Bellême is said to have been Roger of Builli's kinsman, but their exact relationship is unknown.

[41] Grants of land were of course not the only means by which a king might reward his courtiers. He might also dispense such lucrative ephemera as wardships, danegeld exemptions, administrative offices, moratoriums on debts, favor in litigation before royal courts, etc. On Henry I's use of these kinds of patronage see R. W. Southern, *Medieval Humanism and Other Studies* (Oxford 1970) 206-233.

thus transformed from a court dominated by the king and his greatest magnates to a court of middling landholders and household officials in which the chief territorial magnates tended to play a minor role. The contrast is demonstrated by a comparison of Table A (1087) with Table C (1100). Whereas in 1087 seven of England's ten wealthiest landholders were also *curiales* (that is, among the fifteen most frequent lay attestors), in 1100 only one landholder among the wealthiest ten was a *curialis*. [42] Table D makes the same comparison in reverse, listing the ten most frequent lay attestors who were alive at the close of each reign, together with data on their

TABLE D
Relationship between Frequency at Court
and Landed Wealth: 1087, 1101

The 10 leading lay curiales *of Wm. I alive in 1087*					
Names	*Wm. I attests.*	*Addressee*	*Office*	*Land income*	*Norman lands*
Roger of Montgomery	40	1	[earl]	2100	very large
Odo bp. of Bayeux	34	5	[earl]	3000	very large
Geoffrey bp. of Coutances	34	13		780	large
Robt. c. of Mortain	30½	7	[earl]	2100	very large
Robt. c. of Meulan	23	0		220	no (France)
Roger of Beaumont	21	0		77	large
Alan ld. of Richmond	21	1		1100 + waste	no (Britt.)
Eudo *dapifer*	16	0	steward	385	mid.
Hugh e. of Chester	15½	1	[earl]	800	large
Henry of Ferrers	12	2	Domesday commiss.	545	large
Totals:				11,107	

[42] The list of landholders in Table C concludes with three men whose families are absent from Table A. These three did not grow appreciably wealthier between 1087 and 1100; they advance into the select group only because three much wealthier landholding families of 1087 had forfeited their lands (Odo of Bayeux, Eustace of Boulogne, and Geoffrey of Coutances's heir, Robert earl of Northumberland).

TABLE D (Cont)

The 10 leading lay curiales *of Wm. II alive in 1100*					
Names	*Wm. II attests.*	*Addressee*	*Office*	*Land income*	*Norman lands*
Eudo *dapifer*	37	0	steward	415	mid.
Roger Bigod *dapifer*	28	2	steward, sheriff	450	small
Robert fitz Hamon*	21	0		300 + Wales	large
Robert c. of Meulan	16	1		?100	large
Urse of Abitôt	12	5	constable, sheriff	90	very small
Hamo II *dapifer*	9	11½	steward, sheriff	128	no
Wm. Peverel of Nottingham	9	2½	?local justiciar	250	mid.
Hugh e. of Chester	8½	0	[earl]	800	large
Henry e. of Warwick*	8	1	[earl]	325	mid.
Robert of Montfort	7	0	constable	385	large
Totals:				3,243	

*Much enriched under Wm. II

administrative activities (how many royal writs were addressed to them?), their administrative offices and their annual income from English lands. It emerges from this analysis that William I's ten chief lay *curiales* held lands of the king worth almost 3 1/2 times the lands of their counterparts under William II (£11,107 per year versus £3243 per year).[43] William II's *curiales*, on the other hand, were much more apt to be officers of the royal household (5 of 10 versus 1 of 10).

[43] These figures are subject to caution: they are based on Domesday land values in 1086, which had doubtless changed by 1100: e.g., the Beaumont manor of Sturminster (Dorset) was worth £55 in 1086; all the Beaumont lands in Dorset were worth £72 in 1086 (Domesday Book 1.80-80b); but "Sturminster" was worth £140 in ca. 1107 (*Regesta* [n. 29 above] 2, no. 843). Likewise, the values of the lands of Rufus's *curiales* make no allowances for unrecorded gifts of land. Nevertheless, the general implications of the data are clear.

For Rufus to have re-created the close personal bonds between king and magnates would have required a policy of great tact and political artistry, designed to persuade the magnates that their own best interest and advantage lay in working closely and submissively with their monarch. And Rufus lacked the capacity, or the will, to follow such a policy. His *curiales* were typically men of middling wealth, household officials and occasional royalist bishops (as the attestations show), augmented by a mixed bag of young knights of modest origin, entertainers and assorted court followers whose varied activities (on which all the chroniclers dwell) did not include the witnessing of royal charters.[44]

At Rufus's death in mid-1100 the split between magnates and *curiales* remained as pronounced as ever. And there is little to suggest that Rufus would have succeeded, had he lived longer, in drawing the young magnates into his court and administration, or that he was inclined to build a countervailing group of curial magnates through the creation of vast new honors. In the weeks just prior to his death Rufus's confidence and ambition seem to have been immense,[45] but perhaps unwisely so. The peaceful interlude of Curthose's absence on Crusade was about to end, and with Rufus's greatest magnates seldom at court, his regime was dangerously unstable. This view accords with that of Sir Richard Southern who, applying his penetrating insight to very different kinds of evidence, concluded that when Rufus died "the country was ready for a revolution, which might well have swept away much of the structure of royal government."[46]

The revolution very nearly occurred in summer 1101, a year after Rufus's death, when Robert Curthose crossed the Channel to contest Henry I's seizure of the throne and was joined by powerful magnates in England.[47] But the campaign ended with a compromise in which Henry I kept his throne while relinquishing his Norman holdings and promising Curthose a large annuity. The affair was more than simply a struggle between Curthose and Henry I; it was also the climax of the schism between Rufus's magnates and *curiales*.

Table E compares the men known to have supported Curthose in 1101 with those

[44] Walter Tirel, who allegedly fired the misaimed arrow that killed Rufus in 1100, typifies the young knights at the court, though he was better connected than most. Lord of Poix (near Amiens) and castellan of Pontoise, he had only minor holdings in England and Normandy. Having married into the Clare family (by 1086), he joined Rufus's entourage and became the king's intimate friend and constant companion: Orderic (n. 7 above) 5. 288; Eadmer, *Vita Anselmi,* ed. R. W. Southern (London 1962) 27-28. But Walter Tirel attested no known royal charters, nor did the Clare marriage bring him any appreciable lands: cf. Domesday Book 2.41, and *Pipe Roll 31 Henry I* (London 1929) 56, in which his widow, Adeliza of Clare, is recorded as holding one small manor (Langham, Essex: held by Walter in 1086 and valued at £15 per year).

[45] See, for example, William of Malmesbury (n. 12 above) 2.378-379.

[46] Southern (n. 41 above) 231.

[47] C. Warren Hollister, "The Anglo-Norman Civil War: 1101," *English Historical Review* 88 (1973) 315-334 ; see above, chapter 4, pp. 77-96.

known to have supported Henry I.[48] Since, by happy coincidence, exactly nine names can be identified with each party, the totals in all categories in Table E are susceptible to direct comparison. There are many reasons why a baron might have opted for one faction or the other: two members of the Curthose group (Eustace of Boulogne and Ivo of Grandmesnil) had accompanied the duke to the Holy Land; several held extensive lands in Normandy; the leader of the group, Robert of

TABLE E
The Two Factions in the Succession War of 1101

Supporters of Curthose, 1101	Family anti-Wm. II 1088	Family pro-Wm. II 1088	Family anti-Wm. II 1095	Approx. value Engl. lands: £/year	Wm. II attests.
Robt. of Bellême e. of Shrewsbury*	X		X	2365	0
Wm. of Mortain e. of Cornwall*	X			2100	0
Roger the Poitevin c. of La Marche*	X		X	260	2
Arnulf of Montgomery e. of Pembroke*	X		X	200	1
Wm. II of Warenne e. of Surrey		X		1165	2
Walter II Giffard e. of Buckingham				425	1
Ivo of Grandmesnil	X			340	1
Robt. of Lacy ld. of Pontefract	**		**	250 + waste	0
Eustace c. of Boulogne	X			*** 770	0
Totals:	6	1	3	7875	7

*Kinsmen: Robert, Roger and Arnulf were brothers; William of Mortain was their sister's son.
**Roger of Lacy, of the Herefordshire branch of the family, opposed Rufus in 1088 and 1095.
***Not in possession of his English lands in 1100; deprived c. 1088, restored 1101.

[48] The names are drawn from the major English and Norman chronicles of the period. On William of Mortain's role, see also the "Chronica Monasterii de Hida juxta Wintoniam," in *Liber Monasterii de Hyda,* ed. Edward Edwards, Rolls Series (1866) 305-306; see also *Regesta* (n. 29 above) 2, nos. 530-531, 533-536, where the witnesses can almost certainly be identified as supporters of Henry I. Orderic names Robert Malet as a ducal supporter, but probably wrongly: C. Warren Hollister, "Henry I and Robert Malet," \below, ch. 7, pp. 129-36.

TABLE E (Cont)

Supporters of Henry I, 1101	Family anti-Wm. II 1088	Family pro-Wm. II 1088	Family anti-Wm. II 1095	Approx. value Engl. lands: £/year	Wm. II attests.
Hugh e. of Chester		X		800	8½
Richard of Redvers				12	1
Robt. fitz Hamon		X		300	21
Hamo II *dapifer*				128	?9**
Eudo *dapifer*				415	37
Henry e. of Warwick		X		325	8
Robt. c. of Meulan		*		?100	16
Roger Bigod *dapifer*	X			450	28
Urse of Abitôt shf. of Worcs.				90	12
Totals:	1	3	0	2620	140

*Robert of Meulan was in Normandy during the 1088 rebellion; his brother Henry of Warwick supported Rufus.
**There is some confusion between Hamo I *dapifer* and his son, Hamo II *dapifer*. Hamo II probably succeeded in 1087/1091.

Bellême, must have resented Henry's seizure of the strategic Bellême stronghold of Domfront in the 1090s,[49] and Robert probably influenced his two brothers, Roger and Arnulf, and his young nephew William of Mortain. Whatever their reasons for backing Curthose, the nine anti-royalists had much in common. All were sons of great Conquest magnates; all had retained or expanded their lands under Rufus; yet none had entered his court circle.

Henry I's supporters, on the other hand, consisted by and large of Rufus's friends, *curiales* and administrators — men of greater age and experience and of less landed wealth than the Curthose group. Here again, other factors than wealth and service at

[49] Orderic (n. 7 above) 4.256-258, 292; *Anglo-Saxon Chronicle*, A.D. 1094.

court were doubtless involved. Robert fitz Hamon, Richard of Redvers (the only low attestor in the group), and Hugh earl of Chester (the one great magnate) held lands in western Normandy where Henry had exercised lordship prior to his accession. And Henry earl of Warwick is said to have been an old friend of Henry I's.[50]

But regardless of individual motives, the contrast between the two groups remains striking. The nine Curthose supporters held lands valued collectively at nearly £8000; the nine royalists held lands worth less than £3000. The Curthose group had attested Rufus's surviving charters only seven times altogether; the royalist group had attested more than 140 times.[51] The Curthose group included far more men whose families had plotted or rebelled against Rufus than did Henry I's group. Among the royalists were three of Rufus's stewards; the ducal supporters included no officers of the late king's household. In short, the war of 1101 pitted the *curiales* of the previous reign against the non-curial magnates.

Henry I, having survived the invasion-rebellion of 1101, seems to have undertaken a deliberate policy of closing the gulf that produced it, whether by transforming his great magnates into friends and *curiales* or by destroying them and putting others in their places. The vast Montgomery lands of Robert of Bellême and his brothers were forfeited to the king in 1102. Henry I offered his sister-in-law's hand to William of Mortain and, when William refused, gave her in marriage to Eustace of Boulogne. [52] Eustace became Henry I's friend, while William of Mortain defected in 1104 and forfeited his immense English earldom. The faithful and astute royalist Robert of Meulan was raised into the highest echelon of wealth by his acquisition of large portions of the Mortain and Grandmesnil honors. William of Warenne was disseised in 1101, reinstated in 1103, and lured into the royal *curia* (sixty-nine attestations under Henry I as against two under Rufus). And in later years Henry created new magnates and super-magnates from among his own kinsmen and closest associates – Robert earl of Gloucester, Brian fitz Count, Roger bishop of Salisbury, Stephen of Blois.

Clearly, the traditional contrast between Rufus, the "baron's king," and Henry I surrounded by faceless *curiales* whom he had "raised from the dust" requires drastic revision. The data discussed in this paper will, it is hoped, contribute to the needed reinterpretation. Attestation statistics certainly do not tell the whole story. They do not in themselves make clear, for example, the nature of the relationships between the Norman kings and the men who attested their charters. They do not tell us to what extent a king was able to impose his will on his *curiales* or they on him.[53] We

---

[50] Malmesbury (n. 12 above) 2.470. This friendship may well have influenced, or been shared by, Henry of Warwick's brother, Robert of Meulan.

[51] Again, these attestation statistics must be interpreted with caution: some of Curthose's supporters did not inherit or come of age until well into Rufus's reign (see Table C); others spent much time on their continental estates.

[52] "Chronica" (n. 48 above) 306; Florence of Worcester, *Chronicon ex chronicis*, ed. Benjamin Thorpe (London 1848-1849) 2.51.

[53] The chronicles suggest that William I and William II both dominated their courts but that Robert Curthose, as duke of Normandy, did not.

only know that the men most active at the Conqueror's court tended to be of a different sort than those at the court of Rufus, and that Rufus's relations with his greater magnates appear to have been far from satisfactory.

Henry I made an obvious effort to change things. In the days and months just following his accession he presented himself as a reforming king: he directed his coronation charter against Rufus's abuses, filled vacant prelacies, imprisoned the despised Ranulf Flambard and recalled Archbishop Anselm from exile. But Henry's most fundamental effort at reform has largely escaped notice, perhaps because the problem to which it was addressed has not been well understood. According to Orderic Vitalis (whose observation that Henry raised men "from the dust" is so well known),

> From the beginning of his reign he had the wisdom to conciliate all groups, drawing them to himself by his regal munificence. He honored his magnates (*optimates*) generously, bestowed on them riches and honors, and thus won their fidelity by his soothing policies.[54]

As usual, Orderic oversimplifies. Robert of Bellême and William of Mortain, for example, were by no means soothed by Henry's policies. But in time their places as super-magnates were taken by Henry's friends. To determine the degree to which Henry re-created the fusion of magnates and *curiales* that the Conqueror had achieved would require further, very extensive analyses of baronial wealth and attestations during Henry's long reign. For now, suffice it to say that the new king was aware of the problem and was coming to grips with it.[55]

---

[54] Orderic (n. 7 above) 5.296.

[55] The problem is approached very tentatively in Hollister (n. 48 above) 120-122, and (n. 47 above) 331-332.

6

THE MISFORTUNES OF THE MANDEVILLES*

DURING THE REIGNS of the Norman kings of England (1066–1154) the feudal aristocracy held its lands far less securely than in subsequent generations. Never again would royal authority over baronial inheritances be quite so encompassing as in the days of the Conqueror and his sons. Never again would the succession of estates be so fluid or the wealth and power of great landed families so ephemeral. The Norman kings usually allowed family estates to pass from father to eldest son, but only on the payment of an arbitrary relief. They were far less apt to forgive rebellious magnates than their successors were, and baronial revolt—or sometimes merely the intention to revolt—might result in the forfeiture of family holdings and perhaps exile or captivity as well. The Norman age is marked by the fall of great families— the earls of Norwich and Hereford, the Montgomeries, Mortains, Lacys, Baynards, Mowbrays, Malets, Grandmesnils, Abitots, and more. At a less spectacular level, the records of Henry I's reign disclose a policy of tight royal control over baronial marriage alliances and ambiguous inheritances. If a magnate died without a surviving son, the inheritance often depended on the royal will and fell to whoever among the collateral heirs enjoyed the king's favour and was willing to pay the king's price. Many important families managed to keep their lands throughout the period and even extend them— the Warennes, Clares, Beaumonts, Bigods, Ferrers, Giffards, and others— but they succeeded only by remaining faithful to the king or, if unfaithful, winning his forgiveness. Consequently, the Norman age, and particularly the reign of Henry I, was a time when new men often rose into the landed aristocracy through royal service and when the survival and enrichment of the older Conquest families depended heavily on their service to the monarch. In the skilful hands of Henry I, this policy produced thirty-three years of peace in England, and an aristocracy of both old and new families equally devoted to the royal interest—the one sure avenue to their own prosperity. It also produced grumbling exiles and unsuccessful claimants whose grievances fuelled the civil strife that followed Henry's death in 1135.

The insecurity of baronial tenure under Henry I is vividly exemplified in the history of the Mandevilles of Essex, one of the wealthiest and most influential families of post-Conquest England. Geoffrey I de Mandeville, the founder of the family's English fortunes, received from William the Conqueror an

*I am grateful to the American Council of Learned Societies, the American Philosophical Society, the Social Science Research Council, the Fulbright Commission, the John Simon Guggenheim Memorial Foundation, and the Warden and Fellows of Merton College, Oxford, for their help in supporting the research for this paper.

immense fief centering on Essex and including lands in ten other shires, valued collectively at about £782 per year in 1086.[1] He served at one time or another as sheriff of London and Middlesex, and (probably) Essex, and was perhaps also sheriff of Hertfordshire and custodian of the Tower of London.[2] His grandson, Geoffrey II, first earl of Essex, was the subject of a major book by John Horace Round, who portrayed him as 'the most perfect and typical presentment of the feudal and anarchic spirit that stamps the reign of Stephen'.[3] Geoffrey II's sons, Geoffrey III and William II, earls of Essex in succession, were high in the favour of Henry II. Earl William, indeed, was one of Henry II's closest and most powerful associates and was appointed co-justiciar of England by Richard I.[4]

The most obscure of the early Mandeville lords is William I, son and heir of Geoffrey I and father of Round's 'unscrupulous magnate'. William de Mandeville's career, as related by Round and the editors of the *Complete Peerage*, is uneventful.[5] He is said to have succeeded to the Mandeville lands on Geoffrey I's death *c.* 1100 and to have passed them to his son Geoffrey II on his own death *c.* 1129. He appears only once in a chronicle of the period, but in a position of considerable historical interest: Orderic Vitalis identifies him as keeper of the Tower of London in 1100–1 and guardian of the Tower's first known political prisoner, Ranulf Flambard bishop of Durham.[6] In February 1101 Flambard escaped from the Tower and fled to Normandy, serving there as the chief organizer of Robert Curthose's invasion of 1101, which nearly cost Henry I his newly won crown.[7]

We know that in the aftermath of this invasion Henry I punished several barons who had chosen the wrong side, but the chroniclers tell us nothing of William de Mandeville's fate. His career can be reconstructed, however, from an analysis of the charter evidence, with results that differ markedly from the conclusions of Round. William's troubles after Flambard's escape cast light on Henry I's baronial policy, and place the behavior of Round's great anti-hero, Geoffrey II, in a new perspective.

Henry I was by no means prepared to forgive William de Mandeville his behavior in 1101. In a notification to the chief men of Essex and Hertford-shire (1103–5, probably 1103), the king granted to Eudo *Dapifer*, a trusted official and royal favourite, the three Mandeville manors of Sawbridgeworth [co. Herts.] and Great Waltham and Saffron Walden [co. Essex] until such time as William de Mandeville paid Eudo £2,210 3s. which William had owed

---

[1] Geoffrey held of the king in Essex, Surrey, Berks., Middx., Oxon., Cambs., Northants., Warwicks., Suff. and Bucks., and was a sub-tenant in several shires as well.
[2] *Regesta Regum Anglo-Normannorum*, ed. H. W. C. Davis *et al.* (Oxford, 1913–69), I, nos. 15, 39, 93, 111, 181*, 265; III, nos. 275–6. It cannot be confirmed from extant charters of William I or William II that Geoffrey I was sheriff of Herts.; his shrievalty of Essex is mentioned only in a forged charter of William I (*Reg.* I, no. 181*); cf. *Reg.* I, no. 93 (A.D. 1072–6) addressed to Ralph Baynard sheriff of Essex, Geoffrey de Mandeville sheriff of Middlesex, and Peter de Valognes sheriff of Herts.
[3] Round, *Geoffrey de Mandeville* (London, 1892), p. v.
[4] *Complete Peerage* (rev. ed.), V, 116–20.
[5] *Ibid.*, pp. 113–14; Round, *G. de M.*, pp. 37–40.
[6] Orderic Vitalis, *Historia Ecclesiastica*, ed. A. le Prévost (Paris, 1838–55), IV, 108.
[7] See my article, 'The Anglo-Norman Civil War: 1101', above, ch. 4, pp. 77-96.

as a debt to the king.[8] Henry I had evidently seized the three manors as a pledge for William de Mandeville's debt and was now making a gift of the lien to Eudo. The most striking thing about this arrangement is that the value of the three manors, and the debt, are both extraordinarily high. At the time of the Domesday survey Sawbridgeworth and Saffron Walden were demesne manors of Geoffrey I de Mandeville, each valued at £50 per year, and at Great Waltham Geoffrey had demesne lands worth £60 per year. Altogether, these three manors, worth £160 per year in 1086, constituted almost one-third of the total Mandeville demesne in England.[9] Moreover, they lay at the strategic center of Mandeville power and influence—in central and northern Essex and on the Hertfordshire–Essex border. Their loss effectively removed the Mandevilles from the upper stratum of the English baronage.

As for the debt of £2,210. 3s., the editors of the *Regesta* II (who render it incorrectly as £1,210. 3s.) suggest that it was the relief on the lands of William's father, who had died *c.* 1100.[10] But no known relief of Henry I remotely approached £2,200,[11] and one must therefore suppose that other debts were involved as well—perhaps a substantial fine for William's irresponsibility (or worse) in permitting Flambard's escape.[12] The magnitude of the debt was matched by the severity of its collection. The Pipe Roll of 1130 shows us several instances of Henry I's permitting substantial obligations to go uncollected for years without prejudices to the debtor's lands.[13] But in William de Mandeville's case, any hope of paying the debt must have been seriously reduced by the loss of substantial sources of his income.[14]

[8] *Cartularium Monasterii S. Johannis Baptiste de Colecestria*, ed. S. A. Moore (Roxburghe Club, London, 1897), I. 22; *Reg.* II, no. 661: *Donec Willelmus de Magnauilla ei insimul det licencia mea et imperio ipsi Eudoni dico MM. et CC. libras et x libras et iii solidos quas michi debet de debito suo. Quia ego dedi eas omnes predicto Eudoni.* Cf. a similar royal lien in *Early Yorkshire Charters*, II, ed, W. Farrer (Edinburgh, 1915), pp. 326–9.

[9] *Domesday Book*, I, 139b; II, 58a, 62a. Of the total 1086 Mandeville valuation of *c.* £782, *c.* £518 represented demesne lands, according to my calculations. By 1139, and perhaps much earlier, Saffron Walden was the site of an important Mandeville castle (of the motte-and-bailey type): D. F. Renn, *Norman Castles in Britain* (London, 1968), p. 337.

[10] *Reg.* II, no. 661. Geoffrey I was evidently dead in 1100 when his son was constable of the Tower of London. Geoffrey attests or is addressed in several charters of William II (*Reg.* I, nos. 306, 402, 435, 454–5), all of which might be as early as 1087 but three of which might be as late as 1100. Since William de Mandeville is neither a witness nor a recipient of any known charter of William II, it seems probable that Geoffrey I died late in the reign. Some scholars have been misled by attestations of Henry I's charters by 'Geoffrey de Mandeville' [of Marshwood, Devon], who was not related to the Mandevilles of Essex.

[11] The relief on the earldom of Chester, for example, seems to have been £1,000: *Pipe Roll 31 Henry I*, ed. Joseph Hunter (London, 1833), p. 110.

[12] I cannot entertain the view that Henry I himself connived in the escape in order to place Flambard in Curthose's court as a 'secret agent' (see Frank Barlow, *The Feudal Kingdom of England*, London, 1955, p. 176). The invasion of 1101, in which Flambard played the central role, was far too serious a matter to be interpreted as a stage piece to further some complex design of Henry I.

[13] The Chester relief of 1130, for example, appears to have been assessed against Earl Ranulf I *c.* 1121 and to have remained unpaid at his death in or before 1129: *P.R. 31 Henry I*, p. 110.

[14] William de Mandeville's standing with the king is suggested by the fact that he attests only one known royal charter, *Reg.* II, no. 682. He is an addressee in a royal writ of 1100–6 confirming a Mandeville benefaction: *ibid.*, no. 769.

The records of the next three decades enable us to trace the history of the confiscated manors through the remainder of the reign. In *c.* 1105 Henry I ordered the sheriff of Essex and Herts. to reseize Eudo *Dapifer* of the lands and sokes of Great Waltham, Sawbridgeworth, and Saffron Walden 'which William de Mandeville gave or exchanged after his father's death, no matter to whom he gave or exchanged them. . . . And it displeases me that you have not done as I ordered. And see that I hear no further complaint.'[15] The disputes underlying this writ are hidden from us, but it would appear that William may have been trying to sell off his lands in order to pay his debt, and that Eudo *Dapifer's* occupancy of the manors was continuing to receive royal protection.

At some date between 1105 and 1120 at least one of the manors, and probably all of them, passed into the hands of a new holder, Othuer, illegitimate son of Earl Hugh of Chester. A royal writ of 1120–33 records a gift to Westminster Abbey of the church of Sawbridgeworth, in 'the honor that belonged to Othuer fitz Earl'.[16] This person, whose name occurs variously as *Otuer, Otuel, Otwer, Othuer,* etc., was a royal favourite who served as tutor and companion of Henry I's son and heir, William Aetheling, and drowned with him while crossing from Normandy in the White Ship on 25 November 1120.[17] Eudo *Dapifer* had died in Normandy shortly before (February 1120),[18] and Othuer may possibly have obtained the manors on Eudo's death. But if so, he never lived to see them. And the fact that Sawbridgeworth was later identified with 'the honor that belonged to Othuer' suggests something more than an absentee tenure of nine months. It suggests, rather, that Othuer had received the manors prior to Eudo's death and had held them for some appreciable time. But whatever the case, the manors apparently passed to the king on Othuer's death; we find them in royal hands in 1130.[19]

In the meantime, what had become of William de Mandeville? After his single attestation of a royal charter on 13 February 1105, he vanishes from our records. Round, I. J. Sanders, and the editors of the *Complete Peerage*, believe that he died *c.* 1129 on the grounds that his son Geoffrey II had, by

---

[15] *Cart. Colecestria,* I, 24–5; *Reg.* II, no. 688. Eudo *Dapifer* granted a portion of the tithes of his demesne at Sawbridgeworth to Colchester Abbey: *Cart. Colecestria,* I, 3, 6, 15, 68, 85, 146 *et passim.*

[16] J. Armitage Robinson, *Gilbert Crispin, Abbot of Westminster* (Cambridge, 1911), p. 156; *Reg.* II, no. 1884 [1120–33]. Saffron Walden and Great Waltham are probably represented in *P.R. 31 Henry I*, pp. 56, 60, where royal lands in Essex, described as having been 'lands of Otuer', are pardoned 16s. of murder fines and 72s. of danegeld. Cf. *ibid.*, p. 53, where Othuer's former Essex lands are farmed by a royal official for £65. 12d. Since the official would normally expect to realize a profit on the transaction, the farm figure represents only a portion of the actual value.

[17] Orderic, IV, 418. Othuer seems to have crossed to Normandy with William Aetheling in May, 1119: *ibid.*, IV, 347; *Reg.* II, nos. 1204, 1223, 1230–1.

[18] Annales Colecestrensis, in *Ungedrückte Anglo-Normannische Geschichtsquellen,* ed. F. Liebermann (Strassburg, 1879), p. 162; *Historia Fundationis* of St. John's Abbey, Colchester: *Monasticon Anglicanum,* new edition, ed. John Caley, H. Ellis and B. Bandinell (London, 1846), IV, 608–9. This not altogether trustworthy source adds that during the final fifteen years of his life Eudo was blind, apparently residing chiefly at his castle of Préaux in Normandy. He rarely attests royal charters after *c.* 1110. Cf. J. H. Round, 'The Early Charters of St. John's Abbey, Colchester', *E.H.R.*, XVI (1901), 728.

[19] *P.R. 31 Henry I,* p. 62, where Sawbridgeworth is exempted from 46s. of danegeld as a royal demesne manor. Cf. *ibid.*, pp. 53, 56, 60, and above, n. 16.

Michaelmas 1130, apparently paid only two-thirteenths of the relief: 'We may infer,' Round concludes, 'that his father was but lately dead.'[20] But a charter of Henry I, written at the Tower of London sometime before May 1116, discloses that William de Mandeville was dead at the time of its issuance.[21] The charter confirms lands and privileges of the Mandeville priory of Hurley and is a product of Henry I's single recorded visit to the great fortress that William de Mandeville had formerly guarded. William does not attest, nor is his name mentioned. The prior and monks are confirmed in the lands which they have of the fee of Geoffrey [I] de Mandeville, 'and especially in the manors of the honor of Geoffrey de Mandeville that are in the king's hands'. This last phrase might seem to be a reference to the three alienated manors, but since they were then in Eudo's or Othuer's hands, not the king's, it must pertain instead to lands of the late William de Mandeville now held by the king as guardian of the young Geoffrey II.[22]

William de Mandeville's early death requires a re-examination of the Pipe Roll evidence on which Round based his erroneous conclusion. Round assumed that Geoffrey II was charged a relief of £866. 13s. 4d. But in fact we do not know how large the relief originally was; we only know that it stood at £866. 13s. 4d. (1300 marks) in 1129 and that Geoffrey paid £133. 6s. 8d. (200 marks) in 1130, thereby reducing the obligation to £733. 6s. 8d. (1100 marks).[23] Geoffrey's father, as we now know, had died many years before, and even though the relief may not have been charged until Geoffrey came of age, it probably had been carried on the royal rolls for several years at least. The leisurely rate at which Geoffrey was paying it off should serve as a warning against placing too much reliance on Pipe Roll relief data as evidence for the frequently encountered phrase in Anglo-Norman genealogies, 'recently dead in 1130'. A perusal of Sanders' *Baronies* will disclose a suspiciously high number of barons who allegedly died *c.* 1129, and the death dates of several of them should probably be revised backwards. Historians have tended to underestimate the extent to which the Pipe Roll of 1130 can include, without warning, very old debts and very old information. The total amount of money owing to the king in 1130, for example, is a nearly

---

[20] Round, *G. de M.*, p. 40; *Complete Peerage*, V, 113; I. J. Sanders, *English Baronies* (Oxford, 1960), p. 71.

[21] Robinson, *Gilbert Crispin*, p. 150; *Reg.* II, no. 1176. Cf. *ibid.*, no. 1174, a forgery, also from the Tower of London, magnifying the concessions of no. 1176; on the question of its authenticity see Pierre Chaplais, 'The Seals and Original Charters of Henry I', *E.H.R.*, LXXV (1960), 275; *idem*, 'The Original Charters of Herbert and Gervase Abbots of Westminster', in *A Medieval Miscellany for Doris Mary Stenton* (Pipe Roll Soc., New Ser., XXXVI, 1962), pp. 97–98; and Robinson, *Gilbert Crispin*, pp. 153–4.

[22] This is the interpretation of William Farrer: *An Outline Itinerary of King Henry I* (Oxford, 1920), p. 66, n. 6. More recently, Chaplais ('Original Charters of Herbert and Gervase,' p. 98 and n. 1) has impugned the authenticity of this writ (*Reg.* II, no. 1176) on the grounds that it appears to betray the handwriting of a later twelfth-century Hurley scribe. But assuming this to be the case, the writ's unexceptionable form, circumstances and contents (a general confirmation of unspecified Mandeville benefactions), and its irrelevance to the priory's later disputes over lands and customs, suggest the existence of an authentic prototype: see Robinson, *Gilbert Crispin*, pp. 150–1, 153–4. Quite apart from this writ, moreover, there remains independent evidence that William de Mandeville's custody of the Tower had ceased by 1116 at the very latest (*Reg.* II, no. 1175; III, no. 506; below, n. 26), and that he cannot have been alive after 1120 (his widow was widowed for a second time in that year: below, notes 26, 27). [23] *P.R. 31 Henry I*, p. 55.

meaningless figure because it consists of debts accumulated and repeated year upon year.[24]

These debts must be understood not only as sources of royal income but also as instruments of royal control. Henry I might reward a baron for his loyalty and good behavior by allowing his debt to run on indefinitely, accepting nominal payments or none at all. Or, as appears repeatedly in the Pipe Roll, the king might simply pardon the debt in whole or in part. But if the baron should act against the king's interest and lose the royal favour, his debt could provide colourable grounds for legal action—as the case of William de Mandeville so vividly illustrates. Two generations later Henry II would employ this same weapon against Becket.

In all his reign Henry I issued only two known charters from the Tower of London, one of which, as we have seen, concerns the Mandeville foundation at Hurley. Each charter has the same two witnesses: Ranulf the Chancellor and Othuer fitz Earl.[25] Once again Earl Hugh's illegitimate son turns up in connection with the Mandevilles. Hitherto Othuer has not been thought to have had a wife, or offspring, or any relationship to the Mandeville family, but it can be shown that he had all three. Not only did he come into possession of the alienated Mandeville manors; he also succeeded William de Mandeville as constable of the Tower of London. The extreme rarity of the name Othuer, and his appearance with Henry I in the Tower of London, removes any doubt that he is the Othwer mentioned in a record of Stephen's reign as keeper of the Tower under Henry I and immediate predecessor in that office of a certain Aschuill, who guards the Tower in 1136–7.[26] Othuer's connection with the Mandeville family can be deduced, indirectly but conclusively, from a passage in Empress Maud's second charter to Geoffrey II de Mandeville where a certain William fitz Otuel is described as Earl Geoffrey's brother.[27] Round himself was struck by the passage and drew the only possible conclusion: that William fitz Otuel 'was clearly a "uterine" brother of Earl Geoffrey . . ., so that his father must have married William de Mandeville's

---

[24] Total debts in 1130 are *c.* £66,600, but the total collected is only *c.* £24,500. Pipe Roll references to Robert Mauduit, chamberlain of the treasury, have led some scholars to date his death *c.* 1129; he actually died in 1120: *Reg.* II, p. 340; Simeon of Durham, *Opera Omnia*, ed. T. Arnold (Rolls Series, 1882–5), II, 259.

[25] *Reg.* II, nos. 1175, 1176 (A.D. 1107–16, Apr.): *T'. Rann' cancell' per Otuelum fil' comitis apud Turrim Lundon*: Robinson, *Gilbert Crispin*, pp. 150, 153 and above, n. 23. Ranulf the Chancellor attests *c.* 168 charters of Henry I; Othuer attests 13. On the tendency toward particular witnesses occurring in charters with which they have a local or family connection see *Reg.* II, p. xxviii. On the meaning of *Per . . .*, *ibid.*, p. xxvii and n. 34.

[26] *Reg.* III, no. 506: record of a plea *coram rege* between the prior of Holy Trinity, Aldgate, and Aschuill, castellan of the Tower of London: *Othwer(us) quondam regie turris custos. . . . Aschuill(us) etiam succ(essor) Oth(wer)i in turris custodia . . . ad obitum regis Henrici*. The plea is discussed in H. A. Cronne, *The Reign of Stephen* (London, 1970), pp. 265–6. Othuer fitz Earl's connection with London is further suggested by his appearance as first witness to an agreement (*c.* 1111–19) between the canons of St. Paul's, London, and William de Marcy, made in the Chapter House of St. Paul's in the presence of Bishop Richard de Belmeis: *Royal Commission on Historical Manuscripts, Ninth Report*, I (1883), 31b, 66a, misdated *c.* 1127 by the editors. In 1130 the cost of repairing 'houses that had belonged to Otuer' was entered among the deductions from the farm of London: *P.R. 31 Henry I*, p. 144.

[27] *Reg.* III, no. 275 [25–31 July, 1141, at Oxford]: *dedi Willelmo filio Otvel(li) fratri ejusdem Comitis Gaufredi. . ..*

widow—a fact unknown to genealogists'.[28] We can now take the further step of identifying William fitz Otuel's father as Othuer fitz Earl, successor to the alienated Mandeville manors and to the Mandeville wardship of the Tower.

While William de Mandeville was suffering the royal displeasure, Othuer was basking in the royal favor. As the prince's tutor he was well known at court, attesting thirteen charters between 1107 and 1120. Besides the great Mandeville manor of Sawbridgeworth, he held Essex lands which the king farmed in 1130 for £65. 1s. (presumably Great Waltham and Saffron Walden), and lands elsewhere worth £210 at farm.[29] And his possession of Sawbridgeworth suggests that he may have been the intended heir to the entire honor of Eudo *Dapifer* which, including lands that Eudo acquired under William II and Henry I, commanded a cumulative yearly income of at least *c.* £500 in England alone. Othuer was apparently on his way to becoming one of the great magnates of the realm when his life was cut short by the disaster of the White Ship.

The shipwreck that destroyed Othuer's promising career may well have been the salvation of the Mandevilles. Once his favoured stepfather was removed, the young Geoffrey II might hope to recover the three lost manors, custody of the Tower, and perhaps some of the lucrative offices that his grandfather had enjoyed under the Conqueror. He might also hope to inherit Eudo *Dapifer's* vast honor. For the records make it clear that Eudo *Dapifer* was a Mandeville kinsman. The relationship is proven by the wording of Empress Maud's second charter to Earl Geoffrey (1141) in which Geoffrey succeeds to Eudo's Norman estates and his stewardship *ut rectum*—by hereditary right.[30] And the *Genealogia Fundatoris* of Tintern Abbey supplies the final piece in the puzzle: Margaret, daughter of Eudo *Dapifer* and Rohese of Clare, married William de Mandeville and was the mother of Geoffrey, earl of Essex and *dapifer* of Normandy *jure matris*.[31]

Whether William married Margaret before or after he lost the three manors to Eudo we cannot tell. In either case this remarkable marriage, uniting the victim of a substantial confiscation with the heiress of its chief beneficiary, takes on the character of a deft royal manoeuvre to punish a baron while suppressing his motives for rebellion—depriving him of land but not of hope. Henry I, in short, had arranged it that a vested interest in William de Mande-

---

[28] Round, *G. de M.*, p. 169 and n. 1; cf. *ibid.*, p. 229, where a charter of Geoffrey III de Mandeville [1157–8] is attested by William fitz Otuel *patruus meus*; and *Monasticon*, V. 579 n., 580: William II de Mandeville, earl of Essex (1166–89), confirms the grant of William fitz Otuel, *avunculi sui*, to the Cistercian nunnery of Greenfield of 33 acres at Thoresby and Aby [Lincs.], lands that had belonged to Earl Hugh of Chester in 1086 (*Domesday Book*, I, 349a).

[29] *P.R. 31 Henry I*, pp. 53, 133–4. See above, n. 16.

[30] *Reg.* III, no. 275. Othuer fitz Earl's involvement in Eudo's inheritance is perhaps suggested by the fact that Othuer attests royal charters of 1119 and 1120 confirming Eudo's benefactions to Colchester Abbey, and also attests a royal charter of 1120, shortly after Eudo's death, confirming the lands of one of Eudo's tenants: *Cart. Colecestria*, I, 4–10, 21, 23–4; *Reg.* II, nos. 1204, 1230–1.

[31] *Monasticon*, V, 269. The passage was known to Round but rejected by him (and by the editors of the *Complete Peerage*, V, 114) on the grounds that Eudo's lands did not pass directly to Geoffrey de Mandeville but were in Henry I's hands in 1130. This can hardly stand as an objection when one recalls that three former Mandeville manors were also in royal hands, and that Geoffrey's rights were in conflict with those of William fitz Othuer.

ville's disseisin should be enjoyed by William's own father-in-law—the very man from whom the Mandevilles would have aspired one day to receive not only the three manors but an immense additional inheritance as well. These hopes were dampened when, on William's death, Margaret married Othuer fitz Earl. Othuer may well have received the three manors as a marriage portion, and in succeeding to William's wife he succeeded likewise to William's constableship of the Tower. Had he lived on, he might logically have been declared the heir to Eudo's great honor. But his sudden death in 1120 reopened the inheritance question once again.

By 1130 the situation was this: the honor of Eudo *Dapifer* and the three lost manors were in the king's possession.[32] The Tower of London was held for the king by Othuer's successor, Aschuill.[33] Geoffrey II de Mandeville had now come into his truncated inheritance and had received danegeld exemptions in 1129 and 1130 for lands in six shires, but he was indebted to the king for a balance of 1100 marks on his relief.[34] His half-brother, William fitz Othuer, makes no appearance in the Pipe Roll or in other records of the reign. He was doubtless still a minor, and his inheritance probably remained uncertain—yet promising. Some or all of Eudo's and Othuer's lands and offices might one day pass to him, or conceivably to Geoffrey II, or perhaps to neither.[35] In a complex inheritance of this sort everything depended on the

---

[32] Eudo's stewardship may have passed to his nephew, the royal favourite Robert de la Haye (*Gallia Christiana*, XI, 'Instrumenta', col. 233: *Robertus de Haia . . . nepos Hudonis dapiferi Guillelmi . . .*) who attests as *dapifer* in Normandy after 1120: *Reg.* II, nos. 1422, 1688, 1693, 1698; and Archives de Calvados, MS. H. 1833 (1) and H. 1833 (2). Cf. *Red Book of the Exchequer*, I, 355: in 1166 Ranulf de la Haye held 5/6 of a fee of the honor of Eudo *Dapifer*.

[33] *Reg.* III, no. 506. Aschuill, like Othuer, is an extremely uncommon name. I suggest that the person in question may be Hasculf de Tany who attests the royal charter to London c. 1130 (*Reg.* II, no. 1645). In 1141 the Empress granted to Earl Geoffrey de Mandeville, among other things, custody of the Tower of London, and *feodum et servicium terre quam Hasculf de Tania tenuit in Anglia die qua fuit vivus et mortuus, quam tenet Graeling et mater sua . . .* (*ibid.* III, no 274). On the Tany family see L. R. Buttle, 'The de Tanys of Stapleford Tawney', *Transactions of the Essex Archaeological Society*, N.S., xx (1930–1), 153–72; William Dugdale, *The Baronage of England* (London, 1675–76), I, 508–9; Sanders, *Baronies*, p. 4, and Round, *G. de M.*, p. 91, n. 3. A concord between Gilbert abbot of Westminster and William of Bocland [1115–17] is attested by, among others, Othuer fitz Earl, Richard de Mandeville (younger brother of William I de Mandeville), and *Asciulus de Taneyo*: Robinson, *Gilbert Crispin*, pp. 154–5. The names 'Hasculf' and 'Othuer' both occur in the Avranchin family of Subligny; in 1143 Hasculf son of Othuer de Subligny founded the abbey of La Lucerne near Avranches: *Gallia Christiana*, XI, 'Instrumenta', cols. 112–13. Othuer fitz Earl's father, Hugh d'Avranches, had been hereditary vicomte of the Avranchin, and the Tany's came from the same district (Tanis, s.w. of Avranches: Abbé Desroches, in *Mémoires de la Société des Antiquaires de Normandie*, XIV, 1844, 50–51).

[34] *P.R. 31 Henry I*, pp. 55 and *passim*. The peculiarities of Henry I's danegeld exemptions are well illustrated by the fact that in 1129 Geoffrey II had been pardoned a total of £19. 8s. on lands in Essex, Bucks., Warwicks., Berks. and Middx., whereas in 1130 he was pardoned 18s. for lands in Oxford only. Taken altogether, these exemptions exclude the Mandeville Domesday holdings in Suff., Surrey., Herts., Cambs. and Northants., but the apparently erratic nature of the pardons prevents us from drawing any conclusions from these omissions.

[35] Certain of Eudo's lands, however, had already passed to the counts of Boulogne, the lords of St. Clare and others: J. H. Round, *Peerage and Family History* (New York, 1901), pp. 163–4; William Farrer, *Honors and Knights' Fees* (Manchester, 1923–5), III, 167–8. The rival claims of King David of Scotland and Simon de Senlis to the earldom of Huntingdon and Northampton involved a similar conflict between the offspring of an heiress's first and second marriage, and the resolution was likewise dependent on the royal favour: *Complete Peerage*, VI, 640 ff.

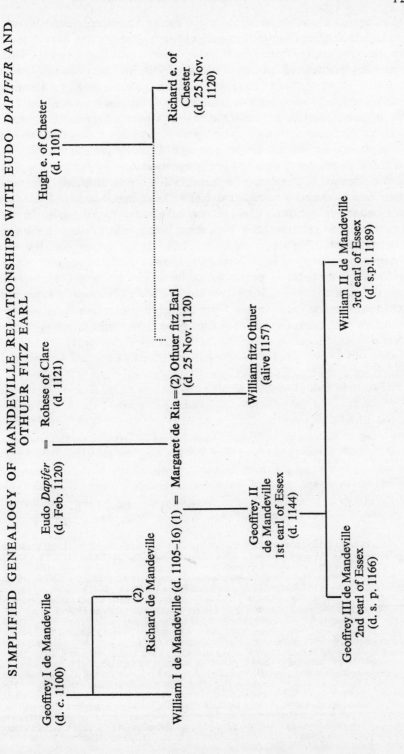

SIMPLIFIED GENEALOGY OF MANDEVILLE RELATIONSHIPS WITH EUDO *DAPIFER* AND OTHUER FITZ EARL

will of the king, and so far as we know, Henry I remained uncommitted at his death in 1135. Perhaps it is significant that in Henry's final year Geoffrey II began attesting royal charters.[36]

Round's portrait of Geoffrey de Mandeville in the opening years of Stephen's reign is that of a powerful, typically acquisitive magnate, hereditary castellan of the Tower, who 'put himself and his fortress up for auction' and played one side recklessly against the other to his own advantage.[37] Professor R. H. C. Davis, by redating Stephen's and Maud's charters to Geoffrey, has provided a needed and convincing revision of Geoffrey's role in the 'Anarchy' —a role that was far more a product of circumstance, far less ruthless, than Round supposed.[38] It can now be seen that in King Stephen's opening years Geoffrey represented a family that had suffered major losses of territory, office and status. Whatever hopes he may have had of recovering his family's fortunes were as yet unrealized. He did not occupy the Tower of London in 1135; indeed, his famous tenure as castellan was far shorter than has been supposed, beginning sometime between 1137 and 1141 and ending in 1143.[39] Geoffrey was probably in possession of the Tower by early 1141, prior to Stephen's defeat at Lincoln,[40] and about midway through the year his occupancy was confirmed by the Empress.[41] But the custodianship was not secured by formal royal grant until Christmas, 1141, when Geoffrey, having defected from Maud, was received back into royal favour. Only then did Stephen state, '*Dedi ei et concessi custodiam turris Lond(onie)*'—words that strongly suggest an original royal grant.[42]

The strife of 1140–1 enabled Geoffrey to recover all his family's losses and more. In 1141, or perhaps shortly before, he regained the long-alienated manors of Sawbridgeworth, Saffron Walden and Great Waltham.[43] Sometime between December 1139 and December 1140 Stephen created him earl of Essex, and in mid-1141 Maud gave him not only the custody of the Tower but also a pardon of all debts incurred under Henry I and Stephen, the shrievalties of Essex, Hants., and London and Middlesex, the office and Norman lands of Eudo *Dapifer*, and much else—all *sine pecuniae donatione*![44] A knowledge of the family's earlier misfortunes lends special significance to

---

[36] *Reg.* II, nos. 1915 (Falaise), 1916 (Argentan), 1917 (Rouen). Geoffrey II was evidently participating in Henry I's 1135 campaign against William Talvas: Orderic, V, 45–47.

[37] Round, *G. de M.*, pp. 98 and *passim*.

[38] R. H. C. Davis, 'Geoffrey de Mandeville Reconsidered', *E.H.R.*, LXXIX (1964), 299–307; cf. *idem*, 'What Happened in Stephen's Reign?' *History*, LXIX (1964), 1–12.

[39] *Reg.* III, nos. 506, 274; Stephen arrested Geoffrey and deprived him of his castles in September or October 1143: Round, *G. de M.*, p. 202. Geoffrey died in 1144.

[40] R. H. C. Davis, *King Stephen* (London, 1967), pp. 59, 63.

[41] *Reg.* III, no. 274: *Concedo illi et heredibus suis custodiam turris Londonie*.

[42] *Ibid.*, no. 276. On this passage Round comments (*G. de M.*, p. 149): 'The latter expression is somewhat strange in view of the fact that Geoffrey had been in full possession of the Tower before the struggle had begun, and, indeed, by hereditary right.'

[43] For Saffron Walden: *Reg.* III, no. 274; for Sawbridgeworth and Great Waltham, *ibid.*, no. 913 [1140–3], and *Monasticon*, IV, 148–9. Henry II, in a charter of January 1156, confirmed to Geoffrey III de Mandeville all the lands of his ancestors, including, specifically, Saffron Walden, Sawbridgeworth and Great Waltham: *Et vadium quod Rex Henricus avus meus habuit super predicta tria maneria sua imperpetuum ei clamavi quietum sibi et heredibus suis de me et de meis heredibus:* Round, *G. de M.*, p. 236; cf. p. 241: 'The release of the lien . . . is a very curious feature.'   [44] *Reg.* III, nos. 274–6.

Maud's words when she granted her earl 'all his holdings, to be held as well and freely as Geoffrey his grandfather held them, or William his father, or whoever afterwards held them, at any time, in fee and heredity by him and his heirs of me and my heirs'.[45] Round remarks on the 'intensely hereditary character' of these grants,[46] but in view of the Mandevilles' earlier troubles one can hardly wonder at Geoffrey's insistence that his tenure, and that of his heirs, be made as secure as words permitted.

Geoffrey de Mandeville was triumphant. The complex inheritance questions of the previous reign had all been resolved in his favour. The chief victim of the settlement was his half-brother, Othuer's son, who had to make do with a fragment of his father's fortune. Maud's second charter to Geoffrey includes a grant to William fitz Othuer of escheated lands worth £100 per year, to be held in fee and heredity. Maud explains with unintended irony that she is giving him this modest estate 'because of her love of his brother, Earl Geoffrey'.[47]

[45] *Reg.* III, no. 275.
[46] *G. de M.*, p. 53 and *passim*.
[47] *Reg.* III, no. 275: *pro amore fratris sui Comitis Gaufredi*—the usual contemporary formula for identifying an intercessor.

7

HENRY I AND ROBERT MALET

Robert Malet, Domesday lord of Eye (Suffolk) was one of the great Norman landholders of post-Conquest England. His father had received from William the Conqueror extensive estates in Suffolk, Yorkshire, and several other counties. As heir to this "honor of Eye," Robert Malet enjoyed an annual income from his English lands of about £600, making him one of the kingdom's wealthier barons.[1] Moreover, he served at times as sheriff of Suffolk and attained distinguished rank in the royal household, becoming the first master chamberlain of England whose name we know, and perphaps the first man ever to hold that title.[2] Robert attests only once as *camerarius*, never as *magister camerarius*, but his possession of the office is established by Henry I's charter of 1133 granting to Aubrey II of Vere the "master chamberlainship of all England" as fully as Robert Malet had formerly held it.[3] At the time of this charter,

I am grateful to the American Council of Learned Societies, the American Philiosophical Society, the Social Science Research Council, the Fulbright Commission, the John Simon Guggenheim Memorial Foundation, and the Warden and Fellows of Merton College, Oxford, for their help in supporting the research for this paper.

[1] On Robert Malet's wealth, holdings and background see *Victoria County History* [VCH] *Suffolk* 1.395-396; Henry Ellis, *A General Introduction to Domesday Book* (London 1833) 1.449-450; *Cambridge Medieval History* 5.510-511; *Dictionary of National Biography* 12.864; Lewis C. Loyd, *The Origin of Some Anglo-Norman Families* (Leeds 1951) 56. The family originated at Graville-Saint-Honorine, Seine-Inf. Robert was a Domesday tenant-in-chief in Suffolk, Yorks., Norfolk, Surrey, Notts., Rutland, Lincs., Cheshire, and Essex, and a subtenant in Suffolk, Norfolk, and Rutland.

[2] See *The Complete Peerage*, rev. ed. 10 app., 47-56: a good summary of the evidence, correcting certain misinterpretations in T. F. Tout, *Chapters in the Administrative History of Mediaeval England* 1 (Manchester 1920) 90-92. See also G. H. White, "The Household of the Norman Kings," *Transactions of the Royal Historical Society*, 4th ser., 30 (1948) 144-147. The *magister camerarius* is listed in the "Constitutio Domus Regis" of ca. 1136 as an officer of the first rank, receiving the same wages and allowances as the master butler, the stewards, the treasurer, and the constables: *Dialogus de Scaccario*, ed. Charles Johnson (London 1950) 133. But these exact arrangements were probably not yet in effect in the early years of Henry's reign.

[3] "Magistram camerariam meam totius Anglie . . . sicut Robertus Malet uel aliquis ante eum uel post eum umquam . . . tenuit": *Sir Christopher Hatton's Book of Seals*, ed. L. C. Loyd and D. M. Stenton (Oxford 1950) no. 39; *Regesta regum anglo-normannorum*, ed. H.

Robert had been dead for nearly three decades, and it is generally believed that he died in exile and royal disfavor. But this view, based on the testimony of a historian writing a generation after Robert's death, is contradicted by more reliable evidence. It will be argued here that Robert's relations with Henry I were quite different from what has been assumed. A reexamination of all the evidence can not only illuminate the career of a major Anglo-Norman magnate but also add to our understanding of Henry I's remarkably success-ful policy toward his baronage, a policy that brought England thirty-three years of unbroken peace.

Orderic Vitalis tells us that Robert Malet, as a consequence of his taking Robert Curthose's side in the civil war of 1101, was disseised and banished by Henry I in 1102.[4] But since Robert Malet attests for Henry as *camerarius* on 13 February 1105, current opinion places his fall in that year or the next.[5] The charter of 1105 is the only known document that Robert attests as *ca-merarius* and is also, apparently, his last known appearance as a living person. It is dated at Romsey *in transitu regis*, as the king was awaiting his crossing to Normandy for a campaign that would see the burning of Bayeux and the capture of Caen. Robert Malet would probably have been crossing with the king, but what became of him afterwards we are not told. We are left only with the traditional view, derived from Orderic, that he was disseised shortly thereafter by a king who had never forgiven him his disloyalty in 1101.

A comparison of Orderic's story with the record evidence discloses more than one inconsistency. The charters of the first three Norman kings make it clear that Robert Malet received the master chamberlainship from Henry I, that Henry may also have reinstated Robert as sheriff of Suffolk—a posi-tion he had held for a time under the Conqueror[6]—and that between 1101 and 1105, Robert was in the inner circle of Henry's court. Robert attested five of William I's charters, none as *camerarius*,[7] and attested no known charters of William II. Indeed, his name does not appear at all in Rufus's charters,

---

W. C. Davis et al. (Oxford 1913-69) 2 no. 1777; cf. the later confirmations of the grant, *ibid.* 3 nos. 634-635. The *Regesta* editors (2.xiii) point out that since there were apparently no English master chamberlains between Robert's death and 1133, the language of the charter cannot be taken to indicate that Robert necessarily had predecessors in the office. G. H. White suggests that William *camerarius* of Tancarville held the master chamberlain-ship of England and Normandy from ca. 1106 to his death in 1129 and passed it to his son, Rabel, whose master chamberlainship was limited after 1133 to Normandy alone: *Peerage* (n. 2 above) 51-53.

[4] Orderic Vitalis, *Historia ecclesiastica*, ed. A. le Prévost (Paris 1838-1855) 4.161, 167.

[5] *Reg.* (n. 3 above) 2 no. 682; *Peerage* (n. 2 above) 51; G. H. White, "The Fall of Robert Malet," *Notes and Queries*, 12th ser., 12.390-391.

[6] VCH *Suffolk* 1.389; *Domesday Book* 2.287b. He did not hold the office at the time of Domesday Book, or at the opening of Rufus's reign: *Reg.* 1 no. 291.

[7] *Reg.* 1 nos. 47, 82, 147, 207, 270.

a fact that precludes his having served in an important office in Rufus's administration.[8] Under Henry I, however, he is twice addressed as a responsible official in Suffolk (probably sheriff), both times, apparently, after the strife of July 1101.[9] Moreover, he attests at least nineteen of Henry's charters, sixteen or seventeen of which seem to have been issued between July 1101 and February 1105.[10] This level of attestation, over a brief span of about three and one-half years, compares favorably with that of such well known royal favorites of later times as Brian fitz Count (forty-three attestations in ten years) and Miles of Gloucester (forty-four in fourteen years).

Robert Malet thus became a major figure in the royal court and administration only under Henry I. Whether he received the master chamberlainship before or after the 1101 crisis cannot be determined—conceivably he acquired it only in 1103 or 1104 when he was apparently replaced as sheriff of Suffolk.[11] But we know that he was chamberlain in 1105, just before he vanishes from our records. In any event, Orderic's suggestion that he was out of favor after mid-1101 seems quite inaccurate. Henry I and Robert Curthose had pledged in 1101 to respect the lands of each other's followers, but such a pledge would hardly have obliged Henry to retain Robert Malet in a powerful, lucrative household position to which he had just been appointed, or, as the case may be, to promote him to that office after the peace. Nor would Henry have felt bound to have Robert Malet incessantly at court. The past or future chamberlain evidently enjoyed high royal favor after the crisis of 1101, and any subsequent forfeiture would have to be ascribed to a second defection on Robert's part rather than to a long-standing royal grudge.

But rather than burdening Robert Malet with a twisting, improbable career of royal favor and twofold treason, it seems preferable to reject Orderic's

---

[8] Rufus's chief administrators attest his charters frequently: e.g., Ranulf Flambard, Urse of Abitôt, and the stewards Hamo, Eudo, and Roger Bigod: *Reg.* 1 (n. 3 above) passim.

[9] *Reg.* 2 no. 655 (Christmas, 1102, '03, or '05; probably 1103), no. 780 (1101-1106, probably 1104, when Ranulf Flambard, who attests, is known to have been in England: Simeon of Durham, *Opera omnia*, ed. Thomas Arnold [Rolls Series 1882-5] 1.260-261; cf. *Reg.* 2 no. 683).

[10] *Reg.* 2 nos. 488(a)-799, passim. Nos. 700 and 702 (both Cornbury) are probably of even date with no. 701 [1101-1105] (Dated at Cornbury, 18 October, and attested by Ranulf Flambard), and with no. 959 (Cornbury) which refers to a royal aid perhaps identical to the aid mentioned in no. 670 [1103-1104] and noted by contemporary writers (e.g., Florence of Worcester and the Anglo-Saxon chronicler, *s.a.* 1104). The Cornbury charters should therefore be dated tentatively ca. 18 October 1104, by which time Henry had probably returned from Normandy. (He returned in 1104 "before winter": Orderic [n. 4 above] 4.201).

[11] He was apparently replaced by Whitsunday 1104 (*Reg.* 2 [n. 3 above] no. 672) but cannot have been replaced, as the editors suggest, before summer 1102: *ibid.* nos. 591, 657n.; but cf. no. 655. Robert, although not addressed in no. 591, is its sole witness. He was with Henry at Hereford on the 1102 campaign against Robert of Bellême and was therefore not called upon just then to do the king's business in East Anglia. He is again sole witness but not addressee in a royal charter for Norfolk and Suffolk of Christmas, ca. 1103 (*Reg.* 2 no. 656), probably concurrent with no. 655 where he is an addressee but not a witness.

story altogether. The historian from Saint-Evroul, writing circa 1135, is far from reliable when discussing Henry's punishment of the 1101 rebels in England. Referring apparently to the year 1102, he writes that Robert of Lacy and Robert Malet were both impleaded at court, deprived of their honors and expelled from the kingdom. We know from other evidence, however, that Robert of Lacy, lord of Pontefract, was not disseised until circa 1112 or thereafter,[12] and whatever the reason, it seems more likely to have been connected with the Franco-Norman wars of circa 1111-1113 than with a crisis long before. Indeed, there is proof that a year after the 1101 crisis Robert of Lacy stood high in the royal favor. Upon the fall of the Montgomeries and their followers in 1102, he received from Henry I the Yorkshire lands of Warin Bussel and William of Say and five additional carucates in Bowland (Yorkshire). At about the same time he seems to have been serving as local justiciar in Yorkshire or possibly even as sheriff.[13]

Charter evidence likewise discredits Orderic's story of Robert Malet's fall. A series of charters of Henry I confirms the lands and customs of the Malet priory of Saint Peter's, Eye, as they were held *die qua Robertus Maleth vivus et mortuus fuit.*[14] Evidently, then, Robert Malet held the honor of Eye until his death, which probably occurred in 1105 or 1106 when his attestations cease.

In contrast, we know that William Malet, who is said to have been Robert's son and heir, did not hold the honor long, if at all.[15] William Malet was alive and holding lands in Normandy in 1117 when Henry I confirmed his gift of Mesnil Joscelin to the abbey of Bec, and in 1121 when the king confirmed his gift of Conteville (Eure) to the same abbey.[16] But sometime between 1105

---

[12] *Lancashire Pipe Rolls*, ed. William Farrer (Liverpool 1902). 383; VCH *Leicestershire* 1.314-315; *Reg.* 2 (n. 3 above) nos. 918, 1030. Robert had lost his lands by the time of the Lindsey Survey (A.D. 1115-1118).

[13] *Early Yorkshire Charters* 3, ed. William Farrer (Edinburgh 1916) nos. 1420-1421; cf. nos. 1418-1419, 1422; W. E. Wightman, *The Lacy Family in England and Normandy* (Oxford 1966) 35-37, 65-66; *Reg.* 2 (n. 3 above) no. 598; cf. nos. 559, 1030.

[14] *Reg.* 2.333, 350 (nos. 1144, 1145, 1147, 1406); *Calendar of Charter Rolls* 5.363-364. See also *Reg.* 3 no. 713: King Stephen confirms a church and its holdings to Redlingford Priory, Eye, *sicut erant tempore Roberti Malet et die qua fuit vivus et mortuus.* Cf. *Reg.* 3 no. 180.

[15] Despite the *Dictionary of National Biography* 12.864, William Malet may have been Robert's nephew, or even his brother, rather than his son. The Malet genealogy remains badly tangled. See J. A. Robinson, *Gilbert Crispin* (Cambridge 1911) 14, and cf. *Monasticon anglicanum* 3.405. Whatever the case, William was almost certainly Robert's heir: below, n. 16.

[16] For the 1117 donation: Bibliothèque Nationale lat. MS 13905, fol. 21v: incomplete transcript by Dom Jouvelin. This donation, omitted from *Reg.* 2 (n. 3 above), is quoted in part, without the reference to Henry I's confirmation, in A. Porée, *Histoire de l'Abbaye du Bec,* 2 vols., (Évreux 1901) 1.334 n. 4, where it is also made clear that the William Malet in question was Robert Malet's Norman heir and a direct descendant of Robert's parents (William I Malet and Hesilia Crispin: *Monasticon* 3.405). For the 1121 charter: *Calendar of Documents Preserved in France,* ed. J. H. Round (London 1899) no. 372.

and 1113 the honor of Eye fell into royal hands,[17] and circa 1113 or not long
thereafter it passed in large part to Stephen of Blois.[18] Most probably Henry
I seized Eye in 1110 when, according to the Anglo-Saxon chronicler, William
Malet, Philip of Braiose, and William Baynard were deprived of their lands.[19]
Henry of Huntingdon adds the information that these three men had wronged
the king,[20] but we are not told the nature of their misdeeds. In 1110 Henry I
was at odds with King Louis VI of France,[21] and at about that time Roger,
son and heir of Urse of Abitôt, was deprived of his lands and his shrievalty
of Worcestershire for having ordered the killing of a royal official.[22] Midway
through the following year Henry crossed to Normandy "on account of the
hostility that some people had against him on the frontiers of France,"[23] and
from then until 1113 he was at war with Louis VI and Count Fulk V of Anjou.
The forfeiture and banishment of William Malet in 1110 was probably connected somehow with these events.

In short, when Orderic speaks of the trial and condemnation of Robert
Malet, he seems to be confusing the master chamberlain with William Malet
and the crisis of 1101 with that of 1110-1113.[24] Orderic is silent on the fall

---

[17] *Reg.* 2 (n. 3 above) nos. 932-933, 1144-1147; charters of Henry I in favor of Eye Priory.
All are A.D. 1106-1116 except no. 933: A.D. 1106-1113.

[18] R. H. C. Davis, *King Stephen* (London 1967) 7; *Reg.* 2 no. 1406 (ca. 1113-1126). Stephen
first appears in Henry's presence in 1113 at St. Evroult (Orderic [n. 4 above] 4.301-302) and
first attests at Henry's court on 28 December 1115 (*Reg.* 2 no. 1102: at St. Albans, as count
of Mortain). The belief that Stephen received Eye in 1113 is entirely plausible but is based
on very slender evidence (*Cal. Charter Rolls* 5.366; *Reg.* 2 no. 932 n.) The Malet Yorkshire
lands passed for the most part to Nigel of Albini and his heirs, at some date prior to ca. 1124:
Yorkshire Charters 3 (n. 13 above) v, and no. 1822 and n.

[19] *Anglo-Saxon Chronicle*, s.a. 1110. Philip of Braiose was later reinstated: *s.a.* 1112;
Pipe Roll 31 Henry I, ed. Joseph Hunter (London 1833) 72, 103, 126, 157. William Baynard's
lands passed to Robert fitz Richard of Clare, probably by 1111: *Reg.* 2 (n. 3 above) nos. 991,
994 and n. Sometime between 1111 and 1119 a William Malet received Flemish lands from
Henry I's enemy, Count Baldwin VII; William had with him in Flanders his wife, *Lismoth*,
and his brother, Robert Malet (II?): *Actes des comtes de Flandre, 1071-1128*, ed. Fernand
Vercauteren (Brussels 1938) xl; nos. 79, 85, 93-94.

[20] *Historia anglorum*, ed. Thomas Arnold (Rolls Series 1879) 237, stating that the forfeitures
occurred at the king's Whitsun court (29 May 1110) at New Windsor. Henry I had encountered difficulties with a William Malet at an earlier time: *Reg.* 2, no. 522 (but possibly the
uncle or father of the William Malet exiled in 1110).

[21] *Louis VI le Gros*, ed. Achille Luchaire (Paris 1890) 39-40: Suger, *Vie de Louis VI le
Gros*, ed. Henri Waquet (Paris 1964) 104-110.

[22] William of Malmesbury, *Gesta pontificum anglorum*, ed. N. E. S. A. Hamilton (Rolls
Series 1870) 253. On the date of Roger's fall (ca. 1110 or shortly thereafter) see *The Cartulary
of Worcester Cathedral Priory*, ed. R. R. Darlington, Pipe Roll Soc., n.s. 76 (1968) xxv, 26-27.
Osbert of Abitôt had succeeded Roger as sheriff of Worcestershire at a date no later than 1113:
Reg. 2 (n. 3 above) no. 1025; cf. nos. 940, 1035, 1062.

[23] *Anglo-Saxon Chronicle*, s.a. 1110: cf. *Historia anglorum* (n. 20 above) 237.

[24] Since Robert Malet is not one of the seven barons whom Orderic (n. 4 above) lists as
ducal conspirators in 1101 (4.103-104), but is only mentioned after the crisis in connection

of William Malet in 1110; the English writers who report William Malet's fall are silent on Robert's. And if Robert Malet's lands had indeed been taken into royal hands in 1105 or 1106 it is hard to understand how William Malet might have acquired English lands of sufficient value to have caught the Anglo-Saxon chronicler's attention in 1110. Orderic notwithstanding, Robert Malet held Eye until his death, probably passing it on to William Malet, his heir, who was subsequently disseised for treason. The king administered the honor for a time[25] and afterwards gave most of it to his nephew, Stephen of Blois.

If this reconstruction is correct it may contribute to our understanding of Henry I's baronial policy in general. Orderic ascribes Henry I's confiscations after 1101 to the king's desire for vengeance.[26] But we must now exclude from Orderic's list of victims both Robert Malet and Robert of Lacy. Of the remaining ducal supporters in 1101, Ivo of Grandmesnil was indicted circa 1102 for waging private war—which would be cause for legal action quite apart from his support of the duke in 1101—and was not disseised but only fined.[27] No action whatever was taken against Walter Giffard, earl of Buckingham, or against Eustace of Boulogne, who was allowed to marry the queen's sister in 1102.[28] There remain, as objects of Henry's vengeance, only William of Warenne, William of Mortain, and the Montgomeries. William of Warenne was deprived of his earldom of Surrey in 1101 but was reinstated and restored to favor in 1103, after which he became one of Henry I's firmest supporters and most intimate counselors.[29] The circumstances of William of Mortain's departure from England are by no means clear, but it seems most probable

---

with the royal reprisals (4.161, 167), his actual role in the 1101 crisis is left in some doubt. His name is not mentioned among those of Henry I's firm supporters (William of Malmesbury, *Gesta regum anglorum*, ed. William Stubbs [Rolls Series 1887-1889] 2.471: cf. Orderic 4.95, 110), nor does he attest with these men at moments of crisis (*Reg.* 2 [n. 3 above] nos. 531, 534-538). Since Henry I's army in 1101 is said by several chroniclers to have contained traitors, potential traitors and waverers as well as friends, it may have been almost as difficult in 1101 as now to determine who was on which side: see Orderic 4.110-113; Eadmer, *Historia novorum in Anglia*, ed. Martin Rule (Rolls Series 1884) 127.

[25] Two charters issued during the royal occupancy of Eye (*Reg.* 2 [n. 3 above] nos. 932-933) are dated tentatively A.D. 1109 by the editors. The limiting dates of both are 1106-1113, and the suggestion of 1109 is merely a guess. Since no. 932 was issued at York, both charters might well be from 1110 when, on 5 July, Henry I was at Stamford (2, no. 950), about half way from London to York on the Roman road connecting the two cities.

[26] Orderic (n. 4 above) 4.161.

[27] *Ibid.* 167-168.

[28] *Ibid.* 104; *Anglo-Saxon Chronicle, s.a.* 1101.

[29] Orderic 4.116, 161-163. William of Warenne attests 69 of Henry I's known charters: *Reg.* 2 (n. 3 above) passim. He later received from Henry the large royal manor of Wakefield, Yorks. (*Yorkshire Charters* 8 [n. 13 above] 9, 67-68, 178) and the lordship of Saint-Saens adjacent to his fief of Bellencombre in Upper Normandy (Orderic 4.292-293).

that he left of his own volition while still in possession of his earldom of Corn-wall. Once in Normandy he defected to Curthose, and only then was he deprived of his English lands.[30] As for the Montgomeries, the destruction of their English power in 1102 was necessary for Henry's pacification of the kingdom. Two of the three Montgomery brothers, Arnulf and Roger the Poitevin, were later restored to Henry's favor—though not to their English lands.[31] The third brother, Robert of Bellême—immensely powerful, and notorious among contemporaries for his violence and cruelty—was taken captive by Henry in Normandy a decade after his banishment, and was never set free.[32]

The motives behind Henry's confiscations and restorations appear to have been dispassionately political. Sentiments of generosity or vengeance were overshadowed by the dominant royal policy of creating a baronage that would be loyal to the king and would participate actively in a strong, centralized regime. A number of key positions in Henry's administration were given to clever, ambitious men of obscure origin,[33] but the chief magnates also had a vital role to play and might themselves serve in high administrative offices, as the career of Robert Malet makes clear.[34] Henry had no wish to eliminate

---

[30] Such is the story told in the *Anglo-Saxon Chronicle*, *s.a.* 1104, and it tends to be sup-ported in general by other sources: e.g., Malmesbury (n. 24 above) 2.473-474; Wace, *Roman de Rou*, ed. Hugo Andresen (Heilbronn 1879) 2.445; and "Chronica Monasterii de Hida juxta Wintoniam," in *Liber monasterii de Hyda*, ed. Edward Edwards (Rolls Series 1866) 306. The Hyde writer adds that Henry I had tried to win William of Mortain's friendship by offering him as a bride the queen's sister, Mary of Scotland, whom William rejected con-temptuously. If the episode is correctly reported it must have occurred prior to Mary of Scotland's marriage to Eustace of Boulogne in 1102: Florence of Worcester, *Chronicon ex chronicis*, ed. Benjamin Thorpe (London 1848-1849) 2.51; cf. 2.53.

[31] *Reg.* 2 (n. 3 above) nos. 919, 965, 1245, 1484; Eadmer, *Vita Anselmi*, ed. R. W. Southern (London 1962) 146-147; *S. Anselmi Opera omnia*, ed. F. S. Schmitt (Edinburgh 1946-61) esp. 426.

[32] Orderic (n. 4 above) 4.304-305, 376-377. On Robert of Bellême and his brothers see J. F. A. Mason, "Roger de Montgomery and his Sons," *Transactions of the Royal Historical Society*, 5th Ser., 13 (1963) 22-24. Another possible victim of 1101, heretofore overlooked, was William de Mandeville, some of whose lands were confiscated by the king. See my article, "The Misfortunes of the Mandevilles," above, ch. 6, pp. 117-27.

[33] See R. W. Southern, "The Place of Henry I in English History," *Proceedings of the British Academy* 48 (1962) 127-156.

[34] Great landholders of Henry I such as Robert earl of Gloucester, Stephen of Blois, and the constable Brian fitz Count were royal intimates and active in the government. These men, however, were Henry I's creations, and most scholars would term them "new men" even though not "raised from the dust." But representatives of important older Anglo-Norman families were also active in Henry's service. Besides Robert Malet and William of Warenne (above, n. 29) one might name such magnates as Hugh, Richard, and Ranulf I, earls of Chester; Robert count of Meulan and his Beaumont kinsmen; the hereditary stewards Roger, William, and Hugh Bigod; Robert fitz Hamon; William and Rabel of Tancarville, *camerarii* (above, n. 3); and Gilbert of Laigle (who attested Henry's charters frequently and served as a royal judge in Normandy: C. H. Haskins, *Norman Institutions* [Cambridge,

the great landholders but only to use them in the governance of his realm. He could destroy rich magnates and raise up others in their place, but he could also forgive disloyal barons when he perceived that they would be useful and trustworthy thereafter. The alleged purge of 1101-1102 was in fact a complex process of evaluating individual defectors with respect to their potential for treason or loyal service in times to come. Some were disseised; others were drawn into the royal government by advantageous marriages, administrative offices, or gifts of land. And, as William of Warenne and Robert of Lacy discovered, the king was prepared to change his mind as circumstances indicated. The handling of barons was an art that Henry understood better than most kings—and far better than the monk of Saint-Evroul.

Mass. 1918] 92). Several of these men were further enriched, some of them significantly so, through Henry's favor. But they or their forebears had been important Anglo-Norman magnates prior to Henry's accession. Setting aside the question of "new men" versus "old men," one is struck by the correlation of landed wealth with royal service—much more evident in the middle and later years of Henry I's reign than in the closing years of William II's, when such major barons as William of Mortain, Robert of Bellême, William of Warenne, Robert Malet, Roger the Poitevan, and Arnulf of Montgomery seldom if ever attested for the king (*Reg.* 1 [n. 3 above] passim).

8

THE TAMING OF A TURBULENT EARL:
HENRY I AND WILLIAM OF WARENNE

King Henry I, the youngest and ablest son of William the Conqueror, was viewed by contemporaries as the greatest monarch of his time — the *rex pacificus* who "made peace for man and beast."[1] Modern historians have stressed Henry's administrative achievements; Richardson and Sayles credit him with the creation of "a carefully-articulated machine" of government.[2] Henry's precocious financial and judicial institutions contributed to the peace of his realm by keeping the royal treasury full and by funnelling many land disputes into the royal courts. But administrative machinery alone does not guarantee peace, as should be evident from the reigns of John, Edward II, and similar unfortunate monarchs. A successful king must, above all else, be capable of dealing skillfully with his subjects. Administrative machine-building is a kind of political science, whereas good personal relationships are a political art. In this sense, Henry I was not merely a scientist but an artist as well.

Interpretations of Henry's reign have heretofore been strongly influenced by Orderic Vitalis' metaphor of new men being "raised from the dust."[3] R. W. Southern, in a characteristically illuminating paper, has shown that Henry's government involved a system of political patronage wherein ambitious climbers received modest but recurring rewards for their service to the king.[4] Southern has thus expanded and re-cast Orderic's metaphor into a perceptive analysis of royal policy towards the middle and lesser *curiales*. It is the purpose

*The author is grateful to the National Endowment for the Humanities, the American Philosophical Society, the Social Science Research Council, the American Council of Learned Societies, the Fulbright Commission, the John Simon Guggenheim Memorial Foundation, and the Warden and Fellows of Merton College, Oxford, for their help in supporting the research for this paper.

[1] *Anglo-Saxon Chronicle*, A.D. 1135.

[2] H. G. Richardson and G. O. Sayles, *The Governance of Mediaeval England* (Edinburgh, 1963) 159.

[3] Orderic Vitalis, *Historia Ecclesiastica*, ed. A. le Prévost (Paris, 1838-55) IV, 164.

[4] "The Place of Henry I in English History," *Proceedings of the British Academy*, XLVIII (1962) 127-69; reprinted with revisions in Southern, *Medieval Humanism and Other Studies* (Oxford, 1970) 206-33.

of this paper to look briefly at another aspect of royal policy — to examine Henry I's relations with the old and wealthy baronial families who were established in England by William the Conqueror.

Henry I has sometimes been pictured as being suspicious of old Conquest families — disseising and exiling them on a systematic scale and thereby creating a dangerous party of "disinherited" to torment England in the next reign.[5] In my own view, Henry was by no means opposed to such families. On the contrary, he was anxious to draw them into closer involvement in the royal court. For Henry was well aware that the success of his reign depended on the cooperation of his greater barons, and he was determined to make such cooperation a practical reality. If a magnate of an old family rebelled or conspired to rebel, he risked forfeiture and exile. But if he remained loyal and frequented the court, he and his family basked in the royal favor. During the reign of Henry's predecessor, William Rufus, the greater barons had attested very few royal charters.[6] They had become dangerously independent of the royal court, and their aloofness lends weight to R. W. Southern's observation that by the time of Rufus' death in 1100 "the country was ready for a revolution."[7] But by Henry I's death in 1135, the greater barons tended to be *curiales* and frequent attestors.[8] Some of them were newly-risen stars, but others were heads of families that had been prominent since the days of the

[5]For a recent critical discussion of this view see Edmund King, "The Tenurial Crisis of the Early Twelfth Century," *Past and Present*, LXV (Nov., 1974) 112-15; and J. C. Holt, "Politics and Property in Early Medieval England: A Rejoinder," *ibid.*, 127-28.

[6]See C. W. Hollister, "The Anglo-Norman Civil War: 1101," *English Historical Review*, LXXXVIII (1973) 317-20 ; see above, pp. 79-82.

[7]*Medieval Humanism, p. 231.*

[8]We lack the evidence on which to construct an exact list of England's wealthiest magnates in *c.* 1135. On the basis of Domesday values, danegeld exemptions in the Pipe Roll of 1130, and later figures on enfeoffments and knights quotas, I would propose, very tentatively, that the wealthiest landholders at the time were Robert earl of Gloucester, Stephen of Blois, Henry bishop of Winchester, Roger bishop of Salisbury, William archbishop of Canterbury, William II of Warenne, Stephen "count" of Brittany, Ranulf II earl of Chester, Robert earl of Leicester, Richard fitz Gilbert of Clare, and Brian fitz Count. Stephen of Brittany spent most of the reign in Brittany and therefore attested scarcely at all. Most of the others were frequent attestors — though Ranulf II, Robert of Leicester, and Richard of Clare attested less frequently than their fathers had done, and Stephen of Blois' attestations were modest in number. A comparison of this group with the chief landholders of 1100 would demonstrate a substantial degree of "curialization" in the intervening generation. The 1135 group includes old families — the Warennes, Clares, Beaumonts, and Breton lords of Richmond — and a cadet line of the 11th-century earls of Chester (whose main line died out with the death of the court-connected Earl Richard in 1120). The Beaumonts attested *c.* 165 of Henry's surviving charters; the Clares *c.* 55; the family of Chester-Avranches-Bayeux, *c.* 55. Another older and wealthy family, the Bigods, attested *c.* 112 of Henry's charters.

Conqueror. Henry seems to have been intent on fusing magnates and *curiales* into a single group. And he worked toward this goal partly by giving new baronies to his *curiales*, partly by making *curiales* of his old barons.

From the beginning of his reign Henry wooed the great families. Among his first acts were the appointments of a Clare to the abbacy of Ely and of a bastard son of Hugh earl of Chester to the abbacy of Bury St. Edmunds. The Clares were favored with gifts of land in 1110 and thereafter;[9] Earl Hugh's son and heir was raised in the royal court; the Beaumonts acquired the town and earldom of Leicester and much besides.

But Henry's courtships with his barons did not consist simply of showering them with gifts. He had no intention of permitting any of his great men to rival him in wealth; he wanted no super-earl, no Thomas of Lancaster on his hands. He gave cautiously and allowed no baron to develop an empire exceeding those of the Conqueror's greatest creations — Odo of Bayeux, Robert of Mortain, Roger of Montgomery, William fitz Osbern. At the onset of Henry's reign, when William of Mortain, earl of Cornwall demanded possession of Odo of Bayeux's vast earldom of Kent, Henry put William off with smiles and evasions, offering him instead the hand of the queen's blue-blooded but penniless sister.[10] Refusing to settle for prestige alone, William of Mortain declined the offer and joined the king's enemies, losing his lands in the process and eventually his freedom. And Henry married the queen's sister to another wealthy magnate, Eustace of Boulogne.[11] Again, when Richard earl of Chester died childless in 1120, Henry permitted Richard's kinsman Ranulf le Meschin to succeed to the wealthy earldom, but in return for the favor Ranulf was obliged to relinquish other lands, including the lordship of Cumberland which Henry had granted him shortly before.[12] In subsequent years, Ranulf's family demanded the return of these lands, and blood was shed over the issue, but Ranulf himself — happy to have become an earl — seems to have accepted the trade in good spirits; his loyalty never faltered. And Henry had forestalled the establishment of a super-fief in northwest England.

[9]See C. W. Hollister, "The Strange Death of William Rufus," *Speculum*, (1973); above, 70-72. Henry's treatment of Robert of Bellême, earl of Shrewsbury, constitutes one major and understandable exception to his conciliatory policy: see C. W. Hollister, "Henry I and Robert Malet," above, 135.

[10]William of Malmesbury, *Gesta Regum*, ed. William Stubbs (Rolls Series, 1887-9) II, 473; *Liber Monasterii de Hyda*, ed. Edward Edwards (Rolls Series, 1866) 306.

[11]Florence of Worcester, *Chronicon ex Chronicis*, ed. Benjamin Thorpe (London, 1848-9) II, 51.

[12]*Complete Peerage*, rev. ed., III, 30, 166. Similarly, when Hugh d'Avranches had received the earldom of Chester from the Conqueror, *c.* 1071, he was obliged to relinquish his earlier holdings centering on Tutbury to Henry of Ferrars: Orderic, II, 222.

Henry's baronial policy was in fact a web of separate, interrelated relationships with individual magnates and their families — the Beaumonts, the Clares, the Bigods, the Mandevilles, the Malets, the earls of Chester, and numerous others. Accordingly, let me illustrate Henry's technique by scrutinizing his treatment of a particular baron from an old and wealthy Conquest family — William II of Warenne, earl of Surrey.

William II of Warenne was active throughout Henry's reign.[13] He inherited in 1088 and lived on until 1138. His father, William I of Warenne, seems to have been the grand-nephew of the Duchess Gunnor, wife of Duke Richard I of Normandy. William I of Warenne had risen high in the service of Duke William the Bastard, acquiring substantial lands centering on the castles of Mortemer and Bellencombre in Upper Normandy.[14] He fought at Hastings and was rewarded with English lands in thirteen counties, including the rape of Lewes in Sussex and extensive holdings in Yorkshire and Norfolk. Their total value in 1086, as recorded in the Domesday Book, was some £1165 a year, making William one of England's three or four greatest magnates.[15] Thereafter he played a substantial role in the English government, particularly during the Conqueror's absences in Normandy. He helped crush the earls' rebellion of 1075, and died of wounds received while fighting for King William Rufus in the rebellion of 1088. It was probably to secure William of Warenne's loyalty in the 1088 rebellion that Rufus made him earl of Surrey.[16] In any event, William I of Warenne profited enormously from his service to his ducal and royal masters, and the lands that he passed on to his heirs were almost princely in scale. In thanksgiving for his good fortune, he and his Flemish wife Gundreda founded at Lewes England's first Cluniac priory.[17]

On Earl William's death in 1088 his lands in England, and perhaps in Normandy as well, passed to his eldest son William II of Warenne, second earl of Surrey, while a younger son, Rainald, received the

[13]The family of Warenne has received thorough attention in the past. My reconstruction follows those of C. T. Clay, *Early Yorkshire Charters*, VIII, *The Honour of Warenne* (Wakefield, Yorkshire, 1949) 1-12, 40-46; *Complete Peerage*, XII, i, 491-6; and William Farrer, *Honors and Knights' Fees* (Manchester, 1923-5) III, 296-300.

[14]Lewis C. Lloyd, "The Origin of the Family of Warenne," *Yorkshire Archaeological Journal*, XXXI (1933) 97-113.

[15]Third or fourth, depending on whether one includes Odo of Bayeux, who was imprisoned in 1082, released on the Conqueror's death in 1087, and disseised and exiled from England in 1088. Orderic (IV, 162) reports the annual value of the Warenne English lands as £1000.

[16]The family held no lands in Surrey, and in the years thereafter they normally styled themselves *Comes de Warenne*.

[17]See David Knowles, *The Monastic Order in England*, 2nd ed. (Cambridge, 1966) 151-2.

maternal lands in Flanders.[18] William II of Warenne, like other second-generation Anglo-Norman magnates, began his career as a much less committed royalist than his father had been. We find the young earl in Normandy in 1090 participating in the sporadic baronial warfare of Duke Robert Curthose's early years. He was no *curialis*: his attestation occurs in only one or two known charters of William Rufus.[19] Sometime in the 1090s he tried unsuccessfully to win the hand of the Scottish princess, Edith-Matilda,[20] and her subsequent marriage to Henry I in 1100 may well have offended the earl of Surrey to the point of his despising the new king. For whatever reason, Earl William responded to Henry's accession with singular lack of enthusiasm, and a later source describes him as ridiculing Henry's obsession with hunting.[21]

Characteristically, Henry attempted to win William's support. There was an effort to marry the earl to one of the king's bastard daughters, but Archbishop Anselm raised the barrier of consanguinity and the project collapsed.[22] When Duke Robert Curthose invaded England in mid-1101, William immediately joined the invasion-rebellion against King Henry, having evidently been involved for several months previously in a secret anti-royal conspiracy. But when Henry bought Duke Robert off with an annuity of 3,000 marks of silver, William of Warenne became a rebel without a cause. For his role in the affair, and perhaps also as a punishment for acts of violence committed by his men in Norfolk, he was deprived of all his English lands and sent into Norman exile.[23]

But in 1103 William recovered his English holdings. While in exile, he had complained to Duke Robert Curthose about losing a fortune in land for supporting the ducal cause and having nothing to show for it. The duke set off impulsively for England, unarmed and uninvited, to plead for William's restoration. On Curthose's arrival, Henry made it known that he was very angry and was considering casting the duke into prison. Terrified, Curthose made the best bargain that he could.

[18] The *Hyde Chronicler* (p. 299) reports that the English lands went to William II, the Flemish lands to Rainald. Nothing is said of the Norman lands, but William II of Warenne was fighting in Normandy *c.* 1090 (Orderic, III, 362). *Regesta Regum Anglo-Normannorum*, III, no. 272 makes it clear that Mortemer and Bellencombre passed to William II's son, William III, and it seems certain that William II was holding Bellencombre in about 1110 or 1111 when he received the adjacent fief of Saint-Saens (Orderic, IV, 292). Rainald died, apparently childless, sometime between 1106 and 1118.

[19] *Regesta*, I, no. 319, and probably no. 260 (William I or II of Warenne). William I of Warenne attests 8 known authentic charters of the Conqueror.

[20] Sometime between 1093 and 1100: Orderic, III, 362.

[21] *Liber Monasterii de Hyda*, p. 305; Wace, *Le Roman de Rou et des Ducs de Normandie*, ed. Hugo Andresen (Heilbronn, 1877-9) II, 446.

[22] *S. Anselmi Opera Omnia*, ed. F. S. Schmitt (Stuttgart-Bad Cannstatt, 1946-51) epistle 424.

[23] *Regesta*, II, no. 542 and p. 306; Orderic, IV, 116.

He relinquished his 3000 mark annuity, and in return Henry agreed to re-admit William of Warenne to England and to restore his lands and title to him.[24]

For a time William of Warenne was apparently unwelcome at the king's court: he attests no royal charters known to have been issued between 1103 and 1107. Meanwhile his brother Rainald of Warenne, the Flemish heir, became an enthusiastic supporter of Duke Robert Curthose in Normandy against Henry I. In 1105, Rainald and other ducal partisans captured and imprisoned Henry's friend, Robert fitz Hamon, and in 1106, in the midst of Henry's campaign to conquer the duchy, Rainald fell into the king's hands in a skirmish at Saint-Pierre sur Dive.[25] Shortly afterwards, at the decisive battle of Tinchebray, William of Warenne apparently served as one of King Henry's chief commanders.[26] Orderic reports that Henry released Rainald just prior to the battle, and that William of Warenne, grateful for his brother's liberation, urged his comrades to fight for the king's cause with the utmost determination. But according to the Hyde writer, Rainald was released after the battle rather than before.[27] Whatever the case, one can well imagine that while William of Warenne was fighting for Henry at Tinchebray, his brother Rainald was under close observation.

1106   After Henry's conquest of Normandy, William of Warenne began to appear at court more frequently.[28] The earl had demonstrated his loyalty at Tinchebray, and, moreover, Henry could afford for the moment to lower his guard. His one great rival to the throne, Duke Robert Curthose, was in a royal prison, and Robert's only son, William Clito, was as yet a harmless child. Henry treated Clito charitably, sending him to the castle of Saint-Saens in Upper Normandy to be reared by Curthose's son-in-law, Elias of Saint-Saens. By 1110, however, Clito was old enough to become the Anglo-Norman pretender in a conspiracy involving the king of France, the count of Anjou, and some of Henry's own barons. Henry had very competent spies, and he was able to ward off rebellion by a series of surprise arrests.[29] But when he ordered the seizure of William Clito, the young prince eluded the royal officers and fled from Normandy with his guardian, Elias of Saint-Saens.[30]

[24] See above, p. 94 and n. 3.

[25] Orderic, IV, 203-4, 222-3.

[26] *Ibid.*, 229. But Orderic's account of the order of battle conflicts with the eyewitness testimony of an anonymous priest of Fécamp who does not mention William of Warenne: C. W. David, *Robert Curthose, Duke of Normandy* (Cambridge, Mass., 1920) 245-8.

[27] Orderic, IV, 229; *Liber Monasterii de Hyda*, p. 307.

[28] *Regesta*, II, Nos. 826-7, 832-3, 875, 877, 885, 918-19, 941.

[29] See above, p. 70 n. 62 and p. 133.

[30] Orderic, IV, 232, 291-2.

Clito's escape caused Henry immense difficulties over the years that followed. For Clito was the only son of the Conqueror's eldest son, and his claim on England and Normandy became the focal point of all subsequent efforts, foreign and domestic, against Henry's rule. But Clito's escape also provided Henry with the opportunity of assuring the allegiance of William of Warenne. The castle of Saint-Saens lies about three miles up the River Varenne from the Warenne castle of Bellencombre. Henry seized Saint-Saens and, in Orderic's words, he "afterwards gave it to his kinsman, William of Warenne, to the end that William would adhere faithfully to the king and firmly resist the king's enemies."[31]

It was an astute move. The castle and lordship of Saint-Saens constituted a valuable and strategic addition to William of Warenne's holdings in Upper Normandy. William knew that if Henry should ever lose Normandy to Clito, Saint-Saens would instantly be restored to Elias — Clito's brother-in-law and devoted companion in exile. William of Warenne, thus became an ardent royalist and active *curialis*. Having attested only one or two known charters of William Rufus, he attested sixty-nine surviving charters of Henry I. In 1111 we find him sitting as a judge in the Norman ducal court.[32] In the crucial years 1118-19, when Normandy seethed with rebellion and a French army was moving almost at will through the regions southeast of Rouen, William of Warenne's loyalty remained firm. In 1119, just prior to Henry's climactic battle with King Louis VI at Brémule, William is quoted as saying to the king, "There is no one who can persuade me to treason . . . I and my kinsmen here and now place ourselves in mortal opposition to the king of France and are totally faithful to you . . . I will support this undertaking, with my men, in the first rank of your army and will myself sustain the full weight of battle." So he did, and Henry won a decisive victory.[33]

Henry's sole surviving pipe roll shows Earl William receiving danegeld exemptions in 1130 totaling £104-8-11, the third highest figure among the English baronage, demonstrating not only the extent of William's lands but also the warm royal favor that he now

---

[31]*Ibid.*, 292-3. On Henry's gift to William of Warenne of the large Yorkshire manor of Wakefield, perhaps in exchange for other lands, see *Early Yorkshire Charters*, VIII, 9.

[32]C. H. Haskins, *Norman Institutions* (Cambridge, Mass., 1918) 91-2.

[33]*Liber Monasterii de Hyda,* 316-17. See also Orderic, IV, 346, 356-7. Among William's kinsmen was his sister's husband (or their son of the same name), Dreux of Mouchy-le-Châtel (in the Beauvaisis), whose rebellion against Louis VI in 1118 diverted a French force about to invade Normandy: *Liber de Hyda*, p. 315. Dreux attested 15 charters of Henry I, most of them after 1120 and some in the company of William of Warenne. He received lands in Sussex, for which he was pardoned 26 s. of danegeld in 1130. But another of William's kinsmen, his nephew Hugh de Gournay, was in rebellion against Henry in 1118-19.

enjoyed.[34] In 1135, when Henry lay on his deathbed at Lyons-la-Forêt, Earl William was at his side and afterwards was one of the five *comites* who escorted the royal corpse to Rouen for embalming.[35] The man who had once ridiculed Henry and rebelled against him, had been transmuted into one of the king's most loyal *familiares*.[36]

William of Warenne's career demonstrates that Henry built his power structure not only by raising men up from the dust but also by luring them in from the heights. The full scope of Henry's policy has not always been perceived by modern historians, but Orderic Vitalis seems to have understood it. "From the onset of his reign," Orderic writes, "he wisely conciliated all groups, and enticed them into his fellowship by his royal generosity. He honored his great men generously, supported them with wealth and honors, and thus won their fidelity by his soothing policies. He favored his common subjects with just laws and protected them by his authority from unfair exactions and robbery. The sublime prince thus stood out among all the lords and monarchs of the West, and merited the favor of everyone, churchmen and laymen alike, who rejoiced at being governed by reason."[37]

Orderic is a little starry-eyed. Perhaps for "reason" one should read "cunning." But he is quite correct in perceiving that Henry favored great barons, at least in moderation. Henry grasped the essential fact that the magnates were necessarily an integral part of any successful monarchy. He realized, too, that most barons — even Norman barons — were by nature neither turbulent nor particularistic, but simply anxious to safeguard their wealth and, if possible, increase it. Henry's great landholders came to discover that rebellion involved high risks but that allegiance to the king and service at his court brought security and enrichment. This was the lesson that Henry taught, and William of Warenne, despite his shaky start, proved to be an apt pupil.

[34]William's exemptions in 1130 surpassed those of Stephen of Blois and were exceeded only by those of Roger bishop of Salisbury and Robert earl of Gloucester.

[35]Orderic, V, 50-1.

[36]*Ibid.*, IV, 163. Having failed in his effort to marry a Scottish king's daughter in the 1090s and an English king's bastard daughter in the early 1100s, William at length won the hand of a French king's granddaughter, Isabel of Vermandois, in or shortly after 1118. Isabel was the widow of Henry I's great *curialis,* Robert count of Meulan (d. 5 June, 1118) whose final years were said to have been darkened by his wife's liaisons with "a certain earl": "Epistola ad Walterum de Contemptu Mundi," in Henry of Huntingdon, *Historia Anglorum,* ed. Thomas Arnold (Rolls Series, 1879) 307.

[37]Orderic, IV, 92.

9

THE ANGLO-NORMAN SUCCESSION DEBATE OF 1126:

PRELUDE TO STEPHEN'S ANARCHY

On 1 January 1127, King Henry I determined the future of the English royal line by having his court swear to accept his daughter Maud as his heir to England and Normandy. John of Worcester states that Henry had taken counsel from his great men,[1] and William of Malmesbury adds that he arrived at his decision 'after deliberating long and deeply'.[2] On the nature of these deliberations contemporary writers are silent; they disclose neither what alternatives were considered, nor what advice the king received, nor from whom. But buried in the sources are certain clues that point to a clash of opinion at the court of 1126 – a struggle between Maud's friends and opponents that divided Henry's *curiales* and foreshadowed the political factions of Stephen's anarchy.

By 1126 the Anglo–Norman succession had become an urgent problem. Henry I, now in his late fifties, had lost his only legitimate son, William Adelin, in the wreck of the White Ship in November 1120. A widower at the time, he had immediately remarried, but as the years passed it became more and more apparent that his second wife, Alice of Louvain, would bear him no children. 'In grief that the woman did not conceive, and in fear that she would always be barren', he was obliged to look elsewhere for an heir.[3]

Maud, Henry's one remaining legitimate offspring, came into the succession picture only in May 1125 when the death of her husband, Emperor Henry V, freed her to return home.[4] She joined her father in

---

[1] *The Chronicle of John of Worcester* ed. J. R. H. Weaver (Oxford, 1908), p.27: '. . . quis . . . in regendi regni statum succedat, communi consilio tractatur' (the normal procedure for major policy decisions); for the date see John Horace Round, *Geoffrey de Mandeville* (London, 1892), p.31.

[2] William of Malmesbury, *Historia Novella*, ed. K. R. Potter (London, 1955), p.3.

[3] *Ibid.* Alice failed to conceive during her fifteen-year marriage to Henry I, for reasons that will always remain obscure. After Henry's death she married William II of Albini (royal master butler and afterwards earl of Arundel) and bore him seven sons. Henry I fathered three children by his first wife (one of whom died in infancy) and at least twenty bastards: *The Complete Peerage*, ed. G. E. C[okayne], new edn., ed. V. Gibbs and others (London, 1910–59), 11: Appendix D. The fact that Robert of Torigny, writing *c.* 1139–42, describes three of Henry's bastards as *adhuc juvenes* suggests that the king was still fit at the time of his second marriage in January, 1121: *Gesta Normannorum Ducum*, ed. Jean Marx (Rouen, 1914), p.307.

[4] Henry V died at Utrecht at the age of forty-four on 23 May, 1125.

Normandy at his command and, it is said, with regret. Now in her early twenties, she had lived in Germany since she was eight and had evidently relished being an empress. To Henry I she had the great advantage of being his own child. For years he had struggled to secure the succession of his son, William Adelin; to have turned now from a direct offspring to a nephew would have been to reverse the direction of his diplomacy. Moreover, Henry's own accession to the throne in 1100, to the prejudice of his elder brother Robert, had been justified by the doctrine of porphyrogeniture: Robert had been born before the Norman Conquest, whereas Henry was born of a reigning king and queen – born in the purple.[5] In 1126 Maud alone, of all possible candidates, could claim porphyrogeniture: she was born in 1102, of a reigning king, and of a queen – Henry's wife, Edith-Matilda – whose ancestors had been kings of the Anglo-Saxons.[6] Edward the Confessor on his deathbed had allegedly prophesied about the grafting of a green tree, and prior to the White Ship disaster many people, interpreting Edward's prophesy as the joining of the Norman and Old English royal lines, had looked to its fulfillment in Maud's brother, William Adelin, *rex designatus*.[7] Henry himself took the idea of the joined lines very seriously, because it provided further justification for the succession of his own children. He would later commend Maud to his barons as the one rightful heir, with Norman kings as her grandfather, uncle and father, and Old English kings in her mother's lineage.[8]

Maud's great impediment was her sex. In this pre-Elizabethan age she could probably not have ruled England and Normandy successfully without a husband to uphold her interests, and the great hope would have been that she might give Henry I a royal grandson. Accordingly, Henry's court swore to uphold the succession not only of Maud herself but also of her legitimate son, if she should have one.[9] In short, the great men of the Anglo-Norman state committed themselves to the rule of the future Henry II some six years before his birth.

---

[5] Orderic Vitalis, *Historia Ecclesiastica*, ed. Marjorie Chibnall (Oxford, 1969–80), 5: 292 and n. 3; William of Malmesbury, *Gesta Regum Anglorum*, ed. William Stubbs (Rolls Series, London, 1887–9), 2: 467; C. N. L. Brooke, *The Saxon and Norman Kings* (New York, 1963), pp.32, 134, 195–6.

[6] Henry's queen, Matilda or Maud, daughter of King Malcolm and St. Margaret of Scotland, was baptized 'Edith'. The hyphenated 'Edith-Matilda' is anachronistic yet useful in distinguishing her from numerous other Matildas of her time. For the same reason the Empress Matilda will be referred to throughout as 'Maud'. Henry I's son, William, is identified herein by the cognomen 'Adelin' (O.E. *aetheling*: heir to the throne) which Orderic gives him.

[7] Malmesbury, *Gesta Regum*, 2: 277; *Vita Edwardi Regis*, ed. Frank Barlow (London, 1962). pp.75–6, 88–90.

[8] Malmesbury, *Historia Novella*, pp.3–4.

[9] John of Worcester, p.27; cf. *Gesta Stephani*, ed. K. R. Potter (London, 1955), pp.6–8.

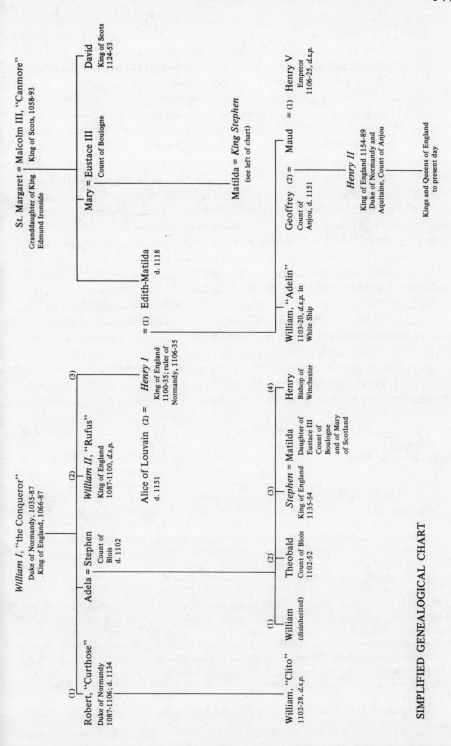

SIMPLIFIED GENEALOGICAL CHART

William I, "the Conqueror"
Duke of Normandy, 1035-87
King of England, 1066-87

St. Margaret = Malcolm III, "Canmore"
Granddaughter of King   King of Scots, 1058-93
Edmund Ironside

(1) Robert, "Curthose"
Duke of Normandy
1087-1106; d. 1134

(2) Adela = Stephen
Count of
Blois
d. 1102

(3) William II, "Rufus"
King of England
1087-1100, d.s.p.

Mary = Eustace III
Count of Boulogne

David
King of Scots
1124-53

Henry I =
King of England
1100-35; ruler of
Normandy, 1106-35

Alice of Louvain (2) =
d. 1151

= (1) Edith-Matilda
d. 1118

William, "Clito," d.s.p.
1102-28, d.s.p.

(1) William
(disinherited)

(2) Theobald
Count of Blois
1102-52

(3) Stephen = Matilda
King of England   Daughter of
1135-54   Eustace III
              Count of
              Boulogne
              and of Mary
              of Scotland

(4) Henry
Bishop of
Winchester

William, "Adelin,"
1103-20, d.s.p. in
White Ship

Matilda = King Stephen
(see left of chart)

Maud = (1) Henry V
Emperor
1106-25, d.s.p.

Geoffrey (2) =
Count of
Anjou, d. 1151

Henry II
King of England 1154-89
Duke of Normandy and
Aquitaine, Count of Anjou

Kings and Queens of England
to present day

Besides Maud, the king and his court might possibly have considered the claims of two or three royal nephews or the eldest and most promising of the royal bastards. The available nephews were Theobald and Stephen, sons of Henry I's sister Adela, countess of Blois; and William Clito, son of Henry's brother, enemy, and captive, Robert Curthose, ex-duke of Normandy.[10] Of these nephews, Theobald count of Blois would have been regarded less seriously than his younger brother Stephen.[11] Henry had favoured Stephen exceedingly, giving him the county of Mortain in western Normandy and vast estates in England,[12] and the Anglo-Norman barons were well acquainted with him. Contemporary writers speak not a word of his candidacy until after Henry's death, but it may perhaps be significant that in 1125, by Henry's arrangement, he was wed to Matilda of Boulogne, daughter and heiress of Count Eustace III.[13] Matilda's mother, Mary of Scotland, was the sister of Henry I's first wife and, like her, a descendant of Alfred and Edmund Ironside. Stephen's children would thus graft the Norman and Anglo-Saxon royal branches no less truly than the children of Henry I and Edith-Matilda. Henry cannot have been unaware of this fact. At the time that he was arranging the marriage (probably 1124 or early 1125) Maud was still reigning in Germany and unavailable. Until she was widowed in late May 1125 Henry may well have taken Stephen's candidacy seriously.

But Henry's primary motive in marrying Stephen to Matilda may well have been the establishment of a trusted nephew in the county of Boulogne rather than a second grafting of the green tree. Boulogne,

[10] William Clito, Robert Curthose's only child, was Henry I's sole nephew on the male side. Adela Countess of Blois was Henry's only sister to bear children. Of her four sons, William, the eldest, had, for some disability, been denied the comital inheritance; Theobald succeeded as count of Blois in 1102 as a child, and inherited Champagne in 1125; Stephen, the third son, became a great Anglo-Norman landholder and count of Mortain and Boulogne; Henry, the youngest, followed an ecclesiastical career (monk of Cluny, then abbot of Glastonbury, bishop of Winchester, and legate for England).

[11] On Henry I's death in December 1135, Count Theobald entered Normandy at the invitation of Norman magnates who wished to place themselves under his authority. He withdrew reluctantly upon hearing of Stephen's accession: Orderic, 6: 454; *The Chronicle of Robert of Torigni*, ed. Richard Howlett, in *Chronicles of the Reigns of Stephen, Henry II, and Richard I* (Rolls Series, London, 1884–9), 4: 128–9. During much of Henry's reign, Theobald had been his ally against King Louis VI of France.

[12] R. H. C. Davis, *King Stephen, 1135–1154* (London, 1967), pp.7–10. Stephen's 1128–30 danegeld exemptions of £132 6s. 4d. for lands in nineteen shires place him among the three wealthiest lords in England (with Robert earl of Gloucester and Roger bishop of Salisbury): *Pipe Roll 31 Henry I*, ed. Joseph Hunter (London, 1929 reprint); my calculation is based on 1128–29 or 1129–30 exemptions, whichever are higher; city aids are excluded. Stephen's Norman county of Mortain was valued at £1000 a year in Henry II's reign: R. W. Eyton, *Court, Household, and Itinerary of King Henry II* (London, 1878), p.102.

[13] *Calendar of Documents Preserved in France*, ed. John Horace Round (London, 1899), no. 1385.

with its active port of Wissant, was strategically situated directly across the Channel from Romney and Dover. It lay southwest of Flanders and just north of Ponthieu, which was ruled in the 1120's by Henry's enemy, William Talvas. William's county was thus caught in Henry's web, with Normandy to the south and Boulogne to the north.

In Henry's eyes the countship of Boulogne would perhaps have seemed more suitable to Stephen's capacities than the throne of England. For already it was becoming clear that statesmanship was not one of Stephen's strong points. His best known political and military failures lay in the future, but it is suggestive that when his supporters were urging his cause in December 1135 they stressed that the assistance of his wise brothers would 'bring to greater perfection whatever is thought to be lacking in him.'[14] During the Franco-Norman wars of 1118–19 – the great military crisis of Henry's reign – Stephen had been entrusted with the governance of a large, vital district on the duchy's southern frontier centering on Sées and Alençon,[15] Stephen's misgovernment drove the inhabitants to ally with Henry's enemy, Count Fulk of Anjou, and to betray to the Angevins the town of Alençon – a vital frontier stronghold guarding the southern approach to Normandy through the valley of the Sarthe. The garrison of Alençon castle held out for Henry, but when Stephen and Theobald tried to resupply it the Angevins repulsed them soundly. Finally Henry himself came upon Alençon with a large army, and in a major battle near the city Fulk routed the Anglo-Normans.[16] The battle of Alençon (December 1118) was the greatest military debacle of Henry's career, and he extricated himself only by bribing the Angevins to break their alliance with France and marrying his son and heir, William Adelin, to Fulk's daughter. The wars of 1118–19 constituted a grave threat to Henry's rule over Normandy, and in later years whenever he recalled the Alençon catastrophe he would doubtless have thought of Stephen. He might have recalled, too, that the justification he had offered for his own conquest of Normandy in 1106 was the incompetence of his brother, Duke Robert.[17]

Prior to Maud's widowhood, Stephen may well have been considered a possible if unpromising successor to the throne. Whatever his shortcomings he was loyal, rich, affable, and well connected, and his marriage to Matilda of Boulogne suggests that his star was rising. But

---

[14] *Gesta Stephani*, p.8.

[15] Orderic, 6: 204–8.

[16] Orderic, 6: 206–8; Sugar, *Vie de Louis VI le Gros*, ed. Henri Waquet (Paris, 1964), p.192; *Chroniques des comtes d'Anjou et des seigneurs d'Amboise*, ed. L. Halphen and R. Poupardin (Paris, 1913), pp.155–61; Josèphe Chartrou, *L'Anjou de 1109 à 1151* (Paris, 1928). pp.10–13.

[17] Incompetence may also have prevented the succession of Stephen's eldest brother, William, to the county of Blois: Davis, *King Stephen*, p.4.

there is nothing to indicate that he was under serious consideration in the deliberations of 1126.

It has been suggested by some that Henry might have settled the succession on his eldest bastard, Robert earl of Gloucester. Robert was able, well educated, immensely wealthy, and a *curialis*-administrator of the king's inner circle.[18] But his illegitimacy ruled him out as a candidate for the royal succession. His bastard grandfather, William the Conqueror, had been the product of an earlier, far different age and had won the throne over the dead bodies of Anglo-Saxons. In 1119 the bastard William of Ypres had failed in his attempt on the Flemish succession and would fail again in 1127, when Flemish townsmen pledged to reject him as their count 'because he is illegitimate'.[19] In England the tradition against bastard kings runs all the way back to the Council of Chelsea of A.D. 787,[20] and in the early twelfth century, with ecclesiastical reform at high tide, the selection of Robert of Gloucester would have been inauspicious at the very least.[21]

There remains William Clito, son of Henry's captive brother Robert Curthose. As the Conqueror's one surviving legitimate grandson in the male line, Clito had the best hereditary claim of all. Indeed, as the only child of William I's eldest son, Clito's claim was better, on the grounds of primogeniture, than Henry's own. In late 1126 Clito was twenty-four years old.[22] Even before his coming of age he had been the focus of opposition to Henry I, and in 1117–19 the French, Angevins, Flemings and dissident Normans had combined in a massive effort to win Normandy for him. The effort failed, and in October 1119 there occurred a little-known negotiation between Henry and Clito in the neighbourhood of Aumale on Normandy's northeastern frontier.[23]

[18] Henry married Robert to the heiress of Robert fitz Hamon and gave him lands in twenty-three shires as well as in Wales, with danegeld exemptions in 1128–30 of more than £125. These lands were later assessed at over 260 knights' fees (at 327 fees including the Welsh lands). Robert was created earl of Gloucester in 1121 or 1122. He attested ninety-six royal charters between 1113 and 1135: *P. R. 31 Henry I*; *Regesta Regum Anglo-Normannorum*, ed. H. W. C. Davis, Charles Johnson, H. A. Cronne, and R. H. C. Davis (Oxford, 1913–69), 2: nos. 1015a–1973 *passim*; I. J. Sanders, *English Baronies: A Study of their Origin and Descent, 1086–1327* (Oxford, 1960), p.6.

[19] Galbert de Bruges, *Histoire du meurtre de Charles le Bon*, ed. Henri Pirenne (Paris, 1891), p.76.

[20] *Councils and Ecclesiastical Documents relating to Great Britain and Ireland*, ed. A. W. Haddan and William Stubbs (Oxford, 1869–78), 3: 453; cf. Eric John, *Orbis Britanniae* (Leicester, 1966), p.33; *Die Gesetze der Angelsachsen* ed. F. Liebermann (Halle, 1903–16), 1: 662; 3: 341.

[21] Rumour had it that Robert of Gloucester was advised to claim the throne on Henry's death but declined to do so: *Gesta Stephani*, p.8.

[22] He was born not in 1101, as was traditionally believed, but on 25 October, 1102: BL MS. Cotton Caligula A. VIII, fo. 41: A.D. 1102: 'Eodem anno natus est Guillelmus filius R[oberti] comitis die sanctorum Crispini et Crispiniani in turre Rotomagensi.'

[23] *Liber Monasterii de Hyda*, ed. Edward Edwards (Rolls Series, London, 1866), pp.320–1; cf. Orderic, 6: 278–80.

Clito pleaded for his father's release, swearing that he and his father would go to Jerusalem and never again trouble Henry's dominions. Henry, victorious over his enemies, refused to free Curthose but promised to enrich Clito in return for his submission. Orderic, reporting Henry's meeting with Pope Calixtus the following month at Gisors, quotes the king as saying that he had offered Clito authority over three English counties and a place at court where he might learn the art of government. Henry alleged that he would favour his nephew 'as a son', or so Orderic tells us.[24] In any event, Clito rejected the offers out of respect for his captive father and resumed his life as a landless wanderer. Had he chosen to become an Anglo–Norman magnate and courtier, the loss of the royal son and heir a year thereafter might well have deflected the succession to him – unless, of course, he had chosen to board the White Ship himself. But even under the best of circumstances, it would have been painful for Henry to offer the succession to the person against whose claims he had struggled so long. And there was always the hazard that, in theory at least, recognizing Clito's right to succeed might have cast doubt on Henry's own right to rule. If Clito were the rightful heir, why should he not be the rightful king?[25]

Even though the negotiations of 1119 failed to produce an accord between Henry and Clito, the two apparently parted without anger. In 1123–24, however, Clito resumed his active role as Anglo–Norman pretender, and the warfare of those two years seems to have embittered Henry deeply. For the second time in his career the peace of Normandy had been broken. The threat was far less serious than in 1117–19, but Henry's severe enforcement of the Anglo-Norman laws against rebels and malefactors in 1124 suggests a mood of angry disillusionment, provoked by the shattering of the 1120 peace.[26] At this moment Henry would hardly have been enthusiastic about settling the succession on

---

[24] Orderic, 6: 288. Orderic puts the offer in the context of a full-scale defense of Henry's policy and may be exaggerating. But that some such proposals were made to Clito is consistent with Henry's goal in 1119–20 to resolve all differences with his foreign and domestic enemies. In 1119 he had allied with Anjou, renewed a money fief with Flanders, and pardoned his rebel barons; in 1120 he purchased peace with France. The homage of his son William Adelin to Louis VI represented an official French acquiescence to Henry's dominion over Normandy.

[25] John LePatourel, 'The Norman Succession, 996–1135', *English Historical Review*, 86 (1971): 245.

[26] Within a period of nine months four rebel knights were blinded (Orderic, 6: 352–4; *Gesta Normannorum Ducum*, pp. 295–6) while in England minters were mutilated (*ibid.*, p. 297; *Anglo-Saxon Chronicle*, A.D. 1125) and forty-four thieves were hanged and six more blinded and castrated (*ibid.*, A.D. 1124; 'more thieves than had ever been hanged before.') A perusal of the *Leges Henrici Primi* (ed. L. J. Downer, Oxford, 1972) makes it clear that Henry did not exceed the letter of the customary law against theft, bad coinage, treason, and slander of the king, but in 1124, as never before, he enforced the law without pity.

the person whose claims had provoked the war.[27] It was probably in 1124 that he began negotiating Stephen's marriage with Matilda of Boulogne.

Nevertheless, Clito's case remained strong, and he continued to find ardent supporters among the Anglo-Normans. Some, like the rebels of 1123–24, would have put him on Henry's throne immediately. But there were others, in no sense rebels, who looked forward to his peaceful succession upon Henry's death. John of Worcester reports that the news of Clito's death in battle in 1128 was received with universal grief.[28] Henry of Huntingdon adds that Clito was the sole rightful heir to the crown and was judged worthy of it by all men.[29] These are strong words, coming as they do from English writers by no means hostile to Henry. They reflect a widespread feeling, following the death of William Adelin, that although Henry merited allegiance as long as he lived, Clito should succeed him. By all accounts, the feeling was sufficiently strong to make William Clito Maud's chief rival in the deliberations of 1126. He is the only claimant apart from Maud herself who is known to have enjoyed substantial support.

On 11 September 1126 Henry I crossed from Normandy to England with Maud and a group of important pro-Clito rebels captured in 1124. Maud was returning to her homeland after an absence of more than sixteen years. Perhaps the succession had already been under discussion at the king's court in Normandy,[30] but now the debate began in earnest. Henry's good friend and former brother-in-law, King David of Scotland, joined the court that fall, along with two other neighbouring princes – Conan count of Brittany and Rotrou count of Perche, vassals and sons-in-law of the English king. And from Normandy came such

---

[27] Henry himself shares responsibility for the hostilities of 1123–24, but their impact on his attitude toward Clito is evident none the less. In 1124 the potentially dangerous and slightly consanguineous marriage of Clito and Sibylla of Anjou was annulled by papal legates under Henry's influence.

[28] John of Worcester, p. 29.

[29] Henry of Huntingdon, *Historia Anglorum*, ed. Thomas Arnold (Rolls Series, London, 1879), pp. 204–5. Orderic (6: 372) adds that when Clito was defending his position in Flanders in 1128, great numbers of supporters came to him from Normandy; cf. the Chronicle of Rouen, A.D. 1128, where Clito is described as 'miles nulli comparabilis probitate': *Recueil des historiens des Gaules et de la France*, ed. Martin Bouquet and others (Paris, 1738–1904), 12: 785.

[30] Henry had assembled a galaxy of distinguished people at Rouen in 1125, including his queen, his three archbishops, and the legate John of Crema: *Regesta*, 2: nos. 1425–7. It is possible (though unlikely) that Henry's regent, Roger bishop of Salisbury, visited Normandy in 1125: Edward J. Kealey, *Roger of Salisbury, Viceroy of England* (Berkeley, 1972), p. 150 n.

major dignitaries as Geoffrey archbishop of Rouen and John bishop of Lisieux, the head of Henry's Norman administration.[31]

The factional conflicts of late 1126 are illuminated by the Anglo-Saxon chronicler's statement that the king had Robert Curthose transferred from Bishop Roger of Salisbury's custody at Devizes to Robert of Gloucester's custody at Bristol. This was done, the chronicler adds, on the advice of Maud, seconded by that of her uncle, King David.[32] Maud was evidently manoeuvring for the succession by assuring that the kingdom's most valuable political prisoner, Clito's father, would be in safe hands,[33] and one can deduce that her succession was already supported by a court faction which included King David and Robert earl of Gloucester, but not Roger of Salisbury.

The *Anglo-Saxon Chronicle* reports the transfer of still another prisoner in late 1126. Waleran count of Meulan, the most important of the captive pro-Clito rebels, crossed the Channel with Henry in September, was incarcerated at the royal castle of Bridgnorth (Shropshire), and was moved to Wallingford shortly thereafter.[34] Bridgnorth was under the jurisdiction of one of Henry's 'new men', Payn fitz John, sheriff of Shropshire, who, after Henry's death, became one of the early backers of King Stephen against the claims of Maud.[35] Waleran's transfer to Wallingford, like Curthose's to Bristol, suggests that Maud was endeavouring to place Clito's chief supporters under the control of her

---

[31] *Anglo-Saxon Chronicle*, A.D. 1126; Hugh the Chantor, *The History of the Church of York, 1066–1127* (London, 1961), p. 129; *Regesta*, 2: no. 1466. Conan of Brittany and Rotrou of Perche were married to illegitimate daughters of Henry I, both named Maud (Rotrou's Maud had drowned in 1120 in the wreck of the White Ship). Also present were Queen Alice, Ouen bishop of Évreux, William of Tancarville the chamberlain, William archbishop of Canterbury, Thurstan archbishop of York (at Christmas and probably earlier as well), and many other magnates and prelates: *Regesta*, 2: nos. 1459–61, 1463, 1466–7, 1475.

[32] *Anglo-Saxon Chronicle*, A.D. 1126.

[33] The safekeeping of important prisoners could be a matter of vital importance. On the almost catastrophic consequence of Ranulf Flambard's escape in 1101 from William de Mandeville's custody in the Tower of London, see C. W. Hollister, 'The Anglo-Norman Civil War: 1101', *English Historical Review*, 88 (1973): 315–34 (above, pp. 77–96), and 'The Misfortunes of the Mandevilles', *History*, 58 (1973): 18–28 (above, pp. 117–27). In 1129–30 a heavy fine was assessed against the *curialis* Aubrey de Vere for permitting a prisoner to escape: *P. R. 31 Henry I*, p. 53.

[34] *Anglo-Saxon Chronicle*, A.D. 1126. Two additional important rebel captives, Hugh of Châteauneuf and Hugh of Montfort, were incarcerated, respectively, in the royal castle of Windsor and in Earl Robert's castle at Gloucester (the castellan of which was Walter sheriff of Gloucester): *ibid.*, A.D. 1124, 1126; Malmesbury, *Historia Novella*, p. 35.

[35] Payn fitz John is recorded as holding his shire court at Bridgnorth: *Regesta*, 2: no. 1473 and p. 356. The *Gesta Stephani* (p. 16) alleges that Payn was slow to support Stephen, but Payn attested for Stephen at Reading *c.* 4 January 1136, less than two weeks after the coronation (*Regesta*, 3: nos. 386, 591; Round, *Geoffrey de Mandeville*, pp. 11–12). Payn died fighting the Welsh in 1137 and thus played no role in the wars between Stephen and Maud. On his career under Henry I see below, n. 74.

own friends. The lord of Wallingford was Brian fitz Count, bastard son of Alan Fergant count of Brittany, and half-brother of Alan's successor, Count Conan, who was just then at Henry's court. Reared in the royal household, Brian fitz Count had prospered enormously in Henry's service. Henry had married him to the heiress of Wallingford and had granted him other lands as well, including an important lordship in Wales. By 1126 he was a trusted counsellor and administrator and would soon rise to the office of royal constable.[36] Brian and Robert of Gloucester were chosen to escort Maud to Normandy in 1127 for her betrothal to Geoffrey of Anjou,[37] and Roger of Salisbury was later to complain that Henry had consulted no one about the marriage except Robert of Gloucester, Brian fitz Count, and John bishop of Lisieux.[38] In other words, among the men on whom Henry and his daughter depended during the delicate marriage negotiations of 1127 were the very persons who had favoured Maud's succession in the debate of the previous autumn. Their dual role as Maud's adherents and as Henry's counsellors on the Angevin marriage casts doubt on the widely accepted chronicle evidence that Maud entered the marriage unwillingly. Roger of Salisbury, on the other hand, was not consulted on the marriage, evidently because he had supported the losing side in 1126. Maud did not trust him.

What was in Henry's own mind in 1126? His inclination toward Maud is evident from the very fact that he summoned her home. But he had not seen her since her departure as a child fifteen years before, and he would likely have withheld his final decision until he could judge at first hand

[36] On Brian's career see R. W. Southern, *Medieval Humanism and Other Studies* (Oxford, 1970), p. 220; F. M. Stenton, *The First Century of English Feudalism, 1066– 1166*, 2nd ed. (Oxford, 1961), p. 236, n.; J. H. Round, *Studies in Peerage and Family History* (New York, 1901), pp. 210–12; J. E. Lloyd, *A History of Wales*, 3rd ed. (London, 1939), 2: 443; *Regesta*, 3: xx. The Pipe Roll of 1130 (pp. 129–31) shows Robert of Gloucester and Brian fitz Count functioning as co-auditors of the Winchester treasury *c.* 1128–29 and also shows Brian enjoying a very substantial danegeld exemption of £72. 9s. 4d. (the fifth highest exemption of any person in England) for lands in eleven shires. He attested more than forty royal charters between 1125 and 1135 (*Regesta*, 2: nos. 1425– 1973 *passim*) and his tenants owed him in excess of 100 knights: *The Red Book of the Exchequer*, ed. Hubert Hall (Rolls Series, London, 1896), 1: 308–10; Sanders, *Baronies*, p. 93. In Henry's closing years, in short, Brian was one of the king's wealthiest barons and most active *curiales*.

[37] *Anglo-Saxon Chronicle*, A.D. 1127.

[38] Malmesbury, *Historia Novella*, p. 5. John bishop of Lisieux, the head of Henry I's Norman administration, was with the king in England in autumn 1126 (*Regesta*, 2: no. 1466). He had reason to favour Maud over Clito, having been at Henry's side in the war of 1123–24 against Clito's supporters (Orderic, 6: 340). Years before, as archdeacon of Sées, he had fled Normandy during the closing years of Robert Curthose's anarchic rule and had found refuge with Henry in England: Orderic, 6: 142–4.

her capacity to succeed him.[39] By 1126 his resentment to Clito might well have slackened. It would have been clear to him that fixing the succession on Clito would not only please many of his subjects but would also ensure peace with France. Louis VI had long been Clito's most powerful friend and had twice disturbed the peace of Normandy in Clito's behalf. But in 1126 Louis seems to have been hoping that Henry would settle the succession on Clito, and as long as the decision remained unresolved Louis made not a move against the Anglo-Norman state. All through the year Clito wandered and waited, and Louis did nothing to help him – or to alarm Henry. In the summer Henry, for the first and last time in his reign, sent troops to serve on a French royal campaign, dispatching a contingent of Norman knights to Louis' expedition against Auvergne.[40] It was a promising sign. As northern Christendom waited, relations between the two monarchs became more amicable than they had been in years.

But at the news of the oaths to Maud, Louis reacted instantly. While Henry's 1126 Christmas court was making final preparations for the oath-taking, rumours of the impending decision prompted Louis to urge the barons of his own Christmas court to consider ways of helping Clito. The oaths to Maud were sworn on 1 January, and before the month's end Louis had married his wife's half-sister to Clito and endowed him with the lordship of the French Vexin. Shortly thereafter, Clito led an armed band to Henry's frontier castle of Gisors to issue a formal claim on Normandy.[41]

Clito's supporters at Henry's court in fall 1126 seem to have centered on the person of Roger, bishop of Salisbury, regent of England and

---

[39] A royal charter attested by Maud in England in 1114–16 (*Regesta*, 2: no. 1174) is clearly a forgery: J. A. Robinson, *Gilbert Crispin, Abbot of Westminster* (Cambridge, 1911), pp. 151–4; *A Medieval Miscellany for Doris Mary Stenton*, ed. P. M. Barnes and C. F Slade (Pipe Roll Society, London, 1962), p. 98 and n. The Waverley annalist alleges that early in 1122 Henry summoned the empress to England, but that she was prevented from completing her journey (so men said) by Charles count of Flanders, who refused to let her cross his lands: *Annales Monastici*, ed. H. R. Luard (Rolls Series, London, 1864–9), 2: 218. Although the Waverley Annals are a late authority, the story may be true: Henry of Huntingdon (p. 244) places Henry I in Kent after Pentecost, at about the time the Waverley annalist has him at Canterbury awaiting Maud's arrival. Count Charles seems to have been on generally good terms with Henry at the time (*Liber Monasterii de Hyda*, p. 320; Orderic, 6: 352–4), but the trouble may have arisen from hostilities between Charles and Maud's husband. Henry V led an army to Liége in 1122 and was strongly supported by Godfrey count of Louvain (Henry I's new father-in-law) who had earlier tried to prevent Charles's succession: A. Wauters, "Godefroid Ier, comte de Louvain", *Biographie nationale: Académie royale de Belgique*, 7 (Brussels, 1883): 846–7; *Actes des comtes de Flandre, 1071–1128*, ed. F. Vercauteren (Brussels, 1938), p. 249; Walter of Thérouanne, '*Vita Karoli Comitis*', *MGH, Scriptores*, 12:542; O. Rössler, *Kaiseren Mathilde* (Berlin, 1897), pp. 61–7; G. Meyer von Knonau, *Jahrbücher des deutschen Reichs unter Heinrich IV und Heinrich V*, 7 (Leipzig, 1909): 273–77.

[40] Suger, pp. 234–6.

[41] Orderic, 6: 368–70.

master of the exchequer. That Roger was disinclined toward Maud has already been made clear. He would later insist that he had sworn to suport the empress only on condition that she not marry outside the realm without the explicit agreement of the king's chief men.[42] William of Malmesbury, who reports these words, obviously doubts the veracity of one 'who knew how to adapt himself to any occasion'. And it can be assumed that Roger, who owed everthing to Henry's favour, would do precisely as the king commanded and render the required oath without conditions. Moreover, Roger and his fellow lords had sworn subsequent oaths to Maud in 1131 and 1133, after her marriage to Geoffrey of Anjou.[43] Nevertheless, Roger's protestations convey the strong implication that he was hostile to Maud in 1126, and the implication is reinforced by Curthose's transfer from Devizes to Bristol.

Roger's opposition to Maud does not in itself imply that he favoured naming Clito as heir in her place. Roger does not seem to have known Clito personally and is nowhere quoted as expressing opinions on Clito's candidacy. Nevertheless, Clito was the most likely alternative to Maud. And Roger's attitude toward him can perhaps be inferred from the glowing accounts of Clito's career in the writings of the contemporary historian, Henry of Huntingdon.

As archdeacon of Huntingdon, Henry was the direct ecclesiastical subordinate of Bishop Alexander of Lincoln. Henry's *Historia Anglorum* was written at Bishop Alexander's request and was dedicated to him.[44] Bishop Alexander, in turn, was Roger of Salisbury's nephew, former ward, and closest political ally.[45]Roger and his kinsmen formed a tightly-knit ecclesiastical family that had risen from obscurity in King Henry's service; they were attacked as a group by Stephen in 1139.[46]

---

[42] Malmesbury, *Historia Novella*, pp. 15–16.

[43] *Ibid.*, p. 10; Roger of Hoveden, *Chronica*, ed. William Stubbs (Rolls Series, London, 1868–71), 1: 187; Ralph de Diceto, *Opera Historica*, ed. William Stubbs (Rolls Series, London, 1876), 1: 246. Round discounts this evidence (*Geoffrey de Mandeville*, p. 31, n.) but unconvincingly: cf. Chartrou, *L'Anjou*, pp. 36–7. Anxious to retain the royal favor, Roger of Salisbury actually supervised the oath-taking ceremony of 1127: John of Worcester, p. 27; Henry of Huntingdon, p. 256.

[44] *Ibid.*, pp. 1–4.

[45] Reared in his uncle's household, Alexander began his ecclesiastical career in 1121 as archdeacon of Salisbury and obtained the see of Lincoln in 1123 through Roger's influence: *Anglo-Saxon Chronicle*, A.D. 1123.

[46] Besides Roger and Alexander, the group included Roger's nephew Nigel, royal treasurer and subsequently bishop of Ely (1133–69); Roger's nephew (or son) Adelelm, King Stephen's treasurer; Roger's son Roger 'le Poer', King Stephen's chancellor; and several archdeacons. Later generations of the family would produce distinguished royal officers such as Richard fitz Nigel – author of the *Dialogus de Scaccario* – and William of Ely: Kealey, *Roger of Salisbury*, *passim*.

On all matters of state they thought as one.[47] While it would be an exaggeration to regard Henry of Huntingdon simply as a spokesman for Roger's family, it is nevertheless suggestive that in the preface to his *Historia Anglorum* Henry entreats Bishop Alexander to praise him when what he writes is fitting and to correct him when it is not.[48] Henry wrote his history to please Bishop Alexander and would not be likely to express views to which the family might object. He heaps lavish praise on Alexander and portrays Roger of Salisbury as a great man in the affairs of the world. Describing Roger's arrest in 1139, Henry resists reflecting on his favourite theme of pride falling, despite its singular appropriateness to the event. He argues instead that Roger was unfairly treated and concludes with a harmless cliché about the turn of fortune's wheel.[49]

Of all contemporary writers, Henry of Huntingdon is William Clito's warmest advocate. Most of the chroniclers and historians withhold their judgment on Clito. Orderic Vitalis describes him as attractive but impulsive and tragically ill-starred. To John of Worcester he is William *Miser* – 'the Pitiable'.[50] But Henry of Huntingdon sees him as the hero of the age, a warrior of irresistible courage, a youth of immortal fame. On no other layman does Henry of Huntingdon lavish such praise. He embellishes his notice of Clito's death with a ten-line eulogy that portrays him as a fallen god.[51] These passages were written between 1128 and 1133, while Henry I still reigned and Roger of Salisbury still dominated the English government.[52] They describe a man who, as Henry of Huntingdon himself admits, had been the king's enemy.[53] Even if Henry of Huntingdon harboured an eccentric personal affection for Clito (whom he had never met), he would hardly have expressed it with such flair unless he anticipated sympathetic responses in high places. A few years later, in his *Epistle to Walter*, Henry of Huntingdon described Clito as a man of supreme worth who remained the one true heir to the crown and was recognized as such by all men. His death destroyed the hopes of 'all those who regarded him as the future king'.[54] Henry of Huntingdon's primary channel into high politics was

---

[47] For example, Henry I was nearly deceived by the efforts of Henry of St. Jean d'Angely into placing the abbey of Peterborough under the authority of Cluny, but 'by the mercy of God and by means of the bishop of Salisbury, the bishop of Lincoln, and other powerful men who were there, the king perceived that he was behaving treacherously': *Anglo-Saxon Chronicle*, A.D. 1132.

[48] Henry of Huntingdon, pp. 3–4: a topos running back to Boethius.

[49] Henry of Huntingdon, pp. 245–7, 265–7, 280, 316. The point must not, however, be pressed too far; elsewhere (p. 256) Henry includes Roger among the oath violators who suffered the just judgment of God.

[50] John of Worcester, p. 29.

[51] Henry of Huntingdon, pp. 249–50.

[52] *Ibid.*, p. xi.

[53] *Ibid.*, p. 247.

[54] *Ibid.*, pp. 304–5.

the court of Bishop Alexander, which he attended faithfully and knew intimately. Roger of Salisbury's hostility toward Maud is mirrored in Henry of Huntingdon's suggestion that her machinations in 1135 may have driven King Henry into his fatal illness, and in his later allusion to her 'intolerable pride'.[55] It seems probable that Henry of Huntingdon's attitude toward Clito likewise reflects the viewpoint of Bishops Roger and Alexander.

Roger of Salisbury's faction may possibly have included, for a time, the archbishop of Canterbury, William of Corbeil. Roger and William seem to have enjoyed a long acquaintance. We know that the future archbishop had earlier studied and taught at the cathedral school of Laon, which was just then serving as a training centre for Anglo-Norman administrators.[56] Roger himself had sent his nephews, Alexander and Nigel, to study at Laon, and he later gave warm hospitality to a fund-raising mission of Laon canons when they visited Salisbury. It was from Laon that Roger drew the master of his own school at Salisbury, Guy d'Étampes,[57] and it may well have been William of Corbeil's activites at Laon that first brought him to Roger's attention. Subsequently William became the first prior of St. Osyth's, Essex, an Augustinian house founded by Roger of Salisbury's close administrative colleague, Richard de Beaumais, bishop of London.[58] Roger's enthusiasm for the Augustinian movement is shown by his founding of St. Frideswide's, Oxford, which, like St. Osyth's was a daughter house of Queen Edith-Matilda's foundaton of Holy Trinity, Aldgate.[59]

Whatever Roger's relationship with William of Corbeil may have been during these years, we are told by the Anglo-Saxon chronicler that William owed his archiepiscopacy to the bishop of Salisbury. During the debates of 1123 over the Canterbury succession, the monastic party had insisted that the new archbishop, like his predecessors should be a monk. But the bishops, led by Roger, were determined never again to have a monk as their primate. The monks held out for two days, 'but it was no use, because the bishop of Salisbury was strong and controlled all England . . . . Then they elected a clerk called William of Corbeil'.[60] Later that year Henry I was told by a legate from Rome that it was uncanonical for a clerk to preside as archbishop over the monks of

[55] Ibid., pp. 254, 275.

[56] See J. S. P. Tatlock, 'The English Journey of the Laon Canons', Speculum, 8 (1933): 454–65; S. Martinet, 'Le voyage des Laonnais en Angleterre en 1113', Mémoires de la Féderation des sociétés d'histoire et d'archéologie de l'Aisne, 9 (1963): 81–92; R. L. Poole, The Exchequer in the Twelfth Century (London, 1912), pp. 53–6.

[57] Kealey, Roger of Salisbury, pp. 48–9, 91–2.

[58] J. C. Dickinson, The Origins of the Austin Canons and their Introduction into England (London, 1950), pp. 112–13.

[59] Ibid., pp. 113–15.

[60] Anglo-Saxon Chronicle, A.D. 1123.

Christ Church, Canterbury, 'but because of his love for the bishop of Salisbury, the king would not annul it'.[61] Immediately after William's consecration, and with his consent, the bishopric of Lincoln was given to Roger's nephew Alexander,[62] and when, in 1125, William journeyed to Rome and won the legateship for Canterbury, Alexander was the one Anglo-Norman bishop to accompany him.[63] They returned early in 1126, in time to participate in the autumn deliberations.

We are not told what role Archbishop William played in the succession debate. But if there was anyone in England who might have raised an effective objection to Henry's plan, that person was the archbishop of Canterbury. As Anselm's career had shown, and as Theobald's would later show, the archbishops of Canterbury enjoyed, at least potentially, a position of considerable independence. Whereas most Anglo-Norman bishops were products of the royal household, the post-Conquest archbishops of Canterbury had all been heads of religious houses before rising to the primacy.[64] According to Canterbury tradition, Lanfranc 'chose' William Rufus to succeed on the Conqueror's death,[65] and Theobald would one day, with papal backing, block the anointing of Eustace as Stephen's heir.[66] Archbishop William's authority was theoretically even greater than Lanfranc's, Anselm's and Theobald's, for William had recently added to his archiepiscopal powers those of the papal legateship. Although he had neither Anselm's fame and connections nor Theobald's opportunity to refuse consecration (which was not at issue in 1126–1127), it was nevertheless his prerogative to swear the first oath to Henry's chosen successor, and his refusal to do so would doubtless have brought the proceedings to an abrupt halt.

On 1 January 1127 Archbishop William exercised his prerogative, swearing the first oath to Maud. It happens that just at that time the

---

[61] *Ibid.*

[62] John of Worcester, p. 17.

[63] Hugh the Chantor, p. 122; Henry of Huntingdon, p. 246. Thurstan, archbishop of York travelled separately. William's party also included John, bishop of Glasgow; Geoffrey, abbot of St. Albans and Thurstan, abbot of Sherborne, a house directly dependent on Roger of Salisbury – who raised it from a priory to an abbey in 1122 (*Regesta*, 2: nos 1042, 1324). The delegation obtained a papal letter confirming all of Roger of Salisbury's possessions: Walther Holtzmann, *Papsturkunden in England* (Berlin, 1930–52), 2: 141, n.

[64] Lanfranc had been abbot of Caen, Anselm had been abbot of Bec, Ralph had been abbot of Sées and bishop of Rochester, William had been prior of St. Osyth's and William's successor, Theobald, was previously abbot of Bec. Ironically, Becket was the first post-Conquest archbishop of Canterbury to rise from the king's household.

[65] 'Acta Lanfranci', in *Two of the Saxon Chronicles Parallel*, ed. J. Earle and C. Plummer (Oxford, 1892–9), 1: 290: 'Mortuo rege Willelmo trans mare, filium eius Willelmum, sicut pater constituit, Lanfrancus in regem elegit, et in ecclesia beati Petri . . . sacrauit, et coronauit.'

[66] Davis, *King Stephen*, pp. 105, 177.

king was manifesting a quite remarkable generosity toward his archbishop. It was very likely at the 1126 Christmas court that Henry agreed to give William of Corbeil and his successors the perpetual custody and constabulary of Rochester Castle with freedom to fortify it as they pleased.[67] At the Christmas court, too, Henry gave William singularly strong support in the long-standing dispute between Canterbury and York. At issue was Archbishop Thurstan of York's right to participate in crowning the king at the Christmas crown-wearing of 1126 and to have his archiepiscopal cross borne before him within the province of Canterbury. Henry owed much to Thurstan – for helping negotiate peace with the king of France in 1120, and for supporting William of Corbeil's bid for the legateship in 1126. Prior to the peace of 1120 Thurstan and the king had been at odds, but since that time they had been on generally friendly terms. Nevertheless, at the Christmas court of 1126 Henry came out foursquare for Canterbury and instructed Thurstan to remain in his lodgings during the crown-wearing. Thurstan was so furious that he refused to speak to William of Corbeil, 'and did not do so for a long time thereafter'.[68] It would have been at about this time also that Henry granted William the privilege of summoning and presiding over a great legatine council. William held his synod at Westminster on 13–16 May 1127, in the presence of multitudes of the clergy and laity and nearly all the bishops of England and Wales (Archbishop Thurstan sent his regrets). The decrees of the synod were afterwards confirmed and ratified by King Henry himself.[69]

All this may be coincidence. One can only observe that when Archbishop William took his oath to Maud, his debt to Roger of Salisbury had been overshadowed by the substantial and recent generosity of the king himself.

In summary, then, the faction supporting Maud in the closing months of 1126 included her uncle King David of Scotland, her half-brother

---

[67] *Regesta*, 2: 356 and no. 1475, dated at Winchester in [January] 1127, 'et hoc consilio baronum meorum.' The 'consilio' probably occurred at the 1126–27 Christmas court, where John of Worcester seems to place the transaction (p. 23). John mentions the gift of Rochester castle (similarly 'consilio baronum suorum') *s.a.* 1126, immediately following his discussion of the oath-taking, and immediately preceding the 1126 obits. The chronicle then continues with the next year date and events of 1127.

[68] Hugh the Chantor, pp. 129–31; John of Worcester, p. 22; Donald Nicholl, *Thurstan Archbishop of York (1114–1140)* (York, 1964), pp. 67–8, 72–4, 95–100.

[69] Hugh the Chantor, p. 130; John of Worcester, pp. 23–5; Henry of Huntingdon, p. 247.

Robert earl of Gloucester,[70] Brian fitz Count, and perhaps John bishop of Lisieux. In the opposing faction were Roger bishop of Salisbury and presumably such kinsmen as Alexander bishop of Lincoln and Nigel *nepos episcopi* (the future bishop of Ely). To this group might perhaps be added Payn fitz John, from whose custody the captive Waleran was removed late in the year, and conceivably Archbishop William, Roger's good friend. We know from charter evidence that all these men were around the king in fall 1126. A royal charter, probably issued at Portsmouth on Henry's return from Normandy, is attested by Maud, Archbishop William, Brian fitz Count and five others.[71] Shortly thereafter the king was at Rockingham with (among others) Robert of Gloucester, Brian fitz Count, Alexander of Lincoln, and probably also Roger of Salisbury, Nigel his nephew, and Payn fitz John.[72] At Woodstock that same fall the king's attendants included Archbishop William, King David, Robert of Gloucester, John of Lisieux, Roger of Salisbury, Payn fitz John, and Brian fitz Count.[73]

The two factions were composed of similar kinds of men – raised to high position by Henry and frequenters of his court.[74] Their differences were neither socio-economic nor ideological but seem to have depended largely on their estimate of their candidate's ability to rule effectively and uphold their interests. The members of both factions had risen high under Henry I, but – excluding King David – their power was too new to be secure and they would have been

---

[70] A further indication of Robert of Gloucester's early attachment to Maud is to be found in *Regesta*, 3: no. 898 (A.D. 1126–31, at London), the only charter known to have been issued by Maud in England before Henry I's death. Its two attestors are Robert, earl of Gloucester and Ranulf (I or II?), earl of Chester. The charter suggests that Henry had given Maud lands in Hampshire. No such lands are recorded in *P. R. 31 Henry I*, but important portions of its Hampshire accounts are missing.

[71] *Regesta*, 2: no. 1448. The charter may, however, be a forgery.

[72] *Ibid.*, nos. 1459, 1461, 1463.

[73] *Ibid.*, no. 1466; cf. no. 1467. Queen Alice, Rotrou count of Perche and a number of others were also with Henry at Woodstock – his favourite hunting place.

[74] Among those reared at Henry's court were King David, Robert of Gloucester, Brian fitz Count, and the captive Waleran of Meulan. On Brian see above, n. 36. Roger of Salisbury, who began as an obscure priest of Avranches, directed Henry's household for some years before Henry's accession in 1100 and was royal chancellor from 1101 to 1102 or 1103 when he received his bishopric. Besides his important work in the exchequer, he served as Henry's regent in England from 1123 onward. He enjoyed danegeld exemptions in 1128–30 of £153 (the highest of any person in England) for lands in fifteen shires (Kealey, *Roger of Salisbury*, p. 277 and *passim*). He attested some 247 charters for Henry I throughout the thirty-five years of his reign. Payn fitz John became sheriff of Herefordshire and Shropshire in the early 1120s. He received valuable lands along the Welsh frontier (*Regesta*, 3: no. 312), attested some sixty royal charters between c. 1115 and 1135, and probably served as an itinerant justice in the west: W. E. Wightman, *The Lacy Family in England and Normandy* (Oxford, 1966), pp. 175–81; *The Cartulary of Worcester Cathedral Priory*, ed. R. R. Darlington (Pipe Roll Society, London, 1968), no. 153; *Regesta*, 2: nos. 1052–1942 *passim*; *P. R. 31 Henry I*, p. 136.

apprehensive about their status under Henry's successor. They were vulnerable and needed a friend on the throne. Hence, a great deal depended on their personal relationships with Maud and Clito. Roger and his kinsmen had never met Clito, but the writings of Henry of Huntingdon suggest a feeling of warm admiration none the less, and messages may well have been exchanged. On the other side, John of Lisieux, Brian fitz Count and Robert of Gloucester had all been involved in warfare against Clito's supporters in Normandy and may well have found Clito himself hard to swallow. Brian and Earl Robert, moreover, would perhaps have feared the return of Clito's exiled, land-hungry companions. As for Maud, she had only recently returned from Germany, but all that we know of her emphatic personality suggests that she was capable of making friends and enemies quickly. And she would have been with Brian fitz Count, John of Lisieux and Robert of Gloucester at Henry's court in Normandy prior to the September crossing. King David and Robert of Gloucester may have been swayed by their kinship with Maud,[75] but their chief motive was probably nothing more or less than personal affection.

The most significant thing about these factions is that they resurfaced in the following reign to become the nuclei of the two contending parties of Stephen's anarchy. Much had happened during the nine years between the oath-taking of 1127 and Henry's death on 1 December 1135: William Clito had died; Maud had been wed to Geoffrey count of Anjou and borne him two sons. But those who had supported the empress in 1126 supported her again in her wars with Stephen, and those who opposed her in 1126 opposed her still.

This is not to say that the rift of 1126 made Stephen's seizure of the throne inevitable. The fact that his first son, Eustace (born ca. 1129–31), was given a name traditional among former counts of Boulogne suggests that Stephen may have continued for some years after the 1127 oaths to see his family's future in that country rather than on the English throne, and that the idea of challenging Maud's succession may not have crossed his mind until the 1130s.[76] Indeed, Maud's opponents in 1126 would probably have had no choice but to accept her in December 1135, had it not been for her violent break with her father

[75] But Robert of Gloucester, Maud's half-brother, was also the first cousin of both William Clito and Stephen. King David, Maud's uncle, was unrelated to Clito but was the uncle of Stephen's wife. Brian fitz Count was distantly related to Maud, Clito, and Stephen: Duke Richard I of Normandy (942–996) was the great-great-great-grandfather of all four.

[76] John LePatourel, 'What Did Not Happen in Stephen's Reign', *History*, 67 (1973): 11, n. Stephen's second son, William, was born sometime between 1132 and 1137: *Early Yorkshire Charters*, 8, *The Honour of Warenne*, ed. C. T. Clay (Yorkshire Archaeological Society, Wakefield, 1949): 14–15.

several months before.[77] A resulting border war between Henry I and the Angevins (August–November 1135) pitted the king and his most faithful supporters – men such as Robert of Gloucester, John bishop of Lisieux and (probably) Brian fitz Count[78] – against a dissident 'Angevin' faction in Normandy.[79] The threat of rebellious Norman barons in league with Anjou had occurred before;[80] it casts considerable doubt on the oft-repeated but oversimplified notion that a deep-set Norman hatred of the Angevins had doomed Henry's succession plan from the start.[81] The problem of December 1135 was not so much a matter of innate anti-Angevin bias as of a bewildering mix-up of allegiances brought on by the mid-1135 war. The clash not only separated Henry from Maud but also produced hostilities and land disputes between Henry's trusted magnates and Maud's and Geoffrey's allies. On Henry's death these hostilities ensured that the very men most inclined to honour his wishes on the succession were politically and militarily at odds with Maud, Geoffrey, and their Norman baronial supporters. The problem was intensified when Maud and Geoffrey, just after Henry's death, launched an ill-considered invasion of Normandy in their own interests and those of their Norman allies, seizing lands in the southern part of the duchy and committing various hair-raising atrocities. The Norman baronial majority was forced to take up arms against the Angevin invasion and to call for the help of Theobald count of Blois, Henry's old friend and Stephen's brother.[82] The overall effect of these events was to paralyze some of Maud's most powerful potential supporters for a brief but crucial period, allowing Stephen to seize the English throne and establish his power. The paralysis is illustrated by the position attributed to Robert of Gloucester

[77] Orderic, 6: 444–6; Henry of Huntingdon, pp. 253–4; *Gesta Normannorum Ducum*, p. 320; C. W. Hollister and Thomas K. Keefe, 'The Making of the Angevin Empire', *Journal of British Studies*, 12, ii (1973): 16 (below, p. 262).

[78] *Regesta*, 2: nos. 1915–16. On Brian's association with Henry during the king's final stay in Normandy (1133–5) see *ibid.*, nos. 1892, 1900–02, 1908, 1911, and (?) 1934. Stephen himself may have served in the 1135 campaign (*ibid.*, nos. 1932, 1934, 1941), but he was in Boulogne at the time of Henry's death: *Chronicle of Robert of Torigni*, p. 127.

[79] Orderic, 6: 444–6: 'Origo igitur maximarum dissensionum inter Normanniae proceres pullulabat. Nam eorum quidam Andegauensi fauebant . . .' (mid-1135). Among these anti-royalist friends of Anjou were William Talvas and Roger of Toeni: Orderic, 6: 444–6, 454–8.

[80] It had occurred in 1118–19 and again in 1123–24: Hollister and Keefe, 'Making of the Angevin Empire', pp. 9–11 (below, pp. 255–6).

[81] In the warfare in Normandy after Henry's death, the Normans seem to have hated Stephen's Flemish mercenaries no less than they hated the Angevins. Their hatred of both arose primarily from atrocities committed by Flemish and Angevin warriors in Normandy at just that time.

[82] *Chroniques des comtes d'Anjou*, p. 225; Orderic, 6: 454–6; *Chronicle of Robert of Torigni*, pp. 128–9. According to Orderic, the invasion began during the first week of December. Robert of Torigny dates the negotiations with Theobald 21–22 December.

just after Henry I's death: he is said to have favoured the succession not of Maud, but of her two-year-old son, the future Henry II.[83] Thus, Robert could support the Angevin succession in theory while, at the same time, holding aloof from Maud and Geoffrey until the situation in Normandy cleared. Yet with Henry Plantagenet in Anjou, Robert could do nothing positive in his behalf until the disputes brought on by the mid–1135 war were reconciled.

Meanwhile Maud's old enemies rushed into action. Having lost their argument in 1126, and their candidate on Clito's death in 1128, they became the earliest supporters of Stephen of Blois. Dashing to England with a handful of companions in December 1135, Stephen was refused admission by Robert of Gloucester's garrisons at Dover and Canterbury,[84] but he was welcomed by his brother Henry, bishop of Winchester, and by Roger of Salisbury. Winchester had been the site of Bishop Roger's exchequer and Bishop Henry's cathedral, and one can presume that the two men had become well acquainted. In 1135 Bishop Henry's partiality for his brother would have blended smoothly with Bishop Roger's dislike of Maud. At Winchester the royal treasure was handed over to Stephen and the fiscal administration was placed at his disposal.[85] It remained to make public some persuasive justification for the violation of the oaths to Maud and her son. The break between Henry and Maud in mid–1135 made it possible for Hugh Bigod, one of the king's stewards, to allege that Henry had changed his mind on his deathbed, repudiating Maud and designating Stephen as his heir.[86] Hugh's oath was supported by Roger of Salisbury, and although many remained unconvinced – for Roger had not been at Henry I's deathbed and neither apparently had Hugh – the story sufficed to persuade Roger's old friend Archbishop William to officiate at Stephen's

---

[83] *Gesta Stephani*, p. 8.

[84] Round, *Geoffrey de Mandeville*, pp. 1–2.

[85] Malmesbury, *Historia Novella*, p. 15. Roger and William of Pont de l'Arche, sheriff of Hampshire and chamberlain of the treasury, delivered the treasure to Stephen. As head of the exchequer, Roger was in a position to sway various administrative officials and sheriffs. For the names of some of Henry's local and court officials who joined Stephen at the opening of his reign see below, n. 98.

[86] The Bigods, a minor family of pre-Conquest Normandy, acquired some English lands after the Conquest. The Conqueror subsequently enriched Hugh's father, Roger Bigod, with lands forfeited by Ralph, earl of Norfolk. Roger Bigod was further enriched by Henry I, who granted him Framlingham, Suffolk. Roger was a sheriff in East Anglia, a royal steward, and an active *curialis* of William I, William II, and Henry I. Hugh inherited the family honour and royal stewardship in 1120 and was frequently at Henry I's court, attesting forty-seven known royal charters between 1121 and 1135. He was apparently with Henry's court in autumn 1126 (*Regesta*, 2: no. 1451), and he was with Henry at Rouen in 1135 (*Calendar of Documents Preserved in France*, no. 590). Ulger bishop of Angers testified at the papal court in 1139 that Hugh had not been present at Henry's deathbed: John of Salisbury, *Historia Pontificalis*, ed. Marjorie Chibnall (London, 1956), pp. 84–5. Hugh shifted his allegiance three times during Stephen's reign and became earl of Norfolk *c.* 1141.

coronation.[87] On 22 December Stephen was anointed and crowned 'in the presence of three bishops (the archbishop and those of Winchester and Salisbury), no abbots, and very few nobles'.[88] A charter issued by Stephen at Reading two weeks later is attested by Archbishop William, Henry bishop of Winchester, Roger bishop of Salisbury, Hugh Bigod, Payn fitz John, and three other laymen.[89] And Roger's kinsmen – Roger the chancellor, Nigel of Ely, and Alexander of Lincoln – likewise turn up among Stephen's earliest attestors.[90] By Easter 1136 Stephen was so well established that the majority of the Anglo-Norman magnates and prelates attended his court.[91] David of Scotland's son, Henry, was there, and so was Brian fitz Count.[92] Shortly afterwards Robert of Gloucester himself arrived and did homage, 'after being many times summoned to the king's presence by messages and letters'.[93] These men, and others like them, had no choice but to join Stephen's bandwagon or forfeit their English lands. But in the first critical weeks of Stephen's bid for power, when his adherents were few and much was uncertain, Roger of Salisbury was at his side. Henry of Huntingdon says flatly that Roger did everything in his power to give Stephen the crown, rendering him greater service than any other person.[94] In March 1137, when Stephen crossed the Channel to establish his control of Normandy, he was accompanied by his chancellor (Roger of Salisbury's son) and by Bishops Alexander of Lincoln and Nigel of Ely (Roger's nephews), while Roger himself governed England in the king's absence and Roger's kinsman Adelelm

[87] *Liber Eliensis*, ed. E. O. Blake (Camden Society, London, 1962), p. 285; John of Salisbury, *Historia Pontificalis*, p. 85; Ralph de Diceto, 1: 248; cf. *Gesta Stephani*, pp. 6–8.

[88] Malmesbury, *Historia Novella*, pp. 15–16. Malmesbury's statement is corroborated by *Regesta*, 3: no. 45: a charter of Stephen's dated 26 December 1135, at Westminster, attested by (only) Archbishop William and Bishops Henry and Roger. The only other charters that may have been issued around the time of the coronation are nos. 270 (attested only by the steward William Martel) and 500 (attested only by Bishop Henry).

[89] *Regesta*, 3: no. 386; cf. nos. 187, 387, 591, 678, and Round, *Geoffrey de Mandeville*, pp. 10–12. The occasion of the visit to Reading was Henry I's funeral. The other attestors are William of Pont de l'Arche (chamberlain of the Winchester treasury), Robert fitz Richard (royal steward and member of the Clare family), and Ingelram of Say (not lord of Clun, as Round alleges, but a member of a cadet branch of the Say family, which held a mesne tenancy under Stephen during Henry I's reign: *Regesta*, 2: no. 1544).

[90] *Regesta*, 3: nos. 99, 255–6, 335, 373a, 465, 585, 716–7, 832, 906, 919, 942, 975.

[91] *Ibid.*, nos. 46, 944.

[92] On Stephen's settlement with King David see Davis, *King Stephen*, p. 21.

[93] *Gesta Stephani*, p. 8; Malmesbury, *Historia Novella*, pp. 17–18. See further J. W. Leedom, 'William of Malmesbury and Robert of Gloucester Reconsidered', *Albion*, 6, iii (1974): 251–63.

[94] Henry of Huntingdon, pp. 256, 265.

served as royal treasurer.[95] And Waleran of Meulan, the captive rebel of 1126, became Stephen's chief adviser.[96]

Contrary to the traditional view that Stephen was raised to the throne by 'the great Conquest baronage' and opposed by Henry I's 'new men',[97] it seems rather that the succession issue divided the court down the middle, with 'new men' on both sides in 1126 and again in the aftermath of Henry's death. Prior to Stephen's great court of Easter 1136 most of his key supporters were officials, *curiales*, and other 'new men' of the previous reign. The only representatives of rich old families among the attestors of his early characters are Hugh Bigod, Robert de Ferrars, and three junior members of the Clare family. The lord of Clare himself, Richard fitz Gilbert, opposed Stephen in 1136; and the Bigods were not merely old established barons but also royal stewards who had served Henry I faithfully and been much enriched by him.[98]

---

[95] Charles Homer Haskins, *Norman Institutions* (Cambridge, Mass., 1918), p. 124; *Regesta*, 3: xix, xxi, and nos. 31, 67, 313, 397.

[96] Waleran was betrothed to Stephen's daughter and in 1136 fought on Stephen's behalf in Normandy, recovering the royal castle of Vaudreuil from Roger of Toeni. Stephen granted Waleran the earldom of Worcester in 1138. He fought on after Stephen's capture in February, 1141, but then shifted to the Angevins in order to preserve his extensive dominions in Normandy: Davis, *King Stephen*, pp. 67–8; H. A. Cronne, *The Reign of Stephen* (London, 1970), pp. 50–1, 169; *Complete Peerage*, 12, ii: 829–37.

[97] J. E. A. Jolliffe, *The Constitutional History of Medieval England*, 4th edn. (New York, 1961), p. 201; Southern, *Medieval Humanism*, p. 220.

[98] The Bigods were not, strictly speaking, an old-line Conquest family: see above, n. 86. The Clares who attest pre-Easter charters of King Stephen are Walter fitz Richard, Baldwin fitz Gilbert, and Robert fitz Richard. All were younger sons of the lords of Clare and all had made their fortunes under Henry I (Sanders, *Baronies*, pp. 107, 110–11, 129). Robert fitz Richard, the most frequent of the pre-Easter Clare attestors, was a royal steward (*Regesta*, 3: xviii; *Monasticon Anglicanum*, 6: 147). Henry I gave him the forfeited honour of William Baynard *post* 1110. The senior Clare, Richard fitz Gilbert, lord of Clare and Cardigan and one of Henry I's great magnates, was in arms against Stephen when ambushed and killed by the Welsh on 15 April 1136 (*Gesta Stephani*, pp. 10–11). Robert of Ferrars was from a middling baronial family of the Conquest whose English lands were valued in Domesday Book at about £543 a year – a Class B family on W. J. Corbett's scale: *Cambridge Medieval History*, 5 (Cambridge, 1926): 510–11. Stephen was also supported from the beginning by the Beaumonts (*Regesta*, 3: xxi), whose English holdings were modest in the Conqueror's days but expanded very significantly under William II and Henry I (*Cambridge Medieval History*, 5: 511; Sanders, *Baronies*, pp. 61, 93). Others whose names occur in Stephen's pre-Easter 1136 charters include administrators and 'new men' such as the steward William Martel, the treasury chamberlain William of Pont de l'Arche, the sheriff and royal justice Payn fitz John, the royal constable Robert de Vere, the constable, justice and sheriff Miles of Gloucester, the chamberlain of the *camera curiae* William Mauduit, and, of course, the most celebrated and successful of all Henry I's climbers, Roger of Salisbury and his kinsmen. William of Malmesbury is clearly correct in observing that Stephen was crowned in the presence of 'paucissimis optimatibus': *Historia Novella*, p. 16.

While Roger of Salisbury, Hugh Bigod and others hastened into Stephen's camp at first opportunity, Maud's friends of 1126 were slow to rally to her support. By about Easter 1138, however, Robert of Gloucester had settled his differences with Maud and Geoffrey.[99] In late July of that year King David led his army into Yorkshire, only to be routed a month later at Northallerton by an English force loyal to Stephen. And by late 1139 Maud was herself campaigning in England, backed by Robert of Gloucester and Brian fitz Count.[100]

From that time onward England was torn by civil war.[101] But through all the confusion, Maud's friends of 1126–27 – David of Scotland, Robert of Gloucester, and Brian fitz Count – fought often for the empress and never against her. King David had declared for Maud and invaded England immediately after Stephen's coronation. Stephen had forced him to terms in early 1136, and Stephen's northern barons defeated him in 1138, but he remained Maud's lifelong friend. He rendered valuable service to her in 1141, raided Stephen's kingdom again in 1149, and knighted Maud's son, the future Henry II, in the same year.[102] Brian fitz Count is described in the *Gesta Stephani* as a person bound to Maud by unbreakable ties of affection: 'Even in adversity, great though the danger might be, they were in no way divided'.[103] As for Robert of Gloucester, from 1138 to his death in 1147 he was Maud's captain and most powerful supporter – the 'life and soul' of the Angevin party.[104]

Roger of Salisbury had complained that Henry I, in arranging Maud's Angevin marriage, had consulted only Robert of Gloucester, Brian fitz Count, and John bishop of Lisieux.[105] In his capacity as a Norman bishop, John played a much more ambiguous role in the years following Henry's death than Robert or Brian. It may be significant that John was one of only two Norman bishops absent from Stephen's

[99] *Chronicle of Robert of Torigni*, p. 136.

[100] Davis, *King Stephen*, pp. 39–40.

[101] See the useful chart of shifting allegiances in *ibid.*, Appendix II.

[102] David's invasions served his own ends well, but he had always kept the peace under Henry I and would almost certainly have continued to do so had Maud succeeded her father. Contemporaries portray David as a man of honour. In the 1140s he was Maud's 'most-favoured friend', a member of 'the hard core' of Stephen's opposition: *ibid.*, pp. 93, 97; R. L. G. Ritchie, *The Normans in Scotland* (Edinburgh, 1954), pp. 257–9; W. L. Warren, *Henry II* (London, 1973), p. 180.

[103] *Gesta Stephani*, p. 89. Brian is said to have written a pamphlet (now lost) in support of the empress's claims: H. G. Richardson and G. O. Sayles, *The Governance of Mediaeval England from the Conquest to Magna Carta* (Edinburgh, 1963), p. 273. A surviving letter of Brian's to Henry bishop of Winchester castigates the bishop and others who had violated their oaths and betrayed Maud: H. W. C. Davis, 'Henry of Blois and Brian fitz Count', *English Historical Review*, 25 (1910): 297–303.

[104] A. L. Poole, *From Domesday Book to Magna Carta*, 2nd edn. (Oxford, 1953), p. 148.

[105] See above, n. 38.

1136 Easter court, along with Richard bishop of Bayeux, Robert of Gloucester's natural son.[106] John had been with Henry I on his anti-Angevin campaign of mid-1135,[107] and after Henry's death John would doubtless have shared the ambivalence of other Normans of the king's inner circle. His opinion of Maud would have declined still further when the Angevin invasion resulted in the burning of Lisieux in September 1136.[108] But whereas John had served as the chief official of Henry's Norman government, he seems to have been permitted no such authority under Stephen. The principal royal deputies in the duchy during the initial months of Stephen's reign were apparently Waleran of Meulan and his twin, Robert earl of Leicester.[109] When Stephen entered Normandy in force in 1137, John joined his court, but before the king departed for England he appointed as his justiciars William of Roumare, Roger of Saint-Sauveur, vicomte of the Cotentin, 'and others'. A charter of 18 December 1138 shows William of Roumare serving as Stephen's Norman justiciar, Roger of Saint-Sauveur having been killed the previous January.[110] But John of Lisieux, despite his removal from the centre of the Norman administration, continued to support Stephen for the next several years. His nephew, Arnulf archdeacon of Sées, argued Stephen's claim before the pope in 1139,[111] and in 1141, when Geoffrey of Anjou was engaged in his conquest of Normandy, John held Lisieux against him for a time, surrendering the city only when it became clear that the Angevin tide was too strong to resist.[112]

As the civil war dragged on, allegiances dissolved and shifted, particularly among Stephen's early supporters. Stephen arrested Roger of Salisbury in 1139 for obscure reasons, perhaps arising from a rivalry between Bishop Roger and Waleran of Meulan. Waleran himself defected in 1141 to save his Norman patrimony from Angevin

---

[106] *Regesta*, 3: nos. 46, 944. John appears in only three of Stephen's charters, all issued during the king's one visit to Normandy in 1137 (*ibid.*, nos. 298, 327, 608; cf. no. 843: John attests a charter of Stephen's queen in 1137 at Évreux). On the attendance of Anglo-Norman bishops at Stephen's 1136 Easter court see Davis, *King Stephen*, p. 22, n.

[107] *Regesta*, 2: nos. 1915–16.

[108] *Chronicle of Robert of Torigni*, p. 131; Orderic, 6: 468, cf. 474.

[109] *Regesta*, 3: xxi. On John's role as head of Henry I's Norman administration see Haskins, *Norman Institutions*, pp. 87–99. Waleran and Robert were of course functioning chiefly as military rather than judicial deputies of King Stephen, and it would therefore be misleading to insist that they literally 'succeeded' John.

[110] Haskins, *Norman Institutions*, pp. 92, 127; Orderic, 6: 494; cf. *Regesta*, 3: xxi–xxii. Haskins (*Norman Institutions*, p. 321) shows John functioning with judicial authority in 1138, but apparently in his capacity as bishop of Lisieux rather than as a vice-regent for Normandy: the case concerned the church of Dives in the diocese of Lisieux and was heard by John in the presence of the dean of Lisieux, two archdeacons, and three other local personages.

[111] Cronne, *Reign of Stephen*, pp. 89–92.

[112] *Chronicle of Robert of Torigni*, p. 142; Orderic, 6: 550.

confiscation. John of Lisieux, tied to his bishopric, came to terms with whoever controlled the duchy – first Stephen, then the Angevins. As circumstances changed, interests and loyalties changed with them. But with all due reservations, it remains clear that the partisan divisions of the anarchy were prefigured by the factions of 1126 at the court of Henry I.

10

HENRY I AND THE ANGLO–NORMAN MAGNATES

To contemporaries, the most striking thing about Henry I's reign was its peace. In an age when violence was brutal and widespread, when the ideal of the *rex pacificus* was cherished but seldom realized, Henry kept England in a state of tranquillity throughout the last thirty-three years of his thirty-five-year reign (1100–1135). Normandy posed a greater problem because of the military threat of hostile and powerful neighbours. Yet even in Normandy the twenty-nine years of Henry's rule (1106–1135) were marred by serious violence only twice: in the crisis years of 1117–1119 when French, Flemish, and Angevin armies, breaking through the duchy's defences, joined forces with rebellious Normans; and again briefly in 1123–1124 when a small group of discontented Norman magnates enjoyed the military support of France and Anjou.[1] Baronial rebellion against Henry I was a hopeless prospect, not only in England but in Normandy as well, unless backed by outside intervention, and royal diplomacy limited such intervention to rare occasions. The Norman monk Orderic Vitalis describes Normandy at Henry's death as basking in abundance after a long peace under a good prince.[2]

Historians of the past two generations, while agreeing that the peace was long, have been less certain that the prince was good. Sir Frank Stenton, in the concluding chapter of his *First Century of English Feudalism*, used evidence from the Pipe Roll of 1130 and elsewhere to argue that Henry I controlled his magnates by extortion and repression. Stenton remarked on 'the fundamental insecurity of a government which, like that of Henry I, had rested on the

---

[1] Hollister, C. Warren and Thomas K. Keefe, 'The making of the Angevin Empire', *Journal of British Studies* (1973), see below, 250-7. The leading 'Norman' rebel on both these occasions, Amaury de Montfort, was at once count of Evreux in Normandy, a major vassal of the king of France, and uncle of the count of Anjou.

[2] Orderic, vi. 472. Similarly, Suger pictures Normandy at Louis VI's invasion in 1118 as a land 'fruitful from a long peace': *Vie de Louis VI le Gros*, ed. Henri Waquet, Paris 1964, 186; the Norman monk Robert of Torigny describes the period from 1124 through 1135 as one of total peace throughout the duchy: Jumièges, 296; and William of Malmesbury credits Henry with giving Normandy 'a peace such as no age remembers, such as his father himself . . . was never able to effect': *De gestis regum*, ii. 476.

enforced obedience of feudal magnates'.[3] This notion has evolved in the writings of formidably gifted historians such as Sir Richard Southern and Christopher Brooke into the sombre portrait of a cold, hard, inscrutable king—savage and ruthless, morbid and unforgiving, terrible and barbaric.[4] Still more recently Henry's regime was described as a 'reign of calculated terror'.[5]

As you will have suspected, I am unconvinced. Given the formidable resources of great magnates in any feudal regime, the notion of a medieval king keeping the peace for a generation by terrorizing his chief landholders seems to me implausible on *a priori* grounds alone. To see Henry's rule as a reign of terror is to miss its central point: that a substantial number of magnates supported Henry's peace and profited from his lordship, that Henry based his success on the shaping of a royalist baronage, bound to him not by fear so much as by gratitude for past and present favours and hope of future ones.

William the Conqueror had created a royalist baronage by sharing with his nobility the prodigious wealth of conquered dominions. As a result, one finds that his wealthiest magnates tended to be the most frequent attestors of his charters. This relationship between landed wealth and participation in the royal *curia* becomes clear when one follows Corbett's methodology of adding up the values of Domesday manors held by the Conqueror's major tenants-in-chief in 1086 and then compares the wealth of such tenants with the totals of their attestations of genuine royal charters between 1066 and 1087.[6] I have presented the results of this comparison elsewhere in tabular form.[7] To put it

---

[3] Stenton, Sir Frank, *The first century of English feudalism*, 2nd ed., Oxford 1961, 257: from Stenton's Ford Lectures of 1929, first published, under the above title, in 1932. Stenton concludes his analysis of English feudalism by contrasting Henry I, whose magnates were suppressed, with Henry II, whose magnates cooperated willingly with the crown.

[4] Southern, Sir Richard, *Medieval humanism and other studies*, Oxford 1970, 218, 231; Brooke, Christopher, *London 800–1216: the shaping of a city*, London 1975, 317.

[5] Mason, Emma, 'William Rufus: myth and reality', *Journal of Medieval History* iii, 1977, 15.

[6] Corbett, William J., in *Cambridge medieval history*, v. 1926, 508–11. I am drawing here from Hollister, C. Warren, 'Magnates and "curiales" in early Norman England', above, 97-115.

[7] Hollister, 'Magnates and "curiales"', 99 (Table A), with some corrections. The ten wealthiest lay landholders in 1087 (with the value of their tenancies-in-chief expressed in pounds per year) are Odo of Bayeux (3000), Robert of Mortain (2100), Roger of Montgomery (2100), William I of Warenne (1165), Alan of Richmond (1100 + waste), Hugh earl of Chester (800), Richard of Clare (780), Geoffrey of Coutances (780), Geoffrey de Mandeville (780), and Eustace II of Boulogne (770). The ten most frequent lay attestors (excluding William I's wife and sons) are

as simply as possible, the ten most frequent attestors of William I's charters include seven of his ten wealthiest lay landholders. Thus, Roger of Montgomery attested more charters of William I than any other layman; Odo of Bayeux, Geoffrey of Coutances and Robert of Mortain were second, third and fourth. In order of wealth, Odo of Bayeux was England's greatest lay landholder (and although a bishop in Normandy, he held as a layman in England); Robert of Mortain and Roger of Montgomery ranked second and third, Geoffrey of Coutances eighth or ninth. In short, William's closest companions in conquest tended to become magnate-*curiales* in the new regime—which is rather what one might have suspected even without the statistics. It will be obvious enough that this wealth-attestation analysis does not in itself encompass the complex details of royal-baronial interaction. Several of William's magnate-*curiales* were also his close kinsmen; neither kinship nor wealth nor frequency of attestations protected Odo of Bayeux from arrest and imprisonment. The Conqueror's creations could mount rebellions against him, and several of them did so in 1074–1075. Nevertheless, William's regime established itself firmly in a hostile land, exercising lordship such as England had never before experienced. And the strength of the new regime was clearly based, to a significant degree, on the intimate associations and community of interests between king and magnates.

William's was a one-time opportunity, never to be repeated. His successors, lacking the advantage of a fresh start, had to deal with powerful landholding families not of their own choosing. His immediate successors faced the further problem of divided baronial loyalties resulting from the separation of England from Normandy between 1087 and 1096 and again between 1100 and 1106. As a consequence of these problems, the relationship between king and magnates shifted drastically at the accession of William Rufus in 1087. A group of Anglo-Norman barons took up arms against Rufus in 1088 with the object of enthroning his brother, Duke Robert Curthose, thereby reuniting England and Normandy. Rufus's opponents included at least six of the realm's greatest nobles—Odo of Bayeux, Robert of Mortain, Roger of Montgomery, Gilbert of Clare, Geoffrey of Coutances, and Eustace of Boulogne—along with other barons of lesser wealth: Roger Bigod, William of Eu, Roger of Lacy and Hugh of Grandmesnil. Rufus was confronted, in short, with the hostility of the very men whom the Conqueror had enriched, or, in several instances, their sons. Only two among England's ten wealthiest magnates—William I of Warenne and Hugh earl of Chester— are known to have supported Rufus. He survived the uprising, thanks in part to Curthose's incapacity, and in 1095 he managed to put down a second rebellion in which

Roger of Montgomery (40), Odo of Bayeux (34), Geoffrey of Coutances ($33\frac{1}{2}$—the half being either William I or II), Robert count of Mortain (23), Robert count of Meulan (23), Roger of Beaumont (21), Alan of Richmond (21), Eudo *Dapifer* (16), Hugh earl of Chester ($15\frac{1}{2}$), and Richard of Clare (14).

he barely escaped being ambushed. The rebellion-conspiracy of 1095 once again involved a coalition of wealthy families—Montgomery, Clare, Lacy, Eu, Mowbray (the rebel Robert of Mowbray was Geoffrey of Coutances' nephew and heir)—whereas the sources name no major magnates who were committed to Rufus's cause.[8]

The split between king and magnates that these uprisings suggest is confirmed by an analysis of the witness lists of Rufus's charters. As we have seen, seven of the Conqueror's ten wealthiest landholders in 1087 were among the ten most frequent witnesses of his charters. To provide a similar ratio of wealth to attestations under Rufus is a bit tricky: as one progresses through Rufus's reign, drawing farther and farther from the Great Survey, one is obliged to supplement Domesday data with much more fragmentary evidence of landed wealth. One thing at least is clear: the ten most frequent attestors of Rufus's charters alive in 1100 include only one representative of the Conqueror's ten wealthiest families, Hugh earl of Chester—that bloated sinner and devoted royalist whom Orderic described so vividly. The heads of the remaining great Conquest families that survived to 1100 attested scarcely at all for Rufus. Some of the honours—those of Odo of Bayeux, Geoffrey of Coutances and (probably) Eustace of Boulogne—had suffered forfeiture. Others had passed during Rufus's reign from seasoned fathers to untried, sometimes adolescent sons. Several such sons were involved in the rebellion-conspiracy of 1095, and it is significant that the eight identifiable conspirators together attested Rufus's surviving charters only nine times.[9]

As far as I can determine from the Domesday and subsequent record evidence, Hugh of Chester, with Domesday estates worth about £800 a year, was Rufus's only frequent attestor whose wealth was comparable to that of the Conqueror's ten greatest magnates—the 'Class A' barons as Corbett called them. The nine remaining men among Rufus's ten major attestors tended to be landholders of middling wealth, often holding royal household offices—men such as Eudo *Dapifer*, Hamo *Dapifer*, Roger Bigod (also a *dapifer*), Urse of Abitôt (constable and sheriff), and Robert of Montfort (constable). Their holdings range between about £100 and £450 a year—comfortable, but not Class A.[10]

Rufus might well have adopted a policy of luring the wealthiest magnates to his court by patronage, but he seems to have made no serious effort in that direction. Alternatively, he might have chosen to bestow vast estates on his *curiales*, making magnates of them. He did of course enrich them, but only

[8] I am again drawing from Hollister, 'Magnates and "curiales"', above, 97-115.

[9] Hollister, 'Magnates and "curiales"', 103 (Table B): Robert of Mowbray (2 attestations for Rufus), Hugh of Montgomery (2), Philip of Montgomery (0), Gilbert of Clare (4), William of Eu (0), Roger of Lacy (0), Odo of Champagne (1), Stephen of Aumale (0).

[10] Corbett's Class A begins at £750: Corbett, 510-11. For the list of Rufus's major attestors see Hollister, 'Magnates and "curiales"', 110 (Table D).

modestly—so far as the evidence discloses. He seized the estates of Odo of Bayeux, Robert of Mowbray and William of Eu, and kept them for himself. At the time of his death he seems to have been supremely confident, but perhaps unwisely so. His brother, Robert Curthose, was known to be returning from the Crusade with a rich wife and enough money to redeem Normandy. Rufus intended to fight for the duchy, but the response of the leading magnates to such a war would have been, to say the least, unpredictable. Sir Richard Southern, on the basis of different kinds of evidence than I have been using, makes the perceptive observation that when Rufus died 'the country was ready for a revolution, which might well have swept away much of the structure of royal government'.[11]

The split between magnates and *curiales* that marked Rufus's reign continued into the early years of Henry I's reign. In the months following his accession Henry did everything possible to win the support of his greatest landholders. The Coronation Charter was only one of many overtures toward the magnates. He appointed a Clare to the abbacy of Ely and a bastard son of Hugh earl of Chester to the abbacy of Bury St Edmunds; he offered his wife's blue-blooded but penniless sister in marriage to William count of Mortain, who rejected the proposal and demanded the earldom of Kent instead.[12] Despite these overtures, Henry's regime was nearly toppled in its initial year when Curthose, invading England in July 1101, attracted active or passive support from most of England's wealthiest magnates.[13] Henry was harvesting what Rufus had sown: the anti-royal coalition of 1101 involved, to a remarkable degree, the families that had been so conspicuously absent from Rufus's entourage and had conspired against him in 1088 and 1095: Montgomery, Mortain, Grandmesnil, Boulogne—the names will be familiar. As I have observed elsewhere, the nine identifiable supporters of Curthose in 1101 differed markedly in wealth and frequency of attestations from the nine identifiable supporters of Henry I.[14] Henry's supporters tended strongly to be the very men who had previously surrounded Rufus—landholders of middling wealth, stewards and sheriffs. Whereas Curthose's nine supporters had witnessed Rufus's charters a total of seven times, Henry's nine had witnessed 140 times.[15] The data on land values become increasingly tenuous

---

[11] Southern, 231.

[12] See Hollister, C. Warren, 'The taming of a turbulent earl: Henry I and William of Warenne', above, 139.

[13] Hollister, C. Warren, 'The Anglo-Norman civil war: 1101', *EHR* lxxxviii, 1973, above, 77-96.

[14] Hollister, 'Magnates and "curiales"', above, 111-14.

[15] The figure of 140 is a corrected total, slightly higher than the figures provided in my *EHR* and *Viator* articles. It is based on the following list of Henry's supporters and their attestations for William II: Hugh of Chester (8), Richard of Redvers (1), Robert fitz Hamon (21), Hamo II *Dapifer* (9), Eudo *Dapifer* (37), Henry of Warwick (8), Robert of Meulan (16), Roger Bigod *dapifer* (28), Urse of Abitôt (12).

as we drift fifteen years beyond Domesday, but according to what evidence is available to me—again, Domesday Book supplemented by subsequent records—Curthose's supporters commanded three times the landed wealth of Henry's supporters.[16] Norman England was clearly experiencing an ominous schism between magnates and *curiales*, and Henry, having survived the crisis of 1101, resumed his attempt to heal it. Magnates who supported his regime and attended his courts would enjoy his favour and profit from his patronage; those who betrayed him risked forfeiture and exile. Trustworthy royalists could always be found to take their place.

Henry appears to have offered such a choice to all his magnate families with the single exception of the Montgomerys, who had conspired against the monarchy in 1088, again in 1095, and still again in 1101. By Rufus's death the bulk of the family's lands were in the hands of Roger of Montgomery's eldest son, Robert of Bellême, whom the chroniclers describe as brilliant, violent, cruel, and sadistic.[17] As earl of Shrewsbury and lord of Arundel he was England's wealthiest magnate in 1100; as heir to his father's Norman lands and his mother's inheritance of Bellême, he commanded tremendous wealth and power in the duchy and beyond its frontiers. To top it off, he married the heiress to the strategic county of Ponthieu, just to the northeast of Upper Normandy. Perhaps the chroniclers exaggerate Robert's villainy; perhaps not. In any event, Henry cannot have regarded him as a promising participant in the new regime. Relations between them would have been embittered by the fact that in about 1092, when Henry was a landless wanderer, the inhabitants of the Bellême citadel of Domfront had withdrawn their allegiance from Robert and taken Henry as their lord. Accordingly, once Henry had weathered the crisis of 1101 he began assembling charges against Robert— forty-five in all, according to Orderic. When Robert, very sensibly, declined to have his case heard at the royal court in 1102, he was disinherited and driven from the kingdom. 'All England rejoiced,' Orderic writes, 'as the cruel tyrant went into exile.'[18] A decade later, having supported Curthose's losing cause at Tinchebray and having subsequently conspired with the French king, Robert was arrested at Henry's court and imprisoned for life. His violent energy and his surpassing wealth, much of it in districts outside the royal control, were altogether incompatible with the kind of regime that Henry intended to build.

There were other forfeitures in the troubled period between Curthose's invasion of England in 1101 and Henry's victory at Tinchebray in 1106, and still others in the years just following, when certain Anglo-Norman barons conspired in behalf of Curthose's young son, William Clito. Some of Curthose's supporters of 1101 were allowed to keep their lands: Robert

---

[16] Hollister, 'Magnates and "curiales"', 112-13. My figures are £7875 for Curthose's nine, £2620 for Henry's nine.

[17] See Mason, J. F. A., 'Roger de Montgomery and his sons (1067–1102)', *TRHS*, 5th ser., xiii, 1963, 1–28.

[18] Orderic, vi, 30.

Malet, Robert of Lacy, Walter Giffard, and Eustace of Boulogne were all forgiven. Eustace married the queen's sister Mary of Scotland (whom William of Mortain had earlier rejected) and became Henry's good friend. Robert Malet was advanced to the master chamberlainship either just before or just after the 1101 crisis and held the office until his death, attesting frequently at Henry's court.[19] William of Mortain, England's wealthiest magnate after Robert of Bellême (his uncle), broke his fealty to Henry in 1104 and joined Curthose in Normandy, thereby forfeiting his English lands. He was taken captive two years later at Tinchebray and imprisoned for the remainder of Henry's reign.

These and other forfeitures gave Henry the opportunity of enriching his followers without excessively depleting the royal demesne. And in the years following Tinchebray, he succeeded by and large in reshaping the magnates into royalists and *curiales*. Despite the forfeitures, Henry lacked the freedom of action—the *tabula rasa*— that had enabled the Conqueror to enrich his *familiares* so magnanimously. The engine of conquest no longer rolled; lands, offices and privileges had to be distributed with caution and finesse. In this connexion, Henry's famous administrative reforms—the exchequer with its Pipe Rolls, the system of justicial eyres, the reorganized treasury and expanded chancery—are to be seen not only as revenue-raising devices but also as means of systematizing the distribution of royal patronage to great and small alike. It was important to modernize the instruments of revenue collection in order to supplement the income from a gradually diminishing royal demesne with new sources of income, or old sources more rigorously audited. But it was likewise important to have exact records of exemptions from danegeld, *auxilium burgi* and *murdrum*; of the marriages of heiresses to royal favourites; of debts that might be collected swiftly or permitted to run on year after year, or pardoned altogether because of the king's love of the earl of Leicester or the lord of Pontefract. The Pipe Rolls are records not only of debts and payments to the crown but also of debts pardoned, taxes forgiven, income relinquished for the sake of patronage. The Roll of 1130 records payments into the treasury of about £24,200, but it likewise records exemptions and pardons totalling £5500.[20]

The great difficulty in comparing Henry I's baronial policies with Rufus's is that the nature of the evidence changes. We have fewer than 200 of Rufus's charters but nearly 1500 of Henry's, which permits a far more comprehensive and sophisticated analysis of Henry's attestors than of Rufus's. Conversely, Domesday Book becomes an increasingly poor index of baronial estate values as Henry's reign progresses. Some impression of baronial wealth can be

[19] Hollister, C. Warren, 'Henry I and Robert Malet', see above, chapter 7, 130-1. He attested nineteen of Henry's surviving charters between 1100 and 1105.

[20] Kaplan, Jonathan D., 'The Pipe Roll of 1130, an English translation and statistical analysis', unpublished Ph.D. dissertation, University of California, Santa Barbara 1971, 203.

derived from the Old Enfeoffment totals in Henry II's *Cartae Baronum*: any magnate who had enfeoffed 100 or 150 knights on his estates by 1135 must have been, to say the least, comfortably well off. Again, the danegeld exemptions on baronial demesnes recorded in the Pipe Roll of 1130 reflect baronial wealth in some instances, but unfortunately not in most. The difficulty is that danegeld exemptions measure not only demesne values but royal favour as well; magnates who were seldom at court received minuscule exemptions, if any.[21] Despite these difficulties, I have constructed a list of Henry's magnates divided according to their landed wealth. The division is based on Old Enfeoffment totals, supplemented by Domesday data when the honours in question seem to have remained very stable, and by 1130 danegeld exemptions when they are high enough to suggest that the entire demesne is exempt. As far as possible, I have tried to follow Corbett's classification system though, to repeat, my data are distinctly less reliable than his. I begin with Class AA: three 'supermagnates'—Robert of Gloucester and Stephen of Blois with about 300 fees each, and Roger of Salisbury whose danegeld exemption total suggests comparable wealth.[22] Next, Class A: eight lay magnates with 100 to 200 fees. Then, Class B: a dozen or so laymen with about 60 to 90 fees. And finally, Class C: about thirty laymen with 30 to 60 fees. The methodology, though admittedly precarious, does provide a valuable general picture—blurred, yet not seriously misleading. And one can hardly arrive at any meaningful conclusions about Henry's policies toward his wealthiest barons without having some reasonably clear notion as to who they were.

Historians have sometimes restricted the term 'magnate' to the heirs of the 'old Conquest baronage'. I prefer the more straightforward definition: a magnate is, quite simply, a very wealthy landholder. The traditional distinction between old and new families raises the question: what do we mean by 'old'? Were there, indeed, any 'old' magnate families in England at Henry's accession? Henry's so-called old Conquest magnates in 1100 were William I's 'new men', or their sons—the beneficiaries of a prodigious land redistribution that had occurred in stages over the previous thirty-odd years.

---

[21] For example, Walter Giffard earl of Buckingham, Robert of Ferrers, and Henry count of Eu rarely attest royal charters; Walter Giffard has no danegeld exemptions, and the exemptions for Robert of Ferrers and Henry of Eu are trivial. Stephen of Blois' exemptions drop, inexplicably, from £134 in 1129 to £66 in 1130: *The Pipe Roll of 31 Henry I*, ed. Joseph Hunter, London 1929, *passim*.

[22] The Pipe Roll of 1130 records danegeld exemptions on Roger's lands in excess of £150, indicating at least 1500 demesne hides or, very roughly, £1500 a year. I have classified Roger as a magnate rather than a prelate because the bulk of his landed wealth was clearly non-episcopal: the total value of the bishop of Salisbury's Domesday manors, demesne and enfeoffed, was £580 a year. Cf. William of Malmesbury, *Historia Novella*, ed. K. R. Potter, London 1955, 31: Stephen arrests Roger not as a bishop but as a royal servant and castellan, much as William I had arrested Odo not as bishop of Bayeux but as earl of Kent.

Moreover, as David Douglas has taught us, the Conqueror's companions themselves represented a Norman aristocracy 'of comparatively recent growth'.[23] Most of the Conquest families had been dominant in Normandy for only a generation or two. William's half brothers, Robert of Mortain and Odo of Bayeux, recipients of tremendously lucrative earldoms in England, were sons of a relatively obscure Norman *vicomte*, Herluin de Conteville, and his wife Herleva, whose liaison with Duke Robert I had had such momentous consequences but who was herself a mere tanner's daughter. Odo became bishop of Bayeux only in about 1050; Robert became count of Mortain in 1055. Accordingly, the forfeitures suffered by Odo in 1088 and by Robert of Mortain's son William in 1104 can hardly be viewed as a ruthless uprooting of ancient families.

Henry's wealthiest magnates of c. 1125–1135 came from a variety of backgrounds. Some were heirs of the wealthiest (Class A) conquest families: Clare, Chester, Richmond, Warenne. Others represented lesser but ascending aristocratic families: Beaumont, Bigod. Still others were younger sons or bastards of royal or comital fathers: Robert earl of Gloucester, Stephen of Blois, Brian fitz Count. Only one among the eleven Class AA and Class A magnates, Roger of Salisbury, had truly risen from the dust.[24] (And I venture to suggest that a political regime so conservative as to prohibit the rise of new men would be neither very successful nor very attractive.)

Four of Henry's eleven wealthiest magnates—Roger of Salisbury, Robert of Gloucester, Brian fitz Count and Hugh Bigod— figure among the ten most frequent baronial attestors of his charters, and three others were bound to the king by ties of kinship, gratitude or both: Stephen of Blois owed everything to Henry; Ranulf le Meschin had been advanced by royal favour to the earldom of Chester; and Robert earl of Leicester owed his substantial Norman honour of Breteuil to Henry, and his English earldom to Henry's generosity toward his father, Robert of Meulan. Seven of the eleven represented families of either the greater or lesser baronage under William the Conqueror.[25] Eight were

---

[23] Douglas, David, *William the Conqueror*, London 1964, 89, and more generally 83–104; Le Patourel, John, *Norman Barons*, The Historical Association, Hastings and Bexhill Branch 1966, 3–25; Musset, Lucien, 'L'aristocracie normande au xie siècle', in *La noblesse au moyen âge, xie–xve siècles. Essais à la memoire de Robert Boutruche*, ed. Contamine, Philippe, Paris 1976, 88–94.

[24] The eight Class A magnates in 1125–1135 are Stephen of Richmond, Ranulf earl of Chester, Robert earl of Leicester, William of Warenne, Richard of Clare, Roger earl of Warwick, Hugh Bigod, and Brian fitz Count. Geoffrey of Clinton, with a demesne exemption of £59, may well have enjoyed almost comparable wealth; although Southern regarded him as a middle-rank landholder, the exemption suggests that his demesne alone may have been worth some £600 a year. Corbett's Class A begins at £750, but the figure includes both demesne and enfeoffed manors.

[25] Stephen of Richmond, Ranulf of Chester, Robert of Leicester, William of Warenne, Richard of Clare, Roger of Warwick, and Hugh Bigod.

receiving substantial danegeld exemptions ranging from £20 to over £150 in 1129–1130.[26] One of the eleven, Stephen of Richmond, was absent for most of the reign attending to his considerable estates in Brittany. He caused no trouble, did no personal service to the king, and received no exemption. Nine of the remaining ten were men, or the sons of men, who had profited substantially from Henry's favour. From the truce of 1101 until Henry's death in 1135, none of the eleven, or their fathers, had opposed the king either in England or in Normandy.

My division of the magnates into classes is obviously fuzzy at the boundaries separating Class A from Class B and Class B from Class C. But the trend toward royalist magnates pierces these boundaries. At the top of Class B one encounters two *curiales* and royal servants, Geoffrey of Clinton and Nigel of Aubigny, along with David king of Scots who owed everything to Henry. Farther down among the Bs are William of Aubigny *pincerna*, a frequently-attesting member of the royal household, Walter fitz Richard who received his barony of Netherwent from the king sometime before 1119, Robert fitz Richard to whom Henry gave the Baynard honour of Little Dunmow, and William Maltravers whom Henry had planted in the forfeited Lacy honour of Pontefract.[27] These last two elevations exemplify a policy, to which Professor Davis has called our attention, of creating royalist magnates by placing them on the forfeited lands of the king's enemies. Robert of Lacy and William Baynard had both been disseised for treason in about 1110–1113, presumably for conspiring to support Curthose's son, William Clito. Should Clito ever prevail over Henry, the Lacy and Baynard honours would doubtless be restored to the families that had held them previously. The new holders thus had a compelling reason to back their king.

Notice, too, that Walter fitz Richard of Netherwent and Robert fitz Richard of Little Dunmow were younger brothers of Gilbert of Clare and Roger lord of Bienfaite and Orbec in Normandy. Gilbert of Clare was a Class A magnate whom Henry had favoured in 1110 with the lordship of Ceredigion in Wales. All Gilbert's lands passed, on his death in 1117, to Richard, his eldest son. Henry's generosity to Gilbert and the two Clare cadets had the effect of putting the entire cross-channel Clare family in his debt. And if any of the Clares had been tempted to betray Henry for Clito, the temptation would have been dampened by the realization that a Clito victory would probably cost their kinsman Robert his lucrative barony of Little Dunmow. At the climactic battle of Brémule in 1119, Roger fitz Richard, the Norman Clare, was in the first rank of Henry's army.[28] As the French were fleeing, William

---

[26] All but Stephen of Richmond, Richard of Clare and Roger of Warwick.

[27] Sanders, I. J., *English Baronies*, Oxford 1960, 110, 129, 138. Of the twelve Class B barons, at least seven were either *curiales* of Henry I or deeply beholden to him.

[28] Orderic, vi. 234–36; 'Chronica monasterii de Hida', in *Liber monasterii de Hyda*, ed. Edward Edwards, RS 1866, 316–17. See 'De libertate Beccensis monasterii', in *Annales ordinis sancti Benedicti*, ed. Jean Mabillon, Paris 1703–1739, v. 604,

Crispin, a baron of the Vexin, struck at Henry's head with his sword; it was Roger fitz Richard who knocked William Crispin to earth.[29]

The conversion of the Clares was an impressive achievement. The family had been involved in the rebellion against Rufus in 1088; they had conspired against him in 1095; they had bullied Henry in the early months of his reign;[30] when Curthose invaded in 1101 Gilbert of Clare apparently sat on the fence while his uncle, Walter Giffard, joined the duke's army.[31] But Henry's gift of Ceredigion to Gilbert and his handsome provisions for Gilbert's younger brothers evidently had their effect. The Clares and Giffards remained royalists for the rest of the reign.

Henry's baronial policy shows to even greater effect in his handling of William II of Warenne, earl of Surrey, whose father's Domesday estates were exceeded in wealth only by those of Odo of Bayeux, Roger of Montgomery and Robert of Mortain.[32] William I of Warenne had fought for the Conqueror at Hastings, helped crush the earls' rebellion of 1075, and died in June 1088 of a wound received while fighting for Rufus shortly before at the siege of Pevensey. In that year Rufus had made him earl of Surrey, either to ensure his loyalty or reward it. William II of Warenne succeeded to his father's new title and English lands and also seems to have inherited the Norman patrimony centring on the castles of Mortemer and Bellencombre in upper Normandy. Like other magnates of his generation, he was not the royalist his father had been. He played his part in the sporadic baronial warfare of Curthose's earlier years in Normandy. Sometime in the 1090s he sought the hand of the Scottish princess Edith-Matilda and seems to have been deeply irritated at her subsequent marriage to Henry I. Master Wace, an untrustworthy but fascinating source, describes him as ridiculing Henry's obsessively systematic approach to hunting. Henry tried to win William over by offering him a royal bastard daughter in marriage, but Anselm blocked the project on grounds of consanguinity. William joined Curthose's invading army in 1101, and Henry responded by seizing his lands and banishing him to Normandy. Two years later, Henry reinstated William in his earldom at the request of Curthose, who, in exchange, relinquished the annuity of 3000 marks that Henry had agreed to pay at the truce of 1101.

For a time William of Warenne was seemingly unwelcome at Henry's court: he attested no royal charters known to have been issued between 1103 and 1107. But he fought in Henry's victorious army at Tinchebray, perhaps inspired by the fact that his younger brother, who had been fighting in

placing Roger fitz Richard at Henry's side at the siege of Brionne in 1124. On the honors of Netherwent and Little Dunmow see Sanders, 110–11, 129.

[29] Orderic, vi. 238.

[30] *Liber eliensis*, ed. E. O. Blake, Camden series, iii. 92, London 1962, 226–7.

[31] Hollister, C. Warren, 'The strange death of William Rufus', see above, chapter 3, 68-73 ; see 69 for the Clare-Giffard genealogy.

[32] This discussion is based on Hollister, 'Taming of a turbulent earl', above, 137-44.

Curthose's behalf, had fallen into Henry's hands shortly before the battle. Whatever the case, William began appearing at Henry's court more frequently in the years that followed. And in 1110 or shortly thereafter, Henry secured William's loyalty for all time by giving him the castle and lordship of Saint-Saens in Upper Normandy. Henry had seized the honour when its previous lord, Elias of Saint-Saens, guardian of the young William Clito, spirited him out of Normandy just ahead of the royal officials whom Henry had sent to arrest him. It happens that the castle of Saint-Saens lies about three miles up the River Varenne from the Warenne castle of Bellencombre. In Orderic's words, Henry gave William Saint-Saens 'to secure his loyal support and resolute defense against enemy attacks'.[33] It was an astute move, for the lordship was a valuable and strategic addition to the Warenne holdings in Upper Normandy, and William would have realized that, should Clito ever return in triumph, Saint-Saens would be restored to Elias—Clito's guardian, brother-in-law, and companion in exile.

Accordingly, William of Warenne now became a *curialis* and ardent royalist. Having attested only once or twice for Rufus, he witnessed a total of sixty-nine of Henry I's surviving charters. In 1111 he was sitting as a judge in Henry's court in Normandy. And in 1119, at the battle of Brémule, William fought alongside Roger fitz Richard in the forward rank of Henry's victorious army. William is quoted as telling the king on the eve of the battle,

> There is no one who can persuade me to treason. . . . I and my kinsmen here and now place ourselves in mortal opposition to the king of France and are totally faithful to you. . . . I will support this undertaking, with my men, in the first rank of your army and will myself sustain the full weight of battle.[34]

William's danegeld exemptions in 1130 came to the tidy sum of £104—the third highest figure among the English baronage—testifying not only to the wealth of his lands but to the warm affection of his monarch as well. When Henry lay dying at Lyons-la-Forêt in 1135 Earl William was at his bedside, and afterwards was one of the five *comites* who escorted the royal corpse to Rouen for embalming.

Henry did not squander lands and privileges on his magnates, for his resources, unlike William I's, were limited and he intended neither to impoverish himself nor to raise magnates to such heights as to rival their monarch. When his old friend Hugh earl of Chester died in 1101, Henry reared Richard, Hugh's seven-year-old son and heir, at the royal court and, in time, arranged a distinguished marriage for him. Richard's bride was Matilda of Blois, sister of Stephen and Count Theobald and the king's own niece. Richard of Chester, like Roger fitz Richard and William of Warenne, was

---

Orderic, vi. 164; by 1150, however, Saint-Saens was back in the hands of Elias's descendants.
Liber monasterii de Hyda, 316–17.

absolutely loyal to Henry in the crisis of 1118–1119.[35] Henry had meanwhile
raised Othuer, Earl Hugh's bastard and Richard's half-brother, to a position
of considerable wealth, entrusting him with the education of the royal
offspring and with the custody of the Tower of London.[36] As it happened,
Richard of Chester, Matilda of Blois, and Othuer all perished in the White
Ship disaster of 1120. Since Richard and Matilda had no offspring, the flexible
inheritance customs of the time would have permitted Chester to revert to the
king.[37] Nevertheless, Henry granted the earldom to Ranulf le Meschin,
Richard's first cousin, a devoted royalist of long standing who had fought
heroically for Henry at Tinchebray and had given him staunch support in the
crisis of 1118–1119.[38] Ranulf was already a wealthy Anglo-Norman baron—
vicomte of the Bessin, lord of extensive lands in Cumberland, and, through his
thrice-married wife Lucy, a major landholder in Lincolnshire. In exchange for
his advancement to the earldom of Chester—England's seventh or eighth
wealthiest Domesday honour—and to Earl Richard's Norman vicomté of
Avranches, Ranulf gave the king most of Lucy's estates, apparently with her
assent, and his own lands in Cumberland.[39] The exchange aroused conflicts in
later years between the monarchy and Lucy's heirs, but Ranulf le Meschin
seems to have accepted the arrangement with good cheer: he had gained a title
and a fortune, and Henry had prevented the formation of a baronial
agglomeration of dangerous proportions.[40] Although not a major *curialis*,
Ranulf attested Henry's charters with some frequency, particularly after his
advancement to the earldom.[41] His loyalty was such that Henry entrusted him
with the defence of Normandy when rebellion and an Angevin invasion
threatened the duchy in 1123.[42] At Ranulf's death in 1129, the earldom passed
quietly to his son, Ranulf II, who is reported in the Pipe Roll of 1130 as owing

[35] Orderic, vi. 222, 304.

[36] Hollister, C. Warren, 'The misfortunes of the Mandevilles', *History* lviii, 1973, 21–4.

[37] The honour of Eudo *Dapifer* escheated at about this time under similar circumstances.

[38] Orderic, vi. 84, 88, 222–4.

[39] *Complete peerage*, iii. 166; vii. 668, 745.

[40] On the vast estates the earls of Chester might have controlled had they made good all their claims, see Jolliffe, J. E. A. *The constitutional history of medieval England*, 4th ed., London 1961, 172. Ranulf seems to have held for a time the lands between Ribble and Mersey that Henry had seized in 1102 from Robert of Bellême's brother, Roger the Poitevin: White, Graeme, 'King Stephen, Duke Henry and Ranulf de Gernons, earl of Chester', *EHR* xci, 1976, 558.

[41] Eleven attestations in the eight years between his advancement in 1121 and his death in 1129: *Regesta regum anglo-normannorum*, ed. H. W. C. Davis *et al.*, Oxford, 1913–1969, ii, nos. 1243–1602 *passim*.

[42] Simeon of Durham, *Opera omnia*, ed. Thomas Arnold, RS, ii. 1885, 267–8.

1000 marks of his father's debt for the land of Earl Hugh.[43]

This Pipe Roll entry is of exceptional interest in that it suggests a form of royal patronage—the deliberate non-collection of a debt—that occurs repeatedly in the pipe rolls of Henry II. The run of annual Pipe Rolls from 1156 onward discloses a pattern on which royal favourites often pay little or nothing on a debt over a long period of years and, in the end, are sometimes pardoned altogether.[44] This kind of policy is virtually impossible to perceive in Henry I's reign, where only the single Pipe Roll survives. Stenton and others have built their theory of Henry I's repression on evidence from the roll of 1130 of baronial debts rather than baronial payments. To quote Stenton, 'the £102 16s. 8d. laid on Simon de Beauchamp because he had been the pledge of a man whom he did not produce in court seems grotesquely severe'.[45] But Simon in fact paid less than a third of the fine (£33 6s. 8d.) and, for all we know, may never have paid the rest. The Chester relief seems to disclose precisely such a policy of non-collection. The round figure of 1000 marks suggests that it may have been the full, original assessment. Earl Ranulf II paid nothing on it in 1130. It is described as his father's debt, which probably indicates that it represented the full relief assessed on the earldom when Ranulf le Meschin received it back in 1121. Further, the designation of the honour as the land of Earl Hugh could be taken to imply that Earl Richard, who acceded to the earldom as a child on Hugh's death in 1101 and grew up in the royal court, had paid no relief at his own death in 1120—probably because the king had the custody of the honour during Richard's long minority. Whatever the case, Earl Ranulf le Meschin was clearly permitted to leave unpaid throughout his eight-year tenure either the whole relief on his earldom or, at the very least, a considerable portion of it. Such was Henry's policy toward a faithful and singularly wealthy earl. It demonstrates how king and magnates could prosper together in the new era of exchequer accounting just as in the land-grabbing, swashbuckling years of William the Conqueror.

Thus far I have been concentrating on the great Domesday honours that remained intact or expanded only moderately under Henry I. Other families, moderately wealthy under the Conqueror and Rufus, were raised to the heights of Class A only under Henry I. Orderic tells us that immediately upon his accession Henry, apparently in contrast to Rufus, eschewed the advice of rash young men and followed the counsel of wise and older men, among whom Robert of Meulan, Hugh of Chester, Richard of Redvers and Roger

---

[43] *P. R. 31 Henry I*, 110. Young Ranulf received danegeld exemptions on 210 demesne hides in addition to his Chester lands, which owed no geld.

[44] Keefe, Thomas K., 'Feudal surveys and the assessment of knight service under Henry II and his sons', unpublished Ph.D. dissertation, University of California, Santa Barbara, 1978, 189–241: William de Mandeville, for example, was assessed £183 over twenty-two years in scutages, aids, pleas, and fines, but paid only £1 of this sum into the exchequer; the remainder was eventually pardoned.

[45] Stenton, 222, from *P.R. 31 Henry I*, 103.

Bigod are singled out by name.[46] The notion of the king surrounded by wise and seasoned advisers is of course a medieval political cliché, and, despite Orderic's implication, three of the four men he names had been *curiales* of William Rufus. Only Richard of Redvers was new to the *curia*. A baron of western Normandy, he had been a loyal friend during Henry's troubled youth and now became a very frequent attestor of royal charters. Henry granted him a Class B barony, chiefly in Devon and the Isle of Wight, carved out of *terra regis* and the vast honour forfeited by Roger earl of Hereford in 1075. Although Roger Bigod and Robert of Meulan had been major attestors for Rufus, it was Henry who catapulted them into the top echelon of the English aristocracy. Roger Bigod's Domesday lands, worth £450 a year, put him in the lower circles of Corbett's Class B barons. But the family prospered, chiefly through Henry I's gifts to Roger, and to such a degree that the Bigod *carta* of 1166 reports the very impressive total of 125 knights having been enfeoffed by 1135. Roger and, later, his son Hugh served as royal stewards and figured among the most frequent lay attestors of Henry's charters.[47]

Robert, count of Meulan and lord of Beaumont, held a Domesday estate of about £250, placing him toward the bottom of Corbett's Class C. Under Henry he was permitted to acquire, through sharp tactics, the considerable Grandmesnil estates centring on Leicester, plus chunks of the forfeited earldom of William of Mortain in the Rape of Pevensey and elsewhere, along with lands from the royal demesne.[48] He became the first earl of Leicester, a notable achievement in a regime that did not create new earldoms with careless abandon, and his successor in early Angevin times answered for 157 knights' fees,[49] a figure that suggests prodigious wealth. Robert earned his fortune by serving as Henry's chief adviser, his most frequent lay attestor, his *alter ego*.[50] Robert's twin sons, Waleran and Robert, were raised in the royal court. The young Robert became earl of Leicester on his father's death in 1118 and, as we have seen, was given the wealthy Norman lordship of Breteuil shortly thereafter. He remained strictly loyal to Henry I, supported Stephen almost to the end, and served Henry II as chief justiciar. Waleran became lord of Beaumont and count of Meulan. Surprisingly, he joined the Norman rebellion of 1123–1124. It was an almost calamitous error, for he was captured at Rougemontier and remained Henry's prisoner for five years. But Henry released him in 1129, following Clito's death, and restored his lands and the royal friendship—though the king's garrisons remained in Waleran's Norman

[46] Orderic, v. 298; cf. Worcester, ii. 57.
[47] Sanders, 46–7; *Complete peerage*, ix. 575–9.
[48] Fox, Levi, 'The honour and earldom of Leicester: origin and descent, 1066–1399', *EHR* liv, 1939, 385–8; Mason, J. F. A., *William the First and the Sussex rapes*, The Historical Association, Hastings and Bexhill Branch 1966, 20.
[49] In 1172; no earlier enfeoffment data exist for the Beaumont earldom of Leicester.
[50] See Walker, Barbara M., 'King Henry I's "old men"', *Journal of British Studies*, viii, no. i. 1968, 3–5; Le Patourel, 12–15.

castles.[51] The Pipe Roll of 1130 discloses the fiscal dimensions of both the royal anger and the royal love. Waleran is charged 100 marks for the recovery of his estates in Dorset (but pays none of it), while at the same time the flow of royal patronage is resumed: he receives danegeld exemptions on forty-six demesne hides in 1129, fifty-two in 1130, and is among those royal favourites exempted from the *murdrum* fine.[52] Waleran learned Henry's lesson well: he attested the king's charters regularly after his release and never rebelled again.[53] The remainder of his career, under both Henry and Stephen, was a model of baronial circumspection.

An important minority of Henry's Class A and AA magnates inherited nothing in England or Normandy and owed their entire fortunes to Henry. Brian fitz Count, with danegeld exemptions on 720 demesne hides, rose through royal gifts and a marriage to the heiress of Wallingford to become one of Henry's wealthiest magnates and most active *curiales*.[54] Robert earl of Gloucester and Stephen of Blois rose still higher, again through royal gifts and strategic marriages.[55] Stephen of Blois' English fortune derived primarily from the forfeited honours of Henry's enemies, William Malet and Roger of Poitou (a disinherited Montgomery), and from his marriage to the Boulogne heiress, the offspring of Eustace's marriage to Henry's sister-in-law, Mary of Scotland.[56]

Henry's three wealthiest landholders—Robert of Gloucester, Stephen, and Roger bishop of Salisbury—were in a class apart. Nobody else approached them in landed wealth. And all three were Henry's creations and unswerving *fideles*. Stephen's ascent has been described as Henry's single act of folly—forced on him by his need of an alliance with Theobald of Blois, Stephen's brother.[57] My own reading of the evidence persuades me that Theobald needed Henry more than Henry needed Theobald, and that the elevation of Stephen and Robert of Gloucester is to be seen as a product of deliberate royal policy, uninfluenced by diplomatic considerations. A comparison of Corbett's classification under William I with my own parallel classification under Henry I discloses a remarkable similarity in the overall distribution of baronial wealth between 1086 and 1125–1135. William I's 'super-honours'—those of Odo, Robert of Mortain, and Roger of Montgomery—had all perished by

[51] White, G. H., 'The career of Waleran, count of Meulan and earl of Worcester (1104–66)', *TRHS*, 4th ser., xvii, 1934, 19–48.

[52] *P. R. 31 Henry I*, 13–16 and *passim*.

[53] *Regesta*, ii. nos. 1607, 1688–90, 1693, 1699, 1702, 1711. Waleran was at Henry's deathbed in 1135 and was one of five *comites* who bore the king's body from Lyons-la-Forêt to Rouen.

[54] Southern, 220.

[55] On Robert of Gloucester see *Earldom of Gloucester Charters*, ed. Robert B. Patterson, Oxford 1973, 3.

[56] Davis, R. H. C., *King Stephen, 1135–1154*, London 1967, 7–9.

[57] Southern, 213.

1104, but by the mid-1120s others had been built in their places. Henry I's 'super-honours' seem to have been of approximately the magnitude of William's. And, significantly, Henry's two greatest hereditary honours were both granted to close kinsmen—a nephew and a natural son—just as two of William's three had been created for his half-brothers.[58] Both kings were, in effect, creating apanages—placing trusted kinsmen in positions atop the baronial hierarchy. The policy had been followed by the Conqueror's ducal ancestors, who entrusted their kinsmen with the great frontier counties of Eu, Évreux and Mortain. It was of course a Capetian policy as well; in one form or another it influenced most of the rulers of medieval Christendom. It often led to difficulties: Odo and Robert of Mortain rebelled against Rufus; Stephen seized the throne after Henry's death and against his wishes. But so long as Henry lived, Stephen and Robert of Gloucester remained the most ardent of royalists.

During the last decade of the reign, Henry's restructured baronage was firmly in place. The forfeiture of honours that marked Henry's early years had diminished after Tinchebray and ceased altogether after about 1113.[59] By 1125 the honours of Robert of Gloucester, Stephen, and Brian fitz Count had been formed. The magnate class was by now solidly royalist and even, to a degree, curialist. The extent of the transformation will be evident when one contrasts the struggle between magnates and *curiales* in 1101 with the backstairs manoeuvering twenty-five years later between the supporters and opponents of the Empress Maud. Two factions appear to have been at odds in autumn 1126 over the question of the Anglo-Norman succession. Maud's candidacy was backed, so the evidence suggests, by Robert of Gloucester, David king of Scots and Brian fitz Count, and opposed by Roger of Salisbury, his kinsmen Alexander bishop of Lincoln and Nigel the Treasurer, and possibly the *curialis* Payn fitz John. The issue was resolved, for the time, entirely within the confines of the court, and with such adroitness that Roger of Salisbury himself was put in charge of the oath-taking ceremony.[60] Maud must have enjoyed that.

The political factions dimly visible in 1126 emerge in the glare of Stephen's early years as the nuclei of the two contending parties of the Anarchy. Roger of Salisbury's group, still opposing Maud, leapt to Stephen's support the moment he crossed the Channel, while Maud's supporters of 1126–1127— Robert of Gloucester, David king of Scots and Brian fitz Count—became the

---

[58] William I's third 'super-magnate' was likewise connected, though remotely, with the ducal family: *Complete peerage*, xi. 682–3.

[59] De Aragon, Gena, 'The growth of secure inheritance in Norman England', unpublished paper, University of California, Santa Barbara, 1978.

[60] On this and what follows see Hollister, C. Warren, 'The Anglo-Norman succession debate of 1126: prelude to Stephen's Anarchy', *Journal of Medieval History*, i, no. i, 1975; above, 145-69.

champions of the Angevin cause. The most interesting thing about these two parties is that, unlike the rival groups of 1101, they were composed of similar kinds of men. All had been enriched by Henry I; all had frequented his court and attested his charters; all were royalists. They made war in Stephen's reign not because they sought freedom from a predatory Anglo-Norman regime (for they had been a part of it), but because they sought effective royal lordship and could find it nowhere.

Why, then, was there a civil war at all? Historians have traditionally viewed Henry's succession plan as unworkable and have attributed its failure to the bias of the Anglo-Norman baronage against Angevins and women (usually in that order). But Stephen's dash for the crown was made possible only by Maud's ill-considered diplomatic break with Henry in mid-1135 and her consequent absence from his court at the time of his death a few months later.[61] Maud and Geoffrey had demanded custody of some of Henry's castles and the restoration of the castles of William Talvas, son of Robert of Bellême. The result was a minor war along the Norman frontier, in which Henry's most faithful magnates—the very group that might normally have been expected to back the Angevin succession—were in arms against Anjou. It was Maud's impetuousness, and a trivial border conflict, that cleared Stephen's path to Westminster. The Civil War was not an exploding furnace of baronial discontent but the product of a political stalemate in which Henry's designated successor, to whom the baronage was oath-bound, found herself pitted against a crowned, anointed king. 'Stephen's reign is so confused and so messy,' writes Edmund King, 'not because the aristocracy was reacting against strong government but because they had accepted it. . . . Having learned to live with a strong king, to accept his peace and adapt their strategy to his power, they found it difficult to manage without one.'[62]

Much more could be said about the men on whom Henry depended for his power and his peace—the bishops and abbots, the *curiales* and royal officials of lesser wealth whom Sir Richard Southern has analysed so brilliantly. Even the magnates have been viewed here in an insular perspective, with no serious attention given to their landed wealth in Normandy (where the evidence is even thinner than in England). Nevertheless, it should be clear that the stability of Henry's regime was based on the support of great landholders. From beginning to end Henry worked to create a royalist baronage. He realized that most barons, even Norman barons, were by nature neither turbulent nor particularistic, but anxious simply to safeguard their family wealth or, better yet, increase it. Henry's magnates discovered that rebellion involved high risks but that loyalty to the king and association with his court brought security and enrichment.

That is the key to Henry's peace. I wish I could claim to have discovered it

---

[61] See Hollister and Keefe, 'Making of the Angevin Empire', below, 262.

[62] King, Edmund, 'King Stephen and the Anglo-Norman aristocracy', *History* lix, 1974, 192.

myself, but it was well known to Henry's own contemporaries. Orderic Vitalis, who understood the Anglo-Norman aristocracy as well as any writer of his time, sums up Henry's baronial policy, and my paper, in these words: 'He treated the magnates with honour and generosity, adding to their wealth and estates; and by placating them in this way, he won their loyalty.'[63]

[63] Orderic, v. 296.

11

LONDON'S FIRST CHARTER OF LIBERTIES:
IS IT GENUINE?

Henry I's charter for London, one of the most celebrated of English medieval documents, has been the subject of numerous scholarly studies over the past century.[1] As London's first charter of liberties it marks the very beginning of the city's long history as an autonomous unit. More than that, it is, in James Tait's words, 'the first great landmark in the development of self-government in the English boroughs.'[2]

Recently, however, the charter's authenticity has been questioned. Christopher Brooke, Gillian Keir, and Susan Reynolds, in a jointly-written article, examined the charter with meticulous care and found it, at best, suspicious.[3] Since then, they have expressed their reservations in works of a much more general scope, and have influenced the views of other writers.[4] They allow that the charter may yet be genuine but regard this possibility as, on balance, improbable.[5] It is my intention in this paper to argue that the charter is in all likelihood genuine after all – that the history of London's autonomy does indeed commence in the reign of King Henry I and by his mandate.

Brooke, Keir, and Reynolds find several aspects of the charter suspicious. To begin with, the original is lost and the first extant copy dates from the early thirteenth century, some seven or eight decades after the purported date of issue. Paleographical criticism is therefore out of the question. It strikes BKR as odd that five of the ten witnesses to the London charter attest no other known act of Henry I. Moreover, the terms of the charter seem uncharacteristically generous for a powerful and notoriously stingy king who apparently had nothing to fear from Londoners, and therefore no reason to placate them. Commonly dated about 1130–33, the charter grants to the people of London, among other things, the perpetual privilege of electing their

---

[1] For example, Felix Liebermann, ed., *Die Gesetze der Angelsachsen*, 3 (Halle, 1916): 302–7; John Horace Round, *Geoffrey de Mandeville* (London, 1892), pp. 347–73; H. G. Richardson, 'Henry I's Charter to London', *English Historical Review*, 42 (1927): 80–7.
[2] James Tait, *The Medieval English Borough* (Manchester, 1936), p. 157.
[3] 'Henry I's Charter for the City of London', *Journal of the Society of Archivists*, 4 (1973): 558–78: hereafter cited as BKR.
[4] C. N. L. Brooke and Gillian Keir, *London 800–1216: The Shaping of a City* (Berkeley, 1975), pp. 207–10; Susan Reynolds, 'The Rulers of London in the Twelfth Century', *History*, 57 (1972): 341–3; Susan Reynolds, *An Introduction to the History of English Medieval Towns* (Oxford, 1977), p. 105; R. C. Van Caenegem, 'Public Prosecution of Crime in Twelfth-Century England', *Church and Government in the Middle Ages: Essays Presented to C. R. Cheney*, ed. C. N. L. Brooke and others (Cambridge, 1976), p. 54.
[5] BKR: 572.

own sheriffs and justiciars, and it reduces London's annual ferm from about £525 to £300. But several years later, in December 1141, King Stephen granted the hereditary shrievalty and justiciarship of London and Middlesex to Geoffrey de Mandeville, earl of Essex,[6] thus nullifying the electoral privileges conceded by Henry I if in fact Henry had actually conceded them. As Susan Reynolds observes, 'It is paradoxical that it should have been the mighty Henry I who made concessions and the weak Stephen who revoked them, apparently with impunity.'[7]

These arguments constitute only a very general summary of BKR's careful and delicate analysis. In the end, the three scholars arrive at no single, dogmatic conclusion but instead offer four possibilities: (1) the charter may after all be genuine, but (2) it may be a forgery of Stephen's reign (not later), or (3) it may be a charter of Henry I with 'improvements' interpolated during Stephen's reign or thereafter, or (4) it may be a charter of Stephen, attributed later on, by design or mistake, to Henry I. BKR offer the cautious conclusion that 'on the whole the balance of evidence slightly favours the second or fourth interpretation'.[8] In short, BKR think it most likely that the charter is either a forgery from Stephen's reign or a genuine charter of Stephen. They suspect that it may have been issued in or around the crisis year of 1141, during the greater part of which Stephen was a captive of the Angevins, or perhaps in late December 1135 when Stephen was in need of London's support for his coronation at Westminster.[9] Whatever the case, BKR find it more reasonable to associate the charter with Stephen, who depended on London's backing, than with Henry I who did not.

I intend now to test these conclusions against the evidence of the charter itself. I shall follow more or less the organization of BKR who examine (1) the manuscript tradition, (2) the protocol, (3) the witness list, and (4) the historical context. But before engaging in such an analysis, it is possible quickly to rule out the supposition that the charter is an authentic product of Stephen's chancery. The witness list is quite out of the question for a charter of Stephen issued either in December 1135–early 1136 or in 1141. Four of the witnesses are impossible for 1141: Alfred fitz Joel of Totnes, lord of Barnstaple, was dead or in exile by then;[10] Hasculf de Tani, William of Albini *Pincerna*, and Robert fitz Richard of Clare – almost certainly identical to the

---

[6] *Regesta Regum Anglo-Normannorum*, 3, ed. H. A. Cronne and R. H. C. Davis (Oxford, 1968): no. 276.

[7] 'Rulers of London', p. 342.

[8] BKR: 572.

[9] *Ibid.*; Brooke and Keir, *London*, p. 209.

[10] *Gesta Stephani*, 2nd ed., ed. K. R. Potter and R. H. C. Davis (Oxford, 1976), p. 82; *Monastican Anglicanum*, new edition (London, 1817–30), 5: 198.

'Robert fitz Richer' of the London charter – were all dead.[11] Nor is the period around Stephen's accession (December 1135) a possible date, for Alfred fitz Joel was hostile to King Stephen at that time and cannot have been at his court.[12] Indeed, the evidence suggests very strongly that Alfred never came to terms with King Stephen and was never at his court. The *Gesta Stephani* shows him in league with Baldwin of Redvers against Stephen in 1136, among a group described explicitly as never having done homage to the king, and it is implied that Alfred subsequently followed Baldwin into exile.[13] By 1141 at the latest, Alfred's lordship of Barnstaple had passed to Henry of Tracy, and there is no evidence that Alfred ever attested for either Stephen, the Empress Maud, or the future Henry II.[14]

The manuscript tradition of the London charter is complex.[15] The earliest copies, dating from the opening years of the thirteenth century, have been identified and skilfully discussed by BKR, and it would be pointless to repeat the process here. One copy, however, merits special attention. Included as part of the early fourteenth-century *Liber Horn*, it bears a series of marginal and interlineated emendations which were closely analyzed many years ago by H. G. Richardson.[16] These emendations result in a more plausible text and a protocol that reflects Anglo-Norman chancery practice much more closely than any fourteenth-century scribe could have deduced. Accordingly, they can only have resulted from the emendor having had before him the original charter, or an early and quite accurate copy no longer extant. It is important to keep in mind, however, that the emendor attempted no changes in the witness list.

A somewhat corrupt list of charters in the London treasury late in John's reign states that W. son of Ren' has in his personal possession one charter *de libertate* of King Henry and that Henry of Cornhill has

---

[11] *Regesta*, 3: xviii and no. 274; *The Chronicle of Robert of Torigni*, in *Chronicles of the Reigns of Stephen, Henry II, and Richard I*, ed. Richard Howlett (Rolls Series, London, 1884–9), 4: 131.

[12] *Gesta Stephani*, pp. 36–42; R. H. C. Davis, *King Stephen, 1135–1154* (Berkeley, 1967), pp. 25–6.

[13] *Gesta Stephani*, pp. 36–8, 42–6.

[14] Cronne and Davis (*Regesta*, 3: no. 388) identify a witness on one of Stephen's charters (A.D. 1135–9) as Alfred of Totnes, but this identification is improbable. The charter is in very poor condition, and of the name in question only the words *de Toten'* have survived. The witness is probably Guy of Nonant, lord of Totnes, who had attested for Stephen in 1136 (*Regesta*, 3: no. 284) and who signed a charter of Henry I in 1123 as 'Guido de Toteneis': *Regesta Regum Anglo-Normannorum*, 2, ed. Charles Johnson and H. A. Cronne (Oxford, 1956): no. 1391, a copy; *Monasticon*, 2: 539; John Horace Round, *Feudal England* (London, 1895), pp. 482–3.

[15] For the text see Liebermann, *Gesetze*, 1 (Halle, 1898): 424–6; and BKR: 375–8.

[16] Richardson, 'Charter to London', pp. 80–7, with a facsimile of one folio.

another (or 'the other': *alium*).[17] BKR speculate as to whether these two charters were duplicate originals of Henry I's charter to London, or Henry II's, or one of each. But we cannot really know, and the evidence does little except to show the plausibility of the original of Henry I's charter having been lost. As BKR point out (561), this evidence may well reflect 'a certain informality in the preservation of the city's records'.

The protocol of Henry I's London charter, as emended in the *Liber Horn*, reflects Anglo-Norman chancery practice but with some striking eccentricities. First, although addressed to all England, it substitutes for the usual *archiepiscopis* (of Canterbury and York) an address to the archbishop of Canterbury only. Second, to the usual *Henr[icus] rex Angl[orum]* it adds *et dux Normann[orum]*, which is most uncommon.[18] There are, nevertheless, other instances of both these eccentricities in authentic, chancery-produced charters of Henry I. Much the closest parallel, as BKR point out, is *Regesta*, 2: no. 1764 (original in the Archives de Calvados), in the hand of Scriptor 13.[19] Here Henry I, as 'King of the English and duke of the Normans', grants properties to the hospital of Falaise and, as in the London charter, includes, in an otherwise general address clause, only the archbishop of the province concerned: *Henricus rex Anglorum et dux Normannorum archiepiscopo Roth[omagensi], et episcopis, abbatibus*, etc. of England and Normandy. The charter was issued at Westminster, and the witnesses and their titles fix its date tightly at June–July 1133. One vital point has not been observed previously: the June–July 1133 date of the charter for Falaise is precisely the date urged persuasively by J. C. Russell on altogether independent evidence for Henry I's charter to London, which likewise issued from Westminster.[20] The two charters share as witnesses Henry bishop of Winchester and Hugh Bigod, and another witness to the London charter, William of Albini, attests a probably concurrent Westminster charter.[21]

Scriptor 13 appears to have left the royal chancery in about 1141 and may then have entered the service of Robert de Sigillo, bishop of London and former master of the king's *scriptorium*, at which time it is possible

---

[17] John Horace Round, *The Commune of London and Other Studies* (Westminster, 1899), p. 256; BKR: 561.

[18] C. W. Hollister, 'Normandy, France, and the Anglo-Norman *Regnum*', *Speculum*, 51 (1976): 214–7 (above, pp. 29–32). See BKR: 562 for the emended protocol.

[19] See *Regesta*, 3: xiii–xiv. Cf. *Regesta*, 2: no. 1742 (A.D. 1132), also concerning the hospital at Falaise, addressed generally to England and Normandy but, again, to the archbishop of Rouen only.

[20] J. C. Russell, *Twelfth Century Studies* (New York, 1978), pp. 94–102; the essay was originally published in 1952 under the title, 'The Date of Henry I's Charter to London'.

[21] *Regesta*, 2: no. 1758.

that he produced at least two forgeries.[22] If this suspicion is correct, it does not of course impugn his work in the chanceries of Henry I and early Stephen, nor are there grounds for believing that his forgeries, if any, ever bore Henry I's name or seal.

The witness list of the London charter roused the suspicions of BKR, whereas I find it altogether plausible. Of the charter's ten witnesses, nine occur unambiguously in the nearly contemporary Pipe Roll of 31 Henry I (A.D. 1130).[23] The list has at least two corrupt readings, but it must be remembered that the *Liber Horn* emendations do not extend to the attestors, and that our earliest texts of the charter are probably copies of copies at the very least. *Roberto filius Richier* (*Richer* in other MSS.) is clearly a copyist's error for Robert fitz Richard, a cadet member of the Clare family with property in London. His name appears very commonly in royal charters of the time as *Roberto filio Ric*, or *Rob' fil' Ric'*, and very likely occurred in some such abbreviated form in the lost original of the London charter.[24] Likewise, *Willemo de Alb' Spina* (or, in other copies, *Alb' Spine, Alba Spina, Albini Spin, Albini*) is plainly a corruption of William of Albini *Pincerna*, Henry I's master butler. BKR find it odd that a common Anglo-Norman name such as Richard should be corrupted into the less common Richer – but we are probably dealing here with an uninformed extension of *Ric* rather than a misreading of Richard. I find it much odder that *Pincerna* should have devolved into *Spina*, but here again a late scribe was probably guessing at a name originally abbreviated and perhaps partly illegible. One encounters in other MSS. innumerable copyists' errors far odder than these, and to inquire why such lapses occurred is too refined a question to be asked of the data available to us. Who knows what a tired scribe might do late of an evening; anyone who has read galley proofs will appreciate the problem. It should be added that the corruptions in the London charter's witness list are insignificant in contrast to BKR's proposal that *Henricus* might mistakenly have been substituted for *Stephanus*.

Three of the charter's ten witnesses – Henry bishop of Winchester, Hugh Bigod, and William of Albini *Pincerna* – are heavily-attesting *curiales* of Henry I. Eight of the ten witnesses occur in or near London in documents of the 1130s. BKR find it suspicious that several of the witnesses attest no other extant charters of Henry I. But the actual existence of nine witnesses at about the time of the London charter can be proven independently, and the tenth, Hubert *camerarius regis*, although not clearly identifiable, is, as I shall argue, entirely plausible. It

---

[22] *Regesta*, 3: xiii–xiv.

[23] I have difficulty with the suggestion (BKR: 567) that a forger might have had access to the Pipe Roll. It would have existed in only a single copy, well guarded in the Winchester treasury.

[24] His name occurs as *Ric'* or *R.* in *Regesta*, 3: nos. 39, 40, 46, 50, 99, 166, 288, 389, 521, 615, 778, 827, 832, 904, 925, 926, 945, 946 and 950.

is not the custom of forgers to invent obscure names, or to insert little-known attestors, unless copied from a genuine original. And if one has problems with the list, they are not eased by transposing the names to another charter, otherwise unknown. None of the names are anachronistic for 1131–3, although some of them are impossible, as has been shown, for late 1135–early 1136 or *post* 1139. It is the business of the forger to convey a sense of authenticity. If the list is unlikely for a genuine charter of 1131–3 (and I do not agree that it is), it is all the less likely in an expert forgery of Stephen's reign. A witness list of powerful *curiales* would have carried more weight than a parade of nonentities, several of them dead by the end of the 1130s.

Now to the ten witnesses themselves. The first, rendered simply as 'the bishop of Winchester', is Henry of Blois (bishop 1129–71), a major attestor of Henry I's later charters. Henry of Blois was with the king at Westminster in mid–1133.[25] His extensive properties included lands in Surrey for which he was pardoned £4 of danegeld in 1130.[26] BKR remark that for Henry of Blois to attest without his name or initial 'is unusual, though not without parallel.' They point to one earlier charter of Henry I (*Regesta*, 2: no. 1262) where Henry of Blois' predecessor, William bishop of Winchester, witnessed by title only. It should be added that Henry of Blois attests as simply 'bishop of Winchester' in no less than seven surviving charters of King Stephen.[27]

The witness list includes two additional *curiales*, Hugh Bigod and William of Albini, both of them major household officials of Henry I. Hugh Bigod, a royal *dapifer* and very frequent attestor, held lands in Norfolk, Suffolk, and Essex, and was pardoned by royal writ from the London city aid in 1130.[28] William of Albini, master butler and another frequent attestor of royal charters, held lands chiefly in Norfolk and was privileged with danegeld pardons in 1130 for his lands there and in Kent. Both he and Hugh Bigod were with King Henry at Westminster in mid–1133.[29].

The seven remaining witnesses are men of lesser wealth and importance. Five of them attest no other extant charters of Henry I, yet the majority of them were involved in some capacity in the royal administration, and most of them held properties in or near London. Robert fitz Siward witnessed no other charters of Henry I, but enjoyed the royal favour none the less. The Pipe Roll of 1130 shows him exempt from *auxilium civitatis* in Winchester and from *murdrum* and

---

[25] *Regesta*, 2: no. 1764.
[26] *Pipe Roll 31 Henry I*, ed. Joseph Hunter (London, 1929 reprint), p. 51.
[27] *Regesta*, 3: nos. 181, 386, 455, 470, 475, 499 and 500; in nos. 609 and 924, copies of apparently genuine acts of King Stephen, Henry's name occurs in some versions as 'Hugh bishop of Winchester' – doubtless a misinformed extension of *H.* in the original.
[28] *P.R. 31 Henry I*, p. 149.
[29] *Regesta*, 2: nos. 1758, 1764.

danegeld in Essex.[30] As BKR point out, he was a protégé of William of Albini *Pincerna*: in 1130 he was paying Henry I for the privilege of marrying the widow of William de Quevilly and inheriting his royal office of usher of the butlery under William of Albini.[31]

Robert fitz Richard attested three other charters of Henry I.[32] A younger brother of Gilbert fitz Richard of Clare, he may have served as *dapifer* under Henry I, and certainly did so under Stephen.[33] In 1111, or perhaps a few years later, Robert was given the forefeited lands of William Baynard.[34] These holdings included extensive estates in Essex and Baynard's Castle in London, which one finds him occupying at the beginning of Stephen's reign, and his heirs after him. It is all but certain that he was holding the castle at the time of the London charter.[35] As lord of Baynard's Castle, Robert received in 1136 the homage of another of the London charter's witnesses, John Belet, who in return was granted fishing rights in the Thames at London.[36] Although John Belet attested no other royal charters, he was active in Henry I's government as sheriff of Berkshire in the mid-1120s and custodian of Battle Abbey during its vacancy of 1124–5. In 1129–30 he was pardoned for danegeld on his lands in Dorset and for forest pleas in Surrey.[37] Like most of his fellow witnesses, he was a royal minister with connections in London or the home counties.

So, too, was William of Montfichet, whose service earned him pardons for danegeld on lands in Middlesex, Hertfordshire, Essex, Surrey, and elsewhere.[38] William attested several other charters of Henry I,[39] and at the time of the London charter he was almost certainly lord of Montfichet castle in London.[40] His wife Margaret was the niece of Robert fitz Richard, lord of Baynard's castle.

[30] *P.R. 31 Henry I*, pp. 41, 56, 60.
[31] *Ibid.*, p. 53; BKR: 566.
[32] *Regesta*, 2: nos. 1204, 1246, 1283.
[33] *Monasticon*, 6: 147.
[34] *The Peterborough Chronicle*, ed. Cecily Clark, 2nd ed. (Oxford, 1970), p. 35; I. J. Sanders, *English Baronies: A Study of their Origin and Descent, 1086–1327* (Oxford, 1960), p. 129.
[35] Mary Bateson, 'A London Municipal Collection of the Reign of King John', *English Historical Review*, 17 (1902): 485–6; cf. *Regesta*, 2: no. 994.
[36] Bateson, 'London Municipal Collection', pp. 485–6; J. S. P. Tatlock, 'The Date of Henry I's Charter to London', *Speculum*, 11 (1936): 461–9.
[37] C. H. Walker, 'Sheriffs in the Pipe Roll of 31 Henry I', *English Historical Review*, 37 (1922): 68–9; *The Chronicle of John of Worcester*, ed. J. R. H. Weaver (Oxford, 1908), p. 160; *P.R. 31 Henry I*, pp. 15, 51.
[38] *P.R. 31 Henry I*, pp. 51, 59, 152.
[39] *Regesta*, 2: nos. 1283, 1401, 1518, 1609, 1719.
[40] Sir Frank Stenton, 'Norman London', *Social Life in Early England*, ed. Geoffrey Barraclough (London, 1960), p. 183. Montfichet castle was probably built during the Conqueror's reign and certainly before 1136: Derek Renn, *Norman Castles in Britain*, 2nd ed. (London, 1973), p. 248.

That the masters of the city's two private castles both witnessed the London charter has not always been given sufficient emphasis. Even more striking is the probability that another witness, Hasculf of Tani, had been entrusted by Henry I with the custody of the Tower of London. Hasculf seems to have acquired his responsibility on the death of the previous custodian, Othuer fitz Earl, in 1120 and to have remained in charge of the Tower until about 1136–1140.[41] Although he witnessed no other extant charter of Henry I, the Pipe Roll of 1130 records pardons of danegeld for his lands in Essex and Middlesex.

The two remaining witnesses present special problems. Alfred of Totnes did not, as far as we know, hold lands in or around London. A major landholder in Devon and lord of Barnstaple (not Totnes), he succeeded his father Joel shortly before 1130. He attests no other charters of Henry I but is addressed in a royal notification of A.D. 1130–5 confirming his father's benefactions at Barnstaple.[42] His father had earlier attested two of Henry's charters.[43] Alfred enjoyed the royal favour to the extent of receiving an exemption from danegeld in 1130 on his Devon lands.[44] He and his father appear to have been involved in a long-standing land dispute with the family of Nonant, which held Totnes after Joel was expelled from the lordship around 1088.[45] Since Alfred is the one witness unassociated with London or its environs, one might be inclined to wonder what he was doing at Westminster in the early 1130s and why he attested the London charter. But these are questions that cannot fruitfully be asked of a man about whose problems, interests, and itinerary we know nothing. It can only be remarked that his brief career as lord of Barnstaple (late 1120s to around 1136) encompasses the probable date of the London charter.

Hubert the king's chamberlain (*camerarius reg'* in the *Liber Horn*: *camerarius regis* in other MSS.) is the most mysterious of our witnesses. He has been identified as Herbert, Henry I's Winchester treasury chamberlain, but that person was dead well before 1130 and his son and heir, Herbert fitz Herbert, did not inherit his chamberlainship.[46] It may be significant, however, that another Herbert *camerarius* was granted a danegeld exemption in 1130 for lands in Bedfordshire.[47] Again, the witness may possibly be Herbert the chamberlain of the king of Scots,

[41] C. W. Hollister, 'The Misfortunes of the Mandevilles', *History*, 58 (1973): 25 (above, p. 124, n. 33).

[42] *Regesta*, 2: no. 1912.

[43] *Ibid.*, nos. 1391, 1569.

[44] *P.R. 31 Henry I*, p. 158.

[45] Sanders, *Baronies*, p. 89.

[46] C. W. Hollister, 'The Origins of the English Treasury', *English Historical Review*, 93 (1978): 265–8 (below, pp. 212–15).

[47] *P.R. 31 Henry I*, p. 104.

whose name occurs in *Regesta* 2: no. 1930.[48] The Scottish Herbert does not appear in the Pipe Roll of 1130 (unless he is the Herbert *camerarius* of the Bedfordshire entry), but his master, King David, had substantial properties in London, Middlesex, and Bedfordshire.[49] Nevertheless, to identify the Scottish chamberlain with the witness to the London charter involves not only the assumption of a copyist's error of 'Hubert' for 'Herbert' but also the improbability that *camerarius regis* in a charter of Henry I might refer to a chamberlain of the king of the Scots. Tatlock and BKR propose Hubert, chamberlain of Stephen's queen Matilda, and BKR interpret his appearance on the witness list as an indication that the charter may have originated during Stephen's reign. But while reverting from the emended 'Herbert' to the original 'Hubert', Tatlock and BKR introduce a new difficulty: Matilda's Hubert was *camerarius regine* (or *r̄gīe*), not *regis* (or *reg'*).

The likeliest answer, I believe, is that the Hubert of the London charter is simply an otherwise unknown chamberlain of Henry I – perhaps a chamberlain of London. BKR consider this possibility and dismiss it as unlikely. But the records of Henry I's reign disclose several chamberlains who occur in that capacity only once,[50] and our knowledge of the chamberlains of London in the final decade of the reign is decidedly clouded: there is a Fulcred, and possibly a Richard, about whom nothing is certain.[51] Quite possibly, two or more chamberlains of London may have served concurrently, on the analogy of the two chamberlains of Winchester, the co-sheriffs of many shires, and the four sheriffs of London. Hubert is a relatively uncommon name, and our witness may yet be the Herbert *camerarius* of the Bedfordshire account. Alternatively, several Huberts can be discovered among the ruling class of London during and just after Henry I's reign. Roger *nepos Huberti* was joint sheriff of London in 1125; he was dead by 1130, but his name occurs several times in the Pipe Roll of that year.[52] His son, Gervase of Cornhill, was subsequently justiciar and sheriff of London. Among their kinsmen was a certain Hubert *juvens*, from whom we can deduce still another Hubert. John Horace Round speculates that one or the other of these Huberts, father or son, may have been the Hubert of whom Roger was *nepos*.[53].

[48] See *Early Yorkshire Charters, 9, The Stuteville Fee,* ed. C. T. Clay (Wakefield, 1952), pp. 213 ff.; and *Regesta Regum Scottorum, 1153–1424,* 1, ed. G. W. S. Barrow (Edinburgh, 1960): 30.

[49] *P.R. 31 Henry I*, pp. 104, 148, 150, 152.

[50] *Regesta*, 2: nos. 684, 1018, 1256, 1365.

[51] Round, *Commune of London*, pp. 121, 124; *Cartularium Monasterii de Rameseia*, ed. W. H. Hart and P. A. Lyons (Rolls Series, London, 1884–93), 1: 256; *P.R. 31 Henry I*, p. 152. The Pipe Roll mentions no currently active *camerarius* of London. A Richard *camerarius* occurs among those pardoned of danegeld in Middlesex, but his name is not among those pardoned of *auxilium civitatis* in London.

[52] *P. R. 31 Henry I*, pp. 144–5; *Regesta*, 2: no. 1653; Round, *Geoffrey de Mandeville*, p. 309.

[53] *Ibid.*, pp. 304–12; Round, *Commune of London*, pp. 107–8, 114.

The evidence for these people being related by blood or marriage is conclusive though their precise interrelationships cannot be coaxed from existing documents. There is some reason to suspect that all these London Huberts were descendants of Hubert de Ryes – steward of William the Conqueror and father of Eudo *Dapifer*, the wealthy and active *curialis* of William II and Henry I. For example, the manor of Chalk in Kent, near London, was held in 1086 by Adam fitz Hubert, Eudo *Dapifer's* brother; it passed subsequently to Eudo *Dapifer* himself and after Eudo's death in 1120 was granted to Roger *nepos Huberti*, who passed it to his son Gervase.[54] It is even possible that Hubert the chamberlain of Stephen's queen was related to this family group, which itself may have had connections with the queen's father, Eustace of Boulogne.[55] The Hubert *camerarius regis* of the London charter may thus plausibly have been any of several related Huberts who were living in and around London at the time, and whose family members were accustomed to holding royal ministries. The witness may even have been the future chamberlain of Stephen's queen, who had strong London connections and could quite conceivably have been serving late in the previous reign as a chamberlain of London.[56] But to identify any particular one of the several London Huberts with the witness of the London charter is obviously sheer speculation. At the heart of the issue is the fact that we cannot hope to have a comprehensive list of Henry I's chamberlains. And for that reason, the appearance of a royal chamberlain, otherwise unknown, in a charter of Henry I does not in itself reflect even slightly on the charter's authenticity.

To summarize, eight or nine of the ten witnesses had interests in London or the home counties. Seven or eight of them were active in the royal court or administration. Several were linked by bonds of kinship or service. Significantly, the list includes men who were in all probability the lords or keepers of London's three major fortifications

---

[54] Domesday Book, ed. A. Farley and H. Ellis (London, 1783–1816), 1: fo. 86; *Victoria County History, Kent,* 3 (London, 1932): 190, 192; *Regesta,* 2: no. 1256; R. W. Eyton, *Court, Household, and Itinerary of Henry II* (London, 1878) p. 77; *A Formula Book of English Official Documents,* 1, *Diplomatic Documents,* ed. Hubert Hall (Cambridge, 1908): no. 13. A royal charter of 1120 suggests that Roger *nepos Huberti* had a special interest in arrangements for the disposition of Eudo *Dapifer's* lands: *Regesta,* 2: no., 1231.

[55] Eustace issued a charter in favour of Eudo *Dapifer's* foundation at Colchester witnessed by Eudo's kinsman Roger de Sumerei and by a certain *Hubertus:* John Horace Round, *Studies in Peerage and Family History* (London, 1901), p. 164. King Stephen granted Barksdon (Herts.), a fee of the count of Boulogne, to Gervase of Cornhill, son of Roger *nepos Huberti,* to be held on the terms granted by Hubert, the queen's chamberlain, and Richard, his son (*Regesta,* 3; no. 344) and later confirmed the grant of Barksdon to Holy Trinity Aldgate by Gervase of Cornhill and Richard fitz Hubert (*ibid.,* no. 515).

[56] For further evidence on the London connections of Hubert *camerarius regine* see *ibid.,* no. 509 and *Monasticon Anglicanum,* 6: 153.

in the latter years of Henry I's reign. Five witnesses attest no other surviving charters of Henry I, but of these five, Alfred fitz Joel was an addressee, Robert fitz Siward was a royal minister with lands in Essex, Hasculf was probably keeper of the Tower of London, John Belet was a former sheriff and royal custodian with interests in London, and Hubert may well have been a London chamberlain of the early 1130s. The very obscurity of some of these witnesses, combined with the singular appropriatenes of most of them to a London charter of liberties of about 1131–3, speak clearly to its authenticity.

Witnesses of the London charter

	Attesting at West-minster mid-1133	Major curialis	Royal official	1129/30 danegeld pardon	Lord or keeper of a London castle	Interests in London/Middlesex	Interests in home counties	No other attestations of Henry I charters
1. Henry of Blois	X	X		X			X	
2. Robert fitz Richard			X?	*	X	X	X	
3. Hugh Bigod	X	X	X	X		X	X	
4. Alfred of Totnes				X				X
5. William of Albini *Pincerna*	X	X	X	X			X	
6. Hubert *camerarius*		X	?			?	?	X
7. William of Montfichet			X		X	X	X	
8. Hasculf of Tani			X	X	X	X	X	X
9. John Belet			X	X		X	X	X
10. Robert fitz Siward			X	X			X	X

Note: Blood or marriage relationships: Robert fitz Richard × William of Montfichet
  Homage or service relationships: Robert fitz Richard × John Belet; William of Albini *Pincerna* × Robert fitz Siward
*Robert fitz Richard's wife received a pardon for danegeld in 1129–30 on her lands in Northamptonshire (*Pipe Roll 31 Henry I*: 85–6).

Although plausible for 1130–3, the witness list raises the most serious difficulties if one argues that the charter was a product of King Stephen's reign. As we have seen, the list is impossible for a genuine charter of King Stephen. The hypothesis of a forgery, on the other hand, is renderd implausible not by the witnesses who died early or eschewed the court, but by those who lived on and remained close to the king. William of Albini *Pincerna*, until his death in 1139, was frequently at Stephen's side attesting his charters; Hugh Bigod likewise attested frequently until 1141; Henry bishop of Winchester, Stephen's brother, was in the king's inner circle during most of the reign and was with Stephen in London at crucial moments between 1135 and 1141. It would have been rash indeed for a Londoner to present to the king a forged charter bearing the attestations of some of Stephen's closest associates – men who might well have been looking over the royal shoulder as the king examined the document and would have been in a position to expose the hoax immediately. Or, if one assumes that Henry of Winchester was so absent minded as to have forgotten whether he had witnessed a notable benefaction of Henry I, there would surely have been treasury officials able to tell King Stephen whether the London ferm had or had not been running at £300 a year since the early 1130s. Such are some of the problems in supposing that the London charter was forged in the years just following Henry I's death. And if one postpones the forgery to the 1150s or thereafter, it becomes progressively more difficult to imagine how a forger could have concocted a witness list such as has just been analyzed.

It is on the grounds of the London charter's historical context, above all, that BKR doubt its authenticity. They find it hard to believe that the powerful, tightfisted Henry I should have granted such generous privileges as the charter embodies – in particular lowering the ferm from about £525 to £300 – and that Stephen, despite his tribulations, should have revoked them without encountering serious trouble from the Londoners. But to pose the problem in this form not only blurs the fine details on which most historical events depend, but also introduces a certain confusion between (1) the reduction of the ferm (BKR's principal worry), and (2) the right to elect sheriffs. The latter concession, however unlikely it might seem on *a priori* grounds, was unquestionably granted by Henry I: the Pipe Roll of 1130 records not only four local Londoners serving as joint sheriffs of London and Middlesex but also a debt of 100 silver marks assessed against the burghers of London for the privilege of electing their own sheriffs.[57] Elsewhere in the Pipe Roll (p. 114) one finds the townsmen of Lincoln paying for a similar privilege: they owe 200 silver marks and three marks of gold that they may hold their city of the king *in capite*. The point that must be stressed is that the concessions which Stephen revoked in 1141 did *not* include the lowered ferm: it was £300 in the London charter and £300 in Stephen's charter of |Christmas 1141 to Geoffrey de Mandeville.[58] What Stephen did, in effect, was to revoke the Londoners' right to elect their sheriffs and justiciars by granting both these offices to Geoffrey and his heirs. In short, evidence

[57] *P.R. 31 Henry I*, p. 148.
[58] *Regesta*, 3: no. 276.

independent of the London charter proves that what Henry I gave to his Londoners in 1129–30, Stephen denied them in 1141.

But one cannot express the matter so simply without leaving loose ends. What evidence is there, apart from the London charter, that Henry permitted the Londoners to elect their justiciars as well as their sheriffs? And can we be certain that Henry did not himself withdraw the privilege of electing sheriffs at some point after 1130? Neither of these questions can be answered conclusively. But what slight information we possess on the names of London sheriffs and justiciars between about 1133 and 1141 discloses local London commerical figures such as Andrew Bucca Uncta (justiciar 1135–9), Osbert Eightpence (justiciar 1139–41?), Gervase of Cornhill (justiciar *c.* 1135 ff.?), and Gilbert Proudfoot (sheriff *c.* 1138 ff.).[59] It is not unreasonable to presume, therefore, that the Londoners' right to elect their sheriffs, embodied in the Pipe Roll of 1130, extended into Stephen's reign – probably to the time of Stephen's charter of Christmas 1141. And if the Londoners were not electing their justiciars in 1130, they appear to have begun doing so soon thereafter: the Oily Mouths and Eightpences and Proudfeet are not the sorts of men whom Anglo-Norman kings normally chose to be their justiciars and sheriffs. This was particularly the case in the early 1130s, when shrievalties and shire justiciarships were being transformed into regional ministries in which a handful of royal *curiales* exercised responsibility for large groups of shires.[60].

In short, Stephen in all probability revoked the electoral privilege granted by Henry I. Unlikely though such an act might seem, it is supported by evidence independent of the London charter. Accordingly, Stephen's concession to Geoffrey de Mandeville, at the Londoners' expense, does not reflect on the authenticity of Henry I's charter to London.

Why should Henry have acted so generously towards London? To begin with, the notion of royal generosity may in this instance be misleading. The Londoners were charged 100 marks in 1130 for the privilege of electing their sheriffs; the burghers of Lincoln were charged

[59] Reynolds, 'Rulers of London', p. 354 with references; H. A. Cronne, 'The Office of Local Justiciar in England under the Norman Kings', *Birmingham Historical Journal*, 6 (1957): 18–38; Round, *Geoffrey de Mandeville*, pp. 110, 141, 167, 398; Round, *Commune of London*, pp. 97 ff. The royal *curiales* Richard Basset and Aubrey de Vere occur in a charter of late Henry I as joint justiciars in London (*Regesta*, 2: no. 1988). The editors date this charter 1133–35, but on the basis of evidence independent of the London charter it should actually be dated 1129–35 and more probably 1130–33 (cf. *Regesta*, 2: nos. 1913–15, 1960).

[60] C. W. Hollister and John W. Baldwin, 'The Rise of Administrative Kingship: Henry I and Philip Augustus', *American Historical Review*, 83 (1978): 884–7 (below, pp. 236-42).

more than twice as much to hold their city 'in chief', that is, without the direct intervention of royal officials. The bishop of Ely owed £240 in 1130 for a permanent reduction of his knights' service and for an exemption from wardpenny for one of his nunneries, having previously purchased a permanent exemption from wardpenny for Ely itself.[61] The Pipe Roll of 1130 bristles with similar instances of payment for royal privileges. It seems most improbable that the hundred marks assessed against the Londoners in 1130 for the right to elect sheriffs included as well the reduced ferm and the other privileges of the London charter. Quite apart from the clear statement in the Pipe Roll, the granting of all these rights for only £100 would have been an extraordinary bargain. It is hardly likely that London could have obtained greater concessions than Lincoln at less than half the cost. Moreover, £9 6s 4d of the London debt were immediately pardoned by the king.[62] Almost certainly, therefore, the broad concessions of the London charter were granted subsequent to those recorded in the Pipe Roll, and at a much stiffer price. The loss of all the Pipe Rolls between 1130 and 1155 makes it impossible to discover what the Londoners paid for their charter, but analogous transactions recorded in the Pipe Roll of 1130 and in the Pipe Rolls of the Angevin kings suggest that they paid a great deal.[63] No further motive for Henry I's concessions need be sought.

But further motives there were. BKR give insufficient attention to the problem of arrears in the 1130 ferm of London and Middlesex. The ferm came to roughly £525 blanch, but of this sum the king actually received only about £215 in 1130; the four sheriffs continued to owe the remaining £310.[64] The urgency of the problem is demonstrated by later entries in the 1130 London account disclosing that the four sheriffs are willing to pay eight gold marks for the privilege of vacating their offices.[65] The previous sheriff of London, Fulcered fitz Walter, was just then paying off the last of his arrears on the 1128–9 ferm (£209 15s 7d) and still owed twenty silver marks on his gersoma – his payment for the privilege of having been appointed sheriff back in 1128.[66] And Fulcered's predecessor in the office, Ralph fitz Eberard, still owed £7 6s

[61] *P.R. 31 Henry I*, p. 44.

[62] *Ibid.*, p. 148.

[63] In 1199 the Londoners paid £2000 to King John 'pro habendo confirmationem regis de libertatibus suis': *Commune of London*, p. 235. John's charter confirmed the £300 ferm and the right to elect their sheriffs and justiciars.

[64] *P.R. 31 Henry I*, pp. 143–4; Tait, *Medieval English Borough*, p. 184. According to the calculations of J. H. Ramsay, the London ferm was £538 13s. 1d. in A.D. 1130: *A History of the Revenues of the Kings of England, 1066–1399*, 1 (Oxford, 1925): 61. Precision is impossible because the ferm included both blanch and *ad numerum* figures.

[65] *P.R. 31 Henry I*, p. 149; they paid three marks and owed the remaining five.

[66] *Ibid.*, p. 144.

11d from the ferm of *c.* 1127–8; the sum was assessed against Ralph's son in Michaelmas 1130 and remained unpaid.[67]

Obviously there was trouble with the London ferm. It was an onerous burden to the sheriffs, and from the king's perspective it was failing to yield what it should to the royal treasury.[68] The back-up in arrears suggests a mounting fiscal crisis: having bought the right to elect their sheriffs, the Londoners may well have found themselves at a loss for candidates. Under these circumstances it is reasonable to suppose that a sensible monarch might consider reducing the ferm, if only for reasons of administrative tidiness. One finds in the 1130 Pipe Roll numerous pardons of debts on the grounds of poverty, which reflect not simply good-heartedness but a realization that the debts would probably never be paid. The analogy between the cancellation of uncollectable debts and the reduction of a ferm in perpetuity is obviously imperfect. But it may well be argued that the London arrears in 1130 bore some similarity to the much more severe and wisespread urban taxation crisis of the later middle ages. 'Throughout most of the fifteenth century,' R. B. Dobson writes, 'the readiness of a financially embarrassed monarchy to make such substantial fiscal concessions [to the English towns] . . . is best interpreted as a reluctant recognition of reality, an acknowledgement that any attempt to enforce payment would produce "no profit to yor gode grace".'[69] Similarly, one reason for Henry I's reducing the London ferm may simply have been its proven unrealistic exorbitance.[70]

J. C. Russell has argued persuasively for a third motive.[71] The chronicler John of Worcester reports that in mid-May, 1133, a great fire destroyed St Paul's cathedral and most of the city of London along with it.[72] A month or two later, Henry I was at Westminster with his court preparing for what would turn out to be his last channel crossing. He was clearly at pains, on the eve of his departure, to settle a great deal of important unfinished business relating to his English realm. Within a period of about two months he ended a five-year vacancy in the see of Durham by appointing as bishop his own chancellor, Geoffrey Rufus; he appointed his treasurer, Nigel, to the see of Ely, vacant since 1131;

---

[67] *Ibid.*; cf. Reynolds, 'Rulers of London', p. 341.

[68] The problem of arrears recurred under Henry II, when the ferm of London and Middlesex was up once again to a figure in excess of £500: Round, *Commune of London*, pp. 230–3.

[69] R. B. Dobson, 'Urban Decline in Late-Medieval England', *Transactions of the Royal Historical Society*, fifth series, 27 (1977): 11.

[70] Cf. Round, *Commune of London*, pp. 231–2; Brooke and Keir, *London*, p. 209.

[71] *Twelfth Century Studies*, pp. 94–102.

[72] *Chronicle of John of Worcester*, pp. 36–7. Compare the king's treatment of the burghers of Durham who owed £5 in 1130 for the pleas of the royal justice, Eustace fitz John: they paid £2 and were pardoned £3 by royal writ because their houses burned: *P.R. 31 Henry I*, p. 132.

he created a new bishopric at Carlisle, and appointed to it his former confessor, Adelulf prior of Nostell.[73] At the same time he reestablished the office of master chamberlain of England after a lapse of twenty-seven years.[74] He granted lands and privileges to Reading Abbey, York Minster, the bishopric of Bath, the hospital of Falaise, Ramsey Abbey, Whitby Abbey, Chertsey Abbey, the bishoprics of Chichester and Lincoln, Nostell Priory, St Augustine's Canterbury, Cirencester Abbey, the canons of Ipswich, Holy Trinity Aldgate, and St Mary's Portchester.[75] He assented to the founding of Missenden Abbey, protected the burial rights of London churches against the claims of St Paul's Cathedral, and confirmed lands of his new master chamberlain, Aubrey de Vere, and of Gilbert Chaylot of Chichester.[76] The evidence suggests strongly that this whirlwind of appointments, benefactions and confirmations, some of them relating to matters of quite major importance, occurred during June and July 1133, just before Henry's channel crossing early in August. And the king managed this administrative torrent while itinerating between Woodstock, Westminster, Winchester, Fareham (Hants), and Westbourne (Sussex).

Some of this evidence was unknown to J. C. Russell. Taken altogether, it adds weight to his hypothesis that the London charter likewise dates from June–July 1133. The hypothesis cannot of course be proven, and the charter may indeed have been granted by Henry I at some other point late in his reign, subsequent to the 1129–30 exchequer year and before his last crossing to Normandy. But it remains altogether plausible that Henry, prompted by the growing arrears in the London ferm, by the great fire of mid-May 1133, and doubtless for a substantial price, issued the London charter along with his numerous privileges to other beneficiaries in summer 1133. If so, the London charter may well have been precisely concurrent with the charter to the hospital of Falaise which, as previously observed, shared with it a common place of issue, a strikingly similar chancery style, and very probably a common scribe.

One is thus at no loss to explain why Henry I should have granted concessions to London. The problem remaining is why Stephen should have withdrawn some of them. There is, first of all, no evidence that Stephen ever raised the London ferm above £300. It was over £500 again early in Henry II's reign,[77] but for Henry II to have raised it well

---

[73] Henry of Huntingdon, *Historia Anglorum* ed. Thomas Arnold (Rolls Series, London, 1879), p. 253.

[74] *Regesta*, 2: no. 1777.

[75] *Ibid.*, nos. 1757, 1759, 1762–4, 1766–73, 1779, 1781–9.

[76] *Ibid.*, nos. 1765, 1774, 1778, 1780.

[77] *P.R. 2 Henry II*, pp. 3–4. The ferm remained at a figure in excess of £500 throughout Henry II's reign (Ramsay, *Revenues*, p. 192). Early in the reign of Richard I the citizens of London purchased a reduction to £300 (*P.R. 2 Richard I*, p. 135; Tait, *Medieval English Borough,*, p. 181). King John confirmed the £300 ferm in his charter of 1199: Round, *Commune of London*, p. 235.

above his predecessor's figure would have been quite in keeping with his early policy of refusing to honour pre-1154 concessions, even those that he himself had made.[78] It might be argued that 1154–5 would have been an ideal moment for the Londoners to produce a forged charter of Henry I, but, as BKR would agree, the precision of the witness list rules out the possibility of a forgery at this late date. And Henry II, who was not celebrated for keeping promises,[79] would not have been above ignoring a concession made late in his grandfather's reign and establishing the London ferm at the level of Henry I's 1130 Pipe Roll. If pressed, Henry II might well have argued that whatever the Londoners had paid in the early 1130s for their 'perpetual' ferm reduction had been more than made good in the intervening decades: this is precisely the kind of argument that Richard I put forth on his return from the Third Crusade in 1194.[80] As Susan Reynolds has observed in another connection, 'Even after charters became a matter of course kings could and did revoke them: political realities mattered more than legal niceties'.[81] We can be quite certain, moreover, that when Henry II issued his own charter to London at the beginning of his reign he modelled it on the charter of Henry I, while deliberately excluding the references in the earlier document to the Londoner's right to elect sheriffs and justiciars and to the amount of the London—Middlesex ferm.[82]

The only concession in Henry I's charter that King Stephen can be shown to have revoked is the Londoners' right to elect sheriffs and justiciars. These two offices he conferred, in December 1141, on Geoffrey de Mandeville whose political and military support he badly needed just then.[83] In 1143, when Stephen's need subsided, he arrested Geoffrey and deprived him of his power and offices.[84] So far as one can tell, the Londoners recovered their rights of election at this juncture. Our list of London sheriffs and justiciars throughout Stephen's reign,

---

[78] William of Newburgh, *Historia Rerum Anglicarum*, in *Chronicles of the Reigns of Stephen, Henry II, and Richard I*, ed. Howlett, 1: 103; *Chronicle of Robert of Torigni*, p. 183; W. L. Warren, *Henry II* (Berkeley, 1973), pp. 61–3.

[79] *Ibid.*, p. 217.

[80] William of Newburgh, pp. 415–6.

[81] Reynolds, *English Medieval Towns*, p. 106.

[82] The language of Henry II's charter for London closely parallels that of Henry I's charter and is obviously derived from it. A careful collation of the two documents makes it clear, as BKR would agree, that Henry I's charter cannot have been a forgery based on Henry II's. The latter harks back explicity and repeatedly to the privileges that London enjoyed under Henry I; the concessions granted in the two charters are strikingly similar, apart from Henry II's omission of the clauses granting the £300 ferm and the electoral privileges. See Round, *Geoffrey de Mandeville*, pp. 367–71.

[83] Davis, *King Stephen*, pp. 63, 69, 80–2.

[84] *Ibid.*, p. 82.

although far from complete, makes the 1141 concession to Geoffrey look like an exceptional and temporary expedient.[85]

Stephen's charter to Geoffrey de Mandeville granted him only such rights and offices in London as the Empress Maud had conferred on him the previous July, at a time when neither Maud nor Geoffrey controlled the city.[86] When Stephen recovered Geoffrey's support later in the year, he would have been under strong pressure to match the empress' privileges. Both the empress' charter and Stephen's concede to Geoffrey the £300 ferm *sicut Gaufredus avus ejus tenuit.*[87] This phrase, if we can trust it, indicates that the ferm of London and Middlesex had been set at £300 back in the days of William the Conqueror and his companion and sheriff, Geoffrey I de Mandeville (died about 1100).[88] If so, then Henry I's concession of the £300 ferm would have amounted to the re-establishment of an earlier custom – the subsequent, higher figure having proved unrealistic. It even opens the possibility that the £525 ferm of the 1130 Pipe Roll may have been a recent, unsuccessful experiment.

In courting Geoffrey de Mandeville, both Maud and Stephen betrayed the interests of the Londoners. That the empress should have done so after having been driven out of London is not surprising. In her charter to Geoffrey she promised to make no peace with the Londoners without his consent 'because they are his mortal enemies'.[89] And Stephen's own dependence on London's support has perhaps been exaggerated. As Edmund King has pointed out, the honour of Boulogne, which Stephen obtained through marriage in 1125, was so situated as to dominate London. It included extensive holdings in Kent, Hertfordshire, Surrey, and, above all, Essex; and Stephen's control of the port of Wissant in Boulogne gave him a tight grip on London's cross-channel commerce.[90] Dr. King's valuable observation does much to explain why Stephen enjoyed the support of the Londoners in 1135, and how in 1141 he could transfer certain of their rights for a time to Geoffrey de Mandeville without stirring them to rebellion.

---

[85] Reynolds, 'Rulers of London', p. 355. Besides those already mentioned, Reynolds' list includes Theodoric fitz Derman (1143–52) and Gilbert (Becket?).

[86] *Regesta*, 3: no. 275; Davis, *King Stephen*, pp. 62–3.

[87] *Regesta*, 3: no. 274; similar language in no. 275.

[88] There is no further information on the amount of the London ferm in William I's reign: London is, of course, not surveyed in Domesday Book.

[89] *Regesta*, 3: no. 275; Davis, *King Stephen*, pp. 305–6.

[90] Edmund King, 'King Stephen and the Anglo-Norman Aristocracy', *History*, 59 (1974): 183, 191–2; cf. Round, *Peerage and Family History*, pp. 147–80. As R.H.C. Davis observed (*King Stephen*, p. 10), 'It was the ships of Boulogne which tended to dominate the channel, and the count's port of Wissant seems to have handled most of the cross-channel traffic'.

12

THE ORIGINS OF THE ENGLISH TREASURY

HENRY ROSEVEARE, in his recent history of the English treasury, declares that its origins are 'as mysterious as the migration of eels'.[1] Roseveare himself suggests that the treasurers of England run back in a more or less direct line to Henry the Treasurer who served under William the Conqueror. In this opinion he is following Richardson and Sayles who, in their much-discussed *Governance of Mediaeval England*, provide a list of five treasurers from the Conqueror through Stephen, beginning with this same Henry.[2] The list can be extended forward to the present day, and Richardson and Sayles believe that it ran back into the reign of Edward the Confessor.[3] Thus they view the treasurership as evolving without any significant break from pre-Conquest times onward. S. B. Chrimes is more cautious: 'The exact origins of the office of treasurer remain obscure; it may have come into existence by gradual evolution, or may have been an entirely new office created by Henry I.'[4] Chrimes is uncertain of the identity of its first holder but thinks that it was probably a lay administrator of Henry I's named William of Pont de l'Arche, whose candidacy for the honour was urged by G. H. White in his study of Henry I's financial administration.[5] Stapleton believed that Henry I's treasurer was Roger of Salisbury; R. L. Poole thought that he was Geoffrey of Clinton; and Liebermann proposed Nigel, later bishop of Ely.[6]

In the face of all this contradiction and confusion, one might be tempted to drop the whole matter and turn to the simpler problem of eel migration. One thing is clear: we cannot understand the origins of the treasury without sorting out the identities and functions of the treasury officials and their subordinates. We cannot begin to understand what they did until we know who they were.

1. Henry Roseveare, *The Treasury* (London, 1969), p. 20.
2. H. G. Richardson and G. O. Sayles, *The Governance of Mediaeval England from the Conquest to Magna Carta* (Edinburgh, 1963), p. 220.
3. *Ibid.* p. 217. For the list of treasurers from Henry II's reign onward see *Handbook of British Chronology*, ed. F. M. Powicke and E. B. Fryde (2nd ed., Royal Historical Society, London, 1961), pp. 99 ff.
4. S. B. Chrimes, *An Introduction to the Administrative History of Mediaeval England* (3rd ed., Oxford, 1966), p. 28.
5. G. H. White, 'Financial Administration under Henry I', *Transactions of the Royal Historical Society*, 4th series, viii (1925), 67–72; *cf. id.* 'The Household of the Norman Kings', *ibid.* xxx (1948), 149.
6. Thomas Stapleton, *Magni Rotuli Scaccarii Normanniae* (London, 1840–4), i. 22; R. L. Poole, *The Exchequer in the Twelfth Century* (London, 1912), pp. 39, 97; Felix Liebermann, *Einleitung in den Dialogus de Scaccario* (Göttingen, 1875), pp. 16–17. *Cf.* E. J. Kealey, *Roger of Salisbury* (Berkeley, 1972), p. 45 and n. 55.

The pre-Conquest treasury is a subject of almost impenetrable obscurity. The influx of revenues from royal manors, and particularly from the danegeld, would have demanded some kind of fiscal system beyond a chest under the king's bed. There is evidence that by Canute's reign (and perhaps even earlier) royal treasure was kept in a storehouse at Winchester, and Edward the Confessor evidently had a financial official named Hugh the Chamberlain and another called Odo the Treasurer or Odo of Winchester.[1] This Odo occurs in Domesday Book as a minor landholder in Hampshire and Devon, and may, indeed, be two separate men.[2]

The fog lifts only slightly as we enter the Conqueror's reign. A certain Henry the Treasurer was active at the time of Domesday Book (1086) but dead by about 1110 when his widow appears as his heiress in Winton Domesday. Henry was a personage of remarkable obscurity. He attests no known royal charters and cannot, therefore, have been an important figure at court. His possessions, all of them in Hampshire, consisted only of three small manors and an odd virgate with a total value of £9.10s., plus two messuages in Winchester itself.[3] He was thus a purely local man of small means and minor political significance – not an important official at the royal court, but merely a keeper of the Winchester treasure storehouse. His office of 'treasurer' was not the great court treasurership of later times, as described in the *Constitutio Domus Regis* of *c.* 1136,[4] but was almost certainly the local Winchester office later called *custos thesaurorum regis*.[5] This officer had direct custody of the treasure house and is described in a later source as holding the keys to it.[6]

1. T. F. Tout, *Chapters in the Administrative History of Mediaeval England*, i (Manchester, corrected ed., 1937), pp. 72–73; Frank Barlow, *Edward the Confessor* (Berkeley, 1970), pp. 186–7; V. H. Galbraith, *Studies in the Public Records* (London, 1948), p. 45. The Conqueror's official, Henry the Treasurer, may possibly have served also under the Confessor: *ibid.* pp. 44–45; Richardson and Sayles, *Governance*, p. 223; *Winchester in the Early Middle Ages: An Edition and Discussion of the Winton Domesday*, ed. Martin Biddle (Oxford, 1976), pp. 390, 467.

2. Domesday Book, i. 49, 52; iii (Exon Domesday), 31. The Hampshire tenant is called Odo of Winchester; the Devon man is Odo 'the Treasurer'. If Odo the Treasurer was connected with the Winchester treasury (which is the only treasury known at the time), it is not unreasonable that he might be identical with Odo of Winchester. See Galbraith, *Public Records*, p. 45.

3. Domesday Book, i. 49; *Winchester*, ed. Biddle, p. 59. Henry had resided in Winchester prior to the Conquest, but did not yet have the three Hampshire manors that he held in 1086.

4. 'Constitutio Domus Regis', appended to the *Dialogus de Scaccario*, ed. Charles Johnson (London, 1950), p. 133.

5. Thus was described William of Pont de l'Arche, custodian of the Winchester treasury in 1135: *Gesta Stephani*, ed. K. R. Potter and R. H. C. Davis (2nd ed., Oxford, 1976), p. 8: 'Fuit eodem in tempore in ciuitate Wintoniensi Willelmus quidam, fidissimus thesaurorum regis Henrici custos et resignator...'. *Cf.* William of Malmesbury, *Historia Novella*, ed. K. R. Potter (London, 1955), p. 15: Roger of Salisbury and William of Pont de l'Arche, 'custodes thesaurorum regalium'.

6. William of Pont de l'Arche is described as giving 'claves thesauri Wintoniae' to William Rufus in 1087 (*recte:* to Stephen in 1135): 'Historia Fundationis of Colchester Abbey', in *Monasticon Anglicanum*, iv. 607; *cf.* Richardson and Sayles, p. 222.

Just preceding Henry the Treasurer's entry in the Hampshire section of Domesday Book is an entry for Herbert *Camerarius*.[1] Herbert's Domesday possessions, although larger than Henry's, were still relatively small and limited to Hampshire: he held two manors *in capite*, worth a total of £3 a year, plus part of a manor of the New Minister, Winchester, worth £5, and two manors of Hugh de Port each worth £1.[2] The Winchester Survey of *c*. 1110 shows that he held extensive property within the city and outside the West Gate, bringing him yearly rents of £27 10s. 9d. How much of his Winchester property represents acquisitions between 1086 and *c*. 1110 we cannot tell, since Winchester holdings are not recorded in Domesday Book. In a charter of Robert *Dispensator* issued during Rufus' reign, Herbert is described as the king's chamberlain of Winchester,[3] and the Abingdon chronicler refers to him as 'the king's chamberlain and treasurer' in passages describing his activities between 1097 and 1100 and again sometime between 1100 and 1130.[4] He is likewise described by later twelfth-century writers as Henry I's chamberlain and treasurer of Winchester, and his name occurs in a charter of Henry I of about 1100 as one responsible for treasury disbursements.[5] He attests four surviving charters of Henry I and is addressed in several more, all of them dealing with financial matters and all dating from the earlier part of the reign.[6] In 1111 he was a member of the Michaelmas treasury court at Winchester.[7] Everything points to the conclusion that Herbert was associated with Henry the Treasurer in the Winchester treasury at the time of Domesday and that by 1100 he had succeeded Henry as treasurer while retaining his former status as treasury chamberlain, thus combining the two offices.

By the later twelfth century the custom was firmly established that two chamberlains of the treasury (later chamberlains of the exchequer) supervised the treasury at Winchester.[8] These two treasury chamberlainships were clearly functioning in the reign of Henry I and perhaps earlier still. During the years of Herbert's ministry, a second, concurrent treasury chamberlainship seems to have been held by a certain Robert Mauduit. This chamberlainship may well have originated with Robert's father, William Mauduit,

1. Domesday Book, i. 48b–49; *cf.* Tout, i. 76–77.
2. Domesday Book, i. 42b, 46, 48b–49; iii. 534–7, 542.
3. J. A. Robinson, *Gilbert Crispin, Abbot of Westminster* (Cambridge, 1911), p. 146: 'Herbertus camerarius regis de Winton'.
4 *Chronicon Monasterii de Abingdon*, ed. Joseph Stevenson (Rolls Series, 1858), ii. 43, 134: 'regis cubicularius atque thesaurarius'.
5. John of Hexham, in *Symeonis Monachi Opera Omnia*, ed. Thomas Arnold (Rolls Series, 1882–5), ii. 317; *Historians of the Church of York*, ed. James Rayne (Rolls Series, 1879–94), ii. 223; *Regesta Regum Anglo-Normannorum*, ed. H. W. C. Davis *et al.* (Oxford, 1913–69), ii. no. 490.
6. *Ibid.* nos. 544, 547, 548, 946–8, 959, 1291, 1379–80.
7. *Ibid.* no. 1000.
8. See J. H. Round, *The Commune of London* (Westminster, 1899), pp. 81–84.

who died sometime between 1086 and 1105, probably during Rufus' reign. William Mauduit attested no royal charters whatever and is not styled *camerarius* in *Domesday Book* or *Winton Domesday*, but a charter of Henry Plantagenet in 1153 states that he had been a chamberlain of the treasury and had passed the office on to his son, Robert Mauduit.¹ William Mauduit was another local Hampshire figure, with Domesday lands in that shire only, worth £37 15s. Significantly, these possessions included the coastal stronghold of Porchester, which was a major transfer point in the shipping of royal treasure from Winchester to Normandy in the twelfth century,² and which the 1153 charter associates with the Mauduit treasury chamberlainship. William Mauduit's possession of Porchester in 1086, and the evidence of the 1153 charter, combine to create a presumption that William held a treasury chamberlainship prior to the reign of Henry I.

However this may be, it is certain that his son Robert held the chamberlainship. Succeeding his father in 1105 or before,³ Robert attested no royal charters, but he is mentioned in the Pipe Roll of 1130 as having shared responsibility for the royal treasure at some undisclosed date prior to Michaelmas 1130, and in 1153 his younger brother was given the office as his heir.⁴ Thus, in the early years of Henry I's reign one can identify two chamberlains associated with the Winchester treasury – Robert Mauduit and Herbert; the latter was also styled 'treasurer', suggesting that he had direct and primary responsibility for the Winchester treasure house and its keys. As will be seen, it is of the highest importance to determine at what date these two men ceased to exercise their offices.

This problem has produced a great deal of confusion. G. H. White, followed by several other scholars, concluded that both men died around 1129 or 1130.⁵ White's argument runs as follows: (1) the 1130 Pipe Roll records a payment of relief by Herbert the Chamberlain's son for his father's lands, indicating that Herbert was recently dead⁶; (2) it appears from other evidence (to be

---

1. *Regesta*, iii. no. 582; see J. H. Round, 'Mauduit of Hartley Mauduit', *Ancestor* v (1903), 207–10, and Emma Mason, 'The Mauduits and their Chamberlainship of the Exchequer', *Bulletin of the Institute of Historical Research*, xlix (1976), 1–23.
2. See D. F. Renn, *Norman Castles in Britain* (London, 1968), p. 285.
3. *Regesta*, ii. no. 729.
4. *Pipe Roll 31 Henry I*, ed. Joseph Hunter (London, 1833), p. 37; *Regesta*, iii. no.582.
5. White, 'Financial Administration', pp. 61–62; *cf.* Richardson and Sayles, pp. 218, 221.
6. *Pipe Roll 31 Henry I*, p. 37; *cf.* p. 104, where a Herbert the Chamberlain is exempted from a pound of danegeld for lands in Bedfordshire. There is, however, no evidence – either from Domesday Book or from later feudal surveys – that Herbert or his family ever held lands in Bedfordshire. There may be a confusion here with an entirely unrelated Herbert the Chamberlain of the king of Scots who is becoming active around this time (*Regesta*, ii. no. 1930; *cf. Early Yorkshire Charters*, xi. 213–15). Herbert the Chamberlain of Scotland cannot be shown to have held in Bedfordshire, but David king of Scots was himself well endowed in that county and is exempted from

discussed shortly) that Herbert's treasury chamberlainship passed on his death or resignation to the *curialis* Geoffrey of Clinton; (3) another 1130 Pipe Roll passage shows Geoffrey of Clinton owing a debt for a loss of treasure while he was on duty with Robert Mauduit in Normandy[1]; (4) thus Geoffrey of Clinton succeeded Herbert before Robert Mauduit left office; (5) but another Pipe Roll entry proves that by 1130 the Mauduit lands had passed from Robert to his younger brother[2]; (6) therefore Robert Mauduit must have died sometime between Herbert's death or retirement *c.* 1129 and Michaelmas 1130.

This is ingenious reasoning. The difficulty is that it builds on the misapprehension that relief obligations in the 1130 Pipe Roll prove that the predecessor was recently dead. In reality Herbert the Chamberlain might have been dead for many years with the relief debt being paid off little by little.[3] The relief on Herbert the Chamberlain's lands in 1130 stands at the odd figure of 353 marks, suggesting strongly that it represents a balance after at least one and perhaps many previous payments.[4] The whole matter is conclusively settled by a passage in Simeon of Durham listing Robert Mauduit as one of the victims of the wreck of the White Ship in November 1120.[5] Simeon's testimony is confirmed by a pair of charters of 1120–2 arranging for the passing down of much of the Mauduit lands from Robert Mauduit to William, his brother and heir.[6] And the Pipe Roll passage showing Robert Mauduit sharing responsibility for the royal treasure in Normandy with Geoffrey of Clinton suggests strongly that Geoffrey had replaced Herbert the Chamberlain sometime prior to the White Ship disaster of 1120.[7] We know from another account that the White Ship was returning to England with the royal treasure after the successful conclusion of Henry I's

---

seventy-five shillings of danegeld in the same 1130 Bedfordshire entry (p. 104). King David had been in England at Henry I's court earlier in 1130: William Farrer, *An Outline Itinerary of King Henry I* (Oxford, 1920), p. 130.

1. *Pipe Roll 31 Henry I*, p. 37.

2. *Ibid.* p. 38.

3. This point is developed more fully in C. W. Hollister, 'The Misfortunes of the Mandevilles', above, pp. 121-2.

4. *Pipe Roll 31 Henry I*, p. 37; Richardson and Sayles, p. 218 and n. 6.

5. Simeon, ii. 259; *cf.* Orderic Vitalis, *Historia Ecclesiastica*, ed. A. le Prèvost (Paris, 1838–55), iv. 419, naming a *Rodbertus Malconductus* as one of the White Ship victims. The family of Mauconduit is distinct from that of Mauduit, but I can find no independent evidence of the existence of a Robert Mauconduit, and I suspect that Orderic intended *Rodbertus Maledoctus*. Whatever the case, Simeon's testimony is decisive.

6. *Regesta*, ii. 340; *Earldom of Gloucester Charters*, ed. R. B. Patterson (Oxford, 1973), no. 152. The charters cannot have been issued after 1122 because Henry I's son, the future earl of Gloucester, occurs in them as 'Robertus filius meus' and 'Robertus regis filius'. Robert became earl of Gloucester in 1121 or 1122 and always thereafter used his title: J. H. Round, *Geoffrey de Mandeville* (London, 1892), pp. 432-4.

7. Independent charter evidence suggests that Geoffrey had succeeded Herbert as treasurer no later than the mid-1120s: *Monasticon*, vi. 221, 223; *Regesta*, ii. no. 1428; *cf.* Richardson and Sayles, pp. 219-20.

greatest Norman war,[1] and it is reasonable to suppose that a treasury chamberlain would have been aboard. The emergency conditions of 1118–20 explain why the chamberlains of Henry I's Winchester treasury, and the treasure itself, would have been temporarily in Normandy.

At the height of Henry's military difficulties in 1118, a frightening though unsuccessful attempt was made on his life by certain un-identified members of his own household, led by a mysterious, unnamed chamberlain. We have two independent accounts of this assassination plot. Suger of Saint-Denis reports that the leader was a chamberlain whose name began with the letter H., who had been closely associated with the king and had been enriched and made famous by him. Henry I afterwards treated the would-be assassin with great mercy, Suger says, blinding and castrating him rather than hanging him as he deserved.[2] William of Malmesbury tells us simply that he was a certain chamberlain of low birth who rose to fame as custodian of the royal treasury. If he was as well known as Malmesbury and Suger assert, his name should appear somewhere in the records of the period, and yet he has never been identified. I suggest that the culprit was Herbert the Chamberlain, who was the only man known to have been styled treasurer at the time and the only known chamberlain in the entire reign to have a name begin-ning with H.[3] Herbert is such an obvious candidate that he would doubtless have been identified long before were it not for the deep-set tradition that he remained in office until 1129 or 1130. In reality we have seen that he had in all likelihood been succeeded by Geoffrey of Clinton in or before 1120. There is no charter or chronicle evidence of his being alive at any time after 1118; indeed, the charter evidence suggests that his lands had passed to his eldest son, Herbert fitz Herbert, by 1121.[4] Herbert fitz Herbert married Henry I's

1. Orderic, iv. 419.

2. Suger, *Vie de Louis VI le Gros*, ed. Henri Waquet (Paris, 1964), p. 190. Two later manuscripts extend the assassin's name, one of them to Hue, the other to Henry. Both seem to be guesses.

3. *Regesta*, ii. pp. xiii–xv. Herbert the Chamberlain acquired some properties in Yorkshire and Gloucestershire under Henry I (*Early Yorkshire Charters*, I, 35–38); at some point after 1086 he or his son acquired three knight's fees *in capite* in Berkshire and Wiltshire and sub-tenancies of the bishops of Winchester and Chichester and the abbot of Abingdon: *Red Book of the Exchequer*, ed. Hubert Hall (RS, 1896), I, 31, 45, 199, 205, 246, 307.

4. The latest definite date at which Herbert the Chamberlain's name occurs is 1111: *ibid*. no. 1000. A charter of Herbert fitz Herbert confirming his brother William's gift of Weaverthorpe Church to Nostell Priory (*Early Yorkshire Charters*, i. no. 26) is con-firmed by Thurstan archbishop of York (*ibid*. no. 27) and subsequently by Henry I in a solemn diploma of 1121–7, very probably 10 Jan. 1122 (*ibid*. iii. no. 1428 and n.; *Regesta*, ii. no. 1312). Henry's confirmation (original lost) is described by Farrer as 'doubtful' (*Itinerary*, p. 110 n. 3) but is accepted as authentic by the editors of *Regesta*, ii. The signators present no problems; Henry I's style, 'dei gratia rex Anglorum et dux Normannorum', although uncharacteristic of contemporary chancery practice, is quite acceptable in a beneficiary-drafted diploma such as is in question here. R. W. Eyton

mistress, Sibyl Corbet,[1] but on Herbert the Chamberlain's disgrace his chamberlainship and treasurership passed not to his son but to Geoffrey of Clinton. Herbert fitz Herbert survived, but in a state of almost total obscurity,[2] though his younger brother, William fitz Herbert, went on to a stormy career as archbishop of York in Stephen's reign and was subsequently canonized.[3]

Thus, after 1120 two new treasury chamberlains are serving the king: Geoffrey of Clinton succeeded Herbert, and William of Pont de l'Arche succeeded Robert Mauduit. Geoffrey is styled royal chamberlain and treasurer in records of the 1120s and appears in the 1130 Pipe Roll paying on a debt for a ministry of the Winchester treasury.[4] Geoffrey is a much more notable figure than his predecessors: he rose from the dust to become a major landholder and *curialis*, attesting ninety-four known charters of Henry I, serving as an itinerant justice, and enjoying a danegeld exemption in 1130 of fifty-nine pounds for lands in fourteen shires that must have been worth some 500 or 600 pounds a year.[5] William of Pont de l'Arche was less exalted but no less busy; he attested thirty-seven royal charters, served off and on as sheriff of several shires and farmed the vast royal estates of Arundel and Bosham.[6] He was exempted from ten pounds of danegeld for lands in seven shires, and he held additional lands in Hampshire which had previously belonged to the Mauduit family. By 1130 he seems to have become custodian

---

(*Antiquities of Shropshire*, London, 1854–60, vii. 149) found it puzzling that Herbert the Chamberlain's heirs could be granting at such an early date while their father lived until *c*. 1129, but this objection begs the whole question.

1. Eyton, vii. 149; *Complete Peerage* (rev. ed.), xi. Appendix D, p. 108.

2. Herbert fitz Herbert is styled *camerarius* in the Winchester Survey of 1148: *Winchester*, ed. Biddle, pp. 70, 73, 108, 127–30, and in a royal charter of 1155 to his son Robert: *Cartae Antiquae Rolls 11–20* (Pipe Roll Soc., 1960), no. 535. But he never attests for Henry I, Stephen or the Empress and is clearly not functioning as a royal chamberlain in these years. He is recorded in *P.R. 31 Henry I* (p. 37) as paying for his father's lands but not for his father's office.

3. Later hagiographical tradition did strange things to the family genealogy, leading more than one historian into the quicksand. See, for example, R. L. Poole, 'The Appointment and Deprivation of St. William, Archbishop of York', *E.H.R.* (1930), 273–81; and G. H. White, 'The Parentage of Herbert the Chamberlain', *Notes and Queries*, clxii (1932), 439–41, 453–5. Between pious legends that Herbert the Chamberlain was a count or earl and married to King Stephen's sister, and confusions with the unrelated family of Herbert the Chamberlain of Scotland, the genealogy has been badly tangled. Herbert the Chamberlain's parents are altogether unknown; for his wife (a daughter of Hunger fitz Odin) see J. H. Round, 'The Weigher of the Exchequer', *E.H.R.* (1911), 725. C. T. Clay disentangles the Scottish from the Winchester family in *Early Yorkshire Charters*, xi. 213–19.

4. *Regesta*, ii, xiii and no. 1428; *Pipe Roll 31 Henry I*, p. 105: Geoffrey pays 100 marks on a balance of 310 marks 'pro ministerio thesauri Wintoniae'. *Cf.* Richardson and Sayles, pp. 219–20. These writers incorrectly identify Geoffrey of Clinton with a Geoffrey who attested as chamberlain early in the reign. See *Regesta*, ii, viii, where the two Geoffreys appear together in a single witness list.

5. On Geoffrey see R. W. Southern, *Medieval Humanism* (Oxford, 1970), pp. 214–18.

6. *Regesta*, ii. *passim*; *Pipe Roll 31 Henry I*, pp. 42 and *passim*. At one time or another he was sheriff of Hants., Berks., Wilts. and Sussex.

and key-keeper of the Winchester treasury, for he is listed in the Pipe Roll as the responsible official during a treasury audit and is described as being in charge of the Winchester treasury at the beginning of Stephen's reign.[1]

William of Pont de l'Arche's Mauduit lands came to him through his marriage to a daughter of Robert Mauduit.[2] On Robert's death he obtained not only the Mauduit chamberlainship but also certain properties pertaining to it, including Porchester Castle – the transfer point for treasure shipments to Normandy.[3] In 1153 Henry Plantagenet returned Porchester to the Mauduit family and the treasury chamberlainship along with it. Richardson and Sayles have objected strongly and at length to the notion, originally proposed by John Horace Round, that the treasury chamberlainships were sergeanties, carrying specified lands with them. But the fact that Porchester, and certain associated Hampshire manors, pass with the chamberlainship from the Mauduits to William of Pont de l'Arche and then back to the Mauduits creates the strong implication that this chamberlainship was indeed a sergeanty. And such is the tenor of Henry Plantagenet's grant to William Mauduit in 1153: Henry gives him 'the chamberlainship of my treasury with its allowances and with all its appurtenances, that is, the castle of Porchester, as I have said above, and all lands pertaining to the said chamberlainship and to the said castle. . .'.[4]

The *Constitutio Domus Regis* of *c.* 1136 describes, among the foremost offices of the king's household, the office of treasurer. The incumbent treasurer is unnamed, but he ranks alongside the chancellor, stewards, master butler and constables as a household officer of the first rank. His livery is the same as those of the master chamberlain and the stewards 'if he is at court and serves in the treasury (*in thesaurio*)'. This ambiguous phrase from the *Red Book of*

1. *Ibid.* pp. 129–31; Round, *Commune,* pp. 76 ff.; above, p. 263, n. 5; Richardson and Sayles, p. 222. William of Pont de l'Arche also purchased the separate office of chamberlain of the itinerant court treasury – the *camera curiae* (*Pipe Roll 31 Henry I,* p. 37); his brother Osbert likewise held an office in the *camera curiae* (*ibid.* pp. 37, 63), as did William Mauduit (*ibid.* p. 134; *cf.* 'Constitutio Domus Regis', p. 133). The rise in status of the treasury chamberlains during Henry's reign is suggested by the prominence assigned by contemporary writers to William of Pont de l'Arche as key-keeper in 1135 (Malmesbury, *Historia Novella,* p. 15; *Gesta Stephani,* p. 8), as compared with the un-named *excubitores* from whom Henry I obtained the keys to the Winchester treasury in 1100: Orderic, iv. 87–88.

2. *Pipe Roll 31 Henry I,* p. 37. William of Pont de l'Arche received all or most of Robert Mauduit's English lands, whereas William Mauduit, Robert's younger brother, received Robert's Norman lands and their mother's lands in England, and was given an office in the *camera curiae: ibid.* pp. 38, 134; *Regesta,* ii. 340.

3. That William of Pont de l'Arche obtained Porchester is proven by the fact that he founded a priory within its walls late in Henry I's reign: J. C. Dickinson, *The Origins of the Austin Canons* (London, 1950), p. 124; *cf. Regesta,* ii. 340.

4. *Ibid.* iii. no. 582. Porchester reverted to the crown soon afterwards. The matter is discussed in detail, but misunderstood I believe, in Richardson and Sayles, p. 432.

the Exchequer is rendered by the somewhat later but more complete Black Book MS. 'if he is at court and serves as treasurer (*ut thesaurarius*)'.[1] Neither version is satisfactory, but it does seem clear that the treasurer is paid while serving at court. And since the basic subject of the *Constitutio* is the composition of the itinerant royal household of the Anglo–Norman state,[2] we are evidently dealing here with a great ministry entirely distinct from the treasury chamberlainships and custodianships discussed thus far. In Henry II's reign the three major fiscal offices are those of the two chamberlainships of the treasury (or exchequer), and the great treasurer himself.[3] The treasurer of the *Constitutio* is a major court figure, presumably with authority in England and Normandy alike, whereas the treasury chamberlains were closely tied to Winchester. The persons of the earlier Anglo-Norman period who bear the title 'treasurer' – Henry, Herbert and Geoffrey of Clinton – are all associated specifically with Winchester: Henry and Herbert held all their properties in or near the city; Geoffrey of Clinton's office is described explicitly in the Pipe Roll as a ministry of the Winchester treasury. William of Pont de l'Arche's office is likewise described as the ministry that had previously belonged to the Mauduits – a local Hampshire family.[4] None of these men can have occupied the high office of court treasurer.

William of Malmesbury informs us that in Henry I's reign it was Roger bishop of Salisbury who controlled the royal expenditure and the treasure.[5] But Roger cannot have been the first court treasurer, because under Henry I household offices were of only moderate distinction and were never occupied by bishops or earls. Chancellors, for example, often rose to bishoprics in this period, but when they did so they invariably vacated their chancellorships. Bishops were enormously active in Henry's administration, but never did they demean themselves by holding household titles. This explains in part why historians have been so puzzled as to whether Roger of Salisbury was Henry I's justiciar, or procurator, or what. As the foremost royal administrator of the last half of Henry's reign, he was described by several informal titles, but his one official title was 'bishop of Salisbury'.

The point must be emphasized that the *Constitutio Domus Regis* describes not the English court or the Norman court, but the single, itinerant royal court that perambulated between England and

1. 'Constitutio Domus Regis', p. 133; *cf*. White, 'Financial Administration', pp. 64–65; Tout, i. 86.
2. White, 'Household of the Norman Kings', pp. 127–55.
3. *Dialogus de Scaccario*, pp. 7, 16–17, 20.
4. William also purchased a ministry of the *camera curiae* (above, n. 42), but if this had been the office of treasurer it would surely have been called so. Nowhere in the records is William styled *thesaurarius*.
5. *Historia Novella*, p. 37.

Normandy. Thus, the treasurer of the *Constitutio* would deal not only with the Winchester treasury but likewise with the treasury at Rouen – where Haskins identified a line of local Norman treasurers[1] – and with other centres where treasury business was done or treasure stored – centres such as London.[2] The one person who fits the description of this ministry is Nigel, Roger of Salisbury's nephew and later bishop of Ely.[3] Since, as Malmesbury tells us, Roger of Salisbury had exercised general supervision over the royal finances, it is natural that he should select his able and well-trained nephew to fill the new court office. Nigel begins to be styled 'treasurer' around the mid-1120s, and he is so titled by his son, Richard fitz Nigel, in his *Dialogus de Scaccario*, by Alexander Swereford in the thirteenth-century *Red Book of the Exchequer*, and by the mid-twelfth-century author of the *Liber Eliensis*.[4] Nigel was almost constantly at court. He begins attesting royal charters around the mid-1120s, and during the remaining decade of the reign attests no less than thirty-one surviving charters, which marks him as one of the fourteen or fifteen most frequent charter witnesses of this period. His activities embraced England and Normandy: he had property at Winchester and in Middlesex (probably Westminster); he attested as treasurer in Rouen and is known to have had dealings with the Norman treasury there.[5] He left the office in 1133 upon his elevation to the bishopric of Ely, but he continued to busy himself with royal affairs in London and at the king's court in Normandy during the final two years of the reign – much to the annoyance of the Ely monks who disliked the deputy he left behind to run the bishopric.[6]

As the court treasurership came into being in the mid-1120s, the term 'treasurer' which had previously been applied in England to the Winchester custodian was now reserved exclusively for the great household officer. It is in this context that Nigel was the first royal treasurer, despite the title having formerly been given to Henry the Treasurer, Herbert, and Geoffrey of Clinton. Nigel's title was old but his office was new. And as its first holder, he began the long

---

1. C. H. Haskins, *Norman Institutions* (Cambridge, Mass., 1918), pp. 106–10: Gilbert, William, and Robert of Évreux. But see the critique by G. H. White, 'Treasurers in Normandy under Henry I', *Notes and Queries*, cl (1926), 59–60.
2. On treasury business at London see *Liber Eliensis*, ed. E. O. Blake (Royal Historical Society, London, 1962), p. 284. One of Henry I's chamberlains, William of Houghton, bore the title 'chamberlain of London': *Pipe Roll 31 Henry I*, p. 145; *Cartularium Monasterii de Rameseia*, ed. P. A. Lyons (Rolls Series, 1884–93), i. 142–4; *Chron. Abingdon*, i. 53, 128; *Victoria County History, Bedford*, i. 197; *Regesta*, iii. no. 746.
3. In advancing Nigel's name I am following Liebermann, pp. 16–17, and Lucien Valin, *Le Duc de Normandie et sa cour* (Paris, 1910), p. 163. *Cf.* H. G. Richardson, 'William of Ely, The King's Treasurer', *Transactions of the Royal Historical Society*, 4th ser., xv (1932), 45–46. For contrary views see above, p. 209.
4. Richardson and Sayles, p. 220; Haskins, p. 108; *Regesta*, ii. xiv and no. 1691; *Dialogus de Scaccario*, p. 50; *Red Book of the Exchequer*, i. 4; *Liber Eliensis*, p. 284.
5. *Pipe Roll 31 Henry I*, pp. 41, 54, 63, 152; *Regesta*, ii. no. 1691 n.
6. *Ibid.* nos. 1902, 1908–9; *Liber Eliensis*, p. 284.

tradition of churchman-treasurers that ran through much of the Middle Ages. He also began a ninety-year tradition of the treasurership being occupied by members of a single ecclesiastical dynasty, founded by Roger of Salisbury.[1]

There is no clear evidence that Nigel had an immediate successor. When he left office in 1133, Henry I may have permitted the treasurership to remain vacant, the duties being performed unofficially by Roger of Salisbury and Nigel, and perhaps also by the master chamberlain, whose office was revived at the exact moment that Nigel vacated the treasurership.[2] But we know that Stephen, shortly after his coronation, appointed as his treasurer Adelelm, another kinsman of Roger bishop of Salisbury.[3] Adelelm lost his office on his family's disgrace in 1139, and we have no evidence of another royal treasurer until about 1158 or 1159 when Henry II appointed Bishop Nigel's son, Richard fitz Nigel. When Richard was later advanced to the bishopric of London, he was succeeded by his kinsman William of Ely.[4] Only when William of Ely left office at the end of John's reign did the treasurership pass from the grasp of Bishop Roger's dynasty.[5]

In short, the treasurership of the *Constitutio Domus Regis* was a new household office, established by Henry I and Roger of Salisbury in the mid-1120s. The Anglo-Norman treasury did not separate gradually from the curia, as household offices would later do. In a sense, the treasurer rejoined the court. The process of reunion was

1. This tradition may have been broken once, briefly, by an otherwise unknown treasurer named William, who occurs in the Pipe Roll of 1156, p. 47 (*cf. ibid.* p. 16 where an unnamed 'treasurer' occurs): H. G. Richardson, 'Richard fitz Neal and the Dialogus de Scaccario, *E.H.R*, xliii (1928), 163.

2. The master chamberlainship, vacant since *c.* 1105, was given to Aubrey II de Vere in mid-1133 as a part of a general household reorganization. The chancellor, Geoffrey Rufus, was raised to the bishopric of Durham at just this time and his office seems to have been left vacant for the remainder of Henry I's reign; the duties of the chancellor apparently passed to the master of the writing office, whose emoluments were increased: *Regesta*, ii. no. 1777; Charles Johnson, 'The Last Chancellor of Henry I', *E.H.R.* (1952), 392. Aubrey de Vere was appointed 'master chamberlain of all England' but was with Henry I in Normandy during the king's last visit, 1133–5: *Regesta*, ii. nos. 1913–15, 1960. A certain 'Roger the Treasurer' attested at Caen in 1135 a charter of Henry I which is also attested by Nigel of Ely (*ibid.* no. 1909). This mysterious Roger may possibly have been Nigel's otherwise unknown successor as court treasurer (conceivably Roger of Salisbury's son, Roger 'the Poor' who became chancellor under King Stephen?); but he may just as likely have been a Norman treasurer only. Haskins, without compelling reason, identifies him as Roger of Fécamp (pp. 107, 110). If Roger the Treasurer is indeed only a local Norman figure, then it may well be that Henry I had no court treasurer during the last two years of his reign. If so, the offices of court treasurer and master chamberlain would never have had concurrent occupants under Henry I, which might explain the peculiar juxtaposition of the two offices in the 'Constitutio Domus Regis' (p. 133).

3. *Thame Cartulary*, ed. H. E. Salter (Oxfordshire Record Society, 1947), i. 2; *Regesta*, iii. xix; Malmesbury, *Historia Novella*, p. 39. Adelelm subsequently became dean of Lincoln Cathedral.

4. *Handbook of British Chronology*, p. 99; Richardson, 'William of Ely', pp. 45–47, 79.

5. *Ibid.* pp. 45–90.

accompanied by a gradual elevation of the early 'treasurers' from local Hampshire nonentities like Henry the Treasurer to chamberlain-treasurers like Herbert and Geoffrey of Clinton, the latter being a considerable landholder and frequent attestor. Finally, the office is altogether transformed into a major household position and filled by the well-educated *curialis*, Nigel *nepos episcopi*, at home equally in Winchester, Westminster and Rouen, but most at home in the king's court, wherever it might be. The later process of depart-mentalization was thus preceded, at least in this instance, by a process of curialization.[1] But this process is actually an illusion, created by tracing the abstraction of the 'treasurership'. The reality is continued curial control throughout most of the Anglo-Norman period, centering on various great court administrators – Roger of Salisbury, and perhaps before him Eudo the Steward and Ranulf Flambard[2] – none of them officially treasurers. Next to them, a Winchester custodian like Henry the Treasurer is a small fish indeed; his role is that of a watchman, not a 'department head'. Henry the Treasurer is a royal servant on more-or-less permanent local assignment from the perambulating court. His *custos* suc-cessors draw closer to the court, gaining in wealth and stature as they do.

At just this time the exchequer process was coming into being, not as a separate office or ministry, but as a semi-annual audit of the sheriffs' accounts, performed by treasury officials joined by other *curiales*. The twelfth-century exchequer was not a department but an occasion. Its staff was the treasury staff; its records were treasury records; and its receipts went directly into the treasury. Henry I's administrators regularly conducted two exchequer audits con-currently, one in England (probably at Winchester), the other in Normandy (at Rouen or Caen). Fiscal administration thus became steadily more complex, and by the mid-1120s it was decided to create a new official to supervise the entire trans-Channel system. By 1130 the pattern of treasurer and two Winchester treasury chamberlains was firmly established, with Nigel serving as treasurer and Geoffrey of Clinton and William of Pont de l'Arche as the two chamberlains.

There is nothing vague about these three offices: they were sold by the king for set amounts and carried fixed emoluments. Chamber-lainships and treasurerships were thus clearly defined, and there can

---

1. *Cf.* the similar process at the papal court: Geoffrey Barraclough, *The Medieval Papacy* (New York, 1968), p. 99.

2. On Eudo's financial role early in Henry I's reign see *Regesta*, ii. no. 490. (Eudo died in 1120 but ceased to be active at court *c.* 1110.) On Ranulf Flambard as William II's *exactor*, or *gastaldus*, or *publicanus* see R. W. Southern, 'Ranulf Flambard and Early Anglo-Norman Administration', *Transactions of the Royal Historical Society*, 4th series, xvi (1933), 99–101. On Roger of Salisbury, see Malmesbury, *Historia Novella*, pp. 15, 37.

TABLE

Treasury Chamberlain 1	Treasury Chamberlain 2	Court Treasurer
Herbert, Domesday *camerarius*; subsequently titled *thesaurarius* (fl. 1086; deprived *c.* 1118)	Henry, Domesday *thesaurarius* (fl. 1086; d. 1086/*c.* 1110)	
	?William Mauduit, Domesday lord of Porchester (d. 1086/1105)	
	Robert Mauduit, lord of Porchester (1086/1105–1120)	
Geoffrey of Clinton, *thesaurarius* (*c.* 1118–1132/3)	William of Pont de l'Arche, lord of Porchester (*c.* 1120–*c.* 1143)	Nigel *nepos Episcopi* (mid-1120s–1133)
		Adelelm (1135/6–1139)
		Richard fitz Nigel (1158/9–1196)
		William of Ely (1196–1215)
Warin fitz Gerold and heirs (*c.* 1155/6 ff.)	William Mauduit and heirs (1153 ff.)	

have been no question at the time as to who held them. But the actual functions of their occupants varied enormously. The financial system continued to function, for example, after the treasurership was apparently vacated in 1133; one of the two chamberlainships seems to have been left unfilled for some time after Geoffrey of Clinton's death around 1132. And at Henry I's own death in Normandy in 1135, we learn that much of the royal treasure had been brought from Winchester to the Norman castle of Falaise, where it was under the control of Henry's bastard son, Robert earl of Gloucester.[1] This information permits us to conclude on a note of humility. After laboriously tracing official treasury titles and their holders, we find the royal treasure at Henry I's death stored neither at the Winchester treasury nor at the treasury at Rouen, and we find it supervised by a man who was neither treasury chamberlain

1. Orderic, v. 50; Robert of Torigny, *Chronicle*, in *Chronicles of the Reigns of Stephen, Henry II, and Richard I*, ed. Richard Howlett (Rolls Series, 1884–9), iv. 129.

nor master chamberlain nor treasurer. Robert of Gloucester was a clever and wealthy man, and the king's favourite bastard – and that tells us a great deal about the actual functioning of the Anglo-Norman government.

13

THE RISE OF ADMINISTRATIVE KINGSHIP: HENRY I

HENRY I, THE YOUNGEST AND ABLEST of William the Conqueror's sons, built an administrative system extraordinary for its day, more effective and, to some, more oppressive than any government the transalpine West had known since the time of the Roman Empire. To a remarkable degree, Henry's government kept the peace in England and Normandy alike.[1] Albert Brackmann has described it as "a new type of political organization" that "set the development of European civilization on a new course."[2] But despite its precociousness, Henry's regime was not the total novelty that Brackmann's enthusiastic phrases suggest. The king and his administrators were as inclined to adapt as to invent, and it is not always easy to distinguish their innovations from their adaptations.

As a son of William the Conqueror, Henry drew on the strong political traditions of both the Norman dukes and the Anglo-Saxon kings. The authority of the pre-Conquest duke of Normandy had surpassed that of all other French princes, including the king of France. The ducal court moved constantly about the duchy dispensing justice, issuing charters, supervising the collection of revenues and the minting of coins. Ducal kinsmen served as counts of the major frontier districts—Mortain, Eu, Évreux—and Duke William commanded their direct obedience as well as that of his regional officials, the vicomtes.[3] The Anglo-Saxon royal administration, which William had seized and perpetuated, was more effective still. As ruler of England the Conqueror inherited a well-articulated system of shires and sheriffs, shire courts and hundred courts, and at the center an ambulatory royal entourage that exercised an unusual degree of control over the kingdom's military and fiscal resources. William gained control of a royal chancery which had developed that potent instrument of monarchical authority, the sealed writ. He likewise took possession of the royal treasury at Winchester, along with a revenue system well designed to keep it filled. The system included set sheriffs' farms, a tight grip on the kingdom's mints and minters, and a unique property tax—the danegeld—collected through a comprehensive assessment network of hundreds and wapentakes, hides and carucates.

---

[1] C. Warren Hollister and Thomas K. Keefe, "The Making of the Angevin Empire," see below, chapter 14: 250-1. William of Malmesbury credited Henry with giving Normandy "a peace such as no age remembers, such as his father himself . . . was never able to effect"; William of Malmesbury, *Gesta Regum Anglorum*, ed. William Stubbs, Rolls Series, no. 90, vol. 2 (London, 1889): 476.

[2] Brackmann, "The Beginnings of the National State in Medieval Germany and the Norman Monarchies," in Geoffrey Barraclough, ed. and trans., *Medieval Germany, 911–1250: Essays by German Historians* (Oxford, 1948), 287–88.

[3] See C. Warren Hollister, "Normandy, France, and the Anglo-Norman *Regnum*," above, chapter 2: 20, references cited therein; and R. C. Van Caenegem, ed., *Royal Writs in England from the Conquest to Glanvill: Studies in the Early History of the Common Law*, Selden Society, no. 77 (London, 1959), 57–58.

In the years after 1066 a tenurial revolution swept away the Old English landed aristocracy and replaced it with a northern French—largely Norman—aristocracy. The English lands of this new aristocracy usually consisted not of compact territorial blocs but of manorial clusters, large and small, scattered across a number of shires. The Conqueror's half-brother Robert, count of Mortain, for example, held lands in twenty shires and Hugh, earl of Chester, in nineteen. This dispersion of great estates, including the king's own, was of fundamental importance to the growth of royal government. As Sir Richard Southern has explained, "It was tenurial complexity that gave royal officials their opportunities, by making all free tenants more or less equal in the royal courts, and inducing all men, however great, to acquiesce in the growth of royal justice."[4]

As a consequence of the dispersion of great estates and of administrative tightening under William the Conqueror and William Rufus, Henry I inherited in 1100 a government considerably more effective than it had been in 1066. The king's control of litigation had grown appreciably through the practice of sending teams of royal justices on *ad hoc* commissions to settle important disputes and the appointment of local justiciars to handle pleas of the crown in the shires and hundreds. Royal revenues were much higher than before, thanks to the doubling of the king's demesne lands during the post-Conquest settlement, the mass of data collected in the Domesday survey, and the fiscal chicanery of Rufus's chief minister, Ranulf Flambard. Immediately after his accession Henry I put the unpopular Flambard into the Tower of London as a highly visible act of public relations. More significantly, however, Henry won the support of virtually all of Rufus's remaining administrators and kept them in office alongside new men from his own entourage.[5] He had no intention of dismissing Rufus's officials and starting from scratch.

THE DOMINATING THEME OF HENRY I'S GOVERNMENT was centralization. Only later would household offices begin to drift out of the itinerant court and settle down as departments. Henry's reign saw the converse trend toward ever-tightening control by the *curia regis*. Both Southern and the collaborators Henry G. Richardson and George O. Sayles refer to Henry's administration as a "machine";[6] if so, it was a machine powered by a single piston. The king's court, incessantly moving across England and Normandy, was the chief source of royal justice, governance, and patronage. Its membership

[margin note: order in source]

---

[4] Southern, *Medieval Humanism and Other Studies* (Oxford, 1970), 229. This fragmentation of holdings probably resulted both from estates being granted at various times during the course of the post-1066 consolidation and from pre-Conquest land patterns often being similarly dispersed, though to a lesser degree. See Reginald V. Lennard, *Rural England, 1086–1135* (Oxford, 1959), 28–39.

[5] C. Warren Hollister, "The Anglo-Norman Civil War: 1101," see above, chapter 4, pp. 80-1; and "Magnates and *Curiales* in Early Norman England," above, chapter 5, pp. 97-115.

[6] Southern, *Medieval Humanism*, 210; and Richardson and Sayles, *The Governance of Mediaeval England from the Conquest to Magna Carta* (Edinburgh, 1963), 163, *passim*.

fluctuated constantly. Some were almost always in attendance, others frequently so, and others occasionally or rarely. Besides officials and servants of the royal household, the court included a less structured group of royal advisers and *familiares*. It also might include visiting foreign princes, royal and comital heirs-apparent and bastards with their tutors and servants, camp followers, and plaintiffs and favor-seekers from the neighborhoods through which the court traveled or, sometimes, from afar.

Until early in Henry's reign, the Anglo-Norman *curia regis* was a disorganized, predatory mob. Eadmer of Canterbury told chilling tales of Rufus's entourage plundering and destroying the countryside, laying waste to all of the lands through which the king passed, taking indecent liberties with local wives and daughters, getting drunk on stolen wine and, when they could drink no more, washing their horses' feet with it and pouring the rest on the ground.[7] Henry I put an end to all this. He issued strict regulations limiting the practice of requisitioning and establishing fixed prices for local purchases. He also established specific offices and allowances for his household and stipends for magnates in attendance, arranging that everyone in his retinue should receive set payments for their subsistence.[8]

At the heart of the *curia* was the royal household staff, whose organization and fixed allowances were recorded in detail in the *Constitutio Domus Regis* of circa 1136. The chief household officers, echoing Continental custom, were the chancellor, stewards, master butler, master chamberlain, and constables. To these traditional ministers Henry added a new one—the household treasurer. Scholars used to dispute whether the *Constitutio Domus Regis* described the English household or the Norman, but they now generally agree that the *domus regis* accompanied the king wherever he might be.[9] The frequency with which Henry's household officers attested royal or administrative *acta* emanating from Normandy and from England supports this conclusion, at least to a degree. When due weight is given to the survival of Henry's English charters in far greater numbers than his Norman charters, it becomes clear that most of Henry's household officials regularly crossed with the *curia* and attested with some frequency on both sides of the Channel (see Table 1). But certain household officials concentrated their activities on one side of the Channel or the other. The steward Robert de la Haye attested a great many royal acts in Normandy but very few in England, and the same is true of the chamberlains William fitz Odo and William of Glastonbury and, to a lesser extent, the steward Robert of Courcy. Conversely, certain household officers attested charters primarily from England: the steward Adam of Port and the con-

---

[7] Eadmer, *Historia Novorum in Anglia*, ed. Martin Rule, Rolls Series, no. 81 (London, 1884), 192–93. Also see the *Anglo-Saxon Chronicle*, A.D. 1097 (Rufus), 1101 (Robert Curthose), and 1104 (early Henry I).

[8] Eadmer, *Historia Novorum in Anglia*, 193; Malmesbury, *Gesta Regum Anglorum*, 487; and Walter Map, *De Nugis Curialium*, ed. M. R. James (Oxford, 1914), 219, 235.

[9] For the *Constitutio Domus Regis*, see Charles Johnson, ed., *Dialogus de Scaccario* (London, 1950), 129–35. And see G. H. White, "The Household of the Norman Kings," *Transactions of the Royal Historical Society*, 4th ser., 30 (1948): 127–59; H. W. C. Davis et al., eds., *Regesta Regum Anglo-Normannorum*, 4 vols. (Oxford, 1913–69), 2: ix–xvii; and, most recently, John Le Patourel, *The Norman Empire* (Oxford, 1976), 135–37.

TABLE 1
Officers of the Royal Household, 1130

Office	Officers of the Household
Chancellor	Geoffrey Rufus* [XE]
Keeper of the Seal	Robert *de Sigillo** [X]
Stewards	Hugh Bigod* [X]
	Humphrey of Bohun* [X]
	Robert of Courcy [XN]ᵃ
	Robert de la Haye* [N]
	(?) William Martel [X]
	(?) Robert fitz Richard (Clare) [X]
Master Butler	William of Aubigny *Pincerna** [X]
Treasurer	Nigel *nepos episcopi** (bp. of Ely, 1133 ff.) [X]
Chamberlains of the Winchester Treasury	William of Pont de l'Arche* [X]
	Geoffrey of Clinton* [X]
Chamberlains of the Camera Curiae	William of Pont de l'Arche* [X]
	Osbert of Pont de l'Arche [X (?)]
	William Mauduit [X]
Chamberlain of England and Normandy	(?) Rabel of Tancarville [N]ᵇ
Norman Chamberlains (?)	William fitz Odo [N]ᶜ
	William of Glastonbury [N]
Constables	Robert de Vere* [X]
	Miles of Gloucester* [E]
	Robert of Oilli [XE]
	Walter of Beauchamp [E]
	Brian fitz Count* (attested as constable in 1131) [XN]
Assistant Constables(?)	Roger of Oilli [E]
	Henry de la Pommeraie [X]
Marshals	John fitz Gilbert [X]
	Wigan the Marshal [N (?)]

NOTE: An asterisk (*) designates a *curialis*; for a definition of a *curialis*, see page 242, below; and, for Henry's *curiales*, see Table 4, below. In their roles as attestors of royal acts, E = 91–100 percent English attestations; XE = 81–90 percent English; X = 51–80 percent English; XN = 50–64 percent Norman; and N = 65–100 percent Norman. (Some adjustment has been made for the greater survival expectancy of charters from England; pre-1106 charters have been excluded from all computations regarding English versus Norman attestations.)

ᵃ Robert of Courcy attested thirty-seven acts between 1113 and 1135 (1.7 per year), but thirty-five of those attestations occurred between 1126 and 1135 (4.1 per year).

ᵇ Rabel "inherited" the Anglo-Norman chamberlainship from his father, William of Tancarville* [X], who died in 1129. But there is no concrete evidence that Rabel performed any functions of the chamberlainship under Henry I. In 1133 the *curialis* Aubrey de Vere received the master chamberlainship "of all England" but he was at times with Henry in Normandy between 1133 and 1135; see *Regesta Regum Anglo-Normannorum*, 2: nos. 1777, 1913–15, 1960.

ᶜ William fitz Odo averaged 1.9 attestations per year, which places him about thirty-second among attestors active in 1130. But the disproportionate loss of Norman acts causes a systematic underestimation of the curial activity of primarily Norman attestors. See Table 4, below.

stables Walter of Beauchamp, Walter and Miles of Gloucester, and Nigel and Robert of Oilli.[10]

This same kind of attestation analysis can help to illuminate the administrative activities of Henry's chancellors: Ranulf (1107–22) and Geoffrey Rufus (1123–33) both attest enormous numbers of surviving royal acts, some from Normandy but far more from England.[11] When Henry was in Normandy, his chancellor was often away from the itinerant court, engaged in administrative work in England. And, since the Anglo-Norman chancery was inseparable from the royal court, the household *scriptorium* must have often functioned without the chancellor's direct supervision. During the latter half of Henry's reign, the chancery staff included about four scribes, under the direction of a subchancellor known as the *magister scriptorii* or keeper of the king's seal.[12] Robert *de Sigillo* occupied this office from 1121 to 1135, and his nearly one hundred attestations, nicely balanced between England and Normandy, suggest that he was regularly with the king's court. The frequency and ease with which the chancery functioned without the chancellor's presence doubtless influenced Henry's decision to leave the chancellorship vacant after Geoffrey Rufus's promotion to the bishopric of Durham in 1133 and may also explain why Henry was willing to double Robert *de Sigillo*'s wages.[13]

That an important minority of royal household officials concentrated their activities on only one side of the Channel is not surprising. Once he had rejoined the duchy to the kingdom, Henry had to depend on some sort of regional governing body to supervise Normandy when he was in England and to administer England when he was in Normandy. His predecessors, William I and William II, faced with the same problem of dual governance, had handled it with a variety of *ad hoc* arrangements. William I left the kingdom in the charge of various great men at different times—men like William fitz Osbern; Odo, bishop of Bayeux; and Archbishop Lanfranc. The Conqueror

---

[10] The responsibilities of Walter and Miles of Gloucester (father and son) included the custody of Gloucester Castle, Walter of Beauchamp's constableship seems to have been associated with Worcester Castle, and Nigel and Robert of Oilli (father and son) were responsible for Oxford Castle; *Regesta Regum Anglo-Normannorum*, 2: xv–xvi. Robert of Oilli, although he attested heavily in England, was rather more active in Normandy than his father had been. Between Henry's conquest of Normandy in 1106 and his death in 1135, he spent about 210 months in Normandy and 140 in England; Le Patourel, *Norman Empire*, 124, 175–76. But, of approximately 980 charters issued during these years, in which the place of origin can be definitely or probably determined, about 765 emanated from England and only about 215 from Normandy. This information, and much that follows, has been drawn from comprehensive (but as yet unpublished) tables prepared by Brian A. Foster that measure the English and Norman attestations of all of Henry I's *curiales*. Foster's study of attestations and crossings will, when completed, provide a far more rigorous analysis of the problem than has been possible here.

[11] Ranulf attested 163 charters, of which 134 are certainly or probably from England and 22 certainly or probably from Normandy; of Geoffrey Rufus's 115 attestations, about 95 are English and about 15 are Norman (a few are of undetermined origin). Even allowing for the much greater survival rate of English charters, it remains clear that both men were often in England while their king was in Normandy.

[12] T. A. M. Bishop, *Scriptores Regis* (Oxford, 1961), 30. From an analysis of scribal hands, Bishop has identified two royal scribes active at Henry's accession in 1100; their number had risen at least to four by mid-reign and seems to have remained at about that level until Henry's death.

[13] For Robert, see *Regesta Regum Anglo-Normannorum*, 2: x; and Johnson, *Dialogus de Scaccario*, 129. Of Robert's attestations 56 percent are from England, 44 percent from Normandy. His contemporary, the chancellor Geoffrey Rufus, attested 86 percent from England, 14 percent from Normandy. On the probable vacancy of the chancellorship after 1133, see Charles Johnson, "The Last Chancellor of Henry I," *EHR*, 67 (1952): 392.

likewise entrusted Normandy to such notables as Queen Matilda, Roger of Montgomery, and Roger, lord of Beaumont. Under William Rufus, whose joint rule of Normandy and England only extended from 1096 to 1100, the first hint of a more specialized English viceregency appeared. Initially, William II's omnicompetent royal minister, Ranulf Flambard, served as coregent with Walchelin, bishop of Winchester; but in 1099 Rufus committed England to Flambard alone, to be assisted by two administrative lieutenants of only moderate wealth—Hamo the Steward, sheriff of Kent, and Urse of Abitôt, sheriff of Worcestershire.[14]

These administrative beginnings, aborted by Rufus's death in August 1100, foreshadowed the development of more stable and elaborate viceregal arrangements in the years following Henry's conquest of Normandy in 1106. From about 1107 onward the Norman viceregal court was headed by John, bishop of Lisieux, whose numerous attestations of royal charters disclose that he was almost constantly at Henry's side in Normandy but seldom crossed with the king to England. His name occurs at the heads of lists of Norman justices, usually followed by that of the seneschal or steward, Robert de la Haye, whose overwhelmingly Norman attestations suggest that his administrative responsibilities were limited primarily to the duchy.[15] He was evidently the chief layman in the Norman viceregal court and its second in command. Others active in the Norman viceregency include the household officials William of Glastonbury and Robert of Courcy, whose names occur chiefly in the Norman records of the reign.[16]

Charles Homer Haskins rigorously examined the personnel of Henry's Norman courts more than sixty years ago, and little has since been added to his fundamental work.[17] But it is now possible, through comprehensive attestation analyses, to sift out the predominantly Norman figures from the cross-Channel *curiales* whose names sometimes appear in Norman documents as judges and administrative officials. A panel of judges hearing a Norman plea of A.D. 1111 included Geoffrey, archbishop of Rouen (who attested chiefly in Normandy), and the Norman "viceroy"—John, bishop of Lisieux—along

---

[14] David C. Douglas, *William the Conqueror* (London, 1964), 185–86, 207, *passim*; and Southern, *Medieval Humanism*, 189. Bishop Walchelin died in January 1098, and Flambard was advanced to the bishopric of Durham in June 1099, before becoming sole regent. The sources are silent on Rufus's viceregal administration in Normandy.

[15] On Henry's Norman viceregency, see Charles Homer Haskins, *Norman Institutions* (Cambridge, Mass., 1918), 88–104; and Lucien Valin, *Le Duc de Normandie et sa cour (912–1203)* (Paris, 1910), 108–09. Of John's attestations, 88 percent are from Normandy, and the percentage would doubtless have been higher still had Henry's Norman charters survived in numbers comparable to those of his English charters. Of Robert's attestations, 96 percent pertain to royal acts emanating from Normandy. He was active in the Norman administration from 1118 or earlier to the end of the reign; see *Regesta Regum Anglo-Normannorum*, 2: nos. 1183–1901 *passim*; and Table 4, below. Lord of La-Haye-du-Puits in western Normandy, he (or possibly a kinsman of the same name) held considerable lands in Lincolnshire worth £78 in 1086 and pardoned £8 of danegeld in 1130. For a brief biographical sketch, see John Le Patourel, *Normandy and England, 1066–1144* (Reading, 1971), 34–35.

[16] Haskins, *Norman Institutions*, 88–89, 120, 307; and *Regesta Regum Anglo-Normannorum*, 2: nos. 1184, 1352, 1422, 1579, 1593. Also see *ibid.*, 1584.

[17] See, however, Jean Yver, "Le développement du pouvoir ducal en Normandie de l'avènement de Guillaume le Conquérant à la mort d'Henri I, 1035–1135," *Atti del Convegno Internazionale di Studi Ruggeriani* (Palermo, 1955), 183–204; and Le Patourel, *Norman Empire*, 121–354 *passim*.

with five lay magnates, at least four of whom held lands and attested substantially on both sides of the Channel. Similar analyses of the other documents that Haskins assembled disclose a Norman viceregal core group that sometimes functioned on its own, sometimes expanded into a larger court of bishops and magnates, and usually merged into the king's traveling entourage when Henry was in Normandy. Even when on its own, the viceregal court was itinerant, meeting sometimes at Rouen, sometimes at Caen, and perhaps, with less frequency, elsewhere in the duchy. Its members spent most of their time in Normandy but on rare occasions one or another turned up in the royal entourage in England, leaving their Norman viceregal duties to subordinates or other household officers.[18]

In England Queen Matilda usually served as regent during her husband's absences, although Archbishop Anselm may have occupied the position on one or more occasions between his return from exile in 1106 and his death in 1109. After Matilda's death in 1118 William Adelin, the royal son and heir, directed the English regency for a year.[19] But these altogether traditional arrangements were supplemented by a clearly identifiable body of viceregal administrators: the witness lists of charters issued by Matilda and William as regents disclose that in England as in Normandy a viceregal court of relatively stable and expert membership was evolving. At its head was Henry's great administrator, Roger, bishop of Salisbury, who attested no less than nine of Matilda's and William Adelin's surviving acts and whose name, when it occurs with others, almost always heads the list. Other figures in the English viceregal group included Robert Bloet, bishop of Lincoln; Richard of Belmeis, bishop of London; Ranulf the Chancellor; the stewards Adam of Port and William of Courcy; the constables Walter of Gloucester and Nigel of Oilli; and the royal justice Ralph Basset.[20] The stewards and constables on this list are among the household officials who attested primarily from England. Indeed, the attestations of almost all of those in the English viceregal core group were very largely limited to royal acts issued in England. Ranulf the Chancel-

---

[18] The magnate-judges were Robert, count of Meulan and earl of Leicester; William of Warenne, earl of Surrey; Gilbert of Laigle, lord of Pevensey; and William the Chamberlain of Tancarville. A fifth judge, William of Ferrars, was doubtless a Norman figure but he did not attest sufficiently to be placed with certainty. Haskins, *Norman Institutions*, 91–92. John of Lisieux traveled to England, for example, in late 1126, presumably to join the deliberations on the royal succession that culminated in the Empress Maud's designation at Henry's 1126–27 Christmas court; *Regesta Regum Anglo-Normannorum*, 2: no. 1466. John of Lisieux and Robert de la Haye were both apparently with the king at York in late 1122; *ibid.*, no. 1338. Both John and Robert were absent because of illness from a Norman court of ca. 1129 where Robert, chaplain to the bishop of Lisieux, and the steward Robert of Courcy seem to have acted in their places; *ibid.*, no. 1584.

[19] On Matilda, see *Regesta Regum Anglo-Normannorum*, 2: nos. 971, 1000–01, 1190, 1198; and R. R. Darlington, ed., *The Cartulary of Worcester Cathedral Priory (Register I)*, Pipe Roll Society (London, 1968), nos. 40, 262. On Anselm, see Eadmer, *Historia Novorum in Anglia*, 197; and F. S. Schmitt, ed., *S. Anselmi Opera Omnia* (Stuttgart, 1958), epistle 407. In early 1109 Henry conferred with Anselm on vital matters of royal diplomacy; *S. Anselmi Opera Omnia*, epistle 461. The queen probably visited Normandy in 1107, but she was with Anselm in England in 1108 or early 1109 when she issued the charter, on Anselm's advice, that established the Augustinian house of Holy Trinity, Aldgate; *Regesta Regum Anglo-Normannorum*, 2: nos. 808–09, 906. On William Adelin, see *ibid.*, nos. 1189, 1191–92, 1201–02.

[20] For Roger, see *Regesta Regum Anglo-Normannorum*, 2: nos. 906, 909, 1090, 1189–90, 1192, 1201; *Cartulary of Worcester Cathedral*, nos. 40, 262. Roger was the first or sole witness to all of these acts except number 906, for which he was the second of three episcopal attestors. For the English viceregal group, also see *Regesta Regum Anglo-Normannorum*, 2: nos. 971, 1001, 1129, 1180, 1191, 1198.

lor was the only official who crossed the Channel at various times in the king's service, but even he attested many more *acta* in England than in Normandy. Clearly, then, the chancellor was in part a cross-Channel *curialis* and in part a participant in the English viceregency.

One extraordinarily illuminating document, as yet unpublished in full, provides a glimpse of the English viceregal court hearing pleas at Brampton, Huntingdonshire, in 1116, apparently in the queen's absence. The "judges" at this Brampton court included several of the men in Matilda's and William Adelin's regency administrations: Roger, bishop of Salisbury; Robert, bishop of Lincoln; Walter of Gloucester; and Ralph Basset.[21] The witness lists of regents' charters, corroborated by the Brampton evidence, thus disclose a select and stable body of England-based viceregal administrators led by Roger, bishop of Salisbury, with functions and membership that closely parallel those of the Norman viceregal body headed by John, bishop of Lisieux.

In England, however, the queen or prince headed the viceregency. But the English viceregal court, and Roger of Salisbury in particular, exercised strong influence on Matilda and William Adelin. Herbert, bishop of Norwich, in begging a favor of Roger during one of Henry's absences, was confident that "you will not find our lady the queen difficult for . . . she takes advantage of your advice in all matters."[22] After Matilda's death in 1118 and William Adelin's in 1120, Roger emerged from the shadows as the officially recognized head of the English viceregency. When Henry departed England in 1123, he appointed Roger to run the kingdom in his absence, and throughout the remainder of the reign Roger was responsible for "the doing of justice in England" not only during Henry's Norman tours but even when the king was in his kingdom. Despite Henry's marriage to the young Adeliza of Louvain in 1121, Roger—not the new queen—presided thenceforth at the English viceregal court.[23] Although Henry always felt free to issue writs concerning England when he was in Normandy (and vice versa), Bishop Roger himself sometimes issued viceregal writs explicitly on the king's instructions.[24]

Neither Roger of Salisbury in England nor John of Lisieux in Normandy appear to have borne an official administrative title. Scholars in the past were inclined to call them "chief justiciars," but their administrative roles were too

---

[21] The two remaining *iudicii* at Brampton were sheriffs of the region; Doris M. Stenton, *English Justice between the Conquest and Magna Carta* (Philadelphia, 1964), 62 n. 46. For a case involving the earl of Buckingham's obligations to Abingdon for a manor which he held of the abbey that Roger of Salisbury, Robert bishop of Lincoln, "et multis regis baronibus" judged, see Joseph Stevenson, ed., *Chronicon Monasterii de Abingdon*, Rolls Series, no. 1, vol. 2 (London, 1858): 133–34.

[22] As quoted in Richardson and Sayles, *The Governance of Mediaeval England*, 151.

[23] *Anglo-Saxon Chronicle*, A.D. 1123; and Malmesbury, *Gesta Regum Anglorum*, 484. Roger's competition was further reduced by the deaths of Robert Bloet and Ranulf the Chancellor in 1123 and the paralysis that struck Richard, bishop of London, that same year. Henry probably made his decision out of dynastic rather than administrative considerations. Hoping that Queen Adeliza would bear him a son, he kept her at his side when he crossed to Normandy. Adeliza's attestations were balanced between duchy and kingdom, whereas Queen Matilda's were chiefly in England.

[24] *Regesta Regum Anglo-Normannorum*, 2: nos. 1472, 1488, 1614, 1814, 1977, 1989. Also see Francis J. West, *The Justiciarship in England* (Cambridge, 1966), 18–19; and Richardson and Sayles, *The Governance of Mediaeval England*, 163. None of Roger's viceregal charters are attested; four conclude with the phrase "per breve regis."

novel to have yet acquired formal names. Their episcopal titles sufficed.[25] At one point Roger titled himself "bishop of Salisbury and procurator of the kingdom of England under King Henry," but no such title was consistently used. Contemporaries sometimes referred to him as "second only to the king" (*secundus a rege*)—surely not a formal office but an indication of his political importance.[26] For Roger's authority in England after 1123 was remarkably comprehensive. As William of Malmesbury put it, Roger "pleaded the cases, controlled expenditures himself, personally supervised the treasure, both when the king was in England and also, without colleague or witness, when . . . the king was staying in Normandy."[27] Roger's control of the kingdom's judicial and fiscal machinery strongly anticipated the power and responsibility exercised by the chief justiciars of early Angevin times. It is not too much to say that the varied responsibilities of both Roger of Salisbury in England and John of Lisieux in Normandy mark the genesis of the chief justiciarship in fact even if not in name.[28]

ROGER'S ADMINISTRATION OF THE KINGDOM'S REVENUES was likewise exercised without formal title. The exchequer, perhaps the best-known cogwheel in Henry's new administrative machine, emerges from the mist around 1110 with Roger of Salisbury clearly in control.[29] Despite extensive investigations, its origins remain obscure. The *Dialogus de Scaccario* from the end of the century implies that Roger did not invent the exchequer but did much to improve and modernize it.[30] Doubtless it evolved out of the ancient practice of sheriffs bringing their revenues annually to the central English treasury, located at

---

[25] For the term "chief justiciar," see, for example, Richardson and Sayles, *The Governance of Mediaeval England*, 159, *passim;* and Haskins, *Norman Institutions*, 87–99. *Capitalis justiciarius* does occur in Anglo-Norman sources but not with its later meaning. Orderic Vitalis used it to describe not Roger of Salisbury but Richard Basset and probably meant simply that Richard's judicial activities were wide-ranging; *Historiae Ecclesiasticae Libri Tredecim*, ed. Auguste le Prévost, 5 vols. (Paris, 1838–55), 5: 68. In 1141 the Empress Maud named Geoffrey de Mandeville her *capitalis justicia* in Essex. The term also occurs in a Norman charter of Henry I's but not explicitly in connection with John of Lisieux; Haskins, *Norman Institutions*, 93–94. Also see, in general, William T. Reedy, "Were Ralph and Richard Basset Really Chief Justiciars of England in the Reign of Henry I?" *The Twelfth Century, Acta*, 2 (1975): 74–103.
[26] "Justitiarius fuit totius Angliae, et secundus a rege"; Henry of Huntingdon, *Historia Anglorum*, ed. Thomas Arnold, Rolls Series, no. 74 (London, 1879), 245. Several of Roger's contemporaries are likewise called justiciars "totius Angliae"; Richardson and Sayles, *The Governance of Mediaeval England*, 174–75. And Henry of Huntingdon himself describes Roger's nephew, Alexander, bishop of Lincoln, as "princeps a rege secundus"; *Historia Anglorum*, 280. On Roger's titles, see Edward J. Kealey, *Roger of Salisbury, Viceroy of England* (Berkeley and Los Angeles, 1972), 70–71, 241–44. On the various unofficial terms used to describe Ranulf Flambard's duties under William II (*exactor, placitator*, etc.), see Southern, *Medieval Humanism*, 184–85, 194.
[27] William of Malmesbury, *Historia Novella*, ed. K. R. Potter (London, 1955), 37–38. Note that Roger's viceregal charters always lack witnesses and that several of his earlier colleagues were dead or inactive by 1124; see notes 23–24, above.
[28] West, *Justiciarship*, 15–23. My position on Roger's "chief justiciarship" is rather less skeptical than that of West but distinctly more so than that of Richardson and Sayles; see their *The Governance of Mediaeval England*, 173–90.
[29] Henry I to *baronibus de scaccario*, attested by Roger of Salisbury and Ranulf the Chancellor; *Regesta Regum Anglo-Normannorum*, 2: no. 963. This, the earliest known reference to the exchequer by name, deals with the aid of 1110.
[30] *Dialogus de Scaccario*, 42.

Winchester since Anglo-Saxon times. Chroniclers alluded to a general administrative and legal reorganization undertaken by Henry on both sides of the Channel in the years immediately following his conquest of Normandy in 1106. This activity, combined with raising a huge aid for his daughter's betrothal in 1110, may have stimulated the accounting reforms that produced what we know as the English exchequer—abacus accounting procedure, court of audit, and pipe rolls recording receipts from the sheriffs and their shires.[31]

From about 1110 onward we encounter mounting evidence of the sophisticated accounting process that appears in some detail in the English pipe roll of 1130 (the one surviving example of the series of fiscal records that were produced annually throughout most of Henry's reign).[32] And, although all of the Norman exchequer rolls from this period have perished, it is certain that an exchequer was functioning concurrently in the duchy. Up to a point, there is general agreement on how the exchequer process worked. Twice each year, at Easter and at Michaelmas, separate groups of royal administrators went to the Winchester treasury and to the Norman treasury to audit the accounts of the sheriffs and vicomtes over the famous checkered boards. Contemporary records referred to the members of these courts of audit as "barons of the exchequer," and the title has given rise to some confusion because it suggests a body of full-time exchequer officials. Indeed, Lady Doris Stenton has referred to Henry I's English exchequer as a "permanent financial bureau," and Francis J. West has viewed it as "the central organ of government."[33] Certainly, it became both in subsequent generations, but at its inception under Henry I the exchequer was merely a semiannual auditing procedure, nothing more or less than a highly effective device for increasing curial supervision over the sheriffs and vicomtes and a means of applying the latest systematic procedures to the collection of royal revenues and the dispensing of royal patronage. The exchequer was not yet a department, not yet an institution, but simply an occasion. Further, it was in essence the viceregal court meeting under special circumstances.

That Roger of Salisbury supervised both the viceregal court and the exchequer has long been understood. That other officials also served simultaneously as viceregal justices and barons of the exchequer has not. But the combined evidence of several of Henry's charters makes it clear that the chancellor was, at least at times, a baron of the exchequer. And the panel of *justitiae regis* who in 1119 heard a plea for the exemption of Abingdon Abbey from danegeld almost certainly represents some of the exchequer barons

---

[31] Orderic Vitalis, *Historiae Ecclesiasticae Libri Tredecim*, 4: 233–34, 269; Florence of Worcester, *Chronicon ex Chronicis*, ed. Benjamin Thorpe, 2 (London, 1849): 57; and Eadmer, *Historia Novorum in Anglia*, 192–93. And see R. L. Poole, *The Exchequer in the Twelfth Century* (London, 1912).

[32] Joseph Hunter, ed., *The Pipe Roll of 31 Henry I, Michaelmas 1130* (hereafter *P.R. 31 Henry I*) (rev. ed.; London, 1929). Annual pipe rolls survive from A.D. 1156 onward and can be used (with caution) to illuminate the roll of 1130. Further illumination—along with some phantom images—is provided by Richard fitz Nigel's *Dialogus de Scaccario* from late in Henry II's reign.

[33] For *barones de scaccario*, see *Regesta Regum Anglo-Normannorum*, 2: nos. 963, 1538, 1584 (Normandy), 1741, 1879. And see Stenton, *English Justice*, 59; and West, *Justiciarship*, 19–20.

TABLE 2

Exchequer and Viceregency Officials, 1111-21

Exchequer Court of 1111	*Exchequer Judges of 1119*	*Viceregency Figures*
Queen Matilda* [E]		Queen Matilda* [E]
Roger, bp. of Salisbury* [E]	Roger, bp. of Salisbury* [E]	Roger, bp. of Salisbury* [E]
Robt., bp. of Lincoln* [E]	Robt., bp. of Lincoln*[E]	Robt., bp. of Lincoln* [E]
Richard, bp. of London* [E]		Richard, bp. of London* [E]
William of Courcy [E]		William of Courcy [E]
Adam of Port [E]		Adam of Port [E]
Thurstan the Chaplain [E]		
Walter of Gloucester* [E]		Walter of Gloucester* [E]
Herbert the Chamberlain [E]		
?) William of Oilli[a]		Nigel of Oilli* [E]
Geoffrey fitz Herbert		
William of Anesy		
Ralph Basset* [E]	Ralph Basset* [E]	Ralph Basset* [E]
Geoffrey of Mandeville [XN]		
Geoffrey Ridel [E]		
Walter, adcn. of Oxford		
	Ranulf the Chancellor* [XE]	Ranulf the Chancellor* [XE]

NOTE: An asterisk (*) designates a *curialis*; for a definition of a *curialis*, see page 242, below; and, for Henry's *curiales*, see Table 4, below. For an explanation of the symbols E, XE, and XN, see page 226 a. (Table 1), above. The absence of such a symbol indicates that the name does not occur elsewhere in Henry I's *Regesta*.

[a] William of Oilli either was a little-known kinsman of Nigel of Oilli or appears on the list as a scribal error for Nigel himself.

sitting at the Michaelmas session at Winchester.[34] Without exception the justices in question—Roger of Salisbury; Robert, bishop of Lincoln; Ranulf the Chancellor; and Ralph Basset—are viceregency figures. An earlier passage from the Abingdon Chronicle preserves a full list of the officials who sat at the Winchester treasury during the Michaelmas exchequer session of A.D. 1111. The exchequer was so new at this point that the justices were not yet termed *barones de scaccario*, and the session itself was described as being *in thesauro* rather than *ad scaccarium*. But there can be no doubt that the account in question is the earliest recorded description of the exchequer court in action. The official regent of England, Queen Matilda, not Roger of Salisbury, presided over the court. But Roger's name appears at the head of the list of judges, and these judges correspond remarkably to the men who assisted the queen and, later, her son in the English viceregency.[35] For the sake of clarity, Table 2 lists the members of the exchequer court of 1111 alongside the

[34] On the chancellor, see *Regesta Regum Anglo-Normannorum*, 2: nos. 963, 1211, 1741. Also see *ibid.*, no. 1514. For the case in 1119, see *ibid.*, no. 1211. The editors propose the date of ca. September 29.

[35] *Ibid.*, no. 1000; and *Chronicon Monasterii de Abingdon*, 116.

names of the exchequer justices of 1119 and those of the men identified with Matilda's or with William Adelin's regency.

Since the order in which the names appear in the Abingdon account of 1111 (and in Table 2) is doubtless indicative of the order of these officials' importance, the common membership of viceregency and exchequer becomes all the more evident. Below the queen, six of the seven exchequer officials of 1111 were viceregency figures, and the one who was not, Thurstan the Chaplain, was a royal chaplain and a canon of St. Paul's under Bishop Richard of London. Of the remaining eight, Herbert the Chamberlain was present as custodian of the Winchester treasury, and Geoffrey Ridel as one of England's most active royal justices. As a "justiciar of all England," Geoffrey probably participated in regency courts even though his name does not occur in the handful of surviving viceregal records.[36] In short, a single administrative-judicial body traveled through England, hearing pleas in the king's name when he was in Normandy and sitting at the Winchester treasury at Easter and Michaelmas for the exchequer sessions. At such times its membership may have expanded to include a treasury chamberlain and perhaps some lesser figures, just as it expanded at the Brampton pleadings in 1116 to include two local sheriffs. Like all courts of its day, the members of the regency-exchequer *curia* shifted, but its core was remarkably stable. And its key figures, despite their English viceregal responsibilities, were frequent attestors of the king's charters. When Henry was in Normandy these officials served him from afar; when he was in England they were at his side.

The single surviving record of Henry I's Norman exchequer discloses a similar identity in membership between the viceregal and exchequer courts in Normandy. Among the barons of the Norman exchequer were the familiar figures of the Norman viceregency: John, bishop of Lisieux; the stewards Robert de la Haye and Robert of Courcy; and the chamberlain William of Glastonbury. One of the nonviceregency figures at the court was the Norman treasury official Robert of Évreux, whose presence paralleled that of Herbert, the treasury chamberlain, at Winchester in 1111.[37]

As occasions rather than institutions, the exchequers had no permanent staffs. The officials of the English and Norman viceregencies, who for a time became "barons of the exchequer," met at their respective treasuries and stored their annual accounts there. Of the two treasuries, the one at Winchester was much the more important, for there Henry kept the bulk of his wealth unless he needed it in Normandy.[38] The Winchester treasury can be traced back to Canute's reign, but little is known of its administration until Henry I's

[36] Donald Nicholl, *Thurstan, Archbishop of York* (York, 1964), 7–10; and Reedy, "Were the Bassets Chief Justiciars?" 80–81. Of the remaining exchequer officials of 1111 who cannot be identified as viceregal administrators, Geoffrey of Mandeville (lord of Marshwood, Dorset) had recently been sheriff of Devon and Cornwall and possibly still was, Archdeacon Walter of Oxford appears seldom in official records and only in England, and the remaining men are altogether obscure. William of Oilli appears in no other contemporary record.

[37] For the one extant Norman exchequer record, see *Regesta Regum Anglo-Normannorum*, 2: no. 1584. Also see *ibid.*, nos. 1184, 1352, 1422, 1579, 1593. On Robert of Évreux, see Haskins, *Norman Institutions*, 108–10.

[38] For much of what follows, see C. Warren Hollister, "The Origins of the English Treasury," above, chapter 12: 209-22.

accession. By then it was under the authority of two royal chamberlains—Herbert the Chamberlain and Robert Mauduit—both of whom were local Hampshire men only infrequently at court. But by the 1120s the two treasury chamberlainships had passed to the *curiales* Geoffrey of Clinton and William of Pont de l'Arche. Geoffrey had risen from obscurity to become a major landholder, sheriff, itinerant justice, and royal *familiaris*. William of Pont de l'Arche served off and on as sheriff in several shires and, in addition to his Winchester office, was chamberlain of the *camera curiae*, the subtreasury that traveled with the king's court.

The real master of the Winchester treasury was, of course, Roger of Salisbury himself, functioning without official title. In the mid-1120s, however, the new household office of court treasurer was created, and its authority extended beyond Winchester to all the treasuries of the Anglo-Norman state. Its first occupant was Roger of Salisbury's nephew Nigel, a frequent attestor of royal charters and the only member of his newly illustrious family to attest substantially from both sides of the Channel. His advancement to the new office represents the final step in the establishment of clearly defined curial control over the treasuries of both duchy and kingdom.

The English and Norman treasuries were depositories of records as well as wealth. Although memoranda of various kinds, now lost, doubtless accompanied the itinerant chancery, the age of major chancery records could not dawn until the chancery ceased traveling and settled down—as it did around 1200. But records had long been accumulating in the Winchester treasury. When Henry seized it in 1100 he must have found there not only Rufus's coins but the records necessary to keep them flowing in: Domesday Book with its comprehensive data on baronial holdings and the hidages and values of manors, pre-Domesday geld rolls, and records of the shire farms and of revenues owed by royal estates and towns. To these materials, Henry's own administration added the annual exchequer accounts—the English pipe rolls and Norman exchequer rolls. The king's two formal treaties with the count of Flanders, which survive in their original chancery hand, were evidently deposited at Winchester, along with early twelfth-century regional surveys that updated the Domesday information for Leicestershire, Northamptonshire, Worcestershire, and Lindsey. There is even scattered evidence that royal writs were sometimes copied and stored at Winchester.[39] Thus, despite the itinerant character of the king's *curia* and viceregency courts, the royal administration was beginning to store in fixed depositories the records necessary to account for what the crown was collecting and what it was granting away.

[39] In general, see Sally P. J. Harvey, "Domesday Book and Anglo-Norman Governance," *Transactions of the Royal Historical Society*, 5th ser., 25 (1975): 175–93. On the Norman exchequer rolls, see Thomas Stapleton, *Magni Rotuli Scaccarii Normanniae sub Regibus Angliae*, 2 vols. (London, 1840–44). For an apparent early reference (ca. 1114) to the preservation of pipe rolls, see Poole, *The Exchequer in the Twelfth Century*, 37–39; and *Regesta Regum Anglo-Normannorum*, 2: no. 1053. Richard fitz Nigel alluded to information that was available "in veteribus annalibus rotulis" of Henry I; *Dialogus de Scaccario*, 42. In ca. 1127 Henry stated that Roger of Salisbury had recognized by charter from the royal treasury ("per cartam de thesauro meo") that Plympton Priory (founded in 1121) was to be free of gelds and other levies; see *Regesta Regum Anglo-Normmannorum*, 2: no. 1515. For similar evidence, see *ibid.*, no. 1488; for other types of royal charters that must surely have been on record at Winchester, see *ibid.*, nos. 1581, 1687, 1691.

THE RIGOROUS EXCHEQUER AUDITS of sheriffs' and vicomtes' accounts did much to solve the problem of controlling local officials, a problem that has beset governments in all ages. And the exchequer was not the only instrument that Henry directed to this end. By the later years of his reign the royal court exercised formidable authority over the shires and hundreds of England through a comprehensive system not only of itinerant curial justices but also of itinerant curial sheriffs. In Normandy the evidence is much thinner because all of the exchequer rolls and most of the royal charters have disappeared. But the surviving records reveal that royal justices were actively at work in the duchy and that the vicomtés of Avranches, Bayeux, Falaise, Argentan, and Exmes were governed at times by royal *familiares*.[40]

How and to what extent Henry centralized English justice are matters of considerable debate. It is generally agreed that the responsibility for pleas of the crown was initially transferred from sheriffs to shire justiciars under William I or William II and that shire justiciarships became an established institution under Henry I. The institution is thought to have grown steadily throughout Henry I's reign and on into the 1150s and 1160s, dissolving only when Henry II's system of judicial eyres made shire justiciarships redundant.[41] Meanwhile, so it is urged, Henry I supplemented the work of the local or shire justiciars by sending itinerant justices out from his court to hear pleas of the crown in various groups of shires. Nevertheless, as William T. Reedy has argued in his careful study of Henry I's itinerant justices, their activities were limited in scope and therefore quite unlike Henry II's "general eyres"; the king continued to exercise his jurisdiction "primarily through his local justiciarate," the history of which is marked, unfortunately, by "little concrete evidence."[42]

Such a reconstruction of Henry I's judicial system is unsatisfactory in several respects. One is struck, to begin with, by the great proliferation of royal justices of all kinds under Henry I—justices of groups of shires, individual shires, hundreds, boroughs, and royal demesne lands.[43] To differentiate among these various sorts of justices can be treacherous, and a certain

---

[40] The *familiaris* Richard, earl of Chester, was vicomte of the Avranchin; the *familiaris* Ranulf le Meschin was vicomte of the Bessin and, after Richard of Chester's death, of the Avranchin as well; John, bishop of Lisieux, served for a time as vicomte of Falaise, Argentan, and Exmes. On the activities of royal justices in Normandy, see Haskins, *Norman Institutions*, 100; and Orderic Vitalis, *Historiae Ecclesiasticae Libri Tredecim*, 4: 439–40, 453.

[41] Henry A. Cronne, "The Local Justiciar in England under the Norman Kings," *Birmingham Historical Journal*, 6 (1957): 18–38; Charles Johnson and Henry A. Cronne, *Regesta Regum Anglo-Normannorum*, 2: xvii; and Stenton, *English Justice*, 65–69.

[42] Reedy, "The Origins of the General Eyre in the Reign of Henry I," *Speculum*, 41 (1966): 688–724. On the justices in eyre, also see Doris M. Stenton, ed., *Pleas before the King or His Justices, 1198–1212* (hereafter *Pleas, 1198–1212*), Selden Society, no. 85, vol. 3 (London, 1967): xlvii–l. On sheriffs, see W. A. Morris, *The Medieval English Sheriff to 1300* (Manchester, 1927), 41–109; and C. H. Walker, "The Sheriffs and the Pipe Roll of 31 Henry I," *EHR*, 37 (1922): 67–79.

[43] L. J. Downer, ed., *Leges Henrici Primi* (Oxford, 1972), 98, 132, 183, 195, 212; *P.R. 31 Henry I*, 91; Stenton, *English Justice*, 57; Orderic Vitalis, *Historiae Ecclesiasticae Libri Tredecim*, 3: 125, 4: 439–40; Kenneth R. Potter and R. H. C. Davis, eds., *Gesta Stephani* (2d ed., Oxford, 1976), 24; Naomi D. Hurnard, "Local Justice under the Norman Kings," in H. W. C. Davis, *England under the Normans and Angevins* (13th ed., London, 1949), 522–24; and Cronne, "Local Justiciar," 22.

confusion persists in the secondary literature between shire justiciars and other kinds of local justices.[44] Contemporaries had not yet developed a technical vocabulary to distinguish shire justiciars from itinerant justices: Henry addressed a writ to Aubrey de Vere and Robert of Chesney as his "justices of Norfolk," but they were also justices in Suffolk, and Aubrey was apparently a justice at about the same time in Middlesex and Nottinghamshire; he was described by his son as "justiciar of all England."[45] None of this would have seemed contradictory to people at the time: a "justiciar of all England," of whom there were several concurrently, did not necessarily hear pleas in every shire or even in many shires. He simply had the authority to do so. And a writ relating to judicial business in Norfolk would be addressed to him in his capacity as justice of Norfolk, as his activities in other shires were irrelevant to the business at hand.[46]

This and other evidence points to the difficulty of separating itinerant justices from shire justices. The distinction, clearly and persistently drawn by modern scholars, was not at all clear to contemporaries. Not until the 1170s was there a technical term for "itinerant justice." Modern scholars have consistently included William of Houghton and Henry of Port among Henry I's justices in eyre, but the surviving pipe roll shows Henry of Port hearing pleas only in Kent and William of Houghton only in Suffolk. Conversely, Geoffrey de Mandeville, earl of Essex, who has been taken by scholars as a prime example of a "local justiciar," was granted judicial authority over three shires.[47] Although King Stephen granted Geoffrey's judicial office "in feodo et hereditate" whereas Henry I's justices seem to have served at the royal pleasure, this distinction is not an altogether satisfactory reason to call Geoffrey's justiciarship "local" and those of Henry of Port and William of Houghton "itinerant." It has been assumed that itinerant justices were sent out from the *curia regis* whereas shire justices were planted in their shires. But

---

[44] Cronne has recognized the danger but not always sufficiently. Having assembled evidence on every sort of English royal judicial official functioning within the confines of a shire, he has concluded that the office of "shire justiciar" was firmly established at the time of Henry I's death; "Local Justiciar," 32, 37–38. And Cronne and R. H. C. Davis have maintained elsewhere, "It must be assumed that every county had its local justice as a matter of course"; *Regesta Regum Anglo-Normannorum*, 3: xxiii.

[45] *Regesta Regum Anglo-Normannorum*, 2: nos. 1714, 1772, 1988. And see Richardson and Sayles, *The Governance of Mediaeval England*, 174. Cronne and R. H. C. Davis have identified Aubrey as a "local justice" of Norfolk and Suffolk, but Stephen's charters are quite ambiguous on this point; compare *Regesta Regum Anglo-Normannorum*, 3: xxv, and *ibid.*, nos. 82, 416.

[46] *Regesta Regum Anglo-Normannorum*, 2: no. 1608; and Barbara Dodwell, ed., *The Charters of Norwich Cathedral Priory, Part One*, Pipe Roll Society (London, 1974), no. 99. In this royal writ relating to Norfolk, Richard Basset and Aubrey de Vere were addressed as *justiciarii;* Cronne and Johnson have dated the charter "1129?" and Barbara Dodwell has suggested a date "probably not long before Michaelmas 1129," on the grounds that Richard and Aubrey became joint sheriffs of Norfolk and Suffolk at Michaelmas 1129; see *P.R. 31 Henry I*, 90. I suggest that the charter should be dated somewhere between 1130 and 1133 and that Richard and Aubrey were sheriffs and justiciars concurrently. Norfolk was among the six shires in which Richard Basset heard pleas ca. 1129–30, and Aubrey probably began serving as an itinerant justice shortly thereafter.

[47] For *justicie errantes*, see R. C. Van Caenegem, *The Birth of the English Common Law* (Cambridge, 1973), 21. For William of Houghton and Henry of Port, see Stenton, *English Justice*, 62; Reedy, "General Eyre," 712; and *P.R. 31 Henry I*, 65, 96. For Geoffrey de Mandeville, see Cronne and R. H. C. Davis, *Regesta Regum Anglo-Normannorum*, 3: xxiii–xxv, nos. 274, 275; Cronne, "Local Justiciar," 21–23; and Stenton, *English Justice*, 66. Geoffrey was granted both judicial and shrieval authority over Essex, Hertfordshire, and Middlesex.

the assumption cannot be sustained when Aubrey de Vere—a heavily attesting *curialis* and joint sheriff of eleven shires—is regarded as the shire justiciar of Norfolk while Robert of Arundel—who seldom attested—is regarded as an itinerant justice in the west.[48]

These problems suggest the need to revise the existing picture of Henry I's judicial system. The belief that shire justiciars, as traditionally conceived, grew and flourished throughout the reign should be reassessed. There were always, of course, minor justices working in the shires and hundreds—men such as "Benjamin" in Norfolk and Robert Malarteis in Huntingdonshire, who impleaded suspected criminals and attended to the king's judicial affairs in various other ways. There were also justiciars of individual shires, but efforts to identify them specifically have resulted in lists of men who were active only in the earlier portion of the reign, and most of the references date from its initial years. Midway through the reign their activities began to blend into those of the "itinerant justices." Ralph Basset, whose judicial activities left their mark in at least eleven shires in the roll of 1130, had earlier been on eyre in two others: Huntingdonshire in 1116 and Leicestershire in 1124.[49] We know of his activities in these years only through isolated chronicle references, but for the period roughly from 1125 to 1130 the pipe roll provides a relatively full picture.

It could be fuller still. Several shire accounts are missing while others are incomplete or mutilated.[50] The roll may, moreover, sometimes conceal the names of itinerant justices under rubrics like "old pleas," "pleas for breaking the peace," or "the old pleas of Holderness."[51] Nevertheless, the roll makes it clear that between about 1125 and 1130 royal justices were at work in all or nearly all of the shires of England.[52] Not every justice was as active as Ralph Basset (eleven shires) or Richard Basset (six shires) or Geoffrey of Clinton (eighteen shires). The names of two justices, for example, occur only in single

---

[48] Stenton, *Pleas, 1198–1212*, xlix; and Reedy, "General Eyre," 720–21.

[49] R. C. Van Caenegem, "Public Prosecution of Crime in Twelfth-Century England," in C. N. L. Brooke *et al.*, eds., *Church and Government in the Middle Ages: Essays Presented to C. R. Cheney* (Cambridge, 1976), 51–61; Richardson and Sayles, *The Governance of Mediaeval England*, 185–87; Cronne and Johnson, *Regesta Regum Anglo-Normannorum*, 2: xviii; and Cronne, "Local Justiciar," 33. For one of many references to *judices* of the county and hundreds, see *P.R. 31 Henry I*, 97. It has been my good fortune to have access to a much fuller and more rigorous list of local justiciars; see Hoc-ming Cheung's unpublished paper, "Local Justiciars under Henry I" (University of California, Santa Barbara). For Ralph Basset, see *Anglo-Saxon Chronicle*, A.D. 1124; and Orderic Vitalis, *The Ecclesiastical History of Orderic Vitalis*, ed. and trans. Marjorie Chibnall, 4 vols. (vols. 2–5) (Oxford, 1969–75), 3: 351. Since the reference to Ralph at Huntingdon in 1116 occurs in Orderic's account of the case of Bricstan of Chatteris, Reedy has concluded that Ralph "did not hear 'pleas' " but only one plea; "General Eyre," 705. But Bricstan's indictment for usury and concealment of treasure was a matter of only routine interest to the *curia regis* and would surely not alone have drawn together the great court that Orderic described.

[50] The accounts for Somerset and several border shires are missing altogether; little is left of the Devon account, and an entire membrane has been lost from the Hampshire account.

[51] *P.R. 31 Henry I*, 3 ("old pleas"), 101 ("old pleas of Richard Basset"), 26 ("old pleas of Holderness"), 25 ("pleas of Blyth"), 27 ("pleas of Geoffrey of Clinton and his fellows of Blyth"), 45–46 (pleas "pro pace fracta"), 74 (pleas of Geoffrey of Clinton "pro pace fracta"), etc.

[52] Reedy has surely erred in saying that "six counties out of those reported were not visited at all"; "General Eyre," 715 n. 164. The pipe roll cannot be used to prove that shires were not visited. Of Reedy's six, Hampshire has only a partial account and Rutland was not a shire in 1130. The accounts for all six include entries that could well refer to the pleas of itinerant justices, even though they are unnamed.

shires, though the scope of their activities may well have been larger.[53] But taken together the pipe roll and charter evidence reveal that shire justiciars had evolved by the 1120s into justices with larger responsibilities—men who would have been described by a later generation as "justices in eyre."[54] The eyre system appears to have collapsed with Roger of Salisbury's arrest and death in 1139, and it was replaced by shire justiciarships and earldoms in the time of civil war that followed. King Stephen granted justiciarships of shires or small groups of shires, sometimes on a hereditary basis, to notables such as the earls of Essex and Lincoln and the bishop of Lincoln as well as to lesser men.[55] Finally, a decade or two into Henry II's reign, the shire justiciarship was swallowed up by the judicial eyres and vanished.[56] I contend that the shire justiciarship was already dissolving under Henry I—and for the same reason.

Henry's policy toward his sheriffs followed a similar pattern. Shrievalties and justiciarships underwent parallel transformations as the king and his *curia* tightened their control. Generally speaking, Henry turned away from his father's policy of appointing magnates as sheriffs and instead appointed less exalted, more pliable men. Sheriffs were shuffled constantly in and out of shires, and as his reign progressed Henry increasingly tended to appoint *curiales* to the office. The pipe roll of 1130 discloses an extraordinary experiment in centralization: two of Henry's most trusted curial administrators, Richard Basset and Aubrey de Vere, were by then joint sheriffs of no less than eleven shires, while many of the remaining shires were in the hands of *curiales* such as the constable Miles of Gloucester and the treasury chamberlains Geoffrey of Clinton and William of Pont de l'Arche. All but the last of these men were active concurrently as itinerant justices and were sometimes to be found on judicial eyres in the very shires that they held as sheriffs (see Table 3).[57] Indeed, the joint sheriffs Basset and Vere were, to all intents and purposes, "sheriffs in eyre." They did not farm their shires in the traditional manner but seem to have functioned instead as *custodes*, responsible to the king

[53] We know of William of Houghton's activity in Suffolk through only a single entry, recording what appears to be a rather old debt; *P.R. 31 Henry I*, 96. But a charter of ca. 1127 shows him working as a royal justice in Bedfordshire; *Regesta Regum Anglo-Normannorum*, 2: no. 1505. Geoffrey of Clinton's work in Sussex is likewise enshrined in a single, barely legible entry in the roll; *P.R. 31 Henry I*, 69.

[54] The single known exception to this trend was Henry I's charter to the citizens of London (ca. 1133) that granted to them the privilege of electing a justice to supervise crown pleas and pleadings in London and Middlesex; *Regesta Regum Anglo-Normannorum*, 2: no. 1645. Although the authenticity of this charter has recently been questioned, I continue to regard it as a genuine act of Henry I: **above, 191-208.**

[55] Cronne and R. H. C. Davis, *Regesta Regum Anglo-Normannorum*, 3: xxiv-xxv, nos. 276, 472, 490. In this last writ (A.D. 1154) Stephen conceded to Robert of Chesney, bishop of Lincoln, "justitiam meam . . . de Lincolnescira" as fully as it had been enjoyed by his predecessors Robert Bloet and Alexander. The pipe roll of 1130 shows that pleas were held in Lincolnshire by Ralph Basset, Geoffrey of Clinton, William of Albany *Brito*, and Richard Basset, but not by Bishop Alexander. Also see the reference to "the pleas of the bishop of Lincoln" in the Lincolnshire account for 1155; Joseph Hunter, ed., *The Great Roll of the Pipe for the Second, Third, and Fourth Years of the Reign of Henry II*, Record Commission (London, 1844), 26.

[56] Stenton, *English Justice*, 68. The eyres of Henry II's later years were not, however, "general eyres" in the sense in which Reedy has understood the term.

[57] Morris, *The Medieval English Sheriff*, 75-104. Miles of Gloucester was both sheriff and itinerant justice in Gloucestershire and Staffordshire, Richard Basset was joint sheriff and justice in Hertfordshire, Leicestershire, Norfolk, and Suffolk, and Geoffrey of Clinton did the same double duty in Warwickshire.

TABLE 3
Sheriffs and Royal Justices

Shires	Sheriffs (1129–30)	Royal Justices (c. 1124–30)
Beds.:	Richard Basset* & Aubrey de Vere*	Geoff. of Clinton*
Berks.:	Wm. of Pont de l'Arche*	Geoff. of Clinton*; Ralph Basset*
Bucks.:	Richard Basset* & Aubrey de Vere*	Geoff. of Clinton*; Ralph Basset*
Cambs:	Richard Basset* & Aubrey de Vere*	? ? ?ᵃ
Cornw.:	Geoff. of Furnell	(?) Robt. Arundel
Cumb.:	Hildred of Carlisle	Walter Espec/Eustace fz. John*
Derby:	Osbert Silvan	Geoff. of Clinton*; Ralph Basset*
Devon:	Geoff. of Furnell	Robt. Arundel
Dorset:	Warin	(?) Robt. Arundel
Essex:	Richard Basset* & Aubrey de Vere*	Geoff. of Clinton*
Glous.:	Miles of Gloucester*	Miles of Gloucester*/Payn fz. John*
Hants.:	Wm. of Pont de l'Arche*	? ? ? [membrane missing from P. R. 1130]
Heref.:	(?) Payn fz. John*	(?) Payn fz. John* [missing from P. R. 1130]
Herts.:	Richard Basset* & Aubrey de Vere*	Richard Basset*
Hunts.:	Richard Basset* & Aubrey de Vere*	Geoff. of Clinton*
Kent:	Rualon of Avranches	Geoff. of Clinton*; Henry of Port
Leics.:	Richard Basset* & Aubrey de Vere*	Ralph Basset*; Richard Basset*
Lincs.:	Rayner of Bath	Geoff. of Clinton*; Richard Basset*; Ralph Basset*; Wm. of Aubigny *Brito*
Mdsx.:	Four Londoners	Ralph Bassett*
Norf.:	Richard Basset* & Aubrey de Vere*	Geoff. of Clinton*; Richard Basset*; Ralph Basset*
Northants.:	Richard Basset* & Aubrey de Vere*	Geoff. of Clinton*
Northumb.:	Odard of Bamborough	Walter Espec/Eustace fz. John*
Notts.:	Osbert Silvan	Geoff. of Clinton*; Ralph Basset*
Oxford:	Robt. of Chesney	? ? ?
Rutland:	Wm. of Aubigny *Brito*ᵇ	? ? ?
Salop.:	Payn fz. John*	(?) Payn fz. John* [missing from P. R. 1130]
Somers.:	Warin	? ? ? [missing from P. R. 1130]
Staffs.:	Miles of Gloucester*	Geoff. of Clinton*; Miles of Gloucester*; Payn fz. John*
Suffolk:	Richard Basset* & Aubrey de Vere*	Geoff. of Clinton*; Wm. of Houghton; Richard Basset*; Ralph Basset*
Surrey:	Richard Basset* & Aubrey de Vere*	Geoff. of Clinton*; Ralph Basset*
Sussex:	Hugh of Warelville	Geoff. of Clinton*; Richard Basset*
Warwics.:	Geoff. of Clinton*	Geoff. of Clinton*
Wilts.:	Warin	Geoff. of Clinton*; Ralph Basset*; (?) Robt. Arundel
Worcs.:	(?) Walter of Beauchamp	? ? ? [missing from P. R. 1130]
Yorks.:	Bertram of Bulmer	Geoff. of Clinton*; Ralph Basset*; Walter Espec/Eustace fz. John*

NOTE: An asterisk (*) designates a *curialis*.

ᵃ Richard Basset and Aubrey de Vere were serving as royal justices in Cambridgeshire sometime between 1133 and 1135; see E. O. Blake, ed., *Liber Eliensis* (London, 1962), 287–88.
ᵇ Rutland was not regarded as a "shire" in 1130; William of Aubigny *Brito* was responsible for its farm but was not, strictly speaking, its "sheriff."

TABLE 4
The Most Frequent Attestors of Royal Acts

Rank	Attestors Active in A.D. *1111*				Attestors Active in A.D. *1130*			
	Name	Total Attested	Year Range	Av./ Yr.	Name	Total Attested	Year Range	Av./ Yr.
1.	Ranulf, Chancellor	168 XE	07–22	11.5	Geoffrey, Chancellor	115 XE	23–33	11.5
2.	Roger, bp. of Salisbury	247 E	00–35	7.1	Roger, bp. of Salisbury	247 E	00–35	7.1
3.	Robt., bp. of Lincoln	155 E	00–23	6.7	Robt. *de Sigillo*	95 X	21–35	6.8
4.	Robt., ct. of Meulan	113 XE	00–18	6.3	Henry, bp. of Winchester	23 E	29–33	5.8
5.	Nigel of Aubigny	148 XE	01–29	5.3	Robt., e. of Gloucester	79 X	21–35	5.6
6.	Eudo the Steward	68 XE	00–15	4.5	Humphrey of Bohun	27 X	30–35	5.4
7.	Geoffrey of Clinton	90 X	10–32	4.1	Miles of Gloucester	43 E	26–35	4.8
8.	Wm. of Tancarville	89 X	07–29	4.0	Geoffrey of Clinton	90 X	10–32	4.1
9.	Queen Edith-Matilda	65 E	00–18	3.6	Brian fitz Count	41 XN	25–35	4.1
10.	Wm. of Aubigny *Pincerna*	120 X	00–35	3.4	Robt. de Vere	49 X	21–35	3.5
11.	Geoffrey fitz Payn	74 XN	11–35	3.1	Nigel the Treasurer	22 X	26–35	3.4
12.	John, bp. of Lisieux	69 N	07–35	2.5	Wm. of Aubigny *Pincerna*	120 X	00–35	3.4
13.	Hamo the Steward	72 XE	00–29	2.5	Hugh Bigod	47 X	21–35	3.4
14.	Henry, e. of Warwick	39 E	00–18	2.2	Thurstan, apb. of York	62 X	14–33	3.2
15.	Ralph Basset	41 E	10–29	2.2	Geoffrey fitz Payn	74 XN	11–35	3.1
16.	Wm., bp. of Winchester	57 XE	00–27	2.1	Payn fitz John	60 XE	15–35	3.0
17.	Wm. of Warenne[a]	69 X	00–35	2.1	Richard Basset	27 E	26–35	3.0
18.	Richard, bp. of London	23 E	08–21	1.8	Wm., abp. of Canterbury	35 XE	23–35	2.9
19.	Walter of Gloucester	31 E	10–28	1.7	Wm. of Pont de l'Arche	35 X	21–33	2.9
20.	Geoffrey, abp. of Rouen	29 XN	11–28	1.7	Hugh, abp. of Rouen	17 N	29–35	2.8
21.	Gilbert of Laigle	29 XE	01–18	1.7	Alex., bp. of Lincoln	34 E	23–35	2.8
22.	Wm., bp. of Exeter	30 XE	07–25	1.7	Bernard, bp. of St. David	52 X	15–35	2.6
23.	Ranulf, bp. of Durham	43 XE	01–27	1.7	Aubrey de Vere	36 XE	21–35	2.6
24.	Nigel of Oilli	23 E	01–16	1.5	John, bp. of Lisieux	69 N	07–35	2.5
25.					Audoin, bp. of Évreux	39 N	19–35	2.4
26.					Eustace fitz John	26 E	21–33	2.2
27.					Wm. of Warenne[a]	69 X	00–35	2.1
28.					Wm. of Aubigny *Brito*	30 E	20–35	2.0
29.					Robt. de la Haye	38 N	16–35	2.0
30.					John fitz Gilbert	12 X	29–35	2.0
31.					Robt., bp. of Hereford	8 E	31–35	2.0
32.					Wm. fitz Odo	26 N	21–35	1.9
33.					John, bp. of Sées	18 N	25–35	1.8
34.					Gilbert, bp. of London	7 E	29–33	1.8
35.					Robt. of Courcy	37 XN	13–35	1.7
36.					Wm. Martel	8 X	28–33	1.6
37.					Waleran, ct. of Meulan[b]	14 X	19–35	1.6
38.					Robt., e. of Leicester	23 X	20–35	1.5

NOTE: Under total royal acts attested, E = 91–100 percent English attestations; XE = 81–90 percent English; X = 51–80 percent English; XN = 50–64 percent Norman; N = 65–100 percent Norman. (Some adjustment has been made for the greater survival expectancy of charters from England; pre-1106 charters have been excluded from the English versus Norman analysis.)

[a] William of Warenne was exiled from England between 1101 and 1103, and these years have been omitted from the calculation of the average.

[b] During the years 1122–28 Waleran, count of Meulan, was first a rebel, then a captive, and those years have been omitted from the calculation of the average.

for the whole of the royal revenues.[58] This intense degree of curialization may have been relaxed slightly during the closing years of the reign, but the sheriffs remained to the end under the strictest royal control.

SUCH ARE THE CONTOURS of Henry I's administrative machine. At its center was the itinerant royal *curia* of household officials and *familiares*. Ranging outward were the English and Norman viceregencies with their semiannual exchequer sessions, and the fixed treasuries with their chamberlains, coins, and records. At the grassroots level were the sheriffs, vicomtes, and local justices whose responsibilities, at least in England,[59] passed more and more under the expert supervision of *curiales* exercising authority over large regions. Overall, the reign was marked by an ever-increasing concentration of authority in the hands of an elite group of *curiales* who gave the system its cohesion.

The growth of curial control can be examined with some precision by making a comprehensive survey of attestations of royal charters. Use of this methodology has helped establish that members of the English viceregency court were very seldom in Normandy and vice versa.[60] The same technique helps identify the royal *curiales*—that is, men whose attestations demonstrate frequent participation in the king's court. For the purposes of this analysis, I have arbitrarily limited the term *curialis* to the thirty-one men active in 1130 who attested surviving authentic charters at the rate of at least two per year, and to a group of twenty-four active in 1111 who attested one and one half or more charters per year.[61] Table 4 ranks these *curiales* in descending order of attestations made per year. These criteria thus enable us to measure the intensity of curial control over Henry's administration in 1130, when the pipe roll casts its shaft of light.

The results are these: of the seven justices in eyre whose responsibilities are known with certainty to have extended beyond a single shire, six were *curiales* (see Table 3). As a consequence of the great centralization of shrievalties disclosed by the surviving pipe roll, *curiales* served as sheriffs in over half of the English shires.[62] Of the fifteen justices of the 1111 exchequer court, the first eight (presumably listed in order of importance) were all *curiales* or household officials or both, and the four (exchequer?) justices of 1119 were all *curiales*. The only extant record relating to the Norman exchequer discloses the same

---

[58] J. H. Round, *Geoffrey de Mandeville* (London, 1892), 297-98; and *P.R. 31 Henry I*, 63.

[59] The disappearance of all Henry I's Norman exchequer rolls leaves the situation in Normandy unclear. A passage from the Troarn cartulary shows the "king's justice" William Tanetin first sitting at Caen with John of Lisieux and later settling the case on his own; Haskins, *Norman Institutions*, 98.

[60] See pages 225-30, and Tables 1, 2, above.

[61] I have not calculated raw totals but totals divided by the span of years across which a person is known to have attested: Roger Bigod, who attested 59 royal charters over seven years, must be regarded as a more active *curialis* than William of Warenne who attested 69 royal charters over thirty-three years. In my calculations of overall appearances at court I have not made allowances for the greater survival rate of English to Norman charters, and the court appearances of predominantly Norman attestors have therefore been systematically underestimated.

[62] Eighteen or nineteen of the thirty-five reported shires were in the hands of *curiales*; see Table 3. The noncurial sheriffs of 1130 are minor or middling landholders and administrative functionaries.

concentration of authority in the hands of household officials and *curiales*.[63] The principal Norman regents—John, bishop of Lisieux, and the steward Robert de la Haye—were both *curiales*. So was Roger of Salisbury, along with the more active of his associates in the English viceregency.[64] The Winchester treasury chamberlains in 1130 were both *curiales*, as was Nigel the Treasurer, and Henry I had the Winchester treasury audited that year by two more *curiales*: his own well-educated bastard Robert, earl of Gloucester, and Brian fitz Count, royal constable and lord of Wallingford.[65] The treasury audit reveals that Henry's *curia* supervised not only England and Normandy but itself as well. The power of the *curiales* was not unlimited, and administrative lapses could bring swift reprisals. Aubrey de Vere was fined for permitting a prisoner to escape his custody; Robert, bishop of Lincoln, who had somehow fallen from royal favor toward the end of his career, lost his tax exemptions and lawsuits along with his influence; and Geoffrey of Clinton was put under arrest for a time.[66] Yet as a group these men basked in the king's favor and prospered enormously. They were the chief technicians and the chief beneficiaries of Henry's administrative machine. By 1130 they ran nearly everything.

What sort of people were they? Historians have previously stressed Henry's policy of creating new men—"raised from the dust," as Orderic Vitalis put it. But the reality is more complex. There is abundant evidence to document Henry's favor toward old Conquest families: Beaumont, d'Avranches, Warenne, Clare, Boulogne, and others. Conversely, the lands of certain other Conquest families were forfeited to the king on grounds of treason: Montgomery, Mortain, Grandmesnil, Abitôt, Lacy, Montfort, Malet. These forfeitures, usually ascribed to Henry's "ruthlessness," can more usefully be viewed as the final phase of a prolonged process of shuffling and reshuffling that constituted the post-Conquest land settlement—a process that involved repeated confiscations and new grants across the years between 1066 and about 1113.[67] Thereafter, the English holdings of baronial families became steadily more secure and entrenched. Henry's *curiales* included members of Conquest families—Warenne, Bigod, and Beaumont—as well as great landholders more

---

[63] Compare Tables 1 and 4, above.

[64] Robert of Lincoln, Richard of London, Ranulf the Chancellor, Walter of Gloucester, and Ralph Basset were all in the curial group; see **pp. 229, 232-34**; above, and compare Tables 2 and 4, above.

[65] *P.R. 31 Henry I*, 130.

[66] Southern, *Medieval Humanism*, 217–19, 224–25; and *P.R. 31 Henry I*, 53.

[67] Orderic Vitalis, *The Ecclesiastical History*, 5: 296. Henry attempted to marry one of his bastard daughters to William of Warenne, earl of Surrey, and later granted him the strategic fief of Saint-Saens in Normandy; C. Warren Hollister, "The Taming of a Turbulent Earl: Henry I and William of Warenne," see above, chapter 8, **pp. 137-44**. The king likewise offered his sister-in-law, Mary of Scotland, in marriage to William, count of Mortain and earl of Cornwall; on William's refusal Mary was wed to Eustace, count of Boulogne, another **English landholder**; *above*, 139. Henry, earl of Warwick, and Robert, count of Meulan, as well as various members of the Clare family grew wealthier through Henry's favor; one bastard son of Hugh d'Avranches, earl of Chester, was raised to an abbacy and another, Othuer, was given extensive lands and a wealthy widow in marriage; Hollister, "Mandeville," **120-3**. Great magnates had been disseised by Henry I's predecessors in 1075, 1082, 1088, and 1095. For a discussion of the gradual nature of the post-Conquest land distribution, see Le Patourel, *Norman Empire*, 40–45; and, for a demonstration of tenurial stabilization in the second half of Henry I's reign, see Gena de Aragon's unpublished analysis, "The Growth of Secure Inheritance in Norman England" (University of California, Santa Barbara).

recently enriched—Robert of Gloucester and Brian fitz Count, "new men" to be sure, yet hardly "raised from the dust." Besides the princely bastards Robert and Brian, the curial group included men of more obscure origins, several of whom Henry had elevated to magnate status by granting them lands and heiresses: Eustace and Payn fitz John, Miles of Gloucester, Geoffrey of Clinton, Richard Basset, and others. The group likewise included great prelates: the archbishops of Canterbury, Rouen, and York and the bishops of Lincoln, Winchester, St. David's, Évreux, and, of course, Lisieux and Salisbury. Many of these curial prelates had themselves risen from the dust—most notably Roger of Salisbury and his nephew, Alexander of Lincoln. But, although the meteoric ascent of such men provoked some contemporary comment and grumbling, Henry's policy was not simply to put down magnates and elevate new men in their places. The scattering of the post-Conquest estates presented him with the opportunity of cajoling and manipulating magnates with rewards and punishments similar to those applied to men of less exalted status.[68] Henry astutely arranged it that a great many of his wealthiest landholders were also royalists and *curiales*, and he accomplished this feat both by making magnates of his *curiales* and by making *curiales* of his magnates—luring them into his court and administration.

Accordingly, it is altogether misleading to view Henry's *curiales* as a clique of smallholding royal administrators pitted against the great landholders. On the contrary, the *curia* included a good percentage of England's wealthiest lay and ecclesiastical tenants-in-chief, some of whom had been reared from childhood in Henry's court or elevated to prelacies from the staff of royal chaplains.[69] By 1130, at least half of the ten wealthiest English landholders were also the king's *curiales*. This meld of wealth and service helps explain the *curiales'* remarkable hold on Anglo-Norman administration and politics and the absence of serious opposition to Henry's government in England. It also suggests a major qualification to the traditional notion of competition among honorial, ecclesiastical, and royal jurisdictions; for many of Henry's wealthiest barons and prelates were also among his more active *curiales*. Drawn to the king's side by the tug of their own ambitions, the *curiales* were, with rare exceptions, devoted royalists. They viewed the advancement of Henry's interests and their own as two sides of the same coin. Long after Henry's death Gilbert Foliot reminded the curial magnate Brian fitz Count of the "good and golden days" when King Henry "reared you from boyhood, educated you, knighted you, enriched you."[70]

HENRY I'S REIGN CONTRIBUTED MUCH to the development of English medieval institutions: it witnessed the origin of the exchequer and justices in eyre, and the concentration in Roger of Salisbury's hands of authority over exchequer,

---

[68] See, for example, Hollister, "Taming of a Turbulent Earl," above, 137-44.
[69] On the royal chaplains' near monopoly of major prelacies during much of the reign, see M. Brett, *The English Church under Henry I* (Oxford, 1975), 104–12.
[70] Gilbert Foliot, *The Letters and Charters of Gilbert Foliot*, ed. Adrian Morey and Christopher Brooke (Cambridge, 1967), 61; and Southern, *Medieval Humanism*, 220 (Southern's translation).

judicature, and viceregency—an authority that prefigured the later chief justiciarship. But subsequent kings, despite the machine's steady growth, had less success with it than Henry I. He was solvent, they were not—at least from the thirteenth century on. He kept the peace as few of them were able to do. And he achieved it not simply by developing the new administrative machinery but by placing it firmly under the control of some twenty or thirty *curiales*. In their hands the machine kept the treasury full for the defense of the Anglo-Norman state against domestic and foreign enemies. Just as important, it enabled Henry I to tighten his hold on his dominions and to enforce royal justice as never before.

14

THE MAKING OF THE ANGEVIN EMPIRE*
(With Thomas K. Keefe)

During the last half of the twelfth century the kings of England ruled a vast constellation of lands stretching from Ireland to the Mediterranean, known traditionally, if not quite accurately, as the "Angevin Empire." While the empire lasted, its rulers were the richest and strongest in Christendom. When King John lost Normandy, Anjou, Maine and Touraine, he also lost much of his income and influence, and the kings of France became the great royal figures of the thirteenth century. It is the purpose of this paper to explore the origins of the Angevin empire, and in particular the union of its two chief components — the Anglo-Norman state and the county of Anjou. Did the empire come about by accident or by political design? And if by design, who was its architect? Was it Henry I, who arranged the crucial marriage between his daughter Maud and Geoffrey, heir to Anjou? Was it Geoffrey, or Maud? Or was it their son, Henry Plantagenet — the ultimate beneficiary of the marriage?

At first glance, the empire would seem to have been conceived in the calculating mind of Henry I, who could hardly have failed to grasp the implications of a marriage joining the Anglo-Norman heiress to the Angevin heir. Indeed, many treatments of the subject, both old and recent, have suggested that the Angevin empire arose from King Henry I's "immensely grandiose designs" to absorb Anjou. But did Henry I have any such desire, or any such intention? The question can only be answered after a careful analysis of Henry I's diplomacy, both in its general contours and in its relation to Anjou.

When Henry I won Normandy from his brother Robert Curthose in 1106, contemporaries observed that this "English conquest of Normandy" occurred forty years to the day after Duke William's landing on Pevensey Beach. The point continues to be made, but its implication is misleading. Henry's victory at Tinchebray was not Hastings in reverse. Despite the Conqueror's dynastic claims, despite the prior settlement of certain Normans in England, and despite the continuity of Anglo-Saxon institutions, the Norman Conquest of England was a conquest indeed. In 1066 and the

*Mr. Hollister wishes to express his gratitude to the American Council of Learned Societies, the American Philosophical Society, the Social Science Research Council, the Fulbright Commission, the John Simon Guggenheim Memorial Foundation, and the Warden and Fellows of Merton College, Oxford for their help in supporting the research for portions of this paper.

years just following, an aristocracy was uprooted and another put in its place. Two previously separate states were now bound together by a common nobility, chancery, court, architecture, and aristocratic language and culture. This *ensemble anglo-normand*, as Professor de Bouard calls it,[1] was far more than a mere dynastic union; when England and Normandy were divided on the Conqueror's death in 1087, their aristocracies remained tightly interwoven. Robert Curthose tried to conquer England, William Rufus went far toward conquering Normandy, and their barons, with lands on both sides of the Channel, could follow one lord only by betraying the other.[2] Eventually Curthose pawned Normandy to Rufus and went crusading, but in 1100, when Henry I succeeded Rufus in England and Curthose returned to Normandy, the Anglo-Norman state was once again two-headed.

In an age when governance was a joint enterprise of prince and feudal nobility, Henry I found himself ruling an unstable kingdom whose chief lords were also major vassals of the Norman duke. In 1100, England's two greatest landholders — William of Mortain earl of Cornwall and Robert of Bellême earl of Shrewsbury — were also the two greatest landholders in Normandy. They were Henry's strongest magnates yet could not be trusted. Duke Robert Curthose, for his part, could hardly have found it satisfactory that Henry's closest adviser, Robert of Meulan, exercised great power in the Risle Valley and the lower Seine with his castles of Vatteville, Pont-Audemer, Beaumont-le-Roger and Brionne, nor could Robert of Meulan regard these castles as secure so long as Curthose ruled at Rouen. So it was that in 1100-1106, as in 1087-1096, warfare between duke and king was endemic and baronial estates were forfeited on a large scale.

England and Normandy, sharing a single ruling class, could not be governed satisfactorily by two independent rulers.[3] Henry

---

1. Michel de Bouard, "Le duché de Normandie," in *Histoire des institutions françaises au moyen âge,* ed. F. Lot and R. Fawtier, *Institutions seigneuriales* (Paris, 1957), I, 23.

2. Ordericus Vitalis, *Historia Ecclesiastica,* ed. A. Le Prévost (Paris, 1838-55), IV, 201 (A. D. 1104): William count of Evreux recalling the biblical injunction against serving two masters, expressed his wish to be subject to one lord only, lest, in being subject to two, he should satisfy neither. cf. *ibid.,* III, 268-69. [Hereafter, Orderic, *Historia.*] On the general subject of Anglo-Norman unity see John Le Patourel, *Normandy and England, 1066-1144* (Reading, 1971).

3. The period 1101-1106 saw an invasion of England, three campaigns against ducal Normandy, attacks by Norman enemies of Henry I against the Norman lands of Henry's friends, and the confiscation of English lands of Curthose's allies. These events are chronicled by Orderic, and by Robert of Torigny in *Gesta Normannorum Ducum,* ed. Jean Marx (Rouen, 1914), pp. 266 ff.

and Curthose both aspired to all their father's dominions, and their personal ambitions to reunite the *regnum Norman-Anglorum*[4] were in step with political reality. This point requires emphasis in the light of recurring tendencies to regard Henry's conquest of Normandy as an unjustifiable aberration or an act of naked imperialism. English historians today, conscious of England's great future as an island kingdom, are too apt to regard the continental domains as an unfortunate distraction. The Norman and Angevin kings, lacking the gift of foreknowledge, regarded their trans-Channel state as a viable unit, and until the disasters of John's reign their point of view was reasonable enough — at least as regards the fusion of England and Normandy. Early twelfth-century England had far more in common with Normandy than with Scotland, Wales or Ireland.

By misinterpreting Tinchebray as simply another product of boundless Norman ambition, one misses the whole point of Henry I's diplomacy. His reign is not a continuation of eleventh-century Norman imperialism but a rejection of it. During the eleventh century great Norman empire builders such as Robert Guiscard, Bohemund, Roger d'Hauteville and William the Conqueror were spreading Norman power all across Christendom — in Apulia, Calabria, Sicily, Antioch, Maine, England and Wales.[5] William Rufus, king of England and son of the Conqueror, was said to have coveted the throne of France[6] and at the time of his death was about to take Aquitaine in pawn, boasting that he would hold his Christmas court in Poitiers.[7] But when an arrow struck Rufus down in August, 1100, everything changed. Henry I, the youngest of the Conqueror's four sons, had grown up with a relatively good education and modest expectations. Now in his early thirties, he seized the unlooked-for opportunity, and six years later he brought an end to the Anglo-Norman civil war with his victory at Tinchebray. Having reunited his father's dominions, he seems to have desired no more.

Well past the age of youthful recklessness, Henry devoted his

---

4. The term was coined by the Hyde chronicler in the 1120s: "Chronica Monasterii de Hida juxta Wintoniam," in *Liber Monasterii de Hyda*, ed. Edward Edwards (Rolls Series, 1866), p. 304.

5. See David C. Douglas, *The Norman Achievement* (London, 1969).

6. See Suger, *Vie de Louis VI*, ed. Henri Waquet (Paris, 1964), p. 10. Rufus' Vexin campaigns of 1097-98 suggest a major effort to expand Normandy at French expense: *ibid.*, pp. 6-12; Orderic, *Historia*, IV, 21-24; *Recueil des historiens des Gaules et de la France*, ed. M. Bouquet *et al.* (Paris, 1877), XII, 5.

7. William of Malmesbury, *Gesta Regum Anglorum*, ed. William Stubbs (Rolls Series, 1887-89), II, 379. Rufus' boast was fulfilled by Henry II in 1166.

remaining twenty-nine years to defending, pacifying, centralizing
and consolidating the state that had, beyond all expectation, fallen
to him. Unlike his bellicose contemporaries — Louis VI, Baldwin
VII of Flanders, William of Mortain, and others like them — he
"preferred to contend by council rather than by sword,"[8] or, to
put it less charitably, he preferred bribery to battle. In short, he
ill-fit the eleventh-century Norman image of the conquering warrior. He disliked war and, beyond the limits of his patrimony, he
had no taste for expansion. "Peace he loved," wrote the archbishop
of Rouen upon Henry's death, and all contemporaries agreed.[9]
It was not peace on earth that Henry sought, but peace in the
Anglo-Norman state, in the furtherance of which he was quite
willing to foment war elsewhere — among the barons of the French
royal domain or the townsmen of Flanders — or to enforce with full
rigor the laws of Normandy and England against treason.

Peace he loved, and peace he kept. It is well known that during
all but the first two years of Henry's thirty-five-year reign England
was placid. It is less appreciated that Henry was also remarkably
successful in keeping the peace in Normandy, where twenty-seven
of his twenty-nine years were free of domestic turmoil.[10] Indeed,
the archetypal rebellion of restless feudal magnates against their
prince was quite out of the question in Henry's reign, except as an
accompaniment to foreign wars against the Anglo-Norman realm.
Of the two Norman uprisings against Henry I, the first, in 1118-19,
followed two years of hostilities between Henry and Louis VI and
occurred in concert with an overt Franco-Angevin invasion of
Normandy; the second, in 1123-24, was a direct outgrowth of
Henry's hostilities with Anjou. It was stirred up by the count of
Anjou's uncle, Amaury de Montfort,[11] and among the troops man-

---

8. *Ibid.*, p. 488.

9. William of Malmesbury, *Historia Novella*, ed. K. R. Potter (London,
1955), p. 14.

10. Normandy suffered warfare for about 1½ years in 1118-19, when hostilities were limited chiefly to the Pais de Bray, the Norman Vexin, the county of
Evreux, and the Maine frontier. Although Henry's control of the duchy was
severely threatened during these months, most of central and western Normandy
remained free of violence. There were, in addition, about five months of hostilities
in 1123-24, confined largely to the Risle valley. Suger remarks that in 1118 Louis
VI invaded a land long accustomed to peace (pp. 184-86); likewise Orderic reports, relative to Count Geoffrey's invasion of Normandy after Henry's death:
"provisions were abundant . . . after a long peace under a good prince . . .:
Historia, V, 73. William of Malmesbury credits Henry with establishing such
peace in Normandy as had never been known before: *Gesta Regum*, II, 476.

11. Orderic, *Historia*, IV, 439-41. Amaury was lord of Montfort l'Amaury
and Epernon in France, Count of Evreux in Normandy, and ancestor of the
thirteenth-century English rebel, Simon de Montfort.

ning the Norman rebel castles were French vassals of Louis VI —
including the king's own cook.[12]

In his pursuit of peace, therefore, Henry necessarily devoted
himself above all else to the security of the Anglo-Norman frontiers.
The long Norman border was protected by a formidable line of
rivers and fortresses.[13] Henry himself built or strengthened no less
than fifteen castles along the frontiers of Brittany, Maine, Perche,
the Vexin Français, the Beauvaisis, and Eu-Ponthieu.[14] More than
once the issue of controlling frontier castles provoked hostilities
with the king of France and the count of Anjou,[15] but on the whole
Henry's fortresses served their purpose well.

No less important than this arc of castles was an encircling ring
of friendly princes bound to Henry I by vassalage, or marriage alliances, or both. Henry, so far as is known, holds the English record
for royal bastards. William of Malmesbury insists that he begat his
twenty or more natural offspring for reasons of policy rather than
pleasure,[16] and whatever the truth of this remarkable observation,
there remains the striking fact that Henry's natural daughters were
wed to princes all along the Anglo-Norman periphery — to Rotrou
count of Perche, to William Gouet lord of Montmirail (Perche),
to Matthew of Montmorency (with interests in the French Vexin),
to Eustace lord of Breteuil, to Roscelin of Beaumont-le-Vicomte
(Maine), to Conan III duke of Brittany, to Fergus earl of Galloway, and to Alexander king of Scots.[17] Both King Alexander and
his successor, King David, were brothers of Henry's queen, Edith-
Matilda, and, like her, were descendants of the Old English royal
line. King David married the heiress of Henry's first cousin and
named his first son after Henry. As earl of Huntingdon through
Henry's favor, David had been an active Anglo-Norman adminis-

---

12. *Ibid.*, p. 448; Achille Luchaire, *Louis VI le Gros: Annales de sa vie et
de son règne* (Paris, 1890), p. cxvii and no. 334.

13. Suger, *Louis VI* pp. 184-86. Jean-François Lemarignier, *Recherches sur
l'hommage en marche et les frontières féodales* (Lille, 1945), pp. 34-72.

14. *Gesta Normannorum Ducum*, p. 309; Orderic, *Historia*, IV, 304 and
passim; The History of the King's Works, I, *The Middle Ages*, ed. R. Allen
Brown, H. M. Colvin, and A. J. Taylor (London, 1963), 35.

15. .Suger, *Louis VI*, p. 106; Orderic, *Historia*, *IV*, 46; below, n. 41.

16. Malmesbury, *Gesta Regum*, II, 488.

17. See *The Complete Peerage* (new ed.), XI, App. pp. 112-20; and, on
the wife of Fergus earl of Galloway, G. W. S. Barrow, *Robert Bruce* (Berkeley,
1965), p. 36 n. 2 (the evidence for this marriage is strong but not conclusive).
A proposed marriage between one of Henry's daughters and Hugh II lord of
Châteauneuf-en-Thymerais, probably *c.* 1113, was blocked on grounds of consanguinity: Ivo of Chartres, "Epistolae," *Recueil des historiens des Gaules*, XV,
167-68. Many of these marriages occurred in connection with specific political
crises or accompanied the conclusion of peace settlements.

trator and courtier, and Anglo-Scottish relations remained unclouded throughout Henry's reign.[18] Finally, Henry cemented relations with the county of Boulogne by marrying his wife's sister, Mary of Scotland, to Count Eustace III and later marrying their heiress to his nephew, Stephen of Blois.

These numerous alliances disclose a single underlying policy. Henry arranged marriages for his kindred with an eye toward strengthening alliances with neighboring princes. After the first two or three years of his reign he strictly avoided marrying his daughters or close female relatives to domestic magnates.[19] His bastard sons, on the other hand, were never married to foreign heiresses[20] nor did he himself, through his own marriages, make any attempt to extend his dominions. His two wives, Edith-Matilda and Alice of Louvain, helped to cement relations with the kings of Scotland and with Godfrey count of Louvain, but neither bride brought any lands with her. Thus, neither through conquest nor through marriages did Henry I endeavor to expand the boundaries of the Anglo-Norman state. Marriages might provide useful alliances or opportunities for the peaceful extension of Norman influence,[21] but Henry did not use them to advance his frontiers. The marriages of Henry's legitimate offspring to the children of Count Fulk V of Anjou were characteristic instances of a general marriage strategy aimed at gaining allies, not lands.

Beyond the circlet of castles protecting Henry's continental frontiers, and beyond the flank of allied princes, were three powerful and potentially hostile states — Flanders, Anjou, and the French royal domain — which could be extremely dangerous when allied with one another. Henry I and Louis VI had serious differences, chief among which were Louis' apprehension of a too-powerful and none-too-friendly duke of Normandy and Henry's disinclination to humble himself, and perhaps compromise Anglo-Norman unity, by

---

18. Henry's relations with Wales were more complex and turbulent than with Scotland, owing largely to political instability among the Welsh, but here, too, Henry's policy was generally non-aggressive: see Lynn H. Nelson, *The Normans in South Wales* (Austin, 1966), p. 124: "Henry's ascendancy in Wales established an era of relative peace which was unparalleled in the history of the region."

19. Henry had attempted unsuccessfully *c.* 1101 to marry a daughter to William II de Warenne earl of Surrey and to marry his sister-in-law Mary to William count of Mortain and earl of Cornwall: *S. Anselmi Opera Omnia*, ed. F. S. Schmitt (Stuttgart, 1946-61), V, ep. 424; *Liber Hyda*, p. 306.

20. Those of their wives who are known were heiresses of lands within the confines of the Anglo-Norman state. See *Complete Peerage*, XI, App. pp. 106-11.

21. As in Scotland under King David: R. L. G. Ritchie, *The Normans in Scotland* (Edinburgh, 1954), pp. 179 ff.

rendering Louis homage for Normandy.[22] As Abbot Suger put it, quoting Lucian, "Caesar cannot abide a superior, nor Pompey an equal."[23]

On four occasions Henry and Louis were at odds — in 1109-13, 1117-20, 1123-24, and 1127-28 — though even then their hostilities were usually carried on indirectly, by supporting one another's enemies rather than by straightforward military confrontation. Henry never launched a serious invasion of France, and Louis invaded Normandy only once (1118-19). After *c.* 1111 Louis supported the pretensions of Henry I's nephew William Clito, son of ex-Duke Robert Curthose whom Henry held captive in England. Louis' goal was to install Clito in Normandy; Henry's was to keep Clito out and preserve the status quo. Since Henry was always triumphant in the end, these wars changed nothing, and historians are not inclined to take them very seriously. To Henry, however, they were wars of survival, important above all else, and unless this fact is kept in mind the policies of Henry's reign cannot be understood.

In the conflicts between the two kings the leanings of Flanders and Anjou were crucial. Both were vassal states of France, and it was essential that Henry devise ways of detaching them from their French allegiance. Thus, he concluded money-fief treaties with the counts of Flanders in 1110, 1119, and 1128,[24] though the success of his Flemish policy owed still more to the fortuitous deaths of hostile Flemish counts in battle.[25] Henry's relations with Anjou were constantly troubled by the issue of suzerainty over Maine, which had long been disputed between the Norman dukes and Angevin counts.[26] William the Conqueror and William Rufus had

---

22. See *Recueil des Historiens des Gaules*, XII, 281, and, for a general discussion, Lemarignier, *Hommage en marche*, pp. 73-100.

23. Suger, *Louis VI*, p. 182.

24. The Flemish money fiefs, or *fiefs rentes*, provided that the counts would render military service to Henry under certain stipulated conditions in return for an annual payment. The arrangement had existed under William I and William II and was renewed by Henry I in 1101 and 1110 with Count Robert II, in 1119 with Count Charles the Good, and in 1128 with Count Thierry. See *Diplomatic Documents Preserved in the Public Record Office*, I, ed. Pierre Chaplais (London, 1964), nos. 1 and 2; *Liber Hyda*, p. 320; Galbert of Bruges, *Histoire du meurtre de Charles le Bon*, ed. Henri Pirenne (Paris, 1891), p. 176; Orderic, *Historia* IV, 483-84; L. Vercauteren De Smet, in *Etudes d'histoire dédiées à la mémoire de Henri Pirenne* (Brussels, 1937), pp. 418-23. In 1134 Henry arranged a marriage between his son-in-law's sister, Sibylla of Anjou, and Thierry Count of Flanders: Orderic, *Historia*, IV, 484 and n. 4.

25. Robert II was killed in 1111 while in arms against Henry's ally, Theobald of Blois; Baldwin VII was mortally wounded in 1118 near Eu; Count William Clito was killed at the siege of Aalst in July, 1128.

26. See the discussions in Kate Norgate, *England under the Angevin Kings*

both struggled to control Maine directly, whereas Henry I contented himself with a loose overlordship and purchased the support of the Manceaux in his 1105-6 campaigns against Curthose. Count Elias of Maine had been a bitter enemy of William Rufus but became a faithful ally of Henry I. He played a significant role in Henry's behalf at Tinchebray and remained on friendly terms with the Anglo-Normans until his death in 1110.[27] But Elias had married his heiress-daughter Eremburga to the young Fulk V, heir to Anjou, and in 1110, when Fulk inherited Maine *jure uxoris*, he refused the homage to Henry that Elias had earlier rendered.[28] Thus did Henry's troubles with Anjou begin.

Already at odds with Louis VI, Henry now engaged in armed conflict with Fulk (1111-13), in the course of which he captured the key frontier fortress of Alençon and extended his control over a number of castles in Maine.[29] The peace of Normandy remained unbroken during these years; Louis VI was distracted by wars against Henry's nephew and ally, Theobald count of Blois, in league with rebellious barons of the Ile de France. But potentially the Franco-Angevin alliance represented a dangerous threat to Normandy,[30] and by 1113 Henry was seeking peace. His method was one that he would use again under similar circumstances in 1119 and 1127-28: he bought off Anjou, separating Fulk V from his French suzerain and settling the issue of Maine by a union of the Anglo-Norman and Angevin houses. In late February, 1113, Henry and Fulk met near Alençon where Fulk did homage to Henry for Maine and Henry betrothed his son and heir, William Adelin,[31] to Fulk's daughter Matilda. The maneuver had precisely the effect that Henry intended; bereft of his Angevin ally, Louis came to

---

(London, 1887), I, 203 ff.; L. Halphen, *Le Comté d'Anjou au xie siècle* (Paris, 1906), pp. 66-80, 178-90; and Robert Latouche, *Histoire du comté du Maine pendant le xe et le xie siècle* (Paris, 1910), pp. 31-53 and *passim*.

27. Orderic, *Historia*, IV, 103, 219, 225, 230; cf. the eyewitness account of Tinchebray in *English Historical Review*, XXV (1910), 295-96.

28. This crucial marriage was the product of negotiations running back into the late eleventh century. Prior to 1098 Fulk IV, count of Anjou (1067-1109), had betrothed his eldest son, Geoffrey Martel, to Eremburga. Geoffrey was killed in 1106, and by 1109 his younger brother, Fulk V, had wed the Maine heiress. Thus, Fulk V succeeded to Anjou on his father's death in 1109 and to Maine on Elias's death in 1110: Halphen, *Le Comté d'Anjou*, pp. 190, 318; Josèphe Chartrou, *L'Anjou de 1109 à 1151* (Paris, 1928), pp. 4-6. On Elias's feudal subordination to Henry I see Henry of Huntingdon, *Historia Anglorum*, ed. T. Arnold (Rolls Series, 1879), p. 237; *Anglo-Saxon Chronicle*, *s.a.* 1110.

29. Orderic, *Historia*, VI, 304-05.

30. The threat would have been even greater had not Count Robert of Flanders been killed in 1111, leaving his county to his youthful son, Baldwin VII; Luchaire, *Louis VI*, *nos.* 121-22.

31. So named by Orderic, from the Old English Ætheling — prince and heir.

terms within a month and conceded to Henry the overlordship of Bellême, Brittany, and Maine.[32]

It has been argued that the betrothal of William and Matilda betrays Henry's designs on Anjou itself. In late February 1113, so it is urged, Matilda of Anjou was the sole offspring and heiress of Fulk and Eremburga, and her future husband stood to inherit the direct lordship of Maine and Anjou upon Fulk's death. But, as has been shown, Henry had a far more immediate motive for the marriage. Even the most optimistic of monarchs can hardly have pinned much hope on the engagement of a nine-year-old son to an infant "heiress" whose parents had been married only a few years, whose father was still in his early twenties, and whose mother was three months pregnant with her second child (Geoffrey, the eventual heir).[33] Moreover, William and Matilda did not in fact marry for six years, by which time Matilda's chances of bringing Anjou to her husband were annulled by the existence of two healthy brothers.

Hostilities between Henry and Louis recommenced in 1117. Early the following year Louis summoned his vassals, Baldwin of Flanders and Fulk of Anjou, to join him in a three-pronged attack against Normandy, to drive out Henry and install William Clito in his place. 1118 and 1119 were the crisis years of Henry's reign. Louis ravaged the Norman Vexin, Fulk attacked from the south, Baldwin invaded the Pais de Bray, and the allegiance of Henry's own Norman barons began to crumble.[34] Campaigning incessantly, Henry managed to keep fairly good order in central and western Normandy. But faced with the steady erosion of his vassals' loyalty and the uncovering of an assassination plot in his own household, he came close to losing his nerve.[35] In 1118, for the first and last time in the reign, Henry faced full-scale invasion by France, Anjou, and Flanders in combination. It was an experience he would never forget.

---

32. Orderic, *Historia*, IV, 307-08. Henry's overlordships of Bellême, Brittany and Maine were inherited from his father, though not without dispute (Lemarignier, *Hommage en marche*, pp. 63-66, 114-21). Thus, at least from the Anglo-Norman point of view, the Gisors treaty represented a return to the status quo.

33. Fulk V, born in 1090 or 1092, married Eremburga sometime between 20 May 1106 and 14 April 1109. So Matilda was born between 1107 and 1111. Geoffrey was born on 24 August 1113: Halphen, *Le Comté d'Anjou*, pp. 190, 318; Chartrou, *L'Anjou*, pp. 1, 4, 15; "Annales de Saint-Aubin," in *Recueil d'annales angevines et vendômoises*, ed. L. Halphen (Paris, 1903), p. 7. Orderic (*Historia*, IV, 439) thinks that Matilda was about 12 in mid-1119.

34. The chief sources are Orderic, Suger, and the Hyde chronicle.

35. See, on the near failure of nerve, *Liber Hyda*, p. 316 and Orderic, *Historia*, IV, 328-29. On the assassination plot, Suger, *Louis VI*, p. 190; Malmesbury, *Gesta Regum*, II, 488.

In September, 1118, Count Baldwin VII was removed from the war by a battle wound of which he later died, but in December Henry suffered the heaviest defeat of his career when his army was routed by Fulk V at Alençon.[36] The battle seldom appears in English histories, having been all but suppressed by the contemporary Anglo-Norman chroniclers,[37] but it was crucial none the less. Combined with the betrayal of Andely to Louis VI shortly afterwards, it drove Henry to seek once again a separate peace with Anjou. In return for rich gifts, Fulk agreed to the marriage of the couple who had been betrothed in 1113. Thus, in June, 1119, Fulk broke his alliance with Louis, and William Adelin married Matilda of Anjou, receiving the lordship of Maine as dowry.[38] Fulk then departed for a visit to Jerusalem, apparently committing the overlordship of Maine to Henry I, to be restored to Fulk when he returned.[39]

Shortly after the marriage Henry routed Louis' army at Brémule, and in 1120 the two kings concluded a definitive peace.[40] Louis received homage for Normandy, not from Henry himself but from his son, and in granting the duchy to William Adelin, Louis in effect rejected the claims of William Clito. The peace might well have endured had it not been for William Adelin's death in the White Ship disaster of November, 1120, nullifying the homage, severing the bond with Anjou, and leaving the Anglo-Norman state without an heir.

As it was, Fulk's return from Jerusalem a year or so later was followed by discord with Henry I over the full restoration of Matilda's dowry. At issue were Alençon and other frontier strongholds which Henry had regained at the time of the marriage but to which he might reasonably allege ancient claims.[41] Most or all of the fortresses had formerly belonged to the lords of Bellême over whom the dukes of Normandy had long claimed suzerainty. Henry refused to give them up, and Fulk responded by marrying

---

36. Chartrou, *L'Anjou*, pp. 11-13.
37. Orderic touches on it (*Historia*, IV, 333) but underrates its importance. Cf. "Annales de Saint-Aubin," p. 7; "Gesta consulum Andegavorum," in *Chroniques des comtes d'Anjou et des seigneurs d'Amboise*, ed. L. Halphen and R. Poupardin (Paris, 1913), p. 155; Suger, p. 192.
38. Orderic, *Historia*, IV, 347; Suger, pp. 194-96; Malmesbury, *Gesta Regum*, II, 495.
39. *Ibid.* Malmesbury alone describes the disposition of Maine and may well be confused. Cf. Norgate, *Angevin Kings*, I, 238-39.
40. Luchaire, *Louis VI*, no. 298 and references therein.
41. Simeon of Durham *Opera Omnia*, ed. Thomas Arnold (Rolls Series, 1882-85), II, 267: *terras, urbes, et castella*. Cf. Orderic, *Historia*, IV, 347-48: the town of Alençon reverted to Robert of Bellême's son and heir, William Talvas, but Henry himself received custody of the castle.

his second daughter, Sibylla, to William Clito, dowering her with Maine.[42] Thus Henry's nephew and rival acquired a territorial base —in a province over which Henry himself claimed suzerainty. There followed a brief war in which Fulk's uncle, Amaury de Montfort, succeeded in generating a Norman rebellion that Henry promptly crushed.[43] On the whole, Henry's warfare in 1123-24 is less interesting than his diplomacy. He held France at bay by persuading his son-in-law, Emperor Henry V, to attack Louis VI, and, through subtle and obscure maneuverings with the pope and his legates, secured an annulment of the Clito-Sibylla marriage on grounds of consanguinity.[44]

By 1125 Henry was once again at peace with France and Anjou, but it was an uneasy affair of unresolved differences and wounds unhealed. The annulment had infuriated Fulk to the point of burning the papal annulment letter, clapping the pope's envoys in prison, and singeing their beards and hair.[45] He submitted at last, under pain of excommunication and interdict, and Clito returned to his landless, wandering life. Fulk's feelings toward Henry can only be imagined.

Henry himself must have been growing more and more uneasy as it became evident that Alice of Louvain, whom he married early in 1121, would produce no heir. The only surviving legitimate offspring was Maud, married since 1114 to Emperor Henry V of Germany. Henry I, now in his late fifties, may even have begun to consider his nephew Stephen, who in 1125 was permitted to marry into the Anglo-Saxon royal line.[46] A number of Anglo-Normans were leaning toward Clito as the most satisfactory successor, and Henry I himself may have given the idea serious consideration. On Henry V's sudden death in May, 1125, Henry I summoned Maud home.[47] But the succession remained fluid until January 1,

42. Chartrou, *L'Anjou*, p. 16.
43. Henry's decisive victory was at Rougemontier on 25 March, 1124: see Orderic, *Historia*, IV, 455-58; *Gesta Normannorum Ducum*, pp. 294-95. The rebellion was accompanied by attacks of William Clito from Anjou: Simeon, *Opera*, II, 274.
44. Chartrou, *L'Anjou*, p. 17 and n. 4; Luchaire, *Louis VI*, p. cvi. Clito and Sibylla were indeed related within the prohibited degrees, but so, to precisely the same extent, were William Adelin and Matilda, and, likewise, Geoffrey and the Empress Maud. On Henry V's abortive invasion of France see Luchaire, *Louis VI*, nos. 348, 349, 358, and references therein.
45. *Recueil des historiens des Gaules*, XV, 251, 258.
46. He married Matilda, heiress of Boulogne, a direct descendant of Edmund Ironside and the Wessex kings. Thus Stephen's heirs would inherit the same Anglo-Saxon royal blood that Henry's own children had inherited from their mother, Edith-Matilda. On the marriage see *Calendar of Documents Preserved in France*, ed. J. H. Round (London, 1899), no. 1385.
47. Malmesbury, *Historia Novella*, p. 2.

1127,[48] when Henry made his magnates and prelates swear to accept Maud as his successor in England and Normandy.[49] There was no question now of a divided succession: to Henry the Anglo-Norman state was an indivisible unit, and Maud, like William Adelin before her, was to inherit it all.

Louis immediately broke with Henry and threw his full backing to Clito, allying the landless Norman pretender to the French royal house. In January, 1127, William Clito married Jeanne de Montferrat, half-sister of the French queen, and Louis invested him with the French Vexin — the land bordering Normandy that Louis himself had held prior to his accession. Shortly thereafter Clito, approaching Henry's frontier fortress of Gisors, issued a formal challenge claiming Normandy as his own, and it is said that some Normans rendered him the respect due their natural lord.[50] In the war that impended, Clito could count on support from Louis and Fulk, though probably not from the count of Flanders, Charles the Good, whose relations with Henry had been generally amicable and promised to remain so.[51]

On March 2, 1127, the situation changed dramatically. Count Charles of Flanders was murdered at mass, and by March 13 Louis was at Arras to help punish the murderers and participate in the selection of the new count.[52] On Louis' advice and command, the Flemings chose William Clito over several other candidates with various claims of kinship to the comital house.[53] Clito, as count of Flanders, was by no means ready to abandon his designs on Nor-

---

48. For the date see J. H. Round, *Geoffrey de Mandeville* (London 1892), p. 31 and n. 1.

49. *The Chronicle of John of Worcester*, ed. J. R. H. Weaver (Oxford, 1908), pp. 27-28.

50. Luchaire, *Louis VI*, nos. 4, 5; Orderic, *Historia*, IV, 472-74.

51. On his accession in 1119, Count Charles had continued the war against Henry I that his predecessor, Baldwin VII, had been waging, but the brief campaign ended with a treaty of peace and friendship: *Liber Hyda*, p. 320; Galbert of Bruges, *Histoire*, p. 176; Malmesbury, *Gesta Regum*, II, 479. In the midst of the 1124 hostilities Charles was a guest at Henry I's court at Rouen: Orderic, *Historia*, IV, 460-61.

52. Walter of Thérouanne, "Vita Karoli," *Monumenta Germaniae Historica, Scriptores*, XII, 557; Galbert of Bruges, *Histoire*, pp. 75-77, 81-84; F. L. Ganshof, "Trois mandements perdus du Roi de France Louis VI intéressant la Flandre," *Annales de la Société d'émulation de Bruges*, LXXXVII (1950), 117-30. On Louis' activities in Flanders see F. L. Ganshof, "Le Roi de France en Flandre en 1127 et 1128," *Revue historique de droit français et étranger*, XXVII (1949), 204-28.

53. Walter of Thérouanne, "Vita Karoli," pp. 557-58; Herman of Tournai, "Liber de Restauratione Monasterii S. Martini Tornacensis," *Monumenta Germaniae Historica, Scriptores*, XIV, 288. Clito's claim was through his grandmother, Matilda of Flanders, wife of William the Conqueror.

mandy.[54] On the contrary, he was in a position to advance them more forcefully than ever before. Henry could now expect a renewal of the Franco-Flemish-Angevin coalition that had nearly wrested his duchy from him nine years earlier.

When Henry heard the news at his Easter court at Woodstock, he was "much distressed,"[55] and in the following months he devoted money, energy, and all his diplomatic ingenuity to the goal of forestalling the impending alliance and shaking Clito's hold on Flanders. Had he merely watched and waited, he would almost surely have faced a Norman rebellion such as accompanied the Franco-Angevin hostilities of 1118-19 and 1123-24. To keep domestic peace and safeguard the integrity of his trans-Channel state it was essential that Henry move swiftly and keep his enemies off balance. Thus, he secretly sent money to various disappointed claimants to Flanders, putting himself nominally at their head, encouraging them all until it could be discerned which one might win sufficient support to unseat Clito.[56] By 1128, through Henry's machinations and Clito's inept handling of Flemish townsmen, the county was in a state of general rebellion.[57] Louis returned briefly in May to support Clito in his need but suddenly withdrew,[58] apparently in response to a military feint by Henry I against the Ile de France.[59]

---

54. Clito's various hopes are suggested by the language of his charter to Saint-Omer of 14 April, 1127: "Si contigerit mihi aliquo tempore preter terram Flandriae aliam conquirere, aut si concordia pacis inter me et avunculum meum H. regem Angliae facta fuerit, in conquisita terra illa aut in toto regno Anglorum eos liberos ab omni teloneo et ab omni consuetudine in concordia illa recipi faciam": *Actes des comtes de Flandre, 1071-1128*, ed. Fernand Vercauteren (Brussels, 1938), no. 127, cl. 7. In his comital charters Clito styles himself *Guilielmus, Dei gratia, comes Flandrie, filius Roberti comitis Normannie* (*Ibid.*, no. 125; cf no. 128). He avoided claiming the Norman duchy as his own because his father still lived. See also *Gesta Normannorum Ducum*, p. 296, where Robert of Torigny asserts that the Anglo-Norman state enjoyed undisturbed peace from 1124 to 1135, despite Clito's doing his best to disturb it during his short tenure as count of Flanders.

55. Henry of Huntingdon, *Historia*, p. 247; cf. p. 312.

56. See Galbert of Bruges, *Histoire*, pp. 78, 146-47; *Recueil des historiens des Gaules*, XV, 341; Walter of Thérouanne, "Vita Karoli," pp. 557-58; Henry actually asserted his own claim to Flanders, as son of Matilda of Flanders (*ibid.*, p. 558; Simeon, *Opera*, II, 282) but made no serious effort to acquire the province for himself. Henry's claim served as a symbol to which other claimants, otherwise mutually hostile, could rally. He put it forward, in Ganshof's words, "moins dans l'espoir de pouvoir s'en rendre maître que dans le but d'en chasser son neveu": "Le Roi de France en Flandre," p. 210.

57. Galbert, *Histoire*, pp. 132-33, 137-51.

58. *Ibid.*, pp. 157-59; *Gallia Christiana*, X, "Instrumenta," col. 192.

59. For eight days Henry sat with his army between Paris and Chartres at Epernon, a castle of Amaury de Montfort, formerly Henry's enemy but now in rebellion against Louis. Henry of Huntingdon, *Historia*, p. 247, provides the year (1128) but not the month. Louis' sudden withdrawal into France can best be explained by placing the Epernon incident in May.

By this time Thierry of Alsace had emerged, with Henry's aid, as Clito's chief rival to the Flemish countship. Hostilities continued in Flanders until late July when Clito was mortally wounded in an assault on Thierry's castle of Aalst.[60] Clito's death brought the crisis, and Henry's troubles, to a sudden end, and the Anglo-Norman state remained at peace with Flanders and France for the rest of the reign. But before Clito met his end, Henry, in the heat of crisis, had negotiated the last of the Angevin marriages.

In 1127-28, as in 1113 and 1119, Henry saw the essential importance of separating Anjou from France, and while he was subverting Clito in Flanders he was also negotiating with Count Fulk. When Henry gave the succession to Maud he had unquestionably planned to find her a husband, for the day was still far off when England could be ruled effectively by an unmarried queen. Henry's real hope would have been that Maud would give him a grandson – a proper heir who, like William Adelin, would join the Norman and Anglo-Saxon royal lines.[61] The effect of the 1127 crisis was to hasten Henry's search for a consort and to determine its direction. The succession was a matter of enormous importance, but the immediate threat to the Anglo-Norman state was more important still. Fulk's son and heir, Geoffrey le Bel, was in a position to render military assistance after Henry's death if Maud should need it. Geoffrey le Bel was still in his early teens in 1127, yet not too young to give Maud an heir. But the real purpose of the marriage was to deflect Anjou from the Franco-Flemish alliance. Contemporary writers agree on this point. In the forthright language of the Anglo-Saxon chronicler, "the king did it to have peace with the count of Anjou and to have aid against William his nephew."[62]

---

60. Galbert of Bruges, *Histoire* p. 171. Thierry had the best hereditary claim as grandson of Count Robert I and first cousin of Charles the Good (*ibid.*, p. xli). On his support from Henry I, see Henry of Huntingdon, *Historia*, p. 249. Succeeding to Flanders on Clito's death, Thierry renewed the money fief treaty with Henry (Galbert, *Histoire*, p. 176). Orderic speaks of a secret alliance between them: *Historia*, IV, 484.

61. Cf. Malmesbury, *Historia Novella*, pp. 3-4.

62. *Anglo-Saxon Chronicle*, s.a. 1127. Cf. *Gesta Stephani*, ed. K. R. Potter (London, 1955), p. 7: "King Henry gave his daughter in marriage with a politic design, that he might establish peace more surely and securely between the Normans and the Angevins. . . . He wanted to make peace in his own time." Likewise, Simeon of Durham, II, 282: "Thus, in order that he suffer no evil from his nephew, Henry sought the friendship of the count of Anjou, to whom he had previously been hostile, desiring to join his daughter, the former empress, to the count's son in marriage." Robert of Torigny (*Gesta Normannorum Ducum*, p. 300) says that Henry gave his daughter to Geoffrey in order to end the long feud with Anjou and to "escape Fulk's enmity and insolence." William of Malmesbury states that William Adelin's marriage to Matilda of Anjou and Maud's to Geoffrey were products of a single motive: Henry's desire "to establish peace between himself and the count of Anjou": *Historia Novella*, pp. 2-3.

The marriage negotiations took place in spring, 1127. Late in May, Maud crossed to Normandy to be bethrothed to Geoffrey, and the king followed in August. The betrothal seems to have occurred in the fall or early winter of 1127 at Sées, or possibly Rouen.[63] On Whitsunday, 10 June, 1128, Henry knighted Geoffrey in Rouen, and a week later Geoffrey and Maud were married at Le Mans in the presence of King Henry and Count Fulk.[64]

At the time of their marriage Maud was a widow of twenty-five and her bridegroom a boy of fourteen. But despite Geoffrey's youth, Fulk immediately associated him in the governance of Anjou. In 1129 Geoffrey became sole count when Fulk departed once again for the Holy Land to marry the heiress of the kingdom of Jerusalem.[65] Meanwhile, less than six weeks after Geoffrey's marriage to Maud its chief cause was unexpectedly removed with Clito's death in battle. The crisis ended, but the marriage endured.

In the absence of any written agreement, one is left uncertain as to exactly what the marriage implied with respect to the succession. According to the customs of the times Geoffrey le Bel would have become heir to England and Normandy *jure uxoris*. But Henry had been known to bend the laws of inheritance among his own barons[66] and there are good reasons to doubt that he intended Geoffrey as his successor. Rather, Geoffrey was, in Orderic's words, to act as a "stipendiary in his wife's behalf,"[67] seeing to it that Maud and her hoped-for heirs received their proper inheritance. He was to provide her with sons, uphold her interests, and, for his own part, be content with Anjou. Simeon of Durham asserts that in the absence of heirs Geoffrey was to inherit the English throne, but given the level of Anglo-Norman hostility toward Anjou Geoffrey could hardly expect to acquire the kingdom without a

---

63. A charter of John bishop of Sées, dated at Sées, A. D. 1127, sixth indiction, Sept. 1127-Sept., 1128), bears the words, *Signum Henrici regis Anglorum. Quando dedit filiam suam Gaufredo comiti Andegavensi juniori*: Gilles Bry de la Clergerie, *Histoire des pays et comté du Perche* (Paris, 1620), p. 106. Round (*Calendar*, no. 1192, n. 5) suggests that this clause may have been added later. Henry was probably in Rouen in the later months of 1127: *Regesta Regum Anglo-Normannorum*, II, ed. H. A. Cronne and C. Johnson (Oxford, 1956), nos. 1545, 1547; a later chronicle tradition makes Rouen the site of the betrothal; *Annales Monastici*, ed. H. R. Luard (Rolls Series, 1864-69), II, 48.

64. The dating of the marriage presents formidable problems which Kate Norgate has satisfactorily solved: *Angevin Kings*, I, 258-60.

65. Chartrou, *L'Anjou*, pp. 23-4. Fulk had been negotiating concurrently with Henry I and envoys from the kingdom of Jerusalem. He took the cross 17 days before Geoffrey's marriage to Maud.

66. Cf. the cases of the earldom of Huntingdon and the honor of Eudo *Dapifer*: *Complete Peerage*, VI, 638-42; C. W. Hollister, "The Misfortunes of the Mandevilles," above, ch. 6, 117-28.

67. Orderic, *Historia*, V, 82.

war, if indeed Simeon's statement is correct.[68] In any event, the success of the marriage as a workable solution to the succession problem depended on the birth of a son, and in this sense the whole plan was a gamble. Maud had borne no children to Henry V, and it could only be hoped that the emperor had been at fault in the matter.

The gamble almost worked. Had it not been for Maud's arrogance and ill-temper she might well have succeeded in 1135, according to plan, as queen and regent for her eldest son, Henry Plantagenet. As it turned out, her temperament betrayed her. In mid-1129 she quarreled with Geoffrey and returned to her father's dominions, thus delaying the conception of the all-important heir. Returning to her husband in fall, 1131, she bore two sons in rapid succession — Henry Plantagenet in March, 1133, and Geoffrey in 1134.[69] In mid-1135, however, she quarrelled with Henry I, with the catastrophic result that at Henry's death in 1135, he had not been on speaking terms with Maud and Geoffrey for several months.[70] Had they been in close communication it would have been vastly more difficult — perhaps impossible — for Stephen to seize the English throne. The succession plan of 1128 might yet have been implemented in 1141 when Maud held Stephen captive and occupied London, only to alienate the magnates, prelates and Londoners by her imperious behavior.[71] Only in 1154, after nineteen years of civil strife, did Henry I's grandson and namesake inherit the English throne, and when he did, England became a part of a vast continental dominion, far more heterogeneous than Henry I's Anglo-Norman state.

---

68. Simeon, *Opera*, II, 282. Simeon's remarks on continental events in 1127-28 are subject to caution. Cf. his clearly erroneous statement (*ibid.*, p. 283) that after Clito's death, and with Louis VI's consent, Henry became suzerain of Flanders and Count Thierry held it as his vassal — a gross exaggeration of the 1128 renewal of the Anglo-Flemish money fief (above, n. 24). In the years following the marriage Henry did nothing whatever to prepare Geoffrey for the throne. Geoffrey received no lands in England or Normandy and, so far as is known, was never at Henry's court after 1128. He received no oaths from the Anglo-Norman barons and was virtually unknown to them.

69. A third son, William, was born in 1136: see Chartrou, *L'Anjou*, p. 37. Maud's irascibility has been ascribed to her resentment at being joined to a boy 11 years her junior and a mere count. But she was obviously aware of Henry I's exalted plans for her and may well have played an important role in the marriage deliberations. Two of Henry's three chief counsellors in the matter were Maud's close associates, Robert of Gloucester and Brian fitz Count: Malmesbury, *Historia Novella*, p. 5; cf. *Anglo-Saxon Chronicle*, *s.a.* 1126.

70. Orderic, *Historia*, V, 45 ff.; Henry of Huntingdon, pp. 253-54; *Gesta Normannorum Ducum*, p. 320.

71. R. H. C. Davis, *King Stephen* (London, 1967), p. 61: "All chroniclers agree that in her hour of victory she displayed an intolerable pride and wilfulness."

That Henry I intended Henry II to inherit the Anglo-Norman state there can be no doubt, yet it is most unlikely that the negotiations of 1127-28 were consciously aimed at unifying England and Normandy with Anjou. Geoffrey was not to be king or duke but consort and, at the very most, co-regent for the hoped-for son and heir. Everything points in this direction. Robert of Torigny, discussing the 1128 marriage and its aftermath, calls Maud Henry I's successor *hereditario jure* and calls her sons *heredes legitimos Anglici principatus;* Geoffrey is merely *marchiatus.*[72] Maud, Henry had argued, carried the blood of English kings from both her father's and mother's side; Geoffrey had no such distinction.[73] In 1131 Henry made his magnates and prelates swear again to uphold Maud's succession, but nothing was said of the husband to whom she was returning.[74] In 1133 a third set of oaths was demanded and received, this time to both Maud and the infant Henry, with Geoffrey once again excluded.[75] In 1141 Maud and young Henry issued nearly concurrent charters in favor of Aubrey de Vere: Maud styled herself (as elsewhere) "Matilda, empress, daughter of King Henry and Lady of England," while her son titled himself, in this his earliest known charter, "Henry, son of King Henry's daughter, and rightful heir to England and Normandy."[76] In 1139 the Angevins took their cause to the pope, pleading the hereditary right not of Geoffrey but of Maud alone, to whom Stephen and the other Anglo-Norman lords had sworn their faith.[77] Throughout the an-

---

72. *Gesta Normannorum Ducum,* pp. 299-300.

73. Malmesbury, *Historia Novella,* pp. 3-4; cf. Robert of Torigny's dauntless attempt to connect Geoffrey's ancestors with the kings of France: *Gesta Normannorum Ducum,* pp. 301-02.

74. Malmesbury, *Historia Novella,* p. 10: at Northampton, 8 Sept., 1131; cf. *ibid.,* p. 13, and Henry of Huntingdon, p. 252.

75. At Westminster, probably in June or July: Roger of Hoveden, *Chronica,* ed. William Stubbs (Rolls Series, 1868-71), I, 187: ". . . fecit archiepiscopos et comites et barones totius suae dominationis jurare fidelitates Matildi . . . et Henrico filio ejus adhuc minimo, et constituit eum regem post se." See also Richard of Hexham, "Historia de Gestis Regis Stephani et de Bello Standardo," in *Chronicles of the Reigns of Stephen, Henry II, and Richard I,* ed. R. Howlett (Rolls Series, 1884-89), III, 145; Ralph de Diceto, *Opera Historica,* ed. William Stubbs (Rolls Series, 1876), I, 246. J. H. Round (*Geoffrey de Mandeville,* p. 31, n. 2) dismisses this evidence, but on insufficient grounds; cf. Chartrou, *L'Anjou,* pp. 36-37. According to the *Gesta Stephani* (p. 8), Robert of Gloucester, Henry I's bastard son and Maud's leading supporter, declared himself on Henry I's death for the succession of Maud's infant son Henry. This view seems to reflect Henry I's own; Robert was very close to Henry in his final years and was at the king's side in his last illness.

76. *Regesta,* III, nos. 634-35: *Henricus filius filie Regis Henrici rectus heres Anglie et Normannie;* cf. Round, *Geoffrey de Mandeville,* p. 186. Note the omission of a claim to Anjou.

77. *Ibid.,* pp. 250-61; John of Salisbury, *Historia Pontificalis,* ed. Marjorie Chibnall (London, 1956), pp. 83, 85. The pope decided against Maud, confirming Stephen in his possession of England and Normandy.

archy, Geoffrey neither claimed the English throne nor so much as set foot in England. According to his biographer, Geoffrey invaded Normandy in 1135 "to effectuate his son's inheritance."[78] Upon his conquest of Normandy in 1141 he assumed the title of duke, but by 1146 he had associated Henry with him in the duchy's governance, and father and son began issuing Norman charters jointly.[79] Geoffrey kept the Norman and Angevin chanceries largely separate, employing both an Angevin and a Norman chancellor. Henry I had employed a single chancellor for his Anglo-Norman realm, and Geoffrey would doubtless have done the same for Normandy and Anjou had it been intended that they be pemanently joined. But Geoffrey had no such intention. In early 1150, while still a healthy man of thirty-seven, he resigned the duchy to his son, retaining only his patrimony of Anjou. His motive was clear enough: Henry, about to turn seventeen and recently knighted,[80] had come of age and could properly receive the Norman inheritance that his father had won for him and exercised in his behalf. In 1151 Geoffrey suddenly fell ill and died, but in 1150 the expectation must have been that Normandy and Anjou would pursue separate though amicable courses for at least another generation.

To what degree does Geoffrey's behavior reflect Henry I's intentions? Geoffrey was a man of normal ambition who might aspire to more than was intended for him but probably not to less. His limited personal goals with respect to the Anglo-Norman state almost surely define the maximum of what Henry I had in mind for him. If Norman-Angevin union was a conscious goal of the 1128 marriage, it was to be achieved not by Geoffrey but by Geoffrey's son. Yet even this conclusion is doubtful. The plan of 1128 clearly involved the succession of the eldest male offspring to Maud's Anglo-Norman inheritance, and the retention of Anjou by Geoffrey. Normandy and England were tightly integrated, whereas Anjou was an alien land from which Henry I seems to have desired friendship, not union. Stephen's seizure of the throne can hardly have been predicted, and the shrewdest calculations of

---

78. . . . *ut filii sui hereditatem vindicet* . . .: John of Marmoutier, "Historia Gaufredi Ducis," in *Chroniques des Comtes d'Anjou*, ed. Halphen and Poupardin, p. 225.

79. C. H. Haskins, *Norman Institutions* (Cambridge, Mass., 1918), pp. 130-32: Geoffrey "had won and held Normandy for his son and not for himself." Cf. *ibid.*, pp. 135 ff; *Institutions françaises*, ed. Lot and Fawtier, I, 30-32, and *Regesta*, III, xxxii-xxxiii. Maud, meanwhile, was absent in England from 1139 to 1148 and could play no role in the governance of Normandy.

80. On Whitsunday, 22 May, 1149, at Carlisle, by David king of Scots. For a good discussion of the event and its implications see Ritchie, *Normans in Scotland*, pp. 295-97.

1128 would have foreseen the Anglo-Norman state passing on Henry's death to Matilda as regent for her son and heir. Geoffrey would have lived out his life as count of Anjou and as protector of his wife's interests until their son came of age.

In restrospect the question instantly arises, who was to inherit Anjou on Geoffrey's death? But to Henry I, in the heat of the Flemish crisis, this question would have seemed far less immediate than to historians of later times. The old king was almost sixty, the bridegroom was fourteen and might with luck survive another half-century. If a son were born soon, as was hoped, he would only be fifteen or sixteen years younger than his father and might or might not outlive him. The outlines of the future could be seen only dimly. Birth and death were equally uncertain,[81] and the ensuing half-century might bring any number of imponderables, including the Last Judgment. Moreover, Anjou was Geoffrey's to dispose of as he pleased, and it might reasonably have been supposed in 1128 that a younger son would someday be designated as the Angevin heir. Perhaps it is no coincidence that the first son of the marriage was named after Henry I, the second after Geoffrey of Anjou.

As matters turned out, Anjou passed in 1151 to Henry Plantagenet, not to Geoffrey the Younger.[82] But in giving his Angevin dominions to the recently-invested Norman duke, Geoffrey le Bel by no means intended a permanent union of the two provinces. In the words of William of Newburgh, the dying count "made a will bequeathing the county of Anjou to his second son; but as the outcome of events in England was still in doubt, he said, 'When Henry obtains his full maternal inheritance, namely, Normandy with England, let him yield his whole paternal inheritance to his brother, Geoffrey.' "[83] Whether this provision reflects a long-standing intention or a deathbed decision,[84] the union of Normandy and Anjou in 1151 was meant to be conditional and temporary, just as in the

---

81. Maud herself very nearly died in childbirth in 1134: *Gesta Normannorum Ducum*, pp. 303-05.

82. See Robert of Torigny, *Chronica*, in *Chronicles of Stephen*, ed. Howlett, IV, 163. Geoffrey the Younger came into immediate possession of three or four Angevin castles (Chinon, Loudun, Mirabeau, and perhaps one other.)

83. William of Newburgh, *Historia Rerum Anglicarum*, in *Chronicles of Stephen*, ed. Howlett, I, 112-14.

84. "Since both the paternal and maternal inheritances would fall to Henry as the eldest son," argues William of Newburgh, "the count was unwilling that provision for the others [Geoffrey and William] should be wholly dependent on their brother's favor, for he knew not what disposition Henry might show towards them." (*ibid.*) William's analysis of the count's motivation in this matter is doubtful. The awarding of Anjou and its dependencies shows a far greater generosity than Henry could ever have been expected to display towards his brother. Likewise, there is no record of any bequest to the third Plantagenet son, William.

years when Geoffrey le Bel had himself ruled Normandy for his eldest son. Geoffrey had resigned the duchy at the proper moment; Henry was now expected to follow a similar course with Anjou.

That Henry received Anjou at all was a consequence of his father's premature death rather than any plan for union. Had Geoffrey le Bel lived to see the reunification of the Anglo-Norman state under his eldest son, there would have been no need of the interim succession arrangement. Geoffrey could then have bequeathed Anjou to his second son directly rather than indirectly. But it was Geoffrey le Bel's responsibility to see that Henry made good his right to the throne of England. And as Geoffrey saw death approaching with England still ruled by the house of Blois, he recognized that his responsibility could only be fulfilled posthumously. Accordingly, he placed the whole of his resources at Henry's disposal — Anjou, Maine, and Touraine — in the hope that these dominions, together with Normandy, would supply revenues and manpower sufficient to gain Henry his English inheritance.[85] Geoffrey may have harbored some doubts as to the outcome of the struggle, but he can scarcely have questioned his son's determination.[86] And if by chance Henry should not recover his grandfather's kingdom, Anjou would at least serve as some compensation for the loss. The union of Normandy and Anjou would thus become permanent only if Henry failed in England, an eventuality that the dying count neither desired nor expected. His hopes are made clear by the terms of his will: that Henry would one day rule an undivided Anglo-Norman state and that Geoffrey the Younger would thereupon succeed to the county of Anjou.

Neither Henry I in 1128 nor Geoffrey le Bel in 1151 was seeking a permanent Norman-Angevin union or consciously laying the foundations of a vast feudal empire. The real architect of both the union and the empire was Henry Plantagenet who, contrary to his father's wish, retained Anjou after winning the throne of

85. See Jacques Boussard, *Le Gouvernement d'Henri II Plantagenêt* (Paris, 1956), p. 8.

86. Henry abandoned England in 1149, reports the *Gesta Stephani* (p. 148), in order to return with the aid of a larger force, enlisting the support of both the Normans and his father. Shortly before his sudden illness, Geoffrey, along with Henry, called for a council to convene at Lisieux on 14 September, 1151, to discuss preparations for the new invasion. Geoffrey died in the week prior to the appointed date and the council never met. Henry scheduled another meeting of the barons in April, 1152, and was ready to embark for England in June with a strong army when hostilities with the king of France delayed him. Finally, in January, 1153, he was able to set out on the long awaited expedition. (Robert of Torigny, *Chronica*, pp. 162, 164-65, 171).

England. The Angevin Empire had its genesis in Henry's actions and policies during the years between 1152 and 1156.

Having become duke of Normandy in 1150 and (conditionally) count of Anjou in 1151, Henry acquired the duchy of Aquitaine by right of his marriage to the heiress Eleanor on May 18, 1152. Upon the annulment of her marriage to Louis VII two months before, Eleanor had become Christendom's most coveted heiress. Among her suitors were the young Theobald V, count of Blois and nephew of King Stephen, and Henry's own brother Geoffrey, whose ardor drove him to the point of trying to capture her and make her his bride. But Eleanor preferred Henry, who was already a great feudal prince and might soon be a king, and the nineteen-year-old Henry found Eleanor and her duchy too alluring to resist.

When Henry was crowned king of England on December 19, 1154, the matter of Aquitaine made it all but impossible for him to relinquish Anjou. The Angevin lands were the essential link connecting Normandy with Aquitaine; if Geoffrey acquired Anjou he would be in a position to sever overland communications between Eleanor's duchy and the Anglo-Norman state. Henry could not afford to take this risk, for his relations with Geoffrey were cool at best. In 1152 the two brothers had been rivals for Eleanor's hand, and later in the same year Geoffrey had joined King Louis VII and Eustace of Boulogne, son of King Stephen and brother-in-law of Louis VII, in an attempt to strip Henry of his continental possessions.[87] Although Henry and Geoffrey had been reconciled afterwards, their relationship remained potentially explosive.

Henry's French suzerain, Louis VII, was no more to be trusted than Geoffrey. Louis had formed the 1152 coalition to punish Henry for marrying the Aquitanian heiress and former French queen without royal permission. Indeed, at the time of Henry's marriage Louis had not yet renounced his own rights to Eleanor's inheritance. He still styled himself "duke of Aquitaine" and regarded Eleanor as his ward. Louis did not easily forgive this encroachment in the south.[88] In an effort to counteract it he arranged

---

87. *Ibid.*, p. 165; "Annales de Saint-Serge," in *Recueil d'annales angevines et vendômoises*, ed. Halphen, p. 101; "Annales de Saint-Aubin," *ibid.*, p. 12. Louis' brother, Robert of Dreux, and his future son-in-law, Henry of Champagne, were also members of the 1152 coalition.

88. Immediately following Henry's departure for England in 1153 Louis launched a series of attacks in the Norman Vexin and kept up this harassment until August 1154 when he reached an accord with Henry: Robert of Torigny, *Chronica*, pp. 171, 172, 174, 175, 180. Between August and November 1154, as a result of this accord, Louis discontinued styling himself "duke of Aquitaine": *Études sur les actes de Louis VII*, ed. A. Luchaire (Paris, 1885), pp. 9-10.

the marriage of his sister to Raymond V count of Toulouse.[89] Henry
and Louis had been reconciled in 1154, but at the time of his
coronation Henry had yet to receive formal recognition of his
lordship over Aquitaine from either Louis or the Aquitanian magnates. His position there remained uncertain, and he might well
have anticipated renewed hostilities from the French king, perhaps in alliance once again with Geoffrey the Younger. In any such
conflict Anjou would be strategically vital.

Henry II was in a dilemma. On the one hand he was obligated
by his father's will to give up Anjou, Maine and Touraine. On the
other hand, even if he were inclined in principle to yield these
rich patrimonial dominions he could not do so without grave risk
to his control of Eleanor's inheritance. His stormy relations with
Geoffrey raised the danger of a renewed Franco-Angevin alliance
such as had earlier caused Henry I such difficulties. And with the
stake in Aquitaine, the hostility of Anjou would be not only dangerous but possibly disastrous. Yet in 1151 Henry had been
maneuvered into taking a solemn oath binding himself to carry out
the provisions of his father's will.[90] Any modification of the will
would require a release from the oath and the approval of the
French suzerain.

Henry sought to resolve his dilemma through diplomacy rather
than force, and although he was obliged in the end to resort to
arms, he had by then managed to isolate Geoffrey from his former
friends. The first, essential step was to secure a papal annulment
of his 1151 oath on the grounds that it had been sworn under
duress. Only thus could Henry gain a semblance of legality for
his retention of Anjou. William of Newburgh reports that Henry
sought the annulment not long after his coronation, and William's
chronology makes it clear that by February, 1156, the annulment
had been obtained.[91] Additional evidence suggests that the crucial
steps were taken in the closing months of 1155. In the second week
of October, Henry sent a party of highly-placed prelates on a
mission to Italy to discuss a variety of political and ecclesiastical

89. Marcel Pacaut, *Louis VII et son royaume* (Paris, 1964), p. 185. Louis'
sister Constance had been formerly married to King Stephen's son, Eustace of
Boulogne, whose death in August, 1153, broke the marriage alliance connecting
Stephen and Louis. Constance's second marriage took place in 1154.

90. William of Newburgh, *Historia*, pp. 112-14; Henry was absent at the
time of his father's death. When he arrived for the funeral ceremony, he learned
that the count had issued instructions to the bishops and magnates present not to
give his body burial until his eldest son had sworn to observe his will. Not
knowing the will's contents, Henry at first refused to take the oath, but the outcry
at allowing his father's body to suffer further corruption caused him to relent.

91. *Ibid.*

matters with Pope Adrian IV. Henry's embassy included Robert de Gorham abbot of St. Albans, Rotrou bishop of Evreux, Arnulf bishop of Lisieux, and William bishop of Le Mans.[92] Since this is the first recorded papal mission in Henry's reign, and since its timing correlates perfectly with William of Newburgh's more general report of the annulment effort, one can assume that the question of the oath was an important item on the embassy's agenda.

While Henry was awaiting news from Italy, his brother acted. In late December, almost exactly a year after Henry's coronation, Geoffrey raised a revolt in Anjou.[93] Perhaps he had discovered Henry's plan, or perhaps he simply concluded that a year was sufficient time to wait for his inheritance. Word of the revolt probably reached Henry toward the end of his Christmas court, and sometime after January 10, 1156, he crossed from Dover to Wissant on the coast of Boulogne.[94] Instead of moving directly against the rebellion he took steps to strengthen his diplomatic position and weaken Geoffrey's. From Wissant he seems to have traveled eastward to Saint-Omer,[95] perhaps contacting the count and countess of Flanders, who are known to have been with him shortly thereafter in Rouen. Sibylla, countess of Flanders, was a sister of the late Geoffrey le Bel, and thus the aunt of both Henry II and Geoffrey the Younger.[96]

By February 2, 1156, Henry was in Rouen.[97] The circumstances suggest that an Angevin family council was to be held in the Norman capital to discuss the fraternal dispute. Within the next week or so, all the Angevins directly or indirectly affected had gathered there: Henry II, William his youngest brother, Maud his

---

92. *Gesta Abbatum Monasterii Sancti Albani a Thoma Walsingham*, ed. H. T. Riley (Rolls Series, 1867-69), I, 126-27.

93. "Annales de Saint-Serge," p. 102. The annalist says that the revolt began at "media hieme." In medieval writings the term "mid-winter" usually refers to Christmas week, the winter solstice arriving on 21 or 22 December. Midwinter Day was 25 December.

94. R. W. Eyton, *Court, Household, and Itinerary of King Henry II* (London, 1878), p. 15. Cf. Robert of Torigny, *Chronica*, p. 186, n. 4 [A.D. 1156]: "Henricus rex in Normanniam transfretavit, prosecutusque est Gaufridum, fratrem suum, qui ab eo dicesserat in Andegavensem pagum."

95. Eyton, *Court, Household and Itinerary*, p. 16; *Recueil des actes de Henri II, roi d'Angleterre et duc de Normandie*, eds. L. Delisle and E. Berger, (Paris, 1909-1927), I, 107-08: charter of Henry II in favor of the hospital of Santingfeld near Wissant, issued *apud S. Audomarum* [1156].

96. Decades earlier Sibylla had seen her marriage to William Clito dissolved by papal annulment and had subsequently married Clito's rival and successor, Thierry count of Flanders. On Count Thierry and Countess Sibylla in Rouen see Robert of Torigny, *Chronica*, p. 186.

97. Eyton, *Court, Household and Itinerary*, p. 16; Robert of Torigny, *Chronica*, p. 186.

mother, Sibylla his aunt, and Geoffrey the Younger.[98] Present also was Henry's trusted Norman official, Arnulf bishop of Lisieux, who had been on the mission to Pope Adrian IV and had now returned in advance of the other envoys.[99] One can presume that Arnulf advised his lord of the pope's decision to nullify the 1151 oath.[100] With papal support, and with his moral position thus redeemed, Henry met Louis VII on the Franco-Norman border sometime in the week of February 3 to 9. The French king, having previously opposed Henry without success, had reached an accord with his powerful vassal in 1154 and was now persuaded, perhaps by the papal annulment, to carry the reconciliation still further. He received Henry's homage not only for Normandy and Aquitaine but for Anjou, Maine, and Touraine as well.[101] As Henry's recognized suzerain for Anjou, Louis could neither support Geoffrey's preten-

---

98. Maud attests a royal charter as "My Lady the Empress" at this time (Eyton, *Court, Household and Itinerary*, p. 17). The third Plantagenet brother, William, is not mentioned as being in Rouen by any of the sources, but he was with Henry at St. Omer and almost certainly accompanied him to the Norman capital (above, n. 95). He was with Henry in Chinon shortly thereafter (*c.* February, 1156: *ibid.*, p. 18; *Recueil des actes de Henri II*, I, 110-11.)

99. Arnulf attested two royal charters at Rouen during this period (Eyton, *Court, Household and Itinerary*, pp. 16-17). Frank Barlow has expressed doubt that Arnulf participated in the mission to the papal court, using a letter of Adrian IV as his evidence: *The Letters of Arnulf of Lisieux*, ed. F. Barlow, Camden, 3rd Series, LX (London, 1939), p. xix, n. 5. The letter, dated 25 April, 1156, mentions Robert of St. Albans and the bishops of Evreux and Le Mans as being present but omits any mention of Arnulf: *Epistolae Pontificum Romanorum Ineditae*, ed. S. Loewenfeld (Leipzig, 1885), no. 228, pp. 124-25. It seems much more likely, however, that Arnulf did in fact go to the pope on Henry's behalf in October but had returned by February. The *Gesta Abbatum Monasterii Sancti Albani* (p. 127), which names Arnulf as one of the envoys, states that Abbot Robert returned to England in June 1156 and that the bishops had gone home earlier. Robert of Torigny places the bishop of Evreux in Normandy on 10 June (*Chronica*, p. 188). Since Abbot Robert and the bishops of Evreux and Le Mans were all with the pope on 25 April, and since the homeward journey would have required six or seven weeks, the appearance of Abbot Robert and the bishop of Evreux in England and Normandy in June suggests that, contrary to the St. Albans writer, the bishops of Evreux and Le Mans did not leave the papal court prior to Abbot Robert's departure. Giles Constable in his article, "The Alleged Disgrace of John of Salisbury," (*English Historical Review*, LXIX [1954], 69), quite properly concludes that the *Gesta* passage actually refers to the previous departure of only one bishop: Arnulf of Lisieux. Evidently Arnulf returned early to inform Henry of the pope's decision concerning the oath, while the other envoys remained to carry on additional business at the papal court.

100. William of Newburgh, *Historia*, pp. 112-14; Henry easily obtained absolution from his oath on the grounds that oaths extorted under pressure are not binding (above, n. 90). Cf. Chartrou, *L'Anjou*, p. 86. The English pope Adrian IV was having serious difficulties at the time with Sicily and with the Roman people, and might have been in an accommodating mood toward powerful potential supporters such as Henry II.

101. Robert of Torigny, *Chronica*, p. 186; Roger of Hoveden, *Chronica*, ed. William Stubbs (Rolls Series, 1868-71), I, 215; The policy of reconciliation was subsequently cemented by the betrothal of Henry II's eldest son to Louis' daughter Margaret.

sions nor aid his revolt. Henry was free to resolve the Angevin question in his own way.

Returning to Rouen, Henry now conferred with Geoffrey himself.[102] Geoffrey's presence in Rouen, at this time of open rebellion, lends further support to the notion of an Angevin family summit. What actually transpired we are not told. Robert of Torigny states that Henry made certain offers which Geoffrey refused to accept,[103] but the nature of the offers remains obscure and the possibilities defy calculation.

Geoffrey's refusal to compromise caused a resumption of hostilities. Not until summer, 1156, did Henry finally force his brother into submission. Thoroughly defeated at last, Geoffrey renounced his claim to the paternal inheritance and received an annuity equivalent to £1500 sterling.[104] With Anjou firmly in hand, Henry journeyed to Aquitaine where the barons rendered him homage.[105] By the end of 1156 England, Normandy, Anjou, and Aquitaine were all under control, and Henry II, at the age of twenty-three, stood foremost among the princes of western Christendom.

Henry now ruled a feudal empire that his more cautious predecessors had neither desired nor clearly imagined — an aggregation of diverse provinces that differed from Henry I's tightly-integrated Anglo-Norman state not merely in size but in fundamental character. It was Henry Plantagenet's own creation, born of his youthful ambition and achieved through his skill and good fortune.

---

102. Robert of Torigny, *Chronica*, p. 186.

103. *Ibid.*, pp. 186-87.

104. *Ibid.*, p. 189. In a letter of spring or summer, 1156, John of Salisbury points out the nature of the rift between the two brothers and Henry's final object when he writes, "Geoffrey has refused to abjure in his [Henry's] favor the whole of the inheritance received from his father.": *The Letters of John of Salisbury*, ed. W. J. Millor and H. E. Butler, revised by C. N. L. Brooke (London, 1951), No. 13, p. 21.

105. Gervase of Canterbury, *Historical Works*, ed. W. Stubbs (Rolls Series, 1879-80), I, 162; Richard of Poitou, *Recueil des historiens des Gaules*, XII, 417.

Funeral plaque of Geoffrey Plantagenet, Count of Anjou.
Copper-gilt and *champlevé* enamelled; 630 x 330 mm. The plaque depicts
Count Geoffrey in a mantle and a tunic holding a sword; on his helmet is a
lion and his shield bears lioncels rampant or on an azure ground. From the
tomb of Count Geoffrey (d.1151) in Le Mans Cathedral. Probably made in
Western France. This is the earliest known example of a shield with a personal
device whose later use by members of the same family can be traced.
   (*H.E.J. Le Patourel*)

15

WAR AND DIPLOMACY IN THE ANGLO-NORMAN WORLD:
THE REIGN OF HENRY I

It has long been understood that the institutional and constitutional history of medieval England was shaped by the fiscal demands of war and diplomacy. As in the later
Middle Ages[1] so also in the Anglo-Norman era, the development of the royal administration is, in J. O. Prestwich's words, 'intelligible only in terms of the scale and the
pressing needs of war finance'.[2] Thus, the familiar administrative innovations of
the Norman kings — exchequer, vice-regency courts, justices in eyre,[3] and much
else — served the needs of a royal policy that was directed primarily toward military
expansion or defence, a policy that required pensions to allies, diplomatic bribes,
and massive outlays for military wages and the construction and expansion of castles.
The immense scope of Anglo-Norman castle building has been made clear by Jean
Yver, Derek Renn, and R. Allen Brown.[4] And recent studies by Marjorie Chibnall
and J. O. Prestwich have disclosed the impressive size and decisive importance of
the Anglo-Norman military household or *familia regis*, a rapid-deployment force of
many hundreds of paid warriors who accompanied the king or garrisoned his strongholds.[5]

Given that military expenses stimulated the precocious growth of Anglo-Norman
government, two related points will be argued in this paper. First, issues of war and
peace were of such overriding importance to the Norman kings as to shape royal
policy not only in the area of fiscal administration but in a great variety of other
areas as well. Second, and I am aware of the anachronism, war and peace in the
Anglo-Norman world occurred in a predominantly 'international' context, by which
I mean that they depended far less on the turbulent barons and feudal rebellions so
dear to our older textbooks than on relations among kingdoms and major principalities. Although baronial rebellions were indeed a continual threat, it has not always
been fully appreciated that many of them, increasingly as one moves from the
eleventh century into the twelfth, occurred in the context of international politics.

[1] See, for example, M. H. Keen, *England in the Later Middle Ages*, London 1973; Michael
Prestwich, *The Three Edwards: War and State in England, 1272-1377*, New York 1980; G. L.
Harriss, *King, Parliament and Public Finance in Medieval England to 1369*, Oxford 1975.
[2] J. O. Prestwich, 'War and Finance in the Anglo-Norman State', *TRHS*, 5th ser. iv, 1954, 19-43.
[3] The profits of justice constituted about ten per cent of all English royal revenues in A D 1130:
Judith Green, 'Praeclarum et Magnificum Antiquitatis Monumentum: The Earliest Surviving
Pipe Roll', *BIHR* lv, 1982, 16.
[4] Jean Yver, 'Les châteaux forts en Normandie jusqu'au milieu du XIIe siècle', *Bulletin de la
Société des Antiquaires de Normandie*, liii, 1955-1956, 28-115; André Chatelain, *Donjons
Romans des Pays d'Ouest*, Paris 1973; D. F. Renn, *Norman Castles in Britain*, 2nd edn, London
1973; R. Allen Brown, *English Medieval Castles*, 3rd edn, London 1976.
[5] J. O. Prestwich, 'The Military Household of the Norman Kings', *EHR* xcvi, 1981, 1-35;
Marjorie Chibnall, 'Mercenaries and the *familia regis* under Henry I', *History* lxii, 1977, 15-23.

The general pattern of political interaction between major power centres is well known. Kate Norgate long ago traced in meticulous detail the prolonged conflicts between Anjou, Blois, Normandy and England, and Walther Kienast provided a masterful account of political relations between the kings of medieval France and Germany together with their major princes.[6] More recently, David Bates and Elizabeth Hallam have provided valuable studies of relations among the French territorial principalities, while David Douglas emphasised the point some years ago that William the Conqueror's path to Hastings was cleared by the deaths, in 1060, of King Henry I of France and Count Geoffrey Martel of Anjou.[7] In later years, when France and Anjou regained political coherence, the Conqueror and his successor William Rufus fought often, and not always successfully, against these powers.[8]

Nevertheless, the defence of the Anglo-Norman dominions has proven less absorbing to historians of our century than to the Norman kings. Neither our current interest in social history nor our traditional interest in national history has encouraged us to linger over the campaigns of English monarchs in France. But when we do attempt to interpret the policies of Anglo-Norman kings in the light of their interests rather than our own, a number of seemingly unrelated events begin to shift focus.

Two of the most celebrated issues in the history of the Anglo-Norman Church, for example, reached their climax and resolution amidst the two greatest military crises of Henry I's reign. The English investiture controversy was resolved in 1105-1106, precisely the years of Henry I's all-out campaigns to conquer Normandy. And the Canterbury-York dispute achieved its greatest intensity and its resolution during the years 1118-1120, when Henry's defence of Normandy against the most formidable coalition of his reign ended in a treaty with France which, but for the subsequent disaster of the White Ship, might well have ensured peace for the next generation.

The best contemporary witnesses of these two ecclesiastical crises, Eadmer of Canterbury and Hugh the Chantor of York,[9] were aware of Henry's concurrent military-diplomatic activities, but dimly so. Their attention was riveted on the affairs of their respective churches and archbishops. Modern church historians have acknowledged the relationship between the ecclesiastical controversies and Henry's wars but without entirely appreciating the paramount importance of these particular wars to the fate of the Anglo-Norman monarchy. It seems clear, however, that although Henry was very interested in both ecclesiastical disputes, he would have viewed them as altogether secondary to his conquest of Normandy in 1105-6, his political survival in 1118-1119, and the recognition of his lordship over Normandy through an international peace settlement in 1120.

---

[6] Kate Norgate, *England under the Angevin Kings*, 2 vols, London 1887, vol. i; Walther Kienast, *Deutschland und Frankreich in der Kaiserzeit (900-1270): Weltkaiser und Einzelkönige*, 2nd edn, 3 vols, Stuttgart 1974-1975: an excessive degree of ethnic-nationalistic ideology does not rob this work of its value; Michel Bur, *La formation du comté de Champagne, v. 950-v.1150*, Nancy 1977, who discusses 'La politique des blocs princiers . . .': 290; and J.-F. Lemarignier, *Recherches sur l'hommage en marche et les frontières féodales*, Lille 1945, 34-72.

[7] D. C. Douglas, *William the Conqueror*, London 1964, 173-5; David Bates, *Normandy before 1066*, London 1982, 65-85; Elizabeth Hallam, 'The King and the Princes in Eleventh-Century France', *BIHR* liii, 1980, 143-56. See also the important articles by Robert Fossier, Marcel Pacaut, K. F. Werner, and Lucien Musset in *Les principautés au moyen âge: Communications du Congrès de Bordeaux en 1973, revues et corrigés*, Bordeaux 1979, 9-59.

[8] Douglas, 211-44.

[9] Eadmer; Hugh the Chantor, *The History of the Church of York, 1066-1127*, ed. Charles Johnson, London 1961.

Operating on this premise, let us first re-examine the Canterbury-York dispute in the years between 1118 and 1120. It is likely that Henry I had no strong convictions about the quarrel. He would have found it, in Frank Barlow's words, inconvenient and embarrassing.[10] It has been said that the Norman kings supported Canterbury over York because of their fear of northern separatism,[11] but in Henry's time, when the north was peaceful and relations with Scotland downright affectionate, there can have been no such fear. Nevertheless, for all his skill at equivocation and creative delay, Henry could not forever evade his responsibility to decide between the primacy of Canterbury and the autonomy of York. To review briefly, Thurstan, on his election to the archbishopric of York in 1114, had refused to profess obedience to Ralph d'Escures, archbishop of Canterbury. Ralph responded in the usual way by refusing to consecrate Thurstan. Under intense pressure from both sides Henry decided for Canterbury, probably because an opposite decision would have earned him more and stronger enemies. After four years of inconclusive manoeuvering, both archbishops were in Normandy where the king was fighting his war. In autumn 1119, Henry permitted Thurstan to visit the papal court which was then touring France. Pope Calixtus II consecrated Thurstan, seemingly to Henry's surprise and against his wishes. Henry thereupon prohibited Thurstan's return to England or Normandy. Thurstan stayed with the papal court, and in March 1120 Calixtus, on the verge of returning to Italy, granted him a written and sealed privilege – a papal bull – permanently exempting archbishops of York from the profession to Canterbury. Calixtus gave Thurstan another bull threatening an interdict on England and the suspension of Archbishop Ralph. At this, Henry relented and, after some further delay, readmitted Thurstan to his see.[12]

Let me now place these events in the context of Henry's military and diplomatic struggles. In 1115, shortly after the quarrel between the archbishops commenced, and immediately after obtaining oaths of fealty from the Norman magnates to his son and heir, William Adelin, Henry I tried to bribe Louis VI of France to make a formal concession of Normandy to William and accept his 'profession' for the duchy.[13] Louis would in effect have been renouncing Henry's nephew and enemy, William Clito, whose counter-claim served as the focal point of all opposition to Henry's rule. After some indecision Louis refused, and his refusal resulted ultimately in all-out war. By early 1118 Henry was engaged in a desperate campaign against the combined forces of Louis VI, Baldwin VII of Flanders, Fulk V of Anjou, and an ominous and growing number of rebellious Normans. There may well have been times when Henry would have regarded his contending archbishops as a pair of flies buzzing around the head of a gladiator fighting for his life. In December 1118, when Hugh the Chantor reports an exchange of icy words between Archbishops Ralph and Thurstan, other sources record the greatest defeat of Henry's career at the battle of Alençon.[14]

---

[10] Frank Barlow, *The English Church, 1066-1154*, London 1979, 41.
[11] Most recently, and with qualifications, by Mary Cheney in her important article, 'Some Observations on a Papal Privilege of 1120 for the Archbishops of York', *Journal of Ecclesiastical History* xxxi, 1980, 430.
[12] For a full account see Donald Nicholl, *Thurstan Archbishop of York (1114-1140)*, York 1964, 57-74, which must now be supplemented by Cheney, 'Papal Privilege of 1120', 429-39.
[13] *Liber Monasterii de Hyda*, ed. Edward Edwards, RS 1866, 309; see, more generally, C. Warren Hollister, 'Normandy, France, and the Anglo-Norman *Regnum*', above, 40-2.
[14] Hugh the Chantor, 60; Orderic, vi, 206-8; *Gesta consulum andegavorum: additamenta*, in *Chroniques des comtes d'Anjou et des seigneurs d'Amboise*, ed. Louis Halphen and René Poupardin, Paris 1913, 155-61.

Archbishop Thurstan, with his attractive blend of holiness and sophistication, was an old friend of Henry's — a veteran of the royal chapel and brother of one of Henry's most ardent supporters in the Norman war, Auduin bishop of Evreux. And Thurstan alone among the Anglo-Norman episcopate enjoyed the affection of Louis VI.[15] This fact may cast some light on Thurstan's otherwise mysterious reply in spring 1119 to Henry's entreaty that he return to England. 'If I stay here until you also return', Thurstan responded, 'I may be able to be of some use to you'.[16] Later in the year, after the decisive Anglo-Norman victory at Brémule, Henry let Thurstan depart for the papal court. The Canterbury sources state that Thurstan promised to refuse papal consecration whereas Hugh the Chantor denies it.[17] Whatever the case, Calixtus consecrated Thurstan at Reims, and according to Hugh the Chantor, Thurstan immediately began working through his friend, Cardinal Cuno of Praeneste, to urge Pope Calixtus to confer with Henry and to do all in his power to arrange the peace with France that Henry so desired.[18] The conference between Henry and Calixtus occurred a month later, in November 1119.[19] Chagrined by Thurstan's consecration without the profession, Eadmer reported a widespread opinion that Thurstan 'could never have presumed to behave as he did in so great a matter had he not noticed that the king was a willing party to it'.[20] Some evidently believed that Henry and Thurstan had an understanding from the beginning, which is possible but unlikely. It is true that Thurstan's consecration was irrelevant to Henry's interests though disastrous to Canterbury's, and that Henry's real advantage lay in appearing to back Canterbury stalwartly while availing himself of Thurstan's diplomatic talents. But in accepting papal consecration Thurstan was defying Henry's will, and even the most astute monarchs can lose their tempers on such occasions. Henry seems to have done so when he banished Thurstan from the Anglo-Norman dominions.

In spring 1120, immediately after obtaining the papal bull threatening England with an interdict and Archbishop Ralph with deposition, Thurstan visited Countess Adela of Blois and her son, Count Theobald II, Henry's nephew and military ally. Adela was Henry's favourite sister, Thurstan's spiritual daughter, and one of the most prudent politicians of her era. According to Hugh the Chantor's eyewitness report, Thurstan 'did not entirely conceal from them what he had done and what he carried'. News of the interdict threat reached Henry, but the papal letter itself was never presented to him; it was later preserved in the church of York as a memento of the victory.[21] Thereafter, Thurstan avoided the company of Louis VI 'out of prudence', because there was still strife between Louis and Henry,[22] but through the mediation of Cardinal Cuno the exiled archbishop is reported to have taken great pains to procure a peace between the two kings, 'being the man on the Norman side in whom Louis had the most confidence'.[23]

Thurstan's itinerary during the weeks following his visit to Adela suggests shuttle diplomacy. He immediately sought out Cardinal Cuno, then returned to confer with the countess while Cuno spent Easter (18 April) with Louis VI at Senlis. Two days

---

15 Hugh the Chantor, 65.
16 Hugh the Chantor, 65.
17 Hugh the Chantor, 68-9; Eadmer, 255, followed by John of Worcester, *Chronicle*, ed. J. R. H. Weaver, Oxford 1908, 14.
18 Hugh the Chantor, 75.
19 Hugh the Chantor, 76-80; Orderic, vi, 282-90.
20 Eadmer, 257; cf. Nicholl, 64.
21 Hugh the Chantor, 91-2, 102-4.
22 Hugh the Chantor, 92.   23 Hugh the Chantor, 97.

after Easter, Thurstan again met with Cuno at Dammartin and then returned to Adela to help arrange for her entry into religious life, while at the same time contacting Henry through messengers.[24] A meeting was then arranged between Cuno and Henry on 30 May at the castle of Vernon on the Norman frontier, where Henry agreed to restore Thurstan to York provided that he would delay his return until Henry had squared matters with Canterbury.[25] Shortly thereafter the peace between Henry and Louis was ratified, and on essentially the terms that Henry had offered in 1115 before the war commenced. One must not permit the subsequent catastrophe of the White Ship to obscure the fact that the peace of 1120 was a dazzling diplomatic triumph for Henry I. And Simeon of Durham agreed with Hugh the Chantor that Thurstan had played the central role in the negotiations.[26] Without inferring deeper secrets than the sources disclose, I will only suggest that the papal interdict, leaked but never delivered, was not intended as a serious threat (for Calixtus, battling with the emperor and his antipope, needed Henry's support) but as a shield with which Henry could — and did — deflect the wrath of Canterbury when he permitted Thurstan to assume his archbishopric without the profession.[27] As the Anglo-Saxon chronicler observed, 'Archbishop Thurstan of York was reconciled to the king through the pope, and came into this country and received his bishopric, though it was very displeasing to the archbishop of Canterbury'.[28] It also seems unlikely that a person as deeply involved in the politics of her age as Adela of Blois would have taken the veil until the terms of a mutually acceptable peace between her son, her brother, and the king of France had been arranged.

Fifteen years earlier, the English investiture compromise was achieved under oddly similar circumstances: the threat of a major ecclesiastical sanction and the mediation of Adela of Blois, against the background of a full-scale military campaign. In 1105-6, Henry was directing all his efforts toward the conquest of Normandy from his bumbling older brother, Robert Curthose. Unlike the Canterbury primacy issue, the papal prohibition of lay investiture and the homage of prelates seized Henry's full attention. They were direct challenges to royal customs that Henry defended on the principle of good stewardship.[29] Pope Paschal retreated early from his opposition to homage,[30] but on the matter of investiture Henry and Paschal seemed equally intransigent. At the papal court at Rome in November 1103, Henry's envoy, William Warelwast, declared (according to Eadmer) that 'the king of the English will not, even at the loss of his kingdom, allow himself to be deprived of the investiture of churches', to which the pope replied, 'not even to save his life will Pope Paschal ever permit such a right with impunity'.[31] As a consequence of this impasse, Anselm, no longer able to function in cooperation with both king and pope, went into exile

---

24 Hugh the Chantor, 92-3.
25 Hugh the Chantor, 95-7.
26 Simeon of Durham, *Opera Omnia*, ed. Thomas Arnold, 2 vols, RS 1882-1885, ii, 258; cf. *De gestis regum*, ii, 496 on the Peace of 1120: 'Veruntamen tam splendidae et excogitatae pacis serenum, tam omnium spes in speculam erectas, confudit humanae sortis varietas'.
27 At Christmas, 1120, Henry explained to Archbishop Ralph and his suffragan bishops the consequences of not readmitting Thurstan: 'Intelligens archiepiscopus sagittam hanc prius in se infigi, episcopi vero ignominiam regi reputantes in regno suo Chriscianitatem interdici, ut eum revocaret et concesserunt et consiliati sunt': Hugh the Chantor, 100.
28 *ASC*, AD1120.
29 See Henry I's letter to Paschal II: *Sancti Anselmi Cantuariensis Archiepiscopi Opera Omnia*, ed. F. S. Schmitt, Edinburgh 1946-61, v, ep. 215.
30 R. W. Southern, *St Anselm and his Biographer*, Cambridge 1963, 171-4.
31 Eadmer, 153. Both positions were overstated, as subsequent events disclosed.

at Lyons.[32]

He re-emerged suddenly a year and a half later and headed northward with the announced intention of excommunicating Henry I. At that precise moment Henry was engaged in his first full scale military campaign in Normandy, which he justified as an effort to save the Norman Church from the violence and anarchy permitted by Robert Curthose's misrule.[33] Amidst spreading rumours of the excommunication threat, and perhaps because of it, Henry's army suffered defections and his campaign halted.[34] Thereupon, through the mediation of the prudent Countess Adela, with whom Anselm discussed his excommunication plan during a long stopover at the court of Blois, Henry met Anselm at Laigle in south-eastern Normandy and negotiated a settlement. Henry retained the right to receive homage from his prelates but surrendered on the central issue of investiture.[35] In 1106 Paschal ratified the settlement, freeing Anselm to return to Canterbury and Henry to complete his conquest of Normandy.[36]

From this sketch, which radically condenses a controversy about which much has been written and much argued, it should be clear that Henry I yielded investitures because he valued Normandy more. Anselm had moved against him at the critical moment, and with the duchy at stake Henry gave in.[37] Anselm's own motive is much less clear, because of the extraordinarily murky explanations provided by Eadmer and by Anselm himself.[38] Perhaps he acted when he did for reasons unconnected with the Norman war, and his timing was a piece of good luck. Professor Sally Vaughn, on the other hand, has argued that Anselm deliberately struck at Henry when he was most vulnerable,[39] and I believe she is correct. Anselm was a great theologian and spiritual adviser; he was also a person of considerable experience in political affairs. He had spent all but the first three years of a long ecclesiastical career in important administrative offices — as prior and abbot of Bec, and, since 1093, as archbishop of Canterbury. He was acquainted with the policies and hopes of both Robert Curthose and Henry I and had twice assumed major military responsibilities in the defence of England against cross-channel invasion threats.[40] During

---

[32] Eadmer, 154-7. As Anselm and William Warelwast neared Lyons on their homeward trip, William told Anselm that Henry would receive him in England only if Anselm renounced the papal ban on lay investiture. Unwilling to ignore a direct papal command, Anselm settled in Lyons.

[33] Orderic, vi, 60-4, 86, 96, 284-6.

[34] Eadmer, 166; Orderic, vi, 78. According to Eadmer, Anselm's threat had prompted many to turn against a sovereign not too well loved.

[35] Eadmer, 166; *Vita Anselmi*, ed. R. W. Southern, Oxford 1962, 134-5; *Anselmi Opera*, ep. 388. Anselm was fully aware of the terms of the compromise (ep. 389); he regarded the settlement as 'so badly needed and so clearly right' (ep. 369) and asked the monks of Canterbury to pray that such concord might be effected between pope and king that he could be reconciled with both (ep. 376).

[36] *Anselmi Opera*, epp. 402, 428, 433; Eadmer, 182-4.

[37] Southern, *Anselm*, 176-7; Barlow, *English Church*, 299; Sally N. Vaughn, 'St Anselm and the English Investiture Controversy Reconsidered', *Journal of Medieval History* 6, i (1980): 73-6. It has often been said that in yielding investitures, Henry I relinquished little or no real power. Anselm himself had pointed this out in a letter to Henry's chief adviser, Robert count of Meulan: (*Anselmi Opera*, ep. 369); and Hugh the Chantor, 14, repeats the point.

[38] Eadmer, 163-4; *Anselmi Opera*, ep. 388.

[39] Vaughn, 'St Anselm', 73-6.

[40] In 1095, in the face of a cross-channel invasion threat, William Rufus had given Anselm the military command of southern England: *Anselmi Opera*, epp. 191-2; and Anselm had brought his knights to Henry I's army and camped with them in the field during Curthose's invasion of 1101: Eadmer, 127. On this last occasion Anselm threatened to excommunicate Curthose and

his exile of 1103-1106, Anselm remained in close touch with England;[41] on one occasion he wrote to his friend William Giffard, bishop elect of Winchester, urging him not to betray a Norman castle to Henry as many others were doing.[42] It is difficult to believe that Anselm could have been unaware of the effect of his excommunication threat on Henry's Norman war. More probably, Anselm did not really intend to excommunicate Henry in 1105 any more than Calixtus II intended to lay England under interdict in 1120. Anselm would surely have realised as clearly as Henry did that the resolution of the English investiture controversy was inseparable from the campaign to conquer Normandy and reunify the Anglo-Norman dominions – a goal that Anselm warmly supported once the investiture issue was resolved.

During the twenty-nine years of Henry I's rule in Normandy, from his triumph over Curthose at Tinchebray in 1106 to his death in 1135, his overriding priority was the defence of his Anglo-Norman dominions, through peaceful diplomacy if possible, and the maintenance of order within them. Historians have credited Henry with maintaining the peace in England but not in Normandy where, as an American writer put it, he was afflicted with 'almost incessant warfare', and, according to a French writer, he battled 'ceaselessly and without definitive success against his perpetually rebelling barons'.[43] But a closer review of the narrative sources and their chronologies suggests that the peace of Henry's duchy was broken only twice – in the period around 1117-19 and in 1123-24 – and that Normandy enjoyed relative tranquillity for all but two or three years of his twenty-nine year rule.[44] Suger of Saint-Denis remarked that in c.1118 Louis VI invaded a land long accustomed to peace. Orderic Vitalis reported that in December 1135, just after Henry's death, Geoffrey of Anjou found abundant provisions in Normandy 'after a long peace under a good prince', and William of Malmesbury praised Henry for maintaining a peace such as Normandy had never before known, even in the days of William the Conqueror.[45]

Nevertheless, Henry's lordship of Normandy was challenged periodically by the hostile coalition of France, Anjou and Flanders, fighting on behalf of Robert Curthose's son, William Clito. It was challenged not only in the war years of 1117-19 and 1123-24 but on other occasions when Henry was obliged to use all his diplomatic talents to keep Normandy free of military violence – in 1109-13 when Louis VI vainly demanded Henry's homage, and again in 1127-28 when Louis installed William Clito as count of Flanders.

In view of these later conflicts, Henry's conquest of Normandy in 1105-1106 was marked by two rather odd circumstances. First, he accomplished the conquest without hindrance from France or Anjou. He evidently purchased the neutrality of

used all his powers of persuasion to convince Henry's magnates to remain loyal to their king. Eadmer (127) went so far as to claim that without Anselm's intervention, Henry 'ea tempestate perdidisset jus Anglici regni'.

41 E.g. *Anselmi Opera*, epp. 330, 337, 355, 357; he continued to attend to Canterbury affairs while in Lyons: epp. 331, 358-60.

42 *Anselmi Opera*, ep. 322; cf. *ASC*, AD1104.

43 Charles W. David, *Robert Curthose, Duke of Normandy*, Cambridge, Mass. 1920, 180; Josèphe Chartrou, *L'Anjou de 1109 à 1151*, Paris 1928, 7.

44 C. Warren Hollister and Thomas K. Keefe, 'The Making of the Angevin Empire', above, ch. 14, 250 and n. 10.

45 Suger, *Vie de Louis VI le Gros*, ed. Henri Waquet, Paris 1964, 184-6; Orderic, vi, 472; *De gestis regum*, ii, 476.

the French monarchy, and in 1105 Geoffrey Martel – eldest son of Fulk IV of Anjou, who had associated him in the governance of the county – was leading a contingent in Henry's army alongside Elias count of Maine. Count Elias withdrew from the campaign around the time that Anselm, his friend and spiritual adviser, was threatening to excommunicate Henry I but returned in 1106 to lead the decisive charge at Tinchebray.[46] The second oddity is that after Tinchebray Henry I, a political realist not given to acts of self-defeating sentimentality, took pity on the three-year-old William Clito, and placed him under the protection of Elias of Saint-Saens, Curthose's son-in-law and devoted follower, whose chief castle was dangerously close to Normandy's north-eastern frontier.[47]

These two oddities can perhaps be explained by the fact that a fundamental shift of long-range consequence was occurring just then in the policies of both France and Anjou – a revival of royal and comital authority which, although gradual, underwent a sudden acceleration with the accessions of Louis VI in 1108 and Fulk V of Anjou in 1109.[48] Both these princes pursued energetically the goals which their fathers had sought only half-heartedly: the extension of control over castles – the all-important instruments of military and administrative authority – and the tightening of bonds of vassalage with their aristocratic subordinates through oaths of homage and fealty. French historians have viewed these policies as efforts to replace the banal authority inherited from the Carolingians, which had been in a state of advanced decay in the Ile de France since the 1030s and in Anjou since about 1060, with new, vertical lines of authority in the form of a feudal hierarchy.[49] Dr Elizabeth Hallam, in discussing the emergence of both the idea and reality of social hierarchy in later eleventh-century France, noted the close connection between the growth of Capetian feudal power and a new, aggressive attitude on the part of Louis VI on the royal lands and beyond them. Olivier Guillot, echoing Louis Halphen, noticed a similar and concurrent process occurring in Anjou.[50]

It would have been difficult for Henry I to foresee in 1106 the surge of French royal authority that began in 1108, or the parallel surge that followed Fulk V's accession in 1109.[51] Although Henry's affectionate treatment of William Clito involved a risk, it would have seemed a small one at a time when the great princes of France smiled benignly while Henry reforged the Anglo-Norman state. But Louis VI, immedi-

[46] Orderic, vi, 68, 78, 88-90; cf. *La chronique de Morigny (1095-1152)*, ed. Léon Mirot, 2nd edn, Paris 1912, 21; Suger, 106; *De gestis regum*, ii, 480. Geoffrey was killed in battle in May, 1106, well before Henry's return to Normandy for the campaign that culminated in his victory at Tinchebray: Chartrou, 3; on Elias's relationship to Anselm see *Anselmi Opera*, ep. 466.
[47] Orderic, vi, 92.
[48] Compare J.-F. Lemarignier, *Le gouvernement royal aux premiers temps capétiens (987-1108)*, Paris 1965, Éric Bournazel, *Le gouvernement capétien au XIIe siècle, 1108-1180*, Limoges 1975; Elizabeth M. Hallam, *Capetian France, 987-1328*, London 1980, 91-7, 111, 114-19; Chartrou, 26 and ff.; Louis Halphen, *Le comté d'Anjou au XIe siècle*, Paris 1906, 133-205; Olivier Guillot, *Le comte d'Anjou et son entourage au XIe siècle*, 2 vols, Paris 1972, i, 124, 352, 428-34.
[49] See in particular Guillot, i, 431-4, and for a valuable summary, Hallam, 'Kings and Princes in Eleventh-Century France', 143-56.
[50] Hallam, *Capetian France*, 95; Halphen, 203-4; Guillot, i, 433-4; cf. Karl Ferdinand Werner, 'Kingdom and Principality in Twelfth-Century France', in *The Medieval Nobility*, ed. Timothy Reuter, Amsterdam 1978, 266-7.
[51] I am using the word 'accession' loosely, to describe their acquisition of full authority over their dominions. Both men had earlier shared their fathers' titles and authority, yet the policy shifts occur just after their fathers' deaths. See Chartrou, 4; Achille Luchaire, *Louis VI le Gros: annales de sa vie et de son règne*, Paris 1890, 289-93 and no. 8.

ately after his father's death, demanded Henry's homage for Normandy, along with the homage of other princes of France, and the neutralisation of two of Henry's frontier castles on the Norman bank of the Epte, Bray-et-Lû and, more importantly, the great stronghold at Gisors − both of which, according to Suger, Henry held in violation of an earlier agreement.[52] It is characteristic of Louis VI's lifelong policy that his initial hostilities with Henry I should result from demands involving castles and an act of homage. But Henry too was avidly interested in castles and homages and offered Louis neither. The two kings met in March, 1109,[53] at Neufles-St-Martin on the Epte, Louis having plundered and burned on the way the French holdings of Henry I's chief adviser, Robert count of Meulan.[54] The meeting resulted in an uneasy two-year truce followed by two years of war in France and Maine.[55]

Meanwhile Fulk V became sole count of Anjou on his father's death in 1109, and inherited Maine *jure uxoris* in 1110 on the death of Count Elias, Henry I's friend and *fidelis*. Unlike Elias, Fulk V rejected Henry's suzerainty over Maine and refused to do him homage for it.[56] Robert II count of Flanders joined the coalition against Henry but died soon afterwards of an injury incurred while campaigning with Louis VI. Indeed, several of the military and diplomatic confrontations between Henry and Louis were affected dramatically by the strange coincidence that four consecutive counts of Flanders − Robert II, Baldwin VII, Charles the Good, and William Clito − suffered violent deaths at crucial moments; but that is another story.

During the truce after the meeting at Neufles (1109-11), Henry in England and Louis in France attended to other matters while apparently encouraging one another's magnates to plot rebellion. In 1111 the struggle flared into open warfare − all of it outside Normandy − followed by a general peace settlement early in 1113 on terms altogether favourable to Henry.[57] That he was able to keep Normandy at peace during these years and win a triumphant settlement is both noteworthy and intriguing. His manoeuverings during these years are well worth examining, for they exemplify early twelfth-century diplomacy at its best. Henry won allies by means of bribes, intrigues and strategic marriages, and he discouraged potential rebels with the aid of a remarkably alert intelligence system. Orderic credits Henry with being so thoroughly familiar with secret plots against him as to astonish the plotters, and he observes elsewhere, in connection with the quarrels of 1109-1113, that Henry swept away the designs of his enemies like cobwebs and crushed them without shedding the

---

[52] Suger, 102-6. Gisors was built as a ducal castle during William Rufus's occupation of Normandy; afterwards Robert Curthose seems to have granted it as a fief to its ducal castellan, Theobald Pain (Orderic, v, 308, 309 n.3), who apparently held it at the time of Tinchebray but returned it to the ducal authority soon afterwards at Henry's urging and perhaps for a price (Suger, 102: Theobald Pain relinquished the castle to Henry 'tam blandiciis quam minis'). From the time that he assumed the governance of Normandy, it was Henry's policy to resume control of previously ducal lands and castles granted away by Curthose (Orderic, vi, 94). Suger's account of the conflicts between the two kings in and after 1109 is badly garbled, but it remains possible that Henry's negotiations with the French monarchy with respect to his conquest of Normandy included a promise not to restore Gisors to ducal control. On Louis' demand for homages, see above, 38 and n. 121.

[53] Or just possibly April: Luchaire, no.72.

[54] Robert was count of Meulan in the French Vexin, lord of the Beaumont lands in Normandy, and earl of Leicester: see Sally N. Vaughn, 'Robert of Meulan and Raison d'Etat in the Anglo-Norman State, 1093-1118', *Albion* x, 1978, 352-73.

[55] See above, 38-9.

[56] *ASC*, AD1110.

[57] See above, 253-4.

blood of his own men.[58]

Following Orderic's hints, one can reasonably suspect that this sweeping of cob-webs was exemplified by the singular abundance of arrests and forfeitures of Anglo-Norman magnates during the troubled years between 1109 and 1113. In 1110, as the Anglo-Saxon chronicler reports without explanation, Henry disseised and exiled William Malet, William Bainard, and Philip of Braose, the last-named being restored in 1112. At about the same time, 1110 or shortly thereafter, Roger of Abitôt, sheriff of Worcestershire and constable of Worcester castle, was deprived of his lands because, as William of Malmesbury explains, with headlong madness he ordered the assassin-ation of a royal official.[59] At about the same time (1109-c.1114) Robert of Lacy was deprived of his honour of Pontefract, while in Normandy Henry ordered the arrest of William Clito, who narrowly escaped capture at Saint-Saens and fled into exile with his guardian, Elias.[60] In 1112 Henry arrested and imprisoned Robert of Bellême and exiled William count of Evreux and William Crispin, restoring these last two magnates in the peace settlement of 1113.[61] The international implications of these moves are suggested by Orderic's assertion that Robert of Bellême was at the time of his arrest serving as an envoy of King Louis VI,[62] and by the kinship ties that linked William Crispin and William of Evreux with Amaury de Montfort and his nephew, Fulk V of Anjou. William of Evreux spent his exile in Anjou, and William Crispin would later turn up in Louis VI's army at Brémule.[63]

Conversely, Henry worked during these years to win the support of magnates in the dominions of his enemies. 'Many of the nobles of Maine', Orderic writes, 'went over to Henry's side, and after doing fealty surrendered their castles to him.'[64] One noble family from Maine may have been won over, or subsequently rewarded, by Henry's grant of the forfeited Lacy honour of Pontefract to Hugh of Laval.[65] Hugh was the uncle and guardian of Guy IV, heir to the Laval estates in Maine, and one piece of evidence suggests that Guy of Laval, perhaps through Hugh's intercession, may have married an otherwise unknown bastard daughter of Henry I's named Emma.[66] Another of the royal daughters was wed at an undiscoverable date to

58 Orderic, vi, 100, 176.

59 On William Malet, William Bainard and Philip of Braose see *ASC*, AD1110, 1112; Huntingdon, 237, adds that the three men had wronged the king but does not elaborate. On Roger of Abitôt's fall see *De gestis pontificum*, 253, and *The Cartulary of Worcester Cathedral Priory (Regester I)*, ed. R. R. Darlington, Pipe Roll Society, London 1968, xxv, 26-7. The most probable date for Roger's fall is 1110; it cannot have occurred after 1114 but might conceivably be associated with Henry's Welsh campaign of May-June 1114. On Henry's arrests during this period, see RaGena DeAragon, 'The Growth of Secure Inheritance in Anglo-Norman England', *Journal of Medieval History* viii, 1982, 385.

60 W. E. Wightman, *The Lacy Family in England and Normandy, 1066-1194*, Oxford 1966, 66-7, 243-4 (Wightman recognises the international context of Henry's dealing with the honour of Pontefract); Orderic, vi, 162 and n. 4, 164.

61 *ASC*, AD1112; Orderic, vi, 178, 180.

62 Orderic, vi, 188 and n.5, 256, 344.

63 Orderic, vi, 180, 198, 236-8.

64 Orderic, vi, 176-7; Marjorie Chibnall's translation.

65 Wightman, 66-7. Wightman inclines toward a later date (1114-1118) for Hugh's acquisition and associates it with the hostilities of 1116-1119. The honour may have been in royal hands for an appreciable time between Robert's forfeiture and Hugh's arrival: Wightman, 243-4.

66 Bertrand de Broussillon, *La maison de Laval, 1020-1605*, i, 1895, 79: '. . . on prétend même que l'abbaye de Clermont aurait conservé longtemps une tombe sur laquelle on lisait: EMMA ANGLORUM REGIS FILIA DOMINAQUE LAVALLENSIS'. The author dismisses this tradition on the grounds that Robert of Torigny excludes 'Emma' from his list of Henry I's daughters, but the list is by no means complete. Emma is absent from the list of Henry's illegitimate daughters in GEC, xi, Appendix D, 112-21.

Roscelin vicomte of Maine and lord of Beaumont-le-Vicomte.[67] The winning of friends in Maine may well have been on Henry's mind when in 1111 he raised Geoffrey Brito, dean of Le Mans cathedral and a favourite of the late Count Elias, to the archbishopric of Rouen.[68] And if Henry did not instigate the rebellion of 1112 in Anjou, he was at least convenienced by the fact that it diverted Fulk V's military resources at the height of the international conflict.[69]

Meanwhile, between 1111 and 1113 King Louis VI was contending, not always successfully, with the largest rebellion of his reign. Henry I's closest friend, Robert count of Meulan, whose county in the French Vexin had been pillaged by Louis in 1109 and again in 1110, settled scores in 1111 by seizing and plundering Paris.[70] In the same year the young Theobald of Blois, perhaps on the advice of his mother Adela, broke with Louis and allied himself with Henry.[71] By 1112 a remarkably large number of French magnates had joined Theobald in an uprising against Louis. The coalition included Lancelin of Bulles lord of Dammartin, Payn of Montjai, Ralph of Beaugenci, Milo of Brai vicomte of Troyes, Hugh de Crecy lord of Châteaufort, Guy de Rochefort, Hugh count of Troyes, and Hugh du Puiset, supported, Suger adds, by an army of Normans.[72] Orderic describes Louis at this time as being too much occupied to disturb the king of England by invading Normandy.[73]

Meanwhile, Henry was winning other allies against France by marrying or betrothing royal offspring to important neighbouring princes. Two such alliances can be dated firmly to the months immediately preceding the peace of 1113. The betrothal early in 1113 of Henry's son, William Adelin, to Matilda daughter of Fulk V drew Anjou from the French into the Anglo-Norman orbit (as would their marriage in 1119, and the betrothal and marriage of the Empress Maud to Geoffrey count of Anjou amidst the Flemish succession crisis of 1127-28).[74] Similarly, the union between Henry's natural daughter Maud and Conan III of Brittany almost certainly occurred just before the peace of 1113 and was intended, as Orderic explains, to establish a bond of peace between the Anglo-Norman monarch and the Breton ducal house.[75]

Henry married a number of his bastard daughters to neighbouring princes across the Norman frontiers,[76] and although none except the marriage of Maud and Conan can be dated securely, it is likely that other such marriages were also designed to win allies during periods of conflict with France and Anjou. We have already touched on the marriages or possible marriages of Henry's daughters to Roscelin of Beaumont-le-Vicomte and Guy of Laval. Another shred of evidence is to be found in a letter of Ivo bishop of Chartres to King Henry protesting the betrothal of one of Henry's daughters to Hugh fitz Gervase of Châteauneuf-en-Thymerais.[77] The letter can be dated loosely by the death of Ivo of Chartres late in 1116, and the fact that Gervase

---

[67] GEC, xi, Appendix D, 116; Orderic, vi, 444 and n.3.
[68] Orderic, v, 236; vi, 172. I am indebted to David S. Spear for the suggestion. Hugh the Chantor, 82, 89, hints that Archbishop Geoffrey was involved in the negotiations of 1119-1120 between Thurstan of York, Louis VI, and the papal curia.
[69] Chartrou, 27.
[70] Luchaire, nos. 72, 103, 111. The episode might possibly be dated 1110; Luchaire favours 12 March 1111.
[71] Luchaire, nos. 117, 121.
[72] Luchaire, no.134; Suger, 146-8.
[73] Orderic, vi, 176-8.
[74] See above, 260 and n. 62.
[75] Orderic, ii, 352; vi, 174 and n.4, 180.
[76] See above, 251-2.
[77] *Patrologia* clxii, cols 265-6.

of Châteauneuf was in arms against Henry during the war of 1111-1113.[78] It looks very much as though the marriage plan that Ivo blocked was intended to draw the family of Châteauneuf into the Anglo-Norman alliance network in connection with the peace of 1113, and that it exemplified the same policy that brought about William Adelin's betrothal to Matilda of Anjou and Maud's to Conan of Brittany.

Not only in 1109-1113 but in later years as well, diplomatic marriages and baronial conspiracies and rebellions tended to coincide with hostilities between Henry, Louis, Fulk, and the luckless counts of Flanders. Viewed in the context of international war and diplomacy, the conventional portraits of Henry I as a menacing, avaricious monarch who arrested and disinherited his barons arbitrarily, and of Louis VI as one who devoted his life to taming the royal principality through constant warfare against the castellans, require a degree of modification. As one browses through Luchaire's annals of Louis VI with a chronology of international politics in mind, one is struck by the close correlation between the rebellions of Louis' castellans and other vassals and his wars with Henry I.[79] An oft repeated example of Louis' persistent struggles with what used to be called 'robber barons' of the Ile de France is his capture and destruction of the castle of Le Puiset on three separate occasions. Intriguingly, the occasions can be dated to the war years of 1111, 1112, and 1118, and on the second of them Louis was able to take the castle only after the departure of five hundred Norman knights who had been assisting in its defence.[80]

Not every French rebellion occurred during the years when Louis and Henry were at war. Public order was less firmly established in Louis' dominions than in Henry's, where the correlation of Norman rebellions and international wars is absolute. But it is during the years of peace that we are apt to find Louis engaged in distant expeditions, such as his campaigns in Auvergne in 1122 and 1126.[81] Returning from the first of these, Louis could regard himself as 'triumphant over all his enemies and in possession of a glorious peace'.[82] Similarly in Anjou under Fulk V and Geoffrey le Bel, there is a tendency (but only that) for rebellions to coincide with wars against Henry I. That the correlation is not accidental is suggested by the complaint of an Angevin chronicler that Henry I was in the habit of buying the support of Angevin barons.[83] The 'turbulent magnates' who loom so large in traditional interpretations of the period are by no means figments of historians' imaginations. But just as the powerful frontier-lord Robert of Bellême, Henry I's premier baronial troublemaker, ended his political career in the service of Louis VI, and Amaury de Montfort, Robert of Bellême's successor on Henry's little list, was an adviser of Louis VI and uncle of Fulk V, so also were Louis VI's hated foes, Hugh du Puiset and Thomas of Marle, allied at crucial moments with Henry I. Thomas of Marle, whose savagery

---

[78] Orderic's reference to the hostilities between Gervase and Henry I (vi, 176) can be dated 1112 and occurs in the context of the larger conflict involving Fulk V of Anjou, Louis VI, and Theobald of Blois. Gervase's wife, Mabel, was a niece of Henry I's enemy, Robert of Bellême. Their son Hugh married Aubrée, sister of Waleran count of Meulan c.1123, to seal a military alliance between Hugh and Waleran against Henry I in connection with the general hostilities of 1123-1124: Orderic, vi, 332 and note 2.

[79] Luchaire, nos. 75, 76, 87, 103, 108, 111, 114, 117, 134, 220, 236, 246, 262, 420.

[80] Suger, 162 and, more generally, 158-68; Luchaire, nos. 114, 134, 236.

[81] Luchaire, nos. 318, 369.

[82] Luchaire, no. 324.

[83] Chartrou, 27-33. Of the nine years in which Chartrou dates Angevin rebellions – 1109, 1112, 1115, 1118, 1123, 1124, 1129, 1130, and 1135 – five are years of warfare with Henry I (1112, 1118, 1123, 1124, 1135). On Henry's policy of buying the support of Angevin barons, see *Gesta consulum andegavorum*, 68.

toward defenceless victims and malicious torturing of prisoners are so vividly described by Suger and Guibert of Nogent,[84] is reported by Walter of Thérouanne to have joined the opposition to William Clito's rule in Flanders in 1127-28 in a coalition designed by Henry I.[85]

The Norman rebellion of 1123-24 provides a useful case study of the interplay between domestic and international politics. Henry of Huntingdon ascribes the revolt to a quarrel between Henry I and his young magnate Waleran of Meulan over some undisclosed issue, and provides no hint that the ensuing hostilities had an international dimension.[86] Orderic Vitalis provides a fuller and more plausible explanation: Amaury de Montfort count of Evreux, being angered at the activities of unscrupulous royal officials in his county, persuaded his nephew, Fulk V of Anjou, to betroth his daughter Sibylla to William Clito and grant the county of Maine as her marriage portion until Clito could recover Normandy from Henry I. Amaury then persuaded Waleran of Meulan and other magnates to rebel in Clito's behalf.[87] Although Orderic's criticism of unscrupulous officials is a topos that runs back to the publicans of the Gospels and beyond, it is not difficult to believe that Amaury, a wealthy and powerful magnate with extensive holdings on both sides of the Norman frontier, could resent the spread of the Anglo-Norman government across his county. Indeed, the castle of Evreux itself had for several years been occupied by a royal garrison.[88] But further information, from the *Anglo-Saxon Chronicle*, makes it clear that Orderic's explanation is romanticised and misleading. The problem must be traced back to the marriage in 1119 of William Adelin and Matilda, daughter of Fulk V of Anjou, and William Adelin's death the following year in the wreck of the White Ship. Fulk V was just then journeying to Jerusalem, and Henry kept Matilda at his court in England until Fulk returned to Anjou and had his daughter brought home.[89] The marriage had been intended to seal a lasting peace, and Fulk had agreed to grant Maine to William Adelin as a marriage portion, to be held of Anjou. William's death broke the seal and raised the issue of Maine once again. Fulk sent messengers to Henry's Christmas court at Dunstable in 1122 to discuss the return of Matilda's dowry, but early in 1123, probably in February, they departed in anger, having failed to persuade Henry to give it back.[90] The following September, Orderic tells us, Amaury, Waleran and others met to plot their rebellion.[91]

It is not to be supposed that Henry's break with Anjou was a product of the royal avarice; indeed, he tried to cheer the departing messengers with gifts.[92] As Simeon of Durham informs us, the dowry consisted not of money but of lands, towns and castles,[93] and they were presumably in Maine. Simeon does not identify

---

84 Suger, 30-2, 172-80, 250-4; Guibert de Nogent, *Histoire de sa vie (1053-1124)*, ed. Georges Bourgin, Paris 1907, 177-9, 198-9; cf. Huntingdon, 308-10 (*De contemptu mundi*).
85 Walter of Thérouanne, 'Vita Karoli Comitis', *MGH* xii, 557. The coalition included Baldwin of Hainaut, William of Ypres, Godfrey of Louvain (Henry I's father-in-law), and Stephen of Blois count of Boulogne.
86 Huntingdon, 245.
87 Orderic, vi, 332.
88 Orderic, vi, 278; William the Conqueror and his successors claimed the right to place their garrisons in private castles at will: C. H. Haskins, *Norman Institutions*, Cambridge, Mass. 1918, 282 ('Consuetudines et Iusticie', c. 4).
89 *ASC*, AD 1121; Chartrou, 13-16.
90 *ASC*, AD 1123; *De gestis regum*, ii, 498.
91 Orderic, vi, 334.
92 *ASC*, AD 1123.
93 Simeon, ii, 267.

them, but Robert of Torigny provides the names of many castles built, strengthened or garrisoned by Henry I, and among them are three major castles in Mayenne in northern Maine: Ambrières, Gorron, and Châtillon-sur-Colmont, all of which were in Henry's hands at his death in 1135.[94] He might well have alleged ancient claims to them — Ambrières was first fortified in 1054 by William the Conqueror[95] — and it looks very much as though they were committed to Henry at the time of his son's marriage and were still garrisoned by his knights in 1123. Robert of Torigny may be providing a further hint when he reports objections from various quarters to Henry's habit of dealing with castles across the Norman frontiers as if they were his own, strengthening them with walls and towers.[96]

The narrative sources, concentrating on the insurrection in Normandy, are all but silent on warfare with Anjou. Simeon of Durham alone mentions military operations on the frontier of Maine, involving William Clito and Fulk V, and he provides no details, while the Anglo-Saxon chronicler alludes even more vaguely to Henry's hostilities in 1124 with Louis, Fulk, and his own Norman landholders.[97] Louis' involvement is suggested by the presence of French knights and magnates, including the king's kitchener, in the garrisons of Waleran of Meulan's Norman castles of Pont-Audemer and Beaumont.[98] And Henry's warfare in Anjou may be echoed in the record of an accord between the family of Thomas of St John and the abbey of Mont-Saint-Michel c.1124 stating that the parties came to terms at Argentan, in King Henry's presence, after Thomas's return from captivity at Gorron.[99] Thomas of St John had fought in Henry's behalf during the Tinchebray campaign of 1106, and in 1118 his brothers, Roger and John, were the hand-picked commanders of Henry's garrison at La Motte-Gautier-de-Clinchamp, a former Bellême castle in Maine.[100] Thomas of St John had probably been commanding a body of knights in Henry's pay — perhaps Breton mercenaries[101] — when he was seized by the Angevins and Manceaux and incarcerated at Gorron. He may, indeed, have been in charge of the castle's defence and captured as a result of a successful Angevin siege, for if his captors had moved him it would likely have been to a more secure rear base.

The victory of Henry's military household over the rebels in March and April, 1124, was accompanied by related events of international scope. In July or August, the Emperor Henry V, by the counsel of his father-in-law Henry I, led a large-scale

94 *The Chronicle of Robert of Torigni*, in *Chronicles of the Reigns of Stephen, Henry II, and Richard I*, ed. Richard Howlett, 4 vols, RS 1884-1889, iv, 107, 128, described as Norman castles taken by the Angevins following Henry's death in 1135. Alençon may also have been at issue: see above, 256.
95 Robert Latouche, *Histoire du comté du Maine pendant le Xe et le XIe siècle*, Paris 1910, 31, 61.
96 Jumièges, 310.
97 Simeon, ii, 274; *ASC*, AD 1124.
98 Orderic, vi, 340, 342.
99 *Regesta*, ii, no. 1422.
100 Orderic, vi, 84, 194, and notes; Jacques Boussard, 'Thomas de Saint-Jean-le-Thomas et l'abbaye du Mont-Saint-Michel', in *Droit privé et institutions régionales: Études historiques offertes à Jean Yver*, Paris 1976, 87-96; on the family, see GEC, xi, 340-6. Thomas served c.1111 as co-sheriff of Oxfordshire; he appears to have crossed to Normandy with the king in 1123: *Regesta*, ii, nos. 1400-1401, 1418.
101 The St John brothers' Norman *caput* was at Saint-Jean-le-Thomas in the Cotentin, and they were important tenants of Mont-Saint-Michel, from which area Henry is said to have often recruited Breton mercenaries: Marjorie Chibnall, 'Feudal Society in Orderic Vitalis', *ante* i, 1978, 47; *De gestis regum*, ii, 478; cf. Chibnall, 'Mercenaries and the *Familia Regis*', 21.

military expedition against Reims.[102] It came too late to help Henry I, who had already restored order to Normandy, though advance rumours of the emperor's project may have discouraged Louis VI from involving himself more directly in the Norman-Angevin hostilities. Whatever the case, the imperial expedition was an utter failure. The Germans turned back, overawed by the size of Louis VI's army, perhaps intimidated by the *oriflamme* banner of Saint-Denis and, just possibly, terrified by an eclipse of the sun.[103]

In the meantime, through complex negotiations between Henry I and the papal curia, Clito's marriage to Sibylla of Anjou was annulled on grounds of consanguinity, very narrowly interpreted, and Henry rewarded the papacy for its good service by permitting Cardinal John of Crema to exercise full legatine powers in England in 1125.[104] As in 1105, Henry was prepared to diminish slightly his control of the English Church when the diplomatic stakes were high, and as in 1120 he was prepared to do so at Canterbury's expense.

International politics clearly overarched the Norman rebellion of 1123-24 no less than the Norman rebellion of 1118-19, the French rebellion of 1111-13, and the epoch-making Flemish rebellion of 1128 against William Clito — during which Henry kept Clito's enemies in his pay and squeezed the Flemish textile towns with a boycott of English wool.[105]

Louis VI had rendered only indirect support to the Norman rebels in 1123-24, and when he installed Clito in Flanders in 1127 and backed him militarily in 1128, Henry's response was similarly indirect — if perhaps more effective. The two kings had not been at blows since 1119, and at Clito's death in 1128 even their shadow boxing ceased. During the seven-year peace of 1128-35 Louis and Henry did not meet, nor were they linked by any known feudal relationship.[106] But both recognised Innocent II in the papal schism of 1130, and both received him at their courts. In May, 1131, Henry met Innocent II at Rouen in a glittering international assemblage that included Peter the Venerable abbot of Cluny, Bernard of Clairvaux, and,

---

102 Suger, 218-30; Luchaire, no. 349 and references.
103 Henry V's expedition cannot be dated precisely. Luchaire, in reviewing the evidence, concludes that it occurred sometime after 25 July and before the end of August, pointing out that Henry V was at Worms on 25 July and that several contemporary writers place the invasion in August. Luchaire further points out that Lambert de Waterlos, writing a generation later, places the expedition *intrante mense augusto* but gets the year wrong; and that, according to the *Auctarium Laudunense*, Henry V withdrew on 14 August. The solar eclipse of 11 August 1124 would have been visible from Reims at about noon (though the path of totality lay to the north of France): Theodor R. von Oppolzer, *Canon of Eclipses (Canon der Finsternisse)*, tr. by Owen Gingerich, New York 1962, 222-3 and Chart 111; Galbert of Bruges reports that the eclipse, even though partial, was an awesome occurrence signifying an oncoming calamity: *Histoire du meurtre de Charles le Bon*, ed. Henri Pirenne, Paris 1891, 5.
104 Helene Tillmann, *Die päpstlichen legaten in England bis zur Beendigung der Legation Gualas (1218)*, Bonn 1926, 27-30; Sandy B. Hicks, 'The Anglo-Papal Bargain of 1125: The Legatine Mission of John of Crema', *Albion* viii, 1976, 301-10; cf. Martin Brett, *The English Church under Henry I*, Oxford 1975, 45-7; Barlow, 109.
105 Walter of Thérouanne, 557; Galbert of Bruges, 146-7; *Recueil des historiens des Gaules et de la France*, ed. Martin Bouquet and others, 24 vols, Paris 1738-1904, xv, 341; Gaston Dept, *Les influences anglaise et française dans le comté de Flandre au début du XIIIe siècle*, Ghent 1928, 18ff.; F. L. Ganshof, 'Les origines du concept de souveraineté nationale en Flandre', *Revue d'histoire du droit*, xviii, 1950, 144, 146 n. 4.
106 See above, chapter 2, 46.

interestingly, Louis VI's chief adviser, Suger of Saint-Denis.[107]

From Suger's own writings, and those of his biographer, William of Saint-Denis, it becomes clear that the father of Gothic architecture was also a French royal envoy to the Anglo-Norman court, visiting Henry frequently and working for peace. Suger had earlier served as provost of the Saint-Denis dependency of Berneval on the Norman coast where he had been generously treated at Henry I's tribunals.[108] Although he later became Louis VI's counsellor and panegyrist, he always remained friendly toward Henry.[109] William of Saint-Denis describes Suger as being on the most intimate terms with the Anglo-Norman monarch, mediating for him with Louis VI to arrange bonds of peace, and frequently coming and going between the two courts.[110] In a letter to Count Geoffrey and the Empress Matilda after Henry's death, Suger himself recalls the honour and love which 'the glorious King Henry' always showed him, running to greet him on both his public and secret visits, and entrusting him with confidential peace negotiations with the king of France.[111] Suger credits himself with settling many wars and intrigues between the two kings, and with having had a hand in every peace negotiation during the final twenty years of Henry's reign. He offers to do the same service to Maud and Geoffrey – if they will keep their hands off Berneval as the good King Henry had done.[112]

Apart from the mere record of his presence at Henry's court in 1131, Suger's diplomatic activities have left no trace in contemporary sources. One faint hint can perhaps be found in a charter of Louis VI issued at Saint-Denis in 1120, sometime before August 3, disclosing that the king was in the company of his queen, his chief household officials, and Cardinal Cuno of Praeneste, Archbishop Thurstan's friend and fellow peace weaver.[113] Suger was not yet abbot, but he was a monk of Saint-Denis and was doubtless among those present. We are left to wonder whether they were negotiating the peace of 1120.

Again, Thomas Waldman and Elizabeth A. R. Brown recently discovered, in a section of a Queen's College Oxford manuscript containing materials that clearly originated at Saint-Denis, a genealogy demonstrating the relationship between an unnamed daughter of Henry I and Hugh fitz Gervaise of Châteauneuf.[114] The genealogy has been copied verbatim from the aforementioned letter of Ivo of Chartres that blocked the projected marriage alliance of c.1113. This letter appears in full, along with some of Ivo's other letters, in a collection of Saint-Denis materials in the Bibliothèque Nationale which contains the bulk of the known writing of William of Saint-Denis and the only surviving copies of Suger's later letters.[115] Clearly, Ivo's campaign against politically significant 'incestuous' marriage alliances was followed

---

[107] *Regesta*, ii, no.1691 n. (Suger did not attest for Henry I but witnessed a concurrent papal letter); Denis Bethell, 'English Black Monks and Episcopal Elections in the 1120s', *EHR* lxxxiv, 1969, 692; *Regesta Pontificum Romanorum*, ed. P. Jaffé, J. Loewenfeld *et al.*, i, Leipzig 1885, no.7472: Innocent II, at Rouen on 9 May, 1131, confirms the privileges and possessions of Saint-Denis at the request of Abbot Suger.
[108] Suger, 'De administratione', in *Oeuvres complètes de Suger*, ed. A. Lecoy de la Marche, Paris 1867, 184-6: Suger was provost of Berneval from 1107 to 1109.
[109] E.g. Suger, 14, 98-102.
[110] William of Saint Denis, 'Sugerii Vita', *Oeuvres complètes de Suger*, 384.
[111] Bouquet, xv, 520.
[112] Similarities between the passages in Suger's letter and William's 'Vita' suggest that William wrote with the letter at hand.
[113] Luchaire, no.289.
[114] Queen's College ms. 348, fol. 48.
[115] BN lat. 14192: for this reference I am again indebted to T. Waldman and E. A. R. Brown.

with keen interest at Saint-Denis in Suger's time. Whatever bearing this may have on Suger's own activities, his service as mediator between Henry I and Louis VI suggests that international diplomacy, both public and clandestine, was a livelier enterprise than the better known narrative and record sources would lead us to believe.

That Normandy and England both suffered widespread violence in the years after Henry I's death might suggest that Henry's peace was a mere oasis, an aberration of no lasting importance. But with the eventual victory of the house of Anjou over Stephen of Blois for the Anglo-Norman succession, Henry I's policy of domestic peace was reestablished and enlarged, and with such success as to make Stephen's reign the aberration.

Yet the 'Angevin Empire' radically reshaped the old Anglo-Norman political world. The unifying concept of the *gens Normannorum*, which G. A. Loud has shown to have been both vigorous and long established in the years of Henry I, began to fade amidst the multitude of principalities ruled by the early Angevin kings.[116] And the vision of a unified, distinctive Anglo-Norman polity, which crystallised under Henry I to the point that one optimistic contemporary could speak of a 'regnum Norman-Anglorum', dimmed in Stephen's reign and all but vanished in Henry II's.[117] With King John's 'triumphs' (as some appear to interpret them), the Angevin dominions dissolved into a new political order more closely resembling the *regnum Franciae* and *regnum Angliae* of later times.

But as Karl Ferdinand Werner has persuasively argued, the road from the Carolingian state to the 'modern' state 'leads through the compact territories of northern France to the great powers of England and France which developed out of them'.[118] The Anglo-Norman era marked the zenith of the older power centres which would be the building blocks of Henry II's 'empire' and Philip Augustus's vastly expanded kingdom, but were still virtually autonomous in the days of Henry I and Louis VI. These two monarchs did much to increase the cohesion of their dominions, as did the dukes and counts who allied with them or fought them. And their achievements in administrative organisation and domestic peacekeeping, of such fundamental significance to the history of Europe,[119] were shaped by the demands of warfare and diplomacy within an international political order soon to be transformed.

116 G. A. Loud, 'The "Gens Normannorum" – Myth or Reality?' *ante* iv, 1981, 104-16, 204-9.
117 John LePatourel, *The Norman Empire*, Oxford 1976; Hollister, 'Anglo-Norman *Regnum*':
118 Werner, 'Kingdom and Principality', 276; cf. 263-4.   above, Chapter 2.
119 For a stimulating general analysis see Joseph R. Strayer, *On the Medieval Origins of the Modern State*, Princeton 1970, and more briefly, 'The Historical Experience of Nation-Building in Europe', in *Medieval Statecraft and the Perspectives of History: Essays by Joseph R. Strayer*, Princeton 1971, 341-8.

16

ROYAL ACTS OF MUTILATION:
THE CASE AGAINST HENRY I*

The subject of mutilations is one I would cheerfully have left to others were it not for its bearing on the character of King Henry I. The sources for his reign disclose a number of instances in which alleged wrongdoers were punished by mutilation, and these punishments have earned Henry a somber reputation among modern historians. Christopher Brooke calls him a "savage, ruthless man"; Emma Mason deplores his "reign of calculated terror"; R.H.C. Davis speaks of his "reputation for brutality." To Sir Richard Southern, "Henry's vengeance was terrible and barbaric . . . . He had a morbid dislike of ridicule and he punished with a Byzantine ferocity already outmoded in the humaner society of feudal France, not only treachery and rebellion but slights to his dignity and honour."[1]

Perhaps the best known contemporary mutilation story comes from the 1125 account in the *Anglo-Saxon Chronicle*, where it is disclosed that Henry had the minters of England castrated and deprived of their right hands. We learn of Henry's morbid dislike of ridicule from an event of about the same time reported by the Norman monk, Orderic Vitalis. Henry had ordered the blinding of three captive rebels when Count Charles the Good of Flanders, who happened to be visiting, protested that it was unjust to mutilate prisoners captured in the service of their lords. Henry replied:

> I act rightly, lord count, and will prove it to you by good reason. Geoffrey and Odard rendered me homage with the consent of their lords, and in violating their faith to me they perjured themselves of their own free will and have thus incurred the penalty of death or mutilation . . . . Luke,

*I am grateful to the National Endowment for the Humanities, the John Simon Guggenheim Memorial Foundation, the American Council of Learned Societies, the Social Science Research Council, the Fulbright Commission, the American Philosophical Society, and the Warden and Fellows of Merton College, Oxford, for their help in supporting the research on which this paper is based.

[1]Christopher Brooke, *London, 800-1216: The Shaping of a City* (Berkeley, 1975), p. 317; Emma Mason, "William Rufus: Myth and Reality," *Journal of Medieval History,* 3 (March 1977):15; R. H. C. Davis, *King Stephen* (Berkeley, 1967), pp. 5-6; and Richard W. Southern, *Medieval Humanism and Other Studies* (Oxford, 1970), pp. 218 and 231.

to be sure, never did me homage, but he was in arms against me at Pont
Audemer, and afterwards when peace was concluded, I pardoned the
garrison and let them depart freely with their horses, arms, and possessions. But Luke rejoined my enemies at once and, with them, raised up
new hostilities against me . . . . And besides, that jesting clown wrote
off-color songs about me and sang them in public to insult me, making
me the laughing-stock of my enemies . . . .[2]

If this is the best defense that Henry can summon up, he would seem at
first glance to be condemned by his own words. But such judgment betrays an over-hasty reading of the text and insufficient appreciation
of its context. Mutilation stories of this kind, however blood-curd-
ling and revolting, cannot always be used to judge the moral character or psychological peculiarities of the rulers who inflicted them.
I will return to the Orderic passage after exploring the wider legal
and perceptual context in which King Henry was functioning.

   Death and mutilation were standard punishments for major crimes
throughout medieval Europe, and in many other societies and times
as well. In medieval Christendom such punishments could be viewed
as appropriate to evildoers who, unless they reformed, would one
day experience the far more horrible torments of hell. These torments were vividly portrayed in contemporary sermons and contemporary art: the suffering sinners in Last Judgment scenes at Conques,
Autun, and elsewhere; the illumination in Henry of Blois' Psalter
showing an angel locking the damned into the mouth of hell—to burn
with Judas "in the devouring flames and blazing tortures in punishment without end."[3] According to popular belief, God could mutilate
sinners here on earth. William of Malmesbury tells of a mason of
Worcester who, refusing to make peace with a fellow townsman, had
his scaffold broken under him by God's power and was crippled for
life.[4] Suger of Saint-Denis reports that the lord of Chaumont, having
disturbed the lands of Notre Dame of Rouen, was struck with a
dreadful malady and died after long and agonizing suffering, "learning even though too late what is owed to the Queen of Heaven."[5]

   The king, by virtue of his holy anointment, ruled as God's regent.
Just as God loved the poor and the good and punished the wicked,
so too was the king expected to protect the defenseless and smite evildoers. St. Anselm spoke for many when he advised Alexander king

[2]Orderic Vitalis, *Historia Ecclesiastica,* ed. A. Le Prévost, 5 vols. (Paris, 1852), 4:460-
61.
[3]These words are taken from a charter of King Athelstan: *Early Yorkshire Charters,*
ed. William Farrer and C.T. Clay, 12 vols. (Edinburgh, 1914-65), 1:no. 1.
[4]William of Malmesbury, *Vita Wulfstani,* ed. R. R. Darlington (London, 1928), p. 40.
[5]Suger, *Vie de Louis VI le Gros,* ed. Henri Waquet (Paris, 1964), p. 194.

of Scots to rule with a blend of gentle kindness and strict justice: "Behave in such a way," Anselm urged, "that the bad shall fear you and the good love you."[6] It was the king's obligation to protect the church, widows, orphans, and other defenseless subjects by acting with severity toward those who would oppress them. Thus, Suger asserts that it is a king's right and duty to repress the boldness of tyrants whenever they are seen to do harm in war, or to rejoice in devastation, or to oppress the poor and destroy churches.[7]

These notions, which recur throughout the Middle Ages, have their roots in the Old Testament. Isaiah's prophecy on the coming of the virtuous king portrays a ruler both compassionate and stern: "His word is a rod that strikes the ruthless; his sentences bring death to the wicked"(2:4). And God himself is made to say, "I crushed the people in my fury, trampled them in my anger, and made the juice of them run all over the ground"(63:6). These Old Testament images recur in the Book of Revelation, where Christ—the "judge with integrity," and "warrior for justice"—is described as wearing a blood-soaked cloak: "From his mouth came a sharp sword with which to strike pagans; he is the one who will rule them with an iron scepter and tread out the wine of Almighty God's fierce anger" (19:11-15).[8]

It was as God's regent, as the figure of the virtuous king wielding his iron scepter, that Henry I promised at his coronation to enforce the laws against treason and felony and to maintain firm peace throughout his kingdom.[9] His sacred obligation to punish wrong-doers in order to protect the weak finds vivid iconographic expression in the seal of his itinerant justice, Richard Basset: an armored knight drives his sword into the face of a griffin who grasps in his beak a naked, defenseless man.[10] Such, symbolically, was the stern duty of a royal justice in the service of a virtuous king.

In an age with few prisons and without police, severe punishment was regarded as an essential deterrent to such serious offenses as treason, murder, rape, arson, and theft. By ancient custom, crimes of this sort put their perpetrators at the king's mercy, and the penalty

[6]Anselm of Canterbury, *Opera Omnia*, ed. F. S. Schmitt, 6 vols. (Edinburgh, 1946-61), 5:Ep. 413.

[7]Suger, *Louis VI*, pp. 172-74.

[8]Cf. *Genesis* 49:9-12; *Jeremiah* 25:30; *Proverbs* 2:22; 2 *Thessalonians* 1:8; and *Revelations* 20:14.

[9]Henry I's Coronation Charter, Chapters 8 and 12, from *Select Charters*, ed. William Stubbs, 9th ed. (Oxford 1913), p. 119.

[10]Sir Christopher Hatton, *Book of Seals, to Which is Appended a Select List of the Works of Frank Merry Stenton*, ed. Lewis C. Loyd and Doris M. Stenton (Oxford, 1950), Pl. III.

was normally death or mutilation. Of the two, mutilation was regarded as the less severe. Suger relates that King Henry acted mercifully toward a chamberlain who had plotted to assassinate him, having the chamberlain blinded and castrated, rather than hanged as he deserved.[11] And Glanvill makes the contrast between capital offenses and lesser crimes which were "to be more leniently dealt with . . . where punishment of the guilty involves only loss of limbs."[12]

In Germanic law, treason against one's lord was the supreme offense.[13] The laws of King Alfred allow no mercy to a person guilty of treason, because Christ himself adjudged no mercy to Judas who sold him to death.[14] Accordingly, the laws of Alfred and his successors assign the death penalty to anyone convicted of plotting against the king.[15] By the time of Athelstan, false minting had come to be regarded as a kind of treason, as it had earlier been regarded in Roman law.[16] For that crime, too, the Anglo-Saxon dooms set the penalty of death or mutilation, as did the laws of Byzantium, Islam, and the other kingdoms of the early and later medieval West: in ancient Rome, counterfeiters were executed; in thirteenth-century France they were regularly boiled alive in a cauldron.[17] More generally, "slander of the king" was unemendable by a money payment. The Leges Henrici Primi, an unofficial treatise reflecting established custom, includes among those crimes punishable by death or mutilation

---

[11]Suger, *Louis VI*, p. 190.

[12]Ranulf de Glanvill, *De Legibus Consuetudinibus Regni Anglie*, ed. G. D. G. Hall (London, 1965), pp. 176-77. The same point was made by the East Roman Emperor Leo III (R.S. Lopez, "Byzantine Law in the Seventh Century and its Reception by the Germans and the Arabs," *Byzantion*, 16 [1942-43]:456.) See also "The Ten Articles of William I," in *The Laws of the Kings of England from Edmund to Henry I*, ed. A. J. Robertson (Cambridge, 1925), p. 242. The laws of the Saxon and Norman kings are published in *Die Gesetze der Angelsachsen*, ed. Felix Liebermann, 3 vols. (Halle, 1898-1916), Vol. 1; more convenient editions, with facing English translations, are *The Laws of the Earliest English Kings*, ed. F. L. Attenborough (Cambridge, 1922), and Robertson, *The Laws of the Kings of England*.

[13]See F.D. Lear, *Treason in Roman and Germanic Law* (Austin, Texas, 1965.)

[14]*Laws of Alfred*, Introduction, cap. 49, in Liebermann, *Die Gesetze*, 1:15-89.

[15]*Alfred* 4, 1-2, in Attenborough, pp. 64-66; 2 *Athelstan* 4, in ibid., p. 130; 5 *Aethelred* 30, in Robertson, p. 86; 6 *Aethelred* 37, in ibid., p. 102; 2 *Canute* 57, in ibid., p. 204.

[16]Lear, *Treason*, p. 189; Glanvill, *De Legibus*, pp. 176-177; and Frederick Pollock and F. W. Maitland, *The History of English Law*, 2 vols. (Cambridge, 1968), 2:505.

[17]2 *Athelstan* 14, 1, in Attenborough, p. 134; 3 *Aethelred* 8, in Robertson, p. 68; Galbert of Bruges, *The Murder of Charles the Good, Count of Flanders*, trans. and ed. James B. Ross (New York, 1967), p. 17, n. 73; Lopez, "Byzantine Law," pp. 448-56. In states in which the prince enjoyed a monopoly on coining, counterfeiting could be regarded as a crime of *lèse majesté* (ibid., p. 449.)

any contempt or slander of the king's person—along with treason, arson, murder, major theft, robbery, and false coining.[18]

The punishment of such crimes by loss of life or limbs likewise occurs in the laws of Normandy, both before and long after Henry's reign.[19] The same penalties are to be found in the laws of France, where death or mutilation for major crimes runs, for example, through the *Etablissements* of St. Louis.[20] One finds these penalties in the assizes of Henry II and in Glanvill, who deals at length with treason and other felonies punishable at the king's will by execution or loss of limbs.[21] Punishment for treason became even more severe in thirteenth and fourteenth century England with the introduction of drawing and quartering, disembowelling, and burning at the stake.[22] As late as 1637 William Prynne and two fellow Puritan writers were pilloried and shorn of their ears for publishing libels against the state.[23]

One encounters similar penalties in the laws of pre-modern China, India, and Islam. The Koran states that those who create violence or corruption "will be killed or crucified, or have their hands and feet on opposite sides cut off, or be expelled from the land"(5:33), and that thieves should have their hands amputated as "an exemplary punishment from Allah"(5:38). (This last punishment was reintroduced by the government of Pakistan in 1977: a police chief in Rawalpindi told an Associated Press reporter, "People are really terrified . . . . Normally we have ten or twelve serious crimes a day but we have had almost none since this announcement.")[24]

Muhammad's views on mutilation would have shocked few medieval churchmen. Gratian, drawing in part from earlier canonical tradition, allows the practice of mutilation and execution even to men

[18]*Leges Henrici Primi*, ed. L. J. Downer (Oxford, 1972), pp. 108 (10, 1), 116 (13, 1, 3.) Cf. ibid., pp. 114 (11, 16a), 164 (49, 7), and 232 (75, 1.)

[19]*Consuetudines et Iusticie* of 1091: 1-2, 8, 13; Charles H. Haskins, *Norman Institutions* (Cambridge, Mass., 1918), pp. 28-29 and 280; Lucien Valin, *Le Duc de Normandie et sa cour* (Paris, 1910), pp. 187 and 247; and *Coutumiers de Normandie*, ed. E.-J. Tardif (Rouen, 1881), p. 64.

[20]*Les Etablissements de Saint Louis*, ed. P. Viollet, 4 vols. (Paris, 1881-86), 2:55.

[21]*De Legibus*, pp. 171-77. See also W. L. Warren, *Henry II* (Berkeley, 1973), p. 355 on the Assizes of Clarendon and Northampton.

[22]Pollock and Maitland, *History of English Law*, 2:500-01.

[23]William Haller, *The Rise of Puritanism* (New York, 1938), pp. 249-54. On the use of torture by tribunals in early-modern Europe, see A. W. B. Simpson, *Torture and the Law of Proof* (Chicago, 1978).

[24]Associated Press report in *The Los Angeles Times*, July 14, 1977, Part 1, p. 13. On mutilation in China, see A. F. P. Hulsewé, *Remnants of Han Law*, 9 vols. (Leiden, 1955), 1:122-28.

in holy orders so long as it is done as a legitimate exercise of political authority: "It is permitted," Gratian writes, "not only to whip evil-doers, but also to kill them."[25] And Suger of Saint-Denis, speaking for the society of feudal France, reports that when King Louis VI, by divine intervention, captured the castle of Crécy he piously massacred the whole garrison, mercilessly beheading them because they themselves had been merciless.[26] Suger makes it clear in this regard that Louis was performing the proper duties of a king who, according to St. Paul, "does not bear the sword in vain."[27] On hearing that Guy lord of la Roche-Guyon had been murdered by his brother-in-law William, "King Louis, by solemn order of the king's majesty, ordered that the crime should be punished by the most humiliating and drawn-out form of death." The punishment was imposed on William and his followers alike. It involved "castrating some, slowly disembowelling others, drawing out their agonies gently and cruelly with the most exquisite tortures. Nor should it be doubted," Suger adds, "that God's hand made such swift vengeance possible."[28]

Not every clerical writer savored the avenging of wickedness quite to the degree that Suger did. But all would have agreed that kings were bound by sacred duty to enforce peace and curb violence and treachery by means that strike us today as brutal. The notion that severe punishment deters criminal acts, although seriously questioned in our own time, was universally accepted in the Middle Ages. Thus, Eadmer of Canterbury lauds Henry I for putting an end to looting and devastation among members of the itinerant royal court by threatening future transgressors with blinding and loss of limbs. Eadmer adds that Henry, at the same time, reestablished the practice of mutilating minters of false coins, which were "harming many people in many ways." Henry took these measures, Eadmer declares, on the advice of Archbishop Anselm and the nobles of the realm, "to alleviate the kingdom's suffering," and from them "great good immediately resulted."[29] Similarly Robert of Torigny—monk of Bec

---

[25]Stanley Chodorow, *Christian Political Theory and Church Politics in the Mid-Twelfth Century: The Ecclesiology of Gratian's Decretum* (Berkeley, 1972), pp. 235-36 and 238.

[26]Suger, *Louis VI*, p. 176.

[27]Ibid., p. 178; and *Romans* 13:4. See also Gabrielle M. Spiegel, *The Chronicle Tradition of Saint-Denis: A Survey* (Brookline, Mass., 1978), p. 45: Suger's Life of Louis VI "presents the Capetian monarch as the realization of the highest ideals and goals of medieval kingship, as an example to present and future rulers . . . ."

[28]Suger, *Louis VI*, pp. 118-20.

[29]Eadmer, *Historia Novorum*, ed. Martin Rule, Rolls Series (London, 1884), pp. 192-93. Eadmer's words on this episode are echoed in Florence of Worcester, *Chronicon ex Chronicis*, ed. Benjamin Thorpe, 2 vols. (London, 1848-49), 2:57.

and later abbot of Mont-Saint-Michel—praises King Henry for keeping the peace in Normandy, preventing his enemies "by the point of
the sword from plundering churches and the poor."[30] The Peterborough monk who reports the mutilation of English moneyers in
1125 adds that "it was done very justly because they had ruined the
whole country with their great false-dealing."[31]

Clerical writers thus accepted without question both the practice of
royal mutilations and their necessity. The Peterborough chronicler
describes in pitiable detail the rampage of destruction that broke out
under King Stephen when wicked men saw that he "did not exact the
full penalties of the law."[32] But these same writers were equally prepared to condemn punishments if they exceeded the limits of the law,
or were imposed upon the innocent. They drew a distinction between
legitimate penalties and atrocities motivated by anger or sadistic im-
pulse. Thus, Guibert of Nogent castigates Thomas de Marle for personally flaying his prisoners and hanging them by their thumbs or
testicles.[33] Orderic charges Robert de Bellême with subjecting his
captives to unheard-of tortures of his own invention, and afterwards
joking about them to his henchmen.[34] These stories, insofar as they
can be believed, suggest that Thomas de Marle and Robert de
Bellême were indeed ruthless and savage men. Orderic finds it start-
ling that Robert preferred murdering his captives through torture to
collecting their ransoms.[35] Torture was not wrong in itself, as Suger's
accounts of Louis VI's reprisals make clear, but torture without just
cause was unacceptable and repugnant:[36] and torture at the expense
of ransom money was the mark of a twisted mind.

Suger himself is prepared to grant his patron Louis VI extraordinary leeway in avenging wrongs. He writes approvingly of Louis'
having a Flemish rebel suspended from a gallows alongside a mad

[30]William of Jumièges, *Gesta Normannorum Ducum,* ed. Jean Marx (Rouen, 1914),
p. 296.
[31]*Anglo-Saxon Chronicle,* A.D. 1125.
[32]Ibid., A.D. 1137.
[33]Guibert, *Histoire de sa Vie,* ed. Geroges Bourgin (Paris, 1907), pp. 178-79. Cf.
Suger, *Louis VI,* pp. 30 and 172-74.
[34]Orderic Vitalis, *Ecclesiastical History,* ed. Marjorie Chibnall, 4 vols. (Oxford, 1969-
75), 4:298; cf. 4:158-60, and William of Malmesbury, *Gesta Regum Anglorum,* ed. William Stubbs, Rolls Series, 2 vols. (London, 1887-89), pp. 475-76.
[35]Orderic Vitalis, *Ecclesiastical History,* ed. Chibnall, 4:298.
[36]Robert and Thomas have both found defenders in our own century: see Le Vicomte
du Motey, *Robert II de Bellême et son temps* (Paris, 1923); and Jacques Chaurand,
Thomas de Marle, Sire de Coucy (Marle, 1963.)

dog and eaten alive.[37] But many contemporary churchmen would have condemned such methods of peacekeeping, even if done by royal command. Despite their sacred obligation to chastise the wicked, great princes too could mutilate unjustly. To give only a few examples, William the Conqueror, as duke of Normandy, punished the townsmen who had defended Alençon against him in the early 1050s by having their hands and feet cut off; Henry II observed the unsuccessful outcome of an expedition into Wales by mutilating and hanging twenty-two innocent Welsh hostages;[38] Louis VII, in a fit of anger, personally hacked off the hands of Queen Eleanor's unfaithful vassals in the Talmont;[39] Richard the Lion-Hearted put out the eyes of eighty Gascon captives;[40] William Clito count of Flanders presided over a seemingly endless chain of grisly tortures and agonizing executions following upon the murder of his predecessor in 1127 —the vengeance extending beyond the murderers themselves to their followers, innocent or not.[41]

Henry I was also accused by contemporaries of unjust mutilations, but only very rarely, and never on the massive scale of the preceding examples. In 1124, when the king was in Normandy, his English justice Ralph Basset hanged or mutilated fifty men for thievery, many of whom, the Anglo-Saxon chronicler believes, were convicted unjustly.[42] Again, Henry of Huntingdon informs us that William count of Mortain, who broke his homage to Henry I in 1104 and became his captive in 1106, was blinded while imprisoned in the Tower of London. The story is not without its difficulties,[43] and blinding was

[37]Suger, *Louis VI*, pp. 246-48.

[38]David C. Douglas, *William the Conqueror* (London, 1964), p. 60; William of Jumièges, *Gesta Normannorum Ducum*, p. 126; and Warren, *Henry II*, p. 164.

[39]Alfred Richard, *Histoire des ducs et des comtes de Poitou, 778-1204*, 2 vols. (Paris, 1903), 2:67.

[40]Achille Luchaire, *Social France at the Time of Philip Augustus*, tr. E. B. Krehbiel (New York, 1967), p. 12.

[41]Galbert of Bruges, *Histoire du meurtre de Charles le Bon*, ed. Henri Pirenne (Paris, 1891), pp. 92, 125-26, 128-29, and *passim*.

[42]*Anglo-Saxon Chronicle*, A.D. 1124.

[43]Henry of Huntingdon, *Historia Anglorum*, ed. Thomas Arnold, Rolls Series (London, 1879), pp. 255-56. After Henry I's death, William of Mortain is reported to have become a monk of Bermondsey Abbey, London, on which occasion nothing is said about his being blind; but this information comes from a brief notice in the Bermondsey Annals, a very late source (*Annales Monastici*, ed. H. R. Luard, Rolls Series, 5 vols. /London, 1864-69/, 3:436). The Bermondsey Annals likewise report that William was freed *c.* 1118 (p. 432), but even if this is correct, he was back in the Tower of London in 1129-30 (*Pipe Roll 31 Henry I*, ed. Joseph Hunter, rev. ed. /London, 1929/, p. 143).

indeed a traditional penalty for treason."⁴ But if the deed was done, and done secretly and without legal proceedings, Henry I must bear responsibility. Although less inclined to outbursts of brutality than Henry II, Louis VII, Richard the Lion-Hearted, William the Conqueror, or—above all—Louis VI, Henry I was capable of acts of cruelty. So, too, were innumerable other successful rulers of pre-modern states across the globe. We can, if we choose, judge them by the standards of modern Western liberalism and deplore them all. But before drawing conclusions about the character or psychological oddities of a pre-modern prince, we must view his deeds in the context of his own age, evaluate them by contemporary standards and contemporary ideas of what was required of a good prince. In doing so, we are confronted with new and interesting problems. For one, medieval writers viewed their society with a pervasive if largely unconscious sense of class distinction: to mutilate poor thieves was a very different matter than to blind the count of Mortain. Aristocrats of the twelfth century would be inclined to rejoice at the execution of a rebellious townsman, but would be shocked at the execution of a rebellious earl. Or again, severity towards traitors and false minters could be seen as the proper response of a peacekeeping prince, whereas the pointless torturing of helpless captives was viewed as an act of wickedness. Henry I is known to have punished by mutilation on a number of occasions during his long and well-recorded reign. I do not intend here to analyze these instances one by one, but only to urge that each of them be interpreted with caution and in proper context. If that is done, it becomes quite clear that Henry I did not punish for the sheer pleasure of it, or for reasons of vengeance alone, or out of a morbid dislike of personal affronts. He is reported to have acted harshly on some occasions, but mercifully on others— in virtually every instance his primary consideration appears to have been the survival of his regime and the keeping of the peace. His punishments provide us no real insight into his psyche or moral character—except to suggest that he was a monarch not to be trifled with. One would have thought twice before violating one's fealty to Henry I. But even this point must not be exaggerated. To view his rule as a reign of terror is to miss its central point—that he based his success on the creation of a royalist baronage, bound to him not by fear so much as by gratitude for past favors and the hope of future ones. In short, with one or two exceptions—William of Mortain and Ralph Basset's thieves—mutilations under Henry I seem to have been

"⁴William the Conqueror blinded many of the men who rebelled against him in 1075. See Henry of Huntingdon, *Historia Anglorum*, p. 206.

generally condoned and often applauded as appropriate to the customs of war and the sacred duties of the peacekeeping king.[45]

To illustrate this point, let me return now to the story with which I began—Henry I's reply to Charles the Good of Flanders justifying the blinding of three rebel knights. It must be understood that Count Charles was not questioning the penalties traditionally assessed against traitors and slanderers. Any notion that Charles was a harbinger of modern penology should be dispelled by the fact that he himself had threatened a disturber of church lands with being boiled in a cauldron—a punishment that his predecessor Baldwin VII had actually imposed.[46] Charles' point was that one could not justly mutilate captives "taken in the service of their lords." Some would have disagreed with this strict interpretation of the law—Suger for one. Nevertheless, Henry addressed himself convincingly to the objection. Two of the three captives were in fact Henry's own vassals. The third—Luke de la Barre—was doubly guilty. He had violated a fundamental custom of medieval warfare: that besieged garrisons, if permitted to depart their castles unharmed, must fight no more against the besieger.[47] Luke, on leaving Pont Audemer, had immediately rejoined Henry's enemies; and by singing his comic songs, he had committed the capital offense of slander against the king's person. Henry's arguments would have carried the day—if in fact he actually uttered them. More probably, the entire scene is a set-piece with invented conversation, intended by Orderic to make clear to his readers that Henry's treatment of the three offenders was beyond reproach. Orderic has Henry conclude his case against Luke de la Barre with these words:

> God has now delivered him into my hands for punishment, so that he may be compelled to renounce his wicked behavior, and so that others, hearing of this punishment of his outrageous conduct, may be corrected.[48]

[45]Such, I suggest, is the purport of such passages as Orderic Vitalis, *Historia Ecclesiastica,* 4:167 and 337; William of Malmesbury, *Gesta Regum,* 2:487-88; and Henry of Huntingdon, *Historia Anglorum,* p. 311. For the usual response to an enemy's mutilation of hostages and prisoners, see F. M. Powicke, *The Loss of Normandy,* 2nd. ed. (Manchester, 1961), pp. 243-44.

[46]Herman of Tournai, *Liber de restauratione monasterii S. Martini Tornacensis,* ed. G. Waitz, in *Monumenta Germaniae Historica, Scriptores,* 14:285. See *Murder of Charles the Good,* ed. Ross, pp. 17, 20 and 45 for Charles' views on crime and punishment. On his attitude toward treason and slander, see Galbert, *Histoire de meurtre du Charles le Bon,* p. 14.

[47]On this tradition, see Powicke, *Loss of Normandy,* p. 245.

[48]Orderic Vitalis, *Historia Ecclesiastica,* 4:461.

Orderic is clearly saddened by the whole tragic episode, but his justification of Henry's measures would have been persuasive to contemporaries even if not to us: "On hearing it," Orderic concludes, "the count of Flanders said nothing, because he had no reasonable objections to offer."

HENRY I AND THE INVISIBLE
TRANSFORMATION OF MEDIEVAL ENGLAND

Historians in the present century have tended to view the reign of Henry I as an historical turning point. Albert Brackmann credits Henry with developing a new type of political organization that set European civilization on a new course.[1] Richardson and Sayles ascribe to Henry's reign the genesis of 'a carefully articulated machine of government' unparalleled in the West since the fall of Rome.[2] 'Looking to the future', Sir Richard Southern writes, 'it is here, we feel, that the history of England begins – a history which is neither that of the Norman conquerors, nor of the Anglo-Saxons, but that of the English crown and aristocracy'.[3]

Southern evaluated Henry's reign by looking to the future, but contemporaries necessarily did so by looking to the past. Like modern historians they regarded his reign as noteworthy, but for altogether different reasons. They cast him in the age-old role of the model king who, with wise, seasoned advisers, restored the good, ancient laws, kept the peace throughout his dominions, and protected the church, the impoverished and the helpless by chastising evildoers. These medieval clichés, echoing well-known passages from Scripture, shaped even the most sophisticated contemporary perceptions of the reign. Henry was praised as a great king, and great precisely because he played the ancient role so well. His royal virtues were old, hallowed virtues. His seldom-mentioned vices – avarice, lust – were older still. How is it that contemporary writers could have missed the big story, overlooking the innovations that contributed to what we now regard as a fundamental reorientation of medieval governance?

Let me be more concrete on the matter of contemporary perceptions. Henry I was viewed, above all, as the embodiment of the *rex pacificus* – an

---

[1] A. Brackmann, 'The Beginnings of the National State in Mediaeval Germany and the Norman Monarchies', in *Medieval Germany, 911–1250: Essays by German Historians*, ed. Geoffrey Barraclough (Oxford, 1948), pp. 287–88.
[2] H. G. Richardson and G. O. Sayles, *The Governance of Mediaeval England from the Conquest to Magna Carta* (Edinburgh, 1963), pp. 159, 172.
[3] R. W. Southern, *Medieval Humanism and Other Studies* (Oxford, 1970), p. 207.

ancient ideal that all kings pursued but few attained.[4] The Anglo-Saxon chronicler praised Henry for having given England 'peace for man and beast'. William of Malmesbury lauded him for 'having established such peace in Normandy as had never before been known, such as even his father . . . had never been able to effect'.[5] 'God grant him peace', wrote Hugh, archbishop of Rouen, on Henry's death, 'for peace he loved'.[6]

In the conventional wisdom of the time, peacekeeping required the king to act severely toward violent subjects – rebels, rapists, arsonists, violators of churches, exploiters of widows and orphans. Accordingly, contemporaries stress that Henry punished such people with exile, forfeiture, death, or mutilation. It is hard for us to read accounts of some of these punishments without concluding that their authors were condemning Henry I for acts of unspeakable cruelty. Yet a careful reading of such passages makes it clear that in nearly all of them he is being applauded for fulfilling the responsibilities of Christian kingship.[7] Isaiah had prophesied the coming of the virtuous king, a ruler both compassionate and stern, whose word is a rod that strikes the ruthless, whose judgements bring death to the wicked (XI, iv). Echoing the old tradition, St Anselm urged the king of Scots to 'behave in such a way that the bad shall fear you and the good shall love you'.[8] Only in this context can one comprehend the passage in which Eadmer of Canterbury, St Anselm's companion and panegyrist, reporting that Henry I reestablished the ancient practice of mutilating false minters, proudly explains that he did so 'on the advice of Anselm and the nobles of the realm . . . to alleviate the kingdom's suffering', and that 'great good immediately resulted'.[9] All contemporaries would have agreed, except of course the minters.

Eadmer's statement displays still another traditional royal virtue: the good king will consult on important matters with his magnates and

---

[4] See, for example, William A. Chaney, *The Cult of Kingship in Anglo- Saxon England* (Berkeley, 1970), pp. 90–94.

[5] *Anglo-Saxon Chronicle*, A.D. 1135; William of Malmesbury, *Gesta Regum Anglorum*, ed. William Stubbs (1887–89), 2: 476; cf. Orderic Vitalis, *Ecclesiastical History*, ed. Marjorie Chibnall (Oxford, 1969–80), 6:472; Suger, *Vie de Louis VI le Gros*, ed. Henri Waquet (Paris, 1964), p. 186.

[6] William of Malmesbury, *Historia Novella*, ed. K. R. Potter (London, 1955), p. 14.

[7] C. W. Hollister, 'Royal Acts of Mutilation: The Case against Henry I', see above, ch. 16, 291-301. Only rarely did a contemporary criticize Henry for his punishments: *Anglo-Saxon Chronicle*, A.D. 1124; Henry of Huntingdon, *Historia Anglorum*, ed. Thomas Arnold (1879), pp. 255–6.

[8] *Sancti Anselmi Cantuariensis Archiepiscopi Opera Omnia*, ed. F. S. Schmitt (Edinburgh, 1946–61), 5, Ep. 413.

[9] Eadmer, *Historia Novorum in Anglia*, ed. Martin Rule (1884), pp. 192–93, echoed by Florence of Worcester, *Chronicon ex Chronicis*, ed. Benjamin Thorpe (London, 1848–49), 2:57.

prelates.[10] The fact that Henry I regularly did so is made clear by repeated and pointed statements in the narrative sources of his reign. But the conventional good king was further expected to select as his closest counselors men of widsom and experience. Thus, Orderic Vitalis assures us that 'King Henry did not follow the advice of rash young men as did Rehoboam' – the son of Solomon whose rash advisers and resulting calamities are chronicled in the book of Kings. To the contrary, Henry 'prudently took to heart the experience and advice of wise and older men'.[11] Employing the same topos, William of Malmesbury speaks of Henry's closest adviser, Robert count of Meulan, as being deservedly a member of the king's inner circle 'because he was of ripe age to counsel'.[12] Other princes were less judicious in choosing their advisers. King Eadwig is said to have been renounced by the Mercians and Northumbrians in 957 because he was misled by foolish counselors.[13] Stephen of Blois, Orderic explains, 'was guided, like Rehoboam, by the fawning of flatterers, not the counsel of older men', and Robert Curthose duke of Normandy was urged by his father William the Conqueror to choose better counselors: 'Have the good sense to mistrust those rash spirits who have shamelessly goaded you on to lawless deeds'.[14] Unlike Stephen and Robert, Henry deferred to men of experience and therefore 'deservedly governed many provinces and peoples.'[15]

Contemporary writers, in short, laud Henry not as a new monarch but as a good monarch of the old school. Orderic sums up Henry's policies in these familiar terms: 'He always devoted himself, until the end of his life, to preserving peace . . . . He shrewdly kept down illustrious counts and castellans and bold tyrants to prevent seditious uprisings, but always cared for and protected men of peace and monks and humble people'.[16] To William of Malmesbury, 'He was venerated by the nobility, loved by the common folk. If it happened that important men, forgetting their sworn oath, drifted from their fidelity, he promptly recalled them to the straight way . . . bringing back the

---

[10] See, for example, Éric Bournazel, *Le gouvernement capétien au XIIᵉ siècle, 1108–1180* (Paris, 1975), pp. 152–54, and, if you can find it, Paul Ward's unpublished and undated paper, 'On the King's Taking Counsel'.

[11] Orderic, 5:299.

[12] *Gesta Regum*, 2:483. Conversely, at the height of the English investiture dispute, Anselm and Paschal II regarded Robert of Meulan as a kind of Wormtongue. Adopting the conventional ecclesiastical fiction of the well-meaning king led astray by wicked advisers, Paschal warned Robert against giving evil counsel and eventually excommunicated him: *Anselmi Opera*, Ep. 353–4, 361, 364, 388.

[13] Vita Dunstani auctore B. in *Memorials of St Dunstan*, ed. William Stubbs (1874), p. 36.

[14] Orderic, 6:207; 3:99.

[15] *Ibid.*, 5:299.

[16] *Ibid.*, 6:99.

recalcitrant to soundness of mind by inflicting bodily wounds'.[17] Suger of St Denis observes that Henry I, with the counsel of wise and skilful men, gave the kingdom of England good order through the law of its ancient kings. He brought order to Normandy, too, imposing peace by force on its ferocious inhabitants, promising nothing less than blinding to thieves or robbers'.[18] Here again, Henry is being pictured not as cruel and savage but as exemplifying the conventional royal virtues, rooted in Scripture.[19] Indeed, all these passages pile topos on topos to such a point that the real, living, breathing Henry I is scarcely visible at all.

When we do catch glimpses of him, we find him playing unquestioningly the role in which contemporaries cast him. Their thought world was also his. He did prefer wise counselors, did avoid rash actions, did inflict severe punishments on traitors, thieves and counterfeiters, did pursue peace and did achieve it to a remarkable degree. 'I establish peace throughout all my kingdom', Henry said in a prophetic and singularly unoriginal clause in his coronation charter, 'and I order that this peace shall henceforth be maintained'.[20]

Was there nothing new in this man? Was he simply a crowned cliché? There is of course his coronation oath from which I have just quoted, and which later served as a precedent for Magna Carta. But as Mlle. Raymonde Foreville has reminded us, similar coronation oaths had been taken, and broken, by Henry's predecessors.[21] William the Conqueror had sworn before the altar of Westminster Abbey, in the presence of the clergy and people, to defend the holy churches of God, to rule his kingdom with justice, to make and uphold just laws, and rigorously to prohibit every sort of rapine and unjust judgement.[22] Henry's only original contributions to the tradition were to make the oath more explicit, and to put it in writing.

Henry I has likewise been credited with raising up new men 'from the dust' through an elaborate system of patronage involving gifts of land, wardships, administrative offices, marriages to aristocratic heiress and the like. But in essence such a policy can scarcely be regarded as innovative. Orderic described the Conqueror as having

---

[17] *Gesta Regum*, 2:487.

[18] *Vie de Louis VI*, p. 100.

[19] Suger frequently applauds his hero, Louis VI, for inflicting far more bloodcurdling punishments on evildoers: see Hollister, 'Royal Acts of Mutilation', above, 291-301 *passim*.

[20] *Select Charters*, ed. William Stubbs (ninth ed., Oxford, 1913), p. 119, cl. 12. Cf. the Coronation Oath of King Edgar: *Die Gesetze der Angelsachsen*, ed. Felix Liebermann (Halle, 1903-16), 1:214-15.

[21] Foreville, 'Le sacre des rois anglo-normands et angevins et le serment du sacre (XI – XII siècles), *Proceedings of the Battle Conference on Anglo-Norman Studies*, 1:1978, ed. R. Allen Brown (Ipswich, 1979), pp. 52-62.

[22] Florence, 1:229.

endowed his closest followers with riches 'that raised them above the station to which they were born'; William Rufus, Orderic tells us, raised up 'underlings whom he exalted by the grant of vast honours as a reward for their flattery'.[23] Indeed, new men are essential to any stable regime, and complaints about them constitute still another medieval topos. A contemporary of Harun-al-Rashid's grumbled about base-born men rising to wealth in the caliph's service: 'Sons of concubines have become too numerous among us; lead me to a land, O God, where I shall see no bastards'.[24] Leopold Genicot reminds us that medieval rulers rewarded their *fideles* with lands, offices, and rich heiresses, 'whether in sixth-century England, eleventh- and twelfth-century Poland, thirteenth-century Hungary or fourteenth-century Castile'.[25]

Nevertheless, the impression lingers that Henry I raised up new men on a scale larger than before, and in an atmosphere of administrative bustle and menaces that contrasted sharply with the quieter, more genial, and more aristocratic environment of Louis VI's France.[26] I myself find Henry's England, with its thirty-three years of unbroken peace, a good deal quieter and more genial than contemporary France with its incessant warfare, urban riots and mass suffering, chronicled in grisly detail in the pages of Suger, Clarius, Guibert of Nogent, Galbert of Bruges, and the chronicler of Morigny. But perhaps more to the point, recent research on royal patronage and charter attestations suggests that Henry's regime included the established aristocracy to a far greater degree than did Louis VI's. Henry favoured and consorted with men new and old,[27] including representatives of such Conquest families as the Beaumonts, Bigods, Warennes, d'Avranches, and Clares. Conversely, as the researches of Éric Bournazel have demonstrated, Louis VI's regime consisted chiefly of ordinary *milites*. It excluded by and large not only the great princes and prelates but even, well into the twelfth century, the castellans of the Ile de France.[28] Henry I,

---

[23] Orderic, 2:190; 5:202.

[24] Philip K. Hitti, *The History of the Arabs,* sixth ed. (London, 1956), p. 333.

[25] Génicot, 'Recent Research on the Medieval Nobility', in *The Medieval Nobility,* ed. Timothy Reuter (Amsterdam, 1978), p. 20; cf. *ibid.,* p. 33 n.38; Franz Irsigler, 'On the Aristocratic Character of Early Frankish Society', *ibid.,* p. 124; Karl F. Werner, 'Important Noble Families in the Kingdom of Charlemagne, *ibid.,* p. 177. Karl Schmid, 'The Structure of the Nobility in the Earlier Middle Ages', *ibid.,* p. 53: 'The first rulers of the Saxon royal house showed their strength by surrounding themselves, as their powerful predecessors had done, with noble families which they themselves had raised up.'

[26] E.g. Southern, *Medieval Humanism,* p. 153.

[27] C. W. Hollister, 'Henry I and the Anglo-Norman Magnates', *Proceedings of the Battle Conference on Anglo-Norman Studies,* 2, 1979, ed. R. Allen Brown; see above, chapter 10, pp. 171-89 ; cf. Barbara M. Walker, 'King Henry I's Old Men', *Journal of British Studies,* 8, no. 1 (1968), 1–21.

[28] Bournazel, *Le gouvernement capétien,* pp. 26–53, 57, 90–91, 94–102, 175–77.

in short, resembles the ideal medieval king surrounded by his great nobles much more closely than does Louis VI.

The community of interests between king and nobility in Henry's England is further suggested by the fact that the tenurial insecurity which had characterized English society since the Norman Conquest came to an end as early as 1113.[29] Baronial honours were remarkably stable throughout the last two decades of Henry's reign, during which the configuration of royal and baronial holdings, with the greatest honours in the hands of royal kinsmen, closely paralleled the configuration disclosed by the Domesday survey at the close of the Conqueror's reign.[30]

Henry I thus had no novel political philosophy but only a cluster of old assumptions drawn from French, Norman and Anglo-Saxon traditions and from the more recent 'tradition' of the Anglo-Norman monarchy. The political abstractions of the so-called Anglo-Norman Anonymous penetrated neither the royal *curia* nor the minds of contemporary historians. Professor Sally Vaughn has shown that Henry's adviser, Robert of Meulan, articulated an early version of *raison d'état*, but we hear of it only once.[31] Much more typically, Henry saw himself as the good steward of his inherited dominions and privileges, responsible to God for preserving them all and passing them on intact to his heirs.

This conception of stewardship was very old. It was shared by contemporary prelates and magnates with respect to their lands and privileges. It governed Archbishop Anselm's views on the lands and primacy of Canterbury.[32] Anselm had gone into exile under Rufus because of having been denied the full restoration of Canterbury's estates along with such traditional archiepiscopal privileges as the right to call synods and to participate in the inner circle of royal advisers.[33] The newly-crowned Henry I summoned Anselm home with the honest intention, so it seems, of conceding everything that the archbishop had formerly demanded of Rufus. Henry must have been flabbergasted when Anselm, on returning, refused to render him the customary

[29] RaGena DeAragon, 'The Growth of Secure Inheritance in Norman England, *Journal of Medieval History*, 8(1982), 381–91. Cf. Southern, *Medieval Humanism*, p. 233.

[30] Hollister, 'Henry I and the Anglo-Norman Magnates', above, pp. 186-7.

[31] Sally N. Vaughn, 'Robert of Meulan and Raison d'État in the Anglo-Norman State, 1093–1118'. *Albion*, 10 (1978), 352–73. Although the statement occurs in a 'quotation' attributed to Robert by Orderic writing many years later, there is reason to suppose that it represents Robert's view rather than Orderic's. Richard of Leicester, a monk of Orderic's abbey of St Évroult at the time Orderic was writing the passage, had earlier served Robert of Meulan as an intimate counselor and major administrator and would thus have been able to provide Orderic with reasonably accurate information on Robert's thinking: Orderic, 5:314–16; 6: 488.

[32] R. W. Southern, *St. Anselm and his Biographer* (Cambridge, 1963), p. 127–8; *Anselmi Opera*, Ep. 452.

[33] *Ibid.*, Ep. 212; Eadmer, *Historia Novorum*, p. 119.

homage and to receive the archbishopric from the royal hands on the grounds that the homage of clerics and lay investiture had been banned at a papal synod that Anselm had attended the previous year.[34] In a letter to Pope Paschal, Henry based his case squarely on custom and the responsibilities of royal stewardship. Echoing an oft-quoted letter of William I to Gregory VII, Henry agreed to pay Peter's Pence 'which blessed Peter had from my predecessors' and to render 'that obedience which your predecessors had in the kingdom of England in my father's time', but only on condition that traditional royal customs remain inviolate. 'So long as I live', Henry wrote, 'the dignities and usages of the English realm shall not be diminished'.[35] These are brave words but scarcely original, and they express a rigidly conservative viewpoint unbefitting a king about to set European civilization on a new course.

The novelty of Henry's reign is to be found neither in his goals nor in his political assumptions, but in the development of new, highly effective means to conventional ends. Focusing on ends, contemporaries seem unconscious of the great administrative innovations of the reign: exchequer, central treasury, systematic judicial eyres, specialized viceregencies. The exchequer system, as we know it from the Pipe Roll of 1130, may well have been developed to assist the collection of an aid in 1110 on the betrothal of Henry's daughter Maud to the emperor Henry V.[36] Contemporary Anglo-Normans saw it as a brilliant stroke of policy that the granddaughter of a bastard duke should marry an emperor; the auditing improvement passed unnoticed. Thereafter the exchequer continued to function, always backstage, as a means of enhancing the collection of revenues to be used for traditional and newsworthy purposes: fortifications, hired knights, diplomatic bribes and the like. Its value is suggested by the fact that whereas Henry seems to have run short of money during his Norman campaign of 1105, he had a substantial treasure in 1120 at the conclusion of three years of heavy warfare, and again in 1135 after having completed a military campaign along the Norman frontier.[37] Predictably, contemporary writers concentrated on the warfare and diplomacy. Their occasional allusions to the royal revenues are limited to complaints about taxes. Similarly, Henry's creation of a central

---

[34] *Ibid.*, pp. 119–20.

[35] *Anselmi Opera*, Ep. 215; cf. *Beati Lanfranci archiepiscopi Cantuariensis opera omnia*, ed. J. A. Giles (Oxford, 1844), p. 32.

[36] *Regesta Regum Anglo-Normannorum*, ed. H. W. C. Davis and others (Oxford, 1913–69), 2, No. 963. The problem of the origin of the exchequer defies precise solution: see *Dialogus de Scaccario*, ed. Charles Johnson (London, 1950), pp. xxii–xxiii; Richardson and Sayles, *Governance*, pp. 157–67.

[37] *Anglo-Saxon Chronicle*, A.D. 1105; Eadmer, *Historia Novorum*, pp. 171–5; Orderic, 6: 306, 448; Malmesbury, *Historia Novella*, pp. 14, 17; Robert of Torigny, *Chronicle*, in *Chronicles of the Reigns of Stephen, Henry II, and Richard I*, ed. Richard Howlett (1884–89), 4: 129.

treasury and viceregency courts were inconspicuous accommodations to the problem of ruling England and Normandy jointly, and his system of judicial eyres constituted a gradual, scarcely visible extension of curial control over the local courts.[38]

The secondary importance of such procedures and institutions to contemporary minds has been obscured by a certain misconception of the role in Henry's regime of Roger bishop of Salisbury, the creator and manager of much of the new machinery. William of Malmesbury and Henry archdeacon of Huntingdon both assert that Roger was Henry I's right-hand man – *secundus a rege* – but both had reason to exaggerate.[39] Malmesbury Abbey was under Roger's jurisdiction and rejoiced in his gifts, while Henry of Huntingdon's archdeaconry pertained to the see of Lincoln whose bishop, Alexander, was at once Henry of Huntingdon's patron and Roger of Salisbury's nephew. There can be no doubt that the king relied heavily on Roger for the administration of England and even for advice on episcopal appointments. But Roger was not a major advisor on matters of high policy – war and diplomacy – as should be clear from the fact that he rarely accompanied the king to Normandy.[40] We have explicit evidence, for example, that he was not consulted on the vital matter of the Empress Maud's marriage to Geoffrey of Anjou.[41] Roger was a brilliant, powerful, indispensable functionary, as was his Norman administrative counterpart, John bishop of Lisieux, who seldom went to England. Roger became the sole regent of England when Henry crossed to Normandy in 1123, but only because Henry, desperate for an heir, wanted his new queen, Adeliza of Louvain, at his side at all times and, presumably, in his bed as often as possible. Henry's advisers on matters of major importance to him were magnates such as Robert of Meulan, William of Tancarville, and, later, Robert earl of Gloucester, Brian fitz Count and Humphrey of Bohun,[42] all of them wise old men – regardless of age.

Yet for all my reservations, these useful administrative mechanisms, these means to ends, betoken a fundamental shift in the style of governance. Sir Richard Southern caught the significance of Henry's reign when he observed that 'these years when nothing happened –

---

[38] On these matters see C. W. Hollister , 'The Rise of Administrative Kingship, pp. 223-45 above; Cf. K.J. Leyser, 'Ottonian Government', *English Historical Review*, 91, (1981), 722: 'The Ottonian writers dwell on the ideals of Ottonian governance. About its means and methods they kept almost total silence. They were not interested in administration and the *munera sordida*.'

[39] Malmesbury, *Gesta Regum*, 2: 483–4; Huntingdon, *Historia Anglorum*, p. 245.

[40] Hollister, 'Rise of Administrative Kingship', above, Ch. 13, p. 241, Table 4; Edward J. Kealey, *Roger of Salisbury* (Berkeley, 1972), pp. 150–51, n. 11.

[41] Malmesbury, *Historia Novella*, p. 5.

[42] *Ibid.*; Vaughn, 'Robert of Meulan'; Hollister, 'Rise of Adminstrative Kingship', above, p. 241, Table 4.

largely because nothing happened – were decisive in the development of English society'.[43]

Let me review some of the half-hidden factors that may provide clues to the decisive yet elusive shift in orientation. Henry's regime marked a drift toward systematization, explicitness, not only in the major administrative innovations already discussed, but as well in such matters as the standardization of measures and coins, the establishment of regulations governing the conduct, wages and perquisites of the royal household, the granting of fixed stipends for barons attending court, the common use of royal writs purged of superfluous verbiage, cast in the most starkly economical style.[44] Royal patronage, while an age-old practice, was now systematized as never before. Writs granting lands and privileges were copied and preserved in the treasury at Winchester. Recent research by Stephanie Mooers has clarified the ways in which Henry's annual Pipe Roll recorded not only income but patronage as well; exemptions from danegeld, *auxilium civitatis* and *murdrum*; pardons or non-collections of debts; wardships, beneficial marriages, and the granting of royal ministries – for a price.[45] Under Henry I the expansion of the Anglo-Norman regnum ceased and, with it, the opportunity to expand the royal estates through conquest and win new lands to bestow on *fideles*. The Anglo-Norman monarchy survived this lowering of expectations by tightening its judicial and fiscal procedures.[46]

The trend toward systematization was accompanied, appropriately, by growing literacy and mastery of Latin among Henry's magnates and administrators, and by a substantial increase in written records.[47] Memory was giving way more and more to documentation, and an illiterate sheriff or royal justice could find himself as incapacitated as a handless minter. Henry's own literacy may have been rudimentary: recalling that William the Conqueror was both illiterate and short tempered, historians have doubted Malmesbury's account of young, bookish Henry remarking in his father's presence that an illiterate king

[43] *Medieval Humanism*, p. 233.

[44] E.g., R. C. Van Caenegem, *Royal Writs from the Conquest to Glanvill* (Selden Society, London, 1959), pp. 252–53; Edward J. Kealey, 'Anglo-Norman Policy and the Public Welfare', *Albion*, 10 (1978), 343; Constitutio Domus Regis, in *Dialogus de Scaccario*, pp. 129–35; Hollister , 'Rise of Administrative Kingship', above, pp. 224-5.

[45] Stephanie Mooers, 'Patronage in the Pipe Roll of 1130', *Speculum*, 59 (1984) 282–307, and, by the same author, 'Familial Clout and Financial Gain in Henry I's Later Reign', *Albion*, 14 (1982), 268–91.

[46] See Judith Green, 'William Rufus, Henry I and the Royal Demesne', *History*, 64 (1979), 337–52.

[47] Richardson and Sayles, *Governance*, pp. 269–84; Ralph V. Turner, 'The *Miles Literatus* in Twelfth- and Thirteenth-Century England: How Rare a Phenomenon?' *American Historial Review*, 83 (1978), 928–45.

is a crowned ass.[48] But whatever the case, Henry saw to it that his sons were well educated. His chief adviser Robert of Meulan is described as a man of extraordinary intelligence, and Robert's sons, Waleran of Meulan and Robert earl of Leicester, while still in their mid-teens, are alleged to have overcome a group of cardinals at the papal curia in a debate on logic[49] – a debate that must surely have been waged in Latin. Robert of Leicester, and perhaps Waleran as well, had been educated at Abingdon under its learned Italian abbot, Faritius, and Richard fitz Neal would later describe Robert as well educated and practised in legal affairs.[50] Another of Henry's rising stars, Othuer, bastard son of Hugh earl of Chester and castellan of the Tower of London, was sufficiently well educated to serve as tutor of Henry's own sons, one of whom, Robert earl of Gloucester, was described by William of Malmesbury as a man of great learning, a book lover.[51] Robert of Gloucester became one of Henry I's wealthiest magnates and most active *curiales*. The Pipe Roll of 1130 shows him conducting an audit of the Winchester treasury along with another of Henry's new magnate-*curiales*, Brian fitz Count, who would later demonstrate his learning by writing letters supporting the Empress Maud's claim to the English throne.[52] The sons and nephews of several of Henry's key administrators were students at the school of Laon.[53] Roger of Salisbury sent his nephews Alexander and Nigel to study there, and both subsequently became bishops and *curiales* of Henry I. Nigel became royal treasurer in the mid-1120's and would later be called upon by Henry II to restore the exchequer system after its deterioration in Stephen's reign. It is suggestive that one of the Laon masters, Ralph, wrote a treatise on the abacus, as did Adelard of Bath, who also taught at Laon and may later have served in Henry's administration.[54]

The pursuit of traditional ends through novel means characterized not only the reign of Henry I but many other facets of twelfth-century

---

[48] C. W. David, 'The Claim of King Henry I to be Called Learned', in *Anniversary Essays in Mediaeval History by Students of Charles Homer Haskins* (Boston, 1929), pp. 45–56; V. H. Galbraith, 'The Literacy of the Medieval English Kings', *Proceedings of the British Academy*, 21 (1935), 211–21.

[49] Malmesbury, *Gesta Regum*, 2: 482.

[50] *Dialogus de Scaccario*, pp. 57–58; *Chronicon Monasterii de Abingdon*, ed. Joseph Stevenson (London R.S., 1858), 2: 229: Robert's education is misdated back to the reign of King William (I or II).

[51] *Gesta Regum*, 2: 518–21.

[52] *Pipe Roll 31 Henry I*, ed. Joseph Hunter (London, 1833), pp. 129–31; Richardson and Sayles, *Governance*, p. 273.

[53] On the connections between Laon and Henry's court, see *Patrologia Latina*, 156: 961 ff.; R. L. Poole, *The Exchequer in the Twelfth Century* (London, 1912), pp. 53–56; Richardson and Sayles, *Governance*, pp. 270–1; Kealey, *Roger of Salisbury*, pp. 48–50. On the school at Laon, Valerie I. J. Flint, 'The "School of Laon": A reconsideration', *Recherches de Théologie ancienne et médiévale* 43 (1976), 89–110.

[54] *Pipe Roll 31 Henry I*, p. 22; Poole, *Exchequer*, pp. 56–57.

civilization as well. In theology, law, monastic life, music and art, no less than in political organization, the twelfth century witnessed a heightened creativity devoted to the service of older ideologies. As Frank Barlow recently expressed it, the new rationalism was neither secularist nor, in the modern sense, sceptical; it implied no criticism or hostility toward the church and its beliefs; logic was applied to theology 'in order better to understand, and display, the teachings of the church',[55] just as a radically new architecture was developed, I would add, to provide a more capacious and appropriate setting for the ancient liturgy (which was itself being developed and systematized). Many historians would agree that during the twelfth century European civilization underwent a change of the most fundamental significance, but the nature and degree of the change is too often obscured by the fact of ideological continuity. Far more visible are the changes that occurred in that allegedly pivotal century between 1450 and 1550, where so many courses and textbooks in European civilization wrongheadedly commence. The cultural transformation of the twelfth century was surely the more fundamental one, but it is marked by no such headline events as the voyages of discovery, the invention of printing, the Protestant Reformation, or Copernican astronomy. Henry I, although a much abler king, will never enjoy the glamour of Henry VIII. In contrast to the revolutionary century of Columbus and Luther, the twelfth century reorientation was subtle, elusive, and imperfectly understood by contemporaries.

Undaunted, medievalists continue to seek the key to what Charles Homer Haskins called 'the renaissance of the twelfth century'. M. T. Clanchy sees it as a vital period in the evolution from memory to written record; Alexander Murray stresses that a major increase in the circulation of money shifted political and economic power into the hands of men trained in reasoning and reckoning.[56] Peter Brown describes the change as a shift from consensus to authority – 'perhaps the greatest single precondition for the growth of rationality'.[57] M.-D. Chenu emphasizes the realization among twelfth-century thinkers that the physical world functioned on natural rather than supernatural principles.[58] Similarly, Charles M. Radding, adopting a biological analogy, sees the century as marking childhood's end: the primitive notion of imminent justice gave way to the adult concept of a natural order – a gradual demystification of

---

[55] Frank Barlow, *The English Church, 1066–1154*, (London, 1979), p. 4, n. 21.

[56] M. T. Clanchy, *From Memory to Written Record: England, 1066–1307*, (Cambridge, Mass., 1979); Alexander Murray, *Reason and Society in the Middle Ages* (Oxford, 1978).

[57] Peter Brown, 'Society and the Supernatural: A Medieval Change', *Daedalus*, 104, no. 2 (1975), 143.

[58] Chenu, *Nature, Man, and Society in the Twelfth Century*, ed. Jerome Taylor and Lester K. Little (Chicago, 1968), p. 6.

what Carolly Erickson has called 'the enchanted world'.[59] Colin Morris credits the twelfth century with the discovery of the individual, Caroline Bynum with the discovery of self through new religious communities.[60]

All these efforts at explanation involve subtle if pervasive changes, many of which are exemplified by the increased systematization of governance that occurred under Henry I: written records, reasoning and reckoning, experimentation, a clear shift, using Peter Brown's terminology, from local consensus toward central authority, more royal administration and less royal charisma in a world of diminishing enchantment. I have little to add to these hypotheses, expect to suggest that we may possess a clue to the twelfth-century puzzle in the character of Henry I himself. Henry's contemporary, the scientist Adelard of Bath, once remarked testily that a person who made no effort to appreciate the rational plan of the universe was as contemptible as one who lived in a house but knew not how it was built.[61] Unlike most of his royal and aristocratic contemporaries, Henry I knew how his house was built. It was an old house, just as Henry wished it to be, but it had new plumbing, the workings of which Henry seems to have understood perfectly. For all his traditional attitudes, Henry was a man of intense curiosity. 'He inquired into everything', Orderic declares, 'and retained all that he heard in his tenacious memory. He wished to know all the business of his officials and dignitaries, and . . . . kept his eye on the many happenings in England and Normandy.'[62] In 1101 we find him personally showing his English foot soldiers how to oppose cavalry charges with their shields and how to return stroke for stroke.[63] At the siege of Pont-Audemer in 1123 he instructed his carpenters on the building of a siege tower.[64] At Woodstock, his favourite hunting park, he displayed his interest in animals not only by pursuing them but also by collecting them: his Woodstock zoo is said to have included lions, leopards, lynxes, camels, and a porcupine.[65]

I shall now hazard the modest proposal that the great mental shift of the twelfth century is epitomized in Henry's approach to hunting. As we all know, hunting was the favoured sport of the medieval

[59] Charles M. Radding, 'Superstition to Science: Nature, Fortune, and the Passing of the Medieval Ordeal', *American Historical Review*, 84 (1979), 945–69; cf., by the same author, 'Evolution of Medieval Mentalities: A Cognative-Structural Approach', *American Historical Review*, 83 (1978), 577–97; Carolly Erickson, *The Medieval Vision* (New York, 1976), pp. 3–28.

[60] Morris, *The Discovery of the Individual, 1050–1200* (New York, 1972); Caroline Walker Bynum, *Jesus as Mother: Studies in the Spirituality of the High Middle Ages* (Berkeley, 1982), pp. 82–109.

[61] Chenu, *Nature, Man, and Society*, pp. 11–12, 57; Radding, 'Superstition to Science', p. 966.

[62] Orderic, 6: 100.

[63] Malmesbury, *Gesta Regum*, 2: 472.

[64] Orderic, 6: 342.

[65] Malmesbury, *Gesta Regum*, 2: 485.

aristocracy. In keeping with the grand old tradition, Henry loved to hunt. Embedded among the concessions in his coronation charter is the stubborn assertion, '. . . I have retained the forests in my own hands as my father did before me'.[66] But Henry seems to have approached the chase in a novel way. Master Wace describes William of Warenne, earl of Surrey, as ridiculing Henry some years before his accession for having studied hunting so thoroughly that he could tell the number of tines in a stag's antlers simply by examining his footprint.[67] Earl William mockingly refers to Henry as 'Stagfoot' for having turned a joyous, mindlessly athletic pastime into a science.

Once again a traditional goal, the stag in this case, is pursued by novel means. In a sense, as in the entire reign of Henry I, as in the whole unfolding of twelfth-century culture, nothing had happened. But the new approach transformed European civilization – not to mention hunting.

[66] *Select Charters*, ed. Stubbs, p. 119, cl. 10.
[67] *Le Roman de Rou de Wace*, ed. A. J. Holden, 3 vols. (Paris, 1970–73), 2: 275–76.

INDEX

Index